THE VANISHING POINT

How did we get here? As the twenty-first century unfolds, several seemingly unprecedented phenomena evoke ghosts of past histories that suggest we may have been here before. Forms and arguments gone acquire new relevance, as retrospective signposts for the contemporary. **India Since the 90s** assembles texts and images from diverse academic disciplines and cultural practices, to look again at the millennial turn that is shaping our present.

Series Editor
Ashish Rajadhyaksha

IN THE SERIES

VOLUME 1 The Hunger of the Republic: Our Present in Retrospect
Editor: **Ashish Rajadhyaksha**

VOLUME 2 Improvised Futures: Encountering the Body in Performance
Editor: **Ranjana Dave**

VOLUME 3 The Vanishing Point: Moving Images After Video
Editor: **Rashmi Devi Sawhney**

VOLUME 4 Cities on the Ground: The New 'Urban' Experience
Editors: **Solomon Benjamin and the Frozen Fish Collective**

VOLUME 5 Another Lens: Photography Practices and Image Cultures
Editor: **Rahaab Allana**

VOLUME 6 Ghosts of Future Nations: Gods, Migrants and Tribals in the Late-Modern Museum
Editor: **Kavita Singh**

Set up in 2010, **West Heavens** (http://westheavens.net/) is an integrated cross-cultural exchange programme aiming to disentangle and compare the different paths of modernity taken by India and China. It promotes several layers of interaction across intellectual and art practices, and social thought, between the two countries. In its ten years of existence, the project has organized numerous forums, exhibitions, film screenings and workshops, and has published more than twenty books.

India Since the 90s

THE VANISHING POINT

Moving Images After Video

edited by

RASHMI DEVI SAWHNEY

Tulika Books

WEST HEAVENS

India Since the 90s
is a collaborative bilingual project between

Tulika Books, New Delhi and **West Heavens**, Shanghai

supported by
Moonchu Foundation, Hong Kong

THE VANISHING POINT: Moving Images After Video

First published in India in 2022 by
Tulika Books
44 (first floor), Shahpur Jat, New Delhi 110 049, India
tulikabooks.in

ISBN: 978-81-947175-8-4

Design, visual concepts, montages: Gauri Nagpal

Printed in India at Saurabh Printers Pvt. Ltd. Greater Noida

INTRODUCTION TO THE SERIES

India Since the 90s

THE VANISHING POINT: Moving Images After Video is the third in our series of six volumes titled *India Since the 90s*. The series is published bilingually, in English and Chinese, and is intended to provide a historical frame for our present. As with the other volumes, almost none of the texts and images used here have been originally created for these books. Many of them are well known. What is new here, therefore, apart from their choice of selection and their assemblage into this particular order, is their re-presentation into something of a cognitive mash-up. This form is intended to give these works an afterlife, attempting both estrangement and refamiliarization, as we seek to re-describe an era that is our very recent past and, in some instances, our actual present.

Over the second decade of the twenty-first century, even as we have seen totalitarian state apparatuses roll out emergency measures of extraordinary control, including nationwide lockdowns, in the name of the public good, we have been incessantly reminded of longer histories – reminded, notwithstanding the radically new nature of various phenomena at play (the new viruses, new technologies, new modes of organization and 'occupation', new systems of regulation), that even 'unprecedented' developments can force larger historical frames with which to view both their time and ours.

As clarity slowly emerges around the 'new normal', to use the phrase of the moment, the uncertainty of our time sees the cover-ups of normalcy occasionally lifted to give us a glimpse into what lies beneath. It is almost as though the growing emphasis on social distancing lies in inverse proportion to the impossibility of *historical* distance. Even as our capacity to imagine stable utopian futures drains away, it is reinvigorated by a textual prescience, as texts and images produced in other times and other places begin to say something in conditions their makers could never have anticipated. We have discovered, it seems, an entirely new ability to read uncanny significances.

Such a definition of the 'normal', this series argues, takes us relentlessly and compulsively back to other moments in time, which too had encountered a similar uncanny everyday. This is not a return to origins. Rather, it is the discovery, in such moments, of the ghosts of other moments. Today's stories, however things pan out, cannot be told without recognizing in them the spectres of the 1990s, the decade that launched a globalization whose end might well be signalled in 2020. And the 1990s cannot in turn be comprehended without accessing yet another equally 'new' moment in history – the 1940s – when the Indian state was imagined, politically and administratively.

The present volume turns to a practice of the moving image that comes after the cinema. It simulates the cinema even as it re-presents – recycles – what used to be the cinema in a radically different medium. As it brings what was once the cinema into a new ecosystem of data storage and circulation, of cutting/pasting (or what one text in this volume refers to as *thundu*, the insertion of 'cut-pieces' of censored-out material) and meme-making, the book also returns the moving image into the garbage heaps and recycled second-hand markets that have been over the years its natural archives. As these archives house what was once the cinema in modes of data manufacture, storage and circulation, they too build their ambitions, define their own manifestos.

Back in 1968, a documentary filmmaker working for the state-owned Films Division had inserted two frames (or a one-twelfth of a second flash inside a film) that said 'F*ck Censorship'. It must have appeared to viewers back then as a hallucinatory 'did-I-really-see-that?' experience of strange ghosts in the celluloid machine. Just under forty years later another filmmaker, clinging to his dead camera for dear life as he was submerged by the all-devouring tsunami wave that hit Tamil Nadu, brought a different value to the ghosts his camera had captured. Two years earlier, numerous all-seeing light-weight cameras with built-in sound recorder and portable editing suites had witnessed the consequences of a massacre that took place in the town of Godhra in Gujarat. The violence inaugurated a new era of state authority with the 'Gujarat experiment', as it came to be known.

The convergences, as political documentary made common cause with the larger world of social media, gave documentary filmmakers a new role within a multi-disciplinary political avant-garde. Such an avant-garde has built on earlier battles, like the famous battle for freedom of speech in the cinema fought by the filmmaker K.A. Abbas in a legendary Supreme Court case in 1970, that was reprised in several other legal challenges to the state in the decades that followed. In 2004 it transformed many of the locales of earlier battles. Concepts that had once defined the cinematic *auteur*, such as the historic binary of realism and censorship, took a new turn as the moving image moved from the centre to the peripheries of the state.

As the decade wore on, the battles too shifted geographically from cities to rural and semi-metropolitan locations (such as, this book shows, Purulia in Bengal, Malegaon in Maharashtra and the villages of Telangana), which saw in musicals, comedies and spoofs the rise of a vibrant, largely unregulated, cinephiliac, no-budget moving-image economy. Over time they included souped-up renditions of once-revolutionary music with communist adherences. They also brought to images and sounds distributed on cheap CDs, pen-drives or local terrestrial cable (or even on regional satellite TV), a political edge that reprised previous battles over linguistic and cultural self-representation that had once defined the nation-states of the twentieth century.

As with other volumes in this series, this one too is framed within the battles for citizenship that defined the millennial turn, when the abstract 'people' of the Constitution of India were re-embodied, in the public domain, as new subjects – new viewers and new makers – in all their desiring, elusive and terrifying immediacy. As also in other volumes, here too there is an emphasis on the way Article 21 of the Constitution, or the right to 'life and liberty', took multiple new turns, as technologies associated with the regulation and ordering of covert space saw battles over state action. Such action has meant something very particular to the moving image. In 2021, shortly before this volume went to press, the Government of India abolished the FCAT – the Film Certificate Appellate Tribunal – to create what many have dubbed a 'super-censor', a parallel arrangement bypassing and potentially superseding the established censorship mechanism. Two months before the abolition of FCAT, a Digital Media Ethics Code was released by the Ministry of Electronics and Information Technology directly targeting 'intermediaries' of digital content, from Twitter to all social media platforms, messaging platforms, all web publishers and OTT platforms.

That was not all. Shortly thereafter, an entire apparatus of state regulation of the cinema was restructured – an apparatus that had been assembled after Independence following the recommendations of the S.K. Patil Film Inquiry Committee of 1951, which included the National Film Archive of India, the Films Division and what would later become the National Film Development Corporation. This mechanism of governance, defined in large measure by the Cinematograph Act, 1952, has been controversial. Whatever its history, or its ambitions to give a new nation its own new cinema in its own self-image, its redefinition in 2021 certainly signals an end, as much to the cinema itself as to the self-identity of the old Nehruvian state.

Each of the volumes exists on its own, as conceived by its editor. A common feature across the texts has been to introduce a glossary of keywords. Several of these are from the Indian languages, some are names of people, yet others are acronyms or abbreviations, while others are English words used in India in ways that divert sharply from dictionary definitions. All are being re-presented here, by way of explanation and for purposes of estrangement and refamiliarization.

Perhaps the only common element across the titles, apart from the interest in the period following the 1990s in India, is an interest in a triad of concepts that we may name *politics*, *space*, *technology*. The pendular movement of the political spaces, until recently spaces of public existence, increasingly turned into spaces of negotiation between *state* and *planet*, a twenty-first-century variation of the old local–global divide, defining both virtual and physically occupied space. Technology is apparatus, frame, mode of mediation and surveillance. Three further terms, in turn, produce the *habitus* for these concepts: *democracy*, the *body* and the *text*. Even as key democratic concepts such as freedom need to be defined anew in times when bodies – both physical and virtual – occupy complex political domains, the text – as *prescient*, as *re-interpreted* and as *meme* – too finds itself bearing new responsibilities.

Ashish Rajadhyaksha
Series Editor
Bangalore, 1 January 2022

CONTENTS

RASHMI DEVI SAWHNEY **2021**

Introduction

On 12 December 2020, thousands of workers at Wistron, a Taiwanese company contracted to manufacture iPhones by Apple Inc. in the Narasapura industrial area, in Kolar district of Karnataka, vandalized the factory. The workers had not been paid for months, it was reported, and in a world only just recovering from the damages of the pandemic, their desperation was screaming out. The losses to Wistron were to the tune of 200 million dollars, and Apple's Public Relations firm had to rush in to do damage control.

The episode speaks to all the contradictions that the 'moving image' holds out to us today. The iPhone symbolizes the most tantalizing fantasies about the moving image in the twenty-first century: sharp high-definition images captured with multiple powerful cameras, easy navigation, clean interface, cutting-edge design, video and sound technology good enough to make professional films, all fitting into a pocket. On the other hand, there is nothing new about the condition of the work force, whose sweat-shop economies represent a very old struggle, even as they manufacture new objects of global desire. The mobile phone as the ubiquitous apparatus of the moving image opens up difficult questions beyond the realm of aesthetics. *The Vanishing Point* glances back at the last three decades from this vantage point, where the analogue and digital worlds create an illusion of convergence.

The term 'moving image' has commonly come to be associated with experimental and expanded cinema. In this volume, it is used to refer to a range of image-

valances, all of which can potentially be accessed through our mobile phones: popular cinema, artists' films and videos, documentary, YouTube videos, and others. One might view these diverse image-types collectively as a demographic marked by commonality and difference, constituting a Republic of Images.

Flashback to 6 December 1992: The Babri Masjid[1] is demolished by a mob of 1,50,000 'volunteers' (*kar sevaks*) led by prominent members of the Bharatiya Janata Party (BJP). Television channels broadcast images of the mob dancing in jubilation, to a vengeful cacophony. The Mediastorm Collective's documentary film, *Kiska Dharm, Kiska Desh* (Whose Country Is it Anyway?) was made just a year before this damning episode. 'We decided to place the Babri Masjid dispute at the centre but sought to understand its reverberations across the country', says Medistorm in their essay in this volume. 'Eleven years after our documentary, we saw the worst carnage ever in the history of independent India – the 2002 pogrom in Gujarat[2] led by the state government. Many asked Mediastorm to rush to Gujarat to make a film on the violence and trauma of the riots. But we just could not. The time for neat analysis was over – Gujarat had rocked the country to its core. We were no longer sure if a documentary could even remotely capture the violence and terror of 2002. *Perhaps a new form was required for this*' (emphasis mine).

Soon after the horrifying pogrom of 2002, the BJP was defeated and a progressive alliance of left and secular parties led by the Congress formed the government in 2004. It was a jubilant respite. Geeta Kapur's essay on the transformative potential of the 'critical documentary' is written in this hopeful moment. She issues a clarion call to artists to essay the role of 'artist-citizens,' referencing a longer trajectory of the avant-garde, and asks provocatively, 'is culture what artists make?' The question bears reflection nearly two decades on, as the populist narrative justifying the destruction of constitutional values, public institutions, mob violence and vigilantism is fuelled by a mediatized propaganda of the seditious desires of an elite class termed variously as 'anti-nationals', 'pseudo-intellectuals', 'painted and dented women' and 'urban naxals'.[3] The answer to Kapur's question – as argued by cultural theorists – is that culture resides within the quotidian and the ordinary, and is created by and belongs to everyone.

The texts and images selected are demonstrative of the making and re-making of culture (through cinema and the visual arts), as practices grounded in complex negotiations with the state, history, memory, capital, desire, technology, prejudice, law, body, power, ethics and hope. In keeping with the objectives of the *India Since the 1990s* series, the anchoring triad of space, politics and technology has determined the logic of selection. The authors, filmmakers and artists who have so generously permitted reproduction of their work will, I hope, also indulge its repurposed use in the volume. Readers are urged to view/read the texts and images in this volume as 'documents of the present', and, notwithstanding the intentional arrangement, are invited to draw their own conclusions.

Other Ways of Seeing

Three sections and two inserts make up the totality of the book. The first insert is a visual essay with a brief commentary on 'the Cinema of Prayoga' by film historian and curator Amrit Gangar, who coined the term in 2005 as a rejection of terms like 'experimental' and 'avant-garde'.[4] An unlikely candidate interrupts the assemblage of filmmakers he usually associates with the term. This is a one-page facsimile of an article by the filmmaker Saeed Akhtar Mirza, published in 1980, where he makes a sensational statement: that 'a certain kind of cinema exists only because a certain kind of State exists.' States are not culturally naive, says Mirza, and exist to perpetuate the interests and rule of certain groups over others. The second insert, 'The Trial', elaborates upon this further by way of a 2004 judgement issued by the Bombay High court on Anand Patwardhan's documentary, *War and Peace*. Patwardhan, a towering figure of Indian documentary, has quite literally taken the state by its horns, turning to constitutional rights time and again, defending freedom of expression, and in the process, expanding the legal interpretation of the term 'freedom of expression' itself.

Gangar, the Prayoga filmmakers, Mirza and Kapur speak to each other's - often divergent - reflections on the relationship between aesthetic form, state control and political art. They are joined by other voices in the second section of the book, titled 'Artist as Citizen'. That these are female voices is an editorial choice I have made. Featured here are multi-media artist Sheba Chhachhi; documentary filmmakers Deepa Dhanraj and Paromita Vohra; theatre director and filmmaker Anamika Haksar; visual artists Pushpamala N. and Sharmila Samant; new media artist Afrah Shafiq; and documentary directors and film theorists, the Mediastorm Collective.

Mediastorm, started in the mid-1980s, was (they say) an 'accidental' formation, created in spontaneous response to the Muslim Women's (Protection of Rights Under Divorce) Bill, enacted following the Shah Bano case (of a 62-year-old woman who claimed alimony after being divorced by her husband under Muslim Personal Law). In 1983, the Yugantar Film Collective was founded by Deepa Dhanraj along with friends. Stills from her films *Molkarin/Maid Servant* (1981, 16 mm), and *Something Like a War* (1991, 16 mm) - now part of a major digitization project by the Arsenal Film Archive, Berlin - feature in the volume. Speaking of another documentary (on the 1984 riots between Hindus and Muslims in the city of Hyderabad), believed lost and now being restored at Arsenal, Dhanraj says it had scratch marks even on the negatives. 'At one point, we were filming a riot, and some men threw a very compact ball of vermilion - they had made it like a little rock, like a missile - straight at the lens. [Cinematographer] Navroze [Contractor] didn't stop shooting. . . . The vermilion entered the lens and the magazines, there were scratches, and we kept it all in. . . . These are material questions, but they're also theoretical questions.'[5]

All major movements in modern history have rallied around the right to representation, the right to 'be seen and heard', none more forcefully than the feminist movement. A consensus that 'the master's house cannot be dismantled with the master's tools' (as Black American writer and civil rights activist Audrey Lorde phrased it) demanded a *new idiom* and *form*, true to the experiences of women (or any other 'identity community'). Paromita Vohra creates a first-person fictional narrator who is often uncertain, vulnerable and even unreliable. 'The idea of a created person, who moreover is a capricious character, strong in personality, overtly performative and hence a bit unreliable, creates, I believe, two dynamics', she says. 'First, it does not compel the subjects in the film to an obvious personal intimacy with the filmmaker. Second, it also demands from those in the audience an intimacy of engagement. . . . This demand also arises from the fact that the narrator is obviously an unreliable, prejudiced or half-informed character who is not grounding the viewer.' Vohra's article is punctuated by multi-media artist Afrah Shafiq's interactive website inspired by the 1905 Bengali short science fiction story 'Sultana's Dream' by Rokeya Sakhawat Hossain. Shafiq's project emerges from her research at the Centre for Studies in Social Sciences (CSSS) archive in Calcutta. Using archival material, she creates an interactive audio-visual account of the infamous 'women's question' in nineteenth-century colonial India with playful, irreverent characters who speak for themselves and join the 'first persons' of Vohra's documentary pursuits.

The mythic depiction of women is often a direct consequence of a denial of individuality, something that defines the work of both Nalini Malani and Pushpamala N. In Pushpamala's *Indrajaal/The Seduction* (2012, b&w, silent, 4 min 30 sec, looped video), the conflict between lead characters of the *Ramayana* (Rama and Ravana) is transferred on to a performative encounter between their siblings, Lakshmana and Surpanakha. In a revenge episode, Lakshmana cuts off Surpanakha's nose, in retaliation for Ravana's abduction of Sita. As blood gushes out of Surpanakha's (performed by Pushpamala herself) nose, the video completes its loop and a dancing Lakshmana appears on screen again. 'I am interested in the citational mode as a way of delving into a kind of collective memory, or modern folklore', explains Pushpamala. 'By being in the work, I insert a specific subjectivity and my own modern sensibility into the picture, and break the codes.[6] One is inside the image, not just outside, looking.'[7] Pushpamala's work has been interpreted in many ways: as postmodern feminist art, and photo-performance and video art, that works variously through 'masquerade', 'gestus', 'fetish', 'citation' and 'iconophilia'.[8]

Malani's use of citation and mythology has been widely written about.[9] Her article in this volume, 'Can You Hear Me?', reflects upon her animation work, ranging from 8 mm film in *Dream Houses* (1969) to iPad animations in *Notebooks* (2017 onwards). 'The many issues that I think of and want to talk about in these *Notebooks* animations come from a wide range of stimuli. This could be daily politics, other people's writings, or something mundane I might have just experienced.' '*Why does Modernism form such a threat in these days of growing orthodoxy? Why limit the freedom of the other?*', Malani ponders, adding, 'In the face of extreme domination by the state there is no way out of the darkness but to find a language in satire even as one squirms around trying to find ways to look for the light.' Her question-statement, 'Can you hear me?' begs a return query: *Who is being spoken to? Who is the audience, the spectator, the listener here?*

The 'spectator' is a densely theorized figure in cinema studies, although art history (not visual studies) has conventionally been more interested in the art and the artist. Multi-media artists Sheba Chhachhi and Sharmila Samant have been invested in taking their work to diverse audiences, the people. Samant, known for her community-based and activist work (along with the late Tushar Joag), started Open Circle, a platform to establish dialogue and collaborate with non-artists, setting up art shows at several unconventional public venues.

Nancy Adajania's essay on Sheba Chhachhi highlights an adventurous trajectory, which she suggests is crucial in understanding Chhachhi's art. Her experiments with 'staged portraits' and her interest in female ascetics and dissident and subaltern spiritual traditions have produced powerful images of women, the women's movement, collectives, and a possibility of articulating resistance on feminist terms. Adajania places this within her own long-standing inquiry into constructing the 'pre-history' of new media or inter-medial art in India.[10] She draws our attention to works produced by Chhachhi, each one experimenting with different modes of exhibition and production, often in public spaces like malls, slums, museums, community centres and highways.

Three Films and a Trip: Gods, Horses, Eyes

Readers are invited to navigate the book as they might an exhibition. While the contents have been classified into three sections, several of the texts and images can be read against the grain, and in a sequential logic completely different to the order of their presentation. The three lead images for each section, for example, form their own parallel narrative. The images are: a still from Mochu's *Cool Memories of Remote Gods* (2017, 14' 48' digital video); a frame from Anamika Haksar's *Ghode ko Jalebi Khilane Le Ja Riya Hoon* (Taking the Horse to Eat Jalebis, 2018);[11] and montaged frames from Avijit Mukul Kishore's film *Squeeze Lime in Your Eye* (2017).

The common thread (I see) running through the three films is that they are psychedelic in their ambition; they straddle reality, fantasy, dreams, desires and memories, blurring them to etch out a sharpened relationship between image and reality, history and the present. Set in the remnants of hippie trails in India, *Cool Memories* documents the fading traces of 1960s counterculture groups as a phenomenon contemporaneous with the development of the personal computer and cybernetics. Mochu sets off on a search to find residues of this spiritual-techno-fictional past. A still from the film opens the Raqs Media Collective's essay in this volume, 'Now and Elsewhere', on the 'contemporary'. The trails reveal a decaying corpse,' says Mochu, 'one with a vampiric ambition.' As computers promised machines to replace the human mind, counterculture desired to recreate mystical experience as customizable 'internal technologies'. The Woodstock generation's dream of universal harmony lay reduced to psychedelic posters, cheap reworks of surrealist paintings and new age mixes of religio-techno-fusion music, as shown in the video.

Anamika Haksar welds together documentary footage, animation, special effects, folk art and devised theatre, to address an incredibly challenging subject: the precarious lives of people living in abject poverty.[12] She explains the complex processes that went into the making of the film, which included seven years of grounded research in Shahjahanabad (Old Delhi), the decision to use theatre and the visual arts (visual artist Archana Shashtri was a close collaborator on the film), and instructions to the editor, Paresh Kamdar, to 'keep the randomness in the edit'.[13] 'The lives of the homeless and marginalized are so unpredictable and precarious, it's impossible to depict them through narrative logic', says Haksar. In the image used in the volume, a Lenin-inspired cart-loader (played by the actor Gopalan) who aspires to be a workers' union leader is seen towering above a city square, unfurling a gigantic red communist flag. In the square stand hundreds of workers, singing revolutionary songs. However, the dream of the great revolution doesn't materialize, and instead the film is strewn with minor acts of subversion, often enacted as dreams or fantasy. Mickey Mouse distributes sweets in a remand home, a pick-pocket runs along an unending parapet, a labourer bottles up his *malik* (master) in a glass jar.

The final image, in the continuum of the three that open each section, is a montage of modified frames from *Squeeze Lime in Your Eye*. Cinematographer and documentary filmmaker Avijit Mukul Kishore turns to Kausik Mukhopadhyay, who migrated from Santiniketan,[14] Bengal, to Mumbai and started making art out of discarded mechanical objects. He collects, fixes and repurposes household objects (toasters, telephones, bulbs, printers, computer keyboards, monitors and so on), bringing them back to life as playful kinetic sculptures. Poet and critic Ranjit Hoskote's catalogue essay on the film states: 'Riffing on the scientific working model and the booby trap as they do, these fantastic, seemingly whimsical ensembles refuse to sit still. . . . Calibrations of speed, an interplay of the regular and the erratic, a counterpoint between anticipation and unpredictability are integral to the performance: for these kinetic sculptures play their role in an eccentric ballet or marionette dance of mechanical and cybernetic objects.'[15] In this volume, Mukhopadhyay (and Mukul Kishore's film) pay homage to the millions of workers in informal and quasi-legal media economies who recycle, repurpose and copy analogue and digital content and media infrastructures, for reasons of passion as well as for livelihood.

Shanghai Express to the Future

The third section of the book, 'Post Cinematic Flows', addresses 'new' media cultures which emerged post liberalization when the flow of goods, technologies and capital began to travel across national borders more easily. The impact of the opening of the media economy – from one national television channel in 1991 to hundreds of options via satellite and cable television – led to radically globalized desires and fantasies of consumption. Concomitantly, it generated an intense anxiety about the erasure of 'cultural values' that popular cinema (rebranded as 'Bollywood') monetized, extending its markets to the diaspora, which now constituted its preferred balcony audience. Two interesting imaginations of cinema's audiences emerged at this time: the 'diaspora film', referring to the large-budget, star-studded film shot in North America or Europe, professing conservative 'Indian' cultural values appealing to nostalgic non-residential Indians (NRIs); and the 'multiplex film', used to describe films, often made in English or Hinglish, displaying an urban-cosmopolitan sensibility, with 'non-star' actors, produced on relatively smaller budgets, for an elite and English-speaking audience small enough to fill a multiplex hall. Unequivocally, the figures representing both these imaginaries of market and audience were Bollywood's biggest star, Shah Rukh Khan, and Calcutta's rugby player, Rahul Bose. The old tussle between Bengal and Bombay (cinema) had returned in a new form.

As Indian cities, and indeed Indian cinema – now well into twenty-first century circuits of global, capitalist aspirations – rushed headlong into a quest for a makeover, both faced the question of direction; where do they want to go next? Urban planners dreamt of a glitzy metropolitan skyline evacuated of slums, as Sharmila Samant's film *Shanghai Tales* (2006) critiques.[16] Inner-city areas of Mumbai, including Girangaon, home to the fierce 1980s textile mill workers' strikes, were lying derelict and seen to be in need of redevelopment. Fearing a piecemeal approach by the development authorities, a group of urban planners and architects began a study of the city's existing infrastructure. The *Gentricity* project by Ranjit Kandalgaonkar, Saurabh Vaidya and Aditya Potluri was produced as a response to this survey, to portray the 'strange contradictions, unique patterns and peculiar forms of existence' that were already in place among the communities residing in these neighbourhoods.

Previously (publicly) undisplayed images from the *Gentricity* series illustrate Ashish Rajadhyaksha's essay, which, in asking searching questions about 'cinema's future', issues a checkmate prognosis to cinema. Bombay cinema, he says, is held back by an 'analogue cultural memory, which prevents it from becoming its VFX-heavy, digital superhero ego ideal'. Referencing Indian cinema's biggest superheroes – Shah Rukh Khan and Rajinikanth – he turns to what he sees as the 'signature achievement of Indian cinema studies', i.e. the link between cinema, everyday life and politics. '*Cinema stands at the cusp of narrative, apparatus and citizenship*. . . . Today, the Indian superhero's ability to walk through walls fundamentally depends on the skill of the *spectator* to manoeuvre the star-hero through them. If the fan fails, the hero too must' (p. 236).

Meanwhile, We the People

In the meanwhile, elsewhere, fans had become cinephiles and producers. Multiple local media industries had begun to flourish across smaller towns in India in the new millennium. These new sites of media production stake their own 'right to representation' on a form of cinephilia.[17] Madhuja Mukherjee's essay describes the production of low-budget films in the districts of Purulia and Bankura in West Bengal. Manbhum, explains Mukherjee, represents both language and land/location, and contrary to popular assumption, a map of 'Bengali cinema' would include videos in the Manbhum, Santhali, Nepali and Rajabhangsi languages, in addition to films in Bengali that 'flow outside cinema theatres, beyond both national and global copyright regulations'. Inserted in Mukherjee's essay are stills from Faiza Ahmed Khan's documentary film, *Supermen of Malegaon* (2012), responsible, perhaps single-handedly, for generating popular and critical interest in Malegaon as a *phenomenon*.[18] The Malegaon film industry, located around 300 kms from Bombay/Mumbai, was subsequently theorized variously as an example of exuberant cinephilia through spoofs and remakes, and as a multi-sited spatial network of trade and economic systems.[19] Manbhum videos, Malegaon spoofs and the meteoric rise of smaller industries – like Bhojpuri cinema after Manoj Prasad's 2001 film, *Saiyya Hammar* (My Sweetheart) – are collectively taken to indicate the growing inability of pan-Indian cinema to address its once-upon-a-time national publics.

Its increasingly dispersed publics include, as we see in S.V. Srinivas's essay, internet and television audiences repurposing cultural forms associated with earlier Maoist movements in Telangana's long history of political struggle from the 1940s. 'How can emerging patterns of media consumption help us to understand today's mass politics?', asks Srinivas, suggesting that, 'What we are witnessing is not the evisceration of the original or the death of the cinema but the transition to a new situation and the emergence of new locations and modes of publicness' (p. 292).

The 'public' is a very special category of film-viewers, quite distinct from the fan, spectator or audience. The spectator can be a singular entity or a part of a gathering; the fan can be an individual but derives agency only as part of a collective club; the audience is always plural and consists of anonymous members which cultural ethnographers have attempted to inject with identity. The public, in contrast, is always multiple, and is perceived to be discerning, all-knowing, and wielding subtle powers over that which they are public of. The gravity of the nomenclature was conveyed in popular idiom by a song from the film *Roti* (Bread, dir. Manmohan Desai), released in 1974, just a year before the Emergency was declared: *'yeh jo public hai woh sab jaanti hai'* (the public knows all). Geeta Patel's text interrogates the sentiment of public protests against the film *Fire* (1996, dir. Deepa Mehta), for its portrayal of a homoerotic relationship. The protests came from a variety of publics: right-wing Hindutva groups who claimed that homosexuality was alien to Hindu culture, and queer groups who stated that the film's portrayal of lesbianism was deeply problematic. Patel reflects upon the opposition the film faced from young female students of Indian origin in North America - the diasporic public - who were outraged by the film's representation of 'Indian masculinity'. Referencing a parallel strand of 1998–99 parliamentary debates on the opening up of the insurance industry to foreign investment and the episodic blows to secularism through the 1990s, she extrapolates the risk, usually attached to the individual body, to that of the body politic now including the public who expresses collective indignation. This, says Patel, forms the idea of the 'culturally immutable' nation, entrusted to protection by the public and, in turn, guarding the public from possible (external) danger.

The Trial

The two major aspects of legislation around cinema are concerned with the regulation of the image itself (censorship and freedom of expression) and the regulation of the circulation of the image (copyright and intellectual property).

Censorship regulations are grounded in a peculiar imaginary of 'another - less able - person' who needs to be protected from 'potential harm, hurt or corruption'.[20] At the root of this imagination is a world divided into adult-like, discerning individuals and infantile others who need to be guarded from a speculative danger. Orders issued in two court cases have been included here as inserts, signifying the judicial courts as performative sites where the aesthetic limits of cinema are shaped. One is the controversial 1970 Supreme Court judgement by Justice Hidayatullah in Khwaja Ahmed Abbas's petition against

The Union of India, for the complete removal of film censorship. The second is a 2003 petition by Anand Patwardhan against the Censor Board. The texts of the two judgements together reveal the subjective mechanisms through which the law is interpreted and its provisions extrapolated. It can be debated *ad nauseam* about whose reason determines the scope of the 'reasonable restrictions' clause in Article 19(2) of the Constitution.

Copyright regulations emerge from the logic of property, with potential for monetization. In April 2008, Warner Brothers Entertainment Inc. filed a case in the Delhi High Court against the proprietor of Cinema Paradiso, on grounds of copyright infringement. Cinema Paradiso, claimed Warner Bros, was violating copyright law by renting out in India, DVDs bought in North America and Europe. Earlier, in 2002, Time Warner Entertainment Company Ltd had filed a case, along with seven of the world's largest media conglomerates, against Arun Kumar Gupta, the proprietor of Lamhe: The Music Shop, a small DVD and CD outlet in Greater Kailash I, New Delhi. The plaintiffs included, in addition to Time Warner, Hollywood's most powerful production houses: Columbia Pictures, Disney, Metro-Goldwyn-Mayer, Paramount, Tristar, Twentieth Century Fox and Universal Studios. What possible threat could a small CD/DVD rental shop in Delhi pose to these media giants? Jeebesh Bagchi's essay refers to the 2002 Time Warner case, citing the affidavit filed by the corporation: 'It is alleged that even a single rental of a film by the Defendant is capable of causing irreparable injury and damage to the plaintiffs. . . . The potential for damage is immeasurable and irreparable' (p. 223). Addressing the paralysing anxiety around the regulation of the cinematic object and, by extension, cinema's publics, he argues that the 'prohibitory sign' curtails lived practices of quotidian creativity in media and technological improvisation within the 'shadow city'.[21] The media, he writes, is haunted by the fear of 'a spectre': the *leaky, rapidly circulating, sensorium of cinematic affect and objects dispersed across material and digital forms, produced by the 'fecund copy'*. 'The vitality, dynamism, conflict and inventiveness visible in this social world demands a more complex description of the entanglement of technologies, subjectivity and desire' (p. 218). Bagchi focuses on informal economies of media production running from makeshift tenements, and the ecology of the 'copy' as digital objects that threaten to escape their legally sanctioned habitat, the copyrighted CD or DVD. Lawrence Liang's essay on the *digileak* picks up precisely this question of the metamorphosis of analogue cinema into its digital avatar.

Archives of History

'As time passes,' say Raqs Media Collective, 'the reasons for remembering other times grow, while the ability to recall them weakens. Memory straddles this paradox. We could say that the ethics of memory have something to do with the urgent negotiation between having to remember (which sometimes includes the obligation to mourn), and the requirement to move on (which sometimes includes the need to forget). Both are necessary, and each is notionally contingent on the abdication of the other' (p. 9). All six essays in the first section, 'Remembrance and Forgetting', are acts of remembrance narrated from points in time in the future. The past is a time left behind, which can only exist in the present through objects that have outlived it, or through memories that struggle to pull it back into consciousness in the form of images and emotions. In another sense, the past is that which has disappeared or 'gone past the eyes'. 'What does disappearance do to the telling of that which has disappeared?' asks Raqs (p. 9). The central object of disappearance posited in this section is cinema (or film) itself. How do we narrate the history of film, after film?

Documentary filmmaker R.V. Ramani asks this question through a moving note on his chance encounter with the 2004 tsunami. Coincidence has emerged as a major aesthetic underwriting Ramani's films, making his work deeply contingent on time. He battled the waves, desperately trying to hold on to his Sony PD 100, as his essay here documents. Seven years later he made a film in memory of his camera, *My Camera and Tsunami* (2011). Ramani's memoir and his *Tsunami* film illuminate crucial challenges that historians of Indian cinema have faced: *how to construct a moving image history in the absence of legitimate documents, of well-preserved prints, of archives themselves?*[22]

Sudhir Mahadevan takes us on a flashback with three possible answers to this potentially paralysing question. The first through Kamal Swaroop's *Tracing Phalke* (2013), which chronicles the filmmaker's journey in search of D.G. Phalke (known as the 'father of Indian cinema'). Merging documentary, re-enactment and archival research, Swaroop creates an experimental film and a historical record. The second protagonist is the Indian-American director Krishna Shah, who dreamt of a cross-over between Hollywood and Bollywood way back in the 1960s. In 1979 he directed *Cinema Cinema*: a flashback of film history narrated through a fictional film screening to impassioned audiences of the single screen theatre, who are 'interactive, haptic, profoundly engaged and resolutely social' (p. 34). The final protagonist is the unremarkable director Hiren Nag, who made a one-film-wonder with *Film Hi Film* (1983). Strung together as a dramatized account of a producer's desperate struggle to make films, it weaves in 'unused' and incomplete sequences from films (recovered from various studios) that were begun but could never be completed or released. It constructs a history of cinema through found footage, repurposing the footage from junk into a meta-narrative. Taking the archive as a heuristic, Mahadevan describes cinema's propensity to make its own past through relentless reuse rather than preservation. *Film Hi Film* reminds us of the possibilities of the 'reserve' – that which is not yet deployed – as outlined by Pad.ma in their sharp manifesto on the digital archive, placed as an Epilogue to this volume. The millions of hours of CCTV footage, says Pad.ma, are not just leftovers of the surveillance machine. They are its constitutive accumulation, the mass that awaits the event. The archive in this sense is sympathetic to practices which sabotage capitalist accumulation, and which have an interest in the future: in the 'unrealized'.

Sebastian Lütgert aka Robert Luxemberg – one of the authors of 'Ten Theses on the Archive' – contributes a cryptic note, densely strewn with references to personal friendships. Along with collaborators, he transforms cinema into both data and painting, in the process of creating an archive that beckons the possibility of property as a commons, generating surplus through distribution rather than accumulation. Lütgert's account within the narrative unfolding in this book can be seen as both a dream and a promise.

Return of the Repressed

Indian cinema, from its infancy, has battled self-doubt and an acute anxiety about living up to an imaginary ideal of 'quality'. Film magazines and debates in newspapers and periodicals are replete with analysis of 'what ails Indian cinema'. This has been an obsession for Bombay cinema in particular, forever fretting about its inferiority to Bengali films. Bengali cinema, on the other hand, has borne the historical burden of 'taste', which, Subhajit Chatterjee's article might suggest, continues to be a legacy it battles. Taking readers into the seedy bylanes of exploitation cinema, Chatterjee's interview with the Ghosh brothers (the most prolific producers of this genre in Bengal) explains the production economy of these low-budget remakes. History here is not told, but retold. Could this be the final fantasy of contemporary Bengali cinema? The pursuit of liberation from its cultural history, possible perhaps only through reincarnation?

In an inverted situation, Darshana Sreedhar Mini writes about Malayalam cinema's desperate attempts to erase its embarrassing past. The dark secrets that must be concealed, in the manner of a *film noir*, refer to soft-porn films from the 1980s and 90s. Her essay deploys K.R. Manoj's film *Kanyaka Talkies* (Virgin Theatre, 2013) as a first-person narrator, telling the story of the irrepressible history of celluloid soft porn.

One of the repeating images used in this volume, and particularly in the article by Raqs, is a frame grab from the famous song from K. Asif's magnum opus, *Mughal-e-Azam* (1960). In this song, Anarkali (played by Madhubala) declares her love for Prince Salim (Dilip Kumar), and has to pay for such audacity of a 'mere slave girl' by being buried alive behind brick walls. Elsewhere one has argued that Anarkali may indeed be the irrepressible uncanny of history, resurfacing repeatedly, sometimes as a meme and at other times as a spectre.[23]

Let us return to the question: what does disappearance do to the *telling* of that which has disappeared? The 'telling' here becomes an act of crucial intervention, keeping that which seems to have gone past the eyes alive in other ways. One of the irrefutable disappearances with the phasing out of celluloid film is the bond between image and reality, what Geeta Kapur suggests one might view as 'spectres without footprints crisscrossing the threshold of objectivity' (p. 139). What is erased is a clearly mapped relationship between world and image. A new contractual arrangement between the material world, image, meaning and representation takes on fluid forms, where the image is larger than life, and life itself is part of and smaller than the image. This creates an 'enmeshed view', comprising multiple components that piece together a perspective that is simultaneously an aerial shot and a close-up, telescopic and microscopic, resting on the surface of the skin and piercing through it.

Kaushik Bhaumik's conversation about Kashmir with the Desire Machine Collective (DMC) gives an uncanny and chilling account of such a sensorium. The conversation is triggered by an art installation about a theatre repurposed as a military camp. Cinema, the site of desire, is transformed into a location of violence. 'The cinematic apparatus is dismantled, but the seats remain . . . a theatre of the absurd is being played out in the dark, without an audience or any reference to time – delirious new ghostly images invoked anew where the flow is disrupted, the past disconnects from the present' (p. 91).

* * *

What new insights can a book on 'the moving image' reveal about history? The answer is in the epistemology of the moving image itself: what is the knowledge of images, what does the image know? In the long trek over centuries to what we have come to understand as 'modernity', the birth of cinema in the late nineteenth century ambushed the project of science; a double agent disguised as technology, or the first child of science. Cinema captured the irrational desires and fears of the modern world, masquerading as both document and narrative. It did so with great flourish and *élan* until its very substance, celluloid film, was overtaken by digital video, and a new relationship between 'world and image' was established. A history of the 'recent past' generated through the moving image as documentary evidence or archival record – as this volume attempts – yields anachronistic accounts saturated with time. Three ways of 'looking' have been demonstrated here. The first is cinema looking back at its own past, the second is women artists looking at and looking back at the world, and the third is the state looking at its publics as they return the gaze. The volume has been a long time in the making, and is marked deeply by the challenges posed to the sustenance of a seemingly normal life during a global pandemic. The characteristics of its time leave traces on any piece of writing, and the surreal rhythm of the two years that this book was in the making is stained across these pages.

A Note on Usage

Permission to reproduce has been received wherever possible. Use of all content here falls within the purview of fair use as stated in Sec. 52 of the Indian Copyright Act, 1957 (together with subsequent amendments). Use intended for research, criticism and review is within Article 13 of the Agreement on Trade-Related Aspects of Intellectual Property Rights (TRIPS), which includes fair use in cases that do not conflict with a normal exploitation of the work and do not unreasonably prejudice the legitimate interests of the right-holder as per Article 9(2) of the Berne Convention for the Protection of Literary and Artistic Works (1967), the WIPO Copyright Treaty and the EU Copyright Directive (1996). Such use is also protected by Section 107 of the Copyright Law of the United States of America as 'criticism, comment, scholarship, or research' that in no way damages the 'potential market for or value of the copyrighted work', and by Britain's 1988 Copyright, Designs and Patents Act (Chapter III, Section 28–29).

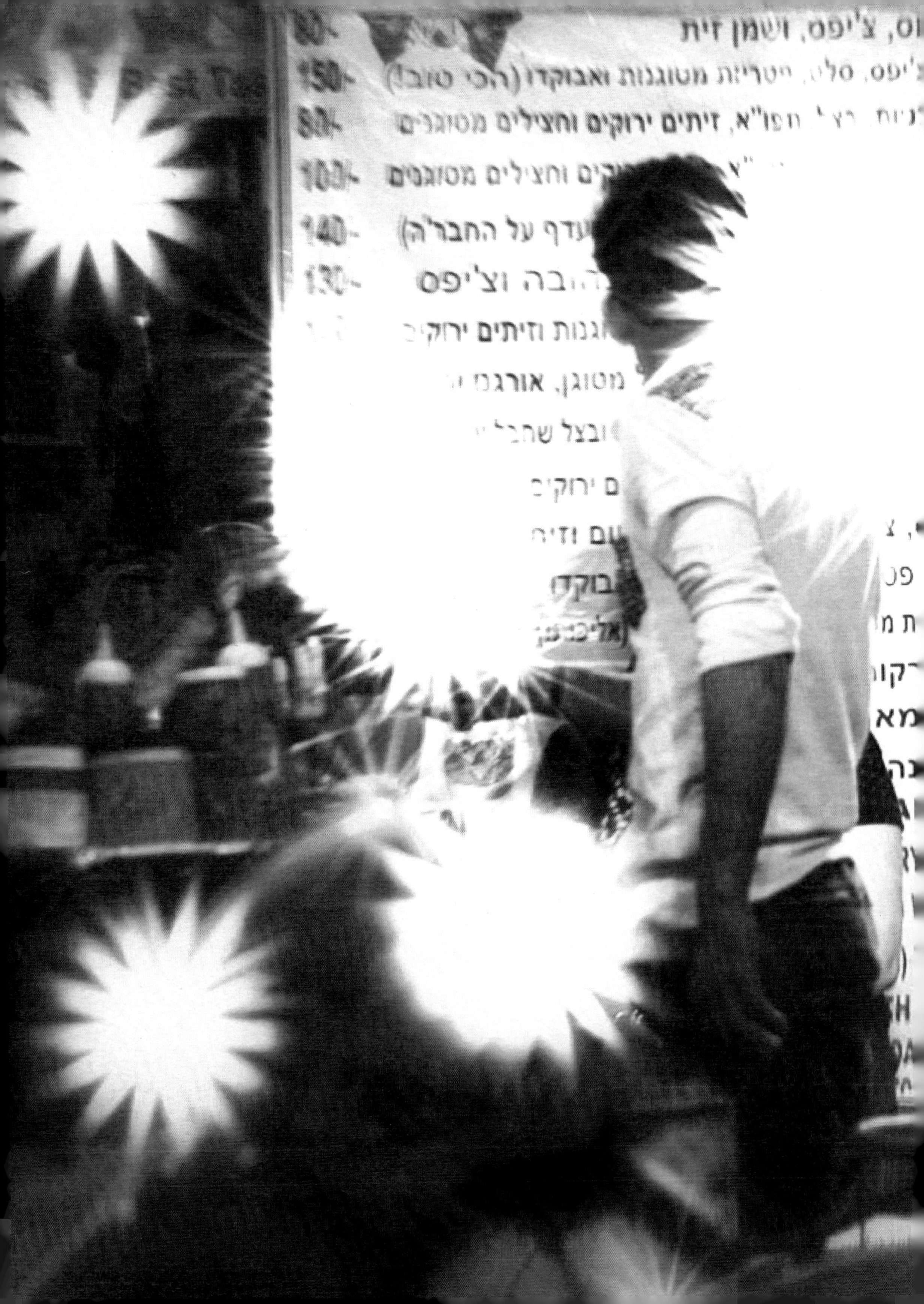

צ'יפס, ושמן זית
150- מטוגנות ואבוקדו (הכי טוב!)
80- זיתים ירוקים וחצילים מטוגנים
וחצילים מטוגנים
140- על החבר'ה)
130- וצ'יפס

remembrance and forgetting

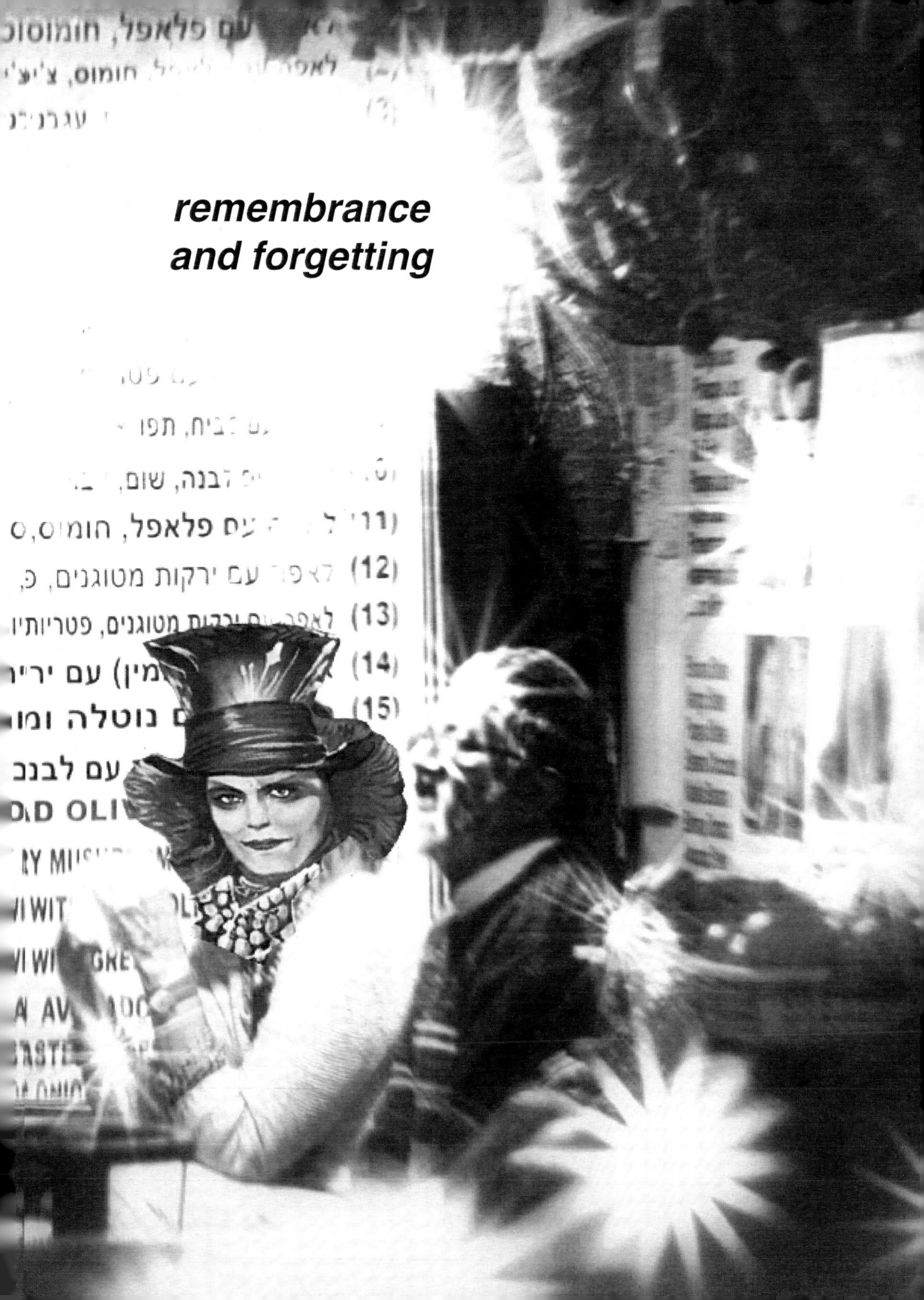

As a relentless chronometric measure of movement imposed for the first time ever on the planet, time places us in a condition that the Raqs Media Collective describes as a 'perennial jet lag'. The moving image is deeply marked by the 'modern experience of time' and 'escapement', a condition of layered plurality that, the authors suggest, allows for other experiences of the contemporary. The contemporary is a 'feeling', a 'thickening', a 'pull', that allows for a 'kinetic contemplation', they write. This text is placed here as a signpost that readers can return to now and again as they browse through the volume.

The essay refers to the Raqs Media Collective's exhibition, *Escapement,* at Frith Street Gallery, London, 8 July–30 September 2009. Originally published in *e-flux*, no. 12, January 2010. Reprinted with permission from *e-flux* and the authors – Shuddhabrata Sengupta, Jeebesh Bagchi and Monica Narula (Raqs Media Collective).

Keywords, Names

Documentary, Escapement, Tactical Media, (Rabindranath) Tagore: See Keywords (pp. 326–44).

Chin Chin Choo: Eponymous dancing girl performing a cabaret with sailors in an unnamed harbour, in Shakti Samanta's noir-crime thriller *Howrah Bridge* (1958). The song, picturized on Helen ('half-Burmese, half-Baghdadi-Jewish star and vamp of vintage Hindi film') speaks of a Chinese heart, a Singaporean youth and a languid grace from Shanghai, while being Alladdin's girl, set in Calcutta's waterfronts and dance bars.

Mughal-e-Azam (King of Kings, dir. K. Asif, 1960): Period film set in Mughal India; a love story between Prince Salim and 'slave girl' Anarkali. The original b&w film includes an extravagant colour dance-sequence inside a Palace of Mirrors, in which the courtesan's challenge to Emperor Akbar is reflected back in hundreds of mirrors.

Tagore in China: Veiled reference to Rabindranath Tagore's controversial 1923 visit to Beijing, where he was received with surprising and unexpected hostility. Tan Chung's writings, from which the authors quote, provide an elaborate account of his visits, his involvement with China, and the founding of the 'China Bhavan' in Santiniketan, the educational institution established by Tagore.

Images

p. 1: Still from Mochu's *Cool Memories of Remote Gods* (2017, 14' 48" digital video) from *Machinic Elixir*, which develops fictions and propositions based on mutations that followed the decay of the techno-utopian impulses of the 1960s and 70s.

p. 4: Montage of dance by Madhubala in *Mughal-e-Azam*, joined by French film director Joris Ivens.

p. 7: The whirling dance, a metaphor for the hallucinations of cinematic time, surrounds Chin Chin Choo.

p. 13: The dance is set against a montage of images defining early Indian cinema, of pleas with the god of death to return loved ones: D.G. Phalke's *Raja Harishchandra* (King Harishchandra, 1913) and Raja Ravi Varma's painting, *Satyavaan and Savitri* (1898). It includes a frame from Chris Marker's *La Jetée* (1962).

RAQS MEDIA COLLECTIVE 2010

The Old Man and the Wind: Joris Ivens's Film

At the very beginning of Joris Ivens and Marceline Loridan's film *Une histoire de vent* (*A Tale of the Wind*, 1988, French), we see a frail Joris Ivens sitting in a chair on a sand dune in the Gobi Desert, on the border between China and Mongolia, waiting for the arrival of a sandstorm.

Elsewhere in the film, an old woman – a wind shaman – talks about waiting for the wind.

Buffeted as we are by winds that blow from so many directions with such intensity, this image of an old man in a chair waiting for a storm is a metaphor for a possible response to the question, 'What is contemporaneity?'

It takes stubbornness, obstinacy, to face a storm, and yet also a desire not to be blown away by it. If Paul Klee's *Angelus Novus*, celebrated in Benjamin's evocation of the angel of history, with its head caught in turning between the storm of the future and the debris of the present, were ever in need of a more recent annotation, then old man Ivens in his chair, waiting for the wind, would do very nicely.

It is tempting to think of this dual obstinacy – to face the storm and not be blown away – as an acute reticence that is at the same time a refusal to either run away from or be carried away by the strong winds of history, of time itself.

We could see this 'reticence', this 'refusal to historicize' as a form of escape from the tyranny of the clock and the calendar – instruments to measure time, and to measure our ability to keep time, to keep to the demands of the time allotted to us by history, our contemporaneity. Any reflection on contemporaneity cannot avoid simultaneously being a consideration of time, and of our relation to it.[1]

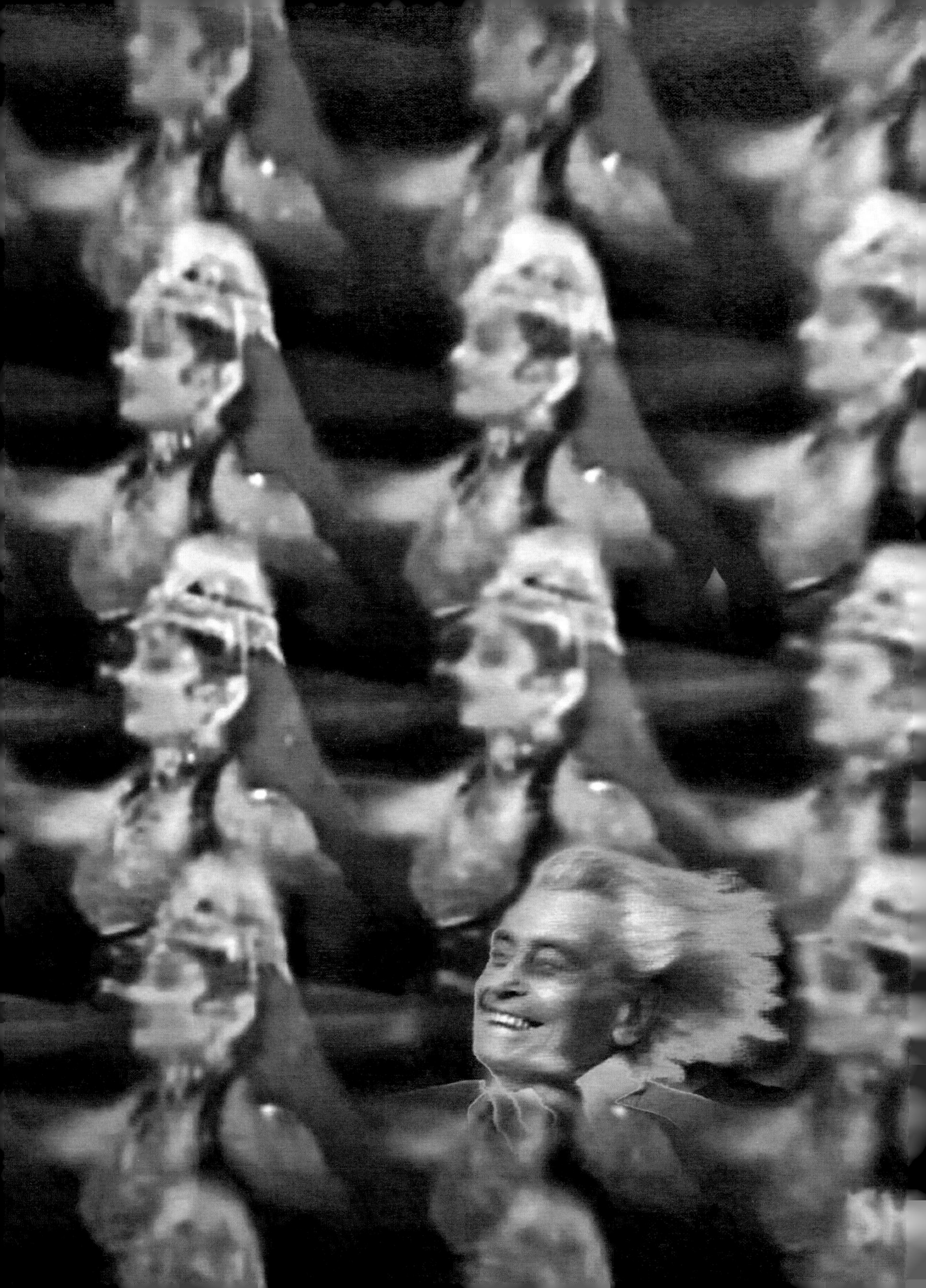

On Time

Time girds the earth tight. Day after day, astride minutes and seconds, the hours ride as they must, relentlessly. In the struggle to keep pace with clocks, we are now always and everywhere in a state of jet lag, always catching up with ourselves and with others, slightly short of breath, slightly short of time.

The soft insidious panic of time ticking away in our heads is syncopated by accelerated heartbeat of our everyday lives. Circadian rhythms (times to rise and times to sleep, times for work and times for leisure, times for sunlight and times for stars) get muddled as millions of faces find themselves lit by timeless fluorescence that trades night for day. Sleep is besieged by wakefulness, hunger is fed by stimulation, and moments of dreaming and lucid alertness are eroded with the knowledge of intimate terrors and distant wars.

When possible, escape is up a hatch and down a corridor between and occasionally beyond longitudes, to places where the hours chime epiphanies. *Escape* is a resonant word in the vocabulary of clockmaking. It gives us another word - *escapement*.

Escapement

Escapement is a horological or clockmaking term. It denotes the mechanism in mechanical watches and clocks that governs the regular motion of the hands through a 'catch and release' device that both releases and restrains the levers that move the hands for hours, minutes and seconds. Like the catch and release of the valves of the heart that allow blood to flow between its chambers, setting the basic rhythm of life, the escapement of a watch regulates our sense of the flow of time. The continued pulsation of our hearts and the ticking of clocks denote our freedom from an eternal present. Each heartbeat, each passing second marks the here and now, promises the future, and recalls the resonance of the last heartbeat. Our heart tells us that we live in time.

The history of clockmaking saw a definite turn when devices for understanding time shifted away from the fluid principles of ancient Chinese water and incense clocks - for which time was a continuum, thus making it more difficult to surgically separate past and present, then and now - to clocks whose ticking seconds rendered a conceptual barricade between each unit, its predecessor, and its follower. This is what makes *now* seem so alien to *then*.

Paradoxically, it opens out another zone of discomfort. Different places share the same time because of the accident of longitude. Thus, clocks in London and Lagos (with adjustments made for daylight savings) show the same time. And yet, the experience of 'now' in London and Lagos may not feel the same at all.

An escape from – or, one might say, a full-on willingness to confront – this vexation might be found by taking a stance in which one is comfortable with the fact that we exist at the intersection of different latitudes and longitudes, and that being located on this grid, we are in some sense phatically in touch with other times, other places. In a syncopated sort of way, we are 'contemporaneous' with other times and spaces.

My Name is Chin Chin Choo

In *Howrah Bridge*, a Hindi film-noir thriller from 1958 set in a cosmopolitan Calcutta (which, in its shadowy grandeur resembled the Shanghai of the jazz age), a young dancer, the half-Burmese, half-Baghdadi-Jewish star and vamp of vintage Hindi film, Helen, plays a Chinese bar-dancer. And in the song 'My Name is Chin Chin Choo', a big band jazz, kitsch orientalist and sailor-costumed musical extravaganza, she expresses a contemporaneity that is as hard to pin down as it is to avoid being seduced by.

The lyrics weave in the Arabian Nights, Aladdin and Sinbad; the singer invokes the bustle of Singapore and the arch trendiness of Shanghai; the music blasts a Chicago big band sound; the sailor-suited male backup dancers suddenly break into Cossack knee-bends. Times and spaces, cities and entire cultural histories – real or imagined – collide and whirl in heady counterpoint. Yesterday's dance of contemporaneity has us all caught up in its Shanghai–Calcutta–Delhi–Bombay–Singapore turbulence. We are all called Chin Chin Choo. Hello, mister, how do you do?

Contemporaneity

Contemporaneity, the sensation of being in a time together, is an ancient enigma of a feeling. It is the tug we feel when our time pulls at us. But sometimes one has the sense of a paradoxically asynchronous contemporaneity – the strange tug of more than one time and place – as if an accumulation or thickening of our attachments to different times and spaces were manifesting itself in the form of some unique geological oddity, a richly striated cross section of a rock, sometimes sharp, sometimes blurred, marked by the passage of many epochs.

Now and Elsewhere

The problem of determining the question of contemporaneity hinges on how we orient ourselves in relation to a cluster of occasionally cascading, sometimes overlapping, partly concentric and often conflictual temporal parameters – on

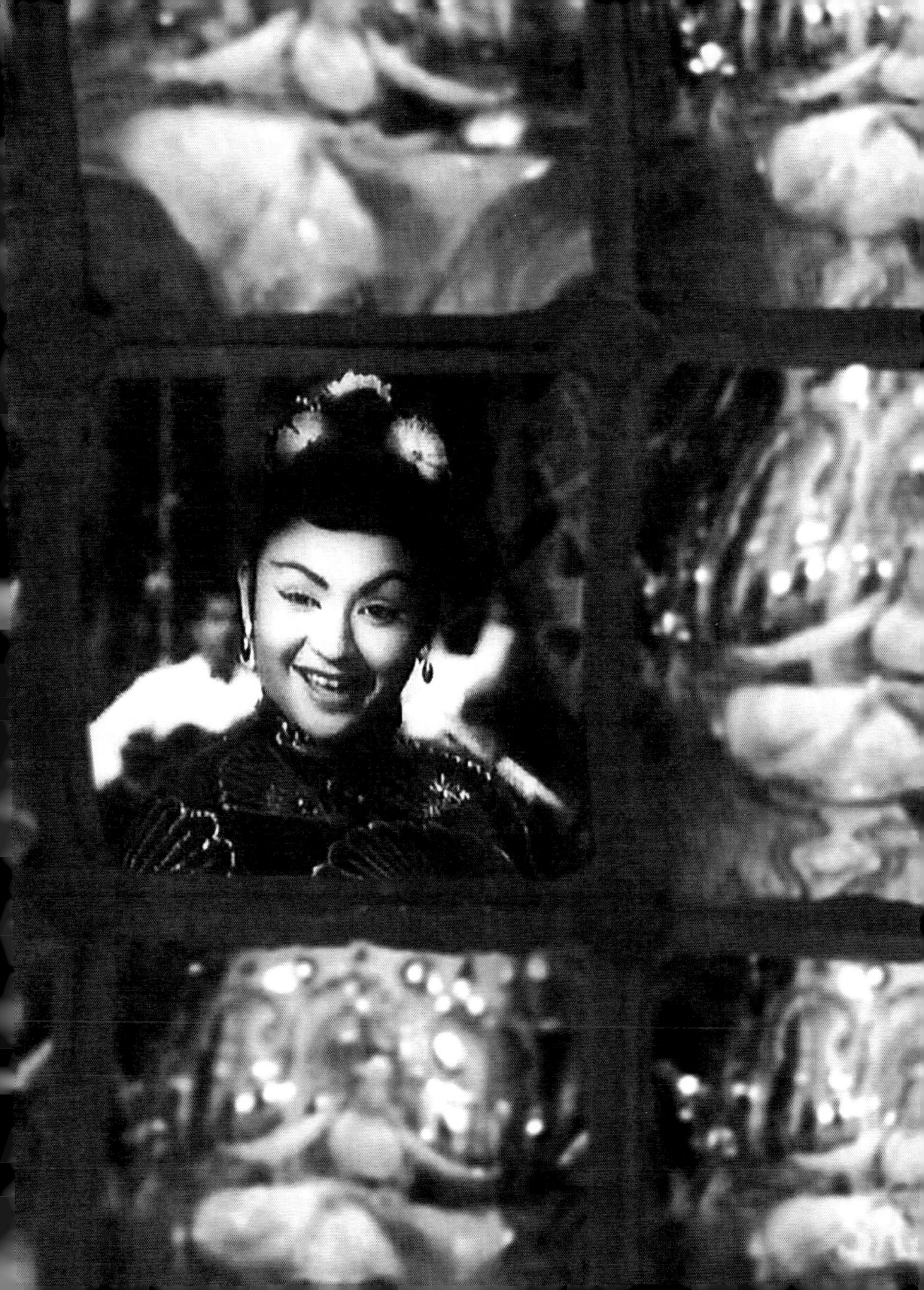

how urgent, how leisurely, or even how lethargic we are prepared to be in response to a spectrum of possible answers.

Consider the experience of being continually surprised by the surface and texture of the night sky when looking through telescopes of widely differing magnifications. Thinking about 'which contemporaneity' to probe is not very different from making decisions about how deep into the universe we would like to cast the line of our query. A telescope powerful enough to aid us in discerning the shapes and extent of craters on the moon will reveal a very different image of the universe than one that unravels the rings of Saturn, or one that can bring us the light of a distant star. The universe looks different, depending on the questions we ask of the stars.

Contemporaneity, too, looks different depending on the queries we put to time. If, as Zhou Enlai famously remarked, it is still too early to tell what impact the French Revolution has had on human history, then our sense of contemporaneity distends to embrace everything from 1789 onwards. If, on the other hand, we are more interested in sensing how things have changed since the internet came into our lives, then, even 1990 can seem a long way away. So can it seem as if it were only recently that the printing press and movable type made mechanical reproduction of words and images possible on a mass scale. One could argue that time changed once and for all when the universal regime of Greenwich Mean Time imposed a sense of an arbitrarily encoded universal time for the first time in human history, enabling everyone to calculate for themselves 'when', as in how many hours ahead or behind they were in relation to everyone at every other longitude. This birthed a new time, a new sense of being together in one accounting of time. One could also argue that, after Hiroshima made it possible to imagine that humanity as we know it could auto-destruct, every successive year began to feel as long as a hundred years, or as an epoch, since it could perhaps be our last. This means that, contrary to our commonplace understanding of our 'time' as being 'sped up', we could actually think of our time as being caught in the long 'winding down', the 'long decline'. It all depends, really, on what question we are asking.

And so, Marcel Duchamp can still seem surprisingly contemporary and Net art oddly dated. The moon landing, whose fortieth anniversary we have recently seen, brought a future of space travel hurtlingly close to the realities of 1969. Today, the excitement surrounding men on the moon has already acquired the patina of nostalgia, and the future it held out as a promise seems oddly dated. Then again, this could change suddenly if China and India were to embark in earnest on a second-wave Cold War space race to the moon. Our realities advance into and recede from contemporaneity like the tides, throwing strange flotsam and jetsam onto the shore to be found by beachcombers with a fetish for signs from different times. The question then becomes not one of 'periodizing' contemporaneity, or of erecting a neat white picket fence around it; rather, it becomes one of finding shortcuts, trapdoors, antechambers, and secret passages between now and elsewhere, or perhaps 'elsewhen'. Time folds, and it doesn't fold neatly – our sense of 'when' we are is a function of which fold we are sliding into, or climbing out of.

A keen awareness of contemporaneity cannot but dissolve the illusion that some things, people, places and practices are more 'now' than others. Seen this way, contemporaneity provokes a sense of the simultaneity of different modes of living and doing things without a prior commitment to any one as being necessarily more true to our times. Any attempt to design structures, whether permanent or provisional, that might express or contain contemporaneity would be incomplete if it were not (also) attentive to realities that are either not explicit or manifest or that linger as spectres. An openness and generosity toward realities that may be, or seem to be, in hibernation, dormant or still in formation, can only help such structures to be more pertinent and reflective. A contemporaneity that is not curious about how it might be surprised is not worth our time.

Tagore in China

In a strange and serendipitous echo from the past, we find Rabindranath Tagore, the Bengali poet and artist who in some sense epitomized the writing of different Asian modernities in the twentieth century, saying something quite similar exactly 85 years ago in Shanghai, at the beginning of what was to prove to be a highly contested and controversial tour of China.

The poet's (and here, all we need to do is to substitute 'artist' for 'poet') mission is to attract the voice which is yet inaudible in the air; to inspire faith in a dream which is unfulfilled; to bring the earliest tidings of the unborn flower to a skeptic world.[2]

Tagore's plea operates in three distinct temporal registers: the 'as yet inaudible' in the future, the 'unfulfilled dream' in the past and the fragility of the unborn flower in the skeptic world of the present. In each of these, the artist's work, for Tagore, is to safeguard and to take custody of – and responsibility for – that which is out of joint with its time, indeed with all time.

On Forgetting

As time passes and we grow more into the contemporary, the reasons for remembering other times grow, while the ability to recall them weakens. Memory straddles this paradox. We could say that the ethics of memory have something to do with the urgent negotiation between having to remember (which sometimes includes the obligation to mourn), and the requirement to move on (which sometimes includes the need to forget). Both are necessary, and each is notionally contingent on the abdication of the other, but life is not led by the easy rhythm of regularly alternating episodes of memory and forgetting, cancelling each other out in a neat equation that resolves itself and attains equilibrium.

Forgetting: the true vanity of contemporaneity. Amnesia: a state of forgetfulness unaware of both itself and its own deficiency. True amnesia includes forgetting that one has forgotten all that has been forgotten. It is possible to assume that one remembers everything and still be an amnesiac. This is because aspects of the forgotten may no longer occupy even the verge of memory. They may leave no lingering aftertaste or hovering anticipation of something naggingly amiss. The amnesiac is in solitary confinement, guarded by his own clones, yet secluded especially from himself.

Typically, forms of belonging and solidarity that rely on the categorical exclusion of a notional other to cement their constitutive bonds are instances of amnesia. They are premised on the forgetting of the many contrarian striations running against the grain of the moment and its privileged solidarity. On particularly bad days, which may or may not have to do with lunar cycles, as one looks into a mirror and is unable to recognize one's own image, the hatred of the other rises like a tidal bore. Those unfaithful patches of self are then rendered as so much negative space, like holes in a mirror. Instead of being full to the brim with traces of the other, each of them is seen as a void, a wound in the self.

This void where the self-authenticated self lies shadowed and unable to recognize itself is attributed to the contagious corrosiveness of the other. The forgetting of the emptying-out of the self by its own rage forms the ground from which amnesia assaults the world. In trying to assert who we are, we forget, most of all, who we are. And then we forget the forgetting.

Kowloon Walled City and its Memory

Nowhere, unless perhaps in dreams, can the phenomenon of the boundary be experienced in a more originary way than in cities. - Walter Benjamin.[3]

A few months ago, we spent some time in Hong Kong, learning what it means to live in a city that distils its contemporaneity into a refined amnesia. We were interested, in particular, by what happened to the walled city of Kowloon and its memory.

Kowloon Walled City and its disappearance from the urban fabric of Hong Kong can be read as a parable of contemporary amnesia. The walled city was once a diplomatic anomaly between China and the British Empire that functioned as a long-standing autonomous zone, a site of temporary near-permanence, an exclave within an enclave.

Kowloon Walled City is not just a border in space; it also marks a border in time – a temporary suspension of linear time by which the visitor agrees to the terms of a compact laid out by the current shape of the territory, a walled compound where a delicate game between memory and amnesia can be played out, apparently till eternity. This is the frontier where reality begins to cross over into an image.

Visiting the 'Memorial Park' that stands on the former site of the Kowloon Walled City today is an uncanny experience. As with all 'theme parks', walking in this enclosure is like walking in a picture postcard spread over hectares rather than inches. The constructed, spacious serenity of the park, its careful gestures to the tumult of the walled city by means of models, oral-history capsules, artifacts, replicas and remains intend to provoke in the visitor some of the frisson in the fact that he or she is standing at what was once both condemned as an urban dystopia of crime, vice and insanitation, and hailed as an anarchist utopia. The neighbourhood itself may have disappeared, but its footprint in popular culture can be discerned in the simulacral sites of action sequences in cyberpunk science fiction, gangster and horror films, manga, and multi-user computer games.

The walled city had approximately 3,000 people living in one-hundredth of a square mile, which amounts roughly to an average population-per-unit-area density ratio of 3.3 million people to a square mile. This makes it the densest inhabited unit of space in world history. If we think of this space as a repository of memories, it would be the most haunted place on earth. Why do such spaces - sometimes crowded, sometimes empty (but apparently crowded with ghosts) - appear in a manner that is almost viral, such that the trope of empty but haunted streets set in the near future of global cities, begins to show the first signs of a cinematic epidemic of our times? Will we remember the cinema of the early twenty-first century as the first intimation of the global collapse of urban space under its own weight? Or is this imaginary appearance of a haunting, suicidal metropolis more of an inoculation than a symptom, an early shoring-up of the defences of citizens against their own obsolescence? How can we remember, or even represent, an inoculation that could be an obituary just as much as it could be a premonition or a warning?

The surrealist poet Louis Aragon, speaking of the disappearing neighbourhoods of Paris as the city morphed into twentieth-century modernity, once wrote that: 'it is only today, when the pickaxe menaces them, that they have at last become the true sanctuaries of the cult of the ephemeral... Places that were incomprehensible yesterday, and that tomorrow will never know.'[4]

What happens when someone from within these spaces that were 'incomprehensible yesterday, and that tomorrow will never know' decides to make themselves known? How does their account of the space square with its more legendary reportage?

I recall the Walled City as one big playground, especially the rooftops, where me and my friends would run and jump from one building to the next, developing strong calf muscles, a high tolerance of pain, and control of our fear, and our feet. The rooftops were our domain, shared only with the jets that passed overhead almost within reach of our outstretched arms as they roared down the final approach to Kai Tak Airport. Among the tangle of TV antennae we hid our kid-valuable things, toys and things we didn't want our parents to know about because, well, most of them were stolen or bought with money we earned putting together stuff in the little one-room 'factories' that were all over the Walled City—if our parents knew we had money, they'd have taken it. We were good at hiding things, and ourselves.[5]

Disappearance and Representation: Haunting the Record

What does disappearance do to the telling of that which has disappeared? How do we speak to, of and for the presence of absences in our lives, our cities?

Ackbar Abbas, in his book *Hong Kong: Culture and the Politics of Disappearance*, meditates at length on disappearance, cities and images:

> A space of disappearance challenges historical representation in a special way, in that it is difficult to describe precisely because it can adapt so easily to any description. It is a space that engenders images so quickly that it becomes *nondescript* . . . we can think about a nondescript space as that strange thing: an ordinary, everyday space that has somehow lost its usual system of interconnectedness, a deregulated space. Such a space defeats description not because it is illegible and none of the categories fit, but because it is hyperlegible and all the categories seem to fit, whether they are the categories of social sciences, cultural criticism, or of fiction. Any description then that tries to capture the features of the city will have to be, to some extent at least, stretched between fact and fiction . . . . If this is the case, then there can be no single-minded pursuit of the signs that finishes with a systematic reading of the city, only a compendium of *indices of disappearance* (like the nondescript) that takes into account the city's errancy and that addresses the city through its heterogeneity and parapraxis.[6]

A parapraxis is a kind of Freudian slip, an involuntary disclosure of something that would ordinarily be repressed. It could be a joke, an anomaly, a revealing slip-up, a haunting.

What does it mean to 'haunt the record'? When does a presence or a trace become so deeply etched into a surface that it merits a claim to durability simply for being so difficult to repress, resolve, deal with and put away? The endurance of multiple claims to land and other scarce material resources often rests on the apparent impossibility of arranging a palimpsest of signatures and other inscriptions rendered illegible by accumulation over a long time, and across many generations. In a sense, this is why the contingent and temporary character of the Kowloon Walled City endured for as

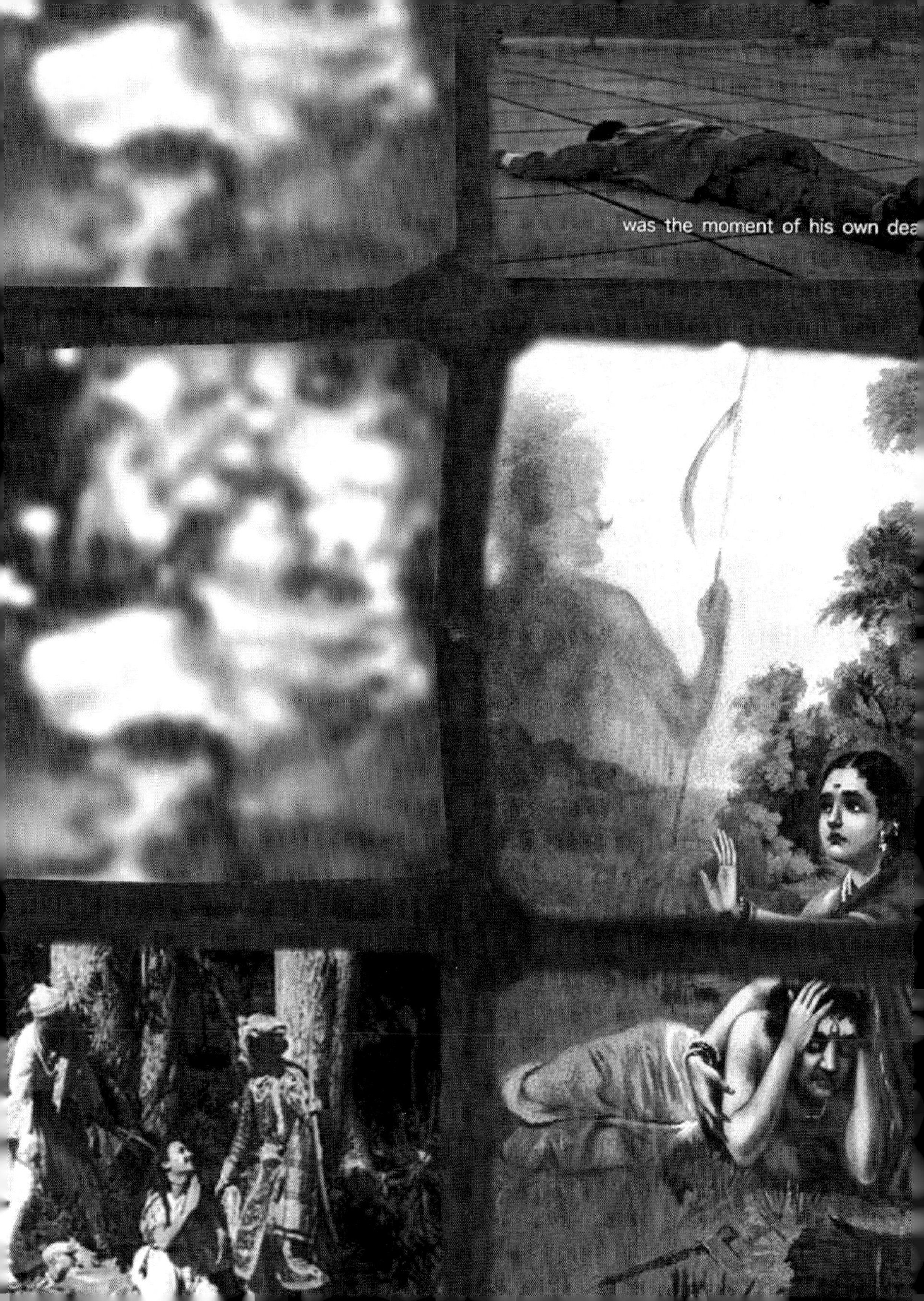
was the moment of his own dea

long as it did. There is of course the delicate irony of the fact that the protection offered by its juridical anomaly with regard to sovereignty – a constitutional Freudian slip with consequences – was erased the moment Hong Kong reverted to China. The autonomy of being a wedge of China in the middle of Hong Kong became moot the moment Hong Kong was restored to Chinese sovereignty. Resolving the question of Hong Kong's status automatically resolved all doubts and ambivalences with regard to claims over the custody and inhabitation of Kowloon Walled City.

A Chinese Sense of Time: Neither Permanence nor Impermanence

It is appropriate to end with a quotation from a Chinese text from the fourth century of the Common Era, a Madhyamika Mahayana Buddhist text, *The Treatises of Seng-chao*.[7]

> When the *sutras* (aphorisms) say that things pass, they say so with a measure of reservation, for they wish to contradict people's belief in permanence.
> (And here we would gesture in the direction of the assumption that this contemporaneity is destined to be permanent; after all, this too shall pass). And when the sutras say that things are lost, they say so with a mental reservation in order to express disapproval of what people understand by 'passing'.
> (And here we would gesture in the direction of the assumption that this contemporaneity is destined to oblivion; after all, something from this too shall remain).

Their wording may be contradictory, but not their aim. It follows that with the sages, permanence has not the meaning of the staying behind, while the wheel of time, or karma, moves on. Impermanence has not the meaning of outpassing the wheel. People who seek in vain ancient events in our time conclude that things are impermanent. We, who seek in vain present events in ancient times, see that things are permanent. Therefore, Buddha, Liberation, He, it, appears at the proper moment, but has no fixed place in time.

What more can we say of contemporaneity? It appears at the proper moment, but has no fixed place in time. In that spirit, let us not arrogate solely to ourselves the pleasures and the perils of all that is to be gained and lost in living and working, as we do, in these interesting times.

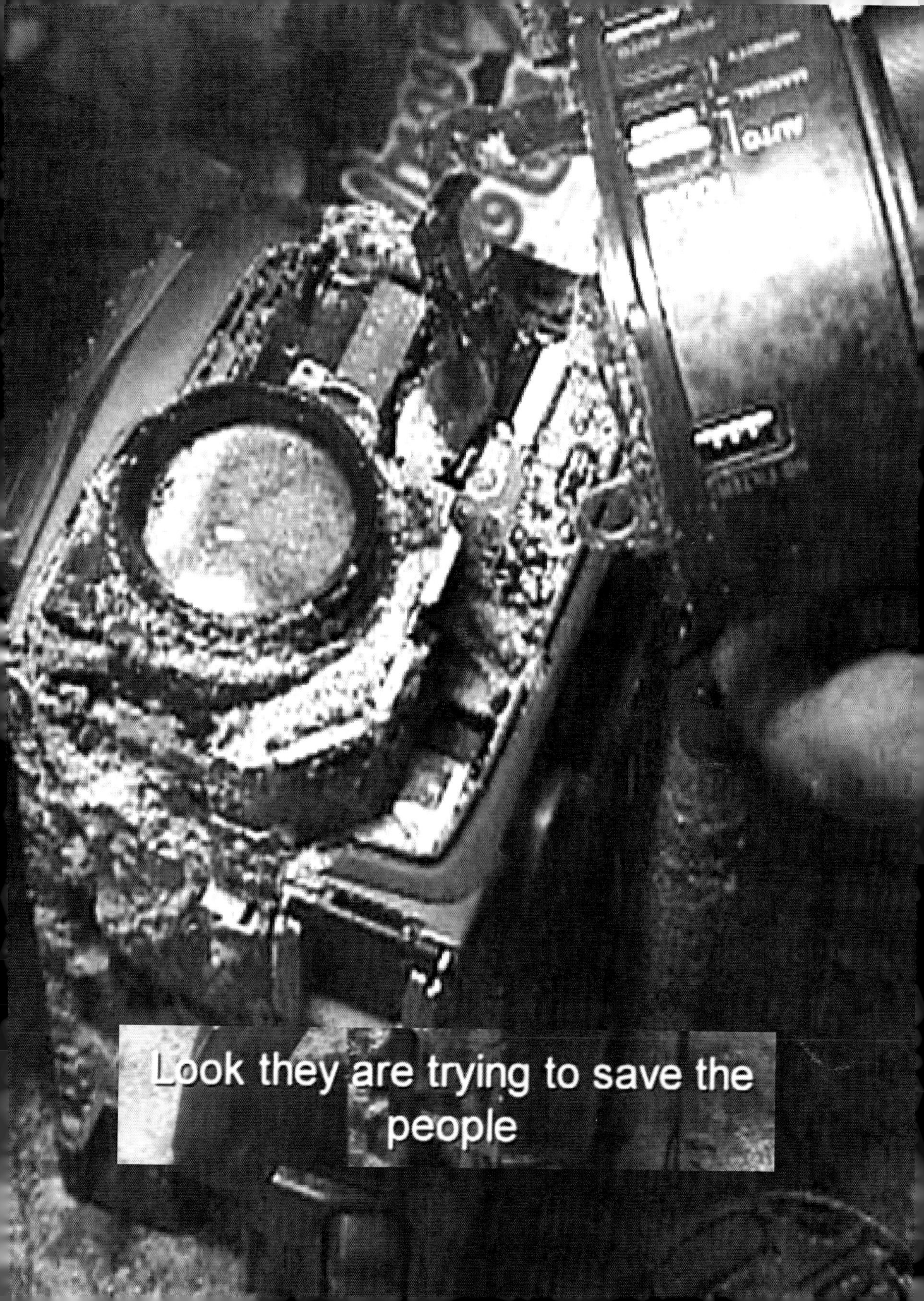
Look they are trying to save the
people

'It takes stubbornness, obstinacy, to face a storm, and yet also a desire not to be blown away by it', said the Raqs Media Collective in the previous essay in this volume. In December 2004, cinematographer R.V. Ramani was visiting Nagercoil in Tamil Nadu, for what was meant to have been a pleasant ceremony – the wedding anniversary of his friend (and noted Tamil writer) SuRa, set to traditional music amid family and friends. Ramani has over the decades compulsively filmed such occasions with his trusty Sony DSR PD 100, his companion since 2000, a faithful witness and able recorder of memories and life. On this occasion, however, he found himself in the midst of the tsunami that hit the Kanyakumari coast.

As the mighty wave lashed, he kept repeating two things to himself: 'Hold your breath, and don't let go of the camera.' This short text is on the ruins that have become a defining feature of the rubble of data, together with the debris of image-technologies gathered in the transition from celluloid and video to the digital. It also frames Ramani's film *My Camera and Tsunami* (2011), memorializing his camera and the image-memories it had once created. Although the physical body of the camera survived, says Ramani, its soul died that day. This text is placed here as an invitation to revisit vexed issues that have marked Indian film historiography: material degeneration, catastrophes, fragmented archives, reconstruction and speculative narratives. It also serves as a way to enter the ruins of the twenty-first century, as a note on the vital impetus of life itself.

A shorter version of this text was published in 2006 as 'Waves of Wrath' in the *Sarai Reader 06: Turbulence*. Reprinted here with permission of the author.

Keywords

Celluloid, *Documentary*, *VHS Tape*: See Keywords (pp. 326–44).

My Camera and Tsunami (2011): R.V. Ramani's well-known documentary homage to his camera, a Sony DSR PD 100, which was destroyed. With no surviving footage left, Ramani had to ponder larger questions of the relationship between image and reality. He says, 'The film emerged from the depth of despair . . . I changed as a filmmaker.'

Images

p. 15: Montaged still of Ramani's smashed camera (*My Camera and Tsunami*, 2011), courtesy the filmmaker.

R.V. RAMANI 2006

02 My Camera and Tsunami

On 25 December 2004, I arrived at Nagercoil to attend a family function at the house of the Tamil writer Sundara Ramaswamy (SuRa) It was his fifth marriage anniversary function. I was making a film on the writer and thought it would be an occasion to do some filming. I had arrived in the morning along with another family from Chennai: Akhila, her two young children, and her parents who are very close friends of SuRa. Though SuRa was against any traditional rituals, just before lunch, they got two garlands and convinced SuRa and his wife Kamala to exchange them. Akhila, a musician and veena player, sang a lovely song. I filmed. In the evening there was a function; many writer friends of SuRa had come.

On the 26th, I had an evening train back to Chennai, which Akhila's family were also travelling by. Since we were free on the morning of the 26th, we decided to go to Kanyakumari on Akhila's suggestion. Just before we set out to Kanyakumari, we received phone calls from friends in Chennai that there had been an earthquake with its epicentre in Indonesia and the tremors had been felt in Chennai too. A little later, we heard that sea water had crossed the Marina beach, reaching up to the roads. Another friend from Chennai called to say the sea water was rapidly receding at Thiruvanmiyur beach and people were rushing to see it.

When we reached the Kanyakumari beach, we found the sea was turbulent. There was a large crowd of tourists but everyone looked disturbed. There was panic in the air as a strange big wave had hit the coast, swallowing up some people standing on the rocks. The boat service to the Vivekananda Rock Memorial was suspended and I could see many tourists stranded on the memorial. Many of the fishing boats were stripped off from their moorings. The fisherfolk looked troubled.

We decided to leave Kanyakumari immediately and go back to Nagercoil. Akhila's little son wanted to take a picture but I convinced him that he could come back another day. On our way back, our driver Iyappan took a different route via Manakkodi bridge. This long bridge is on the backwaters at the edge of the sea, connecting two land parts. We got down on the bridge. The sea had receded and the water from the land was running towards the sea at a very high speed. Our driver then drove via Sothavalai beach, which is a sandy beach. I asked why he came here instead of taking the main road. He said it was less crowded here, and the boy could take a picture. He stopped the vehicle there and asked the boy to take a photograph. My body resisted every bit of it, but we all got down. The sea seemed calm, the water had receded, and it looked like a very low tide. People seated there told us that the sea had been 'misbehaving' since the morning, with the water ebbing and flowing erratically. We spent about five minutes there, and just as we were about to leave, someone shouted, 'A wave is coming.' We saw a wave forming on the horizon, far away.

The wave rose higher and higher – at first, it was a fantastic sight, the entire 180 degrees wave was rising. I heard someone shouting, 'Look! It's a miracle, you can never see such a spectacle again!' It was like nothing I had ever seen or imagined before. It was spectacular. I started filming it on my video camera. The wave was one huge wall – strong, dark and menacing – casting its own shadows. Frothing and fuming, it was advancing towards the shore at a very high speed. Initially, it was just this amazing sight, where the wave was not falling but gaining more and more strength. Soon, the accompanying sound came; a huge thunderous sound. It became apparent that we would have no chance to escape. (We later found out that the speed of a tsunami wave is about 800 kilometres per hour, the speed of an aircraft!)

We ran. Our car was parked about 20 feet behind us. Actually, since the road is much higher than the beach, even at high tide, the waters do not normally reach it. But this wave was different; the height of this tidal wave was almost that of a two-storey building. Before we could reach the car, the wave hit us square. The driver had already got in, while my friend's family was trying to shelter just behind the vehicle. And I ran too, to hide behind the car.

The wave lashed at us, and tossed the car into the air. All at once, we all were separated, drowning and being dragged half a kilometre over a rough surface, crashing through coconut groves, trees, bushes, ditches, rocks, walls. . . . I kept repeating only two things to myself: hold your breath, and don't let go of the camera. Just when I felt I couldn't hold my breath any longer, when I gave up, my head suddenly popped out of the water as the water had dragged me to a higher plane and began to recede. I grabbed a pole, and a broken tree, to stop myself from getting dragged back out with it.

To my amazement, I realized I hadn't suffered any major injuries. I got up slowly, dazed and reeling with disbelief. My camera still remained firm in the palm of my right hand, broken. I clambered onto a hillock nearby and saw three or four more men surfacing and walking about slowly. We could hear moans, cries for help from different directions. The whole place looked devastated; there was water everywhere. Many people were trapped in ditches, seriously injured. Many others had broken legs and arms. Everyone's clothes had been ripped off. We managed to lift five or six people out of the water and place them on a higher spot behind a tree.

And then I started looking for my friend's family. There were dead bodies scattered all around me. I found our car about 100 metres from the road, crushed inside the coconut grove. The driver was lying dead inside. After much searching, I found Akhila, dead, in a small pool of water. There was panic in the air and people were shouting at us to leave the place, as there was a chance of another wave hitting the shore.

I reached the village on the other side, away from the sea, walking through hip-deep water. Akhila's mother had survived too, and she was walking towards the village, dazed, bleeding from her legs and hands. Along with Akhila's mother and many more injured people, I was rushed to a nearby hospital for first-aid.

Later, when we reached the house in Nagercoil, we found out that Akhila's son had survived and was in a hospital with multiple injuries. Many bodies had been brought to the morgue by late evening, and I identified Akhila, her two-year-old daughter Darini and our driver. More than 500 people in that area had perished from the wave. The Manakkodi bridge where we had stopped briefly had been completely washed away by the waves and all those who were standing on it at that time had died. By night, Akhila's father had been found too, but unconscious and in a serious condition. Akhila, her daughter and the driver Iyappan were cremated in Nagercoil. After two days or so, we heard her father had regained consciousness but was still in a critical situation. SuRa and I left for the hospital to see him. The walk down the long hospital corridor was such an intense experience. He became very emotional seeing us and held our hands tightly. Unfortunately, he couldn't recover and passed away after a few days.

I am writing this from Nagercoil, while still recovering from the shock, and am being treated for elbow and knee injuries. Sundara Ramaswamy, his family and his friends are taking care of me. My camera, a Sony PD 100, is broken, clogged with water and sand. I don't know if it can be repaired or if the footage can be salvaged. The images, hitherto unseen on television, would be heart-rending. But no more so than my memories.

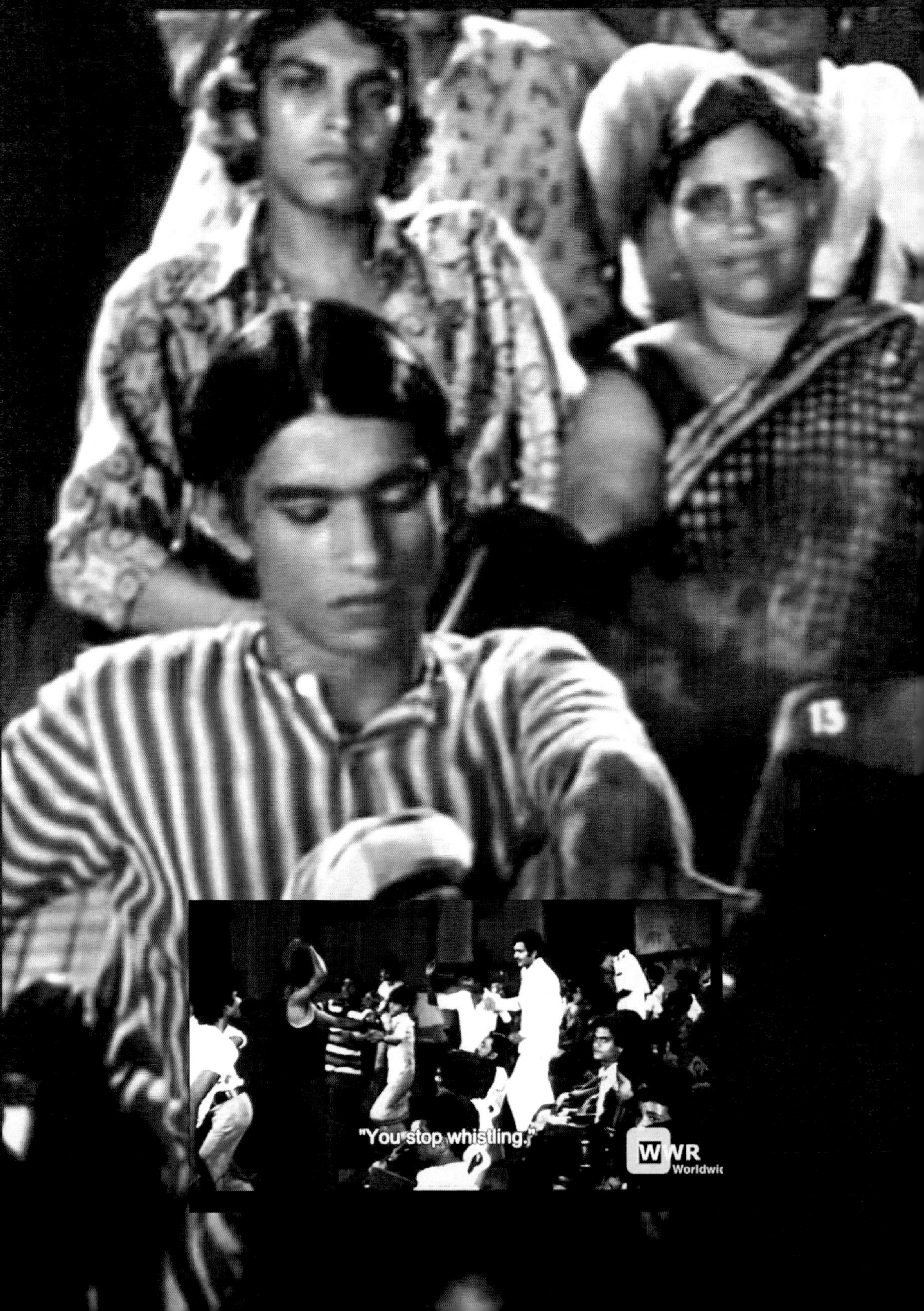
13
"You stop whistling."

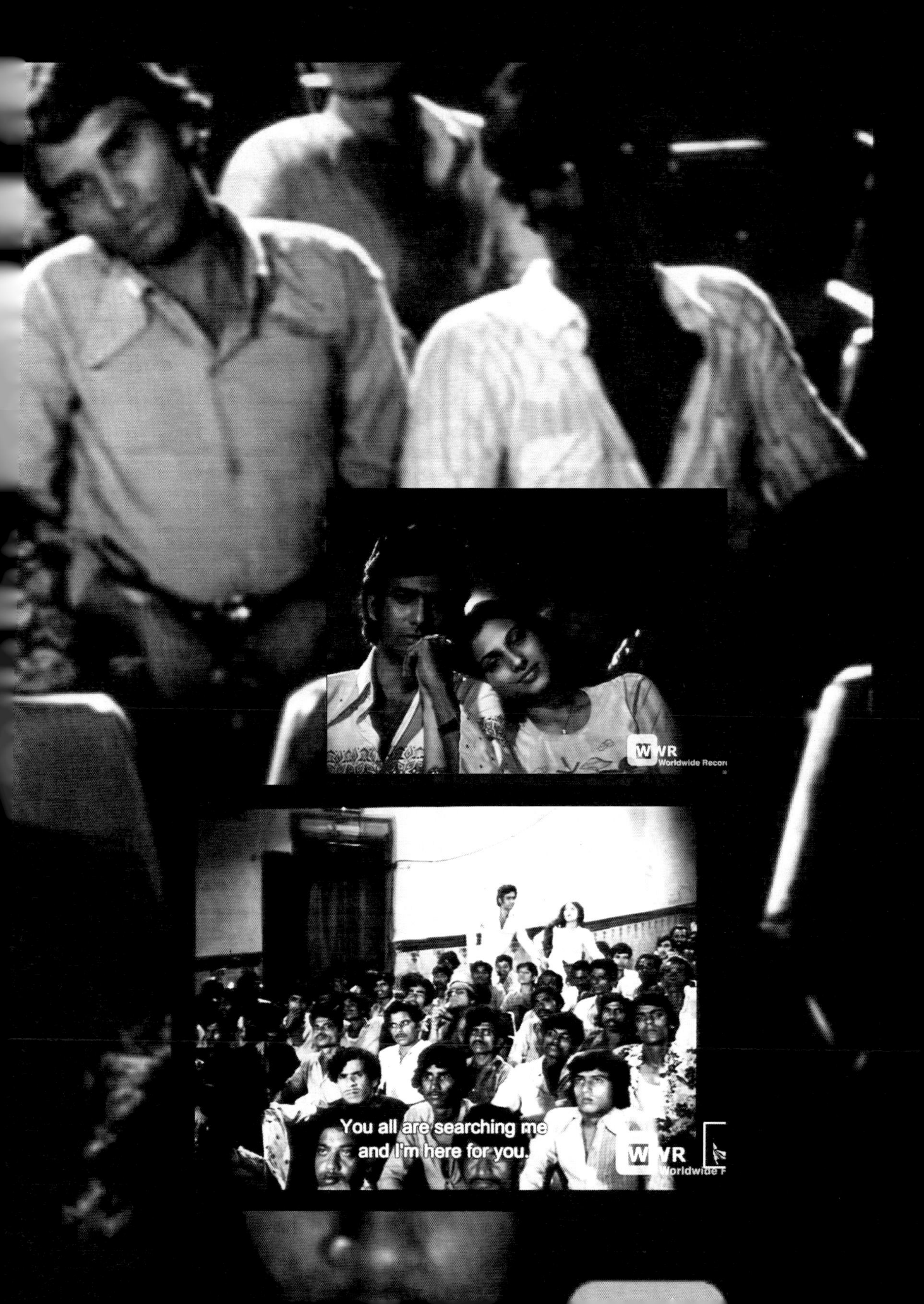
You all are searching me
and I'm here for you.

Making anywhere between 600 and 800 films a year, India's cinema produces 'ephemera' at an impossible pace. Much celebrated as the world's largest producer of films, it also has the smallest number of cinematic survivals. A history of informal durability replaces official systems of film archiving. Media historian Sudhir Mahadevan juxtaposes two seemingly contradictory, and perhaps uniquely Indian, imaginations of archiving. One, an essentially tragic vision of film as ephemera; another, a popular archive of the industry itself, using recycled celluloid. The first is seen in the image of 'Celluloid Man' P.K. Nair, founder of the National Film Archive of India. The second, in the imaginations of avant-garde filmmaker Kamal Swaroop's reconstructs of Dadasaheb Phalke, the 'father' of Indian cinema, through scrapbooks on video and paper, and in compilation films assembled through recycling footage. These are accompanied by popular cinema's own retelling of film history.

Originally published in Sudhir Mahadevan, *A Very Old Machine: The Many Origins of the Cinema in India, 1840–1930*, Albany: State University of New York Press, 2015. Reprinted here with permission from the author and SUNY Press.

Keywords, Names, Abbreviations

Archive, Bollywood, Celluloid, Ephemera in Film, National Film Archive of India, New Media Art, (Dadasaheb) Phalke, (Kamal) Swaroop, Virtuality: See Keywords (pp. 326–44).

Celluloid Man: 2012 film by Shivendra Singh Dungarpur, a sentimental portrait of P.K. Nair, founder of the National Film Archive of India, whose own bodily frailty is linked (by Mahadevan) to the ephemeral nature of celluloid film.

Mughal-e-Azam (colourized): Legendary 1960 epic with two spectacular colour sequences, controversially re-released in full colour and on cinemascope in 2004. Also see Keywords, p. 2.

Film Hi Film (Film, Only Film, dir. Hiren Nag, 1983): Compilation film assembling found footage from incomplete and abandoned films, stringing together a fictionalized narrative of the film industry.

Om Shanti Om (dir. Farah Khan, 2007): Major Bollywood movie reconstructing the history of cinema, itself a purported remake.

Pyaasa (The Thirsty One, dir. Guru Dutt, 1957): Romantic melodrama of a failed poet whose art is sold as trash and recognized only posthumously when the poet is believed dead. The film's extended popularity may well be ironically viewed in the light of its own dark prognoses about survival.

Shah, Krishna: Filmmaker and producer, UCLA Film School graduate, with major plans to make co-productions of Hindi cinema and Hollywood.

Images

pp. 20–21: Montaged stills from *Cinema Cinema* (dir. Krishna Shah, 1979).

p. 27: Montaged stills from *Pyaasa* (dir. Guru Dutt, 1957); out of copyright.

pp. 32–33: Collage from *Tracing Phalke* (dir. Kamal Swaroop, 2013).

p. 39: Still of P.K. Nair inside the National Film Archive of India's vaults, in *Celluloid Man* (dir. Shivendra Singh Dungarpur, 2012); courtesy Film Heritage Foundation.

SUDHIR MAHADEVAN 2015

03 The Protocols of Popular Film Historiography

Ephemera

There is an unresolved contradiction when Indian cinema's prolific output laments its poor archival preservation. The practical size of India's cinematic output poses a challenge for imagining an archive in the traditional sense, of a site of storage and preservation – but that volume is essential to its cinematic imaginary. With anywhere between 600 and 800 films a year, and seen from the vantage point of the films that do become 'visible' by finding exhibition, there is too much 'ephemera'.

One can find a vague echo of this conundrum in the world of film museums entrusted with preservation of film-related materials that ponder over how to collect, catalogue and cross-reference movie ephemera. But it is only a vague echo because the word *ephemera* must mean something quite distinct in India. The challenge isn't to track down and locate ephemera; the challenge is to notice it and figure out what to do with all of it. The ephemeral is what exists in abundance. Or rather, it is ephemeral precisely because it is abundant. Who cares for it when there is so much of it?

The problem seems analogous to that of the countless straight-to-video films in the North American context. Franco Moretti has invoked the 'slaughter-house of literature' – that vast world of literary production that will never be canonized, but nevertheless needs to be excavated and situated alongside existing canons for a more complex view of literary production. With India's cinema, the problem seems doubled. All of it – all of India's cinema (with perhaps the exception of its art cinema) – has been clubbed together, at least until the

1980s, as the 'slaughter-house' of cinema from the vantage point of the western film critic. Moreover, the Indian film industry's mammoth scale produces its own slaughterhouse of movies that disappear into oblivion.

How film history is remembered, memorized, memorialized, preserved in India is a function of the seemingly perpetually emergent temporalities that have shaped its viability. Historians haven't quite acknowledged the implications of a situation in which old and new media seem to coexist to produce an archive that is not yet one, an archive that can never be a stabilized, closed space of storage and predetermined recall. Popular film histories seem to do something quite other than what more sober narrative accounts that count as history proper seem to do. They suggest that not only is the archive of the cinema still in the *making*, it is also for the *taking*.

Laments about the abysmal culture of film archiving and preservation in India, and, indeed, about the state of archives in India in general, have been frequent. The recent release of an elegiac, beautifully shot meditation on India's film history, *Celluloid Man* (dir. Shivendra Singh Dungarpur, 2012) points to this sensibility. The movie melds the biography of P.K. Nair, instrumental in the story of the National Film Archive of India (NFAI), with that of the NFAI itself, and in turn with the story of Indian cinema. Indeed, as the title demonstrates, the end result is the archiving of Nair himself as a scarce and precious object, like the celluloid that is now a metaphor of a scarce sensibility that recognizes the value of film and need for its preservation.

Tracing Phalke

In contrast to *Celluloid Man*, filmmaker Kamal Swaroop's ambitious 'collage' of (Dadasaheb) Phalke's life, titled *Tracing Phalke* (2013), turns Phalke's life into a counter-archive of film and cultural history.[1] *Tracing Phalke* is a dense collage (literally) that, in a cut-and-paste mode, destroys the boundaries between Phalke and his times. As Swaroop puts it in the book's introduction and in interviews elsewhere, the linearity of Phalke's life unravels into an infinite proliferation of inexhaustible threads that turned Swaroop's fascination with Phalke into a decades-long project. Accordingly, *Tracing Phalke* comprises Swaroop's hand- typed 'chronofile' of the developments of Phalke's life, accompanied on the chronofile's margins by 'simultaneous developments in technology and larger historical events'.[2] Swaroop's description of the process is evocative and conveys the impact of media history on film history.

> A pair of scissors and a bottle of glue always with me, I went looking for images to put on my typed pages. These were the pre-internet times; I collected fragments by making Xeroxes from libraries or by mining art catalogues. Soon chimneys sprouted out of the heads of industrialists, underwater turtles nudged a pregnant Dwarkabai

> and an image of Toulouse Lautrec mirroring himself shadowed Phalke's movement into becoming a young man.
>
> When my images began to come together, I no longer knew whether I was putting together or breaking down . . . putting Usha Mantri's face on Ravi Varma's 'Sarasvati', was only making visible the grafting process that had historically taken place in our cinema. But the new collaged 'she' became one of my favourite creatures, a griffin. I began to let griffins live in my book. I let myself cut and shift and paste, I let myself associate and dream and keep in images because I liked them.[3]

Elsewhere, Swaroop has observed that the arrival of VHS was crucial to his ability to conceive of a 'new philosophy of time'.[4] The result is a visually complex experience of Phalke's life that is deeply embedded, in page after page of the coffee-table-sized volume, in a variety of narrative modes, primary sources and images.

It would be difficult to offer an abbreviated discussion of Swaroop's work given the density of visual information, but two points are worth noting. First, in transforming a biography into a series of visual images (including images *of* text) presented to us in the mode of a bound book whose pages we browse, Swaroop offers an intermediated staging of biography. The cinema is far from absent in this vertiginous intersection of the printed photograph with photographed type, typeset reproductions of paintings, woodcuts, engravings, newsprint and frame grabs from movies. Swaroop's 'indiscriminate' collage recalls the 'visual dust' of history captured by the medium of film. As we shall see shortly, the emergence of VHS and its attendant piracies inform the context for the movies I will be examining shortly in greater detail, just as they seem to have shaped Swaroop's own thoughts around Phalke.

Second, we should also note the connections *Tracing Phalke* reiterates between intermediality and topicality. Swaroop is reflecting as much on the origins of a multimedia infrastructure as he is on Phalke's life. My interest in Indian media imaginaries, is an interest in the everyday as a site for the life and times of a medium. Perhaps in this sense, while *Celluloid Man* turns India's pre-eminent film archivist into a precious and receding object, *Tracing Phalke* turns India's pioneering filmmaker into an expression of an everyday imaginary.

Golden Ageing Bollywood

Since economic liberalization and the privatization of media in India, there have been diverse new modes of popular historiography. These have included Bombay cinema's own nostalgic invocations of earlier eras of its history in movies such as *Om Shanti Om* (dir. Farah Khan, 2007). The retroactive colourization of black and white classics such as *Mughal-e-Azam* constitutes a more reflexive industrial stance on the part of a globalizing film industry eager to showcase new resources and competencies – the present technological capacities of recent film and media in India.[5]

Current concerns inflect invocations of the film as a historical artifact grounded in a particular past. Ashish Rajadhyaksha terms these impulses the 'golden ageing' of Bollywood.[6] In contrast to several governmental documentaries which align film history with the history of nationalism,[7] the 'golden age' of Bollywood emerges as such in the post- liberalization era to characterize the films of the 1940s and 1950s. Rajadhyaksha traces this celebration of the 1950s to BBC's Channel 4 programming in the 1980s that showcased the history of Indian cinema in a manner that established the golden-age narrative.

Crucial to this narrative are Nasreen Munni Kabir's prolific publications as well as documentaries for Channel 4 on the history of Indian cinema.[8] There is no small irony in Kabir's celebration of Indian cinema in the first decade after independence (1950s) as the golden age, according to Rajadhyaksha. The 1950s was, after all, the period when the studio system of the 1920s and 1930s broke down because of the influx of independent financiers who lured stars and directors away from studios and inaugurated what would remain the dominant mode of production till the 1990s Bollywood era: a highly disaggregated mode of production reliant on speculative financing (sometimes with very high interest rates) from often less than legitimate sources that turned the film business into a form of money laundering.

The Golden Age thus also ushers in a highly problematic relationship between cinema and the post-colonial state. The distrust of cinema by the post-colonial state as a form of mechanical reproduction can be located in the cross hairs of the uneasy relation between (mass-) cultural politics and the imperatives of commerce and cultural authenticity in the period before Independence.[9] *Pyaasa* (The Thirsty One, dir. Guru Dutt, 1955) can be seen as a consideration of the possibilities and perils of mass-cultural productions. Here, in the context of a discussion on how film history is narrated, *Pyaasa*, along with other films by Guru Dutt, as well as now iconic films by Raj Kapoor, Mehboob Khan and Bimal Roy, became part of a golden age of Hindi cinema.[10]

A third genre comprises historical surveys of specific topics pertaining to the cinema that have become increasingly frequent on television. The Indian television network *Headlines Today* has a series called *An Affair to Remember*. Each episode chronicles a particular notable figure (a playback singer, a star, a director), elements of film form and genre (cinematography, the evolution of the action sequence, horror, double roles), notable films and themes ('100 years of Indian Cinema', 'Stars

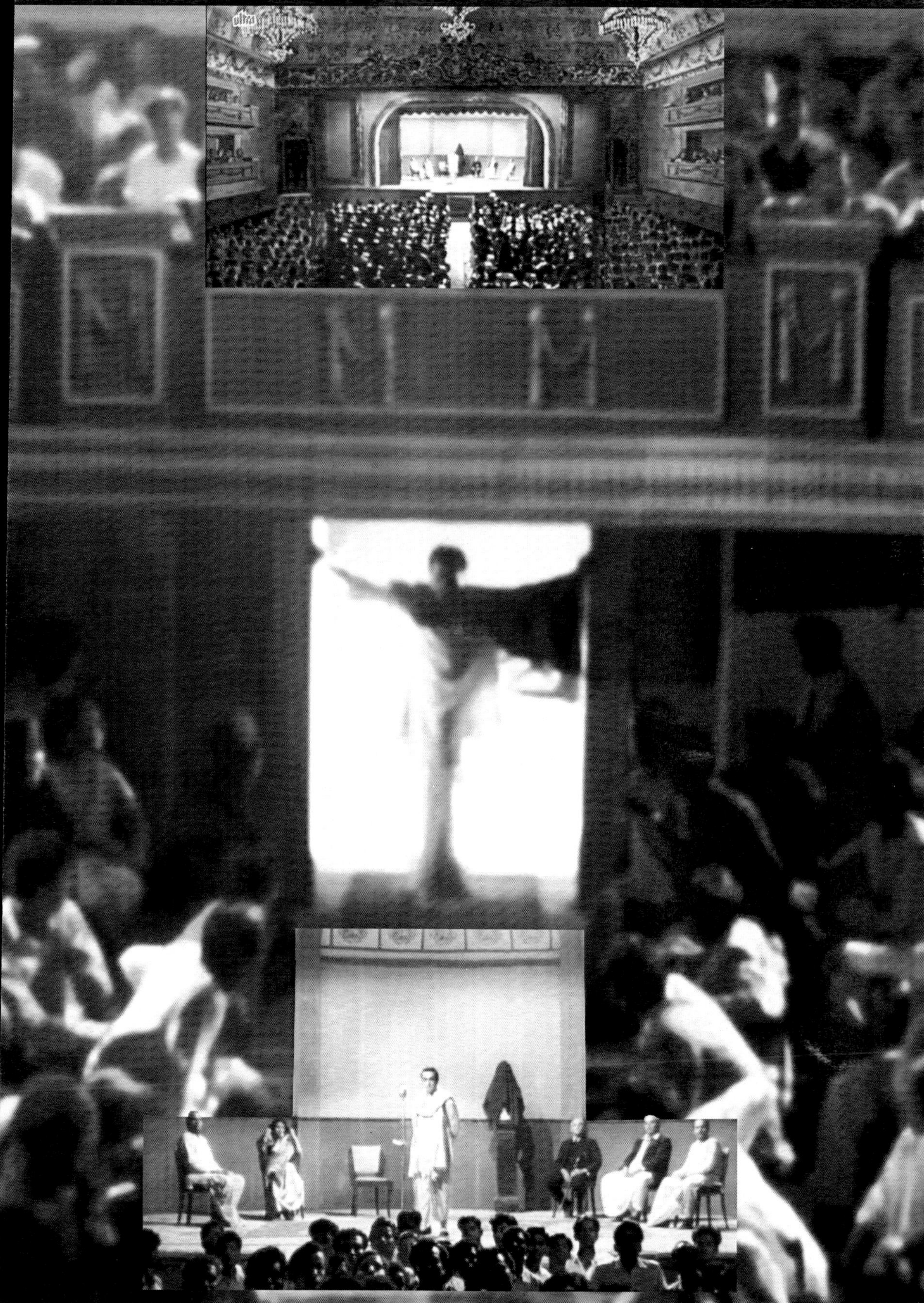

of South in Bollywood', 'Pakistani Artists in Indian Cinema'). This series does not venture beyond a chronology of significant moments, profusely illustrated with clips, voice-over narration, and talking head interviews with relevant film industry figures that alternate between reminiscence and opinion.

All of these genres of film history reveal varying degrees of indifference to the project of a formalized film archive. The absence of an archival imaginary in this conventional sense of respect for the cinema as heritage is not, of course, unique to Indian cinema. Corporate decisions to support archives are often a function of marketing and branding considerations, and television's desire to turn to film history can be seen as a function of cost-cutting practices in relation to producing original content. Obsolescence then haunts considerations of the archive. It informs the aesthetics of celluloid as archival material. And it is a concern not shared by Hollywood or Bollywood. Why mourn, and what is there to mourn, when film history is so easily configured as an immersive and interactive experience with the technological resources of the digital age?

What I am trying to get at here is the possibility that there might be other modes of remembering and preserving the history of the cinema, other protocols whose procedures ought to be considered seriously. Given, on the one hand, the poverty of the archive in its conventional sense, and on the other, the 'heritage' business of the cinema often run by the film industry itself, what other kinds of film historiography might we consider as germane to the possibility of a cinematic archive (which may not be the same as an archive of the cinema-as-celluloid)?

In what follows, I consider two oddities of film history on film that reflect on the history of Indian cinema and produce an unconventional vocabulary of recall.[11]

Cinema Cinema

Cinema Cinema (dir. Krishna Shah, 1979) (henceforth *Cinema*) narrates the history of Indian cinema in the form of a documentary being screened for an audience in a movie theatre. The screening of the diegetic documentary is interspersed with a scripted and enacted picture of an audience. The movie alternates between the history being narrated on screen and the audience in the theatre and their varied responses to what they see on screen. In doing so, the movie experiments with the project of documentary film historiography while retaining its most conventional features: the voice-over narration, the talking heads, the montage of clips of noteworthy films, and a largely linear progression from Indian cinema's origins to the present. It, however, undermines the narrative in the diegetic documentary and its claims to authority by muddling the divide between documentary and fiction. This, after all, is an enactment of a movie screening, a screening that nevertheless presents us with a documentary of Indian cinema. And if that were not enough, the documentary being screened is narrated by the on-screen presence of the biggest Bombay film stars of the time: Amitabh Bachchan, Dharmendra, Hema Malini and Zeenat Aman.[12]

Cinema came in the wake of its director Krishna Shah's earlier big budget flop *Shalimar* (dir. Krishna Shah, 1978), the story of a gang of crooks seeking to outwit each other in acquiring the priceless diamond, Shalimar.[13] Although a flop, *Shalimar* earns the distinction of being one of those rare films in Bombay cinema - perhaps even the first - to be cross-franchised as a novel coinciding with the movie's release.[14]

Who was Krishna Shah? A 2003 article, well into the 'Bollywood' phase of Bombay cinema, described Shah as the 'pioneer of crossover cinema', based in the United States, a Yale and UCLA Film School graduate whose student film had won second place after George Lucas's *THX1138* (1971), and who now had ambitious plans to tap into the Bollywood phenomenon.[15] Shah was not only a crossover pioneer. In the 1980s, he appeared twice in published newspaper reports as a filmmaker warning against video cassette-related piracy of Indian films. One of those appearances included a taped confrontation with an Asian shopkeeper in London over the piracy of his own movie, *Cinema*. The confrontation was later broadcast on a BBC program on the subject of piracy.[16] Another detailed 1980 report and analysis on the impact of video cassettes on piracy quotes Shah saying: 'The signs are clear. This is the last decade of the movies, as we know them. All over the world, the motion picture industry is dying as a result of this unbelievable phenomenon - the video'.[17]

Such portentous pronouncements on the death of cinema in the age of the video cassette contextualize Shah's failed endeavour. *Shalimar*, as well as its follow-up *Cinema*, are symptomatic of the exceptional position of the Indian director who might seek to straddle the worlds of Hollywood and Bombay Cinema in the 1980s. Each of Shah's two movies, *Shalimar* and *Cinema*, is an oddity in its own right. His optimism in the potentials of cross-franchising a movie such as *Shalimar* in India, and his assumption that the form of the Indian film was modular and cross-culturally adaptable (remove the songs and you have its Hollywood version) imagines a cinema reconfigured for a global age, but well before that globalization had become the mantra and zeitgeist in India. Shah's globalism is clearly not in the same epistemic space as British Raj nostalgia. That nostalgia depicts an Indian world filtered through the (fantasy) sensibility of a simpler Anglo-Indian past. Shah instead looked to the United States of the current century and the current moment in the late 1960s, well before India's economic liberalization of the 1990s reconfigured its geopolitical and cultural relationship to the United States.

Shah's desire to actualize a future that was yet to happen - a future characterized by (fantasies of) a complementary synergy between Bollywood and Hollywood - makes his films all the more interesting. *Shalimar* becomes an attempted cinematic rendering of that future with something of a utopian cast to it. *Cinema*, on the other hand, illuminates Bombay cinema's history by localizing its impact at the site of reception, the movie theatre. While one globalizes, the other localizes.

Shah's film also exists at a remove from corporate- and industry-led cinematic records of the history of Indian cinema. In contrast to the TV series *An Affair to Remember*, *Cinema*, as well as the other movie I will discuss here, *Film Hi Film* (Film, Only Film) have not been incorporated as programming into mass media, and have not to my knowledge been broadcast or transmitted on television.

I discovered the two films while browsing an online store selling DVDs of Indian films. One of the consequences of the emergence of online retailers specializing in Indian cinema is the sudden 'appearance' or unprecedented availability of movies that may have barely made it to the theatres on their original release or that have been forgotten over the years. Flops such as *Shalimar*, pre-1950s period films and romances, less well-known films of major stars, and even rarely seen iconic films, now seem to be available in one format or the other. Who owns the rights to these movies? Who is behind the production of the DVDs and VCDs of these movies? Who uploads these films to sites like YouTube?[18]

While answers to these questions can be elusive, and in many cases impossible to obtain, online retail seems to have made the obscure examples of India's cinematic output available. As such, then, the two movies constitute a de-spatialized form of social memory. That is to say, this social memory is no longer rooted in a territorially sited past framed within the parameters of national cinema. Unlike postmodern art that creates and fabricates a new past, here we have an actual past, readymade and prefab, freed from its temporal origins and its locations of significance, to become the object of nostalgia, including for those who may not have even lived it. This is a past that now belongs to no one institution or country and everyone.

As I noted at the outset, *Cinema* enacts the event of a movie screening. The enactment's functions are worth outlining. The particular rhetorical and analytical procedures adopted by the movie bind Indian cinema to the site of its consumption. The chronology is dependent for its meaning and affect not on the intrinsic value of the past but on its present reception in the movie theatre, emphasized through editing and action and given equal if not more time than the documentary itself. The movie is driven by the desire to watch or discover audiences watching. The black box of the theatre is shown darkened only at the outset and at the end to indicate the norm, while it is illuminated through much of the movie as a space of visible social interaction.

In its structure, *Cinema* replicates the act of movie-going. The film opens with an exterior shot of Bombay's Edward Theatre (opened in 1918).[19] A line forms. Tickets are purchased, including from touts that sell tickets in 'black'. Back in the projection room, the projectionist spools the reels of film and a bell rings. The audience takes its seats. A documentary about the history of Indian – but mostly Hindi – cinema commences. The documentary comprises back-to-back clips of notable movies, intercalated with expository narration by four major film stars. The documentary's version of history proceeds chronologically, segmenting the history of Indian cinema into four broad periods and utilizing four stars to introduce each period. In the middle of the screening, there is an intermission. The audience files out. Men line up at the open-air urinal. Others buy snacks while a lady changes diapers. Soon, the documentary resumes. When it concludes, the lights come on and the audience exits the theatre, and the movie too comes to an abrupt end, as if it were running on time borrowed from the documentary nested within it.

Cinema Cinema's nested documentary's archival footage is not restricted to Indian cinema, or for that sake, even to fiction. We see clips drawn from Hollywood and Europe, especially in the pre-sound period, and equally copious use of documentary footage of events in India's freedom movement. Nor is the movie's use of footage restricted to live action. A lengthy discussion of the 1928 Cinematograph Committee report is presented in animation.[20] In this, the movie astutely recognizes the excess of detail demanded by a photographic medium such as the cinema, the challenge it poses to conventional historiography, and compensates for the lack of visual records of a governmental and investigative commission by imagining that event and its complex politics in animated form.

The relation between plot and story in this movie is noteworthy. By definition, the plot refers only to the events we see on screen in the order in which we see them. The story, on the other hand, includes what we see on screen as well as events not seen but inferred by us that allow us to construct a fuller story out of what we are watching on screen. The periodic conflation of the screen *we* are looking at with the screen inside the movie theatre where the documentary is being viewed by our fictional audience complicates the story duration. Like a Chinese box, the movie's 97-minute running time encapsulates its roughly two-hour plotline of events – I am guessing the duration from buying the tickets to exiting the theatre. This two-hour plotline in turn encapsulates the screened documentary's 75-year-long story of Indian cinema. *Cinema*'s running time is less than the duration of its plotline, which in turn is less than the story duration that encompasses the entire history of Indian cinema.

The miniaturized world-in-a-grain-of-sand logic would seem to create a larger-than-life cinema. But it would be more accurate to say that this is reverse miniaturization that accords more priority to the viewing of this documentary by those inside the movie theatre, and also to our viewing of this entire exercise in imaginative historiography. It is not so much that a macrocosm opens up inside a grain of sand. More to the point, the 75 years of Indian cinema are contained and 'tamed' by the event of their narration in a movie theatre, which in turn is

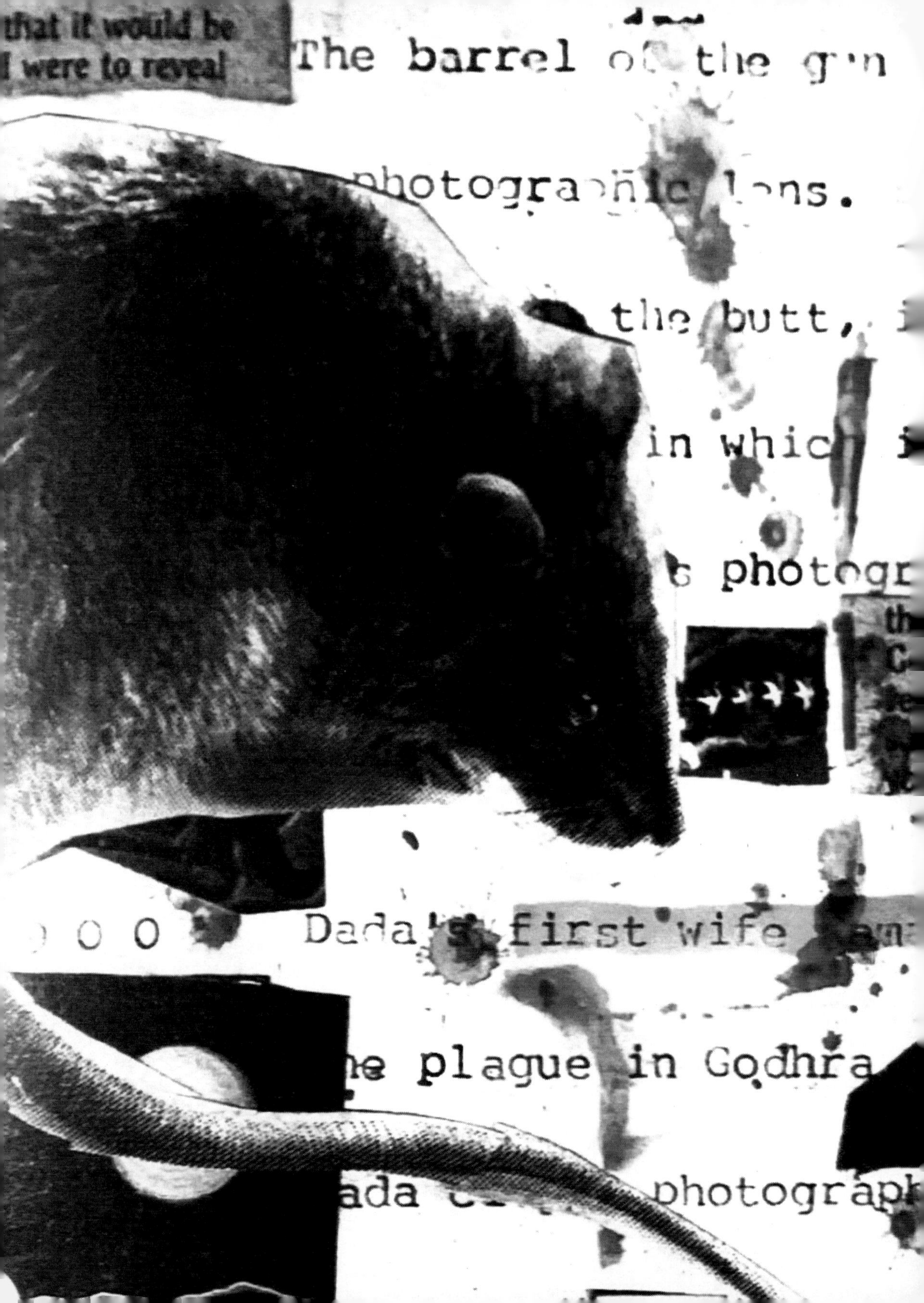
that it would be
I were to reveal
The barrel
the
the butt,
in whic
photogr
Dada's first wife
plague in Godhra
ada
photograph

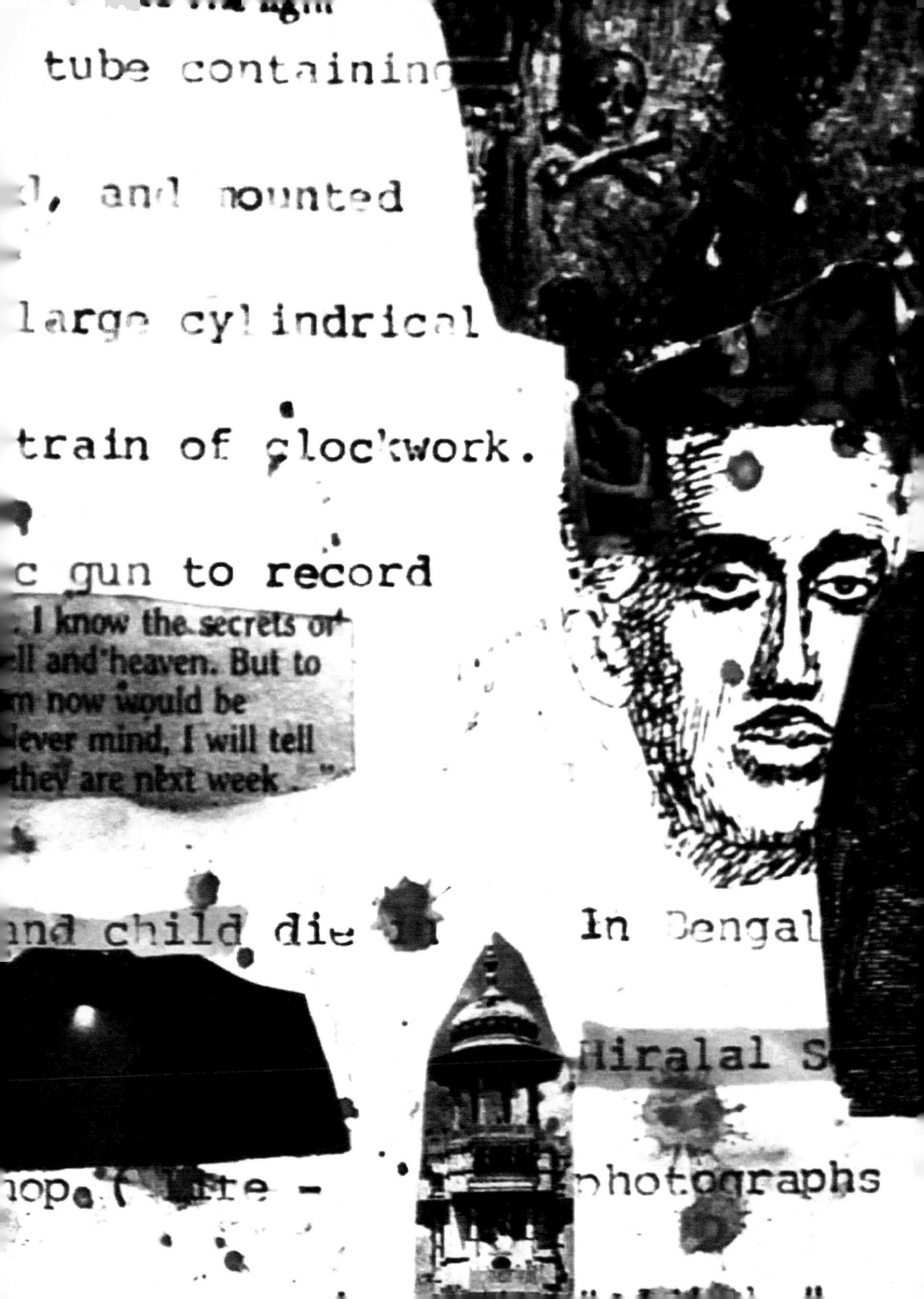
tube containing
and mounted
large cylindrical
train of clockwork.
gun to record
I know the secrets of
ll and heaven. But to
m now would be
ever mind, I will tell
they are next week."
child die
In Bengal
Hiralal S
photographs

contained by our viewing of this imaginative act of historiography. Miniaturization at any rate does not imply reduced significance. On the contrary, the miniature can emblematize a much larger order outside of the container that holds it, and the container itself can serve as a material replication of an orderly universe. Perhaps we ought to think of this movie as producing a microhistory of Indian cinema, one that we are being invited to consume.

The documentary is a collection of elements of the history of Indian cinema – of scenes and fragments of canonical films, dates and personages – whose circumstances are being narrated by major film stars, who may be seen as custodians responsible for the collection or as *sutradhars* (narrators in traditional theatrical forms). In choosing the biggest film stars of the time to narrate the history of Indian cinema, *Cinema* confirms the star-driven nature of Indian cinema. It also situates Indian cinema's history literally and figuratively in the interface – the screen – between spectator and star. Perhaps in the encouragement of star-struck reverie, *Cinema* desires to transform history into an immersive experience.

The public dimensions of Indian cinema emerge in the mode of viewership at work in the theatre, a viewership that is interactive, haptic, profoundly engaged and resolutely social. These dimensions are revealed in the movie theatre. The theatre contains a selective cross-section of Indian society. Among them are young couples in love, married couples with and without children, elderly and youthful single men, specifically marked by sexuality or religion as minorities, the passed-out drunk, and the distracted sports buff balancing the latest sports score on the radio with the movie he is watching. And behavioural types: a man picks his ears, another is fast asleep, a third stares at the camera, and a couple holding hands and cuddled together seem distracted more by their mutual love than by the screen. One young man is dressed in a floral-patterned red kurta, his face made up with eyeliner and lipstick. We witness his determined flirtation with the exasperated married man sitting next to him.

The architecture of the theatre typifies the single-screen theatre in India, with the 'stalls' – where much of the audience interaction occurs – and the 'balcony', where the tickets tend to be more expensive. Shah chooses to situate the entire audience – middle and working class, elite and plebeian – in the stalls, a democratizing impulse, perhaps born out of a US-based director's experience of the cinema and quite unlike the social stratifications of Indian movie-going.

Cinema, in its subject as well as the enactment of that subject, compels us to consider various models of the past, of narrating that past. Is its collection of clips a scrapbook or souvenir that might ask us to remember the origins of Indian cinema? Probably not, since the movie is strikingly free of any aching desire or longing or nostalgia for the past that characterizes the souvenir's *raison d'être*. This is brought home both by the star power that presents this history (a commercial calculation) and by the busy happenings in the hall as the movie plays out.

The activity in the hall, with its frequent insouciance to the project of concentrated spectatorship, tilts the documentary to become a collection of materials from the past, which exist to be utilized as the audience may see fit. Unlike the souvenir, which is a form of antiquarianism, the collection raids the past and arranges selected elements of the past into a new whole. It is a mercantilist disposition, interested in extracting value, in creating something potentially replicable without the charged desire to delve into the origins of the objects in the collection. Even if we judge the documentary to be a presentation of the illustrious patina of film history, its reception in the theatre deflates such an assessment.

Accordingly, the audience responds to old clips in *Cinema* with more complex motivations that exceed nostalgia. An elderly man in the audience laments that the quality of movies in the present seem to have declined compared to these older films, diluting nostalgic affection with qualitative assessment. The young couple argues over Amitabh Bachchan's appeal, the woman in adulation, the man with jealousy. The devout woman treats the image as an iconic one, praying when scenes from devotionals appear on screen. Her husband, meanwhile, sulks and complains, making explicit his preference for 'serious' New Wave cinema, which the wife dismisses offhand. And where there is nostalgic bliss, it is for the tunes being played onscreen, an indication not just of the power and longevity of film songs in India, and therefore the porosity of the filmic text, but also the cinema's ability to cater to auditory pleasures at the expense of the visual.

There are other, more tactile pleasures. One of the final clips is of a risqué song by Helen, Hindi cinema's foremost cabaret dancer, performed in the manner of the *lavani*, a regional genre of popular music in the state of Maharashtra that is often sung to teasing lyrics.[21] The camera's lascivious focus on Helen's swaying hips is intercut with the excited, wide-eyed projectionist in the booth frantically unspooling an entire reel with his hands, as if what is seen on screen could be found and held more concretely in the celluloid in his hands. The past turns into immediately relevant and applicable present.

Yet, to play devil's advocate for a moment, the cinematic image is by default in the mode of a memory quilt, or scrapbook or a souvenir (or a fossil, as Andre Bazin would say). This is, after all, a movie about movies. And as such, the title, with its duplication, perhaps alludes to that fact. It is one of the pleasures of this movie that it not only converts the indexed past into a series of iconic gestures (the extracted scenes) and faces, but also in the process engages in the task of iconoclasm, subordinating film history to the conditions of its possibility - the screen, the projector, the audience, the reels of celluloid, the building, the box office. The movie's wide-ranging dissection of the cinematic apparatus inventively braids the medium's material tangibility (the film reels, the tickets, the building, the technology, the lights) with its affective intensity (the responses elicited by the movie screen).

Film Hi Film

While *Cinema* adopts the conventions of the documentary only to subvert them, *Film Hi Film* (Film, Only Film, dir. Hiren Nag, 1983; henceforth *Film*) adopts, at least at first glance, the conventions of the found-footage or compilation film, in order to tell the story of the film industry.[22] Running almost two hours long, *Film* makes extensive use of scenes from unfinished films. This is not so much stock footage as it is 'found' footage, or more precisely, 'lost' footage being brought to light again.

The footage is alternated with a framing narrative about the troubles of a principled but unfortunate film producer. Gyanchand aka Sethji (played by character actor Pran) is a producer who loses his wealth and his money in a bad investment and is reduced to penury.[23] A French journalist researching the history of cinema comes to interview Gyanchand and makes him a handsome payment for his time. Elated, Gyanchand returns to film production with the money. His former crew of technicians work for him at no cost. Rehearsals and production begin. After numerous other trials, the movie is completed, but distributors show no interest. Frustrated, Gyanchand is about to destroy the reels when, miraculously, a former employee, now a successful distributor, has a sudden change of heart. The movie, titled *Film Hi Film*, is released at a glittering premiere, includes a peppy disco number, new actors who are heralded as exciting new stars and the presence of established film stars from Bombay cinema at the premiere.

This narrative of a producer, whose career, in melodramatic terms, threatens to be an unfinished movie, is interspersed with extended scenes from incomplete movies recovered from film studios.

The relationship of the found footage with the framing narrative is not always explicit, but that seems a function of the fact that the framing narrative is presented as a melodrama of insurmountable hurdles, coincidental occurrences and sudden reversals of fortunes. The interloping scenes from unfinished films comment on the main narrative. Their distinct nature is also visibly clear in that many of the interloping scenes are from black and white films, whereas Gyanchand's story is entirely filmed in colour.

The first found-footage segment appears abruptly, without warning, after Gyanchand has lost all his money and been sentenced to five years in prison. The scenes are from a movie made in 1960, *Reporter*, about a reporter (played by iconic film star Raj Kapoor) with a talking dog for company, one that can predict crimes in advance and gets the reporter in trouble. Following closely on the heels of Gyanchand's reversal of fortune, the scenes perhaps point to good men caught up in unfair circumstances. On other occasions, the footage is supposed to be exemplary or illustrative in a self-evident manner. Gyanchand, asserting to his crew that stars are born, not made, invokes Amitabh Bachchan as an example of an actor who was transformed into a star overnight by the movie *Zanjeer* (Chains, dir. Prakash Mehra,1973). Mention of Bachchan's name motivates the turn to footage of scenes from two incomplete films.

At times, it seems as if the framing narrative wants to satirize the found scenes. In scenes from an unfinished war melodrama, *Shikhwa* (Complaint, 1954), a pacifist hero (Dilip Kumar) is imprisoned as a traitor to the cause of war.[24] To save him from the death penalty, his lover Nutan must abandon him and marry the warmongering general.[25] In the version Gyanchand is directing, this war melodrama is translated by his newbie actors but with Buñuelesque transformations. Shot-reverse-shots of the two characters include the presence of a teddy bear in the heroine's arms and two goats that bear the brunt of the hero's wrath.

Perhaps an explanation is not needed. *Film* bears the markings of its relative anonymity in the history of Bombay cinema in the fact that neither the scenes of its framing narratives nor the found footage appear in the order they ought to. Also obvious is the less than skilful editing in which some scenes close on shots that linger a tad too long on the actors, as if we were watching a poorly timed amateur stage play. The abrupt transitions to the orphaned scenes seem at times to be a function of possibly missing footage or frames of the Gyanchand segments.

Finally, the screen duration of the orphaned scenes is often much longer than the scenes comprising the framing narrative itself, suggesting an economical approach to storytelling where available footage minimizes the need and costs of freshly shot ones. Do these misplacements - and the goats - signal the unknown history of the transfer of this movie from film to cheap VCDs now available online? *Film* may have undergone the randomization of use that underscores the idea of footage lost and then recuperated in entirely new contexts.

Regardless of whether intentional or not, the difficulty of following the plotline does not hamper our understanding of the story. This too may be a function of melodrama, and especially the loose dramatic arc of Indian commercial melodramas that makes a scene-by-scene economy of narration unnecessary and fundamentally foreign to a dilatory unfolding. What then does this movie set out to do?

First, I would contend that *Film* serves to conventionalize an already highly conventionalized cinema. The reclamation of 'orphan' scenes is not motivated by the desire to situate them in a linear and realistic storyline. Writing in the 1980s about the commercial Hindi cinema's own standards or frames of reference, Rosie Thomas observed that in Hindi commercial cinema, the originality of a storyline is less important than the screenplay's emphasis on spectacle and emotion. *What* happens next is less important than *how* it happens. Moral perturbations to be eventually resolved are more important than unsolved enigmas. The audience's familiarity with the depicted cultural universe, and its expectations about the commercial film form, combined with repeat viewings, take precedence over originality. Finally, a succession of ingredients - action, melodrama, song-dance and comedy - is more important than a linear development.[26]

There is, therefore, a certain degree of reflexivity built into the commercial film form of Indian cinema. Considering *Film* as a form of meta theorization of the medium would therefore be misplaced given that reflexivity is a happy confirmation of the established conventions of this cinema. It is not a symptom of - or for that sake, in this instance, a cure for - an epistemological crisis regarding the photographic image, induced by new media.[27]

Second, scholars of found-footage films have often used the metaphor of waste, junk and recycling to describe such footage. Found footage has been termed a form of disposable culture reclaimed from a landfill. However, the impetus that drives this movie's use of found footage is quite unlike in experimental and avant-garde cinema, where the decontextualizing and then repurposing of found footage can be seen as oppositional forms in relation to the capital-intensive Hollywood. Far from stripping away the context, *Film* with its melodrama about a filmmaker seeking to make a commercial film melodrama, restores this found footage to its rightful context.[28] The scenes are from movies that were never completed and, therefore, could be seen as already decontextualized by circumstance, even before the director reuses the material.

Film performs the function of a salvage operation, rescuing what would otherwise be termed as waste. In this function, it serves as an archive in the most literal sense. It is in this sense that we may consider this a movie less about 'found footage' in the sense of fortuitous discovery, and more about 'lost footage' searching for a new cinematic home. After all, the titles at the opening of the movie acknowledge many of the major studios in Bombay at the time as suppliers of these scenes.

Third, the framing device undertakes, however ineffectually, a critique of the film industry as it was in the 1980s. The lack of institutional legitimacy for the cinema is conveyed when Gyanchand takes a principled stand to go to jail on his unpaid debts rather than declare insanity, because he sees himself as the better exemplar of an already reviled industry. The highly disorganized mode of production of Bombay cinema is conveyed in his need to take loans from private moneylenders at usurious interest rates. His inability to afford stars, or find distributors who might want to purchase rights for the film after it is finally done, conveys the picture of a star-driven institution. *Film* writes history in the best possible way: by filtering an orphaned past, self-reflexively, through its own present. It manages to turn found footage into archival footage, where the archive is of the present as well, and not just of the past.

The movie's meta historicity, if it is such at all, derives from the most transparent representational function of the lost scenes as they are incorporated into a larger melodramatic narrative and dramaturgical framework. We are

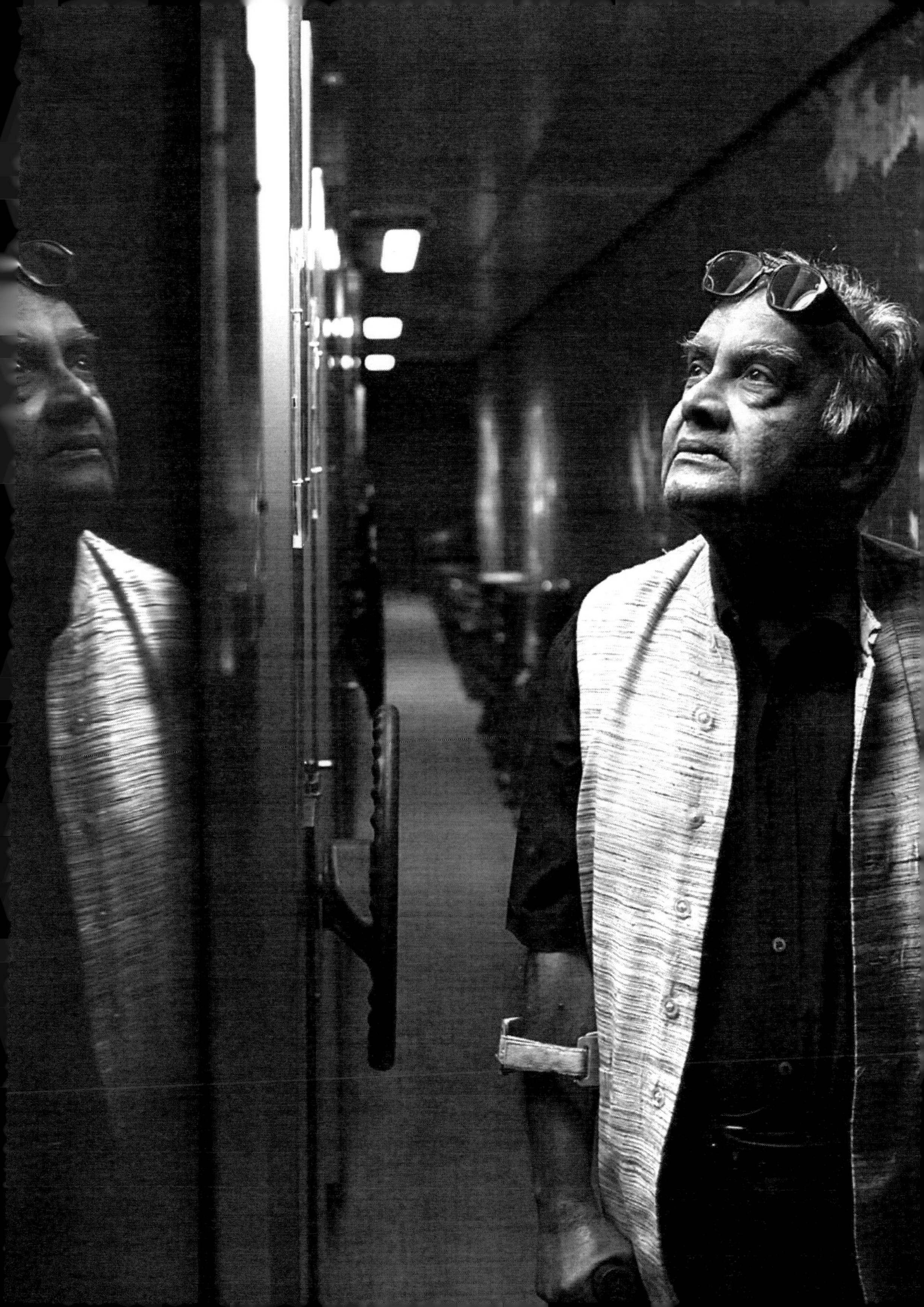

watching a movie about movies. What we are watching is a transparent record, a record of movies as the referents of that record.

Nevertheless, a lingering trace of *detournement* as a secondary strategy is also in evidence in the satirizing of the source material that I described earlier. The footage is frequently employed rhetorically by being decontextualized, repurposed and recombined, as it is also evident in the sly inclusion of news footage of major film stars arriving at a premiere of some other movie, within a montage of shots of Gyanchand being feted at *his* movie's premiere with his cast of unknown non-stars. Inside the theatre of the premiere, we are in for another late surprise. The shots of the theatre are sourced from producer Shabab Ahmed's earlier production, *Cinema*. Where now does this footage - that of the theatre - stand in relation to the movie *Film*?

To unpack that question, we may need to return to an aspect of *Cinema* that I have not touched upon: its status as a 'fictional biography' of a real entity, Indian cinema. In that movie, at intermission, the diegetic audience is treated to an advertisement (with jingle) about Air India. So, the audiences are paying to watch a documentary on the history of Indian cinema as entertainment, where they would otherwise watch a feature-length fiction. During intermission, they watch an advertisement for a state-owned airline - Air India hawking the pleasures of travel and tourism - where they would otherwise watch the state hawking something edificatory and didactic. The intermission was when audiences in post-Independence India would have been invariably treated to the state's pedagogical documentaries on health and civic issues. In a strange reversal, then, commercial cinema adopts the pedagogical documentary mode, while the state adopts the exhortative mode of travel and tourism. The state peddles the consumerist fantasies routinely peddled by commercial cinema. Commercial cinema on its part, presents its own history as edifying in the documentary mode.

Of course, for the diegetic audience and considered within the terms set by *Cinema*, the documentary is entertaining. And promises of entertainment by the state (state-run airlines) are, at best, worthless intermissions. And again, within the terms set by the diegesis, the space of the theatre is the space of real life. However, we also know that the goings-on in the theatre are enacted. *Cinema* confounds, therefore, at least two forms: the mockumentary and the docudrama. It is neither all fiction pretending to be a documentary (the mockumentary), nor is it all fact presented in the manner of a fiction (the docudrama).

It might be more useful to say that the realism at work in *Cinema* is iconic and idealist. As with the commercial Hindi film, it is recognizable and familiar to a narrative community as a cinematic imaginary: the familiar public experience of the cinema (as opposed to an individual spectator and her experience that might be predicated on credulity, or the willing suspension of disbelief). The reuse, then, of the shots of the theatre from *Cinema* in *Film* is possible because those images of the theatre are iconic images of a cinematic imaginary, representative. In other words, those images are not being used - or certainly not solely being used - as indexical records of a movie theatre. They are not being used for the evidentiary power that permits the narrative context to be rewritten while the medium ensures that the evidence remains unassailable. Instead, what we have is a movie with a relation to history where *kuch bhi chalega* (anything will suffice) if it can convey the cinema's iconicity, its practical existence.

Neither *Cinema* nor *Film* is terribly committed to the historicist project. But the two films also attest to a broader principle of popular film historiography. The miscellany, the collection and the compilation have served as the dominant modes of writing and narrating film history in popular culture, not anamnesis or recall in the mode of a fidelity to a certain narrative of the past. Nostalgia turns into recollection and classification, not preservation in its archival or historicist sense. The cinema, removed from elite valorization, state-conferred legitimacy and self-congratulatory industrial nostalgia, becomes a rich repertoire of popular uses in the present.

Through a Different Lens

While the debates around the archiving of Indian cinema's past continue, I have presented here a parallel world of initiatives whose historiographical gestures imply starkly variant perspectives on what would constitute an archive, on the possibility of an archive, and on the necessity of an archive.

Archives are vulnerable to the 'conditions under which they are utilized'.[29] If we think of history as a practice and mode of production, popular visual culture in South Asia is constantly in the practice of producing its history as a vernacular imaginary. The practices of exhibition and image production discussed in this book, therefore, also serve as acts of historiography, of generating a history. At the same time, these practices also constitute open-ended archives, reusing the past and putting past fragments to new or reiterated uses. The question of the cinematic archive may carry its prescriptive, nostalgic and diagnostic elements, especially given the woeful state of India's film archive. But in this essay, I have taken the archive as a heuristic to describe the cinema's propensity to make its past through relentless reuse rather than preservation per se. To reverse my earlier formulation, the archive is not just for the taking in India, it is for the making.

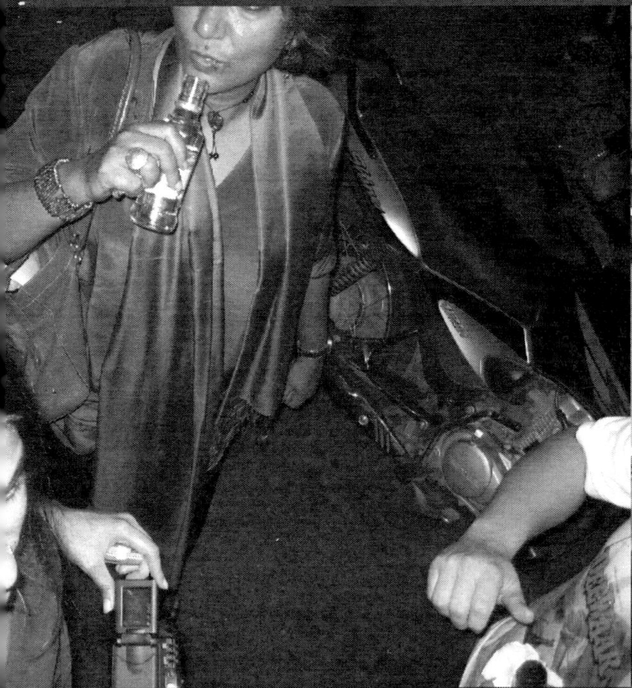

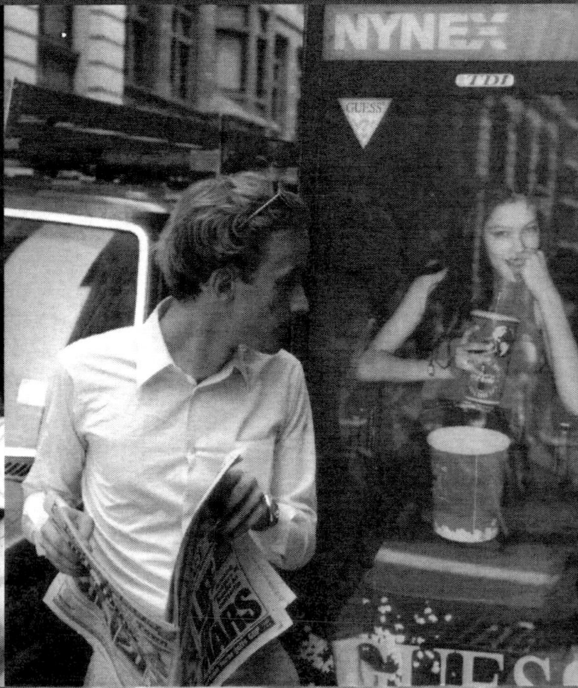
NYNEX
GUESS

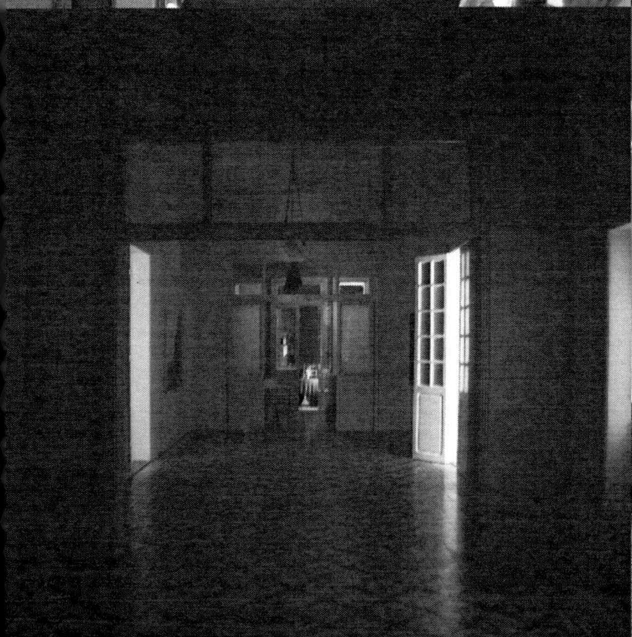

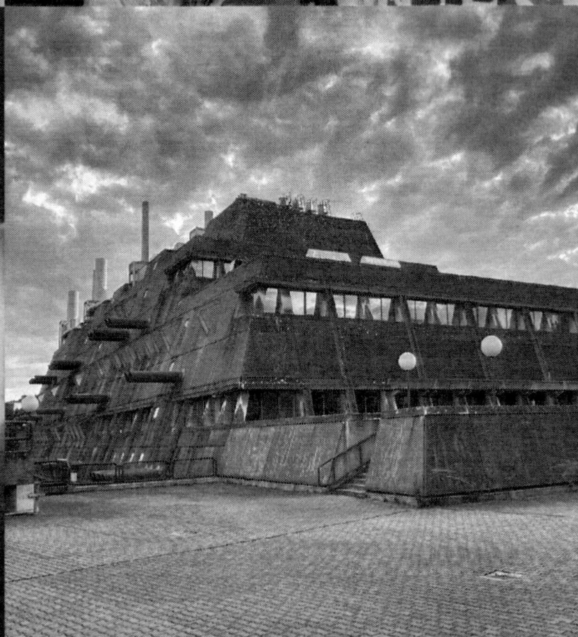

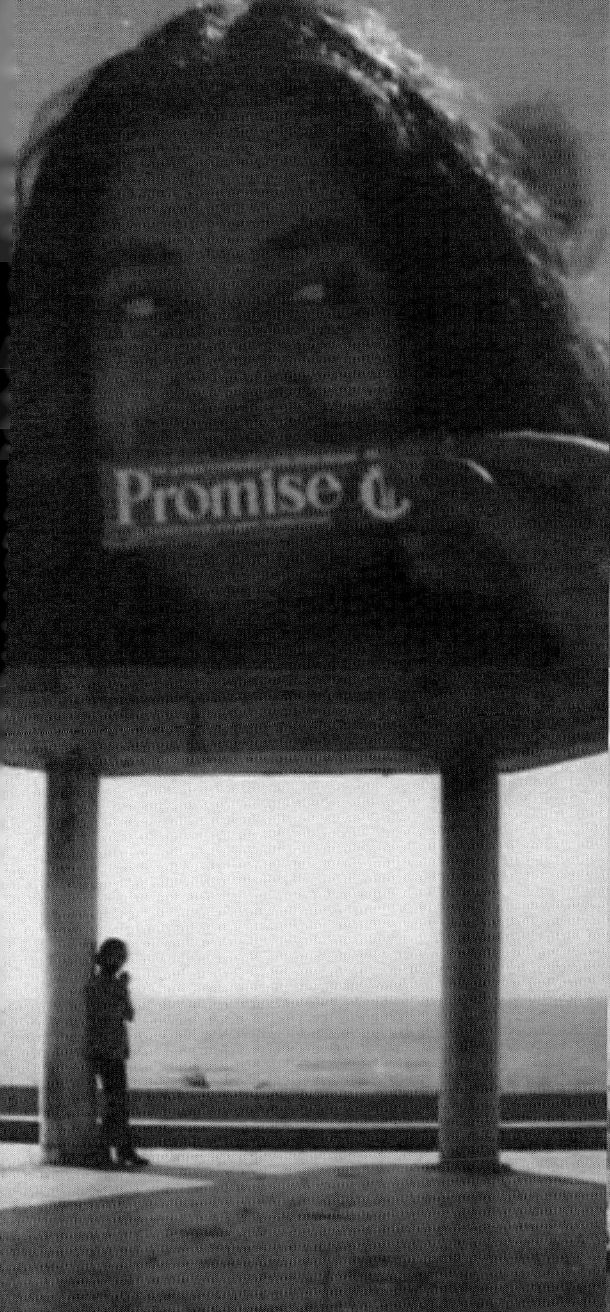
Promise
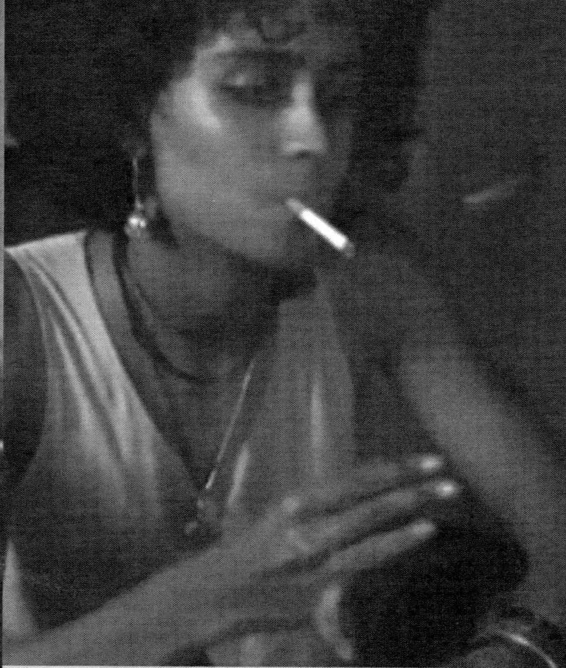
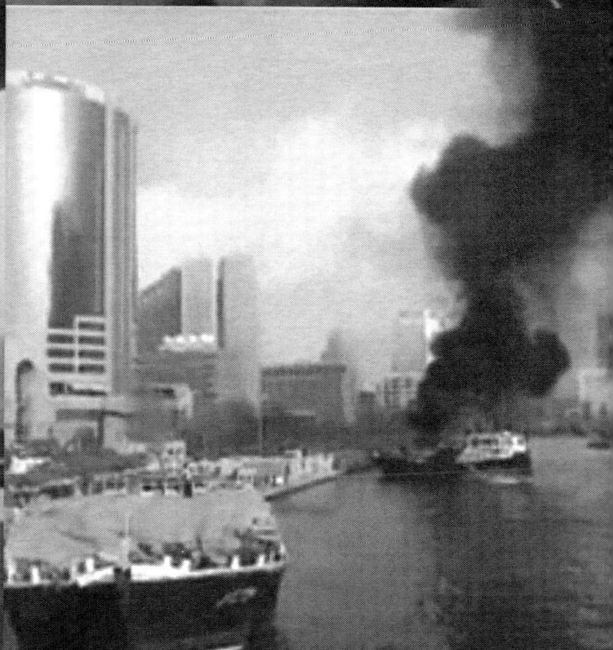

//Sebastian Lütgert and Pirate Cinema, Berlin, learned about Indian cinema through the pedagogic experiment of setting up http://indiancine.ma (an offshoot of Pad.ma and the largest online database of Indian film). Lütgert, aka Robert Luxemburg, works as an artist, writer and programmer with occasional ventures into making films and music. Pirate Cinema, founded in 2004 by Lütgert and Jan Gerber, self-identifies as a bar, cinema and discotheque. Both Pad.ma and indiancine.ma have, through Lutgert's and Gerber's interventions as artist-coders, opened new ways for converting moving images both into data as well as into works of art.

Here Lütgert tries to understand how this strange and sideways engagement with Indian cinema, of which he at once knows nothing and everything, might say something to his enduring interest in developing conceptual and technological possibilities for a radically altered viewing practice. This short text is densely annotated with personal encounters, adding an intimate register to the politics of time, love, archives and cinema.
Thanks to Sebastian Lütgert and Pirate Cinema, Berlin, for their generosity in putting this text together at short notice.

//**Keywords**
Ephemera in Film, Intellectual Property, New Media Art, Pirate Networks: see Keywords (pp. 326-44).

//**Images**
<u>Left page</u>: NW: photograph taken in Bombay (2008); NE: photograph taken in New York (1995); SW: photograph taken in Beirut (2010); SE: photograph taken in Berlin (2020). All photographs courtesy Sebastian Lütgert and Philip Brandts. <u>Right page</u>: NW: *Om-Dar-B-Dar* (dir. Kamal Swaroop, 1988); NE: *In Which Annie Gives It Those Ones* (dir. Pradip Krishen, 1988); SW: *Salim Langde pe Mat Ro* (dir. Saeed Akhtar Mirza, 1989); SE: CAMP: *From Gulf to Gulf to Gulf* (dir. Shaina Anand and Ashok Sukumaran, 2013). All film stills courtesy indiancine.ma (no rights reserved).

// In the Face of Ambiguity, {2021}
// Refuse the Temptation to Guess[1]

// SEBASTIAN LÜTGERT & PIRATE CINEMA, BERLIN[2]

{{

8 // Fragments, as a Teaser for Machine(s) du cinéma: A Voyage with Pirate Cinema through Indian Movies.

This is the interactive online contribution to this book, released at https://indiancinema.org/documents/SIS on 12 February 2021

7 // Please Leave Calcutta as You Found It

Last week, in early June 2020, I came across an old text in the eighth issue of The Journal of the Moving Image, published by the Department of Film Studies at Jadavpur University in Calcutta in 2009. Its appendix was called 'The Future of Hard Drives, a Nod to The Future of Celluloid' that was, and remains to this day, of great concern to some of our friends in India, including Ashish Rajadhyaksha, film theorist and co-editor along with Paul Willemen, of the Encyclopedia of Indian Cinema. To my own surprise – my memories of Calcutta are sometimes hazy – it contained an idea that was immediately applicable to the present moment: a quote by Gordon Moore, co-founder of Intel, more famous as the patron of Moore's Law: 'It can't continue forever. The nature of exponentials is that you push them out and eventually disaster happens.' This is where we are today. Last year in China, a bit of bat shit landed in the mouth of a pig and a few months later, global capitalism as we knew it had come to a standstill. We feel as if we are trapped inside a surreal sci-fi B-movie that tries to educate us about the exponentials of nature. This film about a virus named Corona is a parable, of course, and the exponential it is concerned with is not the spread of a deadly disease, but the rise of global temperatures. In the film we're in, the virus keeps asking us: How do you want to live? In the film we're in, the pandemic is a portal.

My friend replied: Okay, but . . . how did a Pirate Cinema Berlin announcement end up in a film journal in Calcutta? Uh, I said, that's a long story. But if you want the TL; DR: by way of Chinatown ;)

6 // Jagdeep Radio Repairs, Zorawar Singh Marg, Old Delhi, India

One night in late 2005, on my very first visit to India, on a street corner in Bangalore, I came across a small light switch that was attached to a lamppost or electricity pole. I pushed it, and something unforeseen happened.

It was a setup, of course: my first introduction to Indian cinema. To one of its icons even. This would be one of the many possible opening scenes.

5 // Old Bombay Vinyl Junkie

Among the first things 'about India' that our hosts at CAMP showed to us upon our initial arrival in Bombay in late 2007 was *Om-Dar-B-Dar*. This is to say that we got exceptionally lucky, but also formed false expectations: that there would be a lot more of this. In fact, as far as we can see, there is very little. I can say with certainty that I don't 'love Indian cinema', just like, of course, I don't 'like India' – that would be obscene. There are quite a few Indian films that I enjoyed watching, and many more I want to see in the future. But still, I can only list four Indian films that I love. After all these years, that's a low number. Sometimes I think that we've learned surprisingly little about Indian cinema, and one could even argue that we've learned it the hard way.

4 // Egypt Needs More Rain

Part of our voyage through Indian movies takes place on a soon-to-be-retired cruise ship in the eastern waters of the Mediterranean Sea in 2010. This passage addresses a fundamental problem with film studies, not only in India: The primacy of word over image. My 2018 proposition was: 'To shield these images from language'. In 2020, I'm tempted to escalate this to: 'Language is a virus that one day will turn itself against those who speak it.'

3 // Why Does She Not Shower Me with Rupees?

One of the tasks for the new decade could be to collect and ask the questions of Indian cinema. Just like one could do with Iranian cinema (*Where Is the House of My Friend?*), just like the Germans do (*Why Does Herr R. Run Amok?*) and even Hollywood from time to time still has a question (*Who Killed Laura Palmer?*). The point would not be to find answers. Answers are usually not the fun part: they are often banal and sometimes rather unsatisfying.

2 // Kashmiri Queens

Of course, as we all know, there is no such thing as 'Indian cinema'. Indiancine.ma is a Moroccan website for many reasons, the satisfaction our own typographic pleasure is only one of them. Its only peer: Turkishcine.ma. Briefly spotted on the horizon: Korea. And that's because cinema does not align with the nation-state and its borders. Cinema's partitionings and fuzzy margins and enclaves inside exclaves and disputed territories and neighbouring states don't map onto the political geography. 'Indian cinema' is a term like 'Nouvelle vague': It's just a naming convention so that we kind of know what we are talking about. But we need to queer that name, just like Godard did when he insisted that 'Nouvelle vague' didn't only mean 'new wave', but also 'vague news'. We could try the same with the 'moving image'.

1 // Gulf between Us

There was always an obvious water motif in almost everything we were doing. As movie pirates, we already arrived under a seafaring banner. 'Leakage' was among the first English words we learned in India near Civil Lines. Geography was malleable: We travelled the river as archive in Berlin with our main tributary Suzhou River flowing through China. The river of time? In Beirut, we entered it sideways. Later we would spend a month around a river without banks on a rooftop in Bombay. My favourite dive bar at the time? *Yacht*. And in between seasons, to massacre that quote from *Blade Runner*, some of us saw ships burn on the shoulder of Arabia. What did we have in common? BitTorrent.

One issue I always had with Indian cinema: it didn't seem as porous as it could have been. Of course, that mirrors India's geographic isolation. No need to talk about the landlocked north-western or north-eastern regions here. The problem are the Himalayas. There is a German kids' joke: Lets blow up the Alps, I want to see the Mediterranean Sea! The Indian version would be: Abolish the Himalayas, I want to learn more about China! But that's not a joke, since the disappearance of the Himalayas has already begun. They are, among other things, a gigantic body of frozen water that will gradually melt in the foreseeable future and flow into India. The engineering propositions sound a bit scary to me. What would Indian cinema propose?

0 // Lucknow, See Your Error

The year 2020, until the year itself arrived, used to be synonymous with 'perfect vision'. One could argue that the year so far has reinforced this meaning. But why 2020? What about 2000, 2012 or 2620? As every computer programmer (or historian of time) will know, years should be treated as names, not as numbers. There is a hole at the anchor point and below minus 300, all hell breaks loose. The Chinese know this very well: We are in a Year of the Metal Rat.

// Most Quirks (Two Overlapping Authors, All ‘Bombay’ but One ‘Mumbai’, Wink-smiley as Punctuation) are intentional

In 2020, a collaborator who, as an introduction to our software framework pan.do/ra, had just read the ‘Ten Theses on the Archive’ and ‘The Zen of Pad.ma’, asked me: So, are these Ten Theses your Ten Commandments? Are the entries in the Zen of Pad.ma commands that I need to follow on my path to enlightenment? My answer was a bit evasive. I said I was the only person in our collaborative writing group without a catholic education, and also the only one without a clue about Zen Buddhism. But I ended with: Okay, point taken.

The number 10 comes with baggage, from Mount Sinai. The number 12 is not much better: a clique of followers. The number 3, the Holy Trinity, turned upside down, pollutes – as Christian residue – all Marxist dialectics. Four images arranged in a cross will always make a reference to torture. Even monotonically ascending identifiers carry too much meaning.

Maybe one day, we will find images that mean very little, narrate almost nothing, and provide no vision. In fact, a former German chancellor is on record with the bonmot: ‘People who have visions should go to the doctor’. Or, as a friend from Bombay once warned me: ‘If we believe too much in the power of a single image to narrate a story, then that’s the worst thing that can happen.

}}

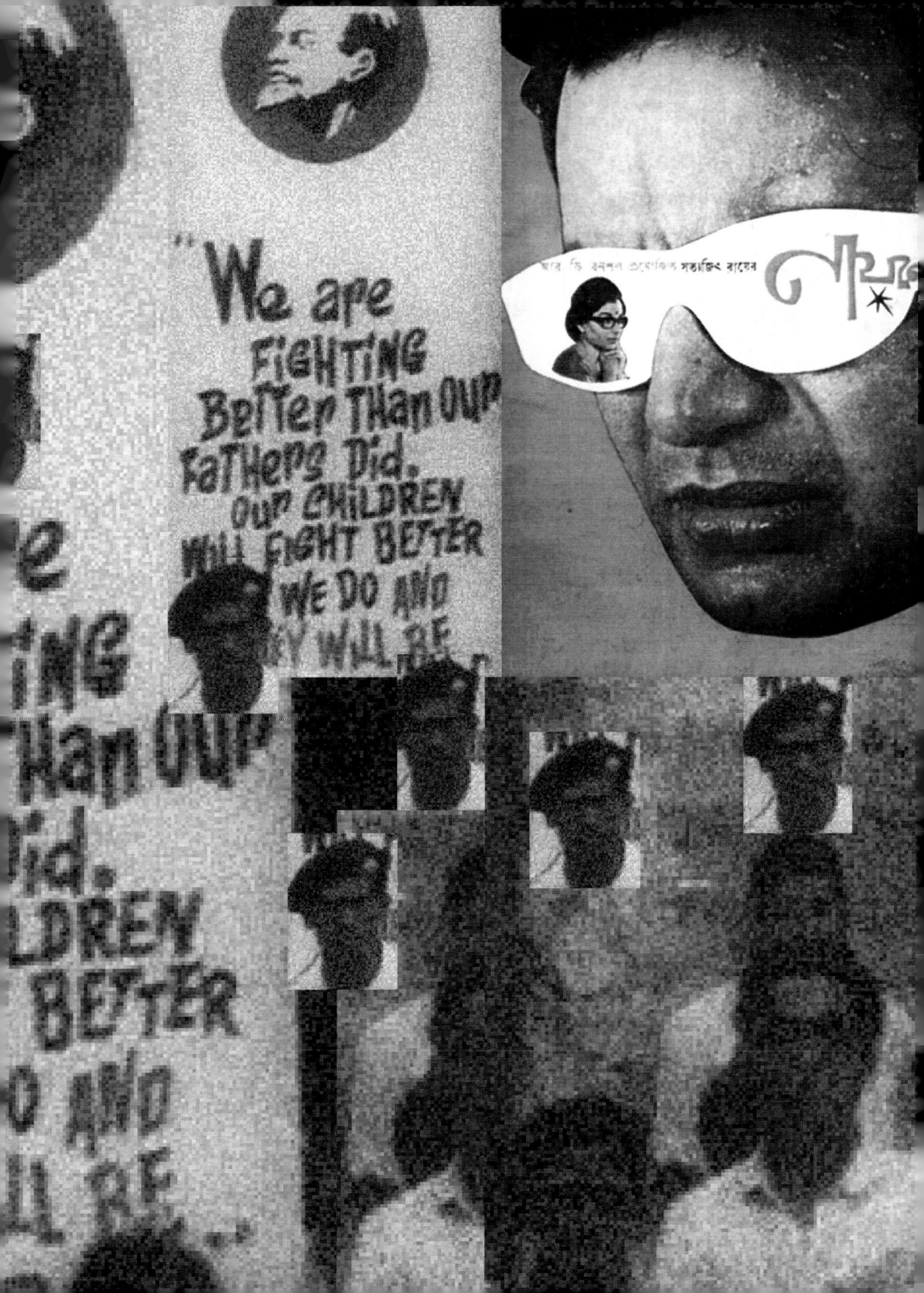
"We are
FIGHTING
Better Than our
Fathers Did.
Our CHILDREN
WILL FIGHT BETTER
WE DO AND

In 2001, sixty years after his death, Rabindranath Tagore's prodigious literary, musical and visual output entered the public domain. Zealously protected by the Visva-Bharati University that Tagore had founded – and after India's copyright law had itself been amended to delay this moment – its eventual release opened some unusual creative floodgates. The process of remaking and reappropriating Tagore was soon followed by a similar obsession with remaking other classic works of literature and poetry, and eventually remaking or producing sequels to famous films by iconic names of Bengali cinema reprised in popular, lowbrow and sometimes explicitly pornographic spaces. Was Bengali cinema haunted by a past it could not shake off? Or was this the under-classes appropriating sites of cultural memory hitherto forbidden to them? Subhajit Chatterjee's interview with the most prolific directors of Bengali exploitation cinema, the Ghosh brothers, charts the cinephiliac tendencies and production networks of the genre.

This is a new version of a text originally published under the title 'A Rendezvous with the Ghosh Brothers: A Sneak Peek into Bengal's Homegrown Exploitation Cinema', *South Asian History and Culture*, vol. 10, no. 4, pp. 397–421. Published with permission of the author.

Keywords, Names

Bhadralok, (*Ritwik) Ghatak*, (*Satyajit) Ray*, (*Rabindranath) Tagore*: See Keywords (pp. 326–44).

Bhansali, Sanjay Leela: Major Bollywood director associated with high-budget period films, including splashy remakes of famous films (e.g., *Devdas*, 2002).

Charulata: Satyajit Ray's 1964 cinematic adaptation of Tagore's 1901 novel, *Nastaneer* (The Broken Nest), marketed in English as *The Lonely Wife* and widely considered one of Ray's most accomplished films; remade as *Charulata 2011*, a soft-porn film, and further remade by Biswajit Ghosh in 2013.

Puruliar Chhau: Dance form associated with the Adivasi/tribal population of Purulia district in Bengal.

Rabindra Sangeet: Songs composed by Tagore. Enormously popular genre of music used extensively in film, especially by Ray and Ghatak.

Visva-Bharati: Arts university established by Rabindranath Tagore in Santiniketan, to which he bequeathed the rights to his collected works; known for rigid policing of Tagore's works – how they are sung, performed or interpreted.

Images

p. 49: Stills from Ritwik Ghatak's *Amar Lenin* (Our Lenin, 1970), made on Vladimir Lenin's birth centenary and briefly banned, montaged with Satyajit Ray's *Nayak* (The Hero, 1966).

p. 56: Frame grab from Satyajit Ray's *Charulata* (The Lonely Wife, 1964).

p. 57: Stills from *Tasher Desh* (Land of Cards, dir. Q, 2012), courtesy the director.

p. 62: Image from *Tasher Desh* juxtaposed with poster of *Disha* (dir. Sanjay Bardhan, 2015), a low-budget Bengali fim about the erotic misadventures of a young woman who hopes to make it big in Kolkata. The poster text bears the suggestive tagline, 'I have seen the city, in the middle of its night'. Photo taken by author in Kolkata, May 2015.

SUBHAJIT CHATTERJEE

2019

05 The Brothers Ghosh

Bengal, Its Art Cinema and its Homegrown Exploitation Genres

> 'Bengalis achieve their orgasm by watching Pather Panchali'
>
> – Q, independent filmmaker

Over the past decade, Bengali cinema has seen an assortment of low-budget features released in the mainstream exhibition circuit, apparently unhindered by the absence of commercial success. Several deploy strategies reminiscent of Euro-American exploitation cinemas, framed by highly localized discourses – especially, in their relationship to both Bengal's urban popular culture and its mainstream film industry. It is a puzzling terrain, and it complicates several neat categorizations that have made up the cinematic map of Bengal.

Writing on Bengali cinema (before academic film studies) was mainly driven by the reformist ambitions of its film society movement.[1] This movement has usually been pivoted around the seminal artistic breakthrough of Satyajit Ray's *Pather Panchali* (Song of the Road, 1955), and has associated the film's realist propensity with socially progressive forces of modernity. From such a view, most Bengali popular cinema – barring a few instances of sporadic artistic flair – was largely viewed as aligned towards archaic, studio-based melodramas in need of transformation.[2] There have been a few revisionist histories of Bengali cinema, locating the modernist-realist experiments of Satyajit Ray and Ritwik Ghatak as being in critical dialogue with a locally rooted, and often aesthetically refined, tradition of popular melodrama.[3]

In contrast, several potboiler melodramas from the 1980s (usually viewed by local intelligentsia as influenced by the Bombay film industry and, thus, as a cultural downfall) attracted a cinephiliac cult audience, not least because of their premeditated distance from highbrow realism.[4] These films are however different from the usual B-Grade, both in how they imagine and use the lowbrow. These films have also bypassed the academic attention recently received by popular Bengali cinema. Here I shall attempt to turn the gaze of the mainstream cinema inward, and will try and explore how specific cultures of fringe production and consumption reveal startling internal dissonances *within* the prevailing Bengali 'high-cultural' ethos.

The localized urban film culture that I shall foreground inhabits a space beyond contemporary Bengali cinema's two dominant incarnations - one, the star-based action-romance dramas banking on time-worn cross regional formulas, including authorized adaptations of Tamil and Telugu films, and two, a new 'urban' cinema claiming high-cultural lineages, seemingly bolder reprising of banal relationship- dramas that thrive on upwardly mobile, middle-class tastes. Since 2010, the former category, the star film, has cost between Rs 1.5 and Rs 2.5 crores (approximately 2 to 3.35 million USD), while the latter category - less lavish, 'new' character-centred urban dramas - has cost around Rs 80 lakhs (1 million USD). Some independent films, usually made with collaborative efforts, have been made with budgets between Rs 25 and 70 lakhs (34,000-94,000 USD). The films to which I refer - and which I classify as a 'homegrown exploitation' sector - are a fraction of even these.[5]

Many of these consciously present themselves as crossbreeds between exploitative genre films (supernatural tales and rape-revenge dramas) and 'mature' entertainment (dramas infused with cautionary or reformist intent). They are usually exhibited at centrally located single-screen theatres in Kolkata, in one-off screenings accommodating three to four different films per day to compete with multiplexes. Their methods are in-your-face amateurish. They sometimes feature mainstream actors, popular musicians and tangential collaborations with industry personalities.

However, their zeal in engaging with social taboos and controversial public debates appear unconstrained by limits of decorum, as content ranges across LGBTQ issues, sex work, social and sexual abuse as reported by television shows and newspaper features. Their publicity is almost distinctively weird, in its shoddy aesthetic and its emphasis on the bizarre. The films' often unresolved narratives, with their ramshackle constructions, alert us to a startling cohabitation of low-grade generic elements with pressing social concerns. Their desperate attempt to find visibility and relevance among an educated middle class that has historically maintained a stark distinction between the reputable and the lowbrow, draws attention to ongoing negotiations across established cultural stratifications in West Bengal.

For all their resemblance to disreputable B- or C- grade cinemas in Hindi and other languages, these films do not easily fit into any existing low-budget networks or premeditated non-urban distribution circuits. Their periodic appearance in prime stand-alone theatres in Kolkata, promotion in urban public spaces and media networks, and the frequent appearance of mainstream artistes in them bear testimony to at least a tangential relationship with the mainstream industry. Further, the amateur auteurs of these films profess inspiration from 'world cinema' and appear driven by genuine aesthetic concerns. Clearly, the fashionably self-aware celebration of 'trash' – which propelled my initial interest in the field – is unsuited to capture what I shall now describe as an obscure but homegrown exploitation phenomenon. This genre aims to communicate to a regional public constituted by the popular media but is opaque to dominant cultural tastes and established social or critical vantage points.

Perhaps the most remarkable figures on this production circuit are the iconic directorial duo of siblings Biswajit and Prosenjit Ghosh. The Ghosh Brothers are from South Calcutta, and they started their career in amateur theatre, shifting into film around 2008 to explore, they say, innovative and socially relevant script ideas for a wider public. As of July 2018, they have completed approximately eight features and are in the process of finishing two more. Working with an entirely amateur crew, with private funding and neighbourhood collaboration through private training workshops, the Ghosh Brothers have a model for cottage-filmmaking that, unlike Hindi or other regional counterparts, bears what I think of as a substantial middle- class psychic investment. Prosenjit, the elder brother and a commerce graduate with work experience in television soaps, usually handles organization and finance. Biswajit, an English literature graduate with a degree in management, handles all creative aspects, ranging from training workshops to script and direction. However, their work roles aren't neatly classified, and are collaborative. Among their significant films are *Kolkatar Doittyo* (The Giant of Kolkata, 2011), a low-budget superhero film featuring a Tamil actor, *Charulata* (2013), a bizarre adaptation of Rabindranath Tagore's seminal novella *Nastaneer* with a queer-feminist agenda, *Chhau* (2015) and its sequel *Chhau 2* (2019), which are reform dramas about traditional dancers of the Purulia district, explicitly quoting Ghatak's documentary on Chhau dancers and also explicitly focussing on disability and violence.

After a long and winding search for this publicity-shy duo, I finally managed to catch up with them during an acting workshop for their forthcoming venture.

The interview was conducted with prior appointment on the evening of 4 July 2018 at the current office-cum-residence of the Ghosh Brothers, in an interior alley of the Dumdum Cantonment area, near the Kolkata airport. The small flat had a sizeable gathering that evening, owing to a script and acting workshop in progress for their latest production *Ami Rabindranath* (I Am Rabindranath) scheduled to go into shooting soon. Biswajit, the younger brother, was the chief respondent to my queries, while Prosenjit made occasional comments and revisions. We were introduced to the gathering, of whom some were playing character roles in various upcoming films, while others were a mix of close associates from the neighbourhood and aspiring actors and actresses. The original interview being in a semi-formal Bengali dialect, I present a translated, annotated and slightly edited version below. However, I have tried to retain some of the informal flavour of the conversation as it captures the ethos of the cinematic culture under discussion.

Subhajit Chatterjee (SC): How old are you both? Where was your original family residence?

Biswajit Ghosh: (BG):(pauses) hmm . . . I am about thirty and my brother is 35–36 years old. We are originally from the Chetla area of South Kolkata.

SC: Have any of your family members ever been involved in filmmaking before you?

BG: No. My mother, who is no more, was a very good Kathak dancer, but as is the case with traditional families she was not allowed to pursue it after marriage. Our father was involved in amateur theatre with his own office colleagues. Our interest in theatre and film stemmed from watching that sort of theatre from a very young age. We staged our first play when I was in the sixth standard. The funds were gathered by selling cheaply printed tickets with false dates, even when the play itself was far from being conceptualized. It was a gimmick. But we got ample buyers at the meagre rate offered. Once we gathered a handsome amount, we decided to hire a room in our own school, the Chetla Boys School, to stage the play. We individually informed all the people to whom we had sold tickets that we were actually staging a play called *Ghumonto Ghumghumi* (nonsensical phrase vaguely meaning 'sleepy mood') but now at a different date. This was a play about ghosts written by me and directed jointly by us. This marked the beginning of our journey.

By the time I was in the tenth standard, we had actually formed a proper theatre group. We used to stage around six to seven shows a month, consecutively. We named our group Alladin Theatre Company and gradually it turned professional. We also started receiving slight help from the Government of West Bengal. Well, then of course, the Left Front themselves lost power. Now, while working in theatre, we got introduced to two personalities – Arati Roy, the popular actress Debashree Roy's mother and the producer Shyam Daga of Daga Pictures.[6] We formed a production house with Arati Roy, APB Films [Arati Prosenjit Biswajit Films]. The first film under that banner was *Ekla Cholo Re* (Let Us March On Alone, 2009). The film was about homosexuality and based on the actual experiences of a homosexual man named Debashish Majumdar who played the main character as well. He had acted earlier in the telefilm *Ushnotar Jonye* (In Search of Warmth, dir.

Kaushik Ganguly, 2003) produced by ETV Bangla portraying the youth of Chapal Bhaduri's character.[7] We asked Debashish about his experiences as a homosexual and he told us in detail about their . . . you know . . . about his feelings. So we based our script on this.

SC: Did Arati Roy, as producer, interfere in any manner with the making of this film?

BG: No, she didn't. She was happy to be a part of the film as chief adviser and in fact contributed some money for production in the form of a charitable donation. We said, 'Aunty, we may not be able to give back the money, so please help us without any expectations.' She also allowed us to use her house near Deshapriya Park [in South Kolkata] for holding our workshops. The film was made on a very low budget. Apart from Debashish, there was a bunch of five to six people who also acted in the film. Frankly, the film did not do well in the theatres, but was received well by the audience. We premiered the film at Chitrabani with help from Father Joseph.[8] Various persons from the film world were present such as Debashree Roy and Dr Shankar Ghosh who was a Professor of Bengali and also an actor. After the premiere, we could release the film in one or two Inox screens but could not recover any money.

SC: I understand that you had made either a film or a play called *Bhoot Kando* (The Affair of the Ghosts). What was this exactly?

BG: It was the second film that we made. It was actually a play that we had written and staged earlier. The story revolved around the fight between humans and ghosts in a village where the former emerges victorious at the end. For this film, we were joined by a person named Samrat Bose, who was very rich. He was from an extremely well-to-do family with feudal inheritance in Chetla. He provided us with everything in terms of location, camera, editing set-up etc. We had shot the film at his palatial house located at Shyam Bose Road in Chetla with newcomers as cast. We made a partnership contract and the film was released under the banner of Biswa Samrat Films at Talkie Show House, and a few *mofussil* halls, and was a commercial success. The satellite rights of the film got sold as well. We were contacted by the television channel Sony Eight, which in those days used to have a program that publicized films the day before their release. They did a nice feature on *Bhoot Kando* due to which it gathered some audience in the halls. The success was moderate actually, after which Samrat moved away from us owing to difference of opinion over several matters. The film was not a huge commercial success either. By then, we had become close to Daga Pictures.

SC: What were the budgets of these two films respectively?

BG: We had made both the films at an extremely low budget. We had a higher budget for *Bhoot Kando* and still it was less than Rs 10 lakh. We shot it with a D55

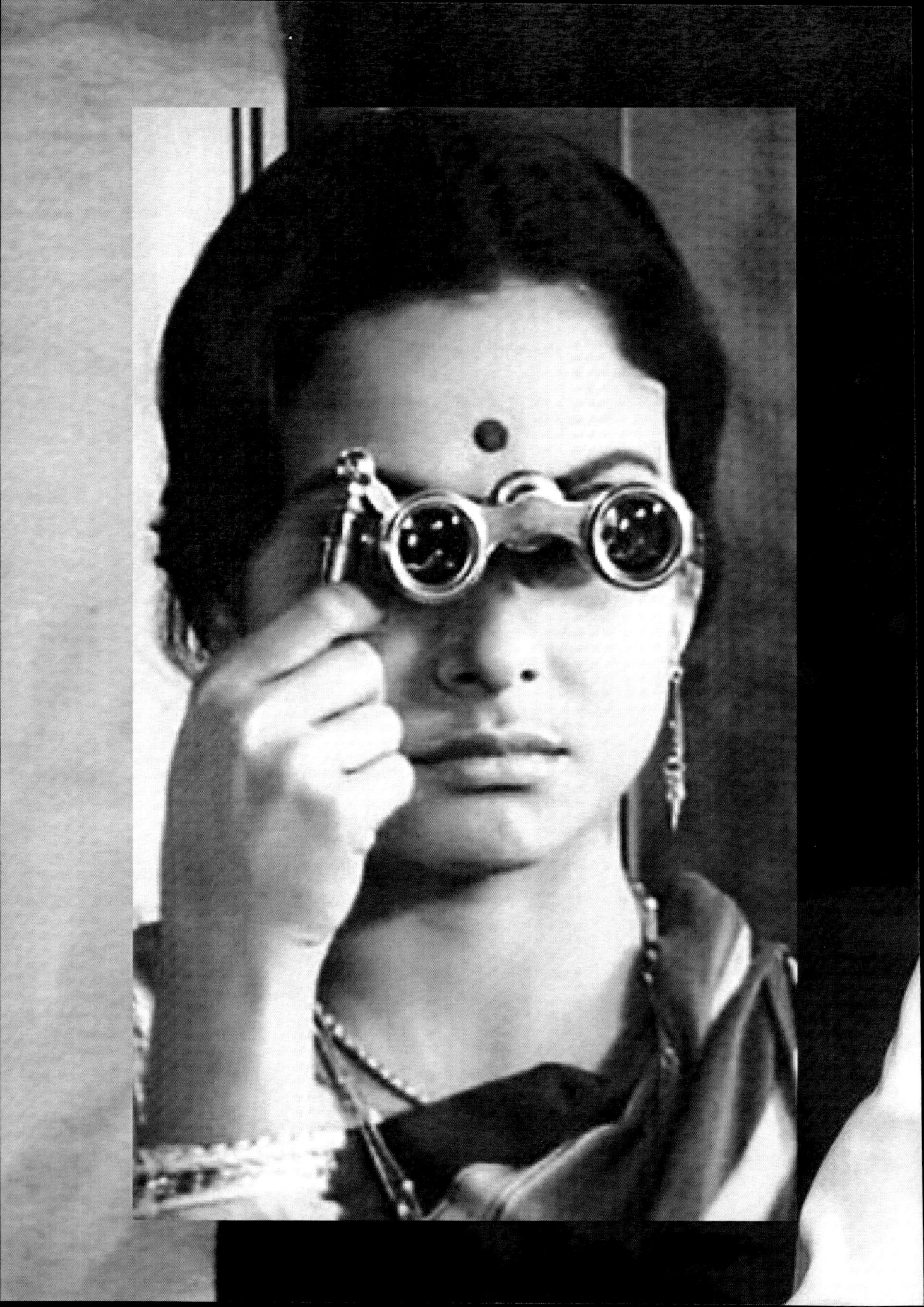

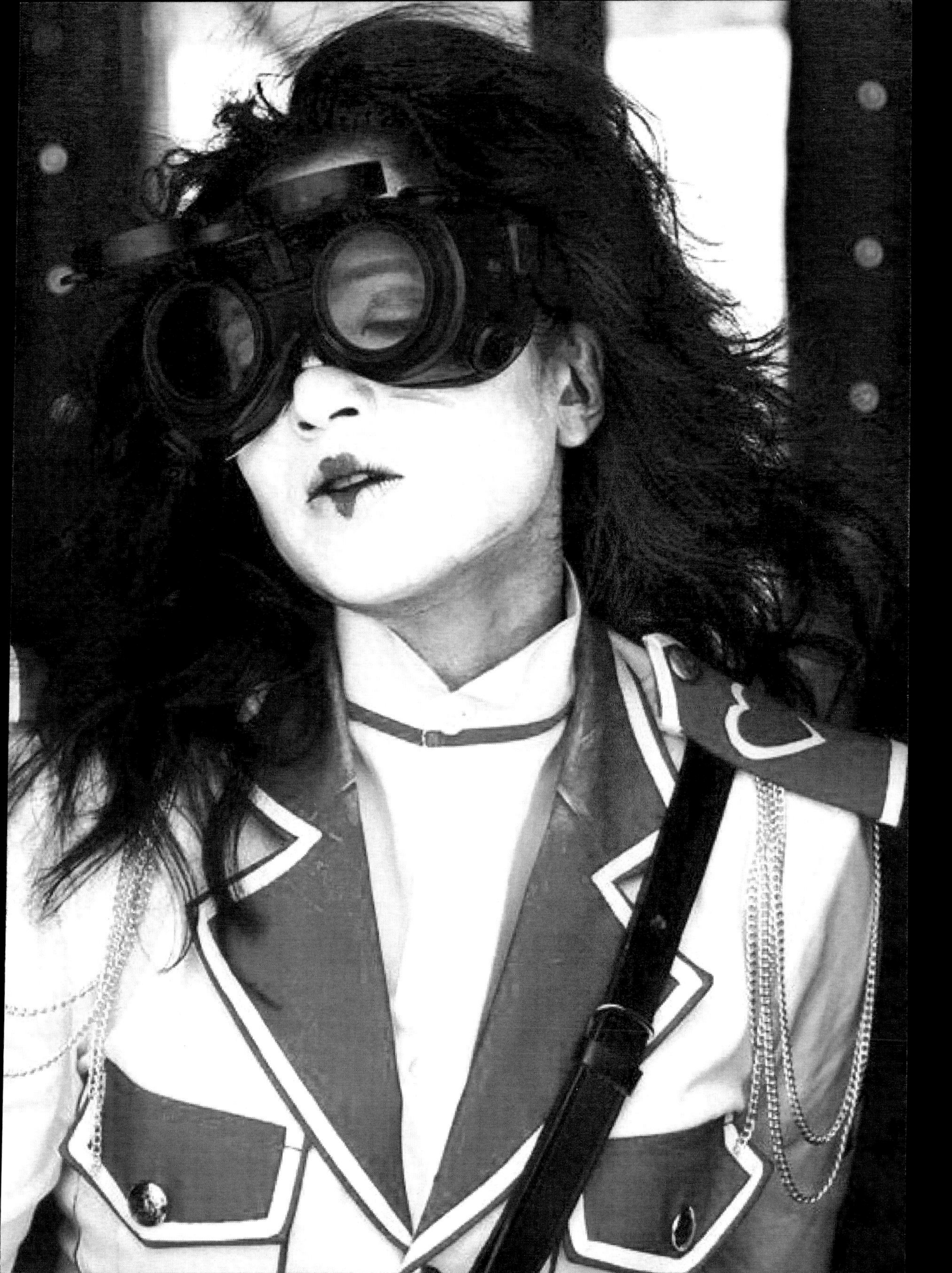

camera and transferred it onto film while releasing. Daga *babu* [a colloquial term of respect often connoting class or social hierarchy] funded that entirely. He also provided for our promotion and distribution.

SC: What about *Kolkatar Doyitto* (*The Giant of Kolkata*, 2011), the superhero film you made?

BG: We then tied up with Daga Pictures and made *Kolkatar Doyitto* with them. The film was released in a large number of cinema halls. It has a unique and different storyline - about an aged, eccentric writer named Arghakamal Dutta who wrote stories all his life which no one would publish. He lives with his widowed daughter-in-law and his dear grandson. The old man is mistreated by the daughter-in-law as she suspects him of leading her son astray with ridiculous stories. Before hanging himself in depression, the grandfather plants the idea of a fictitious character in the young man's mind. It was a man who would roam at night wearing a mask and claws on his hands and would slash criminals. The grandfather's death made a huge impact on the kid, who also goes slightly mad, starts dressing up like this 'giant' character, and roams about in the streets at night fighting crime. On account of his violent activities, he is arrested and produced in court. The court acquits him on the grounds that he had been fighting crime, and he is even awarded a prize for his work. The tagline of this film was that it featured the first Bengali superhero. The film was well-received and ran in theatres. We were able to return some money to the producer.

SC: This was released under the banner White Horse Pictures? When was it established and why such a name?

BG: Yes, see this picture above (a large frame of galloping horses hangs on the wall)? From *Kolkatar Doyitto* onwards we worked under this banner. This was after we broke up with Biswa Samrat Films.

Prosenjit Ghosh (PG): Our mother suggested the name. She was ill and she said, 'Give it a name . . . white horse . . . horses run fast', you know, it is about speed, like about running ahead with your ventures.

SC: So the next film *Charulata* was under this banner? I have watched this film online on the YouTube channel.

BG: Yes. *Charulata*. Many people cautioned us not to go forward with this film. They said such a great man [Satyajit Ray] has done the film, it may be risky. But I had this desire and I was adamant. So we read *Nastaneer* again and again.

SC: Was this film inspired by Ray's *Charulata*, or by the root story *Nastaneer* by Tagore? There is already a remake of Ray's *Charulata*, made in 2012.[9] So why did you plan on making another version?

BG: It was inspired by Ray's film. We really liked the film and have seen it many times. As you may have noticed, our film begins with a tribute to Ray.

SC: But it is also evident from your film that you had read *Nastaneer* and have tried to rewrite the story in a sense.

BG: Yes. We read it multiple times. While reading we felt that Satyajit Ray had shifted quite a lot from the original story in his depiction. We tried to stick to the original story as much as possible. We went through a hard time procuring money for the film. Finally, with great difficulty we finished in a very small budget.

SC: How was the film funded?

BG: Shankar De of Dinesh Chitram helped us out in this aspect.[10] He also provided immense help during the release. We made it amply clear that the money should be treated as a donation, and not like an investment. The film got selected for screening in Nandan and Indira Cinema. As you know, films like this have a dedicated viewership in Nandan.[11]

SC: The posters for this film had started being put up from 2012 but the film ultimately got released in 2013. Why is this?

BG: We had put up the posters earlier, to make publicity about the film. Then we started facing a financial crisis while making the film. The first posters that were released were typeset posters. During the release in July 2013, we had actually put up more banners than posters. We had also put up ads on Kolkata TV and 24 hour TV channels. Angel Video then bought the rights of the film, and the money we gave to Shankar De. We don't know how much exactly we got from the halls. Mr De took care of that.

PG: We had also started shooting *Bishay Pather Panchali* (Subject Pather Panchali) around the same time but we could not release it.

SC: What is this *Bishay Pather Panchali* about? Is it a documentary?

BG: We are very big fans of Satyajit *babu* or rather Satyajit sir. He has greatly inspired our filmmaking. We have learnt filmmaking watching his films. This film was made to foreground the struggles he went through while making *Pather Panchali*. The main source used was *Amader Katha* (Our Story, 1999) by Bijoya Ray [an autobiographical account by Ray's wife] and we also used other sources through internet research. It was entirely a fictional story. However, we had to stop shooting the film because of a tussle with the producer.

SC: Did you have to secure any permission from his son Sandip Ray for making the film?[12]

BG: No. The Censor Board did not have any problem with it either. People can always have different versions of a person's life story.

SC: Did you guys have any problem with the Censor Board regarding *Charulata*?

BG: Nope. It had fetched a 'U' certificate.

SC: What about the kissing scene between Charu and Manda[13] that is there in the trailer?

BG: We had cut it out of the film. We had shown the film for review to the curator of Rabindra Bharati University, I forget Madam's name now, who cautioned us towards possible controversy owing to the huge social stature of the director. She said, 'If you implicate a great man into such obscenity you will be harassed in the censorship process'. Anyway, we plan to take up *Bishay Pather Panchali* again. We want to repeat [remake] the entire film in the future.

PG: Tell them about the film, *Dharshan* (Rape).

SC: Yes. I have seen an extended trailer online. Is the whole film available yet?

BG: No. We have not put up the film as its satellite rights have not yet been sold. People interpreted it as an adult film. We had never made it for such an audience. The film was neither here nor there and it sank at the box office. We could not even sell the satellite rights of the film.

BG: A minor company called Last Dynamic Entertainment sponsored some of it. We then got another project from Sanjeev Nunda who has a dubbing studio. He asked us to deliver film remakes from the south [south India] as directors on hire. The movie that we then started making was of the *nagin* genre[14] and was being shot at a village near Joychandi Hill in the Purulia district. We were forced to make that film for money. We were slowly losing our true selves. Imagine watching films on laptop and repeating them shot by shot! While shooting in Purulia, we met people of the region, intimately mixed with them and got to know about their dance form chhau. One of these lonely nights, we two brothers were standing below the hill. It was a silent moonlit night. At that moment we decided we will learn about the mysteries of this region and its life, about chhau. That is where the idea of the film *Chhau* came from. We moved away from Sanjeev's film. We told him that our mentalities are not matching and this way his film will flop. So we started making *Chhau*.

SC: What is *Chhau*'s story?

BG: The story revolves around a girl and her blind older brother who had chhau in his veins. The girl would keep on urging her brother to dance chhau. In the course of the story, the brother is forced to dance chhau one day to save his sister. The entire village flocks to watch a blind man perform. Gradually, chhau gains popularity in the entire village again. However, a famine spoils everything. People start leaving their village in search of food. Some even go to a faraway village one day, to have the *khichuri* [a basic meal comprising of rice cooked with lentils] being served at someone's last rites. The blind man, Nitai, tries to stop people from leaving the village, but gets abused and beaten up. At the end, everyone returns to the village and resumes the practice of chhau amidst all this misery. The tagline of the film was *mori jabo tobu lach chharbona* (We shall die but won't stop dancing). The Censor Board was very impressed by this film and said that the government might offer some support in view of the subject. They made a recommendation with which we applied to Nabanna.[15] Afterwards we received a call from an officer in the Directorate of Agricultural Income Tax claiming that Nabanna had given them the responsibility to support the film. He asked us to submit the film and all the necessary details, saying that it will be made tax- free only if they deem fit. We were then summoned by the finance department and eventually the film was declared tax-free. The film was even awarded some financial help by the minister in charge of the Department of Paschimanchal Unnayan Affairs (set up by for the development of tribal 'backward areas'). The film was released and was warmly received. We have not sold the satellite rights yet as we are waiting for better offers.

We then made the sequel, *Chhau 2*. The story of this film revolves around an ashram which is a home for physically and mentally disabled people. The home is managed by criminals and is maintained deplorably. These people do not even get to eat properly, so even a scrap of food creates wild frenzy and violence among the inmates. Then a chhau artist, who has been driven out of his village as a suspected leper, comes to this home. The film documents how the artist takes up a challenge to train all these deprived and deformed people in chhau dance.

SC: Who are the actors for this film?

BG: The main character is played by a non-Bengali actor called Shubham Agarwal. Here, we have some of them around us. Jimmy to my right plays the physically disabled person; Pooja sitting there has played the mentally disabled patient; Debasish here plays a character who worked in a graveyard. And, we have here, Debraj Ray who helps us with story suggestions and *kakima* [aunty] who is very talented and who we have resolved to take out of her home into the world of cinema.

Now let's get back to *Chhau 2*. So you see these are people who are thieves and disabled, driven by 'animal instincts' and who beat up humans randomly. The story is how the chhau artist starts training them. Let me describe a scene. There is a dance piece in chhau called *poshu chal*, meaning 'walk of animals', and the artist is confused about how to teach them this dance, for at the very mention of chhau, he is met with obscene verbal abuse. One day, some sweets are sent to the ashram from a zamindar's house. The artist rounds them up across the food and tells them to mimic his movements if they want any sweets. As he runs away with the sweets, the inmates hound him like stray dogs and in the process learn the dance. There is also this situation where he spins a tale about a pot of gold which he promises

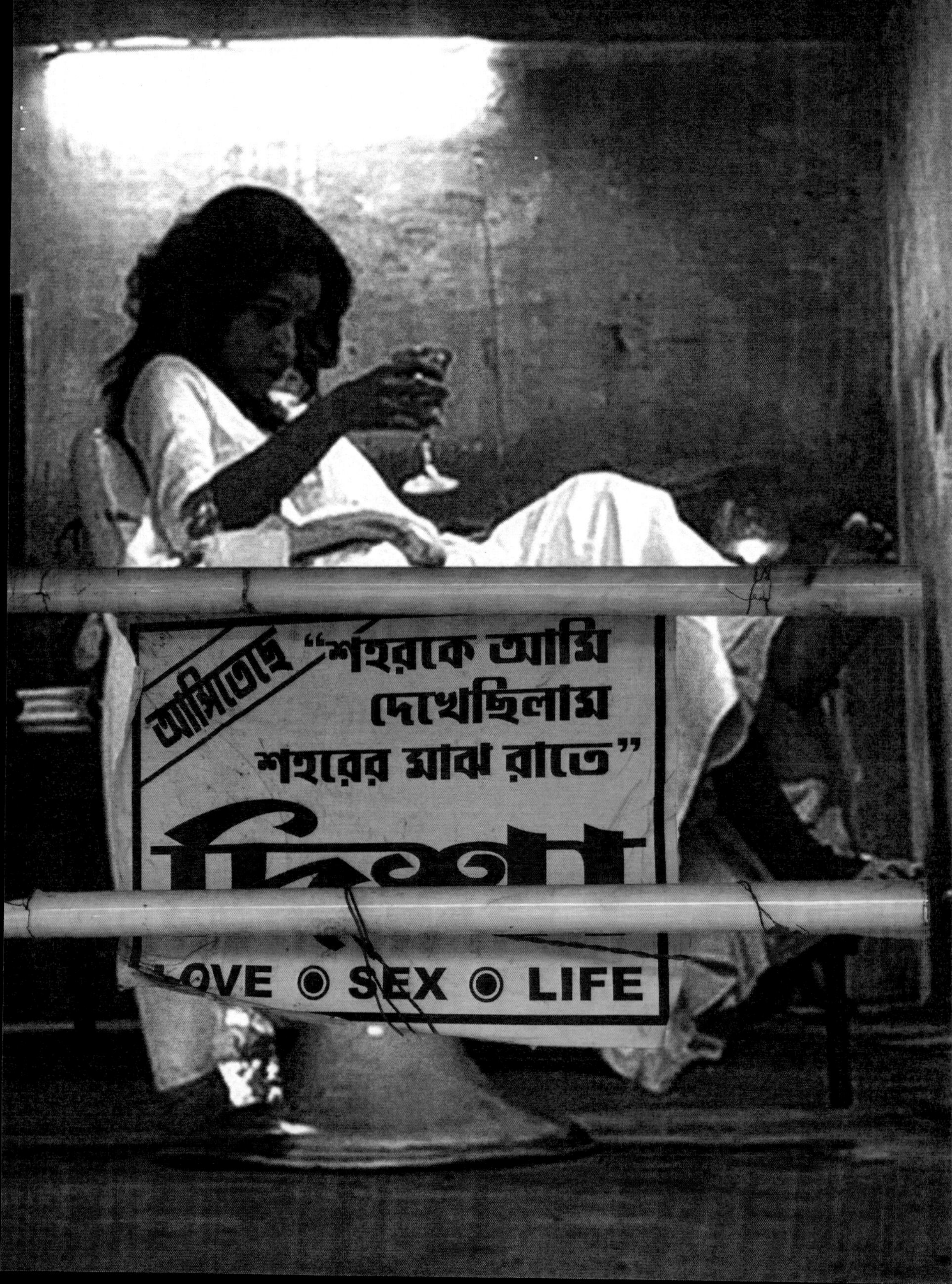
আসিতেছে
“শহরকে আমি
দেখেছিলাম
শহরের মাঝ রাতে”
LOVE ◉ SEX ◉ LIFE

in exchange of discipline in dance training. Eventually, they learn chhau, only to discover that there were no gold coins awaiting them. In rage, the inmates hack and kill the artist. Then realization dawns on them. Chhau has helped them to attain human values again. Finally, they start dancing chhau again.

PG: We also have another unfinished film *Autograph 2*.

SC: My god! What is this one about? Not a sequel to that *Autograph* surely?[16]

BG: No. It is based on the life of the famous director Anup Sengupta (director of mainstream comedy-potboilers often featuring popular stars). His life is very different and we have a close relationship with him.

SC: I am sorry but which Anup Sengupta?

BG: The one who has directed *Chore Chore Mastuto Bhai* (Brotherhood of Thieves, 2005) and *Mama Bhagne* (Uncle-Nephew, 2009). He is also the husband of Piya *di* who is working with us in *Ami Rabindranath* (I, Rabindranath).[17] One day, while chatting, he told us, 'Do you know, Biswajit, I have become a director from a junior artist?' He said that he had started his career playing a junior artist in *Sannyasi Raja* (The Hermit King, dir. Piyush Bose, 1975). I got interested and started documenting these stories. Stories of his experiences, struggle, being cheated by studio personnel – all true stories. That is what the film will be, a document on how he becomes this great director. It is being produced by White Horse as well but we haven't decided whom to get it released through.

SC: Any other unfinished projects in the horizon?

BG: Yes. *Sundarbaner Bhoot* (Ghost of the Sundarbans), which revolves around a lame boy who ventures into a remote village in the Sundarbans mangrove forest area which gets into news for spooky happenings. The boy exposes a racket run by a few dacoits who extort money from people. He gets awarded for his good deeds. This is already shot but lying incomplete. And, there is the film that we are in the process of making, *Ami Rabindranath*, for which I have researched quite a bit.

SC: Could you please elaborate upon the narrative of *Ami Rabindranath*?

BG: We have not started shooting yet. We will start our shooting from July/August 2018 under the White Horse banner. [At this point, PG starts introducing the amateur actors playing the different characters in the film, some of who are present in the room.] Jimmy Das is portraying Rabindranath himself, Pooja Ganguly is playing Jnanadanandini Devi [Rabindranath's elder brother Satyendranath Tagore's wife], Megha is playing Tagore's wife Mrinalini, Saheb there plays Debendranath, and this *dada* here who is an experienced actor with the theatre group Sundaram, will be playing the servant Shyam. There are many more roles awaiting selection. Among the professionals, there is the veteran actor Soumitra Chatterjee who is playing the role of Dwarakanath Thakur [Tagore's grandfather] and Nabanita

Chatterjee is playing the lead, Kadambari Devi, Piya Sengupta is playing Tagore's mother and Pallabi Chatterjee is playing one of his elder sisters. Dr Sankar Ghosh will appear in a special role.[18]

In this film, we are trying to show that the death of Kadambari Devi (Tagore's sister-in-law) actually did Rabindranath good. Rabindranath had lost some of his mental balance after the death of Kadambari Devi. Let me recount the last scene for you. After *bouthan*'s [sister-in-law's] death, Rabindranath is sitting alone on the third floor balcony staring at the sky and muttering to himself. On being asked by his poet friends whether he was planning renunciation, he replies,

I am not unhappy, in fact I am doing much better after Kadambari's death. It is very important for a person not to have any baggage (*pichhutaan*). She used to disturb me day in and day out and I could never work in peace. I have become a free bird now. I can see sky bluer than you can, I can see the trees greener than you can.

All the litterateurs around realize then that Rabindranath's writing has surpassed them. Finally, even Akshay Kumar says, 'we shall never understand Rabi's language as he has risen to a greater height'. The film ends with Rabindranath running on the beach with *ei akashe amar mukti aloy aloy* (my liberation is in the radiance of the skies) playing in the background. It shows the story of constraint and freedom that played out between Kadambari and Rabindranath.

SC: Let's get back to *Charulata*. How did you cast the characters?

BG: The name of the man playing Bhupati, the husband, is Subir Sanyal. Amal was played by Rupam, whom I have observed in amateur theatre for a long time. He was a very dedicated actor and had kept on asking us for the role and we eventually cast him. There is a 'thing' about him, he could attract women. Although he is not conventionally good-looking or fair, he seemed to fit the role of Amal in my directorial imagination. The skin tan is what women like in men. As for Pritha who plays Charu, we found her through an audition and liked her 'look'. We selected her over twenty others though this is her first film and we had to train her carefully. Subir Sanyal used to act in bit roles in television serials earlier. I had felt that he would fit the role of Bhupati well and he has given his best.

SC: Why did you decide to engage with different social issues like homosexuality, deformity, violence etc. in your films? You could have made entertaining films adhering to the general formula, or standard adaptations of Tagore for the small screen. Why make films like this?

BG: Basically to communicate the unknown. We always wanted to gift something new to the audience and we wanted them to engage and discuss our films. We wanted to make films which would be deemed impossible by our audience, say, like *Ami Rabindranath*. We know that this film shall generate controversy.

We wanted to give our audience an everlasting message and a creation that would stand the test of time. If not all then at least a film-literate audience would appreciate, we hope.

SC: Two more things. In *Charulata*, why is there the sound of a whip when the child bride Charu enters her in-laws' house and even in the last scene in which Bhupati departs?[19]

BG: To represent pain.

SC: Whose idea is this? Just a random one or influenced by some other film?

BG: It was the idea of the director. Of course, one has to watch films in general in order to make one film. We watch a lot of films in order to make films – to learn.

SC: What kind of films do you watch?

PG: We watch Ritwik Ghatak, Mrinal Sen.

BG: We don't like the current stuff that is too commercialized. Yes, we have seen Ghatak's *Meghe Dhaka Tara* (The Cloud-Capped Star, 1960), *Ajantrik* (Pathetic Fallacy, 1958); we have seen all of them but we like to watch Satyajit Ray more than any other. We watch his films repeatedly. We love his shots.

SC: Do you watch more of foreign films or Indian films?

BG: Mixed bag – we watch whatever we get access to. I feel watching films is something that we do not only for entertainment but for learning as well. I generally watch films after work that is after midnight on my laptop.

SC: Finally – what are your favourite films?

PG: The two films that we like the most are *Pather Panchali* and *Titanic* (dir. James Cameron, 1997).

BG: I do not think there can be any alternative to these films.

BG: We also love Sanjay Leela Bhansali. Particularly his filmmaking!

SC: Why did you both relocate so far north from Chetla?

BG: We had a flat in a cooperative society in Chetla but we had to face a lot of problems, a lot of internal politics. So we sold that flat and bought this one here. We still have our ancestral house in Chetla which we frequently visit. It's on rent now and soon it will be given to a promoter for redevelopment. We are very happy here.

PG: To tell you the truth, I feel people were moving away from their roots and culture in South Calcutta. That [still being rooted and culturally attached] is still present strongly here in the north. We have found dear people like *kakima* and Jaga *da* – people who can help and support us so well. We have found people like

Debasish and Saheb here who are virtually mad about acting. We now live here with our father.

SC: Have any of you married yet?

BG and **PG**: No, no. Neither of us. We are living with cinema.

Afterword

As the interview bears out, the film industry's marginal sectors have the power to articulate desires and aspirations that remain unsanctioned within dominant cultural discourses. The lack of centralized industrial governance, along with looser norms of censorship, layers the amateurish creative pursuits of this sector with acerbic and ironic energies that indicate potentially significant dissonances within commonly held assumptions about regional cultural identities and their relationship to contemporary social transformations. Here, the work of amateur artistes such as the Ghosh Brothers (among numerous others) becomes a fruitful location to uncover various incongruous currents constituting the shifts in social activism and political culture in the recent past of West Bengal.

Let us consider a few of the links that this preliminary study of 'lowbrow' cinema may go on to uncover. In the post-colonial era, a Bengali highbrow cultural imaginary was essentially defined by the educated middle class's obsessive reverential attachment to the musical and literary tradition of Rabindranath Tagore, and to an art house cinema associated with visionaries like Ray, Ghatak and some of their contemporaries. Tagore's poetry and songs had special resonances among the educated classes in Bengal and gradually became a customary presence in their everyday cultural life. This cultural ethos has undergone a gradual and wide diffusion into the larger public domain producing a set of curious effects.

The taste-culture had a wide recirculation after the 70s through television song–dance programmes, audiotapes, local literary meets, pirated video discs, and finally as an outcome of the lifting of copyright on Tagore's work, thus far held by Visva-Bharati.[20] The cultural imaginary continues to play itself out in the public sphere of politics and communitarian celebrations, as testified by the Kolkata Municipal Corporation's recent redecoration of Satyajit Ray's erstwhile residential area with reproductions of his original film-posters, and the regular evocation of Tagore's songs at major traffic signals or politically sponsored cultural fairs.

This cultural ensemble is unique to Bengal. It is further fostered by the film society movement's internal dynamics and its amateurish mimicry at many regional levels, the numerous small-scale amateur literary publications (the 'Little Magazine' movement) as well as a generalized public desire for producing 'meaningful' art in the digital era. Such circumstances now contribute to many striking encounters between the high and the low, the organized and the haphazard, the refined and the crass - a phenomenon so very familiar yet obscure, which academic research is only beginning to explore. The cinema of the Ghosh Brothers with their intriguing affinity towards cultural esteem and social awareness points towards such complex and startling encounters that could provide an entry into more nuanced accounts of the 'contemporary'.

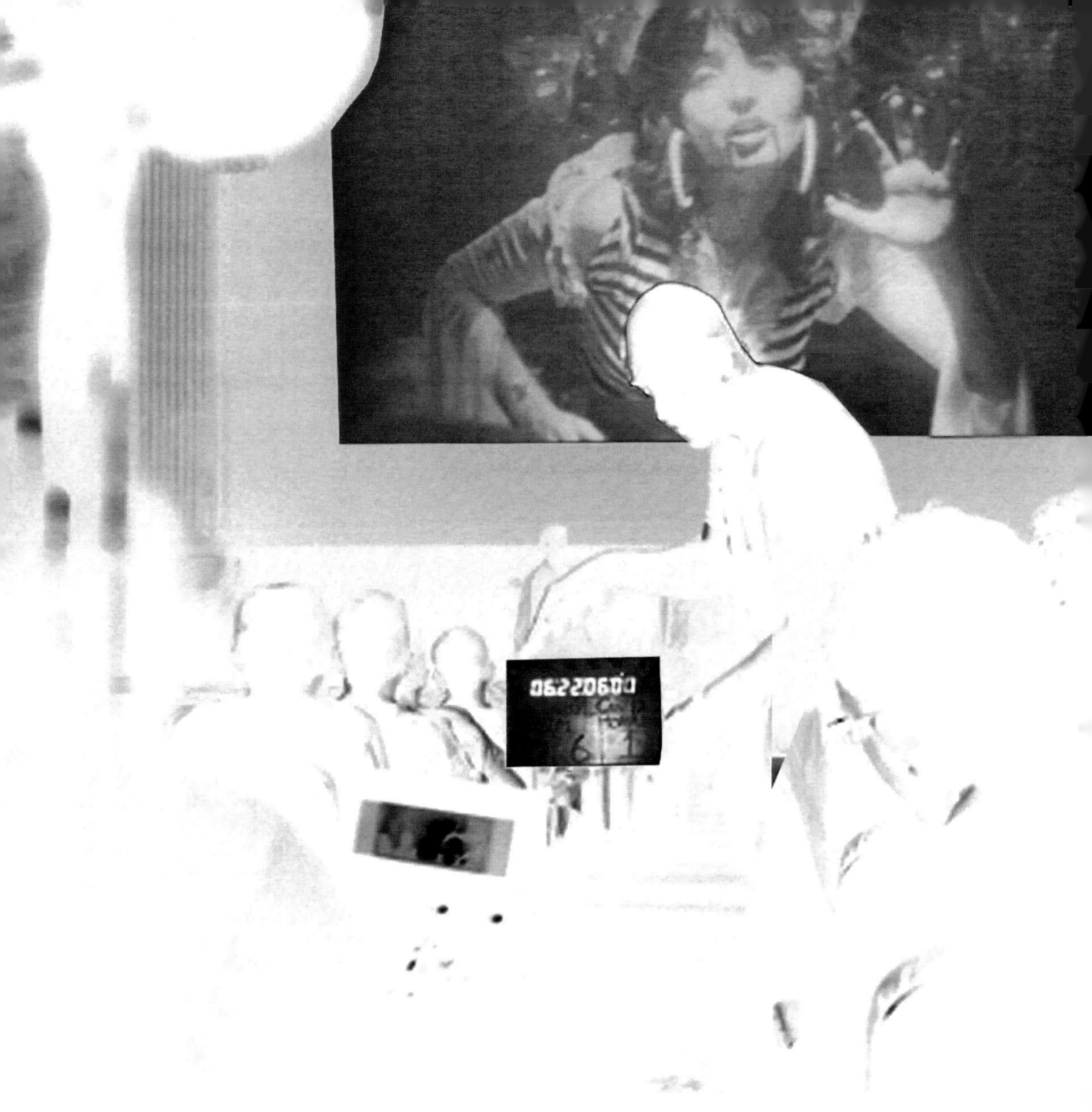

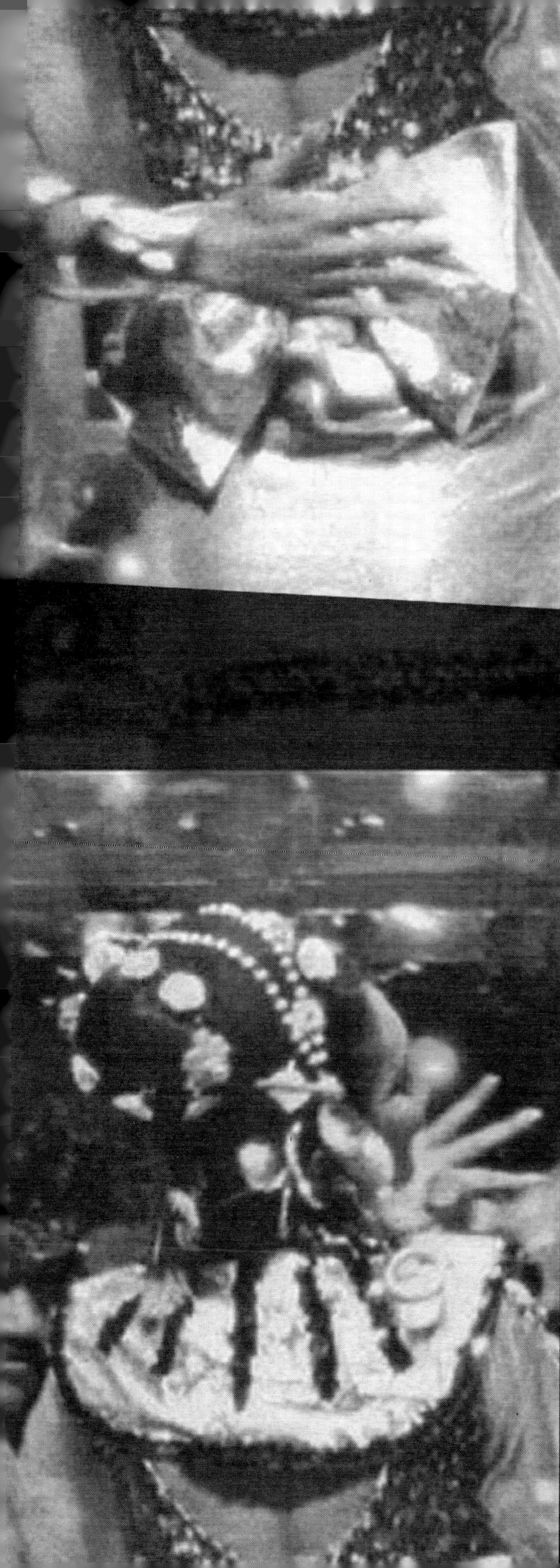
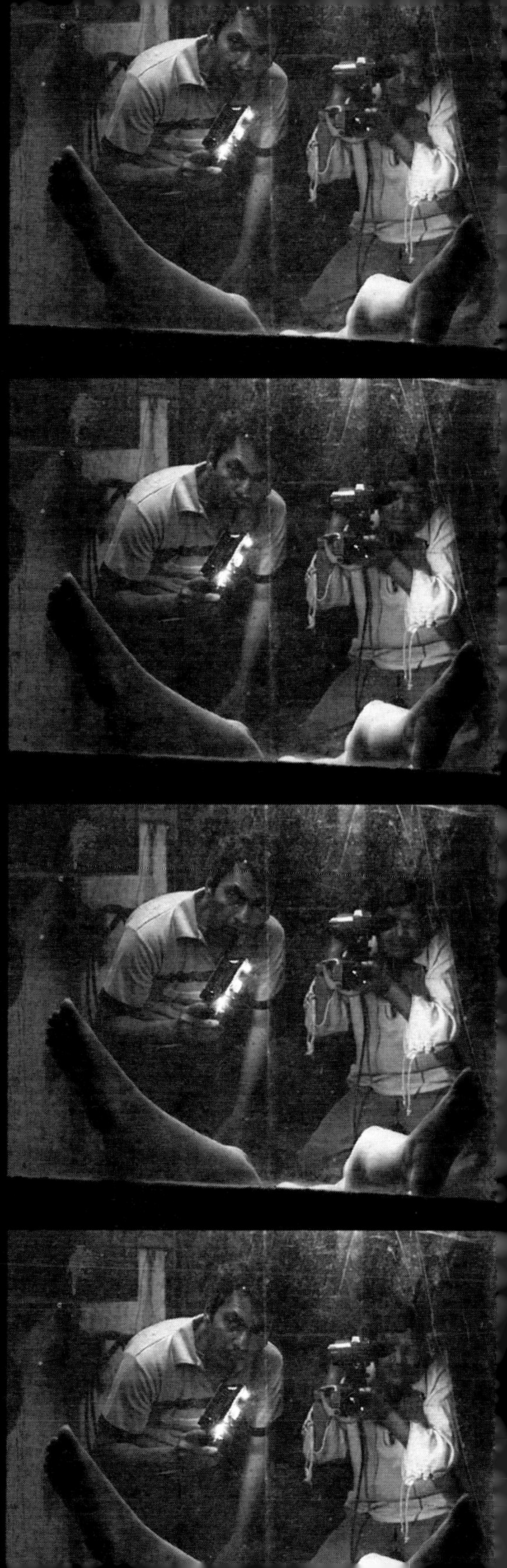

Malayalam cinema's suppression of its soft-porn legacy in the early 2000s led to its reappearance as spectres, haunting theatres and other uncanny sites of memory, resisting subsequent sanitization makeovers. The art-house film *Kanyaka Talkies* (dir. K.R. Manoj, 2013), set in this era, becomes a site for multiple excavations in this essay. Some of the excavations go beyond the film itself. An installation originally made for the film by the artist Priyaranjan Lal became an artwork at the 2012–13 Kochi Biennale. The original movie theatre, briefly converted into a Pentecostal prayer service, reveals its secret history to the author. The memory of soft-porn bleeds into the contemporary as if to retroactively negotiate the end of the celluloid era.

Earlier version published under the title, 'The Spectral Duration of Malayalam Soft-porn: Disappearance, Desire, and Haunting', *BioScope: South Asian Screen Studies*, vol. 7 no. 2, 2017, pp 127–50. Revised version published here with permission from the author and Sage Publications Pvt. Ltd. Grateful acknowledgment to K.R. Manoj for his help and support.

Keywords, Names

Benami Finance, *Censor Board*, *Cinephilia*, *(Adoor) Gopalakrishnan*, *Pornography*: See Keywords (pp. 326–44).

Avalude Ravukal (Her Nights, dir. I.V. Sasi, 1978): Cult Malayalam film about a young prostitute, originally made with arthouse intentions, subsequently reborn into a soft-porn market.

Chitranjali Studios: Unit of the Kerala State Film Development Corporation based in Thiruvananthapuram, set up in part to clean up the film industry.

Gulf boom: Mass economic migration from Kerala to the Gulf countries in the 1970s and 80s, resulting in increased remittances and a neo-rich Malayali diaspora.

Kambikathakal: Erotic stories.

Madakarani: Female figure with unabashed sexuality who uses her charms to her advantage.

Mammootty and *Mohanlal*: Malayalam superstars from the 1980s, often credited with bringing economic stability to the mainstream film industry.

MMS: Multimedia messaging service.

Painkili: Malayalam for vernacular pulp fiction.

Randam-ezhuthukar: Ghost writers who prepare a 'second' script for submission to the CBFC.

Shakeela: Malayalam actress from the south Indian porn film industry and a major sex symbol in the 1990s and 2000s, having acted in over 250 films.

Snapaka Yohannan (dir. P. Subramanyam, 1963): Well-known Malayalam mythological with a Christian theme, telling the story of St John the Baptist.

Swamy Ayyappan (dir. P. Subramanyam, 1975): Hit bilingual mythological based on the cult of the deity Ayyappa at Sabarimala, known for advocating male celibacy.

Thundu: 'Cut-piece', erotic celluloid inserts in films not approved by the Censor Board, spliced together by the projectionist.

Images

pp. 68–69: Montage of stills from Ashim Ahluwalia's *Miss Lovely* (2013), a drama set in the criminal depths of Mumbai's C film industry. A combination of *noir*, documentary and melodrama shot on super 16 and 35 mm, the film is a reflection on the nature of celluloid and the extinction of cinema itself. Images courtesy the director.

pp. 75, 80: Priyanjan Lal's installation, *Kuliyum Mattu Scenukalum/The Shower and Other Scenes*, 2013, mixed media and digital video; images courtesy the artist.

06 Disappearance, Desire and Haunting

DARSHANA SREEDHAR MINI

2016

Introduction

Time is often conceptualized as something heterogeneous, moving beyond clock and calendar. Cinematic time is haunted by an unruliness, as directly evidenced in horror film, which reveals a 'continuous progress of the past which gnaws into the future and which swells as it advances', even as it allows a temporal critique that can '(overturn) the presentism of the contemporary'.[1] Past, present and future coexist as a continuum that refuses the precedence of any one of them over the others.

My essay draws from work on duration and memory to look at the 1980s Malayalam celluloid soft porn. I focus on three sites - the film *Kanyaka Talkies* (dir. K.R. Manoj, 2013), the S.P. Movie Theatre in the city of Thiruvananthapuram, and the art installation *Kuliyum Mattu Scenukalum* (the shower and other scenes) by Priyaranjan Lal (2013). All these reflect the aura of the soft-porn moment and the memory of the era and do so through the figure of the actress Shakeela, perhaps the most recognizable face of the genre.

At their height, soft-porn films were often publicized as 'Shakeela films' even when this particular star did not feature in the cast, so that when she actually appeared it made her into an especially valued commodity. Both Shakeela's on- and off-screen presence becomes a vivid temporal marker in the narrative of both *Kanyaka Talkies* and in debates on obscenity where 'Shakeela' stands in as a synonym for the obscene and desirable sex siren. Her persona, and the space of its manifestation, the soft-porn movie theatre - as we see it as an actuality, in the S.P. Theatre, as well as in its fictional variant in *Kanyaka Talkies* - reveals a spectre of soft porn that gnaws into the present, like a wrinkle on the face of Malayalam film history.

Disappearance becomes a key conceptual node here as it relates to both spectrality and temporality. It has however become something of an absent presence, enabling discussions on temporality and cinematic memory. In the disappearance of the genre, something considerably larger is also lost: an entire way of being, brushed under the carpet of official film histories. The loss is sometimes attributed to the internet, and often to the inability to sustain bonds forged largely on informal and non-contractual arrangements, and inevitably to the dwindling of theatres in the B and C circuits.

Most filmmakers, producers and distributors associated with the form say the term came to be used in production circles only in the 1990s, even though it had earlier been used in journalistic articles since the 1980s to refer to a genre of glamour cinema, by filmmakers like K.S. Gopalakrishnan and Crossbelt Mani.[2] One can see the complexity in the naming of soft porn's origins in the film *Avalude Ravukal* (Her Nights, dir. I.V. Sasi, 1978), especially after a string of copycat productions that followed its success.[3] Although the circulation of *Her Nights* outside Kerala, often with the inclusion of additional footage, has certainly added to its notoriety, there is no evidence to prove that the film was either itself conceived as a soft-porn film or was pivotal to the genre within the state.[4] Some historians have argued as a result that there is no analytical value in reading soft porn as a separate genre.[5] While it is true that there cannot be *one* predetermined and fixed definition of any genre, and that generic definitions are in any case hardly fixed and coherent, to lose the term closes us off from seeing an entire body of films, not all of them pornographic in any conventional sense, that appear to share remarkable similarities. The genre, when named, allows a larger imagination that cuts across media and temporalities, and offers a useful corrective to the tendency to retroactively view soft porn only in opposition to mainstream Malayalam cinema.

In its classical form, the soft-porn film was made on low budgets, and incorporated female figures in the cast of *madakarani* – a figure with unabashed sexuality who uses her charms to her advantage. Although the term implies fleeting sexual pleasure and voyeuristic male consumption, it can also stand in for ways by which gendered demarcations and implacable desires enter the cinema. It has cheaper improvised reiterations of a model once associated with glamour cinema: this time with shoestring budgets, tight production schedules and identifiable features such as continuity errors and stock footage. Its economic marginality often allowed the genre to circumvent certification clauses authorized by the Censor Board. The resistance to legality was mediated through collaborative practices that tapped into loopholes that had allowed the censorship mechanism to function in the first place.

For instance, filmmakers would often employ 'second writers' (*randam-ezhuthukar*) to generate an alternative 'censor' script that would be submitted to the Censor Board. This specialized script would adhere to censorship regulations, even at times addressing the possible oppositions that might be raised by the committee. These 'second writers' sometimes functioned as ghostwriters, but their major task was the ingenious construction of alternative scripts or (what my respondents referred to as) 'Plan B and C'.[6] The insertion of sexually explicit imagery in bits or cut-pieces (locally known as *thundu*) during the exhibition is yet another mode of conveying the presence of the uncanny that can erupt into the screen: a welcome distraction that oversteps a predictable narrative.[7] Another mode of circumventing the system was to shoot large portions in locations far removed from the regional censor-board office (initially in Chennai and later in Thiruvananthapuram) to take advantage of personal connections.[8] Some films also took advantage of the subsidy package offered by the government-owned Chitranjali Studios to promote film production in Kerala, while others made use of shooting locations in the neighbouring state of Karnataka to avail of government subsidy meant for films shot there. Soft-porn films had wide circulation, both as theatrical releases and in the form of DVDs, specially packaged for the diasporic Malayali audience based in the Middle East.

Their emergence in the 1990s marked a considerable shift in production techniques, budgeting, themes and distribution patterns. Even though the genre shared links with earlier cultural modes of sexual expression - such as erotic stories (*kambikathakal*) and vernacular pulp fiction (*painkili*), it emerged as a specifically cinematic genre following a downturn in the box-office performance of mainstream Malayalam films, providing for some years much-needed revenue and employment to many in the film industry.

2001 marked the high tide of soft-porn production: out of the 89 films released, 57 were soft-porn sizzlers.[9] There were anxious responses from the popular press. An article in *India Today* declared:

> Kerala is steaming, and the reasons have nothing to do with the onset of summer. Bare breasts, hairy chests and various other parts of the human anatomy are erupting like a rash across the state's cinema screens and the audience is literally lapping it all up in lascivious delight, unmindful of censors and other sundry guardians of public morality.[10]

By 2005, with the rise of the digital cinema, the trend of soft-porn films started to decline. Many theatres were either shut down or converted into, among other things, wedding halls.

The Cathedral and the Tomb: *Kanyaka Talkies* and the Dying Spaces of Soft Porn

Kanyaka Talkies, based on P.V. Shajikumar's short story '18+' looks back at the soft-porn exhibition, the cultures of its circulation and dierent modes of interaction that existed in the marginal space of the 'B and C centre' theatres.[11] Similar to the critical success of Ashim Ahluwalia's film *Miss Lovely* (2012) also set amid Bombay's B- and C-grade film sector, *Kanyaka Talkies* is marketed as an art-house film made by a credentialled director, and a successful run in festival circuits before it got a theatrical release in 2015 following the Kerala State Film Development Corporation's move to promote independent cinema after the recommendations of the Adoor Committee Report (2014).[12] It was later available as video-on-demand via Kerala Vision Movies and Asianet Talkies, and paid digital download via the portal *ReelMonk*.[13]

The title literally translates as 'Virgin Talkies' and is redolent of the varied layers of memory still alive in the avowedly 'dead' soft-porn culture in Kerala. In overt contrast to the urban 'A' circuit cinema halls, it is set in the rural hinterland, and directly links the term *Kanyaka* to tap into sexual fantasies associated with the closed interiors of the theatre space.

In the film, when the 'Gulf-returned' Yakoob decides to set up a movie theatre in the remote area of Kuyyali in the 1980s, many see him as just an entrepreneur. As his initial business prospects give way to financial setbacks, Yakoob is forced to turn to soft porn. This plot has historical resonances to the 1990s when movie theatres, encountering box office failures even from A-list superstars like Mohanlal and Mammootty, began screening soft-porn films. R. Ayyappan notes that 'of the 73 films released last year (2000), 21 were of the sleaze variety and most of them had covered their cost. But among the remaining 51, there were only three hits and two just-about hits'.[14] This is also echoed in other popular reports of the time.[15]

References to the past glory of the movie theatre repeatedly appear in conversations between Yakoob and with the villagers, in the projectionist's (Saiju Kurup) musings of the good-old days of the family audience. The then-and-now nostalgia spoke to another, more covert, story. The Yakoob character invoked a well-known category of nouveau-riche Gulf emigrants, who entered soft-porn film production to reap profits with limited investment,[16] also often 'fronted' invisible financiers with *benami* (anonymous) funds by floating fictitious production banners.

When the movie theatre 'Kanyaka Talkies' moves from 'family films' to become an exclusive space for male audiences, as women look down upon the theatre as the harbinger of moral depravity, Yakoob's wife rebels. Overcome by Christian guilt, she withdraws from her marriage, declaring that conjugal intimacy shall resume only when the theatre is shut down. When Yakoob refuses to consent to her plea to let go of his business, she becomes bitter and turns to religion for solace. It is only after his second daughter elopes and his wife kills herself, that a remorseful Yakoob shuts down the theatre.

Weighed down by guilt, he now hands it over to the church diocese as a last attempt to cleanse himself of sin. Yakoob's association with soft-porn films is now pitted against ethically upright religion, and the moral decay and disintegration of

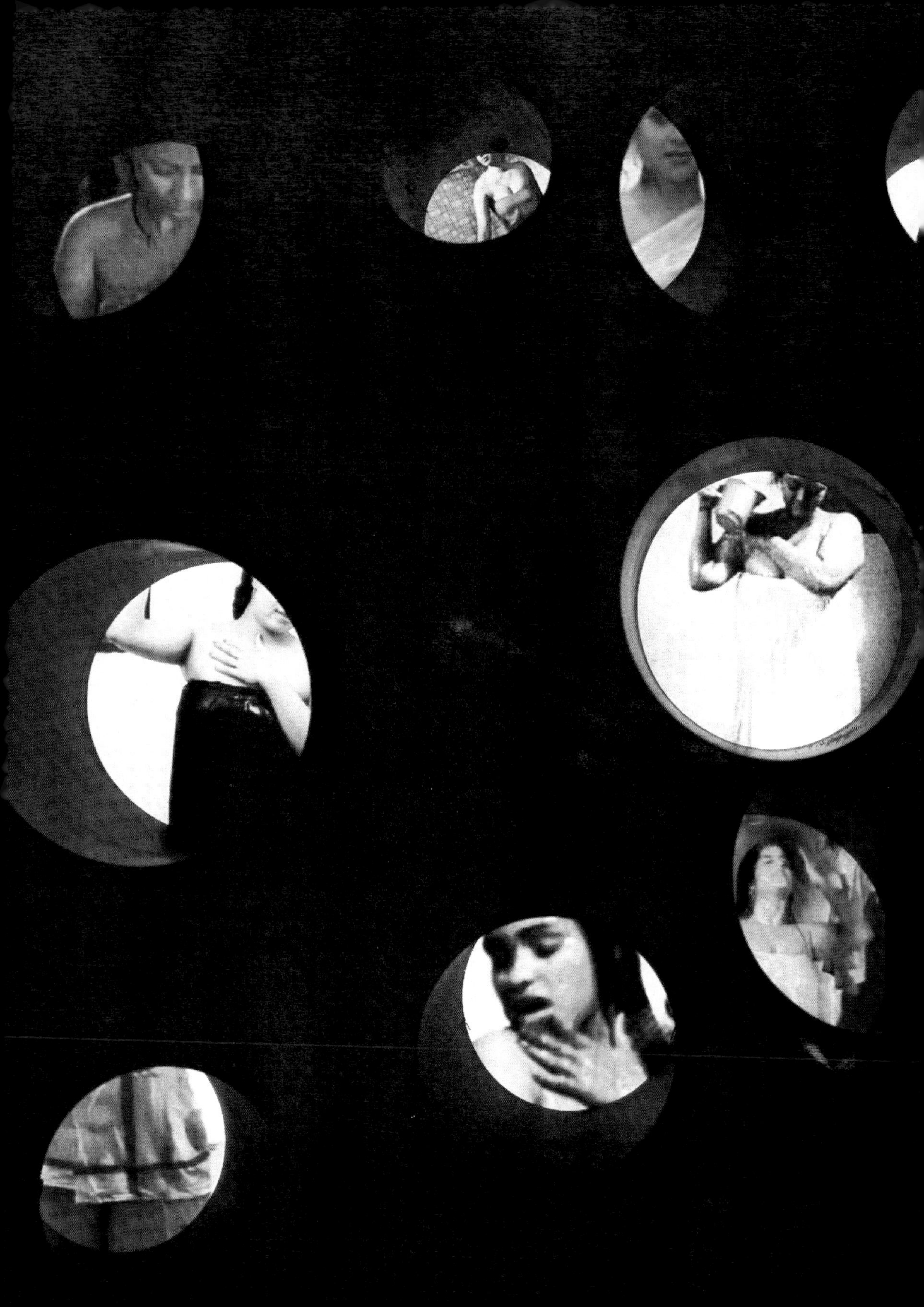

his family are linked to an obsessive love for cinema. This obsession is suggested early on when Yakoob, confronted with the shame of his business, retorts that the cinema business is the only thing he knows and loves. This continues even after he shuts down the theatre, for he continues to be associated with cinema as a distributor. The tag does not deter him from the business he loves, since for him, it is after all a form of cinema.

A crucial aspect of *Kanyaka Talkies* is a transmedia mode of storytelling that underlies its production, bringing together varied artefacts associated with the memory of soft-porn films. This mode is in part to do with factual references, or to memories. The original short story had used an actual movie theatre based in the district of Kasargod,[17] and the film too refers to actual instances of soft-porn theatres later converted to churches (one in the district of Wayanad is specifically referenced). More influentially perhaps, the art-house reputation of both the film and its maker presented the film as a serious ficto-critical account of an era, as we saw at an early screening at the International Film Festival of Kerala in 2013 when several viewers echoed experiences similar to the ones captured in the film.[18]

Such an account is evoked in the opening credits, that intersperse visuals of old equipment and dilapidated interiors with a conversation between a projectionist and a projector repairman. The framing device invites viewers to have a last glimpse of the old technology before it is dismantled for good. The projector repair-technician, as he scrutinizes the worn-out equipment, is accompanied by the projectionist who brushes his hands against the musty exteriors of film canisters. This tactile gesture is imbued with the intimate feel the projectionist has towards the equipment.

Change is inevitable, and obsolete technology with its celluloid culture would soon give way to the digital. As it happens, it is not the influx of new technology that signals the demise of *Kanyaka Talkies*, but its conversion to a church. Notwithstanding his religious faith, Yakoob emulates the course of action a true Christian would take when he is shown the right path and brought back to the fold. Yakoob treats the cinema as though a mistress he belatedly turns down to appease his rightfully wedded wife.

The Church and the Haunting

In spite of Yakoob's bid to remove the last traces of the erogenous air of soft-porn by selling the projector to scrap dealers, and his own physical departure from Kuyyali, the memories refuse to die. Their spectral presence now begins to haunt the space in which it was once housed. Even the priest, Father Michael, seeking to motivate believers to strengthen their faith, is faced with the prospect of strange and inexplicable happenings. Not only does he observe the disruption of the Mass by an unseen third party, he hears moans of lovemaking that evoke repressed desires and stir doubts about his capacity to withstand sinful thoughts. While he strives to meditate and to recover a steadfast sense of purpose to vanquish deviant thought and redeem sin, Father Michael becomes entangled in an existential crisis prompted by this encounter with the uncanny. When he visits a psychiatrist for therapy, the discourse of reason takes over from that of faith: in the process of talking about his disturbing thoughts, Father Michael begins to relate to Yakoob, who he has not met, but whose absence had triggered his psychological crisis. He decides to plunge into a mission to find Yakoob.

The aural environment evokes spatial memory, the movie theatre emerging as a haunted space bringing back repressed desires. Scattered memories associated with soft-porn films echo in an ensemble of stock sounds suggesting seduction and orgasm. The soundtrack of actresses' voices and dialogues, culled from actual soft-porn films, creates a parallel world that collapses time, as Father Michael hears them whisper from their past into his present. One of the acknowledgements in the final credit sequence of the film proclaims some sound elements created through sampling of existing pieces or sound recordings/tracks and layering them with other sounds/tracks.

Sound thus becomes the means by which haunting takes place. The confrontation of the priest with the soundscape of soft-porn films splits the present into two heterogeneous directions, 'one of which is launched towards the future while the other falls into the past'.[19] This oscillation between the temporal moments that confront the priest through the soundtrack is similar to what Deleuze calls 'the vanishing limit between the immediate past which is already no longer and the immediate future which is not yet'. The priest takes these aural hallucinations as an affront to his vows of celibacy: as he hears 'that which a priest like him should never hear'. What we get here is a logic of interruption: indeed, one that bears an uncanny similarity to soft-porn's cut-piece. Just as the cut-piece or *thundu* arrives at unprecedented moments, so now the priest's aural hallucinations also occur at unexpected moments and venues.

The film's strategic restructuring of its soundscape – where sound replaces the old cut-piece – enables a further conflation. Sound assumes a dynamic character as it is mapped onto frontal shots of viewers watching porn films in the theatre. This strategic use of sound also creates both temporal disjunction and an expectation of dramatic turns in the narrative.

Although the building is renovated into a church, the projection room is retained as a warehouse. This liminal space that houses the discarded stuff of the theatre takes on a completely new resonance: an 'architectural uncanny'.[20] Eventually, it is this abandoned projection room and the medium of Yakoob, rather than psychotherapy, that allows Father Michael to believe that he has come to terms with his hallucinatory sensations. Like an exorcism ritual, where the contact with the netherworld can only happen via the shaman, here it is Yakoob's return that allows the locked doors to be opened and for redemption to become possible.

The Installation: The Shower and Other Scenes

The sequence that follows Father Michael's entry into the projection room along with Yakoob is perhaps the most striking sequence in the whole film, featuring a monumental image of Shakeela projected on the wall. This image is rendered iconic by the beams of light that are simulated as projecting from the actress' visage returning the unilateral gaze of the audience as Shakeela emerges as a demigoddess answering the worshipper's prayer. Father Michael's face is also shown framed by strips of celluloid as if to suggest that it is soft-porn cinema *itself* that has been haunting him throughout. This is followed by a multimedia projection of animated images where Shakeela appears with other sex sirens like Silk Smitha, Reshma, Maria and others riding on a horse, with their faces morphing even as the horse gallops.[21]

The multimedia projection used, although commissioned for the film, was in fact part of a larger project by graphic designer Priyaranjan Lal. Lal says, 'The installations were conceptualized as an intervention to counter the neat narratives which structure the history of Malayalam cinema.'[22] Another installation showcases a hundred bath scenes from various soft-porn films viewed through peepholes. Yet another installation showed several 'sex sirens' or *madakarani* figures from Malayalam cinema on cylindrical posts lit from the inside. Not all these actresses were soft-porn stars; many were starlets, like the actresses Jyothilekshmi and Sadhana who had short stints in the industry. Along with the animated horse imagery, the multitude of faces suggest a longer history of sexualized fantasies of which Shakeela is only a part.

These installations had been crafted by Lal, he says, as a rejoinder to the centenary celebrations of Indian cinema. All the video installations were exhibited under the title *Kuliyum Mattu Scenukalam* (The Shower and Other Scenes) as part of the 100-Day Artist Cinema section curated by film critic C.S. Venkiteswaran at the Kochi-Muziris Biennale in January 2015. Even though the installation was publicized as commissioned by *Kanyaka Talkies*, only parts of it were actually used in the film. Lal's work functions as a complementary artistic conversation with the film – a facet of its ficto-critical and transmedial storytelling, so to say, with only some passages of the installation punctuating *Kanyaka Talkies*' narrative.

The installations multimedia images are a departure from the original short story, in which the actual image of Shakeela, or for that matter that of any specific actress, is not central to the narrative. In '18+' the priest only *hears* the voices of actresses and the soundtrack of soft-porn films with no investment in the inner workings of the film industry as such.

There is another significant deviation in the film in addressing the transformation of the priest after his encounter with the soft-porn apparition. If in '18+' the priest is shown to have realized that he is as susceptible to desires as anyone else, and becomes a connoisseur of soft-porn, *Kanyaka Talkies* unravels the contradictory impulses that leave the priest in a state of dismay. The concluding sequence of the film was rewritten over three times as scriptwriters tried to bear in mind the controversies it might provoke in the Christian community, which may not appreciate the possibility of priests, despite their vows of celibacy, being susceptible to worldly desires.[23] In '18+' the priest muses that 'whatever one fears, it comes to haunt you',[24] introducing a new layer of meaning to the repressed desires in his hallucinations. The hallucinations and the moment he inhabits in the present are eerie: dialogue from soft-porn films punctuate his thoughts while delivering mass and hearing confessions.[25] Both the film and the story make an effective investment in Yakoob's return to Kuyyali that cures the priest. In a seemingly magical realist twist, the original short story compares Yakoob to Melquíades who revisits Macondo in *One Hundred Years of Solitude*.[26]

At one point, *Kanyaka Talkies* deviates into a side-story of a nurse named Ancy who aspires to become an actress. Ancy has been duped by a production assistant who casts her in soft-porn films against her wishes and circulates erotic shots he has taken of her. These shots circulate on the multimedia messaging services (MMS) platform made notorious by the genre of 'MMS porn' associated with the 2004 Delhi Public School scandal.[27] Barring this, and one other occasion – when we get fleeting shots of the posters of films released in 2013 (such as *Mumbai Police*, dir. Rosshan Andrrews) on the walls in the background as Ancy waits to meet her agent – the film, unlike the story, does not date its setting. Apart from the problems of historical anachronism, there is one other reason that makes the ambiguity significant. In one way the Ancy episode invokes the widely held view by the mainstream industry and cultural purists, that soft-porn films are 'low-budget' films that exploit women to reap quick profits. There is, however, another aspect to the framing of Ancy as victim in an exploitative and non-consensual arrangement. Many of my interviewees, who were part of soft-porn production, were emphatic when asked if production shots were ever procured against the wish of actors. The filmmaker Thrikunapuzha Vijaykumar says:

> Even though we had access to many 'intimate' shots of the actresses that could have fetched us a good price, we never sold them as 'bits.' There were a few actresses whom we regularly worked with and nobody thought of breaching the trust through any kinds of exposure. After all we all worked for our livelihood

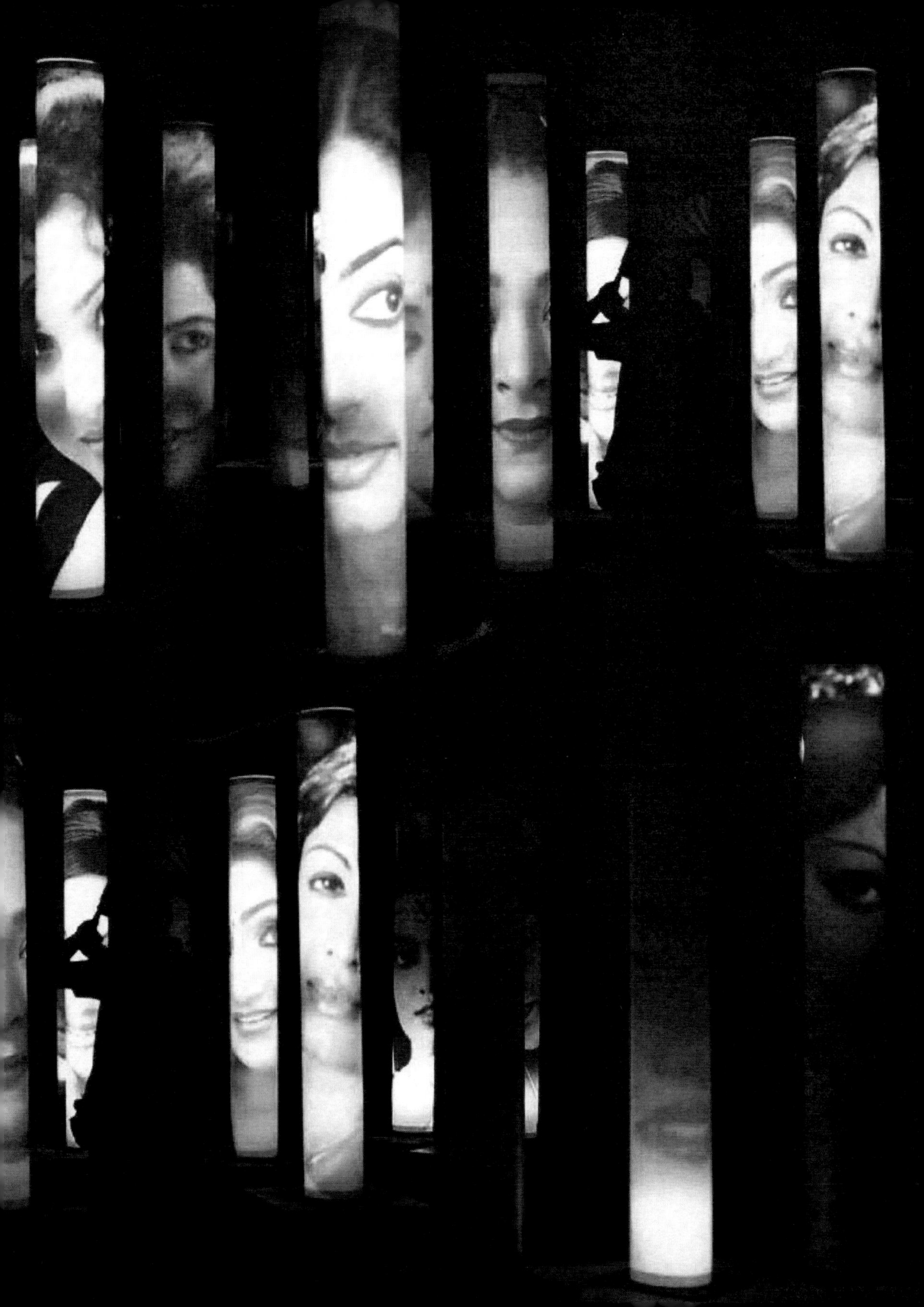

> and there was a clear sense of camaraderie among the cast and crew and no one wanted to compromise that.[28]

It is of course true that accounts on soft-porn production are at best speculative owing to the difficulties involved in tracking the personnel behind the making of these films. Nevertheless, it is worth drawing attention to the relative sense of quasi-anonymity, and its role in supporting many who worked in the industry. And so when respondents spoke of how unused shots of Shakeela were recycled for other films,[29] it appeared increasingly possible to date the collapse of this understanding to the death knell for the soft-porn industry as whole. Actresses who were part of these films disappeared from the public, some appearing occasionally in news columns where their personal lives were compared to the storylines of films that had once featured them.[30]

Even when soft-porn films made it to video-sharing sites, sites that host pornographic material tagged as 'Mallu Aunty films' or 'hot south Indian films', they inhabited multiple temporalities. The insertion of 'Mallu Aunty bits' or 'hot south Indian bits' remains a nostalgic return to the weathered era of celluloid. The insertion into a new digital playground also, however, testifies to their persistence as stubborn, un-erasable residues of that era. One wonders, for example, how the word 'bit' translates in a digital economy that is in any case composed of fragments, where celluloid-era disruption might no longer apply to a pornographic website that is built around distraction.

The Phantom Theatre: Between the Fictional and the Real

While *Kanyaka Talkies* provides an important segue into the discussion of the recently deceased spaces of soft-porn exhibition, the case of S.P. Theatre, a movie theatre with a history of screening soft-porn films, perhaps offers us a close 'non-fiction' equivalent. While *Kanyaka Talkies* sutures its account of the fate of the soft-porn theatres through references to 'real' theatre spaces, it was in fact the S.P. Theatre's interiors in the locality of Peyad in Thiruvananthapuram that stood for the soft-porn theatre in the film. On the way, even as we receive a trace of a 'real' space, another history emerges, where the movie theatre reveals a previous history with an uncanny resemblance to the plot of the film.

None of my conversations with the filmmaker revealed the presence of S.P. Theatre. Indeed, it was only a passing reference by Jayesh L.R., the production executive, that drew my attention to the actual theatre space in which the film was shot. Even though it finds mention in the credits as a shooting location, its crucial significance was never foregrounded in the publicity or otherwise. Reminiscing about the shoot, Jayesh says:

> Except a few production people, the technicians and the cast had no clue about the history of the 'real' soft-porn theatre that was our shooting site. But, as the time progressed we were fascinated by the accounts from the residents nearby. Some of them even thought that the story of the film was inspired by the theatre. It was indeed true that Shakeela films were part and parcel of the film culture of Peyad, and at one point S.P. Theatre was jokingly referred to as being located in Shakeela junction.[31]

When S.P. Theatre began its career in 1980, it catered to family audiences and even on occasion doubled as a place of religious congregation. Devotional films were re-released here, including *Snapaka Yohannan* (dir. P. Subramanyam, 1963) based on a Biblical tale and *Swamy Ayyappan* (dir. P. Subramanyam, 1975) based on the Hindu deity Ayyappan. Both films invited religious devotees, and the theatre became a site of worship and prayer. As the first movie theatre in the locality of Peyad, Gladys, the owner, reaped enough profits to stop renting projectors and buy his own equipment. As in the fictional film, it was the crisis of the 1990s that forced Gladys to start screening soft porn.

When I visited it in June 2014, I was surprised to see that the space had become a venue for a Pentecostal prayer service. The devotees, comprising men, women and children wearing white dresses and carrying Bibles, were certainly surprised to have an intruder entering the sacrosanct space. When I was asked about the purpose of my visit, I thought it wise and strategic not to share with them my 'not-so-pure' intentions that involved tracking a history of what had once had been cheekily called a 'sperm bank'.[32] It is fitting, then, that the narrative of *Kanyaka Talkies* deals with an 'exorcism' of the suppressed ghosts of the soft-porn years. If the movie theatre became a haunted space where the spectres of past actresses screamed out to the living, the actual S.P. Theatre was home to a slightly different form of haunting after it was closed to the public on 18 June 2013 shortly after the shooting of *Kanyaka Talkies*.

For nearly a decade, even after soft porn declined and 'Shakeela camps' (theatres which screened Shakeela films) went 'clean' either with mainstream films or as converted marriage halls, S.P. Theatre survived. Demands for digital upgradation had wiped out most remaining B and C circuit theatres, but S.P. Theatre continued until 2013 without going digital. Indeed, until it was shut, it remained the only movie theatre projecting older soft-porn films to dedicated audiences visiting it out of sheer nostalgia. Apart from being a favourite hangout of male filmgoers, it was also a key local hub of entertainment. Many recounted a roadside tea shop that sprung up after the theatre became a hot spot to cater to the crowd during the 'interval', the short break of five minutes. In fact, both the interval's interruption of the narrative and the splicing in of the erotic 'cut-piece' were carefully calibrated to suit both the projectionist and the tea-stall owner. Since most films screened at S.P. Theatre were only of ninety minutes unlike the mainstream feature film length of two-and-a-half hours, it was the projectionist who decided when to break for the five-minute interval.

Nanukuttan, who had run the canteen for S.P. Theatre for more than twenty years, narrated how he had to poke the projectionist to remind him of the 'interval':

> The canteen was on the side of the exit door and diametrically opposite to the projectionist's room. I was in one way the link between the projectionist and the audience. I waited for the jeers and hoots from the audience demanding *thundu* (cut-piece), some of whom would come to the canteen to whine about the repetition of the film of the same type and lack of interesting stories.[33]

Nanukuttan's intervention (on behalf of the audience) might not always translate as a fruitful one as the insertion of *thundu* was not after all an arbitrary exercise, but a carefully planned one. Speaking about old times, Vasu, one of the apprentices who was perceived as the cut-piece expert among the B-circuit cinemas, said:

> It is the projectionist who has the final say as to when and where *thundu* could be spliced in. He has to be good at his job, and inserting/splicing isn't as mechanical as people might think. We try various options to achieve an effect on the viewers, sometimes really whacky ones.[34]

The location of S.P. Theatre on the outskirts of the city had helped Gladys get substantial returns from the sale of tickets. The theatre came under B-circuit classification, which meant the entertainment tax slab was much lower than the A-centre theatres. Balcony and front circles cost Rs 10 and Rs 7 respectively. Augmented by the profit-sharing arrangements forged with the distributors, the business was a lucrative one. For Gladys, the day when the theatre was shut down remains still fresh in his memory. He recounts:

> While I knew all along that like all clandestine deals, this also has to come to an end, it was difficult to think of a day when I would wind it up for good. On June 18, 2013, when the decision was taken to wind up my business, I decided not to mourn the parting, but to make the last day of the theatre an eventful one. The evening show was shown free and I invited my regular viewers to participate. I still have the last entry of the collection and the ticket stubs.[35]

My encounter with Gladys was a crucial moment in my research, as he was one of my few respondents who were willing to take me down memory lane, to the time when soft porn had once flourished in Kerala. Methodologically, this was crucial, as the veil of anonymity cast over such productions had made any attempts to find the 'real' personnel behind these films next to impossible. Barring a few prominent directors, and some actresses such as Shakeela, Reshma and Maria, the arena of soft-porn cinema was flooded by pseudonyms, or names of 'lost' or disappeared actresses. In spite of the availability of many of these films on DVD format, uploads on media-sharing sites, and even sites exclusively meant for Malayalam pornography, there is a strange way in which the details of production, including the technicians, production banner and even shooting locations are hard to come by. Curiously, for a form once so popular, references to my object of study were at once everywhere and nowhere: soft porn as a form appeared predisposed to spectrality.

My interactions with Gladys reconnected many technicians, distributors, and exhibitors whom both of us had known at different points in time. Sharing memories and information, we found, uncannily, as in the manner of a play with shadows and mirrors, that some of Gladys' close associates were also my respondents. It was through Gladys and the connections he had that I could put together the last piece of the puzzle of their careers. Gladys became excited when I showed him my field diaries in which I had sketched rough diagrams to link what appeared to be disparate connections.

The recollections set in motion by my own research triggered a moment of remembrance for Gladys as he revisited his stint with soft porn. In turn, a further register of collective remembrance emerged when Gladys invited a few people from the locality of Peyad to share their recollection of the heyday of the theatre. While many of them remember how S.P. Theatre was a vibrant space where local men gathered for chit-chat, others evoked their viewing experience through anecdotes of the cinema's exhibition practices. Even after the cinema's closure, there were times when men who visited the locality of Peyad made a stop-over at the theatre to 'breathe the air of the old times'.[36] Despite its metamorphosis into a prayer hall, the built structure of S.P. Theatre continues to haunt its patrons, conjuring up memories of another time when the space was emblematic of a thriving cinematic culture.

Conclusion

When I first met Gladys, we were both ignorant of the intersecting histories that connected us. Gladys had no clue that the plot-line of *Kanyaka Talkies* shared such similarity to the history of many theatres of the time, including his. On seeing the photograph of Shakeela in the projection room, I initially thought that the photo was a remnant that was left hanging after the film shoot, especially since it was prominently used as publicity material for *Kanyaka Talkies*. When asked whether this was part of the production design of the film, Gladys sent for his son to get a photo-album that showcased the varied phases of the theatre. One of the photographs that had the same Shakeela image was taken in the 1990s – something that Gladys referred to as his 'Shakeela phase'. Gladys showed me this photograph as evidence that proved that the Shakeela image was part of the theatre's topography for a long time. However, it was his use of the phrase 'Shakeela phase' that struck me the most, especially as a suggestive remark on the spectrality of soft porn. S.P. Theatre no longer screens soft porn, but its history signified in that image will be retained even when the same space will be converted to a wedding hall. The physical space itself begins to take the form of a palimpsest with multiple layers of use, motivation and experience etched into its skin. Curiously it is not the spatialization of time that is at work here – as in the homogenous notion of time – but a *temporalization of space* that harks back to the Bergsonian notion of a duration that gnaws into the present. In conclusion, there are perhaps two senses in which the duration of soft porn is spectral.

First, being everywhere and nowhere, buried beneath the surface of a 'respectable' film history, soft-porn cinema's predilection to anonymity and disappearance makes it fertile ground for the release of spectral images in its afterlife. And second, as a form that is recently deceased, the residue of soft-porn culture in the contemporary haunts Malayali public culture in a sort of a phantom-porn syndrome, whose spirit is conjured up both in recent debates and controversies around obscenity (as, for instance, in the case of the recent reality TV show *Malayalee House* which was likened to a 'Shakeela Film') and in the discussions around the actual spaces of screening. In both these senses, there is a spectre truly haunting Malayalam film history – the spectre of soft-porn cinema.

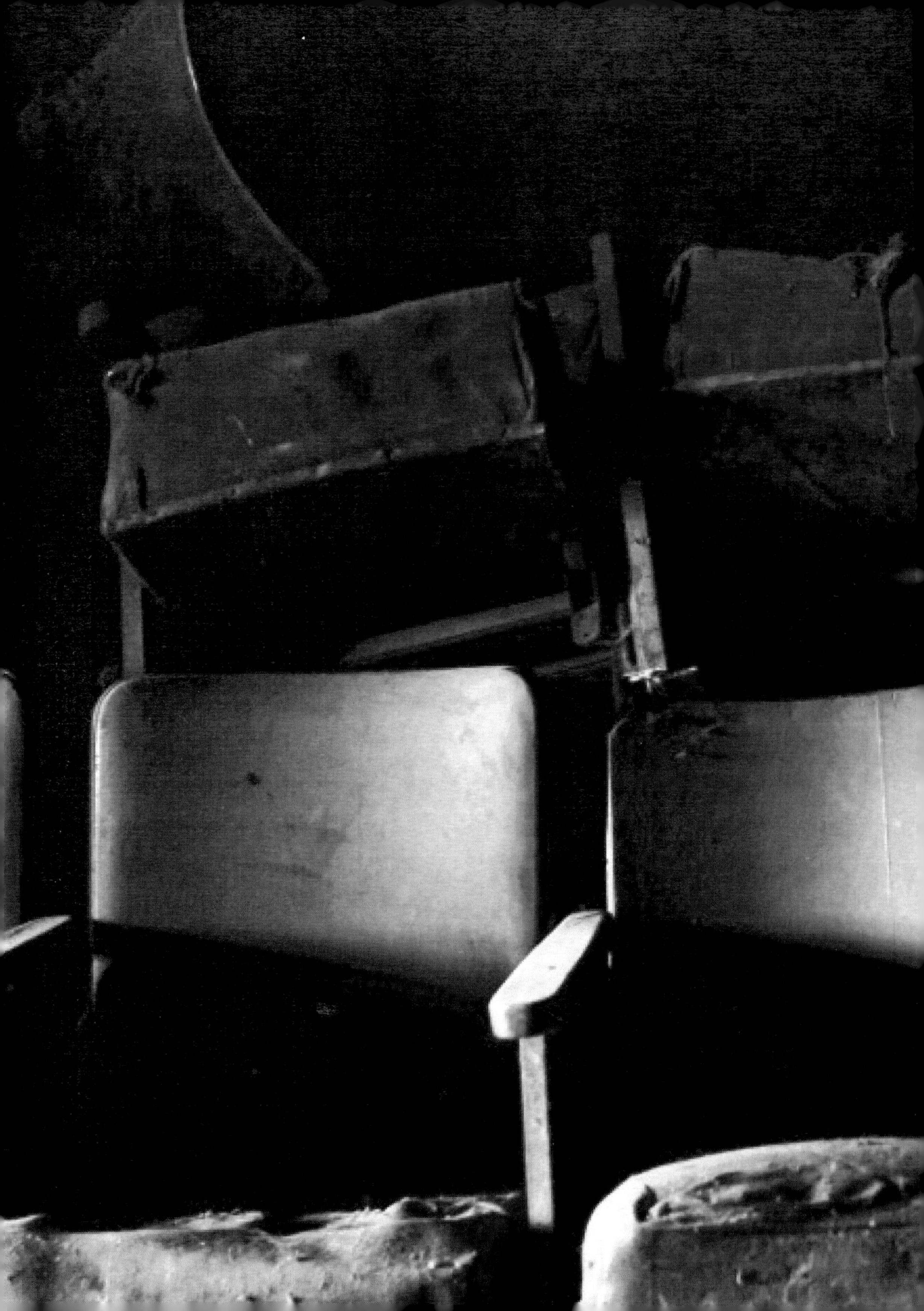

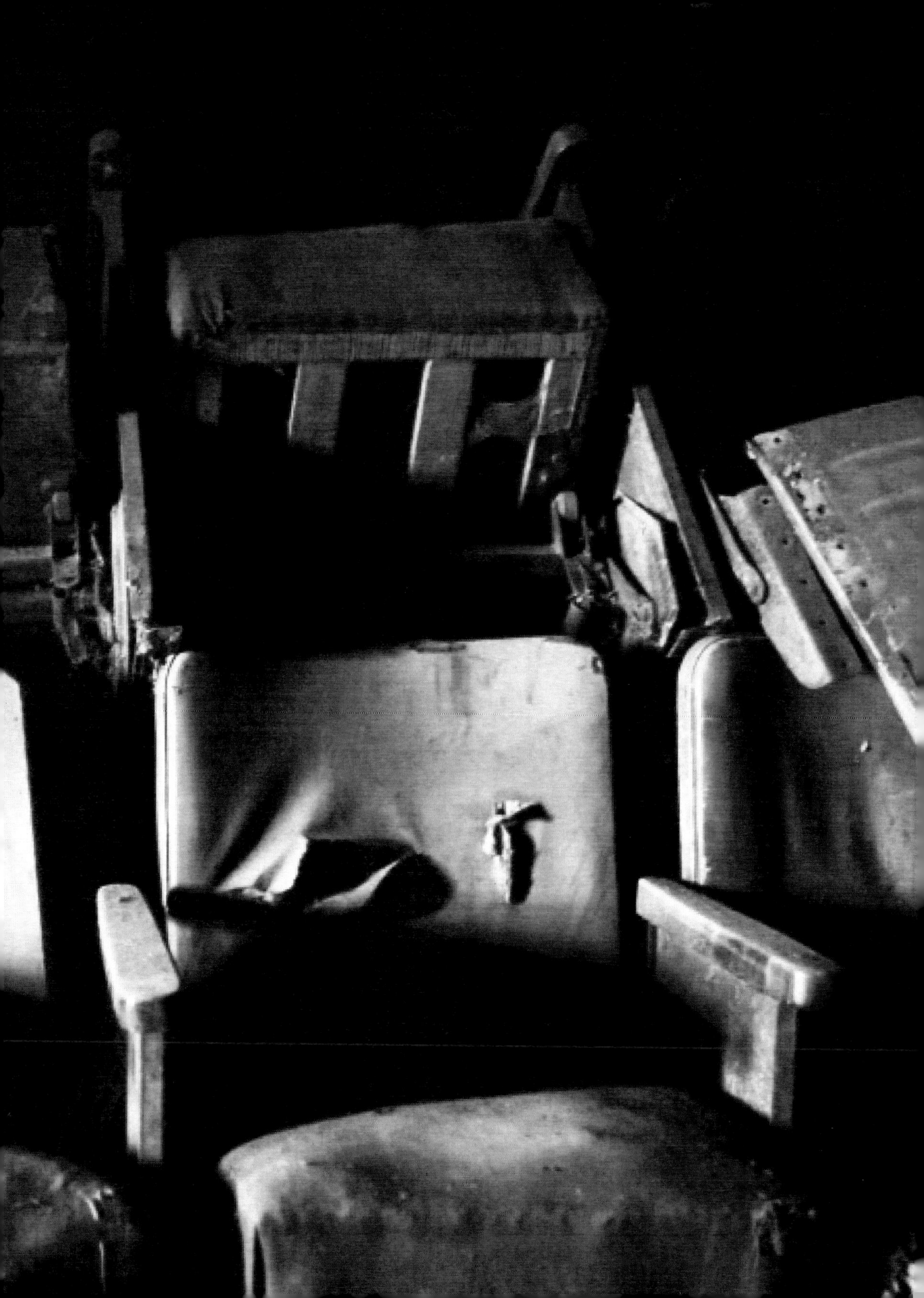

The Desire Machine Collective's (DMC's) multichannel video, *Nishan I* (2007), is located inside a derelict movie theatre, Firdous, in Srinagar. Firdous (Paradise), refers to Mughal emperor Jehangir's famous declaration of Kashmir, as well as a more recent cinematic paradise. Firdous showed popular Hindi films, including early colour romances set in idyllic Kashmir landscapes. The theatre was closed in 1989 when Islamic doctrinaires enforced a ban on films in the Valley, and was converted into military bunkers by the occupying Indian armed forces who used it as barracks, interrogation centre and ammunition dump.

DMC, influenced by French philosopher Gilles Deleuze, seek to 'disrupt the neurotic symptoms arising from constricting capitalist structures with healthier (schizophrenic) cultural flows of desire and information'. *Nishan I* was shown in 2012 at the *Being Singular Plural* show at the Guggenheim Museum, New York, curated by Sandhini Poddar. Here, Mriganka Madhukaillya and Sonal Jain of the Collective discuss their work, Firdous – the once-upon-a-time movie theatre, Kashmir and art in war zones, with film historian Kaushik Bhaumik.

Originally published in *Synoptique: An Online Journal of Film and Moving Images Studies,* vol. 3, no. 1, 2014, Spring, pp. 99–116. Thanks to DMC, Kaushik Bhaumik, and journal editors Ylenia Olibet and Lola Remy, for permission to reprint.

Keywords, Names, Abbreviations

Avant-garde, Citizenship, Documentary, (Kamal) Swaroop, Kashmir insurgency, New Media art: See Keywords (pp. 326–44).

AFSPA: Armed Forces Special Powers Act, a controversial Act enacted in 1958.

Article 370: Category under which the Indian Constitution gave 'special status' to those parts of Jammu and Kashmir (J&K) which had acceded to India in 1954. It was withdrawn on 5 August 2019.

CRPF: Central Reserve Police Force.

Eastmancolor: Kodak colour stock introduced into Indian cinema in the early 1960s enabling lush productions in full colour associated with 1960s modernity, the rise of air travel and domestic tourism.

JKLF: Jammu and Kashmir Liberation Front, a political organization fighting for a secular and independent Kashmir.

Kashmir ki Kali (Flower of Kashmir, dir. Shakti Samanta, 1964): Colour musical and the best known of Shammi Kapoor's Kashmir films.

Roja (dir. Mani Ratnam, 1992): Iconic Tamil film set largely in Kashmir, generating a controversial political argument on nationalism, militancy and gender.

SEZ: Special Economic Zone, governed by economic laws different from the rest of the country.

Shammi Kapoor: Major Hindi film star primarily associated with colour musicals of the 1960s.

Images

pp. 86–87: Still from *Nishan I* (DMC, 2007), digital video; reproduced with permission of the artists.

p. 93: Modified still from *Kashmir ki Kali.*

pp. 98–99: Montage of Sanjay Kak's seminal documentary on the Kashmir insurgency, *Jashan-e-Azadi* (How We Celebrate Freedom, 2007), framed from architectural space of the derelict *Nishan I.*

KAUSHIK BHAUMIK and DESIRE MACHINE COLLECTIVE

2014

Kaushik Bhaumik in conversation with Desire Machine Collective

Kaushik Bhaumik (KB): Could you tell me a little about Firdous and about the manner in which its spaces were employed by the army?

DMC: Prior to the insurgency in 1989, Kashmir had many well-attended movie houses. Firdous - then one of Srinagar's most popular theatres - was closed down, as the Bollywood films being shown there were considered anti-Islamist. It was taken over by the Central Reserve Police Force (CRPF) in 1989. Over the years, militants have carried out dozens of attacks, including a suicide attack on the cinema hall. The premises were also under occupation of the Border Security Force (BSF), which replaced the CRPF to fight militancy in 1993, before it was again handed over to the CRPF in 2003. After almost twenty-one years of occupation, the hall was vacated by the CRPF in 2011. It was used for years as a military interrogation centre, primarily targeting Kashmiri youth suspected of militancy. During this time, people were executed inside quite regularly.

The many cinema halls in Srinagar are all fortified and act as bunkers for the army. They use Firdous as their bunker and barracks, and as cookhouses, bathhouses, mess rooms, living quarters and ammunition dumps. The balcony of the auditorium is not used, while the lower section of the auditorium serves as a store and accommodation space. The smaller rooms and landings on the sides are also converted into living quarters, while the foyer is the recreation area where there is a television that the soldiers can watch in their spare time. There was a Hindu temple on the landing of the projection room.

KB: The ironies of an army interrogation centre in a cinema hall called Firdous are many. *Firdous*, or paradise, is, of course, the word that appears in Jahangir's famous exclamation about Kashmir being paradise on earth. And then, Bombay cinema shot Kashmir endlessly in the 1960s and 1970s as a cinematic paradise. And, of course, cinema itself is an apparatus that is often used to promise us paradise in our imperfect lives.

DMC: It is perhaps not ironic that the favourite cinema 'location' for Bombay cinema through the 60s and 70s quickly turned into a battlefield set, out of bounds to civilians. The same cinematic voyeurism with which the directors filmed the landscape of Kashmir in numerous films, with its lakes, snow-clad mountains, valleys and rivers, infiltrates certain discourses of the desire of the nation-state to retain control of Kashmir as a paradise that defines Indian nationhood (as can be evinced from the lyrical tone of Films Division coverage of life in the Valley in Nehruvian times). There was an anthropological voyeurism involved, of the kind displayed by anthropologists like Fürer-Haimendorf, who were obsessed with the beautiful body of the tribal.[1] They were expressing their own sexual desires through their writings and photography. A similar thing seems to have happened to Kashmir with Bombay cinema. Sometimes we might be too much in the thrall of 'structural' issues affecting Kashmir. It might be interesting to see the problem in Kashmir as 'auteur-driven' by the fantasies of discrete individuals – filmmakers, politicians, intellectuals etc. – fantasizing about Kashmir as an Edenic locale for playing out desires that cannot be actualized on the plains.

KB: There is an excess of plains' histories that played out in infantile regressive forms such as we see in the Bombay cinema of the 1960s. Even then, the excess created a certain kind of 'target' of the Kashmiri, especially women, in the eyes of the hero seeking to work out his plainsman excesses in a landscape where he was free from social and cultural surveillance. This target-creation as 'compensation' for the asceticism of a violent historical society, is a structural function of discourse creation coeval with social constructs such as 'frustrated soldiers in sexual denial over long periods, raping women'. Audiences, too, are interpellated through the filmic apparatus to run rampage over Kashmir in compensation for their anxiety-ridden lives on the plains. Of course, Kashmiri women were 'hyper-fair', making this option even more attractive to plainsmen obsessed with obtaining fair brides abetted by their familial fantasies. Plains' histories need the carrot and the stick, the stick of hard 'civilizational' life oset by the carrot of 'holidays in the mountains', cybernetic on–off codes that confuse the mind, create anxiety. We have been made to see Kashmir as the carrot, as paradise – we never saw the underlying history of frustrations on the plains that fuelled such a fantasy. Now if the local population reacts against this run of fantasy, the tendency would be to want to sweep away such reaction through the application of a nomadic force equivalent to the force of the total mass fantasy that India has about Kashmir.

DMC: We don't think there is any difference between the Shammi Kapoor films of the 1960s with its voyeuristic tourism, and a film like Mani Ratnam's *Roja* (1992).[2] The premise is the same except that now the gaze cannot penetrate the landscape so easily – the paradise has turned sour due to political issues. The militarization of Kashmir can then be seen in some senses as some kind of a sublime castration carried out on the object of fantasy that no longer fulfils one's desires. Cinema produces new concepts that change how we perceive and interact with the world.

KB: When the military interrogation replaces cinema in Firdous, in some senses the interrogation of our desires by cinema is suddenly replaced by an interrogation of our sensory capacities by the military. This double meaning of interrogation in the irony that Firdous comes to embody over the decade probably relates to your formulation about war and cinema.

DMC: Paul Virilio's understanding that 'war is cinema and cinema is war'[3] foregrounds what is fairly transparent – the long historical relationship between war and cinema. From the early days of the development of cinema, war and cinema share the same technologies – telescopic lenses, freeze frames, virtual reality, point-and-shoot – mutually inspire each other's narratives, and, in turn, construct the realities of their audiences. Going back to the origins of cinema, we could speak of Marey's first chrono-photographic 'rifle'.[4] This association continues with the pilotless drone, an aircraft whose camera can take two thousand pictures and whose onboard television can broadcast live to a receptor station 240 kilometers away.

At Firdous, what is fascinating is that one form of cinema, utopian fantasy films, are replaced by another kind of film – the interrogation. The cinematic apparatus is dismantled, but the seats remain. It is as if a ghost audience seated in the hall is being interrogated through the spectacle of the interrogation of individuals. We feel the after-images of this movie of army interrogation every time we are in Firdous. In terms of the early conception of photographic mediums as a 'ghost industry' where ghosts were phenomenon of electrical energy, this absence of image and light in the cinema halls with soldiers living, sleeping, dressing and eating in that space seems like an apparition and some kind of residual after-images of films that have happened here. A theatre of the absurd is being played out in the dark, without an audience or any reference to time – delirious new ghostly images invoked anew where the flow is disrupted, the past disconnects from the present. But now all this will be whitewashed.

KB: Yeah . . . it is as if one film was followed by another, which now will give way to the 'next release'. One is reminded, from your metaphor of whitewashing the spectacle, of the replacement of the poster of a just-gone film by that of the new one . . . the older film is 'whitewashed' in favour of the new one.

DMC: Modern political cinema begins from a very different position, premised not on the 'already there' of the people, but on their absence. The stakes involved in proclaiming the people 'missing' is nowhere more evident than in the post-colonial cinema of (Glauber) Rocha and (Ousmane) Sembene.[5] These filmmakers, Deleuze argues, understand that what is required is not simply an assertion of an identity counter to the one proposed in colonial rule. They thus resist the urge to evoke dubious notions of 'origins' - a true identity, a unified people prior to colonialist domination - and, instead, actively seek to forge a new collectivity, a people who belong not to the past, to history, but to the future - the people as future conditional.

KB: Cinema operates in particular ways in the timecode of spaces like Kashmir, where life, until recently, was pastoral and non-industrial. Suddenly, modernity comes along and seeks to discipline such a society. The lyrical presence of cinema is suddenly withdrawn by state diktat to announce the end of a certain historical timecode for populations.

DMC: Just as war does, cinema also takes place in time, as the primary commitment we make to experience it is time-sensitive, not place-sensitive, and as space disappears in the cinema when scenes are flattened onto a screen. We are transported quickly, in our railway-car-styled theatre through a one-dimensional celluloid topography. Fittingly, the 'cinematic' functions occasionally as a form of 'kinematic', and kinematics. Cinema simulates the feelings of movement, speed, and immediacy.

A similar thing is achieved by the spectacle of the military, a certain kinematic effect where the spectacle forces us watchers to 'move'; it produces effects of speed and immediacy within people watching it. An essential dimension of trauma is the breaking up of the unifying thread of temporality. Trauma results in a dissociation and multiplicity, which leads to a disruption in the sense of being-in-time and a consciousness of duration. Trauma is pre-verbal and timeless - still and silent. The body used to be confined in space, and now it is time that imprisons us. It is the body in time - in a space-time - too infinitely compressed for man not to feel a fundamental claustrophobia.

KB: Yes, one is reminded of cinema's endless fascination with filming military drills . . . the Riefenstahl films.[6] Indeed, one wonders whether the kind of disciplining of bodies that military surveillance is carrying out on Kashmiri bodies through the exercise of what Foucault called bio-power, a vast reality TV show if you wish, does not have something in common with the manner in which Bombay cinema today focuses on fit bodies, the script as fit narrative etc. After all, classical Hollywood cinema could only happen after certain docile bodies were made possible through military-industrial discipline.

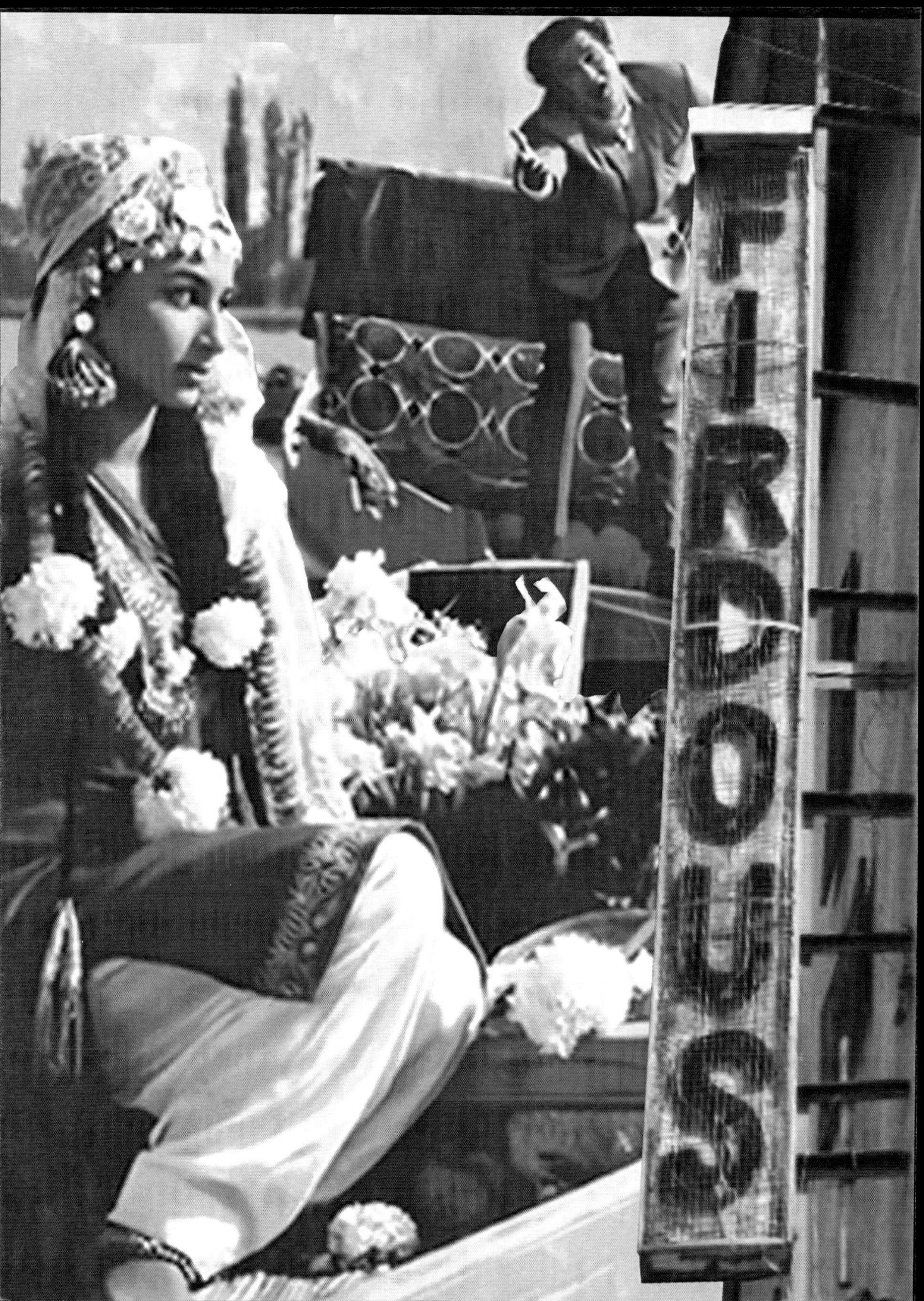
FIRDOUS

DMC: Exactly! Something of that kind is happening. Controlling time is essential to war – the activity of the narrative consists in constructing coherent temporal ensembles in order to configure time and the role of nation-state in disrupting the linear assemblages of time of the local people. Disrupting communal activities of yore – watching movies in a cinema hall, weddings that traditionally took place at night and so on – is essential to military control of Kashmir. Against the earlier cinema of Kashmir as paradise, filled with good, easy-going people, a new kind of cinema of military discipline is being imposed. Indians on the whole take the army's presence in Kashmir for granted. There is, in a lot of popular media discourse, an unquestioned patriotism which flows through cricket, commerce, media and pro-army stands in Kashmir, and this, I guess, produces a certain kind of cinema of discipline towards a space like Kashmir.

KB: Could you please say a little about the temple shrine placed in the space where the cinema screen once was in another of the Srinagar theatres?

DMC: Cinema halls have been read as cathedrals and the speed effects of light as creating a form of collective experiences and memories in these new temples. The Hindu temple replacing the screen in Shiraz Theatre does lend easily to the feeling of a ritualistic function of purification and purging of the space in progress. It also seems to function like an exorcism of the many ghost images that lie suspended in the dark auditorium and a substitution for the dark screen. It is a fascistic thing that is happening: the shrine coming into the cinema hall, the suppression of all signs of Islamic culture all over Kashmir in favour of Hindu cultural symbols, invokes for us some kind of Nazi swastika marching in. All this is deeply disturbing. The only functional movie theatre in Srinagar, Neelam, which does screen films right now, is also under army occupation, and moviegoers have to pass through intense security checks to enter. The body is being disciplined by such measures to some kind of military routine. So paraphrasing Virilio, cinemas were training camps which bonded people together in the face of death agony, teaching them to master the fear of what they did not know.

KB: Before continuing with cinema, a little about *Nishan I*, the video installation that Sonal made in Srinagar, out of which the experiences of Firdous also come out.

DMC: *Nishan I* looks at sensory disorders that result from a disruption of 'organic flows' due to sustained conflict. It looks at interior spaces of a derelict apartment, with traces of absences of that which is repressed, while daily life goes on with apparent normalcy in the streets and canals outside. A departure from reality, that war produces, opens up many more dimensions puncturing the discourse of normalcy. The interior of the house unfolds in a complex labyrinth both in space and in time. Multiple geometric planes collude and liner perspective collapses in the fractured mind, and only fragments are left to us with which to make structures.

Concealed behind the foreground (layers of dust) present only in the form of absence, in the threatening unknown, is that which is expressed. The layers of time that don't fit at the seams create a dissonance, a discontinuity – and it becomes a cause of discomfort. In this contraction – of time and the disappearance of territorial space in times of war – multiple temporalities converge into one space, breaking chronological continuity. In the fissures that are produced by the senses coming apart, perceived reality is destroyed and new realms of perception open up – the mundane everyday assumes the realm of myth and fairy tales.

Linear perspective invented during the European renaissance abstracts from psycho-physiological space. This space is an unpredictable flow of visual phenomena, it is a homogeneous, unchanging infinite space – purely mathematical. It is an abstraction on which the camera is also based. It depicts the individual gaze. In *Nishan I*, many perspectival planes collide, breaking the illusion of a single homogeneous, unchanging space and the single position for the viewer. The horizontal monumentality of the work also works against vertical modernity, and one has to navigate the space and change one's position to experience the work. It is about the freeing up of perception, and from being bound to a single standpoint and an immobile eye. Also, *Nishan I* goes against the perspectival 'stable view' – that of the viewer looking out of the window – which creates an absolute distinction: between the grounded viewer and the world in flux out there, brought to focus from this point of grounded vision. The widow, however, has to be left out, as it is the location of the gaze. In *Nishan I*, however, the window and interior space is also revealed, referencing the subject himself/herself and also making evident his/her centered gaze to the world outside. In this case, the house was used by the army as a bunker. A viewer who loses his gaze and is drawn into the continuous flow of sensory phenomenon loses this subject position and can merge with the object he is experiencing – the perceptual flow.

KB: This, of course, then loops back to the Virilio equation between war and cinema through the idea of common use of visual devices that home in on a target. *Nishan I* thus seeks to interrupt the habits of the vision that homes in and targets. Back to cinema then. How do you think the love triangle between the Indian state, Bombay cinema and the 'regional' actually function?

DMC: The triangle relation you mention is quite a perverse one. Nation-state and Bollywood cinema conspire and create identity and wipe out multiplicity of the regional by appropriating them as stereotypes or zones or a fantasy land. There are instances of films like *Dil Se* (From the Heart, dir. Mani Ratnam, 1998) . . . or *Tango Charlie* (dir. Mani Shankar, 2005) which need to be seen in this light.

In Kashmir, we think, what happened was that a certain generation progressively got alienated from mainland India in a political sense. Then, the same films that entertained Kashmir in the 1960s were seen to be an alien point of view – say, where a Kashmiri is portrayed as a villain and is bashed up by a north Indian hero, this would be seen as some kind of negative gesture made by the Indian nation/Bombay cinema towards Kashmiris. It is with politicization that critiques of stereotyping Kashmir and Kashmiris arose. Then, of course, the Islamists brought in the logic of Bombay cinema as being anti-Islamic. But then there are other things. There is deep resentment amongst the Kashmiri young that young men from Kashmir cannot get into the Bombay film industry despite being so good-looking by cinematic standards. It is always the women who are coveted by the industry.

KB: That brings us to the ironic historical loop that marks the passage of Kashmir in Bombay cinema in the 1960s into something like Firdous, and it involves the issue of the unemployed young. After all, one may argue that the Shammi Kapoor films set in Kashmir mark a decisive break in the relationship between Bombay cinema and the nation-state ideal, with the stern task of nation-building giving way to frothy youth culture playing itself out freely in the margins of India. A logic of 'unemployment' is written into the content as well as the economics of such films. And somehow the events that lead to what happens in Firdous passes in substantial ways through discourses about the unemployed young.

DMC: Society is not able to quench the desires of youth. Cinema steps in, but over time this fantasy fails. 1980s youth culture in India wanted to open up to liberal culture, but India was not liberal enough. A story of a young Kashmiri man seducing a Bombay girl was never made. The image is not liberated. Older images open up minds and bodies, but images that follow cannot answer the sensory needs of the young. National fantasy has no place for the Kashmiri youth or the young for that matter.

A narrative that we come across very frequently here in Kashmir is about young men who became militants after being unsuccessful in love – love defined by the logics of Bombay films watched in the cinema halls. Here, the energies of cinema turn so easily to insurgency. Indeed, we should be only making horror films given the levels of sexual repression the young have gone through.

KB: People die for the loves inspired by cinema seen inside theatres, and here we have people being executed inside cinema halls. Sublime castrations seem to abound in a nation perpetually in the grip of melodramatic throes of either repressed love or authoritarian patriotism. Yes, there is horror cinema all around the idea of Firdous – the interrogation film, the execution film, the military spectacle kinematics.

DMC: The fact is that in spaces like Kashmir, Assam or Meghalaya, there is no culture of the film screen onto which people living in these regions can project their fantasies. Bombay cinema can step into the absence of indigenous screen cultures for a time, but it can never satisfy these regions' local people's fantasies about themselves. Cinema is about projecting one's thought onto a moving image, about contrasting one's experience with those depicted in cinematic images to figure out one's life's experiences. The cinema screen is some kind of prosthesis for perception. It teaches us what the contemporary is, what friendship and love are, etc. This is missing in Kashmir.

There is no space for fantasy. A similar thing is happening all over India, where multiplexes are rooting out screens. There is no representation of the desires of the people – art-house cinema from 'regions' focus too much on village life, and Bollywood is urban only in a certain way. There is no representation of the contemporary youth experience on screens in these regions. This connects strongly with the ban of Hindi cinema in Manipur and the huge popularity of Korean cinema and now Korean fashion in the state and slowly in the region.

KB: In a sense, militarization of regions precisely produces the abolition of the 'cinematic' within populations. Militarization is aimed against the fantasies of sensory freedoms of the people. In a profound sense, militarization abolishes the cinema screen and what we call the 'cinematic' within our lives. Of course, the youth suer most from the abolition of the 'cinematic'.

It is interesting to think in this respect about the situation in urban contexts from the 1970s onwards around the world, where a certain confused interface emerges between sensory radicalisms produced by cinema and political confusions of the time. For Kashmir, I have heard this story of an erstwhile JKLF (Jammu-Kashmir Liberation Front) leader trying to woo a contemporary academic by singing Hindi film songs to her on the phone through the night. You have lived through similar turbulent times in Assam in the same period. In some ways what happens in Kashmir and Assam after the 1970s is precisely the Indian state's inability to handle this new kind of youth sensory radicalism arising on the interface between cinema and politics.

DMC: I [Mriganka] am an accidental becoming. In Guwahati, while I was growing up, I had an abundance of choices. Calcutta was a major reference point for Guwahati, sending films and books accessible to the middle class. We loved Bombay cinema. But I also saw Bergman films in 16mm in a hot room in Cotton College where I studied. Cinema was a space for meeting people, where we discussed our desires and fantasies. Before a place globalizes, cinema is already there to de-territorialize you; it expands the horizons of experience, where you are in the world, utopian desires. Youth needs utopia. Radical politics was possible because choices were available in what you read, what you saw and what you experienced. After 1989, the space for such politics went missing.

Today, there is this SEZ (Special Economic Zones) model-riven homogenizing happening. Guwahati has been taken over by Delhi. New citizens are coming in

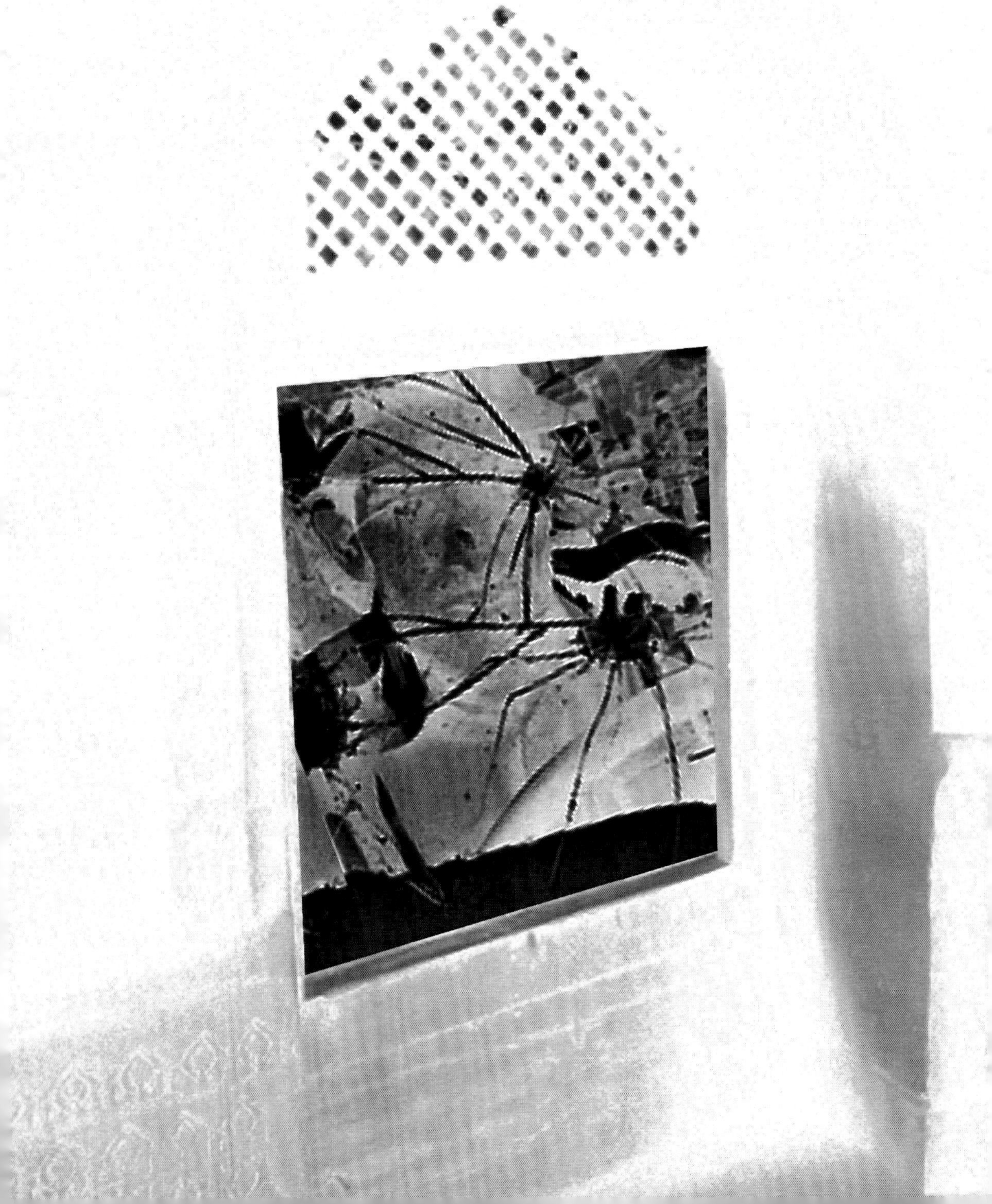

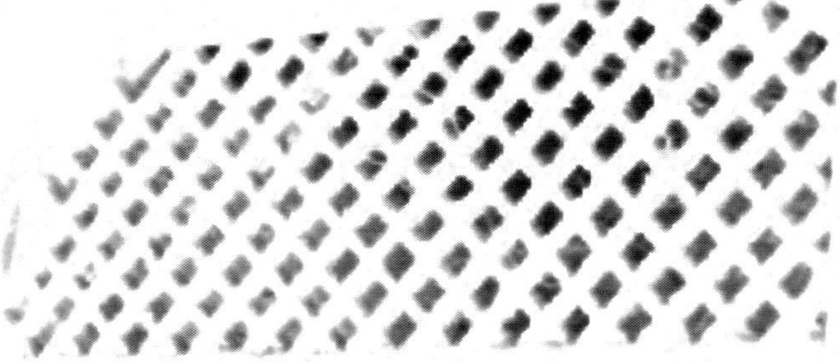

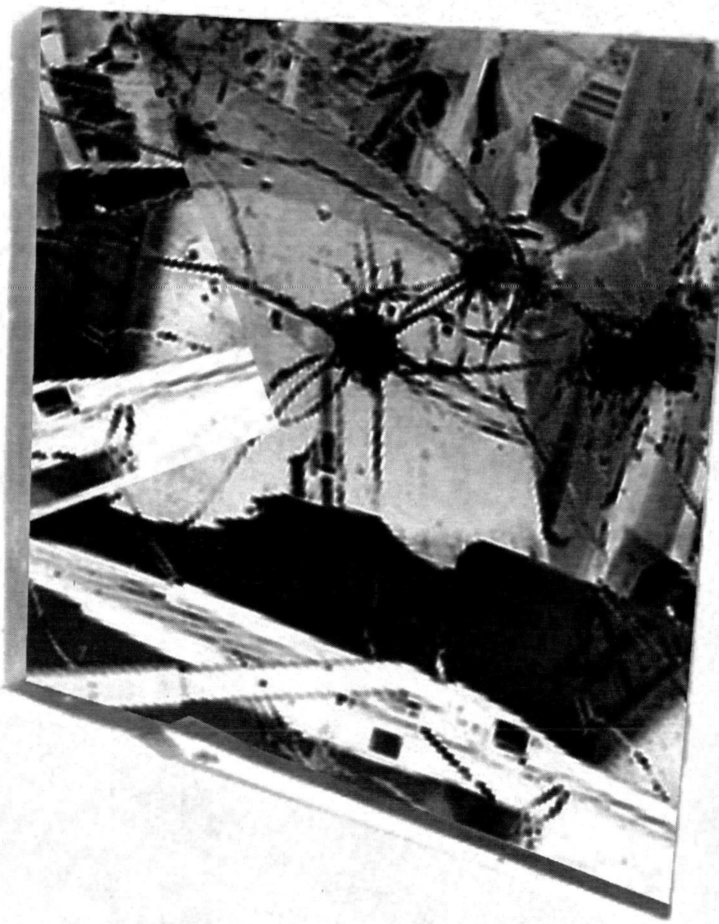

who want to live and consume as the rest of India. Identical houses are being built all over India, and media decides how you live. We are becoming like an island. We are living life televisual on a 70mm LCD screen.

KB: The dynamism of what Deleuze calls 'any space whatever',[7] where anything connects with anything, gets curtailed in media-driven consumerist lives. There is this illusion that the world is at your doorstep on your television screens – a false 'any space whatever'. We are back to surveillance, but this time authored by Karan Johar,[8] where the new Indian patriotism is wearing branded American clothes. It is ironic that it is in this time of standardization that, more than ever before, one needs films – of the kind (Jacques) Rivette makes or like (Pier-Paolo) Pasolini's *Trilogy of Life* – set in 'any space whatever' to capture the complexity of Indian experience, but also to challenge that spurious and false discourse of 'unemployment' (something that a film such as Kamal Swaroop's *Om-Dar-B-Dar* was).[9] I am reminded of *Nishan I* challenging the Renaissance single-point perspective through the invocation of miniature paintings and the plural nature of religious architecture in Kashmir.

Finally, a meditation on the perception of the Bombay industry as a well-oiled machine productive of pleasure that wants to steamroller into quiet frontier regions and shake up such regions into industrial excitement. Sometimes, there would be resistance to this noise (as in Manipur), sometimes magical success (as in the case of the JKLF leader I referred to above). For the Kashmiris, I guess Indian colonialism probably produced conditions fraught and pain-ridden akin to the 'intimate enemy' situation that Ashis Nandy speaks of with respect to British colonialism in India.[10]

DMC: We see Bombay cinema as some kind of a neighbourhood cinema where there is a voyeuristic eye that goes around peeking into houses to see what's going on there. Kashmir is one such house that Bombay cinema peeks into – there are many others. The North East has had no place in Bombay cinema – so culturally alien is the North East to mainland sensibilities. This kind of neighbourhood cinema cannot respond to a multicultural society like India. Its vision is too unidimensional. Bombay cinema is not nomadic enough, like French cinema revealing new lives after May 1968 or like Asian cinema. It cannot imagine producing cinema in any space whatever. Ronnie Screwvala will produce *Dev D* (2009), but it is anchored in the production of a patriotic film such as *Swades* (2004).[11] There is today a tyranny of nationalism in India and an idea of the global filtered through this patriotism. It is possible that the images of Kashmir from 1960s Bombay cinema would have satisfied the father of this JKLF leader of whom you speak, but for the son's generation such images were not enough. They did not correspond to reality around the younger generation. That's when the questioning of representation begins.

KB: One thing that has always intrigued me about current Bombay cinema is the manner in which it can make films about spaces alien to its imagination only when some kind of popular marketable framework is provided for that space. So *Udaan* (Flight, dir. Vikramaditya Motwane 2010) set in Jamshedpur post the 'nationalist' stardom of the Indian cricket captain whose domicile it is, *Peepli Live* (dir. Anusha Rizvi, 2010) when there is enough 'national' media focus on farmer suicides.[12] Media popularity in the 'national' register of certain issues might be providing a new framework for the nation–Bombay cinema connection that was very feeble from the 1960s through the 1980s. Here, Mani Ratnam is a pioneer. He brings Kashmir back into Bombay cinema and Bombay cinema back into the nation–cinema nexus precisely when Kashmir becomes a media event. Firdous then becomes, ironically, a laboratory - a metaphor for the transformation of Indian lives, Bombay cinema and of everything in between, where bodies trained to live under the conditions of an earlier Bombay cinema are now being disciplined to a new regime of bio-power driven by media-fuelled consumerism and standardization of life towards a new order of productivity, failing which they shall be executed.

By its very nature, says film historian, writer and curator, Amrit Gangar, cinema is like a river. Her eternal *prayoga* is to flow, to move in time and space. 'The Cinema of Prayoga' is a term he coined in 2005 to refer to the work of a small group of filmmakers influenced by the aesthetic philosophy of Mani Kaul, seeking an indigenous cinematic theory and aesthetic. Euro-centric terms such as experimental, avant-garde, or underground, says Gangar, are inadequate for comprehending the complexities at the radical margins of Indian cinematographic modernity. The Cinema of Prayoga proposes a theory of film that locates the radical evolution of Indian cinema as part of a continuous tradition of artistic innovation. A visual essay has been attempted here to translate some of the possibilities evoked by 'prayoga', from the time-based-movement of cinema to the time-based-stillness of painting or photography. Zoomed-in landscapes are inserted with, and juxtaposed against, frame grabs of 'stilled movement' from films of the Prayoga canon, including by Ashish Avikunthak, Kabir Mohanty, Amit Dutta, Vipin Vijay and the late Arghya Basu (1971–2012).

Excerpts from 'Looped to be Mukt', originally published in *Moving Image Review and Art Journal*, vol. 1, issue 2, 2012. Reprinted here with permission from Intellect and the author.

Keywords

Celluloid, (Mani) Kaul, (Kumar) Shahani: See Keywords (pp. 326–44).

Images

pp. 102–04, 106–17: Montages of frame grabs and stills from the following films:

Kalkimanthankatha/The Churning of Kalki (dir. Ashish Avikunthak, 2015, 79 mins): Set against the backdrop of the Maha Kumbh mela (a crowded religious gathering on the banks of the Ganges) and inspired by Samuel Beckett's *Waiting for Godot*, the film reflects on the idea of God in the modern world.

The Kali of Emergency (dir. Ashish Avikunthak, 2016, 79 mins): A metaphysical contemplation on times of perpetual emergency, through the many incarnations of Goddess Kali.

Vakratunda Swaha (dir. Ashish Avikunthak, 2010, 21 mins): A requiem for a friend who committed suicide, a deeply personal contemplation on life after death, shot over twelve years.

Death, Life etc. (dir. Arghya Basu, 2009, 80 mins): A poetic documentary on the paradoxes of 'development' in the stunning landscapes of Lachen, Sikkim, shot during the Lossar (New Year) festival as people await an icy winter.

Song from an Ancient Land (dir. Kabir Mohanty, 2006–12, 4 hrs): Four-part durational video of an hour each, depicting everyday life in Bandra, Mumbai, rendering the plasticity of video and seamlessness of time, inspired by mathematician and historian D.D. Kosambi's idea of 'history at the doorstep'.

Nainsukh (dir. Amit Dutta, 2010, 90 mins): On the life and work of the eponymous, style-shaping painter of the eighteenth century, Nainsukh, shedding light on that era in art history.

Hawa Mahal/ Palace of the Winds (dir. Vipin Vijay, 2003, 58 mins): Poetic video essay on the phenomenology of the medium of radio through criss-crossed stories, evoking the very act of listening and cognition through a spectrum of auditory hallucinations.

Video Game (Vipin Vijay, 2005, 30 mins): Video journey about the act of 'becoming', exploring themes of love, home, and future, and a commentary on the evolution of cinema, the automobile, and the filmmaker himself.

All images courtesy Amrit Gangar and the filmmakers.

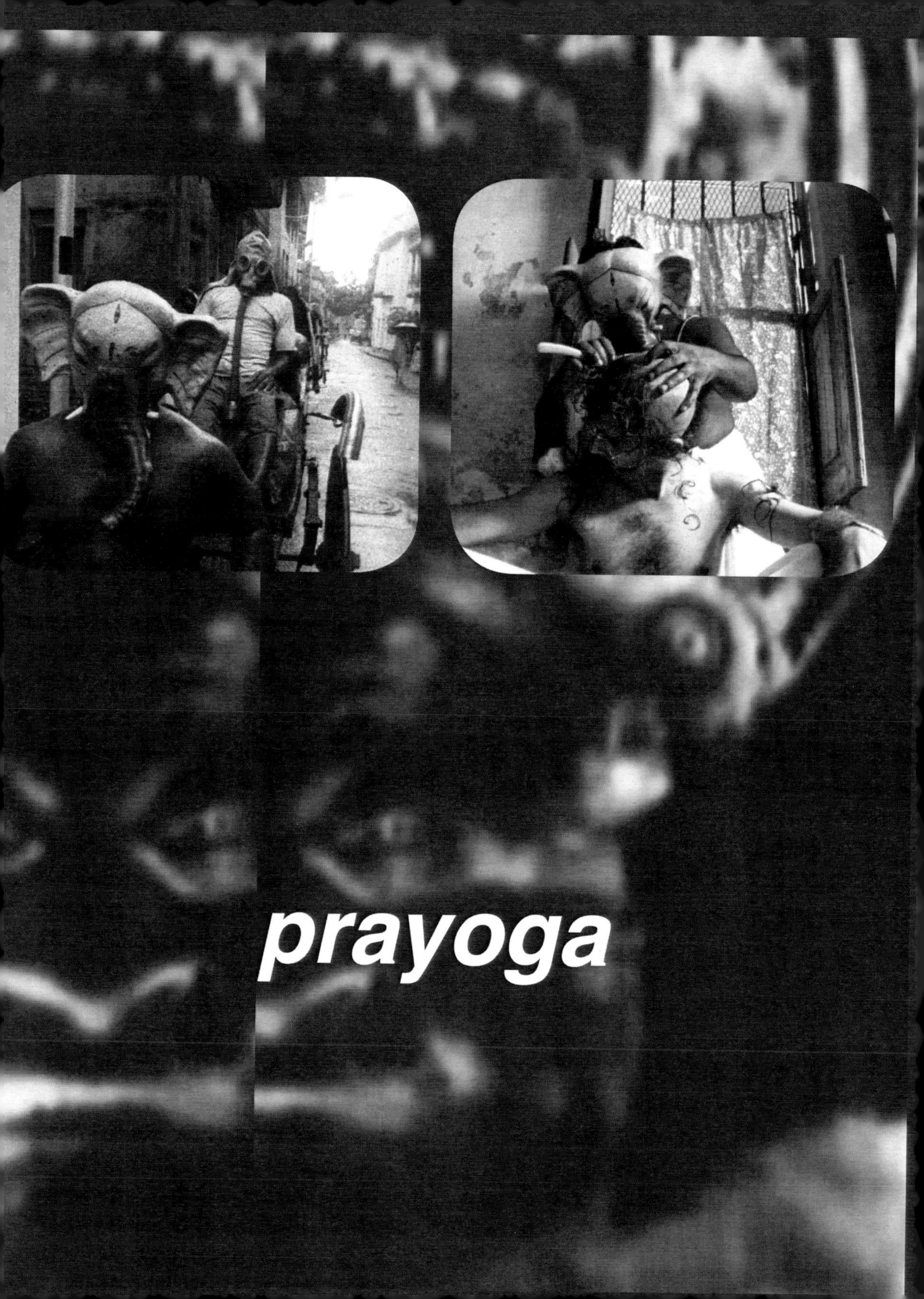
prayoga

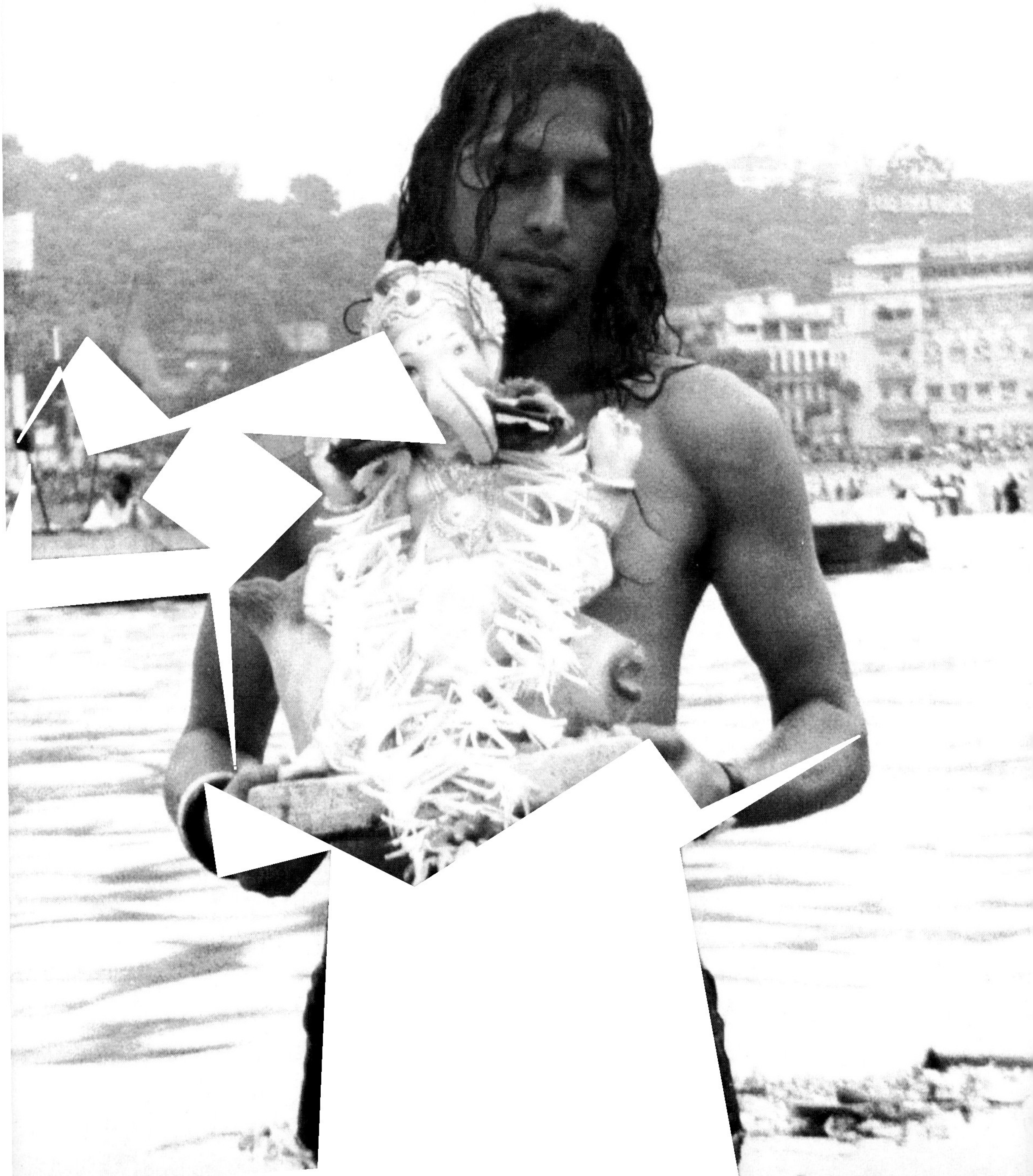

AMRIT GANGAR 2012

By its very nature, the moving image is like a river. Her eternal *prayōga* is to flow, to move in time and space, being *mukt* (**Ed:** unfettered), free, beyond the stagnant cesspool of the loop, of stasis, gathering an unprecedented mass of moss, the unrecyclable digital waste of our times. This sense of stasis has become so all pervasive that we no longer enjoy the real image of the moon on the move or the clouds in the sheltering sky. The omnipresent electronic moving image that keeps surfacing before our eyes is eternally looped, actually and virtually, materially and metaphorically, and in the final analysis, its monotony nullifies its movement. It stops being a moving image in the true sense of the term. In fact, we have before us a mass of inert moving images, all the time, 24×7, on television, on video, in our homes and studios, on airplanes, computers, mobiles, iPhones or iPads. It is the restless viewer who, through constant surfing, offers a semblance of movement to the apparently moving image. What is constantly lost in this 'movement' is *laya* [**Ed**: cadence] absorption of the mind, deep concentration, and this loss, in turn, opens the way for *pra-laya* [**Ed**: Sanskrit word for dissolution] the contemporary tsunami (of moving images).

Euro-America-centric terms such as avant-garde, experimental or underground are inadequate for the full comprehension of the complexities occurring at the radical margins of Indian cinematographic modernity. In their talks or writings, neither Mani Kaul nor Kumar Shahani have used these terms for their work, although reviewers in the media have often called them avant-garde. However, there is an inherent critique of the avant-garde among Indian practitioners. According to Shahani, the basic contradiction of the cinematographic form arises from its capacity to replace the object of its contemplation with its image. The commercial cinema has used this phenomenon to create not only dreams that substitute reality, but also its commodity gods known as stars.

Even montage has, with the best of intentions, led to the necessary juxtaposition of icons, which totally replace reality instead of evoking or analysing it, thus creating a structure close to myth with all its falsehoods. Avant-garde experiments, borrowing syntax from the other arts, have merely been attempts at achieving a kind of respectability for the cinema.

Indian film epics depict events that elaborate on their general themes. European filmic traditions find their origins in the discovery of 'perspective' during the European Renaissance, whereas Indian film has been used more generally

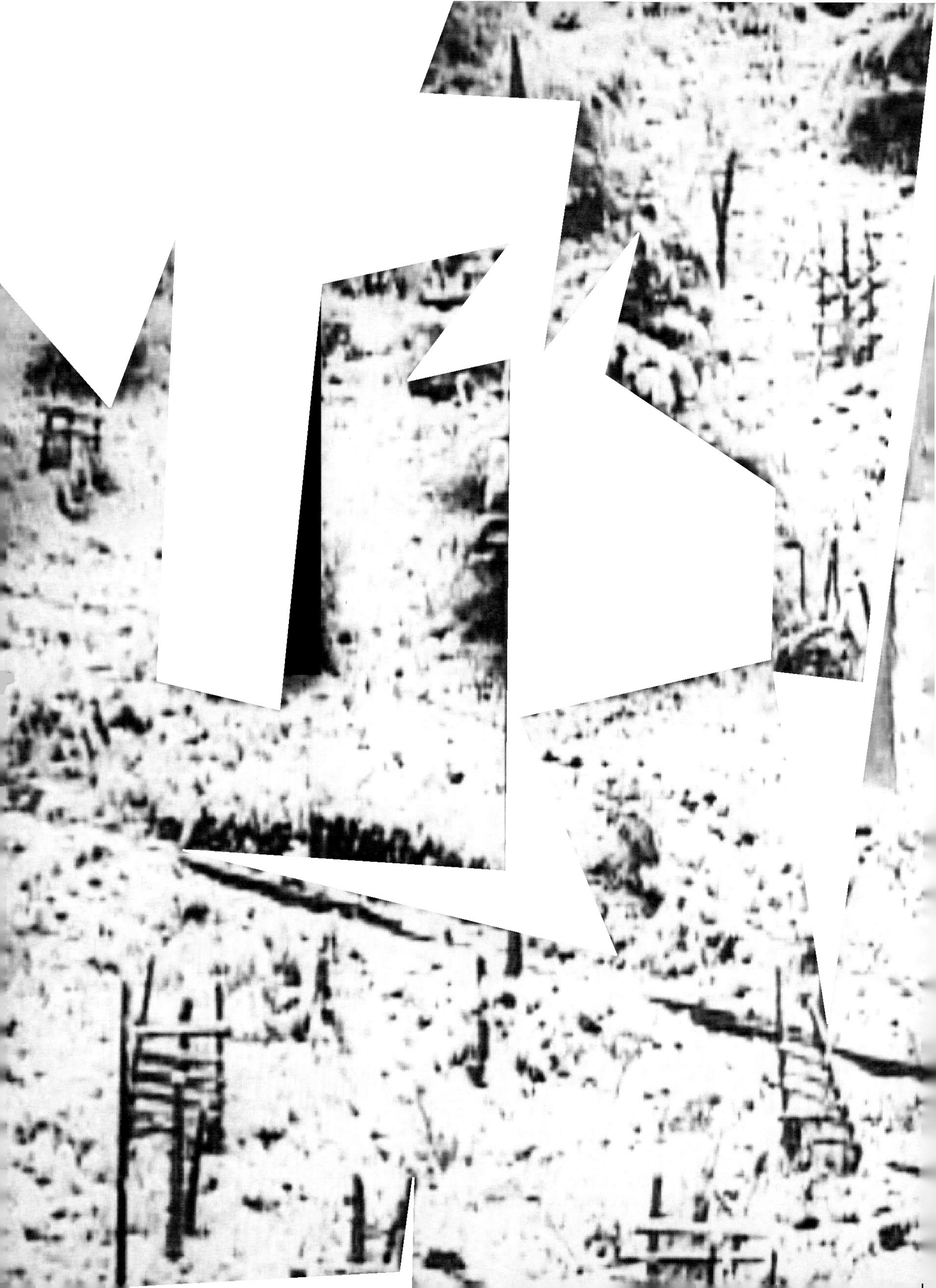

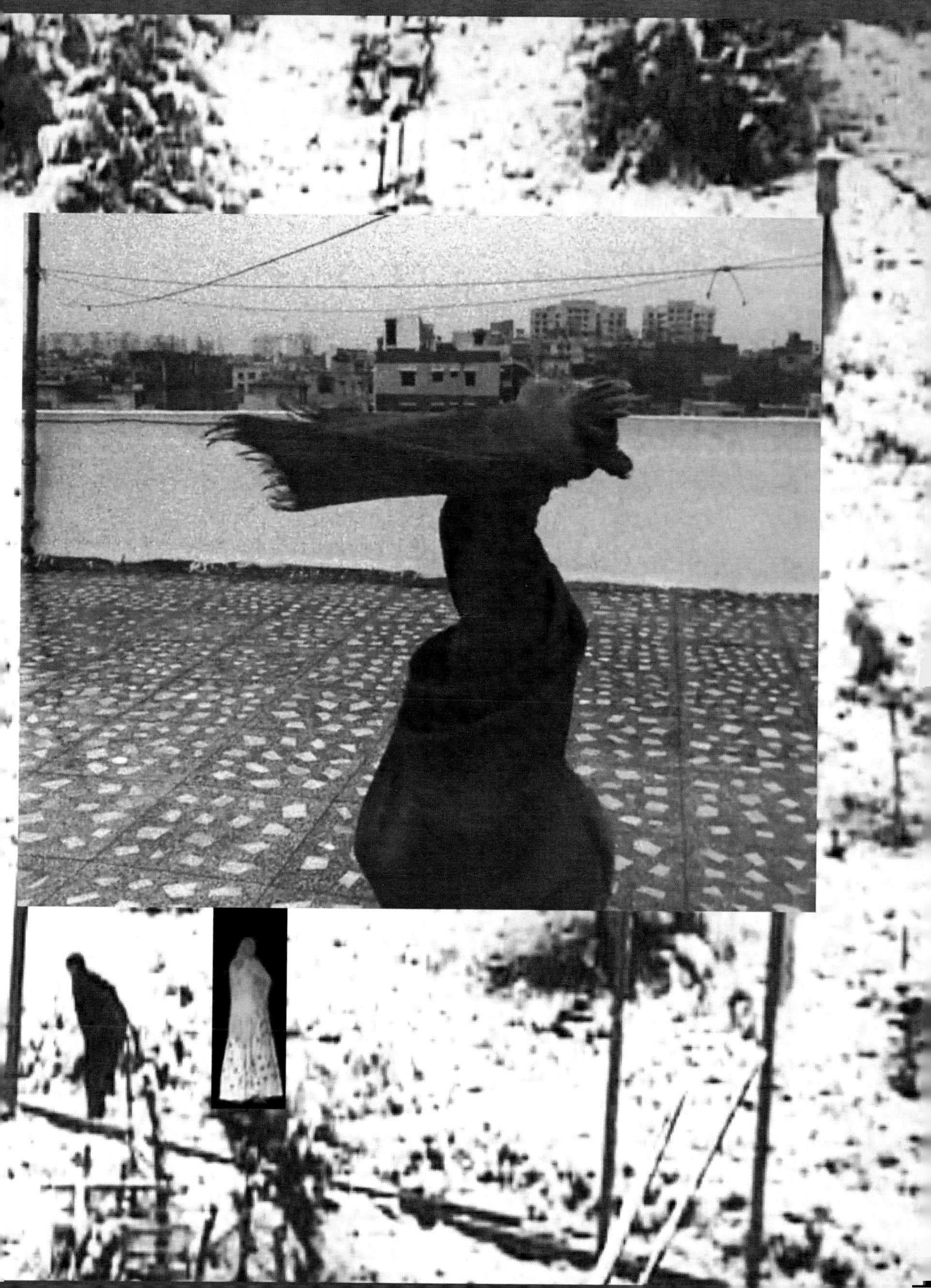

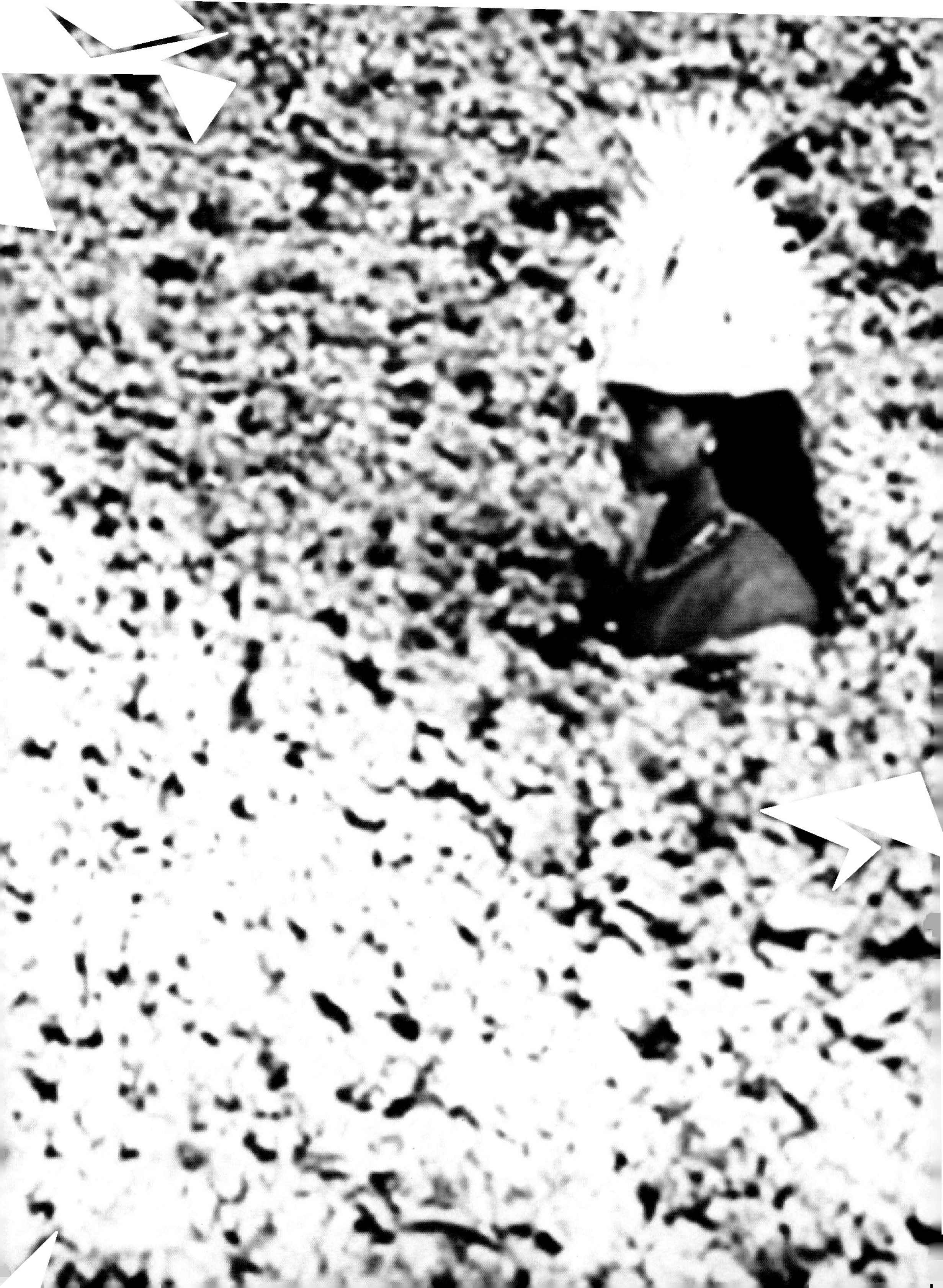

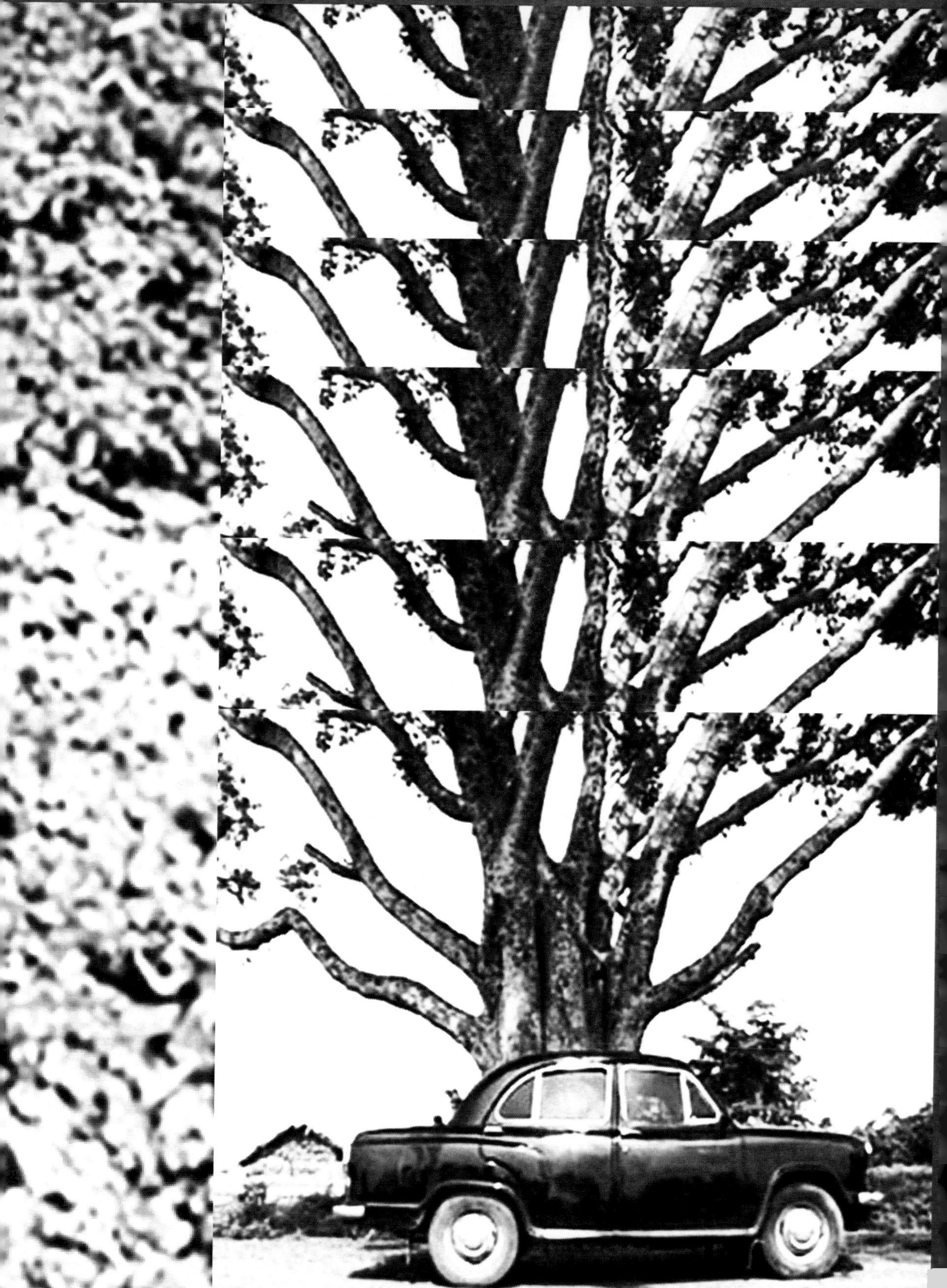

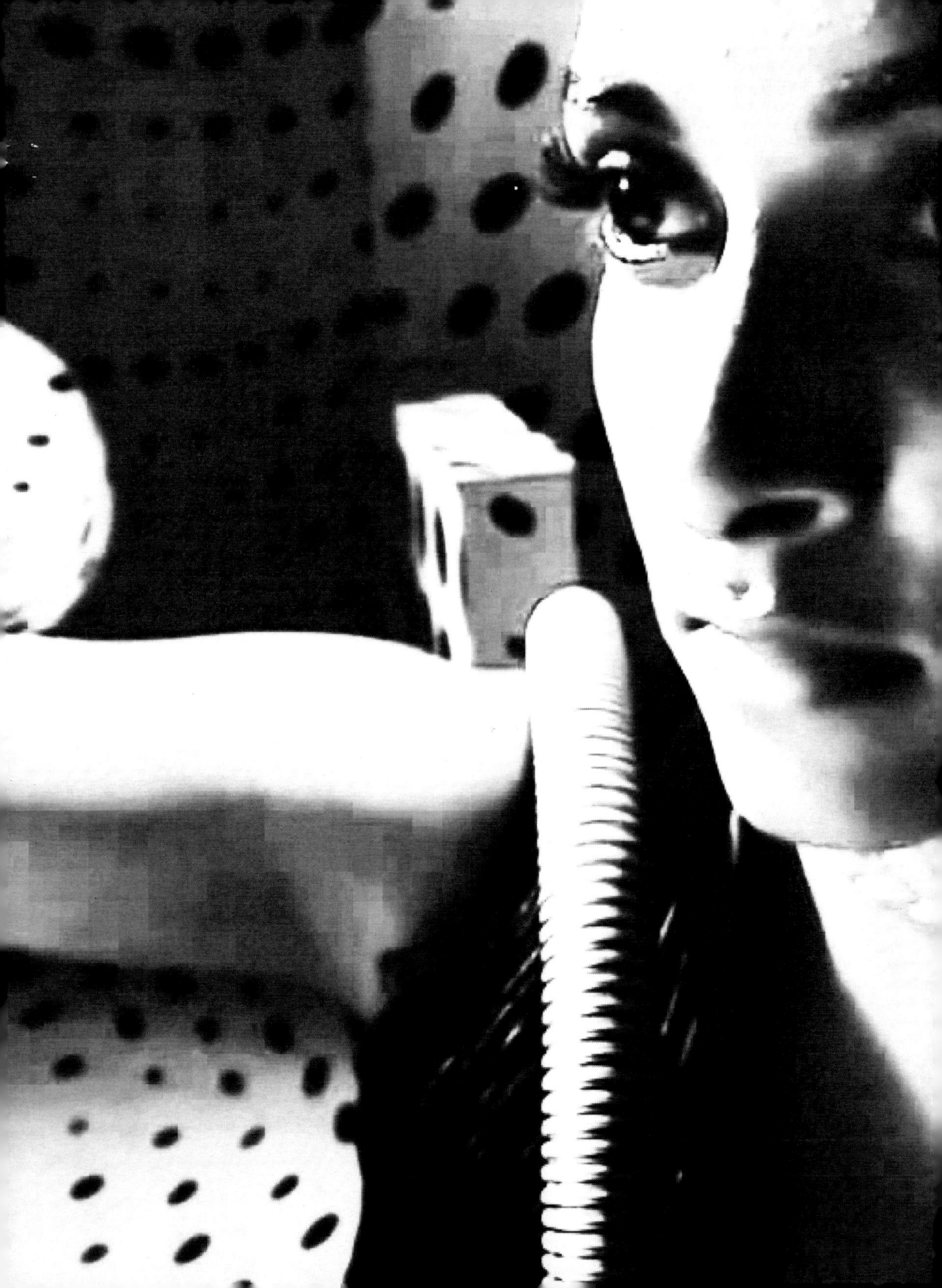

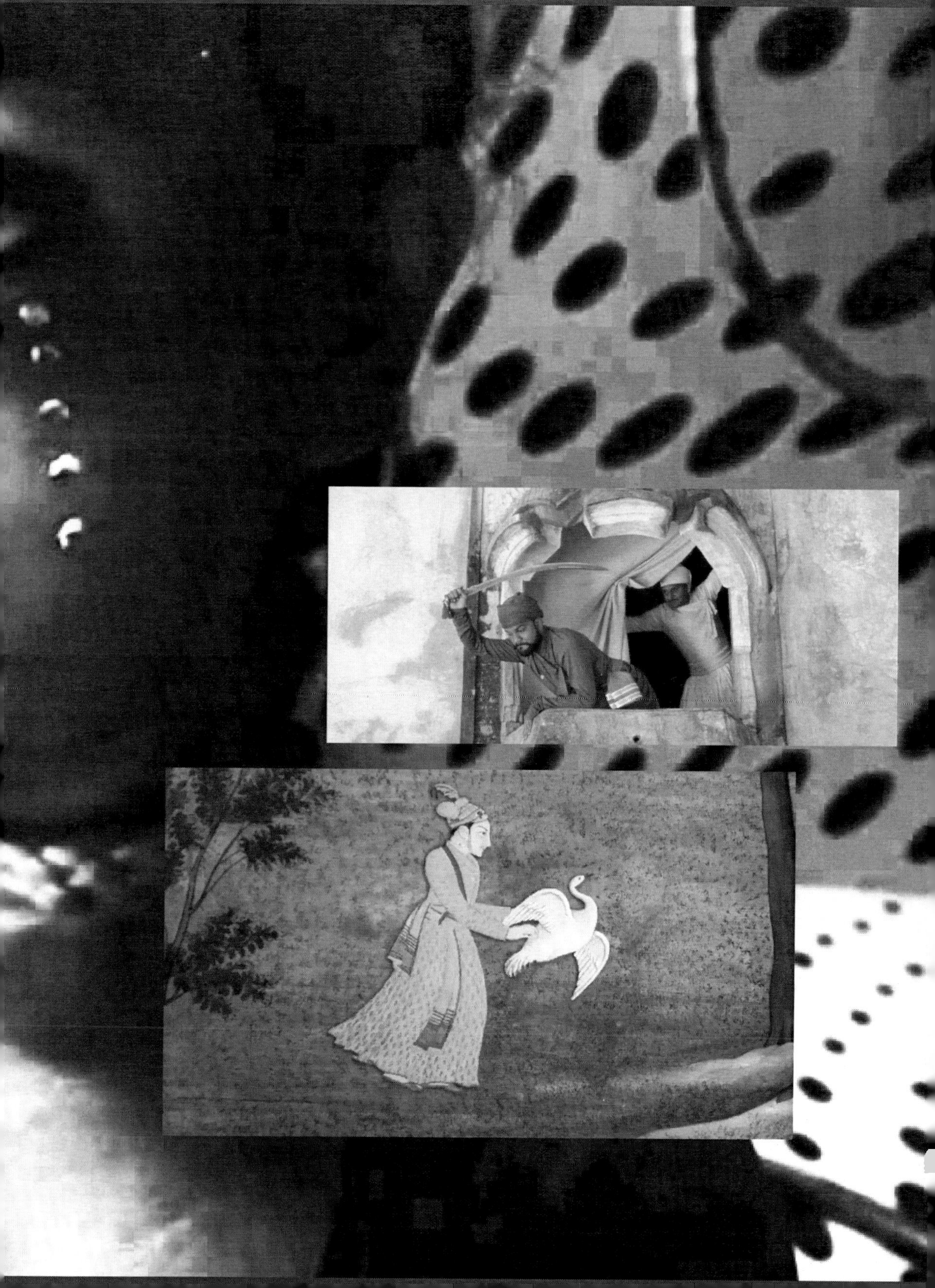

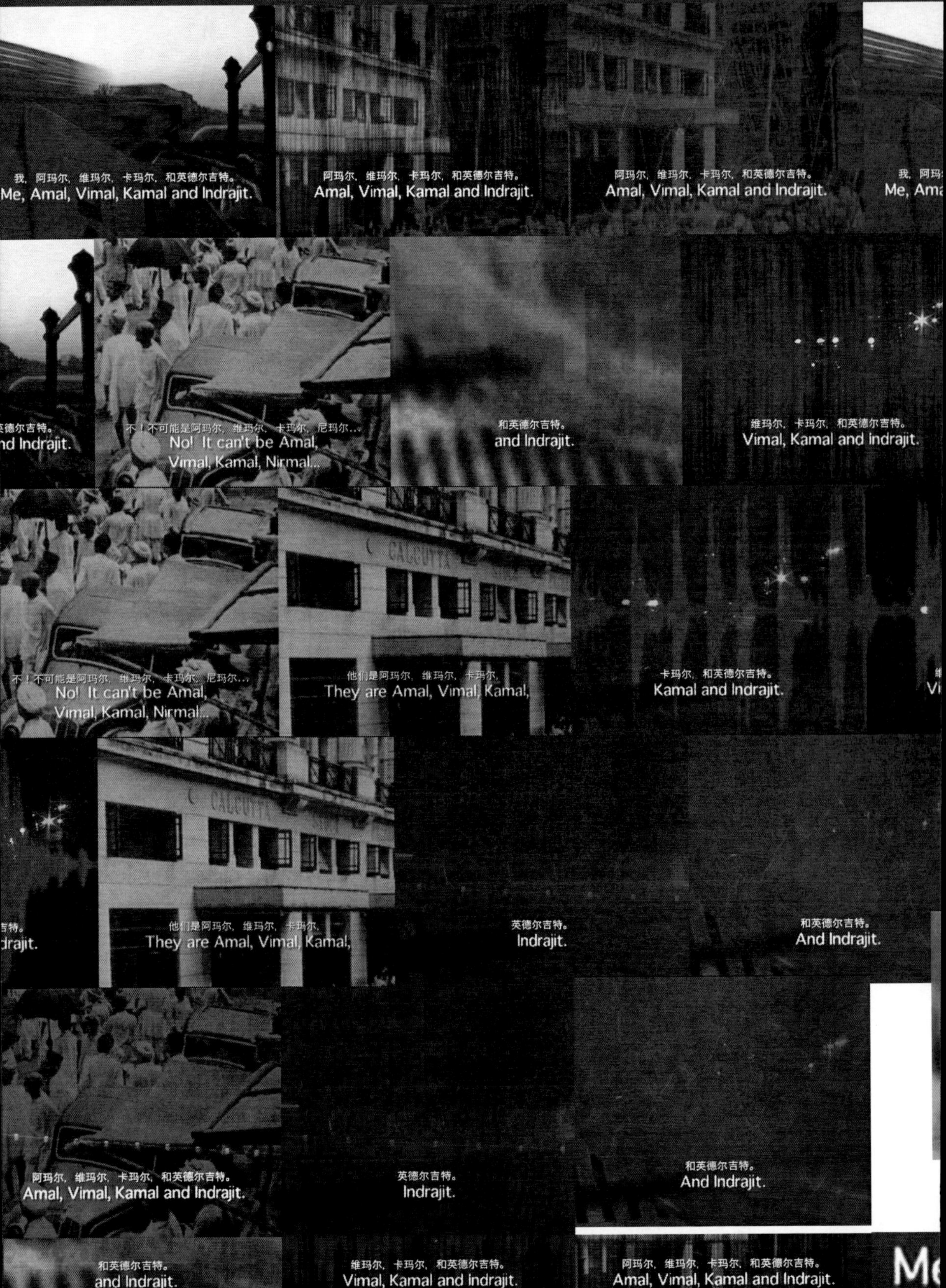
我，阿玛尔，维玛尔，卡玛尔，和英德尔吉特。
Me, Amal, Vimal, Kamal and Indrajit.
阿玛尔，维玛尔，卡玛尔，和英德尔吉特。
Amal, Vimal, Kamal and Indrajit.
阿玛尔，维玛尔，卡玛尔，和英德尔吉特。
Amal, Vimal, Kamal and Indrajit.
不！不可能是阿玛尔，维玛尔，卡玛尔，尼玛尔…
No! It can't be Amal, Vimal, Kamal, Nirmal...
和英德尔吉特。
and Indrajit.
维玛尔，卡玛尔，和英德尔吉特。
Vimal, Kamal and Indrajit.
不！不可能是阿玛尔，维玛尔，卡玛尔，尼玛尔…
No! It can't be Amal, Vimal, Kamal, Nirmal...
他们是阿玛尔，维玛尔，卡玛尔，
They are Amal, Vimal, Kamal,
卡玛尔，和英德尔吉特。
Kamal and Indrajit.
他们是阿玛尔，维玛尔，卡玛尔，
They are Amal, Vimal, Kamal,
英德尔吉特。
Indrajit.
和英德尔吉特。
And Indrajit.
阿玛尔，维玛尔，卡玛尔，和英德尔吉特。
Amal, Vimal, Kamal and Indrajit.
英德尔吉特。
Indrajit.
和英德尔吉特。
And Indrajit.
和英德尔吉特。
and Indrajit.
维玛尔，卡玛尔，和英德尔吉特。
Vimal, Kamal and Indrajit.
阿玛尔，维玛尔，卡玛尔，和英德尔吉特。
Amal, Vimal, Kamal and Indrajit.

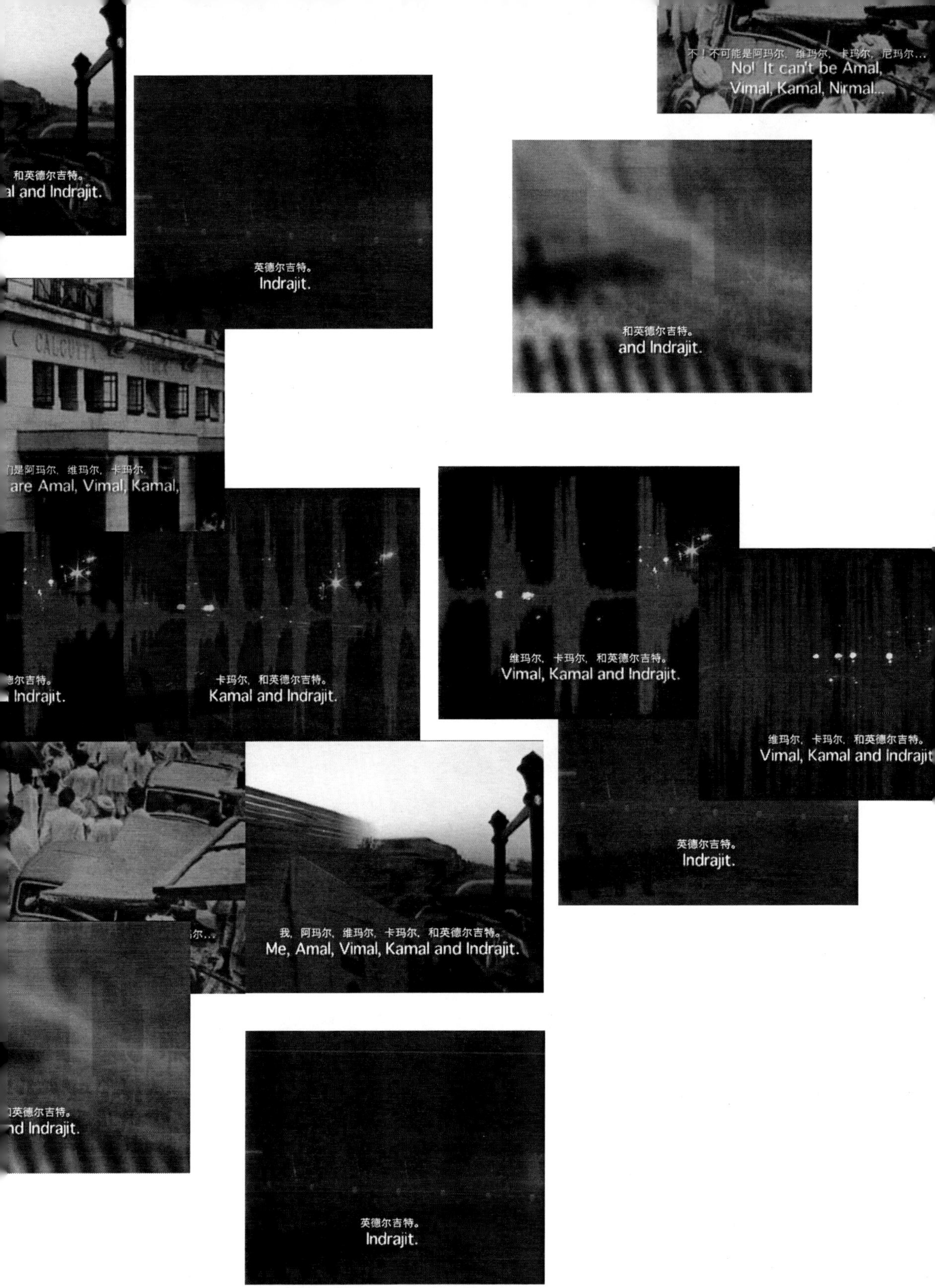
不！不可能是阿玛尔、维玛尔、卡玛尔、尼玛尔…
No! It can't be Amal,
Vimal, Kamal, Nirmal...
和英德尔吉特。
l and Indrajit.
英德尔吉特。
Indrajit.
和英德尔吉特。
and Indrajit.
are Amal, Vimal, Kamal,
卡玛尔、和英德尔吉特。
Kamal and Indrajit.
Indrajit.
维玛尔、卡玛尔、和英德尔吉特。
Vimal, Kamal and Indrajit.
维玛尔、卡玛尔、和英德尔吉特。
Vimal, Kamal and Indrajit
英德尔吉特。
Indrajit.
我，阿玛尔、维玛尔、卡玛尔、和英德尔吉特。
Me, Amal, Vimal, Kamal and Indrajit.
英德尔吉特。
nd Indrajit.
英德尔吉特。
Indrajit.

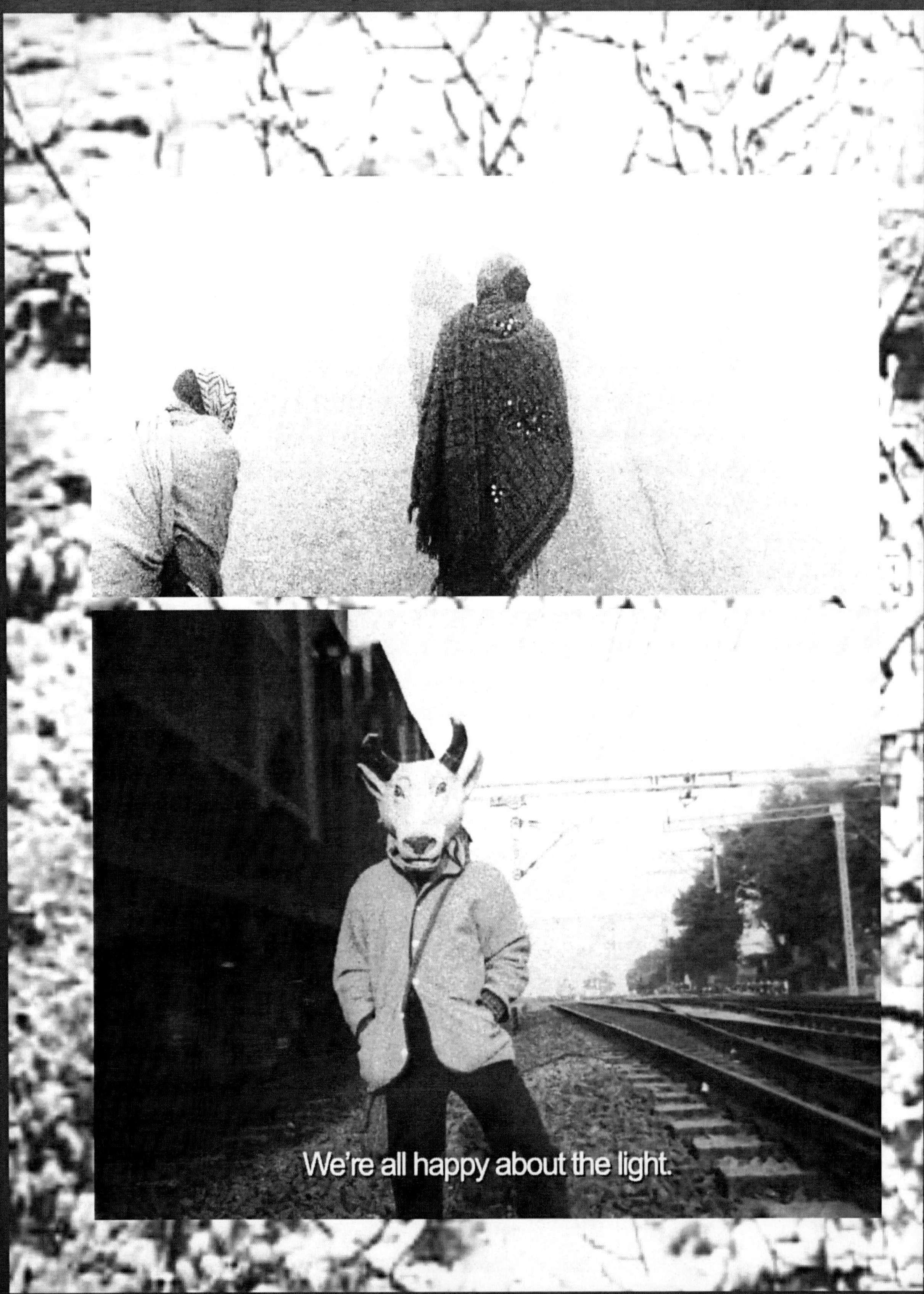
We're all happy about the light.

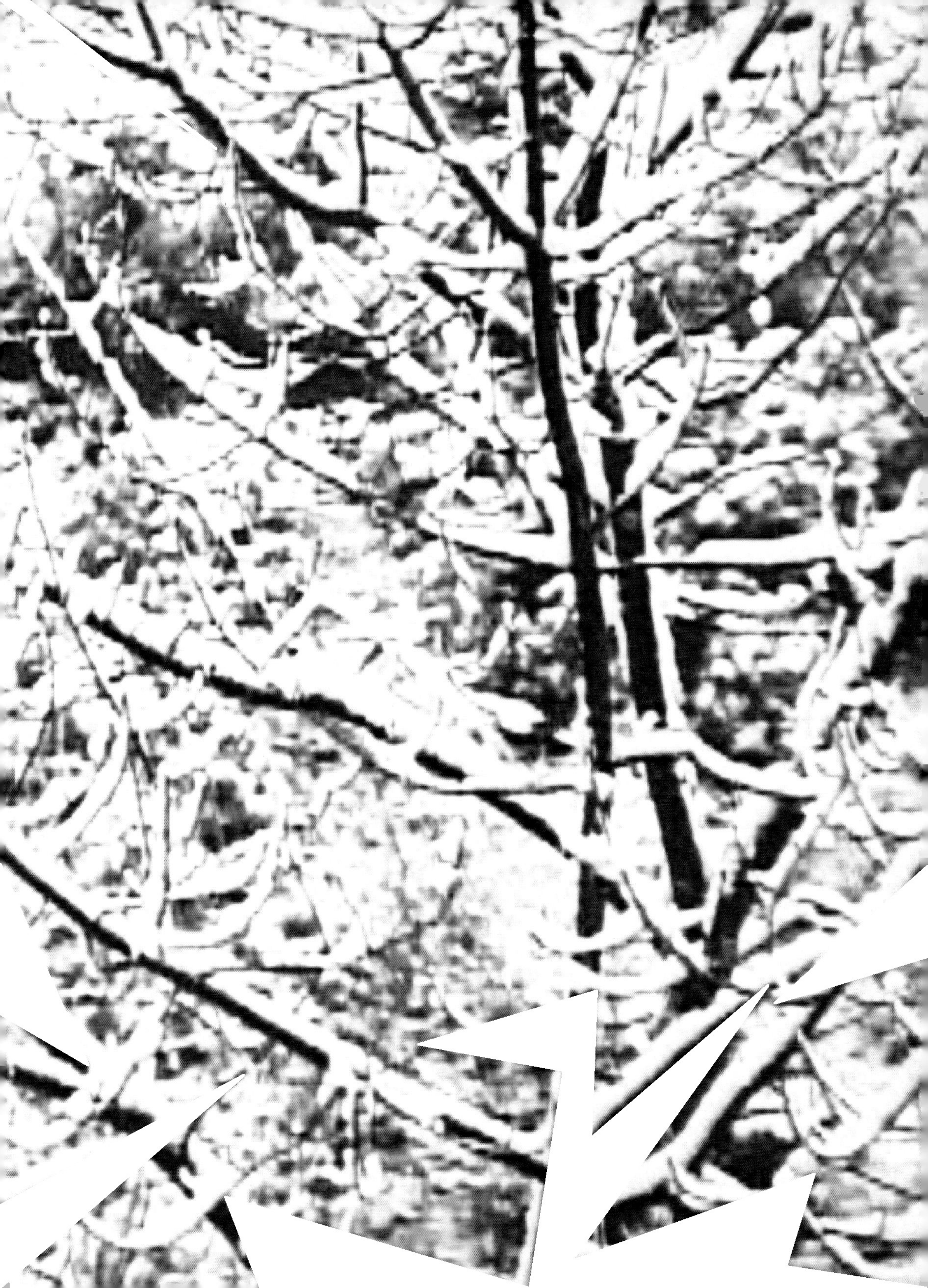

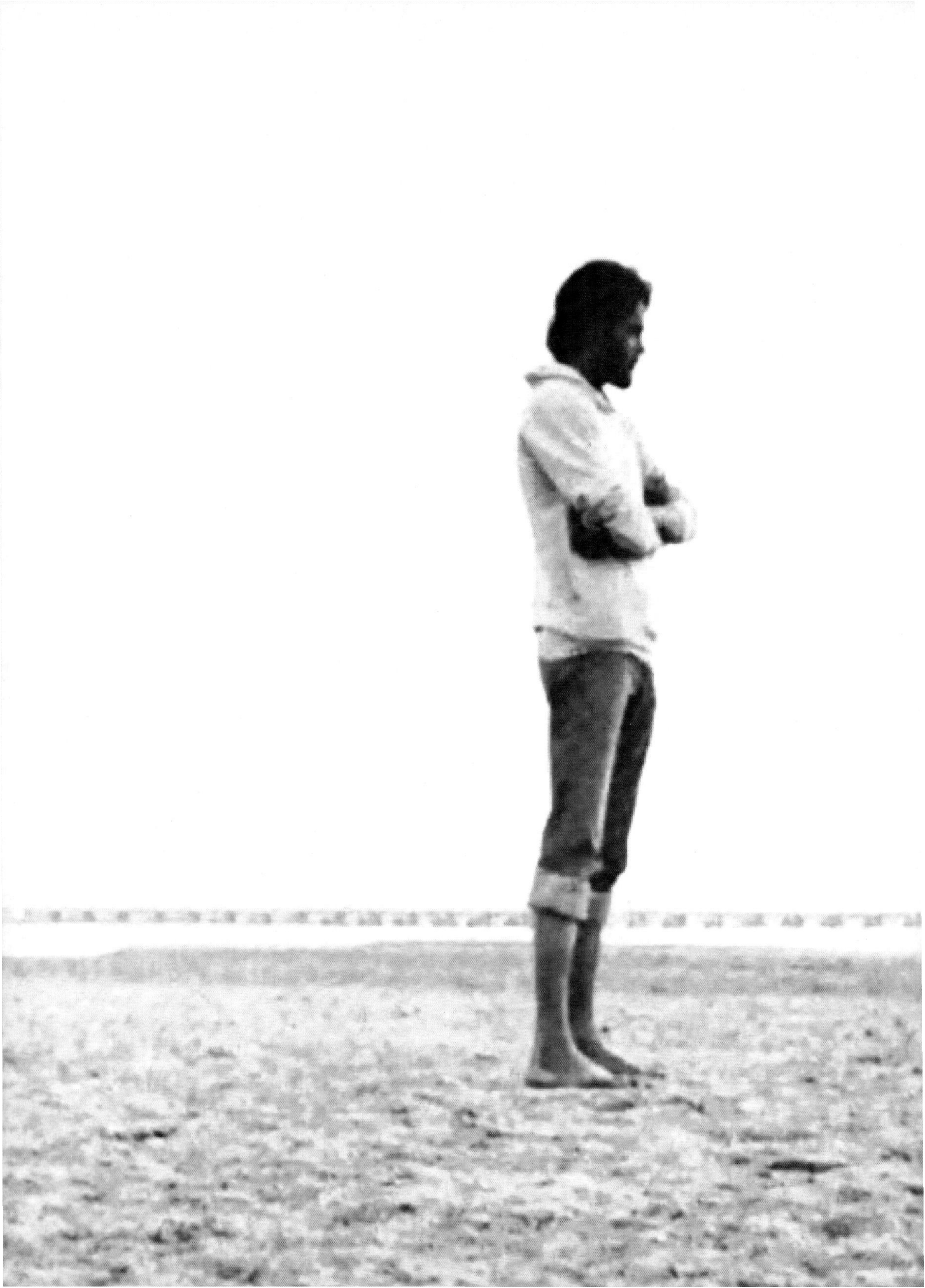

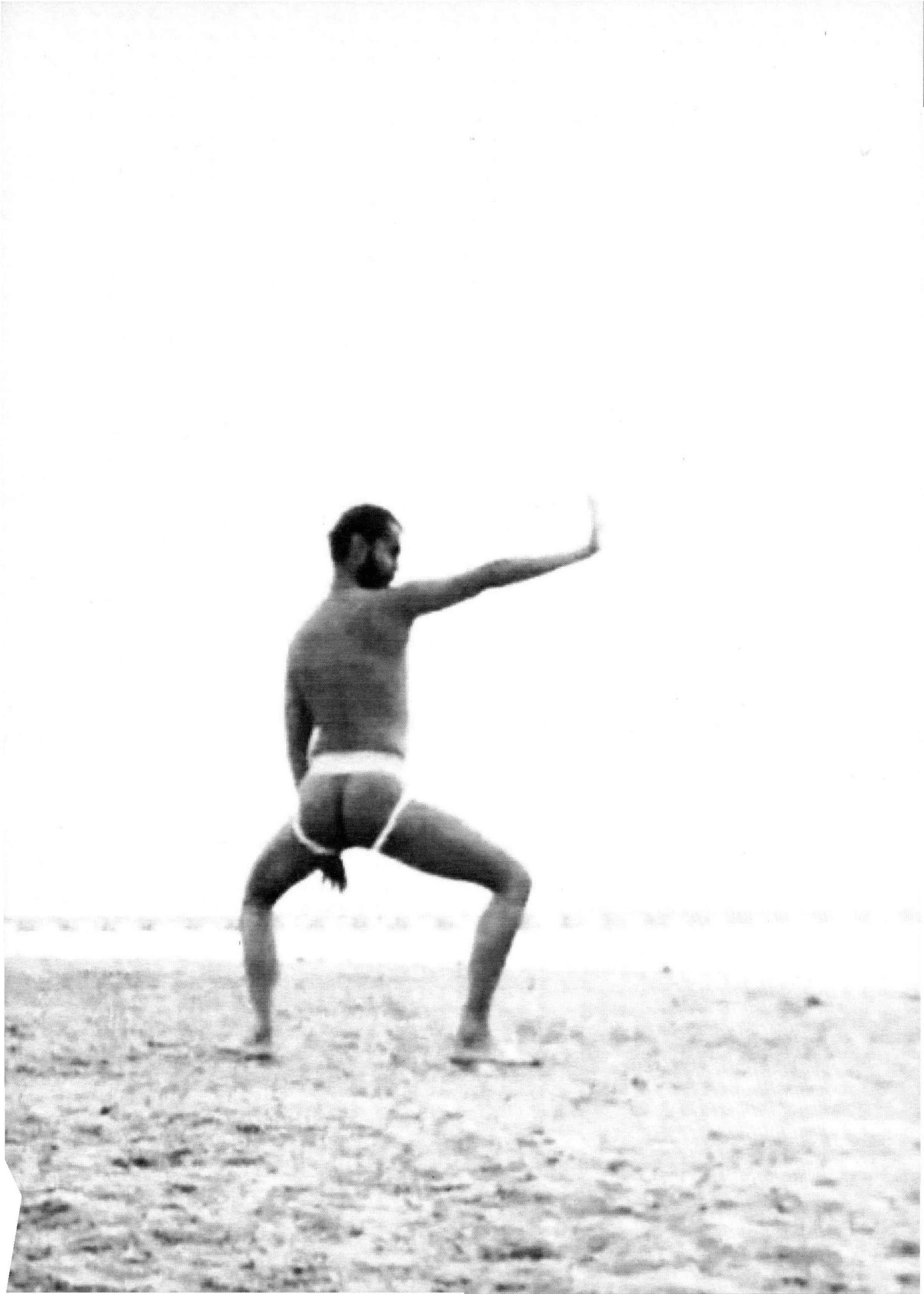

for the transmission of musical and philosophical knowledge. *Cinemā Prayōga* therefore draws on earlier India.

Within such an epic universe of impressions and feelings, the idea of substituting and expanding 'experimental' by a much more profound and inclusive notion, one that takes in both classic Indian cinema and more contemporary art cinema (if one may call it so without being divisive), should prove a productive enterprise. And as filmmaker-academic Ashish Avikunthak rightly believes, *Cinemā Prayōga* proposes a theory of film for Indian cinematographic modernity that attempts to provide an interpretative framework for understanding the radical evolution of Indian film not just as a mimetic outcome of western derivatives, but, crucially, as part of a continuous tradition of innovation in Indian film-making practices.

In general terms, *Cinemā Prayōga* has the quality of being intuitive and congenial, capable of achieving a certain unity of emotions that is profound, both formally and metaphysically. Avant-garde to me is a military word. *Prayōga*, on the contrary, is artistic and meditative. As the loosely equivalent Sanskrit word for the English 'experiment', *prayōga* has several different connotations, including design, device, plan, application, employment (especially of drugs and magic), use, exhibition (of dance), representation (of drama) and recitation. If we deconstruct the word *prayōga*, we get Pra + Yoga, where the prefix 'pra' in a way is an engine. As a prefix to verbs, it means 'forward', 'forth', 'onward', 'before'. In other words, it carries the sense of vanguard.

The notion of *Cinemā Prayōga* also accommodates the idea of imperfection as it is practised in Indian classical music (as against the conventional or habitual quest for perfection), and introduces an element of randomness, not as dysfunctional but as functional.

As long as there is a world in flux, the journey will go on and the artist's work is never complete. As Ritwik Ghatak (Bengali filmmaker: see **Keywords**) says, artists will secretly keep alive their capacity for dreaming, their ability to capture phenomena out of that continuous flux.

Art lies in snatching at something that has just happened, has never happened before, and will never happen in exactly the same manner again. Art conserves this happening of an extraordinary moment forever as an example. It is for art to keep its eyes and ears open, to snatch like a hawk at the ineffable at its core and illustrate the forces of growth operating within it so that a route to the future defines itself, however partially, and a golden line is somehow charted out.

Saeed Mirza on the Cinema of Struggle & the Cinema of the Status-quo

How Far Can A Filmmaker Go?

IT seems strange to me that in the voluminous writings of filmmakers, critics, and other kinds of journalists in India, one very basic point is never mentioned or referred to: that a certain kind of cinema exists only because a certain kind of State exists. In other words, there is a direct co-relation between the quality of cinema and the quality of the State. And this fact exists all over the world.

What do I mean by quality of films? By quality I mean the underlying structures, content material, and form which determine the films. By quality of State, I mean its political, social and economic structure and, through that, its cultural pretensions.

When 'new wave', 'parallel', or 'avant garde' filmmakers talk about the lack of an alternative channel of distribution which forces them into the existing market-place, which necessarily means conforming to its basic structures, they are missing the point. They are performing the function of the State — and the status quo. Because the existing channels of distribution with their odious dealings exist *because* of the State and *not* despite it.

To expect a State to be culturally naive and therefore open to reform is perhaps, to use a cliché, putting the cart before the horse. Most states are clearly defined politically and exist to perpetuate the rule of a group, or groups, of interests over the interests of other groups — no matter how developed, underdeveloped or undeveloped they are. And therefore it follows that to maintain the interests of the group, or groups, in power, a certain kind of cultural philosophy exists. Any philosophy outside the official version is doomed to be flung to the remotest fringes of the existing social order, if not outside the frontiers of the State.

Which brings me back to our filmmakers. Those who feel that they are more pragmatic and level-headed and have a polite contempt for their 'idealist' colleagues let them know, that despite their protestations of the nature of the State, despite their 'commitment' to change, by the very fact of their accepting a certain existing form of presentation, they are part of the very state that they are vociferously wanting to change. They are performing for the State and not against it. They

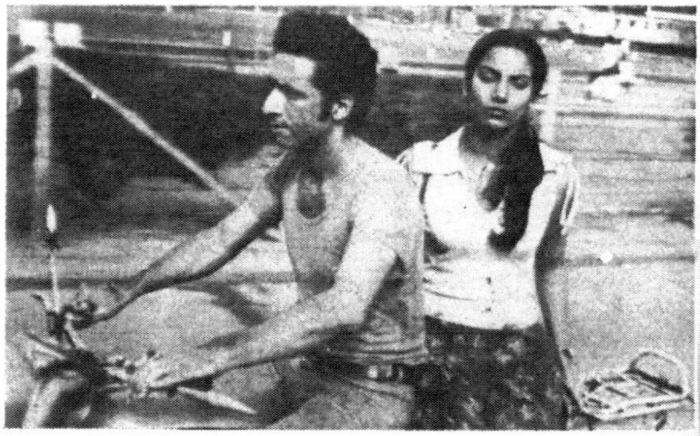

Naseeruddin Shah and Shabana Azmi in 'Albert Pinto'

have become merged with the interests of the ruling groups and serve as the escape valve which the State requires from time to time.

There will be some filmmakers who perhaps feel that there is nothing basically wrong with the State and if there is any dissonance it can be restored through persuasion and consensus. I wish them luck. History is full of such people who thought there was an easy way out. I believe there is no such way. There are only two kind of films — the cinema of struggle and the cinema of the status-quo. By struggle I mean of form, content material, music, structure, lighting, colour. *Pather Panchali* and *Aparajito* were one of the first few films of struggle — before they were co-opted in various third-rate imitations of artists sponsored by the State.

I feel that it is the duty of the artist to change the structure of his or her work before the State (or filmmakers of the status-quo) can co-opt and neutralise them. They must keep one step ahead of a State that needs to reduce them to insignificance. Now is the time to experiment with myth, legend, the epic, the lyric, signs and symbols, and a whole host of other inputs like sociology, anthropology and history, to create a cinema that will perform its basic function — that is to question everything that exists. Because when the artist fails to perform his or her duty, they have failed as artists. They have become court jesters.

Sounds depressing, doesn't it? The real tragedy is that despite any harsh statements, I belong (in a roundabout way) to the category of the pragmatic filmmakers. Hopefully I'll have the courage of breaking away and *not* be accepted in the eyes of the State. Because despite my films, which I feel were honestly made, what bothers me is the circles in which they are accepted. *That* sets me thinking. Those circles really represent the status-quo, oppression, smugness and ossified thinking — which need to be destroyed.

Originally published in *Cinema Vision*, India, vol. 1, no. 3, 1980, p. 72.

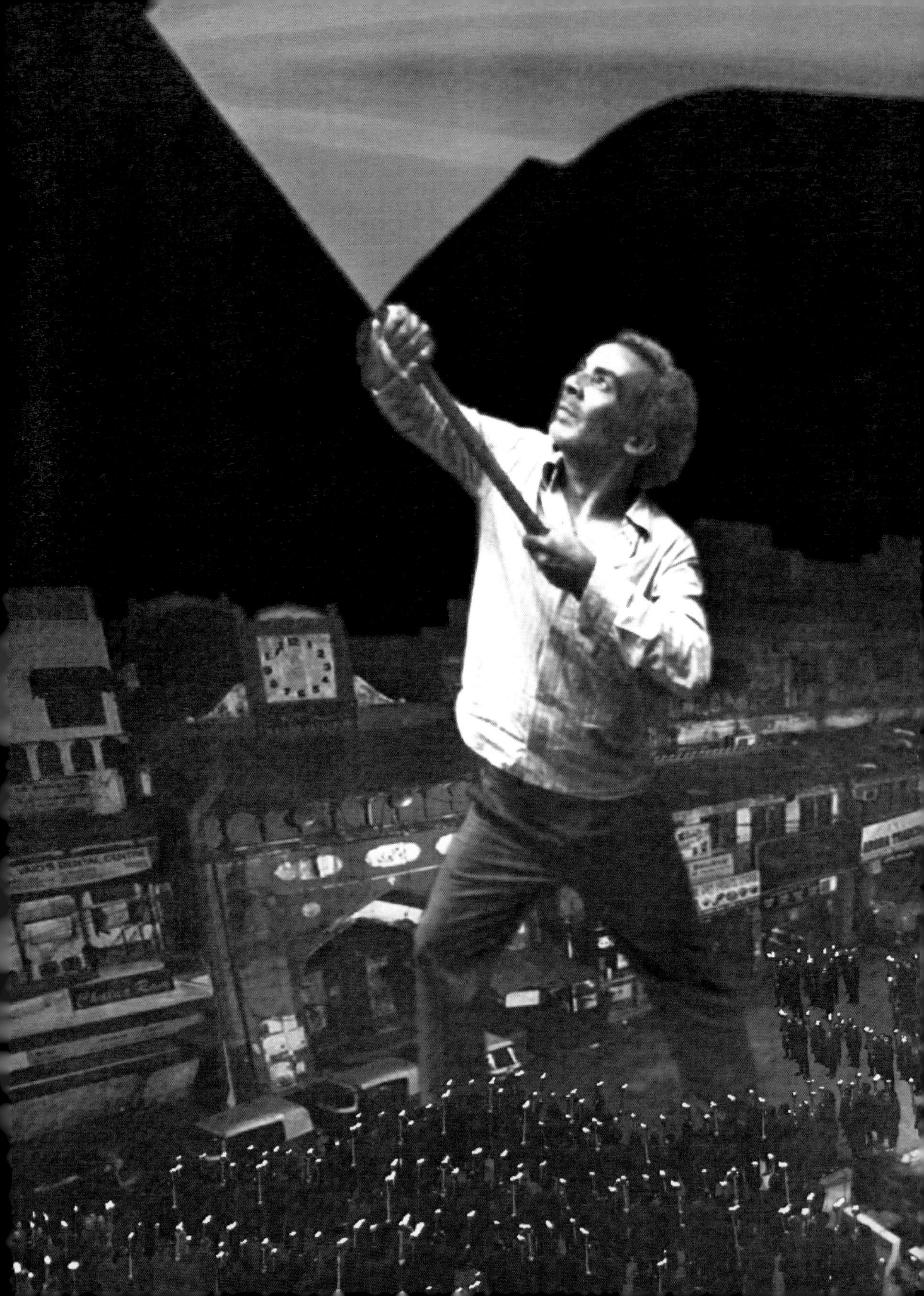

artist as citizen

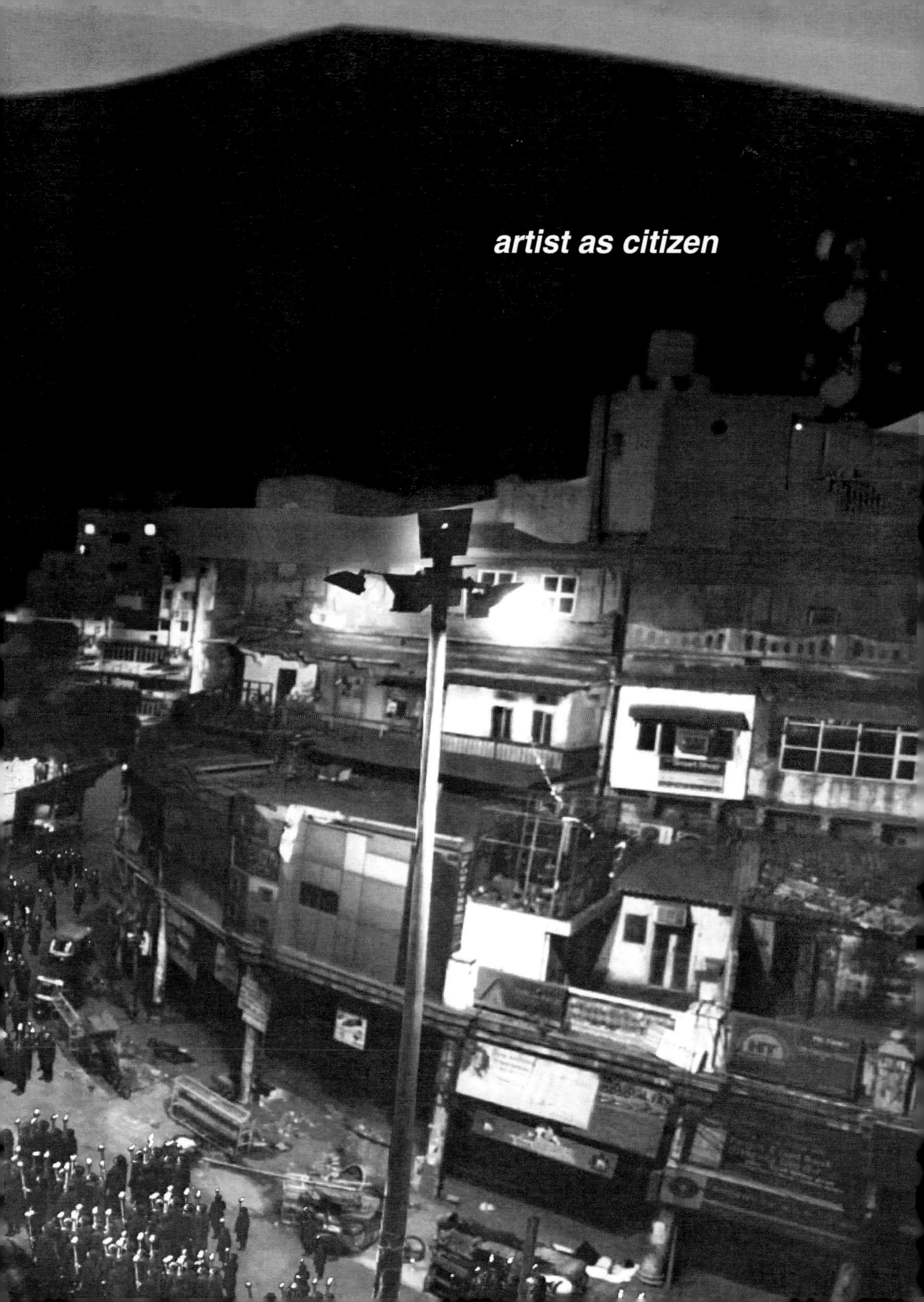

The state-supported genocide in Gujarat in 2002 was India's holocaust moment, etched in public memory as the haunting photograph of Qutubuddin Ansari pleading for life with his hands folded. Activists and artists responded with urgency to this devastating episode, and independent documentary filmmakers in particular took on a range of political responsibilities, including providing legal evidence. The 2004 election, bringing to power an unusual alliance of left and secular parties, allowed for a sigh of relief.

Setting her argument in that victorious moment, Geeta Kapur sees an aesthetic juncture: a moment of possibility for what she has theorized previously as an Indian avant-garde. Expanding her thesis, she points to ways by which 'radical elements . . . (can) be drawn . . . as much from within the "classic" binaries of high and low, genre and avant-garde, as from the conceptual, the mediatic, the documentary and the mythological.' Subsequent political history – with Hindutva parties securing majority mandates in 2014 and 2019 – certainly belie the optimism of 2004, yet Kapur's proposed conjunctures have only strengthened, as artists, writers, activists, students and intellectuals have drawn from 'high' art, popular culture, poetry, new media, the anti-colonial movement and performance, creating work and staging protests to protect constitutional values.

The essay, originally written in 2004, was published as a longer text in Terry Smith, Okwui Enwezor and Nancy Condee, eds, *Antinomies of Art and Culture: Modernity, Postmodernity, Contemporaneity*, Durham: Duke University Press, 2008. Much gratitude to Geeta Kapur for granting permission to publish this abridged essay.

Keywords, Names

2002 Gujarat, Avant-garde, Ayodhya, Dalit, (Deepa) Dhanraj, Documentary, Hindutva, (Amar) Kanwar, (Anand) Patwardhan, Sovereignty, Vikalp, Yugantar Collective:
See Keywords (pp. 326–44).

Images

pp. 120–21: Still from *Ghode ko Jalebi Khilane Le Ja Riya Hoon/Taking the Horse to Eat Jalebis* (dir. Anamika Haksar, 2018). Haksar's genre-breaking film about migrant labourers in Old Delhi draws upon devised theatre, documentary cinema, animation, special effects and painting. Image credits: Saumyanand Sahi (cinematographer); K. Gopalan (actor); Paresh Kamdar (editor); Archana Shastri (visual artist); Soumitra Ranade (VFX); Anamika Haksar (Mise-en-scène). Image courtesy Anamika Haksar.

p. 127: Frame from Pushpamala N., *Indrajaala/Seduction*, 2012, video installation: single channel or three channel video, b&w, silent, 4 min 30 sec. The installation, referring to early ethnographic and animation films, depicts a famous revenge episode from the *Ramayana*. Image courtesy Pushpamala N.

p. 132: Still from *Shanghai Tales* (Sharmila Samant, 2006), video documentary critiquing the indiscriminate Mumbai–Shanghai development plan. Scenes of a slum demolition shown from the point of view of a young boy, while city planners dream of a glitzy Shanghai skyline. Image courtesy Sharmila Samant.

p. 137: Frame from *Molkarin* (Deepa Dhanraj, 1981), 16 mm, b&w. Cinematography: Navroze Contractor. Part of the Yugantar film collective's early work, the documentary shows the oppressive working conditions of women domestic workers in the city of Pune who come together to form a workers' union.

GEETA KAPUR **2004**

I

Introductory: Is Culture what Artists Make?

The unexpected turnaround staged by the Indian electorate in 2004 released extraordinary possibilities for re-examining the coordinates of citizenship, culture and art practice. This essay follows from that event, the implications of which continue to unfold. Challenging the flourishing right-wing ideology of middle-class India, the election demonstrated with remarkable élan the power of the democratic vote, the maturity and astuteness of the (still largely rural) electorate, the possibility of overthrowing an anti-people right-wing government, and of giving a subtle mandate that requires a long-surviving centrist party to seek support from regional, under-caste/Dalit, socialist and left parties to form a mixed (and balanced) government. The 2004 churning of the Indian democracy can be seen as reconfiguring a secular public sphere capable of exposing the vileness of a majoritarian ideology (like Hindutva), but, further, as throwing up a debate on the rights of representation within the increasingly fraught and complex paradigm of the nation.

The proceeding argument is poised on the fragile hope that a democratic election can also change the economic destination of a nation - an extrapolation worth maintaining for the sake of its discursive potential if not its political certitude. Symbolically, the wager of the vote is that the Indian state and the government in power must return to certain key principles guaranteed in India's constitution. Specifically, that economic security is an inalienable right of the citizenry and the responsibility of the state - to fulfil which, it must guide the national-global compact through and beyond a contemporary that is overdetermined by the consolidation of a new empire.

If this democratic assertion is to be read across a preceding series of political disjunctures (I mean people's resistance movements and the left parties' emancipatory pedagogy that exert direct, even extra-parliamentary, pressure on government and state), the consequent electoral change reflects the convergence of a people's representational drive. It signals the need to define a radical version of citizenship, one that goes beyond the protocols of civil society. It precipitates a cultural conjuncture in the contemporary, which, in turn, needs to be transcribed into a calibrated account of subjectivities specific to the practice of the arts. The framing thematic that reflects on the antinomies of art and culture is held in suspension here in order to suggest that they are both driven by the same set of contradictions in any given historical circumstance; but that they nevertheless parody the rules of interdependency. I pose a riddle to condense and problematize the relationship: *Is culture what artists make?*

There is a straight answer: culture is a field made up of opposing representational interests that require to be kept in a workable relationship of consensual norms. Traditionally a containing matrix, culture at its most persuasive acquires a hegemonic status inviting non-coercive and participatory allegiance. On the other hand, art is always made up of a set of paradoxes nurtured in the imaginary and working with, but also against, the norm – to undermine its authority in favour of a new configuration of symbolic meanings. We place artists, like other cultural practitioners, among 'organic intellectuals' or the committed intelligentsia, as a 'class' that can be seen to translate the people's representational drive into the norms for a civil society, and these norms, in turn, into an immanent expression of individual subjectivity. It is this last embodiment that remains the elusive part of the mediated relay. The language of the arts draws equally from a socialized as from an (existentially) estranged subjectivity; it refracts and defers and conceals meaning to mark its radical variance from instrumental reason as operative in the political domain.

If, on the other hand, we claim provocative sets of contradictions *in* and *between* art and culture, it makes the above question tendentious, but still not redundant. It is asking to be answered in the double negative but with the slippages read into the negation serving as critical clues in a failed equation. Even traditionally, culture has seeds of dissent inscribed into its interstices that can be interpreted as confrontational cultures/cultures of protest. Modernist art, for all the autonomy it claims, acquires an avant-garde status at the juncture where it goes outside the institution of art and connects with the more radical political movements of its time or, at any rate, with the subversive aspects of the cultures in opposition.

Not wanting to repeat the methodology of contextual readings made too familiar by sociology, I propose that art can be read as an index (of the hot-footed process of globalization), as symbolic (of persistently hypothesized national cultures) and as a sign (of the surplus value and, with it, of unsolicited pleasures generated beyond commodity exchange). I want also to steer clear of the culturalist euphoria sometimes encouraged within cultural studies discourse; or, rather, its pointedly postmodern misrepresentations with a weak (and faulty) politics. I refer to such ruses that suppress the economic to cushion the impact of corporate globalism, that deploy a rhetoric playing on the political with the perverse purpose of celebrating failures in class confrontations and national projects.

Neither do I, for obvious reasons, want to revert to the culturalist ideologies favoured in countries with rich surviving traditions such as India. This feature requires special alertness and flexibility on the part of cultural practitioners. For example, modern art as an 'institution' does not have a stable status within the matrix of civil society in India, which means that contemporary Indian artists have no buffer against the social, against social reality, nor perhaps against the ideology of the state. To compensate for this 'lack' – of autonomy – the politics of civilizational plenitude and cultural synchronicity, and, in conservative times, of a homogenizing cultural nationalism, is played up. Representational drives are translated into a programmatic plotting of identities; a minority polemic that further marginalizes the culturally disenfranchised is foregrounded.

It may also be that the institutional autonomy of art, supported by the luxury of a liberalized economy, does not suffice within the post-colonial condition; that the chimera of a self-sufficient aesthetic, too quickly appropriated by the market (booming with the recent, neoliberal, turn), robs the art scene of a substantive equation: between a hypothesized institution of art and art's agonistic function in what is, in a country like India, a valid public sphere.

My riddle is posed both to counterbalance the risky option of (economic and political) overdetermination with which I pitch into this paper, as well as to ensure that we are not left with what are at once soft and spurious options for a reified (transnational/transcultural) exchange of spectacular, consumer-driven signs. This twin skepticism changes both the definition of radicalism in art and the expectation from an avant-garde – about which more as we go forward.

Artists as Citizens

During the twentieth century, all through the national movement and up until the immediate contemporary, Indian artists (including, for this argument, visual artists and filmmakers, literary and theatre practitioners, with specific examples drawn from the two former categories) have represented, both euphorically and critically, the imagined community, even perhaps the state embodiment, of the nation. Deriving from the hundred-year-long national movement for independence, artists, as members of the intelligentsia, have found forms of critical affiliation with what can justifiably be called the national-state.[1] They have devised genres and styles, and figural types, as well as aesthetic strategies, for the purpose.

While, at this level, artists may identify with 'accredited' members of a national elite and seek to wield power with and through institutions of the state, at another, they support the more contestatory values of a democratic polity by positioning themselves in the public sphere. When faced with assertive aspects of state power, artists, like the large left-leaning intelligentsia of India, have tried to step outside the orbit of coercions, to recognize the changing contours of a democracy addressing itself to political dissent beyond the protocol of (a covertly state-administered) civil society.[2] Further, there is a history of artists operating from within explosive group formations, collectives and movements, and taking on a forthrightly antagonistic role. Foregrounding their view from a subaltern locus, Dalit writers in particular challenge, defy and mock the ideology of the ruling class (and caste), the hegemony of the state and the very legitimacy of the national.[3]

On a broad plane Indian artists, in terms of their aesthetic, have tended to function much like the 'universal' moderns: with the liberty of projected identification of the 'other'; with a language sensitive to the ethics of such embodiment; with strategies for displacement, subversion, gender transgression.[4] In a more philosophic sense, they have tended to assume the privileged, if ironical, status of a sovereign-subject, corresponding to but more self-valorizing than that of the citizen-subject. They have sought allegories or otherwise deconstructed signs of the national whereby they can be both inside the nation and outside the state in their interpretative rendering of the political.[5]

With globalization, new factors have emerged to alter the role of artists as citizens. The retreat of the state within a global capitalist economy means that we must look for not only new notions of citizenship, but also for new subjectivities that develop among young aspirants within the urban – among, say, the new 'class' of youth gambling on livelihood chances in the outsourcing economy of global capital. I am thinking of the seemingly vacuous masquerade played out by Indian youth within internationally hooked call centres, or of young cyborgs interpellated into a global network of info-technology within altogether new space-time coordinates. Younger artists tend to identify with these expanding realms of indeterminacy and often adapt a mediatic version of the avant-garde – turning the rupture in the institutional associations of nation and state into a trans-subjective 'free zone' of democratic exchange.[6] Dissolution of causative trajectories of purposes and interests, a vertigo of disconnection, produces a shredding and restringing of material connectivities, a spin into a vortex of anxieties and desires, and thereon, an aggravated condition of metropolitan entropy. 'All that is solid melts into air'[7],

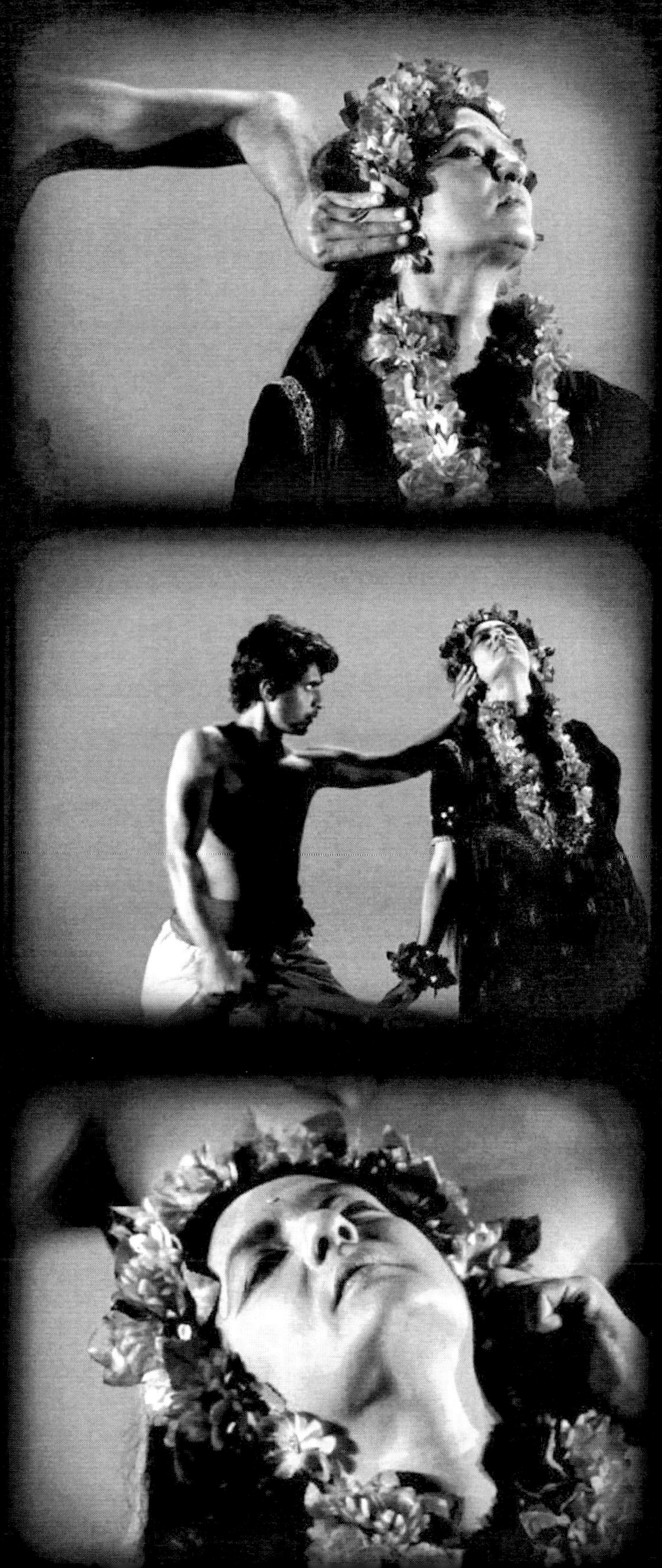

and the surreal fragments of the unredeemed Real ask to be theorized (perhaps) in cultural terms; to be rendered (perhaps) into new aesthetic practices.

When the national state, claiming custodianship of its peoples' economic interests, is handicapped and eventually even crippled by capitalist globalization, the widespread travail is accompanied by the emergence of fresh affiliations in the form of affirmative or, more properly, partisan action at the grassroots, some of which is 'documented' in the very process of formation by filmmakers and videographers working in solidarity with national and international NGOs. Covering the sub-terrain of a nation's neglected populace, this makes, in some ways, common cause with the idea and emergence of 'multitudes', and it looks to establish human rights and good governance in the constitution of a global citizenry.

A Documentary Mo(ve)ment

The recent groundswell in the Indian documentary scene is politically compelling in that it helps to explore how spontaneous resistance to reactionary ideologies can bestow upon scattered practitioners the status of a movement that is virtually 'underground' at the same time as it is fully public.

The context is the five-year rule (1998–2004) of the right-wing government led by the Bharatiya Janata Party, which peaked to a ruthless logic in 2002 when a state-supported pogrom against the Muslim community in Gujarat consolidated Hindutva ideology as fascist. Almost a dozen films dealing directly with the Gujarat genocide of 2002 have been made; earlier riots and massacres saw hardly one or two. Documentary evidence assumes access to citizens as co-witnessing spectators. Not surprisingly, therefore, a confrontation on the censorship law became the actual occasion for the documentary movement to erupt. During a routine selection procedure for the Mumbai International Film Festival (MIFF), the requirement prescribed by the state for all Indian films to obtain a censor certificate became a sudden rallying point and developed, in 2004, into an alternative film festival with a travelling circuit. By now, nearly 300 short and documentary filmmakers are associated with this action platform, a majority of who have opted to exhibit their films without the censor certificate, sometimes under threat from the authorities.

After the May 2004 election, the actual situation in the country is less grim. Yet the need for solidarity continues in anticipation of the need to assert the constitutional right to freedom of speech and expression (a useful euphemism to win the right of dissent and confrontation). The constitutional right is of course bracketed with other provisos that constrain that right. This well-marked battle involves legal interpretation and a complex political discourse; it involves a proactive definition of rights of representation as much as those of expression and information, and of all these in relation to theories of spectator address and reception.

We should note that the rejection of censorship arises as much from a precipitate political moment as from video and digital technology itself, which, by its immediacy, informality, constructs a different private-public interface, suggesting what it means to function in and shape a contemporary public sphere. Place this development within the twin frames of the nation and the state - both based on privileged identities, legal sanctions and hierarchy of command - and the grant of official freedom through a censor board certificate begins to appear at best gratuitous. It is the mood of the moment to foreground these issues in disregard of, and in opposition to, the mediating institution of the state. Thus, these hundreds of filmmakers seek a mandate under the title 'Films for Freedom 2004'.

The upsurge in the production and reception of documentary films in India has to do with 'a crisis in democracy', says the filmmaker Amar Kanwar;[8] equally or, rather, inversely, one might say that it is the result of a more extensive democratic consciousness that reveals gaps and losses and translates these into a language of intervention. '[I]n some ways', Sudipta Kaviraj says, 'it is better not to treat democracy as a governmental form. . . . A better strategy . . . is to treat it, more problematically, as a 'language', as a way of conceiving, and in more propitious circumstances, of making, the world'.[9] Indeed, if democracy, as Kaviraj suggests, is something like a 'narrative contract' between identifiable nationalities and group formations, then the documentary form confirms the contract, whether it adopts the activist mode connected to political ideologies/organizations/movements (such as the century-old Indian labour movement), or whether it links with anthropology-driven, grassroots politics that prioritizes the immanent nature of community structures and seeks legal visibility and self-definition within the local context. Either way, political space is sought to be captured by the direct access assumed by its communicational ethics. And while any one documentary unravels the issues piecemeal, the synergy of many eyes, hands and expositions at work with the camera provides a peculiar 'narrative' positioning of the medium in the above contractual sense of the term, at the present juncture.

But let me backtrack a little. If we mark 2003–04 as a moment when the Indian documentary movement names itself, it is preceded by nearly two decades of interventionist documentary film practice. Take a major protagonist in this battle, the pugnaciously political Anand Patwardhan, who has been at the forefront of the documentary scene since the late 1970s/early 80s.[10] He has confronted the major issues during these decades: the Emergency (*Prisoners of Conscience*, 1978); the demolition/displacement of 'slum' habitation in a city like Bombay caught between the ordering regime of urban development and devouring real-estate sharks *Hamara Shahar* (Bombay Our City, 1985); and the people's movement against the big dam project on the Narmada river that has destroyed a large (tribal and peasant) population, and the story of its decades-long opposition that finally lost to a bitterly fought juridical order (*Narmada Diary*, 1995). Here, we focus on Patwardhan in the year 1992, when the Babri Masjid was demolished, an event signaling the victory of the right wing straight through to the parliamentary elections of 1998-99. Patwardhan's *Raam ke Naam* (In the Name of God, 1992) was made during and after the Babri Masjid demolition; it was followed by *Father, Son and Holy War* (1994), which traces the origin of the fascist tendency to a pathological regret over lost manhood perpetrated by the false ideology of 'modernized' Hindutva.

Patwardhan's films are based on a rationalist, cause-effect dialectic; their spirit is entertaining, volatile, provocative; their form is pedagogic and associated with avant-garde moments in culture and politics: the revolutionary vigour of the early Soviets through to the Third Cinema movement in Latin America during the liberationist decade of the 1960s (and early 70s).[11] Patwardhan is contextualized within a documentary movement based on historical rupture of a momentous scale; a movement coming in the wake of political and cultural decolonization that proposes nothing less than a third world aesthetic whereby artists lay simultaneous and rhetorical claim on realism, modernity and the avant-garde, and, more specially, on documentary 'truth' *as* an avant-garde strategy of resistance and renewal. Within India, Patwardhan runs into trouble with the state and fights with guerrilla tactics and legal aplomb, repeatedly claiming that the state is a reality, that it can be fought and made to bend and, at best, even taught by citizens' initiatives to rectify its ideological (mis)understanding of a living democracy.

The much younger filmmaker Amar Kanwar,[12] in what he calls more activist documentaries such as *The Many Faces of Madness* (2000) and *Freedom...!* (2002), presents a morally pitched interrogation of problematized subject-matter ranging over agricultural labour, Dalits, ethnic minorities, dispossessed tribal communities fighting the devastation wreaked on their living environments by the development policies of independent India, accompanying this with a philosophical discourse on human (and environmental/planetary) survival.

Hereon, the signal differences between Patwardhan and Kanwar emerge.[13] The 'objective' interlocutor that Patwardhan foregrounds in his films is, in Kanwar, an extension of the very person of the speaking subject - the filmmaker himself. Working in the interstices of the social, Kanwar develops a 'documentary' form of intersubjectivity, but through a ruse. He displaces social issues on to more philosophic, aesthetic, *affective* planes of thought and feeling. Using poetry and reflexion above argument and dialectics as his preferred style - manifestly in his 2002 film, *Night of Prophecy* - Kanwar advances the idea of freedom and ethics as natural correlates of film practice, and defers any programmatic definition of praxis. Kanwar's films ask that we undertake critical rethinking of the two supposedly contradictory categories of interrogation and affect. And to thereby rethink action, especially action inducing (as it often does) the spectre of violence.

In *A Season Outside* (1998), the slowly materialized, sensuously held image arrests the attention of the spectator until it reaches the stage of what Walter Benjamin calls 'mimetic innervation'. In this film, several narratives crisscross and plot the iconic moments of valiant militancy in the communitarian identity of the Sikhs of India. Folding the medieval into the modern, the sacrifices of the legendary gurus into the community's fraught honour today, Kanwar uses visual allegory in such a way that the travesty of masculine violence is interrogated from within the beauty and pain of martyrdom. Kanwar's own vulnerable passage into contemporary history brackets the film: an autobiographical reference to his family's journey at the time of Partition; a documentary quotation of Gandhi walking to quell communal riots at the time of partition. The film ends by consciously adopting a form of social 'mourning' that becomes, by the deployment of a deliberate default, political in the manner of its righteous reflexivity.

Thus, what I schematically designate as two alternatives in documentary film practice in India may, equally schematically, be seen as a generational change in the nature and pursuit of politics itself. Patwardhan courts history; Kanwar's is an exploration of the ground reality by a filmmaker who prefers to hold a premium on subjective knowledge, and on a doubting, tarrying discourse over means and ends set apace by history. In an increasing number of films, the subaltern figure is seen working with a subversive (more secessionist than cumulative) strategy of survival, inhabiting a fragmented map of the social that no longer coincides with that of the nation.

What is gained and lost by this change in the documentary genre and in the genre of politics itself is arguable. Even today, beyond the successful and failed revolutions, post-colonial realities and their corresponding cultural imperatives continue to be crucial; and a conscious representational drive, with the dynamic of an evidentiary aesthetic, erupts in clusters across the new empire. In any case, current ideological preferences hold no absolute privilege over the future and I would think the balance is tipped by the degree to which different styles of cultural articulation support confrontational alternatives that are being rapidly disempowered by the consolidation of global capital.

II

The Sphere of Art: Where the Compass Points

I describe, now, what I call a full circle of manifold art practices, and position 'high' art and 'low' art on the polar points of a vertical axis, particularizing these rough categories as modernist art and popular art. I position a horizontal axis across the vertical and polarize two opposing categories, genre and avant-garde, particularizing genre with reference to the powerful drive for realism and the

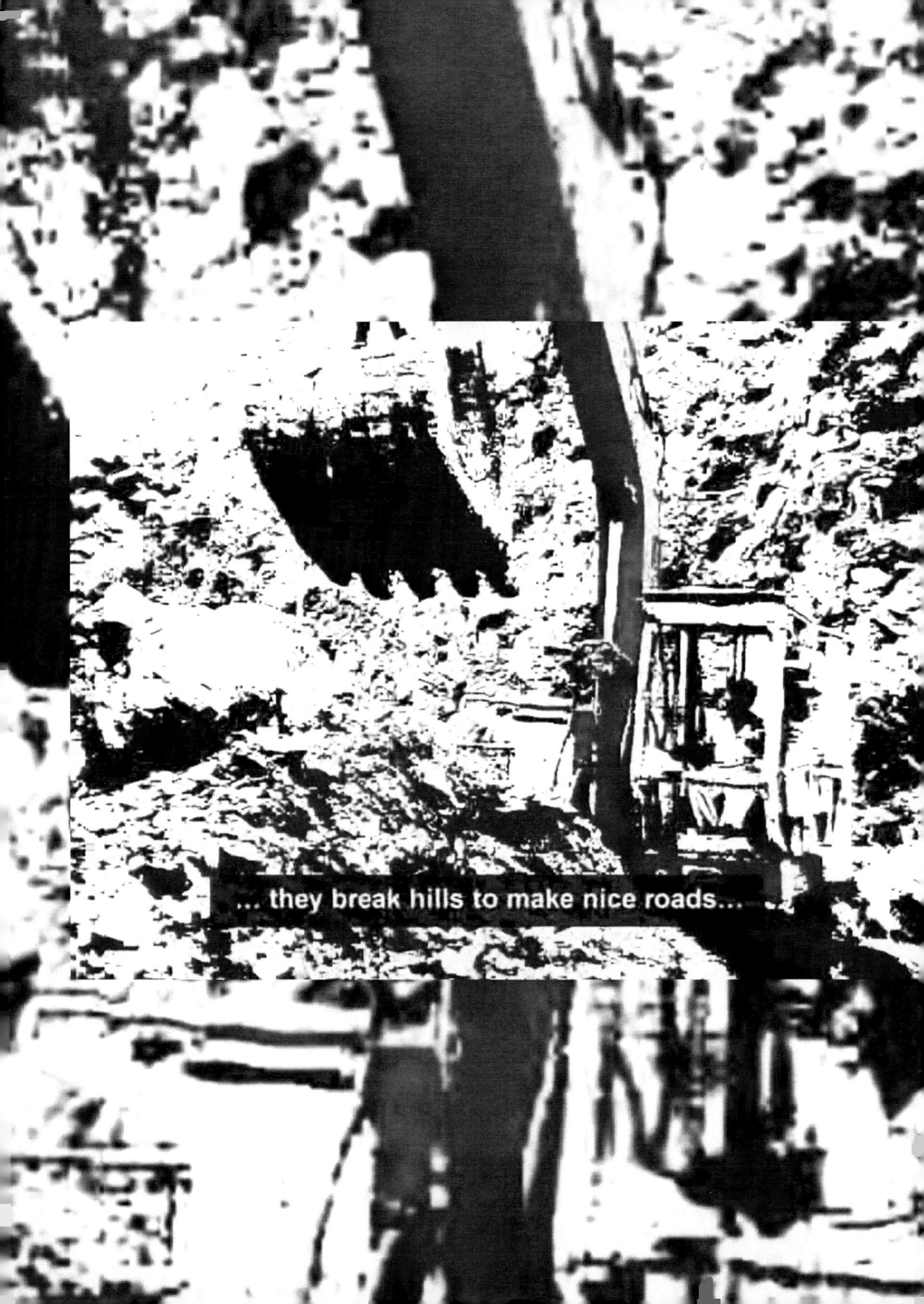
... they break hills to make nice roads...

avant-garde as a contemporary site of radicality (related to but not exhausted by the 1920s' historical avant-garde that spelt extreme rupture).

The vertical and horizontal axes support a full circle. Navigating the top half of the circle's circumference, a picture of sanctioned reciprocity between the categories of realism, modernism and the avant-garde is obtained.[14] Positioned at the southern pole with 'low' art, I reach up, somewhat more willfully, to the avant-garde – gaining agency for the popular/urban in mockery of Clement Greenberg's puritanical separation of avant-garde from kitsch. Indeed, the two-way equation confirms, precisely, the wit exercised by avant-garde practice in drawing from high and low art at once. On the opposite side, I extend the reach of low art to the comprehensive category of genre in its realist (and quasi-realist) aspect – what the Bombay films, for example, manipulate with such élan.[15]

In this full circle, my compass points, first, to auteur-based high art, seeing it sustaining its stakes in subjectivity, sovereignty and utopia. Modernism in its reflexive moments has offered pedagogies for the advancement of a counter-culture (as for example with 'Dada'). And it has provided a framing aesthetic for 'an immanence of the concrete' in consonance with a materialistic dialectic during the revolutionary decades of the twentieth century: I am referring to the Constructivist movement in the visual arts; the insurgent cinema of the Soviet revolution; Brecht's epic form in theatre that played, along with Sergei Eisenstein's montage aesthetic, a foundational role in defining what we mean by socialist radicalism in art. In a finer analysis, there is reason to separate the Soviet-led historical avant-garde from European high art designated as modernism, but here the conjunction will hold simply as a way of designating the conceptual complexity and linguistic innovations in the advanced arts of the early twentieth century. It also explains why I so privilege the consolidated ground of high art in the spherical diagram of manifold art practices.

The compass then points, symmetrically, to the popular, which helps unpack the modernist norm, showing not only how it may end up going awry through reification within bourgeois ideology but offering, more positively, performative manoeuvres in the imaginative rendering of the stratified social. Interestingly, this is done by none other than Eisenstein and Brecht themselves – which is why the distinction between mainstream modernism and the socialist avant-garde needs to be drawn – and then by the intrepid radical of the 1960s, Jean-Luc Godard. Further, the popular foregrounds the politics of pleasure lodged in the unconscious; it submits the symbolic to a vulgar, faux-surreal decoding procedure, and offers up an almost grossly rich signification. I am thinking of Hollywood's *film noir* and Bombay cinema's most affective sub-genre, the melodrama, both of which become also tools used by film theorists to build a semiotic and psycho-social critique of what is considered after the 1960s as the precious culture of auteur-based art cinema.

The location of the popular is considered to be methodologically more useful in today's culturalist debates. Popular cultural studies offer a different, broadly anthropological, interpretation that is more hybrid than deemed respectable in art history proper. Placed within the frame of the postmodern, popular culture lends theory the daring to force a passage into the very obscenities of the Real, thus, as it were, blasting open the more discreet transaction between the imaginary and the symbolic conducted on the ground of a purer aesthetic. More specifically, in India, recognition of the now near-ubiquitous cinema effect triggers styles of contemporary acculturation that complicates the argument in favour of popular Indian cinema's corrupt and stubborn forms of realism. And, by a kind of generic twist, this cinema offers, as film theorist Ashish Rajadhyaksha shows in his many writings, a politically canny take on shifting power relations between the citizen and the state.[16]

I am not, however, inclined to give over the ground of contestation to the anti-high art/anti-modernist formations that often dominate today's cultural studies discourse. I do not believe that a people's democratic impulse must essentially be read into the consensual reception of popular forms. There is sufficient critique of the image-based culture industry *and* the culturalist ideology itself as it develops in late capitalism, as of the phenomenon of a fatally spectacularized culture and its strategies of subsumption, to require any reiteration here. My argument rests on the possibility of keeping up the tension in the high–low binary: to keep up the cognitive ambitions and the epistemological value of art's transformative structures in high art, and to keep alive visual and other pleasures through the subversive agency of low art. The argument suggests that a strategic makeover of modernity's utopian drive may, in certain ways, enter and imbricate the everyday common culture. But, equally, that by accommodating popular culture's ruder features, the (class) barriers between genres may come down and do some all-round good.

We are, by this stage of the argument, looking towards the avant-garde, but the compass is now volatile. Its oscillation activates the sphere's entire circumference: so, what is the message?

While the four main nodes – high and low, genre and avant-garde – are well-formed compounds, there are differentiated sub-categories stretched along the cusp of the sphere's four segments. Modernist high art pushes towards the avant-garde position via conceptual art or, more broadly, the conceptual approach, which is translated today into the predominantly lens-based options of photography, film, video and the digital. Between the avant-garde and the popular lies the more amorphous category of new media art, involving a digital, computer-based research-and-play repertoire of intelligent games that offer mediatory transformations of the everyday.

On the opposite side, between high art and (the realist) genre, I suggest placing the critical, self-reflexive form of the documentary, carrying a mandate for raising the subjective pitch in proportion to the political partisanship of the maker. And, on the cusp of realism and the popular, I place the documentary as a recording genre dominated by an information-ethnography ethics and aspiring to enrich a 'common culture'. Such documentaries use popular representational means and even, at times, mythologized fable structures that prod the political by decoding the icons, rituals, caprices and prejudices of everyday culture through a playful semiotics.[17]

My diagram proposes – in a cunning fit that serves, let me admit, my own purpose – that radical elements are now to be drawn from all round the circumference of the sphere: as much from within the 'classic' binaries of high and low, genre and avant-garde, as from the conceptual, the mediatic, the documentary and the 'mythological'.

Documentary Re-take

Since the establishment in 1989 of a unipolar world, a substantial number of documentary 'films'[18] aim to break into routine accounts of war, disaster, torture, genocide, as delivered by the 'world news' syndrome; to invert the gross and homogenized televisual spectacle into a discreet exposure of those multiplying targets of destruction, coercion and subjugation that lead to the suffering of large parts of humanity within the globalizing process. More ambitiously, these documentaries want to address the absolute power of capitalism as embodied by the most belligerent, blighted, blatantly criminal nation-states, led by the United States of America. The compounding of corporate, militaristic and trade sanctions decreed upon the besieged economies of the world, the worldwide control over people's civil and political rights in the name of western-style (neoliberal) democracy, and the abuse of democracy by these same super-imperialist powers produce, above all, a desperate urgency to forge a corresponding *language* for oppositional 'truth': for enduring testimonies, for witness accounts, for collective strategies of spontaneous resistance through people's action.[19] And, for imaging/voicing the sustained work of organized political movements.

As my two examples from India show, the 'new' documentary addresses the many struggles of the citizens and the populace against global capital, against national governments and their respective states, against class (and caste), and against the forces of the right that align with religious and communal violence as they do with anti-people policies in favour of the ruling classes.[20] Appropriately, the language of the new documentary is tuned to the conditions (the cultural intricacies, the contour and rhythm) of life in specific societies, just as they are, of course, to the ideology and style of the documentarist.[21]

Today, the power of the moving image and of the political pedagogy embedded in it depends on a recognition of the critical apparatus developed by cultural and creative practices (for example, the rich dialogue for and against realism in auteur cinema), and the knowledge archive, the discursive output, within history and the other social sciences since (especially) the 1960s. I have already juxtaposed Patwardhan and Kanwar in some detail; the work of Madhushree Dutta (*I Live in Behrampada*, 1993), Rakesh Sharma (*Final Solution*, 2004) and Lalit Vachani (*The Boy in the Branch*, 1993 and *The Men in the Tree*, 2002),[22] on the same ground - on the communal, majoritarian ideology of Hindutva - is instructive in terms of the very definition of documentary form: is it to be (gross) mimesis or social analysis; is it to be insurgent or investigative, hostile or compassionate, polemical or reflexive?

The women's movement has provided the groundwork for a good number of feminist films: Deepa Dhanraj's film against brutal, nationwide policy of family planning, in *Something Like a War* (1991); Surabhi Sharma's exploration in *Jari Mari: of Cloth and Other Stories* (2001) of the unorganized sector of the small-scale industry (in Mumbai) where women's labour still earns them no working-class rights. Concerning women and sexuality, there is Reena Mohan's film on anxieties and bad faith around female beauty in *Skin Deep* (1998); Shohini Ghosh's witty articulation of and by the female sex workers of Calcutta in *Tales of the Night Fairies* (2002); and Paromita Vohra's take on the pop pedagogy of post-feminist feminism in *Girls Unlimited* (2002). Rahul Roy's modest and compassionate portrait of working-class urban youth in *When Four Friends Meet* (2000) contrasts with Amar Kanwar's exploration of the vulnerable and voracious aspects of male sexuality in the Indian metropolis in *King of Dreams* (2001). The emancipatory agenda is fulfilled on a more personal and eccentric note by Ruchir Joshi's film journey with itinerant Baul[23] singers, the 'mystic' minstrels of Bengal in *Eleven Miles* (1991); while *A Night of Prophecy* (2002) by Amar Kanwar 'narrativizes' songs of protest from different regions of the Indian republic to echo an anarchist ring of liberation.[24]

Documentarists understand that even as they work within the tropes of the document, the archive and a *verité*-based realism; even as they respect the ethics of indexicality - the relationship between representation and a pro-filmic 'reality' - the ruse of representation must be fully addressed. As also the transitive, durational and deferred nature of the narrative fragment in the short film format. That these make up the very poetics and politics of what is staked as the bare 'truth-value' of the documentary project.

It follows that recognition of the inextricability of subject and history, widely accepted in critical discourse, allows contemporary documentarists to interject anxiety and memory in the everyday, to test promises and betrayals in civil society by tracking forms of mortality in the biographical (and autobiographical) mode. Wary of a political 'method' and polemical pronouncements, the new documentary offers data that have a premium on the condition of indeterminacy and loss. It could in some ways hope to realize what was so poignantly addressed in one of Susan Sontag's last texts: a compact with the world *Regarding the Pain of Others*.[25]

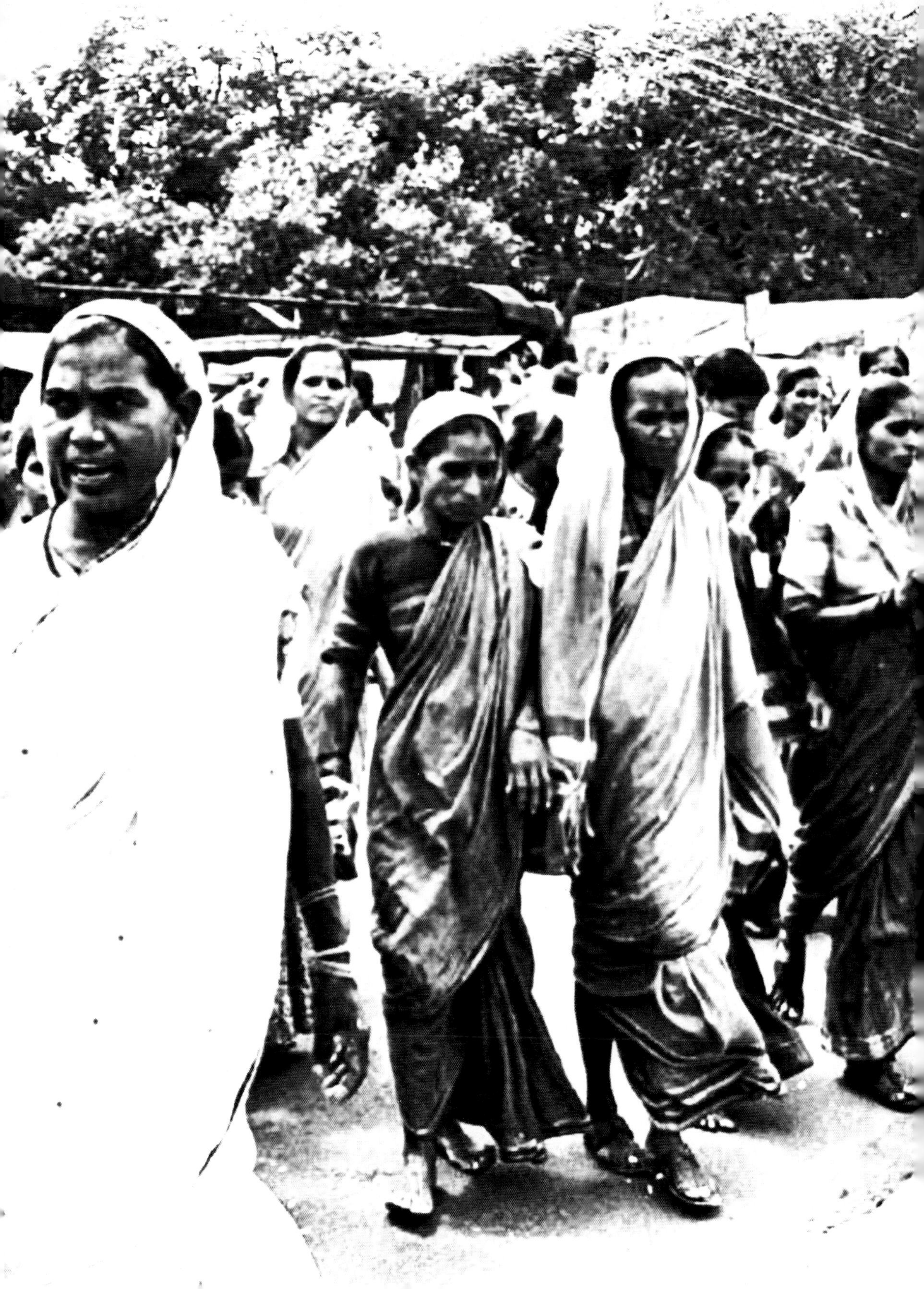

While the documentarist cannot, perhaps, answer to the overtaken ideal of a 'people's culture' in the socialist sense of the word, it may be possible to hypothesize, on the basis of a worldwide documentary upsurge, a common culture of the 'multitudes' with a 'be against' slogan in the manifestos of hope that the new global empire supposedly yields[26] – in the form of a nemesis or, indeed, as a demonstration of the dialectic. This claim postulates that cultures of protest find spontaneous communicability across and beyond communitarian and national boundaries. Further, that the extrapolated forms of historical knowledge translate as collective creativity, as evidentiary articulation, pushing the promise of democracy and even perhaps approximating, in their enunciation, in their disinterested passion, to a version of an aesthetic. Can this agenda proxy for the avant-garde? Can it actually be, in our time, what the vanguard was for the twentieth century: an inquiry into the wide parameters and present conditions of praxis premised at once on refusal, risk and utopia?

Mediatic, Critical, Avant-Garde

Leaving these questions suspended, my next move is to refocus on the sphere of art; to reiterate the significance of establishing, and then blurring, mediums and art-historical categories.[27] To let the needle oscillate and 'encompass' segments of my proposed sphere, rather than fix the direction for the avant-garde. 'I have chosen to think of the contemporary work in film and video that shares . . . a kind of lifeline between the received categories of the documentary and avant-garde, each of which has been discursively and institutionally cloistered to its disadvantage.'[28]

Beyond the conditions that made it a rigorous phenomenon in the 1920s, the avant-garde reinvents itself in the present through two new channels: one, the witnessing aesthetic of the documentary – *verité* films, as well as reflexive accounts of lived lives, autobiographical or fictional; and, two, the multiplying media technologies expanding the realm of the virtual. These tendencies are together but differently driven by the challenge global capitalism throws at existing formations of state, nation and community; and, consequently, on culture, communication and intersubjectivity.

If the radical documentary is infused with the courage to 'undo' the righteous claim on reality and to re-map the world on the basis of global deprivation, experimental media artists can be seen, on the other hand, to rework the symbolic in the light of new subjectivities in the emerging global citizenry. Artists will interject political issues of loss and reparation in a monologic form. Personal fictions are set apace within the non-narrative schema of, say, an ethnographic account. In terms of structure, both documentarists and artists have developed an aesthetic of the fragment – psychic fragmentation, as well as fragmentation owing to the disaggregation of life-worlds that corresponds, metonymically, to physical displacement all across the world.

This is the place to interject a hitherto deferred fact: in terms of technology, the post-celluloid media[29] has far-reaching consequences on the meaning and effect of the moving image. The ontological/indexical bond between image and reality is disturbed (if not broken), setting off what we might call spectres without footprints crisscrossing the threshold of objectivity. The sanctity of a Bazinian realism[30] is relativized, affecting all forms, whether documentary or experimental, narrative or avant-garde. There is an insistence on the 'now' – because of the 'ubiquity, endless receptivity, and ephemerality' of video and digital media.[31] Live signals, shallow and often degraded images, destabilize received settings and pitch the mediatic encounter into something of a semiotic crisis.[32] In the stake-sweep of media-technology, what is the relay between a formal aesthetic of the moving image, the evanescence of the virtual, the speed on the information highways of cyberspace? To what extent does this technology yield a democratically constituted 'commons' and what kind of hackers' ethics, what liberationist attitude, do media gift to youthful entrants?[33]

Unlike a classic documentarist who will, very likely, want to re-establish an indexicality for the new medium, an artist will use the eminently erasable image produced by electronic and digital media for more fantastic, more elusive, purposes. The media seem to provide an interface not only between the private and the public, but also between semiotic crises and extreme conditions in the social. It is not surprising, therefore, that these media have lodged themselves (belatedly but) so rapidly in precisely such societies as have witnessed the most radical changes in the globalized political – changes that push the fraught and fragmented narrative of national citizenship to the brink, that produce conditions for subjectivities *in extremis*. A deeply visceral response translated into visual allegories at once sublime and cannibalistic (using that term in recall of 'anthropophagia', a Brazilian 'modernist' trope, valorizing a devouring instinct to fulfil a 'perverse' form of transcendence) comes across in an increasing number of videos/installations by non-western artists, especially the Chinese.[34]

Pushing the argument further: artists as media practitioners, working out the relationship between the imaginary and the symbolic, are prepared – by the medium? – to face up to what one might call the residue of the abject, and the obscene, in the material substratum that is the Real. Think of the highly subjectivized video performances that have allowed the body in all its excess to surface via the virtual in a vision of the soul at once spectral and carnal.[35] This could be the unreconstructed self; or, on the other hand, it could be the estranged other, grossly designated, lovingly recuperated, in terms of class, colour, race, ethnicity and gender.[36] It is the peculiar pulse of an unstable subject-position that makes the contemporary artist function at all – and in experimental video it becomes, one might say, a mediatic compulsion, even as the odd and varied presentational formats of video installations establish a vulnerable ephemerality, a desired 'unknowing', reinforced by a disorienting multiplication of monitors and screens in a maze of black-box projections within the exhibition space.[37]

But here, I want to recall a counterpoint played throughout the argument. The terms of reference between documentary, narrative and avant-garde – as between the indexical and the virtual, and between analog and digital – are so upturned that artists, as much as they may be attracted by the ineffable, are drawn, by way of compensation, to the vastly variable reality-effect. When the global flux within the mediatic and the political accelerates, the stakes on the truth-value that artists are required to uphold are raised.[38] My argument thus moves towards translating the cleft genres and crossed languages now being adopted by art and media practitioners into an equation framed by the critical.

> 'Vision, whether blind or seeing, is always invested with a function of apprehending the visual in a manner far more extensive and complex than what the eye ultimately sees. And what truth can images tell us when they are drowning in the continental drift set up by modern media industries?'[39]

Today's interactive art practices (including video, digital and new media technologies, installations and performance) are volatile, they are driven by contradiction. At their most alert, these practices make a judicious alignment with the critical. This move provides access by proxy to the dialectic once given over to the all-conquering new that the earlier, more self-possessed, protagonists in the vanguard put forward.

Okwui Enwezor asserts: 'The propagators of the avant-garde have done little to constitute a space of self-reflexivity that can understand new relations of artistic modernity not founded on Westernism'.[40] He is targeting radical art that has allowed itself to be subsumed within modernism's superior claims to artistic autonomy and the avant-garde in general for its rigid alignment with the European grand narrative of permanent innovation. Tellingly, therefore, he titles a section in the exhibition catalogue of Documenta 11, 'What is an Avantgarde Today? The Postcolonial Aftermath of Globalization and the Terrible Nearness of Distant Places'.[41] He then positions himself across the divide in the era of postcolonial globalism which must, by historical necessity, introduce what he calls the condition of aterritorial instability, defy totalization and encourage what he further calls a non-integrative discourse resulting from the ongoing deconstruction of western democracy, as from the vast, diasporic displacement of populations across the continents. He demands that the avenues of post-colonial politicality structure the road map of art history in a way that you gain direct access to the vexed issue of a citizenship-ethic (complicit with or critical of the new concept of global sovereignty); and so that the springs of new subjectivities already unleashed by the great rupture of decolonization are uncovered.

Critical art privileges theory, ideology, critique of the aesthetic - and the imaginary is not suspended in such practice. The structural relationship of the imaginary and the symbolic may be weighted in favour of an interrogative mode in critical art, but the unexpected subversions nurtured in the imaginary are fully at play if we mean, by critical art, something distinctly other than plain discourse or polemics. Critical art bends the claim of radicality in favour of reflexion through a subverting aesthetic, through formal innovation and a conceptual recoding of 'artistic' materials, and it is this that sets apace a vanguard within the contemporary.

In Conclusion

To end on an ideological note: this criticality is not only what is useful for investigating the theoretical antinomies of art and culture, it is what is most forcefully deployed in interrogating the hegemonic presumptions of the west. More particularly, I refer to the confrontation between the 'institution of art' serving as an invincible citadel of aesthetic and ethical value in the western world, and the complex matrix of practices (cultural, aesthetic) produced in the still explosive conditions (as against institutions) of post-coloniality within and outside the west. To the degree that the post-colonial is both a global and postmodern phenomenon, it gives to these two brittle categories their more historical and multifaceted profiles. I, therefore, suggest that when we work through larger sets of (economic and social) antinomies characteristic of late capitalism, we must move to a situational analysis of cultural production within vastly heterogeneous geopolitical realities. I would, thus, argue for the necessity to constitute a space for self-reflexivity not only outside that of westernism, but also, indeed, in what Enwezor calls 'distant places' that are, in my argument, both terribly near - and terribly far. The post-colonial global in Enwezor's reckoning is characterized by the expanding diaspora; in mine, it is situated in locations geographically outside the west - Japan, Latin America, Africa, Asia - that offer at different times and for quite different reasons, a conjunctural dynamic propitious to radical, critical art that we may still choose to conjure in the form of an avant-garde.

Wary of what is now being called 'transcultural extraterritoriality', I suggest we gauge the holding power of the contemporary within the global 'time of now', but vis-a-vis named entities: nation-states, social and political formations, and all the territorially contained yet cruelly exposed sites of cultural production wide across a political topography.

In my ongoing argument, this is what provides the impetus for artists to set apace a vanguard: in dispersed locations, in displaced contemporalities. This is not to relativize the avant-garde out of existence, it is to give it a redoubled contextual value. The efficacy of the claim on the radical, as, indeed, the worth of the praxis achieved, depends on the locus of operation, the historical moment and the discursive position the practitioner is seen to (made to) occupy. It depends on the particular historical conjuncture and the degree of responsiveness of the 'artist' in the face of exigent forces that spell the contemporary.

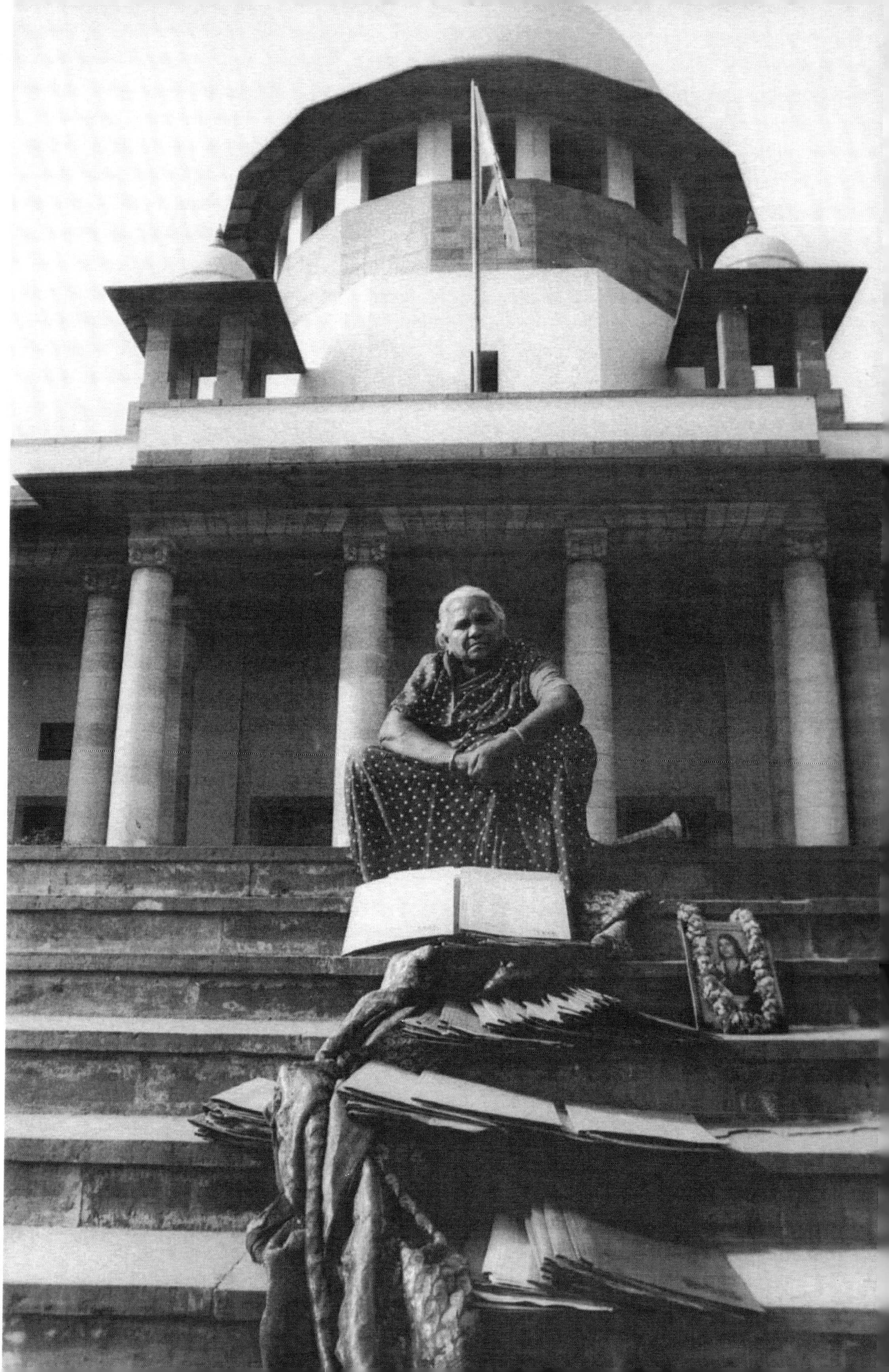

Long before the 1980s, the moving image was of interest to several practitioners who were not filmmakers. Artists, photographers, designers and activists saw possibilities in the cinema that do not feature in any standard history of Indian film. Nancy Adajania has written about the experimental film and media work of artists who were, for example, associated with the landmark Vision Exchange Workshop (VIEW), as well as the innovative transmedia and photographic work of artist and designer Dashrath Patel for Montreal's Expo '67 and the painter Krishen Khanna for Osaka's Expo '70. In this essay, she locates the artist Sheba Chhachhi's body of work through her involvement in the autonomous women's movement, technological experimentation, interest in female mystics, formative influences at the National Institute of Design, Ahmedabad, and, importantly, her investment in extending exhibition and 'art viewing' beyond the site and publics of the art gallery.

A longer version of this essay was published in *Moving Image Review and Arts Journal*, vol. 7 (2), 2018, pp. 204–20. Reprinted here with permission of the author, Sheba Chhachhi and Intellect publishers, UK.

Keywords, Names

Babri Masjid/Ayodhya, Craft, Jugaad Aesthetics, New Media Art, Progressive Artists Group, Video, Vision Exchange Workshop, Women's Movement: See Keywords (pp. 326–44).

Bhau Daji Lad Museum: Museum of the industrial arts set up in colonial Bombay in 1855, now known for showing major contemporary art alongside its permanent collection of late colonial materials.

Kaleka, Ranbir Singh: Artist known for dense and complex moving image video art, projecting video on to large-scale paintings extended to multi-channel installations.

Khoj: Delhi-based artist-run organization and collective started in 1997, in the city's Khirki area that is home to a diverse migrant workforce.

Kumari, Meena (1933–72): Major movie star of the 1950s and '60s, known for her tragic roles.

Narayan, Govind: Mid-nineteenth-century author famous for descriptions of Bombay.

National Institute of Design (NID): Iconic design school founded in Ahmedabad in 1961, emphasizing an aesthetic of developmental indigenism.

Patel, Dashrath (1927–2010): Designer, photographer, sculptor and founder-secretary of the National Institute of Design.

Parthan, Baiju: Artist whose work is at the cusp of painting, digital and hybrid intermedia installations, exploring cyberspace and digital flows.

Sundaram, Vivan: Artist who works across different media including painting, sculpture, photography and installation. Among the earliest Indian artists to start using video.

Syzygy (1969): 11-minute, 35 mm abstract film made by Akbar Padamsee for Vision Exchange Workshop with animation artist Ram Mohan.

Images

p. 143: Sheba Chhachhi, *Sathyarani*, 1990, staged portrait; part of *Seven Lives and a Dream*, 18 silver gelatin prints, 1990–91.

p. 149: Sheba Chhachhi, *The Mermaid's Mirror*, 2005, 36 toy televisions, film stills, sound, text, elliptical wooden structure; an immersive installation about cinema, intimacy and tropes of femininity constructed around the figure of the tragic-romantic heroine Meena Kumari.

pp. 154–55: Sheba Chhachhi, *Initiation Chronicle*, 1998–2001, silver gelatin prints; documents an initiation process at Juna Akhada at the Kumbh Mela, Allahabad. Women are divested of gender and other markers of social identity to be reborn as androgynous ascetics.

pp. 160–61: Sheba Chhachhi, *Winged Pilgrims: A Chronicle from Asia*, 2006, installation with 8 animated duratrans lightboxes, two layers; 2 animated duratrans lightboxes, three layers; 5 silk and fibreglass objects; 5 motion lamps; sound 4' (looped); black box. It maps migrations of culture and inter-species relationships since the sixth century, through the figure of the birds, robes of Buddhist pilgrims and the 'plasma action' toy TV.

All images courtesy Sheba Chhachhi.

10 The Ecologies of Technological Experimentation

Sheba Chhachhi's Multimedia Environments

NANCY ADAJANIA **2018**

If you wish to contextualize new media practices in India from the 1990s onwards, you would be better advised to look in the wrong places. Places that are either too hallowed to be subjected to profanation such as the artistic legacy of the Progressives,[1] usually perceived narrowly, in terms of painterly achievement. Or considered too profane to be allowed to rupture the boundaries of conventional art history: such as the technological innovations in the audiovisual medium in the world's fairs of the 1960s and 1970s or the much-reviled Festivals of India exhibition cycle in the 1980s.[2]

In the early 2000s, I grew more and more impatient with a consensual, even formulaic reading of new media practices in India. It usually attributed the emergence of video art or intermedia installations solely to two factors. The first was economic liberalization which opened up the protectionist socialist economy and ushered in, over time, new technologies such as S-VHS cameras, VCPs and VCRs (video cassette players and video cassette recorders), 24-hour television and eventually the internet. The second was the upsurge of a reactionary majoritarianism. Alongside the political and economic forces of globalization, the counter-modern forces of the Hindu right vitiated the Indian public sphere with their exclusivist agendas. While this reading can be applied to the early works of the pioneers of video art such as Nalini Malani and Vivan Sundaram[3] made in the 1990s, how would we account for the intermedia works of artists such as Ranbir Singh Kaleka and Baiju Parthan[4] from the late 1990s, early 2000s? The former produced an interface between painting and video projection and the latter between painting and the internet. Kaleka and Parthan were clearly not reacting to any external stimulus, but rather extending their painterly language to explore the intersecting phenomenological encounter between old and new media, between the enchantments of everyday reality and the cosmic realm.

There is no single narrative of new media art in the Indian context. There are as many narratives as there are practices, each distinctive in its own right, layered with its own aesthetic and political urgencies. In my search for a more substantial genealogy for new media art that is inflected by an affirmative stance rather than a reactive causality, I developed what I have called a 'pre-history' for new media art in India.[5]

Elsewhere, I have charted this pre-history through the experimental films and photographs of Akbar Padamsee, M.F. Husain, Tyeb Mehta, Nalini Malani and Krishen Khanna[6] from the late 1960s/early 1970s, as well as the multimedia installations and exhibition design of Dashrath Patel[7] for the world's fairs of the 1960s and 1970s and the Festival of India exhibitions of the 1980s, as also his development of DIY audiovisual technologies to aid grassroots activists.[8]

This is part of my commitment to retrieving the lost histories of Indian art, and to writing art history against the grain of received narratives. During the 1960s and 1970s, when these experiments were being conducted, the art world in India was fixated on painting as the premier form, so these were seen as aberrations if they were noticed at all. Art criticism was still obsessed with the questions of modernism, indigenism and authenticity, and had not expanded to be able to embrace such experiments. There was no critical framework or cultural context for them. That is why I have analyzed the history of Indian new media art as a passage from 'no-context media' from the late 1960s to 'new-context media' of the 1990s.[9]

More significantly, even when I have analyzed, say, the experimental films of Padamsee or Patel's multimedia installation in Montreal's Expo '67, I have adopted a confident, capacious transcultural perspective that neither valorizes the nationalist narratives of post-colonial Indian art nor does it feel crushed by the constraints of a time-lag or a lingering sense of belatedness, especially in the case of new media art and the consequent need to catch up with the west. For instance, my reading of Padamsee's film *Syzygy* goes beyond the standard reading of Paul Klee's pedagogical diagrams, Sanskrit aesthetics and mathematics to make connections with the international experiments in art and music as manifested in the works of John Cage, Xenakis and Rauschenberg.[10] In an interview with me, Padamsee corroborated the fact that he was acquainted with the works of these figures; and I have critically analysed Patel's interventions in the Montreal world fair against the backdrop of the contradictions and collusions between competing narratives of nationalist self-representation and Cold War politics.[11]

In this essay, I shall concentrate on the multimedia installations of the feminist artist Sheba Chhachhi. I have situated Chhachhi's new media art practice in diverse ecologies of pedagogic and technological experimentation:

such as her sharing of visual communications skills with urban and rural activists in the women's movement, presenting her photographs in slums and women's workshops, and later her video installations in a gallery setting, a mall and community centre. Secondly, I shall investigate the historic multimedia environments produced by the National Institute of Design (NID) (Dashrath Patel was the founder-secretary of NID and a mentor figure to Chhachhi). And third, the *jugaad*-oriented entrepreneurship of artisans in India's street-markets whose creative improvisations modify the techno-kitsch that washes up on our shores as the flotsam of globalization.

In Medias Res

To stand at the barricades is to learn the art of precariousness, to position oneself between the juggernaut of authority and the upsurge of protest. It is an art that Sheba Chhachhi has mastered and refined since the early 1980s, when she joined the autonomous women's movement in India.[12] At the barricades, she acted as a documentarian, photographing newly insurgent women who were claiming public space, articulating their position as citizens subjected to social and political oppression. At the opportune moment, Chhachhi would vault into demonstration, slipping from the observer-documentarian's role into those of partisan and participant. Early lessons learnt in the tough school of activism - of observation, infiltration, and collaboration, as well as tactical mobility - stood her in good stead when she decided to engage with the art world in the 1990s.

My concern here is with the artist, who, through the labour of the imagination, engages with the ground of material conditions, realized and relayed across a spectrum of sites such as documentation, art, law, institutional reform, or as a collaborative activity. I will consider how the term 'transcendence' itself has been variously parsed in the fields of feminist activism and in India's dissident and subaltern spiritual traditions, from which a number of Indian feminists have drawn ideological and cultural sustenance.

A Spectre Had Begun to Haunt India

While aligning itself with a broad left understanding of social and political formations, the autonomous women's movement in 1980s India worked largely independently of any political party and government. The movement was manifested in the public domain through street demonstrations, agitprop theatre and interventions in the media. It turned issues such as dowry, rape, female infanticide, domestic violence, sexual harassment, communalism, environmental degradation, land rights, urban and rural poverty into subjects of legal vigilance and public debate. Both as documentarian and protagonist, Chhachhi became a chronicler of these historic events.

Chhachhi's engagement began in the post-Emergency period, a time of introspection and regrouping for Indian dissident groups. The state could no longer be relied upon to act as a guardian of civil freedoms. This led to the formation of a large number of self-organized citizen's committees, women's groups and workers' unions, which fought for legal and social reform both together and separately.[13]

Chhachhi, then a student of design at the Visual Communications faculty of NID in Ahmedabad, heard about these struggles against patriarchal violence from her sister Amrita Chhachhi,[14] a gender and labour studies scholar and activist, and one of the founders of the women's group Stree Sangharsh ('Women's Struggle').[15] In 1980, Chhachhi began to work, together with designer Jogi Panghaal,[16] with the women's movement in Delhi. They worked particularly closely with the feminist collective, Saheli ('Woman Friend'), being part of its inception in 1981, and with Action India/Sabla Sangh, which works in resettlement colonies and shantytowns.[17] Chhachhi was also a co-founder of Jagori ('Awaken, Woman'), established in 1984 'to spread feminist consciousness for the creation of a just society'.[18] Like others in the collectives, Chhachhi was involved in diverse ways – as a photographer and designer, but also in planning campaigns, analysing and debating issues, doing casework, and sharing visual communication skills.

The most prominent strain within Indian feminism was an activist one, confronting the executive and judicial establishment on issues of manifest violence against women, especially rape and dowry killings. According to the historian Radha Kumar, the activist aspiration, whether Gandhian, Maoist, Socialist or Communist (most feminists belonged to one or another of these ideological camps), was to 'transcend' the self. At the same time, some feminists critiqued such an idealization of selflessness and sacrifice as a vestigial reflex of the patriarchal structure of consciousness; they wished, also, to secure a field of ludic autonomy, of intimacy and pleasure, which neither the patriarchy nor the activist orthodoxy would sanction. This conflict between achieving social-juridical reform and ensuring ludic autonomy was pushed into 'abeyance', as Kumar phrases it.[19]

This is borne out by the transitions in Chhachhi's work from the 1980s to the 1990s. If we compare, for instance, her activist photographs of the 1980s with her 'staged' photographic portraits in the series, *Seven Lives and a Dream: Feminist Portraits* (1980–91) and the photo-based installations, *Ganga's Daughters* and *Wild Mothers 2: The Mirror Is the Witness* (1994) of the 1990s, the latter are more able to pursue questions related to the production of an expanded subjectivity, the assertion of sexual desire or control over one's sexuality.[20]

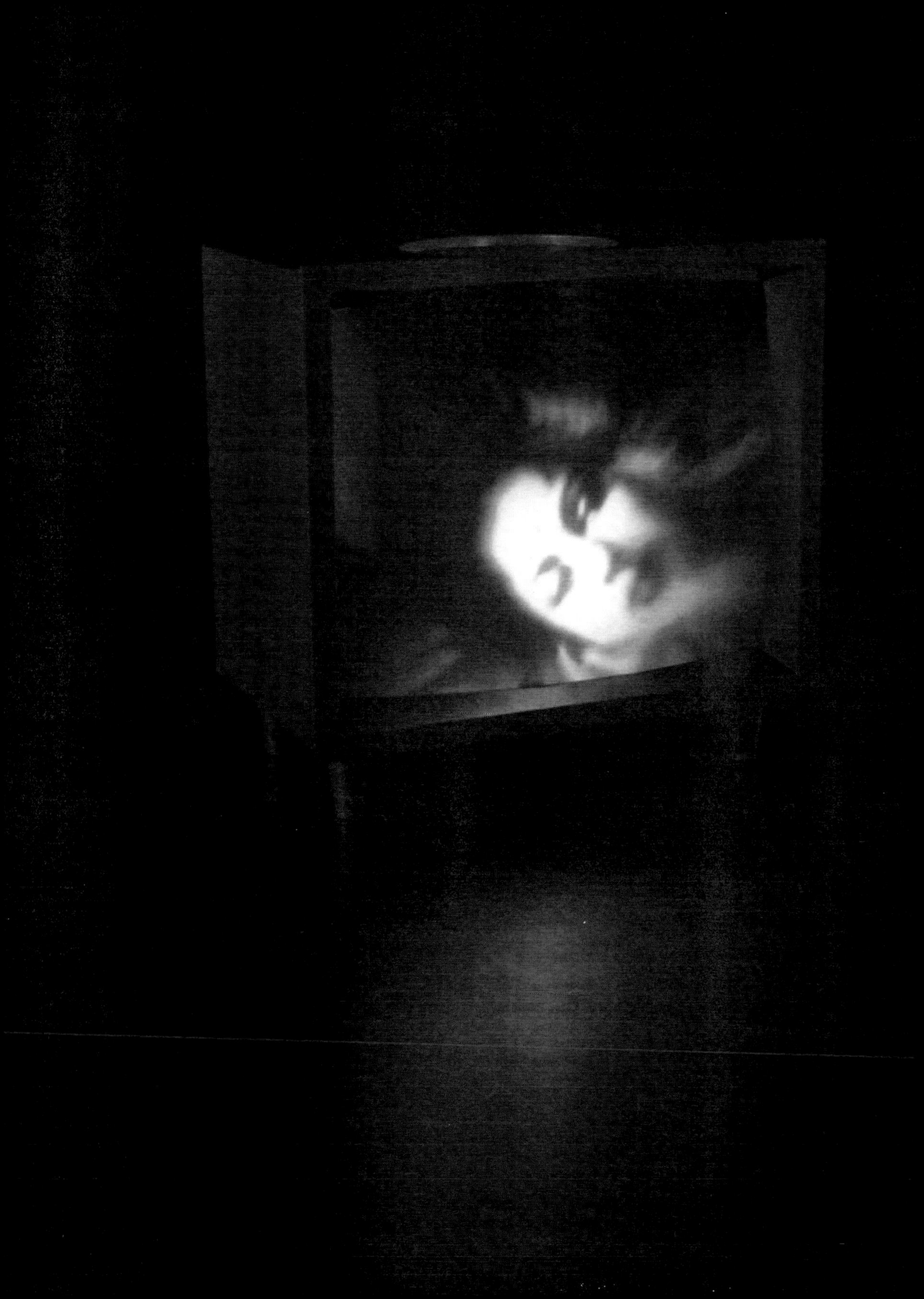

Precariousness at the Barricades and amongst Nomadic Renunciates

Through widespread hate speech and large-scale mobilization, the Hindu right unleashed a campaign of suspicion and antagonism against the Muslim minority, which culminated in the destruction of the Babri Masjid on 6 December 1992. India would never be the same after this cataclysm.

The women's movement too was irrevocably altered. While it focused its energies on resisting the scourge of communalism, the positions on religion within it were anything but consensual. Critical positions ranged from those who saw religion as inherently oppressive, patriarchal and anti-women, to those who believed that the interweaving of religion, culture and identity had to be appropriately addressed, to others who felt that heterodox and dissident practices, philosophies and cultural forms could be recuperated and scrutinized for contemporary deployment. Chhachhi has come to favour the third of these positions:

> While I agree with the feminist critique which exposes the oppression of women as coded into institutionalized religion, I believe that plural interpretations of Hinduism are an important form of countering the attempt to manufacture a monolithic Hindutva.[21]

Reminiscing in 2008 about her exploration of the 'rich and complex negotiations of gender and womanhood in the heterodox world of female mendicants', Chhachhi wrote of how at the same time:

> . . . the Hindu woman was being actively re-inscribed within upper-caste orthodoxies. Many of the gains of the struggle for women's rights were appropriated via television serials, the valorization of *sati* and the invocation of Shakti within Hindu right-wing discourse. Myth and history were being rewritten, as the attempt to construct a homogenized Hinduism was forged in the fire of violence, intolerance and sectarianism.[22]

Even before Chhachhi joined the women's movement, she was intrigued by the lives of mystics and renunciates that she had encountered. Precariousness can be located at the barricades, but also amongst renunciates whose nomadism is a protest against the material acquisitiveness that defines worldly life.

Ganga's Daughters (1992–2002) merits discussion here. She 'hung out' with the women-ascetics for years before she decided to take their photographs, in consultation with them. She was especially looking at indigenous, pre-modern forms of feminism, irritated by the constant accusation of feminism being 'western'. My own cultural knowledge indicated that this was not necessarily true.[23]

In Chhachhi's representation, individual women-ascetics loom large on the horizon of the eye. We may wince in their presence but cannot look away. We are mesmerized by Jater Ma's matted hair, cascading to the ground, throwing out roots like a banyan. Kotwal is framed vertically by the bamboo staff she holds and the power she wields, 'but, look, the self that hovers/in between/is neither man/nor woman'.[24] *Bhadramahila* lifts her hand – to bless or say goodbye, we cannot say.[25] A teardrop runs down her cheek. These women have sloughed off the conventional roles of wife, mother and daughter. As the Virashaiva poet Akka Mahadevi, who wandered naked with only her long hair to cloak her body, sang: 'Take these husbands who die/decay, and feed them/to your kitchen fires!'.[26] Her husband is Shiva, 'white as jasmine', her soul's *doppelganger*.

In the monochromatic series *Initiation Chronicle* (1998–2001), the renunciates discard their old selves and are reborn as Ganga's daughters.[27] Here we see long shots of women engaged in an act of ritual rebirth: water baptizes and heals bodies scarred by too many inhibitions; cloth unfurls like a sail to wrap itself securely around the women's bodies. A single moment of solidarity asserts itself as two women in renunciate clothing tenderly hold hands.

The destabilization of social, political and spiritual expectations – and the roles, identities and locations that attend them – animate the representation of ascetic subcultures in *Ganga's Daughters*. What did we expect: beatific faces glowing with spiritual illumination? What we find is a psychological theatre of women who are mutilated and whole, variously calm, aggressive, aggrieved, or infused with melancholia so deep that it infects us. For, though the woman-ascetic is no longer a 'woman', she still inhabits a para-society with its own hierarchic norms. Here, androgyny can pale in the presence of women who perform as 'honorary' males, carrying all the attendant ills of oppressive patriarchal politics. How does the woman-ascetic negotiate the tension between freedom and unfreedom, stricture and choice, caught as she is in the double bind of heterodoxy that can act as orthodoxy by other means?

The complexity of this double bind is best conveyed by two scenes that are contrapuntally held together in *Ganga's Daughters*. In the first scene, one of the photo-frames in the installation suddenly stirs with movement. Chhachhi animates found photographs of an early twentieth-century woman-ascetic, Yoginiamman. The sackcloth-robed ascetic, standing in the midst of thick foliage, leaps, hovers before descending, and then in one fluid movement achieves ascension and exits the frame. The empty frame opens to yet another scene, with a distinct shift in energy. Instead of a beatific, waif-like ascetic, we encounter Mahant Mira Puri of the Juna Akhada[28] – the head of her religious order, whose expansive girth is manipulated digitally to balloon out until it fills the frame. Both ascetics are shown as resilient women playing with gender, but their resilience connotes very different values: the first is a questor hungering for freedom, while the second is an aspiring political figure swaddled in saffron, hungering for power. It is not surprising that Mahant Mira Puri – who takes on an aura of male authority – went on to share the stage at the World Sadhvi Meet with Sadhvi Rithambara, the female ascetic and Hindu right-wing ideologue who castigated Hindu men for being effeminate and instigated violence against Muslims during the Ramjanmabhoomi agitation of the early 1990s.[29]

For Chhachhi, Yoginiamman as well as Buri, Jater Ma and others are 'wild mothers', women perceived as social deviants, whose heady combination of revelry and defiance captivated her: 'I have always been drawn to such women, for their marginality, their 'craziness', their freedom, their 'oddness' in terms of social conventions.'[30]

A year later, Chhachhi decided to link the photographs of the activists and the renunciates in a palimpsestual manner in *Wild Mothers 2: The Mirror Is the Witness*. The installation took the form of an ellipse, accessible on all sides: viewers who approached it could see, through the translucent photograph that they were viewing, the presence of other photographs. Further, the mirror-like surface on the ground threw back reflections of the photographs, and the viewers themselves. The image of the renunciate Buri may have appeared as a fragile stain of water and light, but we could not help being hypnotized by those eyes, deep as a well. In a surreal moment, even as we look at her, activists march across Buri's high forehead. Unresolved questions of activism and faith fold into one another, conjoining different forms of struggle and resistance, whether in the questor's retreat or the politics of the street. The marginality of these resilient women is transformed into a signature of solidarity.

An Infinity of Traces

Chhachhi's artisanal building up of patterns of images, myths, songs, stories and reportage in her artistic practice is often transhistorical and transcultural as she vaults across histories, topographies and temporalities, dealing with an infinity of traces. The inventory is crucial. Through a continuous relay of the intuitive and cognitive, these plural cultural resources must consistently be brought to the light of consciousness and thus into the active process of self-making, to play their role as vital self-historicizing strategies. *Winged Pilgrims: A Chronicle from Asia* (2006) could be read as one of the most accomplished examples of this line of investigation and exploration.

The swan, the phoenix and Garuda (eagle) rotate in an endless loop on animated lightboxes in a penumbral room.[31] Their slow, hypnotic repetition across a garland of screens evokes a monk chanting a rosary. Symbolizing purity, wisdom and regeneration, these birds dominate Asia's mythic narratives: in Chhachhi's *Winged Pilgrims*, they transit across phantasmagoric digital tapestries, backdrops attesting to the cultural exchanges staged across the region. In these composite backdrops, there are traces of Persian and Mughal miniatures, Chinese brush painting and the Buddhist 'Heart Sutra', but also the scruffy reality of environmental degradation as conveyed by documentary photography.

Chhachhi proposes an Asia that embodies a conversation crafted from cross-fertilizations among cultures. *Winged Pilgrims* reminds us of the storytellers, image-makers, merchants and monks who crossed the Silk Route for centuries, creating a rich Asian cosmopolitanism. Historically, this is how artists in various Asian locations have worked. The painters in Akbar's ateliers drew on Safavid and Chinese influences, while artists in Jehangir's atelier adapted scientific realism from European sources to accommodate the emperor's fascination with documenting flora and fauna, as for instance in the celebrated image of the turkey brought as a gift from the Americas by an envoy.[32]

Ironically, India and China – which once traded in silk, jade, ivory and turquoise, cherished both by merchants and by pilgrims as sacred treasures – are today linked by the circulation of techno-kitsch dumped in the mass market. And something is amiss here: the unnaturally slow movement of the winged pilgrims signals their fate. They move in one direction only, like prisoners of a mind that, at best, can mimic flight. Chhachhi organizes her artistic journeys with the discipline of a yogic practitioner. She adapts a toy that carries the look of the 'Now' – a plasma TV – but works like a lightbox, albeit with an electronic roller. In an age of consumerist aspiration that reveres speed and novelty, she prefers the pleasures of an aesthetic of slowness, contemplation and beauty made from paradox. Even the warbling and lament of the birds are scored in a single female voice, a *cappella*.

In one of the digital tapestries, a row of parrots – that ambidextrous symbol of wisdom and the erotic – crosses a nondescript urban cityscape, like misplaced totems in a land that has forgotten to read the signs. But this could also be a literary allusion to the *Tutinama*, the 'Tales of the Parrot', a legendary fourteenth-century Persian story-cycle adapted from the Sanskrit *Shukasaptati*,[33] which revolves around a parrot that entertains a merchant's lonely wife with stories so that she will not embark on amorous diversions while her husband is away on his travels.

Many artists have been attracted to shamanic techniques of ecstasy, prophecy and clairvoyance. Chhachhi, a wandering mystic at heart, gently warns her viewers not to be blinded by the flash of agonism and greed, not to 'destroy their belief in a higher self – the *achin pakhi*, the unknown bird, the unrecognized inner, spiritual self'.[34] I trace the trope of the *achin pakhi* to a song by the Baul bard,[35] Lalan Fakir: *Khanchar bhitor achin pakhi komney ashey jay*? (How does

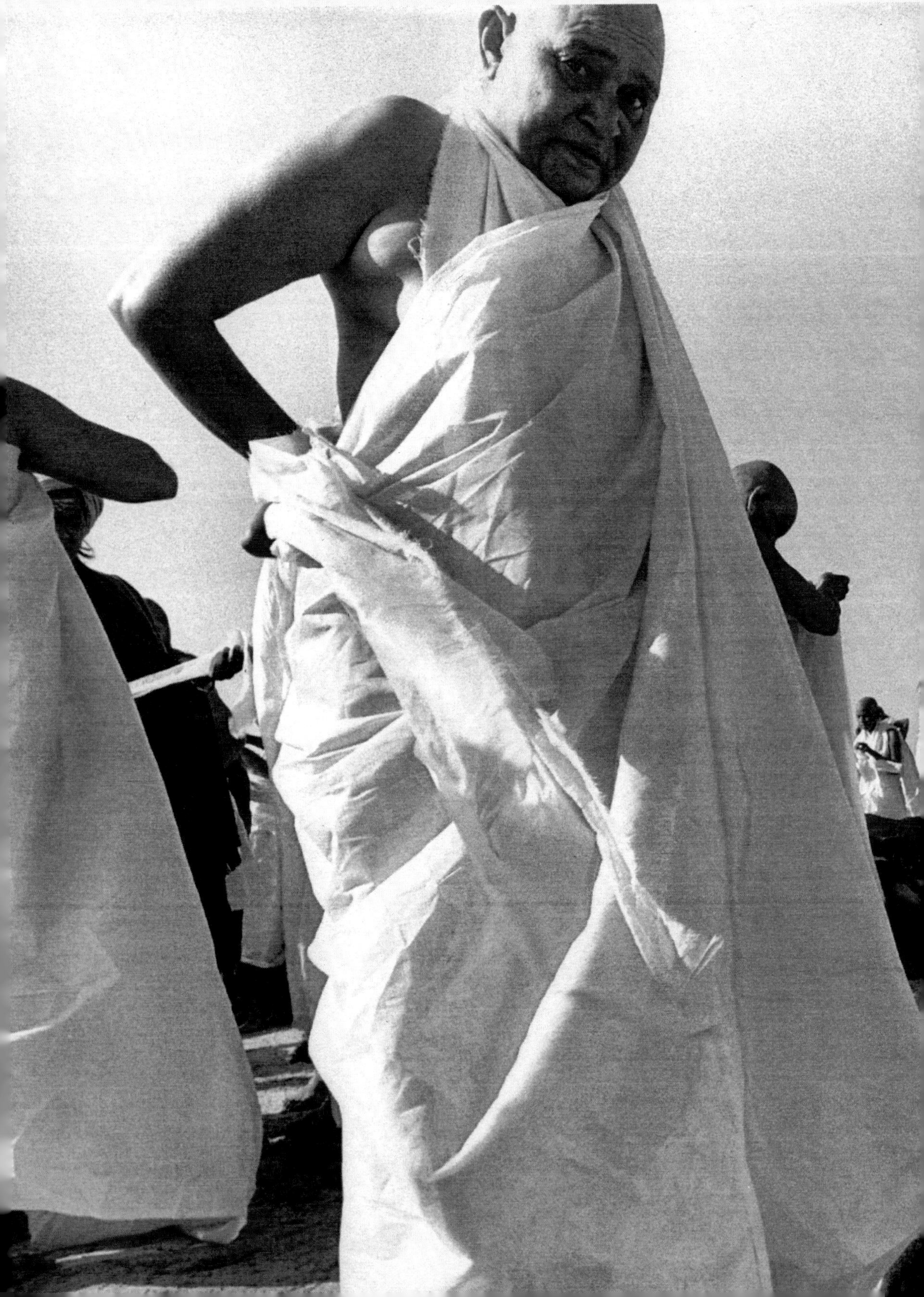

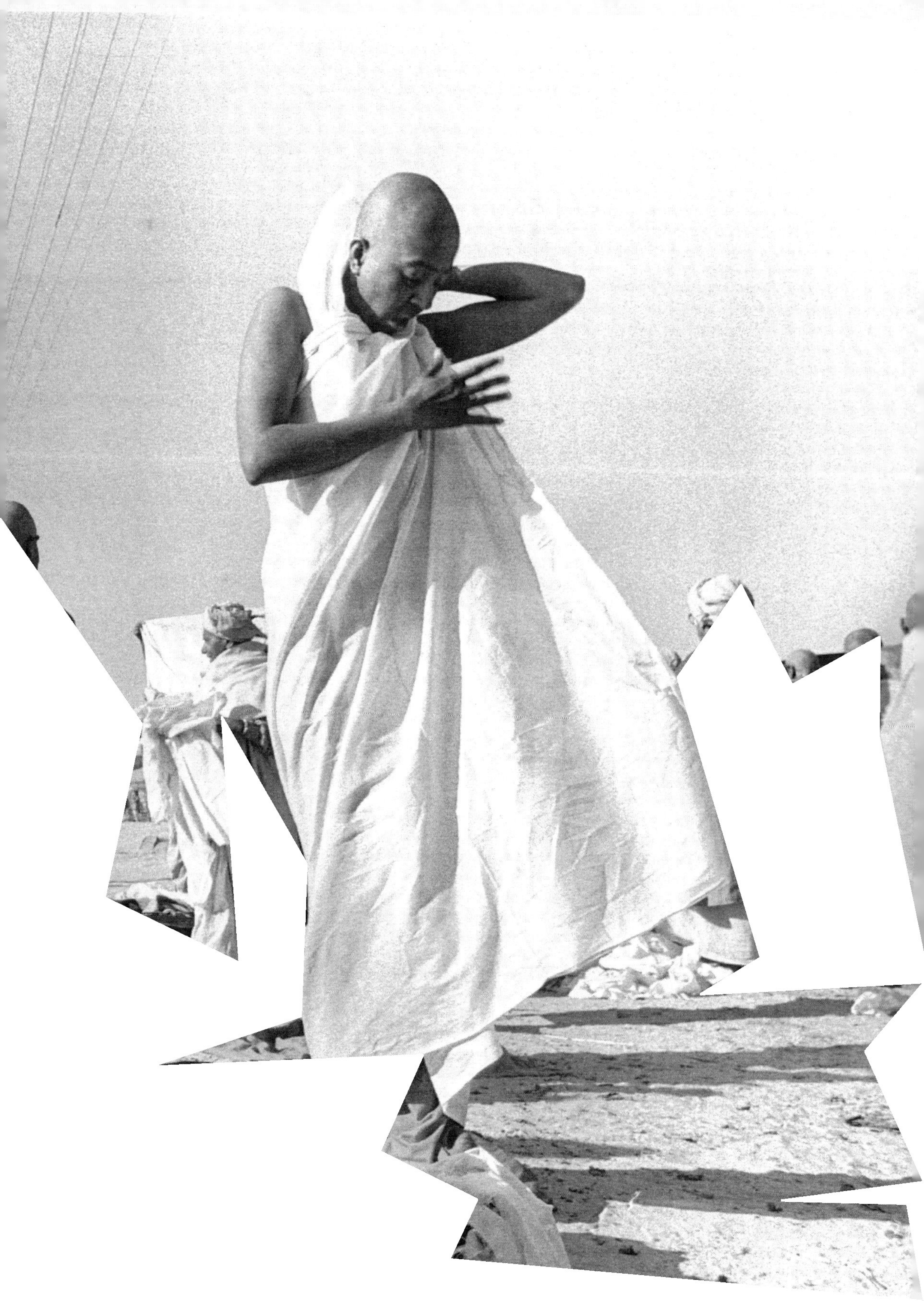

the unknown bird come and go in the cage?). Lalan's bird, beyond name and form, manifests itself through the mortal, ephemeral body. However, the mystic argues, it would be a mistake to identify it with the body, which is a cage. The pure self is a bird liberated from the constraining vestments of identity or belonging; its flight leaves no mark.[36]

But if the *achin pakhi* is *achinha* (without sign or mark), how do we make sense of the dense accretions and traces, art-historical, political, economic and spiritual, left behind by the avian protagonists of Chhachhi's *Winged Pilgrims*? I would contend that there is a productive friction in her art between two kinds of transcendence: on the one hand a spiritual transcendence, and on the other, secular transcendences, emancipatory affordances gained in and through contestation with material realities. It is on the latter that all initiatives of revolution and resistance, including feminism, are premised.

Just as in the subaltern religious poetics from which Chhachhi draws artistic inspiration, art offers a possible 'transcendence' through the imaginative gesture of liberating a brief zone of space-time from the prevailing canon of conformity and field of authority. This transcendence remains grounded in determinate material experience and is not an escape from it. In a Buddhist tenor, the artist ruminates: 'My own philosophical ground is closer to a conception where matter is a manifestation of energy, which is mutable, can be transformed and, in fact, is in continuous transformation, dependent on causes and conditions, void of inherent existence.'[37]

The Art of Immersion

At this juncture, it is necessary to explore the variety of media deployed by Chhachhi to translate her research trove – of mythology, history and literature – into an artistic practice; one that highlights her ideological preoccupations while producing a sensorium of effects. I would like to study her choices in relation to organic materials, as well as analogue and digital media, with reference to the design pedagogy at the NID where she studied, alongside her socialization in the women's movement.

In the late 1970s, when Chhachhi joined NID, 'design or communication skills were either market-oriented or within a developmental frame. There was no engagement with gender issues per se.'[38] NID was established in 1961, on the basis of 'The India Report' (1958) which the Nehru government had commissioned Charles and Ray Eames, renowned architects and exhibition designers, to prepare.[39] NID's goal was to create innovative industrial design solutions to serve the needs of a newly developing economy. One of the chief collaborators of the Eames' report was that extraordinary figure Dashrath Patel, painter, sculptor, ceramicist, photographer and exhibition designer. Having imbibed the Eamesian design ethic, which emphasized both qualitative excellence and social usefulness, Patel pioneered NID's design pedagogy and practice programme in the early 1960s. He also designed the Indian pavilions for international trade fairs in New York, Tokyo, Montreal and Osaka in the 1960s and 1970s.

Like the Eameses, Patel set up exhibitions as large-scale immersive environments with film and multimedia projections. For the India Pavilion at Montreal's Expo '67, critic Sadanand Menon recalled, Patel resourcefully 'creat[ed] a nine-screen 360-degree projection of 'A Journey in India'... with no access to high-tech equipment. Faced with the task of having to create a 'Circarama' effect, he devised a plywood housing for nine cameras which he would wear around his neck.'[40] I have argued elsewhere that Patel's energetic experimentations in multimedia form a long-forgotten pre-history to contemporary new media art practices in India.[41] I will now show how Patel and Chhachhi's paths met and intersected in ways that both surprise and illuminate.

Within Patel's personality and choices - this is true of many Indians of his generation and location - the strikingly different approaches of Nehru and Gandhi regarding the use of technology competed for attention and fulfilment. In 1980, Patel left NID to work at the micro-level for activists and NGOs on 'need-based programmes' in 'small, negligible economies', improvising low-cost screen-printing technology and DIY projectors.[42] Prompted by the Gandhian activist Vikasbhai, he set up the Rural Design School in Sewapuri, Varanasi, to train children of local artisans. Chhachhi was also associated with Sewapuri and Vikasbhai. Like Patel, she shared visual communication skills with rural activists. Chhachhi and her designer colleague Jogi Panghaal, with whom she co-founded 'Lifetools', a design studio focused on social needs, visited Sewapuri annually where Marxists, Gandhians and feminists met to network and forge alliances, 'to hold workshops, developmental debates, political gatherings - anchored around Vikasbhai - an amazing Gandhian with an extremely open mind and heart'.

Chhachhi's multimedia installations can be seen within the NID-Eames-Patel genealogy, with the crucial difference that she was not projecting a spectacular national image of Nehruvian India, whether aligned with a utopian nationalism as with Patel or calibrated as an element of Cold War 'soft power' strategy as with the Eameses. Instead, as a post-Emergency feminist artist, she trained her eyes to critique the nation-state's political and social lapses and to account for its disenfranchised citizens.

And yet a family resemblance connects these three figures, a certain typology of exhibition-making sustained by a desire to democratize the protocols of viewing. Multimedia installations allowed for a transdisciplinary breaking of boundaries where text, image, light and sound could exist as independent media, but were also filtered through each other. By assembling diverse media in a non-linear, polyphonic and performative manner, the artist allowed the viewer multiple possibilities of entry into the work.

Early in her practice, Chhachhi assembled her installation *Wild Mothers 2: The Mirror Is the Witness* as a layered narrative, using translucent photographs to create a complex ontology of protest.[43] Her design pedagogy and activist background enabled a flexibility of approach and an ethic that required viewers not to be alienated. In her multimedia installations, the viewers are by degrees immersed, enthralled, made complicit in the action and encouraged to levitate on the wings of imagination. But equally, they are forced to take a step back and look the stereotype in the eye, and to recognize the dense accretions of history for what they are, separating vital questions from dead habits of the mind. They become active participants in Chhachhi's dark and luminous theatre, implicated as they are in the phenomenological experience of an art not separated from life but permeated with it.

Chhachhi does not necessarily choose the most advanced technology in her multimedia installations; she may be happier rummaging through markets in Delhi for street toys or working out artisanal solutions for a lightbox that combines still and moving images, just as Patel developed a slide projector for rural activists using cardboard and torches.

In 1996, Chhachhi produced an immersive environment by installing an ellipse of toy televisions, video sculptures glittering like jewels in the melting dark (A Box of Shards/*The Mermaid's Mirror*). Fragmentary images of the iconic Hindi film actress Meena Kumari of the 1950s and 1960s, brimming over with pathos, disintegrate on the TV screens.[44] These liquid images, accompanied by dialogues quoted from legendary Hindi films, mirrored the actress's on-screen persona of the wounded, self-sacrificing wife, lover, prostitute or widow. These dialogues are in turn intercut with Meena Kumari's recitation of her own poetry: a fine Urdu poet, she was unable to release herself from the socially sanctioned role-playing in which she was trapped.

Mounted on cylinders wrapped with film positive with nothing more to drive them than the heat of an incandescent bulb (Chhachhi's tribute to the *jugaad* aesthetic), Meena Kumari's images move slowly, perspiring in their toy cages. By 1996, state television had lost its monopoly of broadcasting to the nation. The early years of globalization had given rise to private TV channels competing for TRPs. At such a moment, Chhachhi, instead, slowed down televisual reception by taking viewers into an early technological mode of seeing and feeling, an apparently lost history of sentience before the tyranny of the cathode ray tube.

There is something uncanny about the presentation of *The Mermaid's Mirror*. We know intuitively that the work is more than just a commentary about the stereotypical representation of gender in popular culture. While it is not easy to put the subjective experience of this work into words, I would borrow a term from the vocabulary of spiritual experience to approach it: such work provokes *bhaavashru*, literally 'tears of feeling', a sign that one has been transported into a space of spiritual bliss or ecstasy.

Chhachhi's multimedia installations often produce powerful affective states: images disintegrate, colours bleed, light liquefies, sound emerges from a place abandoned by language. We sense this surplus of feeling in the leaking blue atmosphere of *Neelkanth: Poison/Nectar* (2002), the ominous red translites of *Rakt-Pushp* (Blood Flower, 1997), the orange flames of light licking the *yoni* (vulva) in *Black Waters Will Burn* (2011).

'Our People are Capable of a Very Wild Imagination'

Earlier in this essay, I sketched out the mutable relationship between the viewer and the artwork as it shifts emphasis and switches interpretative codes across the course of Chhachhi's experimentation with multimedia environments. This mutability is conditioned, as I have sought to demonstrate, by the varied, not immediately visible or available, deep histories of her work – for example, the artist's osmotic absorption of the Eames-Patel NID design legacy.

At the '48° C Public.Art.Ecology' festival curated by Pooja Sood in Delhi in 2008, Chhachhi had the opportunity to point a dowser's rod at a city whose memory has been clouded by colonial erasure and post-colonial amnesia.[45] Descending into the basement of the Delhi Public Library to experience *The Water Diviner* was like following Tarkovsky's *Stalker* into a sealed zone. A public art festival, at least theoretically, acts as a liminal rupture in the city's official narrative of securitization and surveillance, re-sensitizing its citizens to their environment, allowing them to roam freely and even drift into forbidden spaces. But mere access does not automatically guarantee engagement with the city's hidden memories. The artist created an intense psychic 'situation' within the bowels of the public library, to steer her viewers away from their habitual reflexes of seeing without looking, and to enchant them with a cosmology of water, albeit under threat.

The basement was flooded in blue light, perhaps subliminally referring to the nocturnal blue associated with Krishna.[46] Once a swimming pool for British officers, an attempt at converting it into a conference room had been abandoned and finally, it became a dump for unwanted books rotting behind cobweb curtains. Chhachhi piled the books up so as to create a thoroughfare furrowed between the heaps, and punctuated these with book-shaped lightboxes: illuminated books carrying images from miniature paintings depicting riverine songs and stories juxtaposed with contemporary ecological dystopias.

At one end of the basement, black water flows from a lion's head, the remains

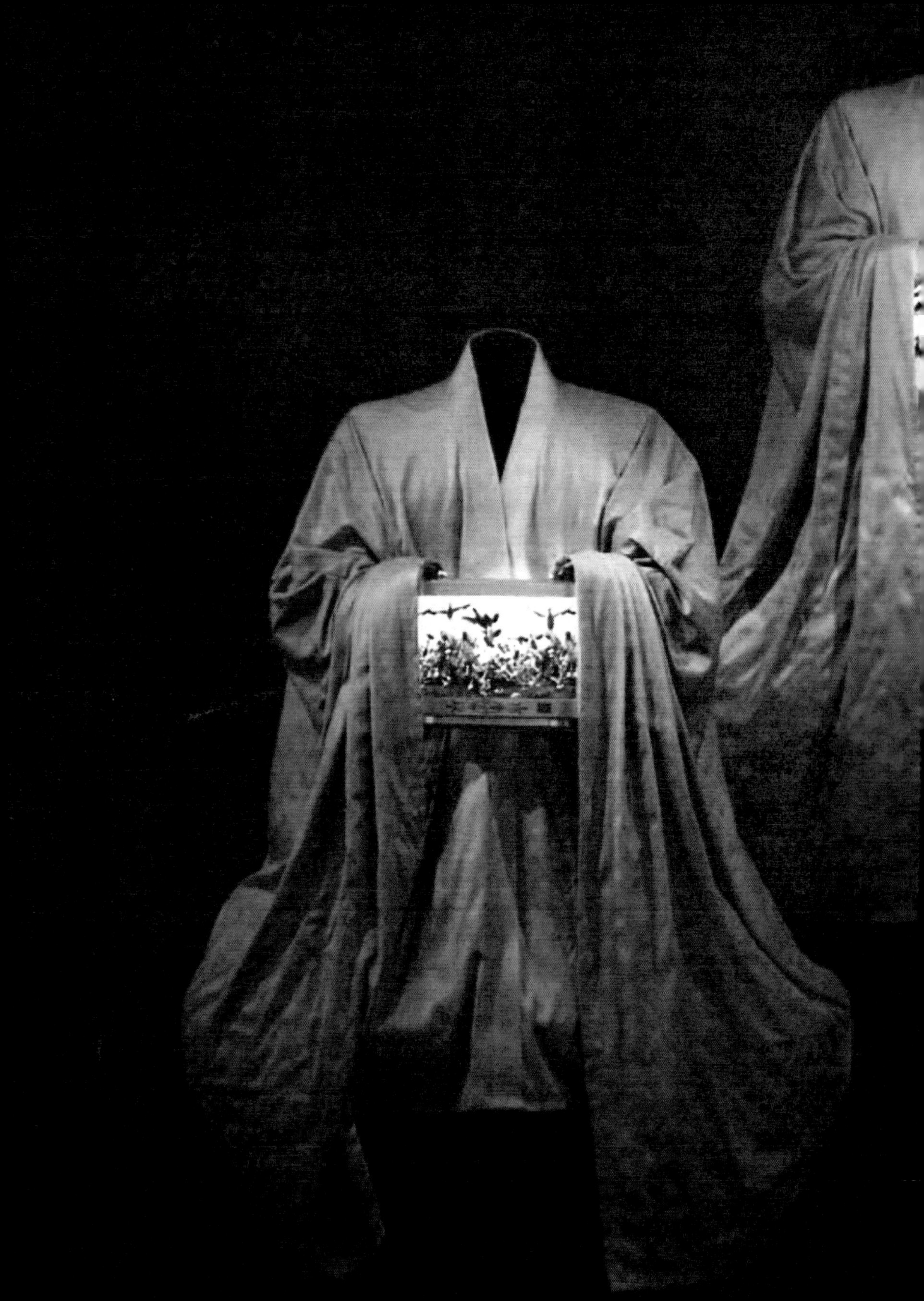

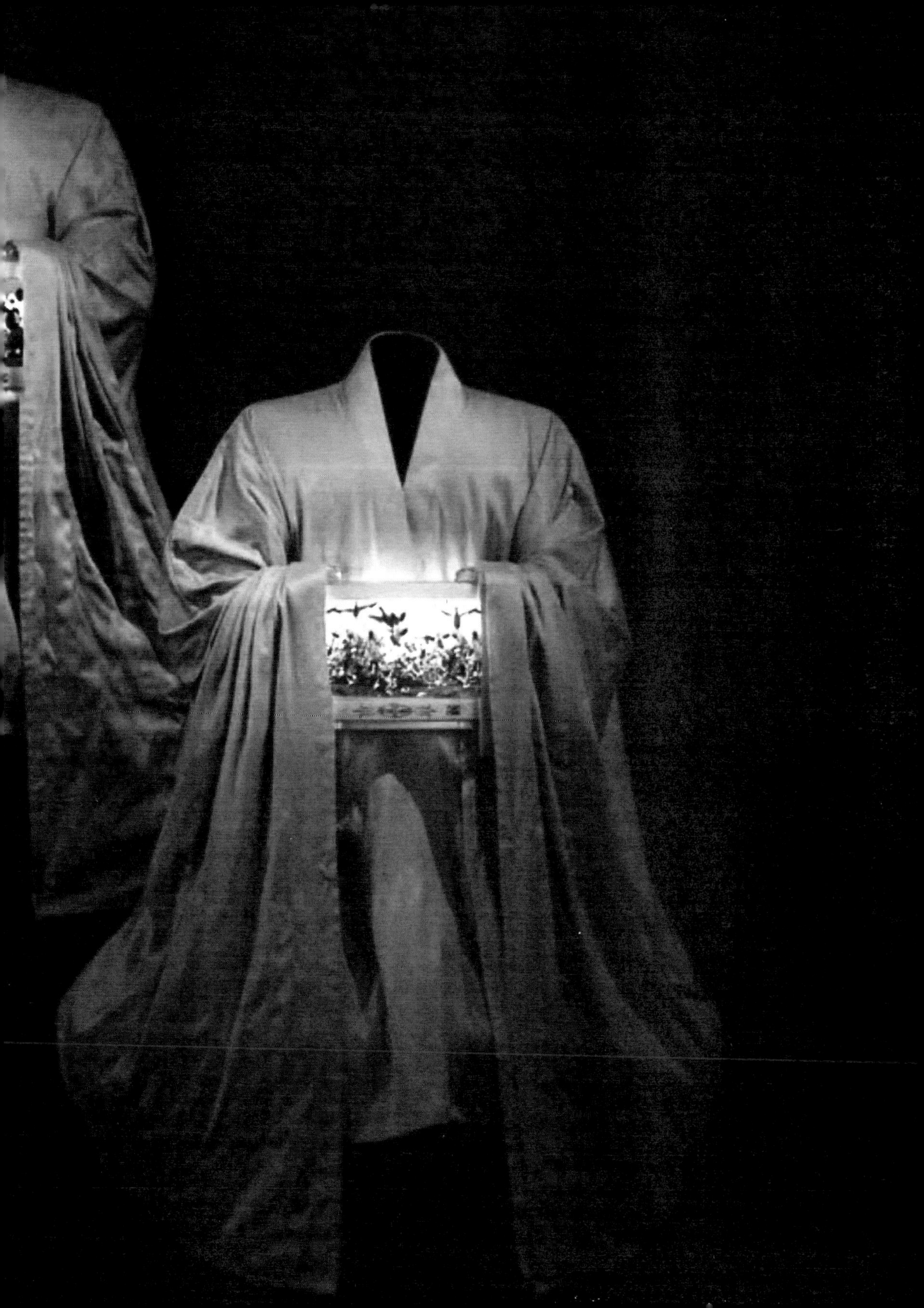

of a colonial water fountain. At the other end, an elephant dives in pristine blue waters. Could this be an apparition generated by the mind? And what is this illuminated map on the ground? A suggestion that the street above us was once a waterway. We draw closer to the elephant, that gorgeous creature swimming gracefully in a liquescent video projection. It dissolves gently into a cloud of particles and gradually reconstitutes itself, signalling cycles of dissolution and regeneration. The coming apart and reconstitution of the elephant within the installation could be seen as a metaphor for Chhachhi's reconfiguration of the 'psycho-geography' of the Delhi Public Library, activating hidden reserves of memory associated with the sacred and cosmic wholeness, but also with the fracture and loss of these.[47]

The 'psycho-geographical' experience produced by Chhachhi in *The Water Diviner* was one of excruciating beauty alternating with psychic disturbance, and of sensory knowledge and enchantment held in tension with criticality. Thus the people who marched in purposefully or drifted into the basement of the Delhi Public Library were provoked into a new form of 'reading' their urban neighbourhood. At a subliminal level, it could not have been lost on them that the river Yamuna that courses through Delhi is black and polluted, but it could be a pulsating blue. With *The Water Diviner*, Chhachhi brought the cosmological face to face with the ecological crisis. It is intriguing to note that etymologically, the words 'crisis' and 'critique' share a common root – *krinein* in Greek means 'to make a choice'.

In her interactive 2011 video installation *Bhogi/Rogi* (Consumption/Disease), shown at Select Citywalk Mall in Saket, Delhi, Chhachhi chose to work with a sophisticated technological interface. Distracted viewers in the mall could walk casually into a booth and find their image captured on a two-way screen projecting the viewers' activities inside the booth on the outside and thereby beckoning the attention of passers-by. Produced in technical collaboration with multimedia designer Thomas Eichhorn, and commissioned by Khoj, the artist wanted to implicate the viewer's body in this critique of genetically modified food. Their narcissistic urge to look at themselves on the screen would by default suck them into a high-key, toxic environment where aubergines and tomatoes sizzle like eerie creatures. The artist had produced a purgatory for conspicuous consumers, the genetically modified foods boiled and bubbled on screen. We are what we eat, the artist seemed to warn us, even as we flailed our arms and performed antics in front of the screen. Chhachhi chose this interactive and performative format of presentation over a didactic and discursive one, to build a direct personal relationship with the dangers of biotechnology.

Apart from being shown in a shopping mall, *Bhogi/Rogi* was presented in a community centre and a gallery. Chhachhi observes:

> 'Inside the mall, 9,000 to 10,000 people went through the work

> in a day. It was extraordinary! However, fifty per cent of the people stopped at the first level. Once they realized that while you see yourself on the screen, you are also being seen from outside, they would get people to photograph them and it would be over. So, in a sense, the work was re-consumed.'[48]

On the other hand, when *Bhogi/Rogi* was re-installed at the community centre, young working-class people interacted with the installation repeatedly and were far more engaged with it; they asked searching questions. Meanwhile, in the conventional white cube, the viewer was presented with the appropriate 'ritual' circumstances to receive the work.

All these varieties of audience encounter seemed to converge at the Dr Bhau Daji Lad Museum in Mumbai.[49] where Chhachhi was invited to present her works in 2011. She was aware that her viewers there would represent a heterogeneous mix of classes, ethnicities and levels of education. Many of them, visiting the museum with a general intention of gleaning information on the city's history, would be surprised by the interpolations of contemporary visual art in its ethnographic collection. The Bhau Daji Lad Museum, formerly the Victoria and Albert Museum, opened to the public on 2 May 1872. Craftsmanship and the role of the artisan were inscribed into the museum's foundational charter. The nucleus of its collection was constituted from duplicates of exotic specimens of the colony (geological, archaeological, stuffed animals and local crafts), which were sent to England for the first 'Great Exhibition of the Works of Industry of all Nations' in 1851. This exhibition was meant to showcase the most innovative industrial design products from the colonies, and thereby encourage trade and increase industrial production.[50]

George Birdwood, one of the early curators of the museum, corroborated the economic dimension of this exhibition-making practice when he wrote: 'it [the museum] will be a standing agency for the organization of periodical exhibitions of the industries of India and of the countries in commerce with Bombay'.[51] But this ardent champion of India's craft traditions also proclaimed that there was no 'Fine Art' in India. This dogma was responsible for the creation of a curious situation: while craftspersons were drafted into making 'economic products' for the empire, the 'Fine Art' artists who were trained at the schools of art established by the colonial administration in India were reduced to draughtsmen who would illustrate the empire's ethnographic and archaeological surveys.

By a productive irony and in an act of poetic justice, Chhachhi's intervention in the museum defied and deflated the Birdwood doctrine. It rescued the artisan from the romanticism of the traditional oriental ware-turner, while also demonstrating the imaginative energy of the modern Indian artist. Of course, as we have seen, Chhachhi's journey into art is not the classical art school route but, rather, consists of a series of engagements with the asymmetries of power, articulation, expression and recognition, which are encoded into the very fabric of the Bhau Daji Lad Museum. When Chhachhi made her intervention, the museum had been newly restored by an army of artisans who had repainted and gilded it to a fine finish, in collaboration with heritage conservation experts. In the midst of the exquisite high Victorian architecture stood a statue of Prince Albert, Queen Victoria's consort, who was responsible for the initial museum collection and the promotion of Indian crafts at the Great Exhibition of 1851. In front of the statue, Chhachhi laid a new set of tiles on the floor, stamped with the hands of an artisan (*mistri*) and factory worker who had been laid off. Even as the gestures of colonial empire-building and a post-colonial corporate state were made to confront each other in *Itbari Khan ke Haath* (Itbari Khan's Hands) we were compelled to reflect on the uneasily hyphenated relationship between citizen and subject.[52]

Chhachhi's site-specific installations at the Bhau Daji Lad Museum employed irony to tweak temporality, location and gaze. For instance, an excerpt from the powerful *Ganga's Daughters* suite was placed in a room displaying vitrines filled entirely with puny figurines of male ascetics suspended in contorted yogic poses. The marginalized male ascetics could not help but elicit laughter. The space in the room was also shared by the academic painter M.V. Dhurandhar's twentieth-century paintings, a large theatrical watercolour painted in the western tradition of history painting (*A Court Scene*, 1928) and another depicting a coy group of traditionally attired women.[53] Configured together with the women-ascetics in a single space, they seemed to warrant a meditation on the philosophical questions of truth, beauty and justice.

Walking through Chhachhi's exhibition at the Bhau Daji Lad Museum, observing the baffled but intrepid viewer who hesitantly picks up the pedagogical handout to begin decoding the artwork, I was reminded of an account by the late nineteenth-century Bombay writer Govind Narayan. In *Mumbaiche Varnan* (A Description of Bombay, 1863: 235),[54] Narayan describes an exhibition comprising objects ranging from pythons, birds, animals and clothes from various parts of the world held at the Town Hall in 1856 (this was before the museum collection came to be housed in its current building in Byculla). While many native philanthropists supported the idea, some naysayers reportedly said: 'This is just the madness of the English and an utter waste of money.' Narayan brushed these sceptics aside with judicious sarcasm: 'Our people are capable of a very wild imagination.' His own support for the colonial educational programme was unequivocal: 'A museum is the principal place for education and entertainment. People are motivated to industry and diligence when they see the skilled work of people from various parts of the world.'

Curiously enough, colonial-era Indian opinion-makers seemed to have great clarity about what constitutes museum culture. We cannot say the same today with regard to state-controlled museum infrastructure, its collections or its public, but what we can say with certainty - although in a quite different register from Narayan's - is that 'Our people are capable of a very wild imagination'! Can artists create the appropriate conditions for the production and reception of art such that 'wildness' can be nurtured and sustained?

* * *

Having taken several detours in this essay to understand Sheba Chhachhi's multimedia environments, I have arrived at a discontinuous continuity between her earliest interventions of showing her documentary photographs on a clothesline in a slum (a proto-history of her multimedia works) to her later insertions of video installations into varied contexts such as a museum, a community centre, a mall or a gallery. We are certain that Chhachhi is preparing herself to engage with the barricades of a new historical moment, one dominated by surveillance, censorship, mob lynching and heightened aggression towards women and the disenfranchised.

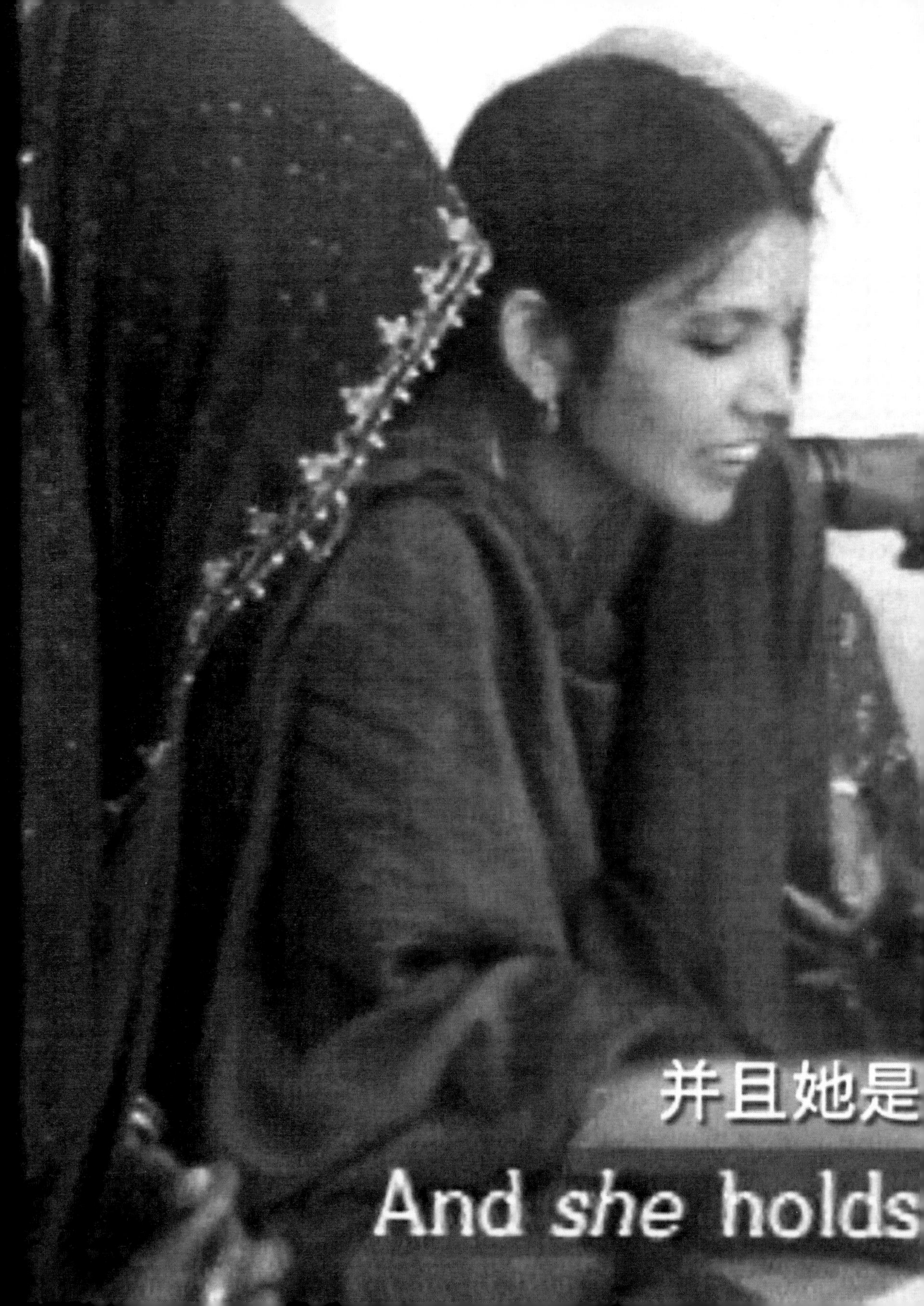
并且她是
And *she* holds

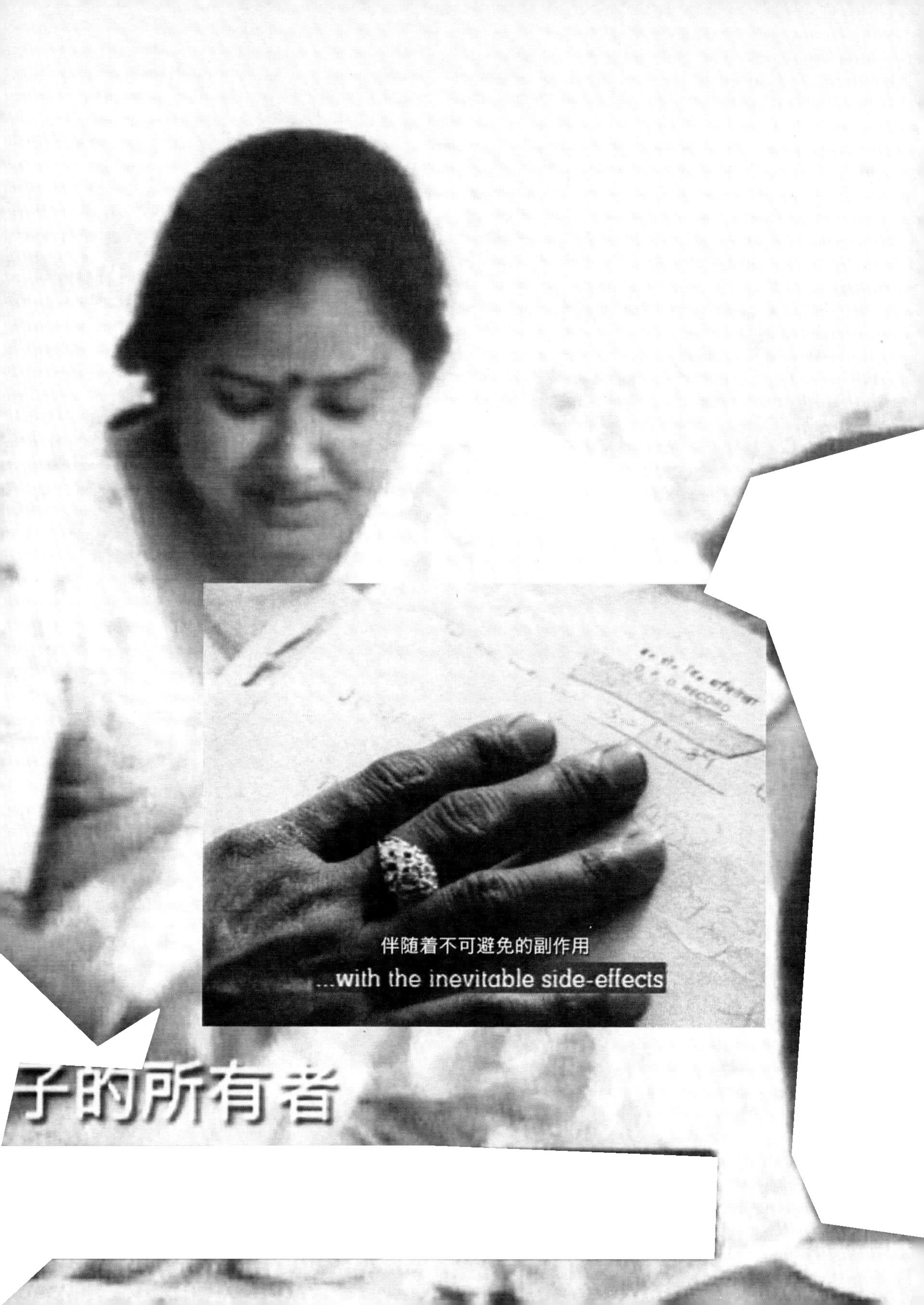

子的所有者

Established in 1984, Mediastorm was among India's first film collectives, one of several founded in that decade, defining a documentary practice almost entirely removed from the conventional histories of Indian film. Set up by a group of women graduates from the still-new Mass Communications Research Centre in Delhi's Jamia Millia Islamia University, Mediastorm's films were shot on video and edited (they write here) in a friend's studio at night, when the equipment was free. This era of nascent video technology, post-Emergency, is defined as much by the growth of terrestrial (and later satellite) television as by tactical media practices using lightweight, portable equipment. It is significant that the group views the 2002 Gujarat massacre, which saw a major upsurge in independent documentary filmmaking, as constituting an end of their work, defining new priorities and fields for the group's members.

This essay was first written for the 1991 Chameli Devi Jain Award catalogue. In 2017, a version was presented at 'The New Medium', curated by Shaina Anand for the Mumbai Academy of the Moving Image (MAMI) film festival, performed as a media archaeological excavation alongside Anand's effort to digitize Mediastorm's films. Reprinted here with permission from the Mediastorm collective.

Keywords, Names, Abbreviations

2002 Gujarat Riots, Documentary, Doordarshan, (Anand) Patwardhan, Street Theatre, Tactical Media, Video, Women's Movement: See Keywords (pp. 326–44).

Beveridge, James (1917–1993): Canadian documentary filmmaker, one of the founders of the National Film Board of Canada, and a leading figure in the tradition of John Grierson's (1898–1972) documentary idiom.

Hamara Shaher (Bombay, Our City, 1985): Landmark documentary by Anand Patwardhan on slum evictions in Bombay. See Keywords, p. 338, for Patwardhan.

Hashmi, Safdar (1954–1989): Theatre director, actor, author, and major figure in street theatre in India as founding member of the Jana Natya Manch, murdered for his political views in 1989.

MCRC: Refers to the A.J. Kidwai Mass Communications Research Centre at Jamia Millia Islamia, Delhi, founded in 1982, whose alumni led a major documentary film movement from the 1990s.

Muslim Women's Bill: Controversial bill granting Muslim women the right to alimony post divorce. Enacted after the 1985 *Ahmed Khan v. Shah Bano Begum* case in which the Supreme Court issued a judgement supporting Shah Bano's claims to alimony. Subsequently, due to protests by the Muslim orthodoxy, a watered down Muslim Women's (Protection of Rights on Divorce) Bill of 1986 was passed.

Sati: Hindu tradition of widow self-immolation, and a major issue defining social reform in the nineteenth century. In 1987, after a woman named Roop Kanwar died through an act claimed to be voluntary self-immolation, India enacted the Commission of Sati (Prevention) Act, 1987.

Images

pp. 166–67: Modified screen grabs from Deepa Dhanraj's documentary, *Something Like a War* (1991, 16 mm, colour), cinematography: Navroze Contractor; courtesy Deepa Dhanraj. The film exposes the biopolitics and coercive nature of the state's family planning programme enforced upon women, and intertwined questions of reproductive rights, sexuality, patriarchy and poverty.

SHOHINI GHOSH, SABINA KIDWAI, SHIKHA JHINGAN, RANJANI MAZUMDAR, SABEENA GADIHOKE and CHARU GARGI[1]

1991

The Mediastorm Collective was formed in 1985, when we were final-year students of MA, Mass Communication, at the Mass Communication Research Centre (MCRC) in Jamia Millia Islamia, New Delhi. We were the second batch of students to study at MCRC, which was to become over the next two decades, one of the most prestigious media institutions in India. The founder of MCRC, Anwar Jamal Kidwai,[1] was a dynamic visionary who sought to build a media institute that would provide hands-on education to media practitioners who would 'think with their heads and work with their hands'. Born out of an Indo-Canadian collaboration, MCRC aspired to be a production school that sought to create media practitioners devoted to sociopolitical concerns.

A.J. Kidwai's collaborators in this project were James and Margaret Beveridge.[2] Jim Beveridge was a famous Canadian documentary filmmaker and a close associate of John Grierson, often called the 'The Father of the Documentary'. Margaret, his wife, was a talented and highly regarded editor. The founding trio ensured that MCRC was frequently visited by filmmakers of different persuasions.

One of the filmmakers who visited MCRC and left a lasting impression on us was Anand Patwardhan who screened his hard-hitting documentary, *Hamara Shahar* (Bombay, Our City, 1984),[3] about the city's slum-dwellers. The film opened up a new world to us. Here was a documentary that was observational in nature, without a voice-of-god narration, and one that was driven by passion and politics in equal measure. We were blown away!

The forming of Mediastorm Collective was accidental and emerged out of the controversy around the Muslim

Women's Bill, following the now famous Shah Bano judgment. Shah Bano, a sixty-two-year-old woman, was divorced by her husband according to the procedures of the Muslim Personal Law.[4] After the divorce, she had no means to support her children and she moved the courts to claim alimony from her husband. It took seven years for the case to reach the Supreme Court which, after several hearings, ruled in her favour. Although it was not the first time that the court had passed such an order, the court's comments on the Quran caused a furore. The Muslim orthodoxy reacted with cries of religion being in danger, and the Congress government responded to this crisis by reversing its stand on the judgment. Instead, it supported an independent member's Bill, thereby enacting the Muslim Women's (Protection of Rights on Divorce) Bill in May 1986.[5]

All of us were quick to see that in the entire controversy, it was going to be Muslim women who would suffer the most, not to mention the fillip that it would provide to religious fundamentalists on both sides. The women's movement had reacted sharply and several vocal protests were organized outside the Parliament House in New Delhi. The anti-Bill movement received another fillip when Arif Mohammed Khan, a minister in the Congress government, resigned. Eight of us got together and decided to make a documentary on the Bill. We felt that it was important to document the movement using the video technology that had empowered us at MCRC. The tentative permission granted to us was withdrawn when the university was drawn into the vortex of the controversy. A.J. Kidwai informed us that Jamia would not be able to support this controversial film. However, he said, the film was important to make and, therefore, he would help us make it independently. Among other people, he requested the well-known wildlife filmmaker Mike Pandey to support the film.[6]

Mike generously extended to us his technical facilities. But we could only work when the facilities were free, so *In Secular India* (1986) was made as the city slept. We would edit in shifts throughout the night, taking turns to work and sleep on the studio floor. As film production entails a number of expenses, we undertook a frantic fund-raising drive and approached like-minded individuals. With the generous help of many individuals (whose names appear on the credits), the film was made and shown to a packed auditorium on 14 September 1986.

In Secular India received much press and public attention. Prior to media liberalization and the advent of cable and satellite television, the regular source of news and current affairs (apart from newspapers) was Doordarshan. It was common knowledge that Doordarshan was the mouthpiece of the government, so, predictably, the national debate on the Muslim Women's Bill had found no place there. That so many showed up to watch a film made by eight unknown students was evidence that people were ready for a dissident visual media. Our collective was formed as a voluntary, non-profit organization. We relied entirely on the massive support and solidarity of various fellow travellers and well-wishers since funding for political documentaries has never been easy. But the mood for intervention was in the air. We also sensed, like A.J. Kidwai, that a new media culture was gathering storm. This premonition was contained in naming the collective 'Mediastorm' - that, indeed, we were part of a new moment.

In 1987, the country exploded with news from Deorala village in Rajasthan. Roop Kanwar, a young Rajput widow, had decided to burn herself on the funeral pyre of her husband. The 'sati' event had taken place in the presence of the villagers and the police did nothing to prevent it. What was horrifying was that powerful Rajput groups along with the family of the in-laws had decided to organize a *chunri mahotsava*[7] glorifying the sati, turning the *sati sthal*[8] into a pilgrim spot. The government responded initially with some ambivalence as it probably did not want to risk alienating the powerful but conservative Rajput lobby in the coming state assembly elections. Women's groups in the country, on the other hand, were outraged.

One of our members was not in the country, but the other five decided to take a train to Jaipur. Packed into one car and armed with a hired studio camera, we travelled to Deorala. As we emerged from the car, the desert stretched endlessly in the distance, broken only by the sight of a stream of people - men in colourful turbans and veiled women circling the *sati sthal* in silence. Occasionally, there were cries of *Sati Mata ki jai* (glory to mother Sati). In retrospect, we must have looked very odd to them, wearing ethnic *salwar kameez* (knee-length shirt and loose trousers commonly worn by women across north India) in an attempt to 'merge in' (that misplaced assumption and attempt has been laid to rest since!). We were immediately cornered by a gang of men, subjected to interrogation, and asked to leave.

We never got to Deorala again, but our filming in Rajasthan sought to explore the socially restrictive world of Rajput culture where women had no status without their husbands. One of the moments in the film, *From the Burning Embers* (1988), that we were very happy with was a discussion with Jat women who spoke out without fear against the restrictions of their upper-caste sisters.[9] The big question in the print media was whether Roop Kanwar had taken this step voluntarily. For us, after our experience of shooting at a school run by the Rani Sati Mata Temple in Jhunjhunu,[10] there was no doubt that Kanwar's actions were mediated through social circumstances. We shot a sequence where young girls prayed every morning to the Sati Mata. Needless to say, the school authorities asked us to leave immediately.

During our shooting trips in Rajasthan, we managed to generate a major archive of footage. Not all of it was used in the film, but we preserved the footage. A few years later, when Kalyan Singh Kalvi got elected from Barmer district and became the minister for energy, we found an old interview by him in our archive, where the politician had not only defended sati but also placed it as one of the major aspects of Indian culture that had to be defended. Women's groups used the footage to hold a press conference since, in his new avatar, Kalvi was denying his role in defending sati.

The film was also enriched by a street play performed by Jana Natya Manch (JANAM), which we shot in MCRC. A.J. Kidwai always managed to find ways to help the collective, and shooting a play with a multi-camera set up in a studio was not something we could have done without his help. One of the richest memories of working as a collective was the way people helped us in whatever way they could. The singer Vidya Rao sat through the night to sing a song that was composed by musician Kajal Ghosh. The songs for the film were penned by the writer Kalindi Deshpande.[11]

In Secular India was the only film that was made by the eight of us, because two members soon got married and left the country. The remaining six became the core group. To this day, we have stayed friends and collaborators in our many different pursuits. Moreover, as a group of filmmakers, we made many allies and some of them became friends for life. But one friend and ally we lost very early was the talented playwright and street-theatre activist Safdar Hashmi.[12]

Safdar was a friend and we had asked him to write us a song that would be a leitmotif in *In Secular India*. Initially, Safdar was a bit reluctant because he said he had never written a song before. Then one day, in a tea shop, he sat and wrote the whole song. Sung by a friend, for the film *Ek Pardanashin* (The Veiled One), it remains, for many of us, as moving today as it was then. Safdar would also write some powerful songs for Mediastorm's second film, *From the Burning Embers*. In 1988, an organization working for communal harmony decided to honour Mediastorm and Safdar's theatre group, JANAM along with some other writers. The award carried a plaque and a cash prize of Rs 15,000.

Having accepted, we discovered that the person to give the awards away was going to be the Information and Broadcasting minister, H.K.L. Bhagat.[13] Mediastorm and JANAM were in a quandary because we did not want to take the award from a man who was allegedly one of the prime architects of the Sikh genocide following the killing of Indira Gandhi in 1984.[14] After discussions with Safdar, we decided to respect the jury (that had impeccable credentials) without legitimizing Bhagat. We would accept the award, but not attend the ceremony. Our MCRC class-fellow, Akhtar Ali Khan accepted the award on our behalf and read out a statement. JANAM followed the same strategy, but issued a statement that categorically held Bhagat responsible for the pogrom against Sikhs. Within ten days of the award function, hoodlums armed with iron rods bludgeoned Safdar in Sahibabad. He was rushed to the hospital where he succumbed to his injuries. The thousands who accompanied Safdar's slain body on his last journey were a testimony to his immense popularity and people's growing outrage with the cynical politics of the Congress.

Soon after, our documentaries on the Muslim Women's Bill and on sati were recognized by the Chameli Devi Jain Award in 1991. *Kiska Dharm, Kiska Desh* (Whose Country is it Anyway?) made in 1991, was Mediastorm's most difficult and ambitious project. The film sought to track the rise of the Hindu right wing and the deepening communal divide in the country by forces unleashed by the Ram Janmabhoomi movement.[15] We decided to place the Babri Masjid dispute at the centre but sought to understand its reverberations across the country. It is for this film that we travelled the most – we went to Bhagalpur, Ahmedabad, Bombay, Faizabad, Lucknow and Ayodhya. The last leg of the shooting covered the bricklaying ceremony at the Babri Masjid and L.K. Advani's inflammatory speeches, which had wreaked havoc across north India.

The mosque, as we saw it during our several trips, was heavily barricaded with barbed wire and virtually inaccessible to the media. Only Hindu devotees could go in and offer prayers at the Ram *chabutara*[16] where an idol had been kept. It seemed like a lost battle. Even the policemen on duty to protect the mosque did not see anything wrong in the festivities and rituals offered by the devotees. They probably thought our camerawoman was harmless and let her go through. The camera was on and, subsequently, we were the few who had footage of what was happening inside.

Kiska Dharm was shot before the demolition actually happened. Everywhere, we noticed how memories of violence had marked the site. In the village Logain, close to Bhagalpur, a woman described the frenzy of the violence and how people were buried in the fields.[17] It is with *Kiska Dharam* that we began to see the limits of just focusing on the 'event'. We had to access a subterranean world of memories, suspicion and hatred. It is for this reason that the film, which originally began with the dispute at the Babri Masjid, became something much larger in its scope. Whether we succeeded or not is a different matter and, in hindsight, we may have been hasty in the way we analysed communalism in the film. But sometimes, strange things can happen when we least realize it.

The film has been our most widely shown documentary and everywhere the screening was followed by a discussion. We enlisted the composer, singer, lyricist, and film theorist, Madan Gopal Singh for the main song of the film which added a different kind of layer to the documentary.[18] Many told us how valuable the documentary was in generating discussions. Though we do see the problems in our film today, we also came to recognize how difficult it was to analyse the complex experiences of communal conflict. Eleven years after our documentary, we saw the worst carnage ever in the history of independent India – the 2002 pogrom in Gujarat led by the state government.[19] Many asked Mediastorm to rush to Gujarat to make a film on the violence and trauma of the riots. But we just could not. The time for neat analysis was over – Gujarat had rocked the country to its core. We were no longer sure if a documentary could even remotely capture the violence and terror of 2002. Perhaps a new form was required for this.

It has been a long journey since the last film. Many ask why Mediastorm has never made another film as a collective. The answer to that one is that there is a moment for particular kinds of formations, and our moment of collective work was in the late 1980s and early 1990s when the media scene was different. A year after we had made *Kiska Dharm Kiska Desh*, the Babri Masjid was demolished. Jubilating mobs danced in joy over the ruins of the mosque. Something in India had changed, something in us also changed; we were overwhelmed by the force of history. Our utopic faith in the will of people to resist the tide of right-wing authoritarian forces had been brutally overturned. The political coherence and interventional certitudes that had driven our documentary work had been put in crisis. New journeys had to begin for each one of us. In the decade of the 90s, globalization radically transformed the mediascape. New modes of making and disseminating documentaries had emerged all over the world. Documentary filmmakers were experimenting with the language of cinema; we began to move further and further away from the form of the three documentaries we had made. Documentaries were no longer just about the content; they were just as much about the form and style. Each one of us engaged with this moment in our own ways. A number of us took up teaching while simultaneously pursuing higher studies. The canvas of our individual interests widened, our notion of collective practice also changed. We continue to share a common politics but film-making today with portable equipment is much more of an individual exercise in creativity. We continue to collaborate with each other on various other projects and remain the closest of friends. Our shared history marks us as the 'Mediastorm women' even today.

CHAPTER ONE

an inner world of their own

अंदर की बात

It is the earlier part of the nineteenth century, and you have landed into an andarmahal/ a zenana/ the innermost quarters that women from an affluent house were confined to.

Completely secluded, the only link that women from these households had to the world outside were working women who accessed the andarmahal to do household jobs and had the freedom to roam the world.

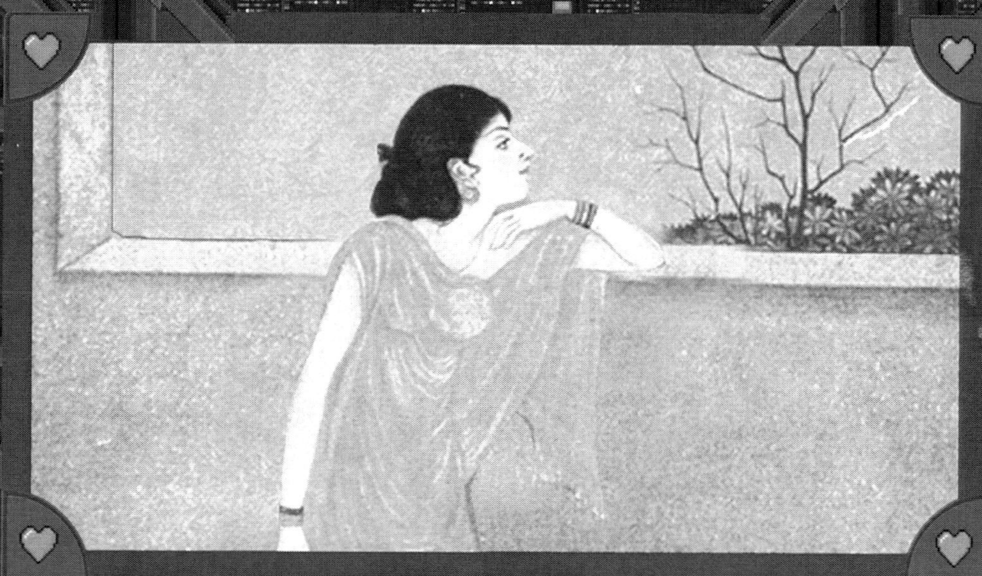

Author and documentary filmmaker Paromita Vohra examines the history of the 'speaking subject' of India's documentary cinema, including in its more radical independent strain. Her own filmmaking strategy, Vohra writes, emerges from her discomfort with this history. She traces her chosen aesthetic lineage to the documentary filmmaker S.N.S. Sastry, who managed – together with a small number of other filmmakers (S. Sukhdev, Pramod Pati) – to make experimental documentaries from inside the state-run documentary propaganda behemoth, Films Division. In the fashion of Sastry's now cult shorts such as *And I Make Short Films* (1968) and *I Am 20* (1968), Vohra strives to create a 'highly particular narrator, a fictional persona who is unique and not an Everywoman, and who necessarily is a bit unreliable through this peculiarity of being a persona with clear characteristics, prejudices and idiosyncratic expressions'. Vohra has done this in a series of well-known documentaries, notably *Unlimited Girls* (2002), *Cosmopolis: Two Tales of a City* (2004) and *Morality TV and the Loving Jehad: A Thrilling Tale* (2007),

A different version of this essay was earlier published as 'Dotting the I: The Politics of Self-less-ness in Indian Documentary Practice', *South Asian Popular Culture*, special issue: 'Beyond Borders', edited by Ananya Jahanara Kabir, vol. 9, no. 1, 2011, pp 43–53. This version is published here with the author's permission.

Keywords, Names, Abbreviations

Dalit, (Deepa) Dhanraj, Documentary, Emergency, Films Division, (Amar) Kanwar, (Anand) Patwardhan: See Keywords (pp. 326–44).

Film Advisory Board: Board set up to persuade the Indian film industry to make propaganda documentaries for the war, in the mode introduced by the British Ministry of Information, and long-term ancestor to the Films Division.

Mir, Ezra (1903–1993): Major wartime and post-war documentarist, part of the Film Advisory Board and its successor, Information Films of India; set up the Indian Documentary Producers Association in 1956 when he was appointed as Chief Producer at Films Division of India.

Pati, Pramod (1932–1975), *S. Sukhdev* (1933–1979), *S.N.S. Sastry* (1930–1978): Documentary filmmakers who developed a distinct idiom of experimentation while working in the Films Division, when it was dedicated to state propaganda. Sometimes this was directly subversive, such as Pati's flash frames saying 'Fuck Censorship'; mostly, it was an individualized modernist idiom that took on independent ideologies.

Images

pp. 175, 181, 186: Screen grabs from Afrah Shafiq's interactive website, *Enter Sultana's Reality*, which leverages the title of Begum Rokeya's feminist utopian short story titled 'Sultana's Reality', originally published in 1905 in *The Indian Ladies Magazine*, Madras. Shafiq is a new media artist who intertwines archival findings, history, memory, folklore and fantasy to create a speculative world born of remix culture. Here she uses photographs and documents from the archive of the Centre for Studies in Social Sciences, Kolkata, presenting debates around the infamous issue of 'women's education' in colonial India as a digital interactive website using sound and archival material.

PAROMITA VOHRA **2011**

12 Who Is the First Person?

On Making Documentaries

I

Let me describe my work briefly. An essential part of a phase in my filmmaking has involved working with the idea of fictional personae who are the narrators of my films. That is to say: someone says 'I' in the film, but that person is not the filmmaker Paromita. Rather, it is someone (often played by the filmmaker) whom we know only through various identities assumed in the film. For example, in my film about feminism, *Unlimited Girls* (2002), the narrator is known only by her chat identity, 'Fearless' – indeed, she could as easily have been called 'Aimless' from the way she appears in the film. 'Fearless' is seen only as a shadowy presence – hands, feet, a smudgy reflection on a granite wall or on a dark computer monitor. Likewise, in a short documentary about food politics in Mumbai, *Cosmopolis: Two Tales of a City* (2004), the narrator is 'Annapurna', a rather vain and foolish, if likeable and fat, goddess of food whose every opinion is countered by another better-looking and reasonable-sounding goddess, played in the film by the well-known television actress Renuka Shahane.[1] And in the film *Morality TV and the Loving Jehad: A Thrilling Tale* (2007), the narrator is not played by the filmmaker, but is an even more shadowy and slippery character who speaks in the tendentious phrases of a pulp novel.

To discuss the reason for these choices, it would be important to examine their inheritance, so to speak. This inheritance is a history of the tension that has surrounded the idea of the narrator and the use of the first person pronoun in Indian documentary practice, and how it has been influenced either by documentary theory, or by the economics and politics of production and circulation.

In 1947, the Indian government formed the Films Division (FD), which was essentially a renaming and reinstating of the Film Advisory Board.[2] FD described itself as 'the official information organ of India'.[3] Producing newsreels and short documentaries about the development of a new nation, FD made over 500 films in its first decade, mostly under the directorship of Ezra Mir.[4] These were films about issues as diverse as 'how to vote', 'terrace farming', or 'the nuclear family' – basically, topics in keeping with the goals of Jawarharlal Nehru's Five Year Plans,[5] themselves framed by the larger aims of the new Indian Constitution. FD was by no means the only producer of documentaries; films were produced outside of the government framework as well, notably Burmah Shell's film producing unit which made a series of films on the people and cultures of India.[6] Nevertheless, it is safe to say that a huge part of documentary production was tied to the style and goals of FD and that a large enough, educated elite identified with the prevailing ideas of Nehruvian socialism – development and 'upliftment' of the masses through various progressive projects.

This mandate of the government films was not different from the prevailing liberal ideas of the time: that is, that there should be an understanding of the diversity that is India, its customs and its traditions; that this diversity should be unified through these films; and that, furthermore, through films the poor should be uplifted. This idea of 'uplift' has remained a part of documentary intent ever since, and we can see it was immediately influenced by the ideas of Grierson as also those of his student, James Beveridge, who worked in India with Shell and with the Films Division.[7] He later helped set up Delhi's Jamia Millia Islamia University's Mass Communications Research Centre, which was intended as a masters course with a focus on politically engaged documentary filmmaking.[8]

II

I consider this act of setting up a government body for documentaries, defined as films meant for national upliftment, as having set up a literal films division, so to say: the division of purpose between 'films' and 'documentaries'. This is a distinction that has lasted to the present day, and that has endowed documentaries with a defined purpose – the carrying and fulfilling of social responsibilities. They were removed from the realm of commercial or popular circulation, and were produced within an economy of patronage, state or foundation funding. This development also meant that those who made documentaries were choosing to do so for very little money, and were choosing a purpose higher than that of profit. In this oblique way, documentaries became connotatively liberal. They entered into the creation of a curious mask of the self. So, if one chose to speak as a documentary filmmaker it automatically meant that the filmmaker in question cared, was liberal and committed, and, in some sense, could not be countered. It made the documentary filmmaker part of an alternative elite, because it identified him or her with the political elite of the time right up to the 1980s, even though, following the declaration of Emergency rule in 1975,[9] many of these films were critical of the government. Although called a 'people's cinema', they were not, in fact, made by the people whom they were about, but a quite separate, educated and relatively privileged elite speaking on behalf of those they saw as oppressed. This consequence bestowed a hidden value on documentary films. At the same time, their surface value was one of nobility and higher purpose, which justified the films – no matter what kind they might be. There was a feeling among practitioners as well as those who constituted their audiences that their choice (both of making and of viewership) was a *self-less* choice.

By extension, and literal though it may seem, we can see in countless examples of documentary films produced even into the 1970s no evident 'self'. In the majority of these films, the first person pronoun was never used – neither by the voice in the film, nor by the people who were in the film, since they never spoke. As a general consensus around the socially concerned purpose of documentary filmmaking, and due to the limitations of existing technology, the films all ended up with the same disembodied form. Regardless of who produced them, they rarely had a distinguishing individual style. They never included interviews, and the only voice to be heard is a commentary in an elite, usually male, voice, speaking over illustrative or symbolic visuals. All of us growing up in India before the 1980s encountered this combination of voice and visual at some point. The style had a unitary quality: that is, it seemed like the performance of a unitary being who had gathered knowledge and then processed it for our benefit into bite-sized bits. It implied, therefore, that the one who was speaking knew more than they were telling you and was somehow qualified to speak thus. The 'I' was absent because, perhaps, it was a version of the royal 'We' that spoke.

In the 1960s, a startling stylistic break happened within the Films Division under the directorship of J. Bhownagry.[10] He encouraged a great deal of experimentation, and the important work that happened in that period was influenced by discussions around *cinema verité* taking place in Europe, the US and Canada. Wolf Koenig,[11] a director and cinematographer working with the National Film Board of Canada talked about 'openness to the moment that reveals'.[12] According to his position, the intellect is the enemy; reality is about a theatre in which the camera is a catalyst. Karel Reisz spoke about how he wanted audiences to identify with detail as opposed to polemic and conclusions;[13] the British filmmaker Richard Leacock (*A Search for the Feeling of Being There*, 1997)[14] spoke of the possibilities of intimacy and what he called the feeling of 'being there'. This was a vanguard of film theorists and practitioners who believed in the observational method of documentary – one popular to this day – in which the observer's identity, while not obscured, was minimized.

We can see the appeal of this form in reaction to the formal straitjacket that had ruled so far. The documentary form was now seen as having new possibilities –

a development that also spread to India. There were three main stars of this phase of FD helmed by Bhownagry through the 1960s: Sukhdev, who made films in a mould we are familiar with today – political documentary broadly in the tradition that Anand Patwardhan furthered through his films from the mid-1970s onwards; Pramod Pati, a highly experimental, radical filmmaker; and S.N.S. Sastry, who combined diverse styles in his filmmaking, favouring cinematic collage, or what we would today call a remix style – and, of the three, the one with whom I'm most concerned for the purposes of discussing my practice.[15]

These filmmakers revolted against what they saw as the stultifying form of filmmaking of the time and their films were full of an individual personality. Both Pati and Sukhdev were very outspoken as filmmakers. Pati inserted flash frames within his film *Explorer* (1968) that said 'Fuck Censorship', while Sukhdev made political documentaries criticizing the state of the nation (though not directly the then government). There was no performance of objectivity, and Sukhdev even appeared in his own films in various ways, both fictional and non-fictional. For me, the most interesting of these three, however, was Sastry, because he was perhaps the first filmmaker in India who freely used the first person pronoun in his films. In fact, the titles of his two most famous films both feature the word 'I': *And I Make Short Films* (1968) as well as *I Am 20* (1968).

I think it is significant that Sastry, as we see from his films, is highly uncomfortable with both the forced patriotism of official films as well as with the 'angry young rebel' feel of films that counter the government agenda. In my reading, he uses the concept of 'I' to express this sense of ambivalence. He is very concerned with art and form as embodying politics, which he explores in *And I Make Short Films*, and his irritation with the discussion of whether documentaries are art or politics, and, indeed, with this division itself, is clearly stated in the film; he is also very interested in individual experience or feeling, which he explores with intelligence and humour in *I Am 20*, a film made to commemorate the twentieth year of Indian Independence (1967), in which Sastry interviews a series of people born in 1947 about their relationship to the idea of India. In both films, he complicates the sense of the 'we' that was unproblematically implied in films to mean, 'we, the people of India' (the opening line of the Indian Constitution), through the use of an 'I'. But Sastry's 'I' is a fragmented one.

In *And I Make Short Films*, Sastry builds a sound and picture collage, made up of material from other FD films. The narration of the film is in the first person, but rather than the unitary narration of one person, it is a construction made up of sound quotes from various peoples' speeches and interviews – all of whom use the first person pronoun. Some of the people 'quoted', or whose quotes construct the narration, are Picasso, Nehru and Jean Bhownagry. In the other film, *I Am 20*, on the one hand, 'I' is India, for the film is made to celebrate the twentieth year of Indian Independence. But that idea of India is split into a number of

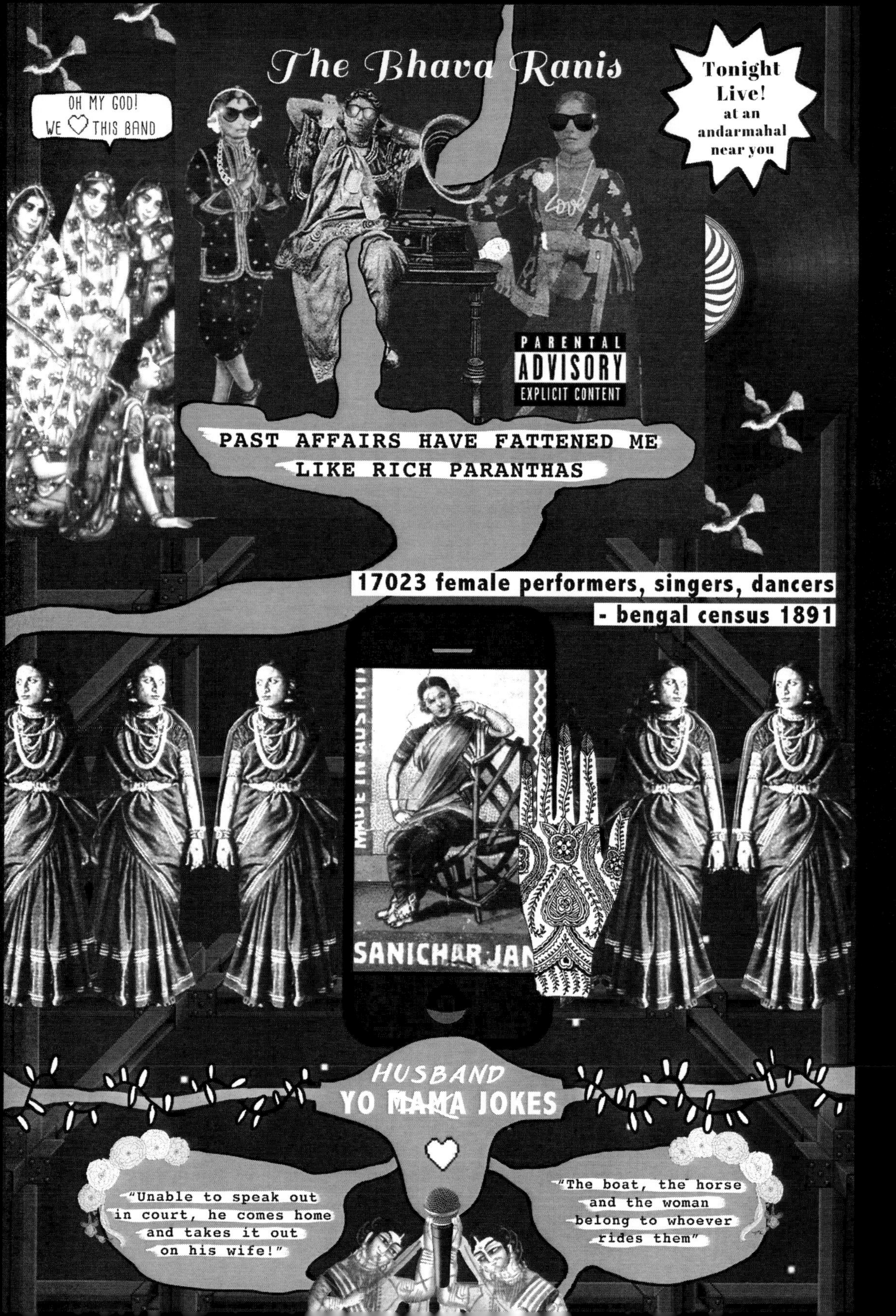
The Bhava Ranis
OH MY GOD! WE ♡ THIS BAND
Tonight Live! at an andarmahal near you
PARENTAL ADVISORY EXPLICIT CONTENT
PAST AFFAIRS HAVE FATTENED ME LIKE RICH PARANTHAS
17023 female performers, singers, dancers - bengal census 1891
MADE IN AUSTRIA
SANICHAR JAN
HUSBAND
YO MAMA JOKES
"Unable to speak out in court, he comes home and takes it out on his wife!"
"The boat, the horse and the woman belong to whoever rides them"

different kinds of people – farmers, air force pilots, Elvis-loving young men, flight attendants, Bengalis, Christians, Tamils, men, women. Also startling about the film is something people were not yet used to seeing in a documentary: the interview, which could be used as a result of the creation of synchronized sound equipment. As a result of all these innovations, the film creates a certain passion of feeling and viewpoint, but also an ambiguity about meaning and message.

III

However, this was a very brief period in documentary history. All of these filmmakers died young (which is a whole other narrative) and there was a heavy restriction of freedom in FD and very soon of freedom of all expression, when, in 1975, the Indian government declared a state of emergency. At this time, the production of serious documentaries shifted completely from FD to the independent space. The most visible idea of the documentary was realized in the political films of the 1970s and 1980s – most notably the films of Anand Patwardhan and Deepa Dhanraj.[16] These films were strongly influenced by the Latin American Third Cinema movement,[17] and, in fact, a lot of the films from then until the 1980s were made in the context of people's movements or left-of-centre movements. These movements had peaked between the late 1960s and 1975, when the optimistic dream of a newly independent nation had already gone sour and poverty, unemployment and tremendous inequity were being protested. The repression, censorship and political excesses of the Emergency which was declared in 1975 further strengthened these movements and the volume of related discussions. The dominant idea was that a people's cinema was needed – a complete rejection of the government; and although this also happened in the parallel fiction cinema of the time, it happened faster in documentary (because, perhaps, fiction films were also made with state funding, unlike documentaries). What began to emerge amongst the films made in the context of these discussions was a template, an idea of a 'correct' style of filmmaking, which would function as 'the voice of the people'.

To quote the filmmaker Deepa Dhanraj from an early 1990s interview:

> We saw films as a way of documenting and expressing a certain thinking. Why we chose films specifically as the medium as opposed to the theatre, we really were not clear about. We were unhappy with the films around us and we did feel the need to reach out and generate images to counter the negative portrayals in the media. India having such a strong audience tradition, films seemed to be a good medium to enable us to go into community and draw people together. That we were not going to screen these films to a neutral audience was very clear, so our audience was fixed. The whole

> process was an alliance with the people who helped us to make the film. So both in production and conception, the themes and concerns of these films originated with the activists of that area.[18]

This desire to be 'the voice of the people' created, in a sense, a new kind of *self-less* film. Usually, it meant that the film contained no commentary or a very bare commentary, and used instead interviews with affected communities or sometimes their leaders in order to transmit a clear message without ambiguities and confusion. The notion of the individual subjective filmmaker, or individual subject, was strongly rejected, and films now had to be about collective identities at all times - although these identities were not as amorphous as the 'Indian' identities of FD films. Rather, they were now marginalized voices and identities. There were several heated debates around this issue over the years during which this new form was endorsed, one which was keen to mask the idea of an individual speaking the film, and discouraged quite openly any experimentation or the introduction of filmmaker subjectivities as being, to put it crudely, a bourgeois indulgence or, in the Indian context, Brahminical (upper-caste) approaches.

To quote Deepa Dhanraj from the same interview again:

> In India, what has also happened is that we have got stuck with the form of socialist realism without the environment of revolution which bred this form in the first place... (as in say Chile, or the USSR. ... Many film forms created (in those contexts) have become radical genres which 'political' filmmakers have used and are still using in toto. Here in India, the prevailing ideological climate is reactionary and we seem to have got stuck with these forms without the specific historical circumstances that bred them in the first place. Today, by and large, these films only illustrate the individual film-maker's politics and don't move into the realm of political activity.[19]

One could restate Dhanraj's comments to say that there was a performance of liberalism that was being carried out through the act of making a certain documentary, and there was high anxiety in stepping away from this performance for fear of seeming unqualified to speak in this process of what the nation should be or how it should be, and perhaps of revealing and unmasking an identity of privilege. This absence of the 'I', however, allows for a fixed performance from the subject, the filmmaker and the audience, who also proceed along fixed lines of victimhood, fervour, anger or indignation. Therefore, for instance, the only way a filmmaker can prove he or she is 'secular' and so authorized to speak about this subject is by constantly speaking about communalism in his or her films. Similar paradoxes prevailed for feminism and issues of caste. In these sometimes radical, and sometimes supposedly radical films, too, there is no presence of the 'I' from the filmmaker's perspective – who is supposedly a revolutionary – nor from that of the subjects', the revolutionary oppressed who, in fact, express themselves as 'we'.

In the post-liberalization 1990s, with the falling away of many of these movements, documentary film practice underwent a huge transformation. In response to a very fragmented political context, and correspondingly a fragmented context of circulation, where the usual audiences for documentaries – those who identified with certain movement politics and organizations – were now dispersed, Indian documentary practice underwent an upheaval and a proliferating experimentation. This period resulted in diverse simultaneous practices. An overall acceptance of the subjective in documentary and the personal in filmmaking produced the presentational work of Mani Kaul, the personal essay films of Ruchir Joshi, and later, the political essay films of Amar Kanwar; the use of intimate biographies as history by Reena Mohan and Sameera Jain; films incorporating theatrical performance and the theatre of performance by Madhusree Dutta – to name just a few styles that emerged.[20]

It may be too much of a simplification to say that the earlier forms of filmmaking, which were impatient with the ideas of subjectivity and intimacy, and even of ornamentation, were more masculinist styles. While an overwhelming number of documentary practitioners and theorists have been men, women have certainly practised documentary in this way as well. But what is discernible is that, many of the shifting approaches to documenting reality did come from feminist theory and discussion: the re-examination of modes of power in conversation/ interview, the idea of oral histories, a comfort with personal viewpoints and approaches, all of which, while easily accepted in the practice of art itself, have always been a matter of unease in the world of documentary practice.[21] In fact, a number of schisms along these lines – how to define what is political or worth taking seriously in political activism – did take place within the world of organizational left politics through the 1980s and 1990s. During these decades, feminists broke away from Marxist groups, Dalit feminists challenged the feminist movement on its non-reflexivity vis-à-vis caste or religion, and sexuality movements challenged other movements on account of heteronormativity and prudery. These upheavals of discussion around the idea of political tone led to the many new approaches that began to emerge in Indian documentary practice.

While these approaches are diverse, they have collectively achieved a strong breakthrough: no longer do we make films in terms of a fixed reality; there is a recognition that often the subject performs an aspect of themselves for an aspect of you, the filmmaker at the time; there is also an incorporation of this element of mutual performativity into the form of the film and its claims to reality and truth. In these films, the first person is sometimes stated, and sometimes implicit. This ease has brought in its wake fresh anxieties. During the 2000s, practitioners have become more comfortable with the idea of documentary as creative endeavour, one where there can be formal excellence or experimentation along with political engagement – in fact, a somewhat opposite movement to the idea that roughness in form signals authenticity of politics, or discussions which privilege unedited material as having more revolutionary resonance. However, this development has not always been a perspective that those funding documentary have unequivocally shared.

Till today, in fact, a large amount of funding sources for the documentary, with very few exceptions, remain tied to a programmatic agenda. For a film that does not fall into an interpretation of that agenda, funding often has to be sought from outside India. Thus, a significant number of documentaries are now funded by European, British and, to a lesser extent, US broadcasters. Interestingly, there is a preference and encouragement here for the use of the first person in the narration of these films. The use of the 'I' happens here within a very different programmatic context. Foreign commissions often ask for a 'compelling personal story' following a single character and placing the filmmaker as an 'I' looking for a personal connect, an emotional story. The 'I' of this narrative is not a complicated one, but carries in fact with it an uncomplicated notion of intimacy and simplicity. Since these are 'international stories' not playing to an informed audience, it is felt that complicated narratives, and idiomatic styles of filmmaking, via the personality of the filmmaker, in which the film embodies the subjectivities of the filmmaker, would make the film impenetrable.

Here, the 'I' becomes a sort of eyewitness narrator who simplifies and leads the viewer through the labyrinth of a foreign reality to create a unitariness of narrative and narrator. It displaces the gaze onto a visible point – the fixed narrator – and thereby controls how it is deployed. So the first person becomes an uncomplicated and uninterrogated mask of the self; but also a disingenuous one. The idea that there is personal investment in making a film about anything – a famous female hijacker for a Palestinian immigrant, the exiled Queen of Iran for an exiled Iranian in France, the president of Pakistan for a progressive Pakistani woman, the domestic help for an urban Indian feminist, a little boy in a slum for a compassionately curious observational filmmaker – is one that allows us to elicit intimacy from the subject, for the audience, without necessarily granting it of ourselves, although there are always extraordinary exceptions. Somewhere, this smoothening 'I' confirms the political reliability of the narrator, affirms their *locus standi* to tell us a general story about their culture.

This shifting journey of the first-person pronoun through the history of Indian documentary in many ways tells the changing story of how documentary practitioners strive to be political beings – and to what extent they are able to negotiate the power equation between the subjects of a documentary and the filmmaker/narrator of that documentary. One cannot claim that one way of being political is superior to another, but we do understand that the act of making a non-fiction film carries implications for reality and responses to that reality, which are

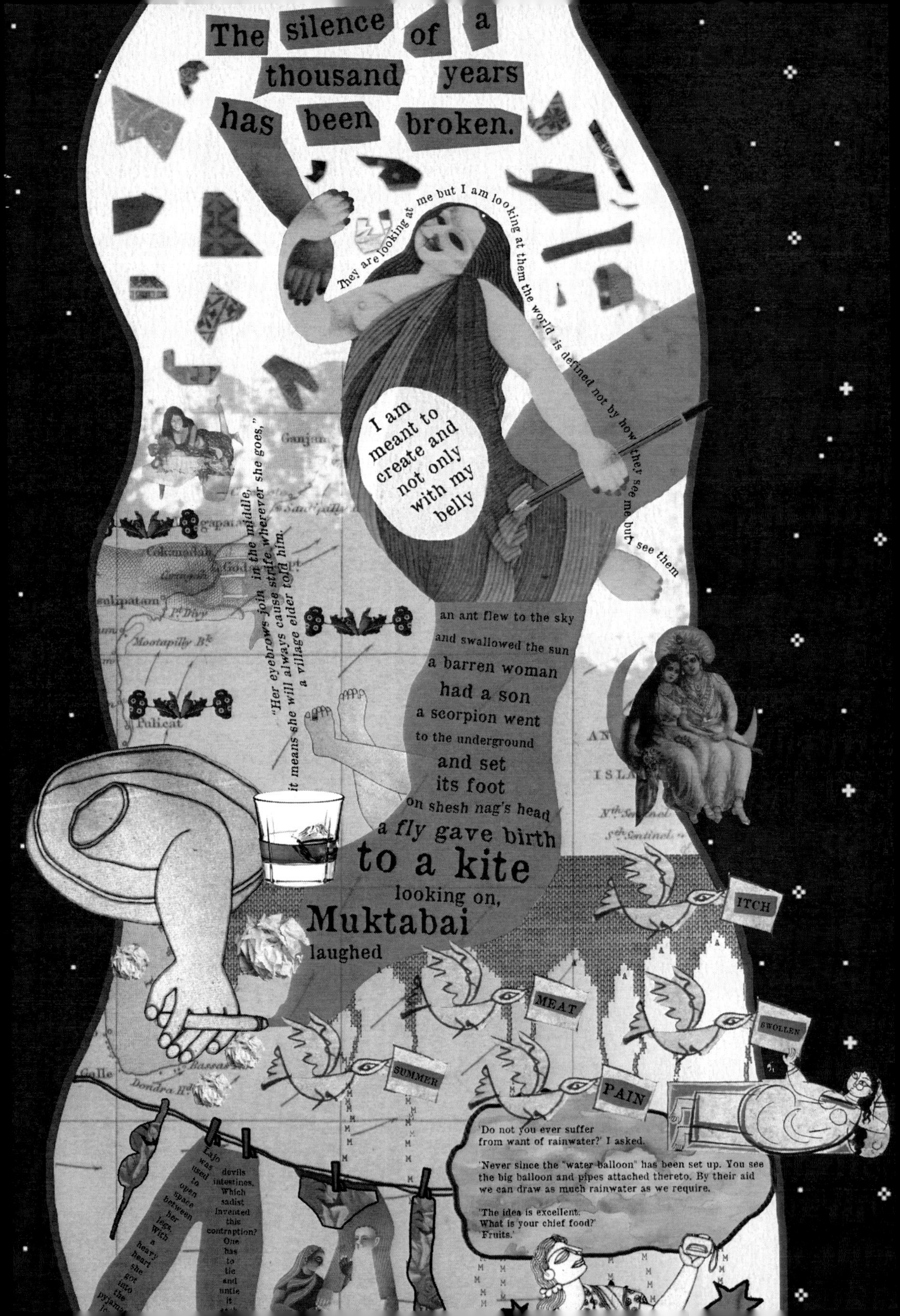

The silence of a thousand years has been broken.
They are looking at me but I am looking at them the world is defined not by how they see me but I see them
I am meant to create and not only with my belly
"Her eyebrows join in the middle, it means she will always cause strife wherever she goes," a village elder told him.
an ant flew to the sky
and swallowed the sun
a barren woman
had a son
a scorpion went
to the underground
and set
its foot
on shesh nag's head
a fly gave birth
to a kite
looking on,
Muktabai
laughed
ITCH
MEAT
SWOLLEN
SUMMER
PAIN
'Do not you ever suffer from want of rainwater?' I asked.
'Never since the "water balloon" has been set up. You see the big balloon and pipes attached thereto. By their aid we can draw as much rainwater as we require.
'The idea is excellent. What is your chief food?'
'Fruits.'
Lajo was used to open space between her legs. With a heavy heart she got into the pyjama
devils intestines. Which sadist invented this contraption? One has to lie and untie it

very different from fictional and abstract forms. It is not, in that sense, a simple act; it is an engagement with the idea of truth and falsehood, good and bad, right and wrong that hopes to influence the public conversation around something.

For me, personally and politically, as a filmmaker and a citizen living in times where we cannot take any political ideas and identities for granted, these engagements and negotiations have largely centred around detailing the kind of 'I' who narrates the films I make. My strategy (and I reiterate that I don't consider it superior to other strategies, just preferable for me. Eventually, the political and creative strategies employed by any filmmaker are also particular to her biographical and aesthetic preferences besides her political intentions) is to create a highly particular narrator, a fictional persona who is unique and not an Everywoman, and who necessarily is a bit unreliable through this peculiarity of being a persona with clear characteristics, prejudices and idiosyncratic expressions. One of the reasons I feel strongly about this element is because, while I'm not against seductive pleasures in a film for the audience to enjoy itself – in fact, I feel this enjoyment can be a trustworthy guide, something that encourages the viewer to trust their instinct and judgement rather than that of the narrator; put them in the mood, so to say – I am suspicious of a seductive ease of understanding, the automatic assumptions of the political categories and values that some themes or issues might carry for audiences.

The idea of a created person, who moreover is a capricious character, strong in personality, overtly performative and hence a bit unreliable, creates, I believe, two dynamics. First, it does not compel the subjects in the film to an obvious personal intimacy with the filmmaker, although there may well be a performative or an intellectual intimacy, and even a public intimacy as in conversation, which is replete with hesitation and doubt rather than assertion. Second, it also demands from those in the audience an intimacy of engagement, with itself but not necessarily with others, because the audience has to rely a bit more on its own sense while watching the film. This demand also arises from the fact that the narrator is obviously an unreliable, prejudiced or half-informed character who is not grounding the viewer, either through a personal claim of having witnessed, or through making the audience a witness through seemingly close observation, but rather leaving the viewer to arrive at some conclusions on their own. By confusing and complicating the 'I' in the films, I think I reflect some of Sastry's discomfort with form turning into a political orthodoxy and thereby proving its value, rather than through the immediate experience and understandings it hopes to provide or catalyze.

At a more specific aesthetic level, I have chosen a voice or persona which emphasizes popular culture, humour and the quality of the trickster as, at first, an intuitive and later, a conscious political response to what I consider a pompous tendency in talking about politics, a paternalistic declamatoriness that is constantly employed to denote seriousness – and thereby dominate the political discourse, designing a disguised elitism. In laughing at this tone that takes itself so seriously, I want to be able to democratize, for want of a better word, how audiences relate to the idea of politics and, in fact, by offering no superior standpoint of experience or knowledge, but only the experience of having watched one person's film, with its attendant flaws and flourishes, perhaps compel them into political and philosophical reflection. At the risk of sounding paternalistic (or maternalistic), I would say this sort of 'I' presents the intimacy of uncertainty and gives the audience a certain self-confidence with which to engage in the political. I believe these forms of the personal and the popular tap into existing vernacular audience traditions – for instance, of identifying with the trickster, while being aware and alert that she might, at any time, turn her laughing gaze upon you and involve the audience in a project of reformulating the terms of the political discussion – but also that they reformulate the idea of the documentarian as an artist, not an activist above art (and, by implication, artifice).

Through these aspects of my practice, I hope to erase earlier divisions – not only those that are about where we must find politics and how it should be presented and, by implication, who is qualified to speak of the political and the way they must speak of it, but also divisions that dictate how documentaries are watched as cultural products. In this revisionism, I dare say that along with many of the filmmakers working through the 1990s and in the contemporary moment, I am also engaged in constructing or reconstructing more indigenous theories of documentary practice and language which might eventually contribute to a more self-sustaining and enlivened (and, from the filmmaker's point of view, enlightened) funding, creating, viewing and exhibition context than has existed for some time. These formal responses are an acknowledgement of the reality that there are many contending voices in political ideology, and that there is no unquestionable progressive position to be taken. These practices also intentionally cast doubt on the assumed superiority and value-free narrative tendency of an 'international' language of documentary, which is essentially a European or an Anglocentric language of documentary.

The watching of a film is eventually a ritual, as so much of it is so publicly experienced. The desire to make films with a fragmented or elusive first person narrator in some ways arises from the desire to interfere with a monotony that sets into a ritual, and to reinvigorate it in the process. But also, in an age where public viewing is increasingly replaced by individual private viewings on computers or TV screens, a heightened awareness in negotiations with the 'I' who narrates a film holds the possibilities for a more personal, reflective ritual of watching reality and making sense of it.

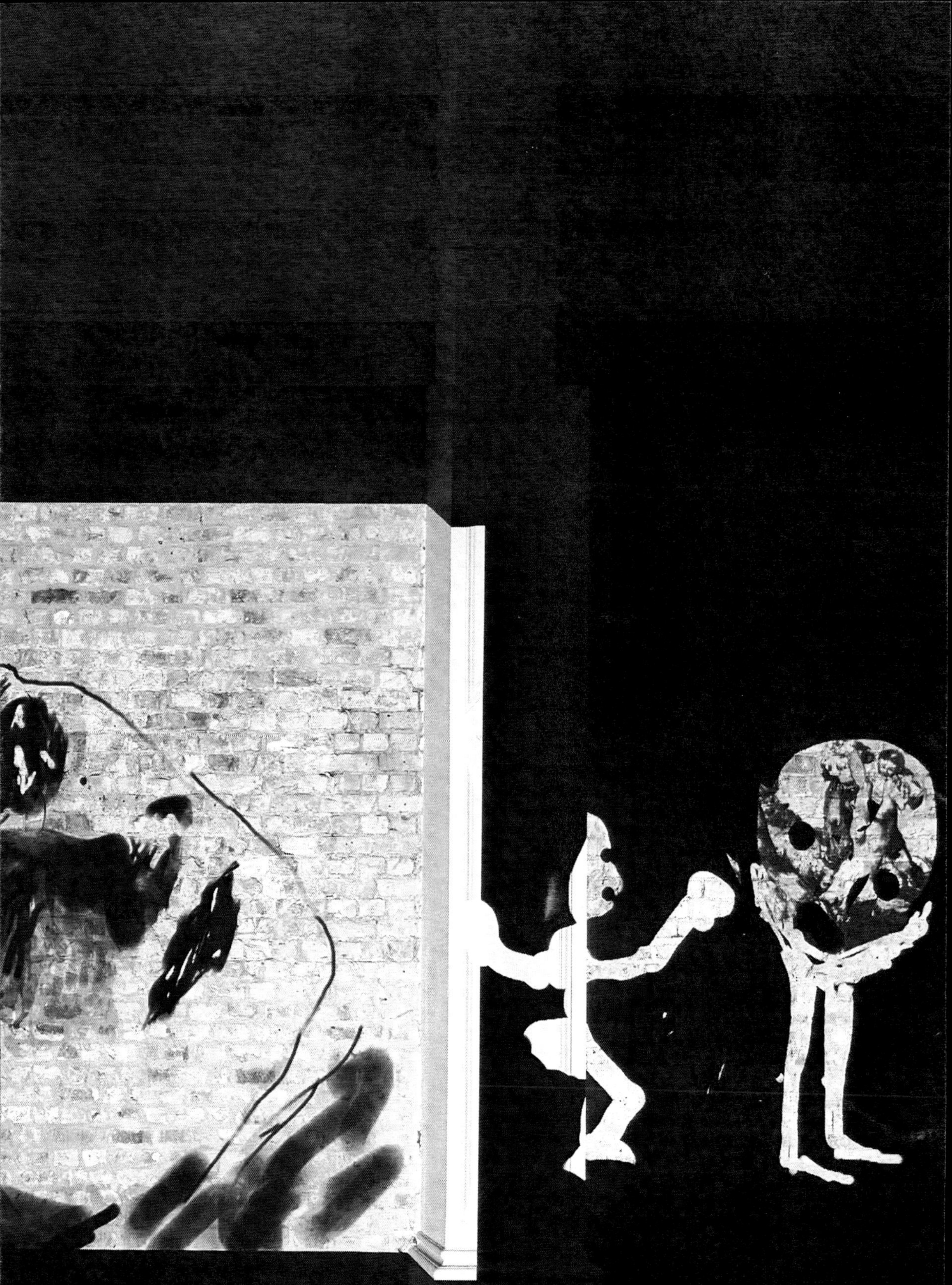

Nalini Malani's paintings of the 1980s, followed by her 1990s turn to video art, and thence to large installations and performance art projects, has been a well-charted trajectory. In 2014, when Malani showed, for the first time, her early experiments in 8 and 16 mm celluloid reversal stock that she had made as far back as 1969 at the Vision Exchange Workshop, this linear trajectory – from painting to film via installation – was disrupted, and a new way perhaps opened of approaching the genealogy of the moving image. Malani's experimental short, *Dream Houses*, was made first by building a maquette of black cartons, then shot with still images using different lighting, in turn projected using varied filters, and repeatedly exposed on an 8 mm camera. Her recent work in theatre, stop-motion animation and iPad animations, reveals a distinct and perhaps unique history of the filmed moving image.

This text was written for the catalogue of the exhibition, *Can You Hear Me?*, Goethe Institut/Max Mueller Bhavan, Mumbai, in 2019. Reprinted with the permission of the artist.

Keywords

8 mm/Super 8 mm, Celluloid, New Media Art, Reversal Stock, Video, Vision Exchange Workshop: See Keywords (pp. 326–44).

Images

pp. 186, 196–97: Nalini Malani, *Can You Hear Me?*, 2020, 9-channel animation chamber with 88 animations, sound. Courtesy Nalini Malani and Whitechapel Gallery. Photographer: Luke Walker.

Thought Bubbles

The exhibition title, *Can You Hear Me?*, is about not being heard. In the list of titles of the recently made animations, called *Notebooks,* this title has two variations. The words may be similar but, in fact, they address two different types of concerns. *Can You Hear Me?*, with a question mark, is the scream of a minor girl who is being violently raped but nobody hears her cry. *Can You Hear Me*, without the question mark, is a strident command, and has to do with exerting 'power'.

In this exhibition, I have juxtaposed a series of more than fifty iPad animations, made between 2018 and 2019, with the very first animation, *Dream Houses* I, made in 1969 on 8 mm film. A juxtaposition that is similar to the double-projection film installation *Utopia*, 1976, in which I placed *Dream Houses II* next to my 16 mm black and white film of a disillusioned young woman as protagonist.

In both juxtapositions, in *Utopia* and in this exhibition, *Can You Hear Me?*, the leitmotif is a question: What has the idea of Utopia given us? This in turn raises others: How did we start out and what are we heading towards now? With the death of Modernism and the progressive socialist state, what is our excuse for the present state of affairs and the future? It reminds me of the poem *Nothing Twice* by Wislawa Szymborska:

> *Nothing can ever happen twice.*
> *In consequence, the sorry fact is*
> *that we arrive here improvised*
> *and leave without the chance to practice.*[1]

We come improvised. There is no time to rehearse life, and nothing can be redone.

In a span of 50 years, I have made three types of animations. In the first one, *Dream Houses*, 1969, began with a physical object in different light configurations shot on 8 mm reverse stock. In the period between 1996 and 2017, the animations were of my paintings /erasures sessions, shot with a photo camera, the stills were then edited on to video. The most recent ones, called *Notebooks*, are made digitally on an iPad.[2]

The animations that I have made since 1996 are like 'Thought Bubbles' in their character and function. When I see or read something that captures my imagination, I have a need to react with a drawing or drawings in motion. Not exactly in its mimetic form but more as a 'Memory Emotion'. I feel like a woman with thoughts and fantasies shooting from the head. Each of them can have different ideas and may not feel like it is from the same person. Each of these voices in my head needs therefore a different penmanship.

These iPad animations as a set of works have a sense of the abject. For this I have developed a language that is funny, sad, modest, energetic, hysterical and acute. But within it also appears the satirical, comic and the absurd. How else to make sense of life?

Stop Motion Animations, 1969

In the entrance passage of the newly opened VIEW (Vision Exchange Workshop) in May 1969, Nuruddin, Akbar Padamsee's brother, had made and placed a series of boards showing a grid of squares with about twenty scales of grey.[3] It triggered my mind to use such a grey scale as the basis of my first animation. I wanted to try to transform the black-and-white scale into colour, as I had read about in Johannes Itten's publication *The Art of Colour*, and also wanted to experiment with additive colour through light and movement.

My ideas in those days were first of all inspired by my architect friends, from whom I learned about and discussed the ideological possibilities of modern architecture, of the Bauhaus for example, in the work of Walter Gropius and Mies van der Rohe, and that of Frank Lloyd Wright and Buckminster Fuller. As I had studied Graphic Design and Typography, I frequently did the lettering for their maquettes. These represented a visionary world, which I wanted to visualize in the form of an animation film. Around this time, architect Charles Correa, a close friend of Padamsee's, came almost weekly to VIEW to talk about his ideas on social architecture.[4] That's when I met the legendary Buckminster Fuller.

For *Dream Houses*, I built a maquette from black cartons, which was available at the stationery shops outside the J.J. School of Art. This maquette I shot with a Mamiyaflex camera on 6 x 6 cm slides, which came in rolls of 12. For each slide, I changed the angle of the light source. These slides were projected on the wall, and recorded with an 8 mm film camera, on reverse stock. In front of the camera, per section, I placed different additive primary colour filters. After I shot with green, for instance, the film was rolled back, and for the second time it was shot with red. This superimposition gave the colour yellow in certain parts of the grey scale on the film. It was a painstaking process that although I had calculated and proofed in advance, much was also happening by chance. The registration was essential and that is the reason why there came about two variations of *Dream Houses*, with the first one a few frames off.

The film was developed at the Kodak Laboratory in Worli, which took about ten days. After this, I started the process of editing on the Moviola at VIEW. *Dream Houses* was made all by myself, without assistance. On the part of the senior artists at VIEW, there was no interest in my work or in the final result. If there was anybody I discussed it with, it was Nandan Kudhyadi,[5] who was then a student at the art school in Baroda, and who after VIEW went to the Film and Television Institute of India (FTII) in Pune. As I had no money to make a negative for screening copies, *Dream Houses* remained in its tin box in my different studios until 2011, when it was discovered by my partner Johan Pijnappel[6]. As an art historian, he understood the importance of this early work, and organized to have it professionally cleaned and digitally scanned in Amsterdam.

In the brief period since its rediscovery, *Dream Houses* has been recognized as an important icon in the canon of Indian Modernism when it was shown in my retrospective, *You Can't Keep Acid in a Paper Bag* at the Kiran Nadar Museum of Art in New Delhi in 2014. Soon after that, the work found place in international museum collections, and was included in major exhibitions such as *From the Collection: 1960 - 1969*, Museum of Modern Art, New York (2016), *The Collection - Stedelijk Base*, Stedelijk Museum, Amsterdam (2017), *The Rebellion of the Dead*, Centre Pompidou, Paris (2017), *Awakenings: Art in Society in Asia 1960s - 1990s*, National Museum of Modern Art, Tokyo (2018), and *Mud Muses*, Moderna Museet, Stockholm (2019).

Erasure Animations, 1996–2017

Although not featured in this exhibition, I would like to say a few words on the second form of animations made in the period between 1996 and 2017, as this gives a better overview on how I work with animations, and for what purpose. The first one from this period was *Memory: Record / Erase* made in 1996.[7] This work was part of the theatre play *The Job* for which I collaborated with theatre director Anuradha Kapur.[8] It was my second theatre production with the Max Mueller Bhavan in Bombay - the first one was *Medeamaterial* in 1993 for which I collaborated with performer Alaknanda Samarth.[9] In the 1960s, when I had a studio at the Bhulabhai Desai Memorial Institute, I had helped theatre director Satyadev Dubey with backstage work,[10] but it was only in 1992 that I actively got into theatre through Alaknanda.

When she came into my wall drawing/ erasure installation *City of Desires* at Gallery Chemould in 1992,[11] she immediately said, 'This calls for a performance'. It was a time when due to the rise of orthodoxy and right-wing politics that had begun in the late eighties, I felt that if I wanted to be heard as an artist, I had to break out of the painting frame, or, in the case of theatre, had to go beyond the stage.

Therefore, *Medeamaterial* was performed without a stage, where the public followed the protagonist from room to room in the Stuttgart Halls of the Max Mueller Bhavan.[12] This in contrast to *The Job* which was developed for the Experimental Theatre (part of the National Centre for Performing Arts) on a kind of proscenium arch, to be able to address a larger public.[13] However, I did not want to let go of the idea of direct confrontation with the public, and added a series of installations around the stage, which were separated by a wall of carton boxes. We wanted the atmosphere of a warehouse. Half an hour before the start of the play, the visitors were invited to walk around and interact with these installations following the performer, Ritu Talwar. In two of the six installations animated elements appeared: these included a zoetrope, and the animation *Memory: Record/Erase.* I wanted to extend certain aspects onto the thought processes of the protagonist. These animated thoughts were like 'Thought Bubbles,' which work for me as a 'Memory Membrane'. The idea of animating thoughts came to me while making the wall drawing, *City of Desires*, at Gallery Chemould. When I wiped parts of the charcoal drawings, it occurred to me that I could make this into animations.

Memory: Record/Erase was made in one night at Chemould with a full setup, including a camera person and light assistants. It was to be painted on paper. To give the recorded image more brightness, Alok Upadhyay, the cameraman came up with the idea of pasting the paper on the glass entrance door, and to use a backlight. It was one long session from 8 pm until 8 am. I worked without a storyboard, where one drawing followed by traces of erasure led to the next idea. For this, I had to be totally concentrated, especially when there were so many people around me. And, with the wet paint dripping, there was no time for pause. The level of concentration and focus was like that of a singer rehearsing a *raga* - a total immersion in a stream of thought. This same kind of painting/erasure process, as a 'one-time performance', has been used for all my animations in the period of 1996 to 2017.

The title of this first type of erasure animation, *Memory: Record/Erase*, refers not only to how it was made but to the type of video technology used as well, and on a political level how our memory is manipulated by politicians. It was shown for the first time at the Second Asia-Pacific Triennale of Contemporary Art, at the Queensland Art Gallery in Brisbane in 1996. For my solo exhibition, *The Job* at the Max Muller Bhavan in 1997, I used the animation as part of a new video sculpture, also called *The Job*, in which a monitor stands for the head of the female protagonist lying on a hospital bed. On that occasion, my first monograph *Nalini Malani: Medeaprojekt*, was published, in which the film historian Ashish Rajadhyaksha wrote the first article on my moving-image art.[14] After that exhibition, *Memory: Record Erase*, was shown at the Mumbai Film Festival in 1998. Initially the work was rejected by a jury member, the well-known animation specialist Ram Mohan,[15] the same professional animator with whom Akbar Padamsee had worked to make his film *Syzygy* in 1969 at VIEW.[16] In Mohan's opinion, my work was not an animation as the movement jerked too much. It was eventually accepted because another jury member, the film scholar and historian Amrit Gangar made a case for the originality of the work.[17]

The possibility of creating these erasure animations, and using them in various formats, opened up a whole new field. Soon after, the World Wide Video Festival in collaboration with the Prince Claus Fund gave me the opportunity to make the immersive video installation *Remembering Toba Tek Singh* as a response to the nuclear experiments by India in 1998.[18] I did not call this a video installation but a *videoplay* as it was actually my intention to continue making theatre plays. However, it was clear to me that the costs of traveling and availability of actors would limit me too much, so I turned the whole theatre play, actors and backdrops included, into video. The work consisted of four projections and 12 monitors placed on the floor in tin trunks. The main images on the walls were of two female protagonists, one Indian and one Pakistani, trying to fold a sari across the room. In the main projections, appears the documentary footage with the explosion of the nuclear bombing of Hiroshima and Nagasaki. On this footage is superimposed an animation of monsters.

This collaging of my erasure animations within video, and later in video/shadow plays, became a way of working wherein I could insert personal expressions within the images, such as in *Gamepieces* (2003), *Unity in Diversity* (2004), *Mother India: Transactions in the Construction of Pain* (2005), *Remembering Mad Meg* (2007) and *In Search of Vanished Blood* (2012).[19] I wanted certain motifs to come back in these works, and with animation I had full control. With animated drawings and paintings, my fantasy world could take over. In *Mother India* for instance, I collaged part of the animation *Stains* in the belly of the cow.[20]

In *Remembering Mad Meg*, the videos are only animations. This work grew from a two-channel projection, when it was first presented at my solo show at the Irish Museum of Modern Art in 2007, to a four-channel projection in the retrospective at the Centre Pompidou in 2017. The world of Pieter Breughel the Elder, from which this is inspired, together with that of Jeroen Bosch, gave me a tremendous range from which to create nightmarish fantasies in the form of animated metamorphoses. What interests me is the metamorphosing as I work along, as if my mind is out there on the paper or the wall. My concentration is on that stain or mark and what can come out of it. It is a bit like automatic writing as in Henri Michaux's work.

As a four-channel video/shadow play, *Remembering Mad Meg*, brings the visitor inside a chamber; a curious all-encompassing overwhelming array of sight and sound.

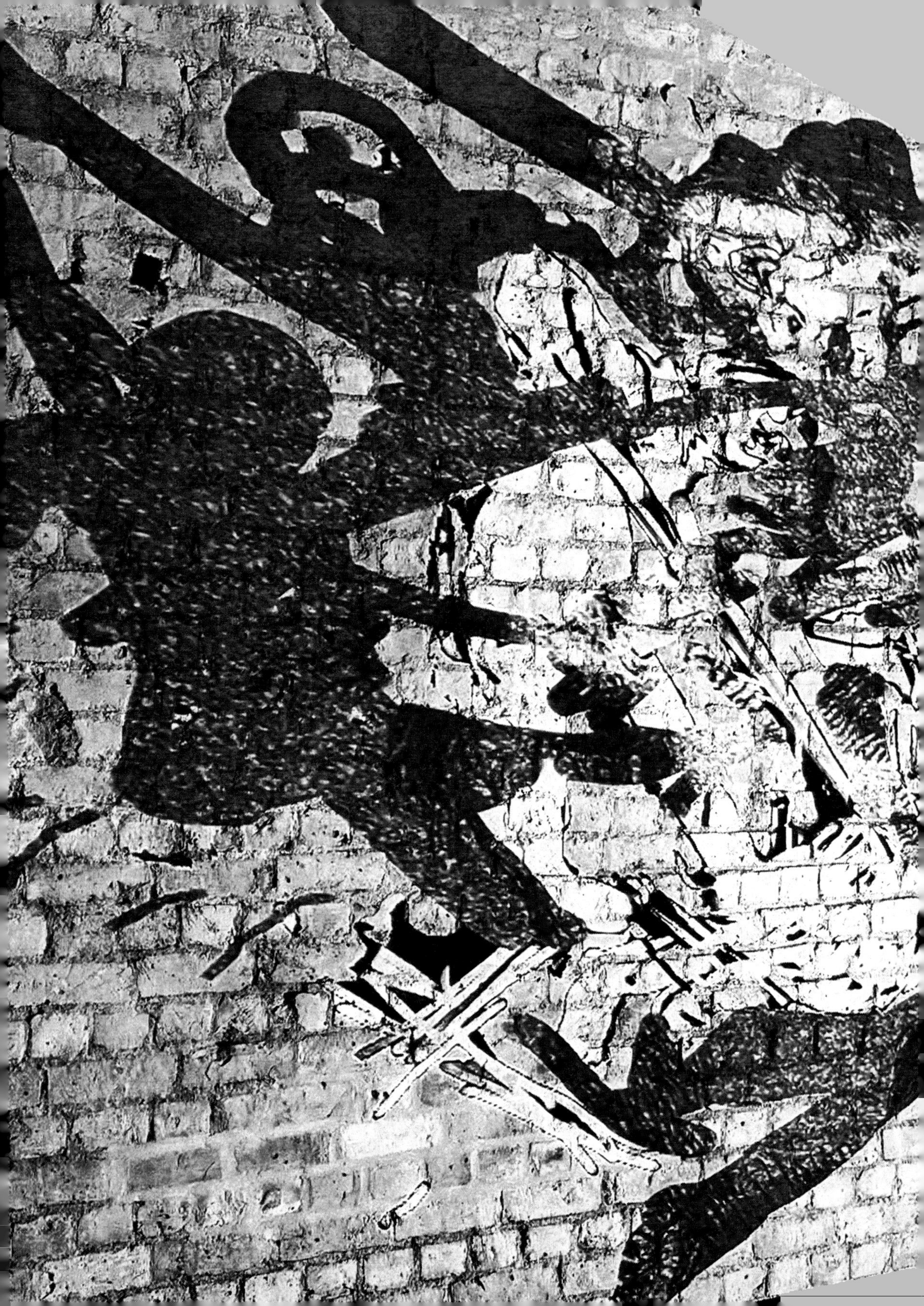

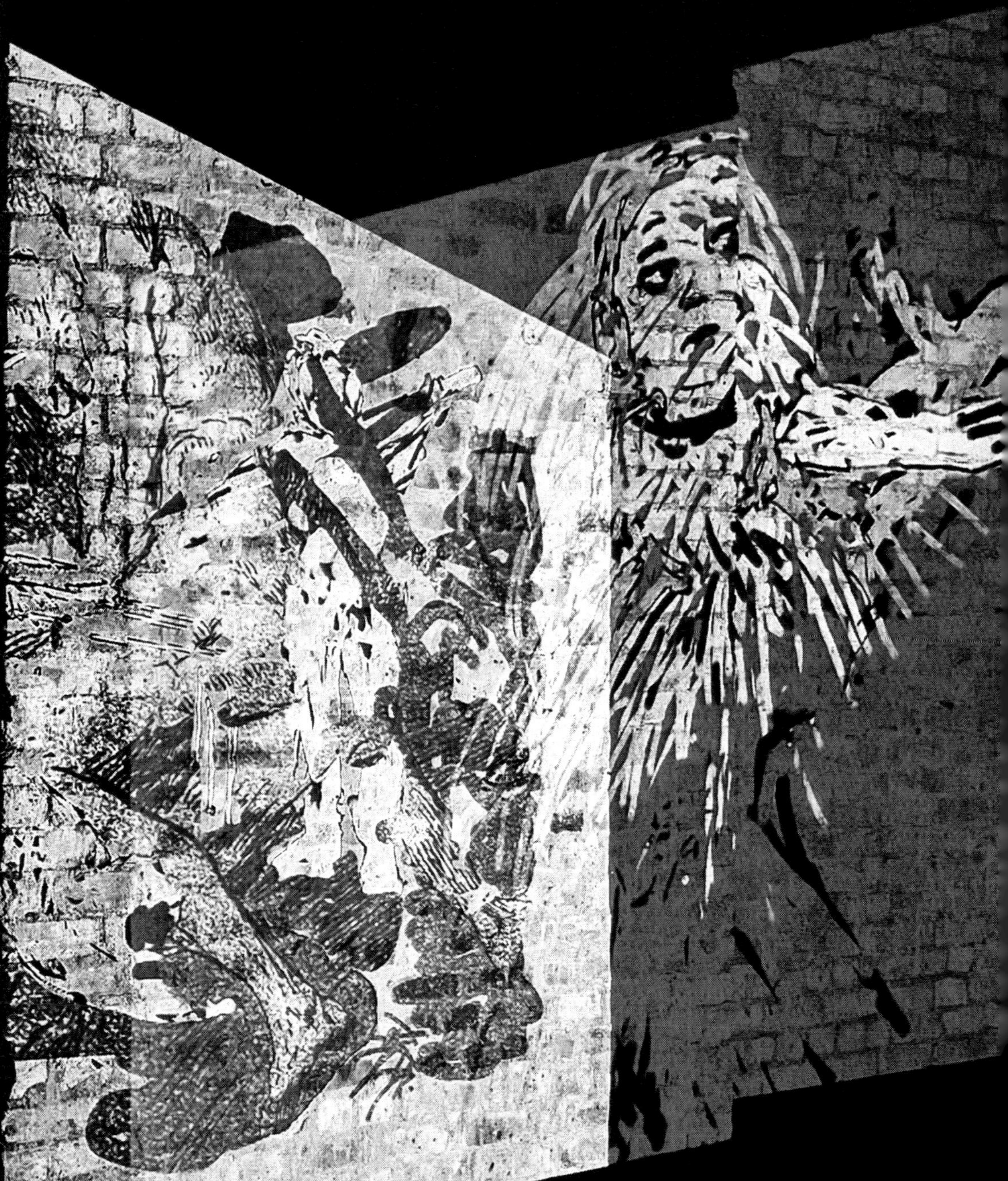

After a while, one notices the different constantly changing layers, where the image in a shadow is of a different timbre as the one of the painted image. Superimposed, these animations and shadows evoke many thoughts that fall in different places, depending on what you are looking at. As such these video/shadow plays recreate the complexity of thought the way time works at any given moment. It is the simultaneous nature of what a human mind can do in the unconscious. It is like when you sleep and have no control on what you dream, on the nightmare or other absurdities.

iPad animations, 2017–19

In 2017, I was constantly in the middle of work for retrospective exhibitions at Centre Pompidou and Castello di Rivoli. It was difficult to plan long sessions of painting so I decided to focus on iPad animations, a medium that I taught myself in 2015, including the sound. As there is this deep inner urge to draw every day, and I am obsessed with the moving image, I decided to make 'moving drawings'. For this, I found an animation app which provided me with several tools. I threw out the Apple Pencil, and started to draw with my index finger. There is a sensitivity of fingertip on plate that is so direct and has its own inner workings. This is totally different from using a pencil. There is something more erotic, something very raw and direct about the process of drawing, rubbing, scratching and erasing, to do with messing around in one's mind, which then comes out at the tip of one's finger.

The many issues that I think of and want to talk about in these *Notebooks* animations come from a wide range of stimuli. This could be daily politics, other people's writings, or something mundane I might have just experienced. There is the daily inner urge to examine them through my drawings, to question them, to show a different angle, to laugh about or to protest. Why does Modernism form such a threat in these days of growing orthodoxy? Why limit the freedom of the other? How can the alpha male tap into his female side of thought? Is there a way to understand the contradictory language that politicians use?

In my reaction to what has triggered or irritated my mind I often start out with a quote from a wide range of writers, whose texts I have been reading for decades such as, Hannah Arendt, James Baldwin, Samuel Beckett, Bertolt Brecht, René Crevel, Veena Das, Faiz Ahmad Faiz, Milan Kundera, Saadat Hasan Manto, Heiner Müller, George Orwell, Toni Morrison, and Wislawa Szymborska. It is a kind of graffiti that I get from these writers. A similar kind of graffiti comes from images of artists like Goya or Grosz, Japanese prints of the floating world, or Kalighat paintings,[21] and even from my own earlier works. From there on, the making of the animation flows as if by itself and goes in any direction with different levels of transparency and opacity. I have no control over the style, nor do I work towards 'a' style, as style is a market-driven idea. It is the subject that decides or governs the form.

In a period of two years, more than seventy animations were made: some are longer than the 1-minute Instagram limit, and some have never been shown online. If I would categorize this weekly growing collection of iPad animations, there would be the socio-political, the more 'abstract' ones, the feminine/masculine, the satirical and the personal ones.

The socio-political ones are an expression of frustration and anger with the decisions that are made by the powers that are operating in this world. I feel we now live in very confusing times compared to my youth. The absurd decisions made by the powers around us may lead to the most dangerous and horrific ends. The democratic model has changed from a vehicle of hope into one of helplessness. For example, the animation *Blind Man's Bluff*, has to do with powerful heads of state and the regressive results of their actions. Similarly, in *Megalomania* I and II, the head of a state breaks the world into smithereens. In *Dystopia*, we are in the land of the absurd. With *Ubu Roi*, where I satirize power, greed and the insensitive practices of the complacent, haute bourgeoisie abuse their success.[22]

The more 'abstract' animations have to do with my own quirky thoughts and fantasies. In *Hysterical Bird*, I quote an image from Goya's *Los Caprichos* - something that happened over hundred years ago and whose absurdity resonates even today. The hysterical bird also evokes Walter Benjamin's book *Thesis on the Philosophy of History*, in which he speaks of Klee's *Angelus Novus*. In my animation, I chose to have a bird that is rendered helpless – she flaps her wings unable to fly. The bird would like to sing 'to awaken the dead and make whole what has been smashed'.[23] Reading Hannah Arendt's statement, 'The earth is the very quintessence of the human condition', struck me.[24] When you have the earth as a vast territory and the heart is the microcosm, what the earth yields and what the heart makes of it, might equal art? Hence the animation title *Heart - Earth - Art*. *Nothing Twice* is inspired by the poem of the same title by Wislawa Szymborska in which she tells us: 'In consequence, the sorry fact is that we arrive here improvised and leave without the chance to practice'.[25]

In the animations dealing with feminine/masculine ideologies, there is one where these very words became the title itself. I believe femininity and masculinity reside in both men and women. It depends what part of the person is activated in a given moment. The problem is that the feminine part is mostly denigrated. Veena Das's quote reflected exactly what I have been talking about for years. She writes, 'There are feminine regions of the self that reside in both men and women. . . .'[26] The portraits in this animation are built up in a barcode line configuration. But can this advanced reading program identify the regions of the feminine or the masculine? *My Secret Flower* is about a young girl's awakening sexuality and her freedom to feel within the flower. In *Portrait of a Girl I* and *II*, the childhood of a girl collapses into the life of a young woman, such that the past is not erased but constantly present. Recalling girlhood feels pleasurable and joyous.

In the face of extreme domination by the state there is no way out of the darkness but to find a language in satire even as one squirms around trying to find ways to look for the light. In *Double Speak I*, a little puppet figure is trying to run away from an aggressive lecturing male head. It is seen with a quote from a poem by René Crevel, a communist and a surrealist, that dwells on the freedom to dream and fantasize. In *Double Speak II*, a large figure is the prosecutor. His body consists of two legs with a huge head that is completely filled with violence. The head is an image quote from *Disasters of War* by Goya. From Samuel Beckett's play *Endgame* I have two players Hamm and Clove, who want to end their lives but they cannot. They are trapped in the physical room while simultaneously being trapped in their self-conscious cages.

Relatively few animations from the *Notebooks* are personal as I feel it is difficult to put this out there in the public. *Thoughts* starts with the text 'People's voices in my head' after which a cluster of image quotes appear turning into each other. Are these bad thoughts, good thoughts, complicated thoughts? *She is Gone my Mighty Bird* is about missing my mother - who passed away this year at the age of 97 - the beautiful bird under whose wing I lived for 72 years.

Can You Hear Me?

Fifty years have gone by. *Dream Houses* came alive after remaining in the dark for forty-five years. This animation reminds us of glowing expectations, coming from a shared ideology for all, into a better - nay - into a humane social future. How intense is the contrast with the installation *Notebooks* fifty years later, where a multitude of 'Thought Bubbles' have a sense of the abject. Within these phantasmagoric illusions, there is place for the satirical, the comic and the absurd. With these animations, I am still exploring what the Dada art movement started - the idea of the absurd. The most mundane circumstances can lead to thoughts which go everywhere, in a million directions. A whole range of feeling can spring up at any moment. The absurdity of life, how little value it has, during which people can be taken away from you anytime. It feels as if life has no validity or precious meaning. Similarly, nature and ecology are treated with disdain and one feels helpless with the catastrophes around. Has the world gone crazy? If Nature dies, we die.

Who will listen?

Hello. Can you hear me?

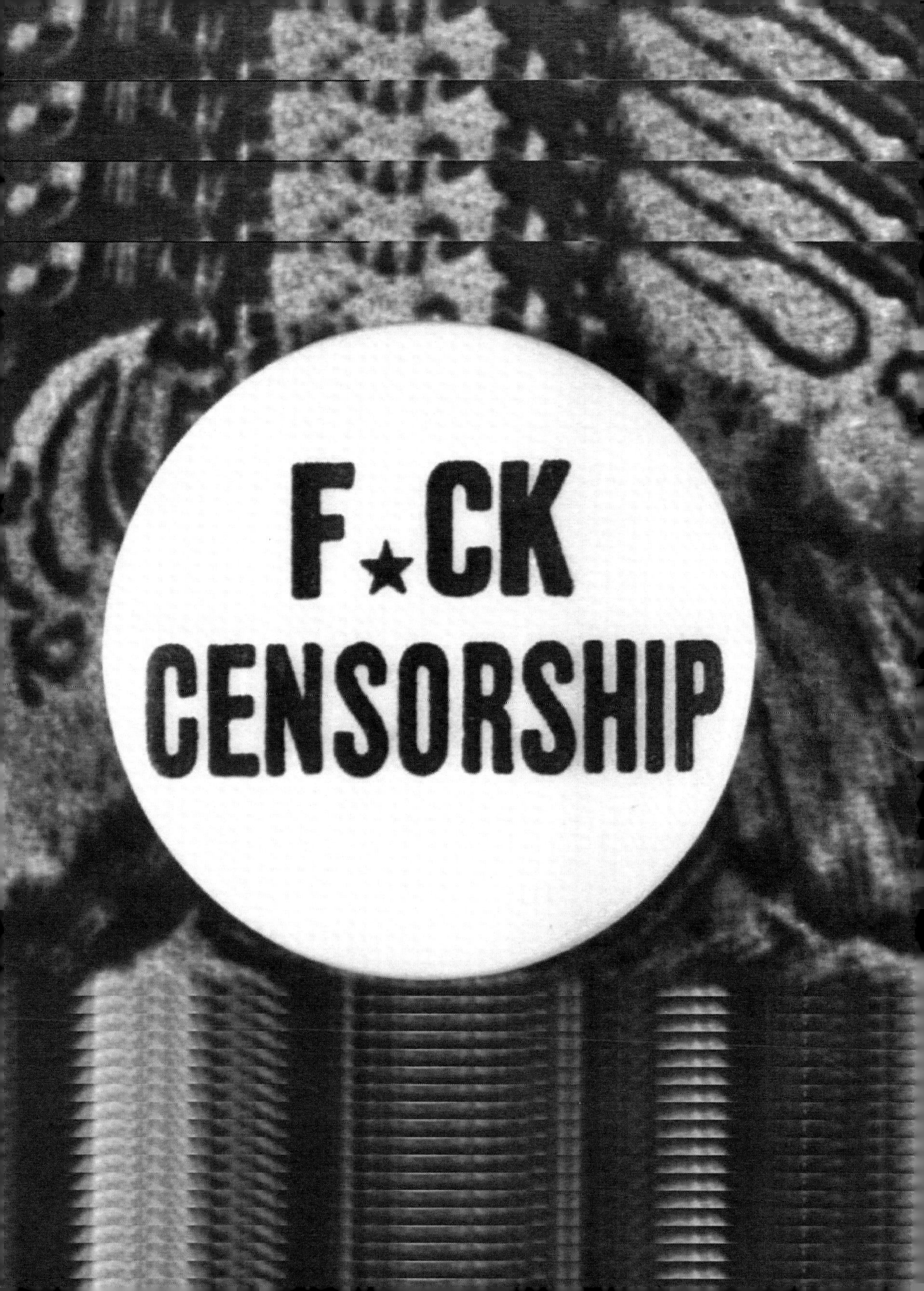
F★CK
CENSORSHIP

An open letter to the Information and Broadcasting Ministry, Government of India, against proposed amendments to the 1952 Cinematograph Act was signed by 1,400 influential film directors, actors, producers and academics in July 2021. The amendments, they believed, would severely endanger freedom of expression and democratic dissent. The bill sought to empower the central government to revoke a certificate previously granted to a film, if found to violate Section 5B(1) of the Cinematograph Act, 1952. That is, if a film is found to be 'against the interests of [the sovereignty and integrity of India] the security of the state, friendly relations with foreign States, public order, decency or morality, or involves defamation or contempt of court or is likely to incite the commission of any offence.' The state's move trampled underfoot the long battle against censorship led by filmmakers.

Two judgements are included here as an insert. The first is a 1970 Supreme Court order issued by a bench headed by Justice Hidayatullah, in response to a petition by director, writer and journalist, Khwaja Ahmed Abbas, demanding the complete removal of film censorship. The second is a 2004 Bombay High Court judgement issued by Justice Hemant Gokhale and Justice Ranjana Desai, in Anand Patwardhan's petition against the Central Board of Film Certification (CBFC), which had superseded orders issued by the Film Censorship Appellate Tribunal (FCAT), in the cuts demanded of Patwardhan's documentary, *War and Peace* (2003). The film, made in the wake of the nuclear tests carried out by India and Pakistan in 1998, was pro-peace and anti-violence, said Patwardhan, refusing to accept even a single cut. Excerpts from the judgments included here demonstrate that the keen deliberations around film aesthetics and public sensibility generate an alternative theory of the language of cinema. 'The delicate task of deciding what is artistic and what is obscene has to be performed by courts and in the last resort, by the Supreme Court and so, oral evidence of men of literature or others on the question of obscenity is not relevant', proclaimed Justice Hidayatullah.

Images

p. 201: Flash-frame from Pramod Pati's film *Explorer* (1968, 7 mins), produced by the Films Division.

pp. 206–07: A still from Chaitanya Tamhane's 2014 film, *Court*. The Kafkaesque trial of anti-caste activist and folk singer Narayan Kamble, accused of abetting the suicide of a dalit sewer cleaner, runs parallel to the absurdity of the lives of advocates in a Mumbai trial court. Image courtesy Chaitanya Tamhane.

Supreme Court of India 1970

K. A. Abbas vs The Union Of India & Anr on 24 September, 1970

Author: M Hidayatullah
Bench: Hidayatullah, M. (CJ), Shelat, J.M., Mitter, G.K., Vaidyialingam, C.A., Ray, A.N.

ACT: Constitution of India Article 19(1) (a) and (2)-Pre-censorship of films – If unconstitutional – Cinematograph Act,1952, s. 5-B-Provisions of-Directions under s. 5-B(2) – If vague and therefore unconstitutional.

The petitioner is a journalist, playwright and writer of short stories. He is also a producer and director of cinematograph films. He was a member of the Enquiry Committee on Film Censorship (1968) and is a member of the Children's Film Committee. He has produced and/or directed many films some of which have been well-received here and abroad and even won awards and prizes.

The petitioner produced in 1968 a documentary film in 2 reels (running time 16 minutes) called *A Tale of Four Cities*. In this film he purported to contrast the luxurious life of the rich in the four cities of Calcutta, Bombay, Madras and Delhi, with the squalor and poverty of the poor, particularly those whose hands and labour help to build beautiful cities, factories and other industrial complexes. The film is in black and white and is silent except for a song which the labourers sing while doing work and some background music and sounds for stage effect. The film, in motion sequences or still shots, shows contrasting scenes of palatial buildings, hotels and factories – evidence of the prosperity of a few, and shanties, huts and slums – evidence of poverty of the masses.

These scenes alternate and in between are other scenes showing sweating labourers working to build the former and those showing the squalid private life of these labourers.

Some shots mix people riding in lush motor cars with rickshaw and handcart pullers of Calcutta and Madras. In one scene a fat and prosperous customer is shown riding a rickshaw which a decrepit man pulls, sweating and panting hard. In a contrasting scene the same rickshaw puller is shown sitting in the rickshaw, pulled by his former customer. This scene is the epitomisation of the theme of the film and on view are the statutes of the leaders of Indian Freedom Movement looking impotently from their high pedestals in front of palatial buildings, on the poverty of the masses.

On the boulevards the rich drive past in limousines while the poor pull rickshaws or handcarts or stumble along. There is also a scanning shot of a very short duration, much blurred by the movement of the photographer's camera, in which the red-light district of Bombay is shown with the inmates of the brothels waiting at the doors or windows. Some of them wear abbreviated skirts showing bare legs up to the knees and sometimes a short way above them. This scene was perhaps shot from a moving car because the picture is unsteady on the screen and under-exposed. Sometimes the inmates, becoming aware of the photographer, quickly withdraw themselves.

The whole scene barely lasts a minute. Then we see one of the inmates shutting a window and afterwards we see the hands of a woman holding some currency notes and a male hand plucking away most of them leaving only a very few in the hands of the female. The two actors are not shown.

On July 3, 1969, the Central Government decided to give a 'U' certificate provided the following cuts were made in the film:

> Shorten the scene of woman in the red-light district, deleting specially the shot showing the closing of the window by the lady, the suggestive shots of bare knees and the passing of the currency notes. Dir. IC(iii)(b)(c); IV.

The mystery of the code numbers at the end was explained by a letter on July 23, 1969 to mean this:

> I. It is not desirable that a film shall be certified as suitable for public exhibition, either unrestricted or restricted to adults which 45 1 C(iii) (b) deals with the relations between the sexes in such a manner as to depict immoral traffic in women and soliciting, prostitution or procuration.
>
> IV. It is undesirable that a certificate for unrestricted public exhibition shall be granted in respect of a film depicting a story or containing incidents unsuitable for young persons.

The petitioner raised four points: (a) that pre-censorship itself cannot be tolerated under the freedom of speech and expression, (b) that even if it were a legitimate restraint on the freedom, it must be exercised on very definite principles which leave no room for arbitrary action, (c) that there, must be a reasonable time-limit fixed for the decision of the authorities censoring the film, and (d) that the appeal should lie to a court or to an independent tribunal and not the Central Government.

This is the first case in which the censorship of films in general and pre-censorship in particular have been challenged in this Court, and before we say anything about the arguments, it is necessary to set down a few facts relating to censorship of films and how it works in India.

The Government of India appointed a Committee on March 28, 1968 to enquire into the working of the existing procedures for certification of cinematograph films for public exhibition in India and allied matters under the Chairmanship of Mr. G. D. Khosla, former Chief Justice of the Punjab High Court. The report of the Committee has since been published, and contains a valuable summary of the law of censorship not only in India but also in foreign countries. It is hardly helpful to the determination of this case to go into this history, but it may be mentioned here that it is the opinion of experts on the subject that Indian film censorship since our independence has become one of strictest in the world.[1]

In 1966 Mr. Raj Bahadur (who succeeded Mrs. Indira Gandhi as Minister for Information and Broadcasting) said that the Government would 'continue a liberal censorship' and was considering certain expert opinions on the subject. He also suggested to the film industry that it should formulate a code which would be the best from all standards so that the Government may be guided by it in formulating directives to the censors. See *Journal of Film Industry*, February 25, 1966, also quoted by Hunnings at page 18 of his book. This suggestion came to nothing for obvious reasons.

Film industry in India is not even oligopolistic in character, and it is useless to expect it to classify films according to their suitability as is done in the United States by the Motion Picture Association of America (MPAA) founded in October 1968. There, the film industry is controlled by eight major producers and private control of film-making is possible with the assistance of the National Association of Theatre Owners and Film Importers and Distributors of America. Having no such organisation for private censorship or even a private body like the British Board of Film Censors in England, the task must be done by the Government if censorship is at all to be imposed.

The delicate task, of deciding what is artistic and what is obscene, has to be performed by courts and in the last resort, by the Supreme Court and so oral evidence of men of literature or others on the question of obscenity is not relevant. It is clear that expressions like 'seduction', 'immoral traffic in women', soliciting prostitution or, procuration', 'indelicate sexual situation' and scenes suggestive of immorality', 'traffic and use of drugs', 'class hatred', 'blackmail associated with immorality' are within the understanding of average men and more so of persons who are likely to be the panel for purposes of censorship. Any more definiteness is not only not expected but is not possible. [471 G]

We may now illustrate our meaning how even the items mentioned in the directions may figure in films subject either to their artistic merit or their social value, over-weighing their offending character. The task of the censor is extremely delicate and his duties cannot be the subject of an exhaustive set of commands.

Direction is necessary to the censors so that they do not sweep within the terms of the directions vast areas of thought, speech and expression of artistic quality and social purpose and interest. Our standards must be so framed that we are not reduced to a level where the protection of the least capable and the most depraved amongst us determines what the morally healthy cannot view or read. The standards that we set for our censors must make a substantial allowance in favour of freedom thus leaving a vast area for creative art to interpret life and

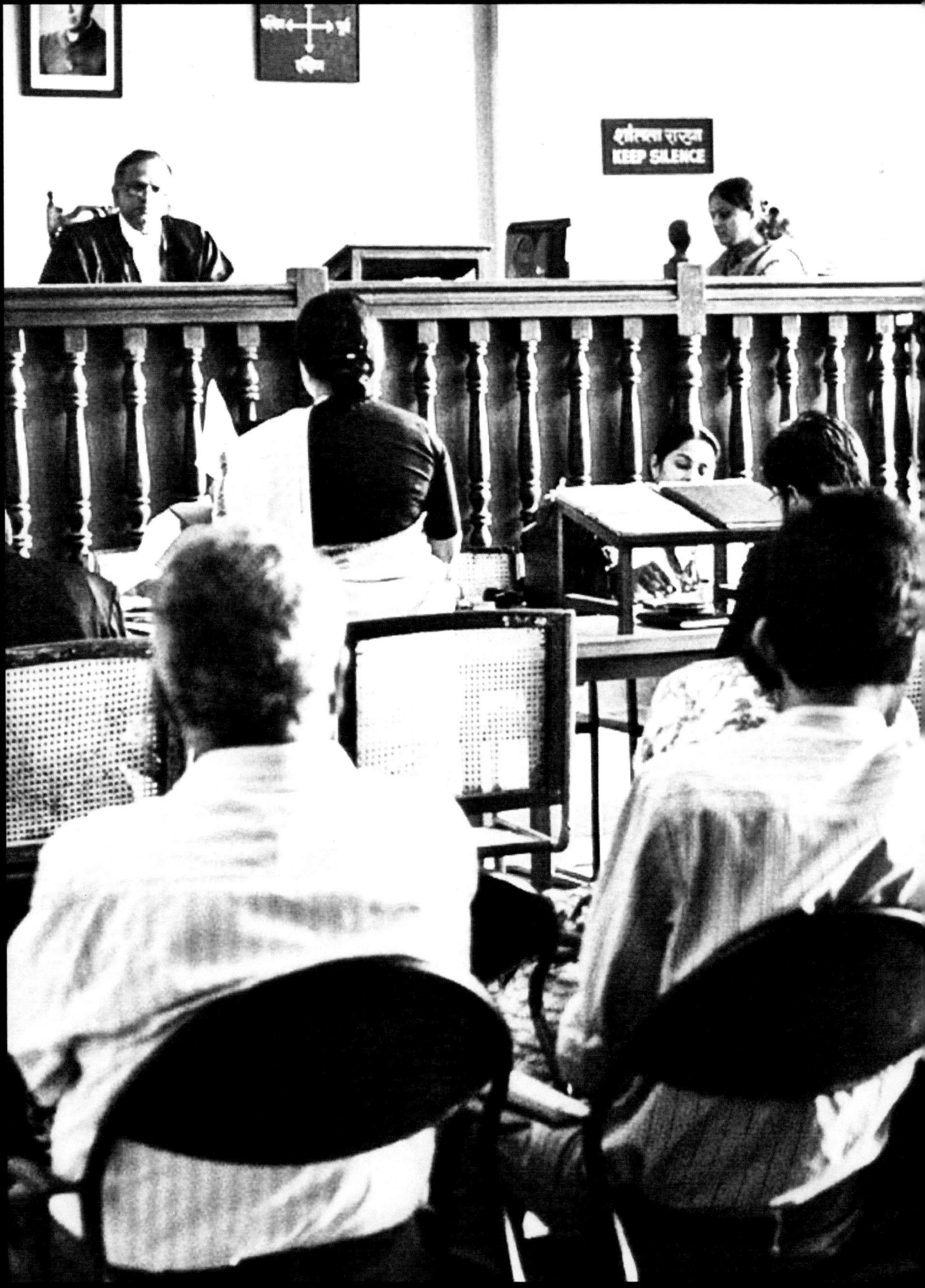
KEEP SILENCE

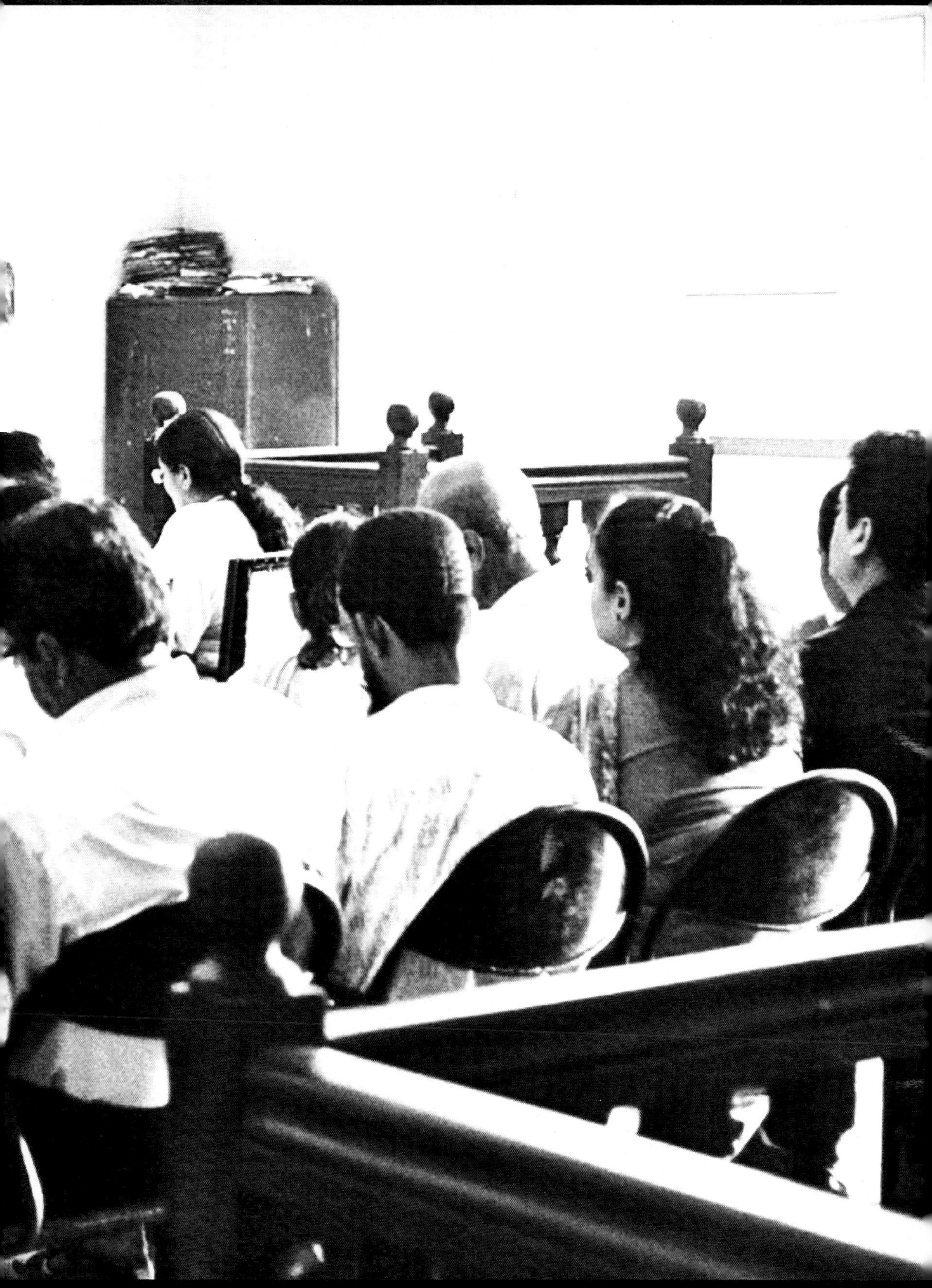

society with some of its foibles along with what is good. We must not look upon such human relationships as banned in toto and forever from human thought and must give scope for talent to put them before society. The requirements of art and literature include within themselves – a comprehensive view of social life and not only in its ideal form and the line is to be drawn where the average man begins to feel embarrassed or disgusted at a naked portrayal of life without the redeeming touch of art or genius or social value.

If the depraved begins to see in these things more than what an average person would, in much the same way, as it is wrongly said, a Frenchman sees a woman's legs in everything, it cannot be helped. In our scheme of things, ideas having redeeming social or artistic value must also have importance and protection for their growth. Sex and obscenity are not always synonymous, and it is wrong to classify sex as essentially obscene or even indecent or immoral. It should be our concern, however, to prevent the use of sex designed to play a commercial role by making its own appeal. This draws in the censor's scissors.

Thus, audiences in India can be expected to view with equanimity the story of Oedipus, son of Latius, who committed patricide and incest with his mother. When the seer Tiresias exposed him, his sister Jocasta committed suicide by hanging herself and Oedipus put out his own eyes.

No one after viewing these episodes would think that patricide or incest with one's own mother is permissible or suicide in such circumstances or tearing out one's own eyes is a natural consequence. And yet if one goes by the letter of the directions the film cannot be shown. Similarly, scenes depicting leprosy as a theme in a story or in a documentary are not necessarily outside the protection. If that were so, Verrier Elwyn's *Phulmati of the Hills* or the same episode in Henryson's *Testament of Cresseid* (from where Verrier Elwyn borrowed the idea) would never see the light of the day. Again, carnage and bloodshed may have historical value and the depiction of such scenes as the sack of Delhi by Nadirshah may be permissible, if handled delicately and as part of an artistic portrayal of the confrontation with Mohammad Shah Rangila. If Nadir Shah made *golgotha*s of skulls, must we leave them out of the story because people must be made to view a historical theme without true history? Rape in all its nakedness may be objectionable, but Voltaire's *Candide* would be meaningless without Cunegonde's episode with the soldier, and the story of Lucrece could never be depicted on the screen. Therefore, it is not the elements of rape, leprosy, sexual immorality which should attract the censor's scissors but how the theme is handled by the producer.

It must, however, be remembered that the cinematograph is a powerful medium and its appeal is different. The horrors of war as depicted in the famous etchings of Goya do not horrify one so much as the same scenes rendered in colour and with sound and movement, would do. We may view a documentary on the erotic tableaux from our ancient temples with equanimity or read the *Kamasutra* but a documentary from them as a practical sexual guide would be abhorrent.

Bombay High Court 2003

Shri Anand Patwardhan vs The Central Board Of Film Certification on 24 April, 2003

Equivalent citations: 2003 (5) BomCR 58, 2004 (1) MhLj 856
Bench: H Gokhale, R Desai

The facts leading to this petition are as follows:

The Petitioner is a well-known figure in the field of documentaries in India and has been making socially relevant documentaries for nearly three decades. In the past, he has made films which have won national and international awards, wherein he has dealt with various subjects like street dwellers (*Hamara Shahar/ Bombay Our City*, 1985), religious fundamentalism (*Ram Ke Naam/In the Name of God*, 1992), the connection between machismo and sectarian violence (*Pita, Putra aur Dharmayuddha/Father, Son and Holy War*, 1995) and the plight of those displaced in the name of development (*A Narmada Diary*, 1995).

The subject of the present petition is a documentary called *War and Peace (Jang aur Aman)*. It deals with the journey of peace activism in the face of global militarism and war, and has been filmed over a period of three years in different countries such as India, Pakistan, Japan and USA.

FCAT (Film Certification Appellate Tribunal) directed two deletions and one addition. The first deletion is with respect to a demonstration which is being held at Hutatma Chowk, Mumbai.[2] The demonstrators are giving slogans 'Hindu Bomb, *hai hai* (Hindu Bomb, shame shame) and Muslim Bomb, *hai hai* (Muslim Bomb, shame shame). The FCAT has directed that the slogans be deleted. The second deletion is from a speech of a Dalit Leader Bhai Sangare.[3] This Shri (Mr.) Sangare is seen giving a speech after the explosion of the atomic device by India.[4] The speech records anguish of the speaker on the device being exploded on the day of Buddha Jayanti.[5] The speaker says that Buddha gave the message of love and, that being so, why was the bomb exploded on his birthday? And then the speaker says 'Why didn't you do your blasts on Rama's birthday? It's your culture. All your gods are fully armed. Rama has an arrow, Shankar has a trident, Vishnu has a chopper.[6] All have weapons. So when it's the birthday of armed ones, do your bomb blast. Our Buddha is unarmed.' This second deletion directs the deletion of the sentence 'It is your culture.'

Then FCAT has directed an addition where there is a reference to the Tehelka Tapes. The FCAT order states 'And lastly the so-called Tehelka Tapes. Let Mr Patwardhan show the tapes but let him mention in the commentary and display at an appropriate place that the tapes are under the scrutiny of a Judicial Commission.'

In order to decide the question raised in the petition, it is necessary to refer to some of the provisions of the Constitution and the Cinematograph Act, 1952. Article 19(1)(a) of the Constitution grants all citizens of India the right to freedom of speech and expression. This right of the filmmakers has come up for consideration in various judgements from time to time. One of the earliest judgments is that of a Constitution Bench of the Apex Court (Per Hidayatullah, CJ.) in K.A. Abbas v. Union of India.[7] That was a matter wherein the petitioner therein had made a documentary entitled *A Tale of Four Cities* (1968). It had a scene showing the red-light district in Bombay, and the Board of Film Censors had directed a cut regarding some of those scenes. This decision was challenged in the petition filed to the Apex Court.

For our purpose, what the court has observed in para 49 and 50 of the aforesaid judgement is relevant and those observations are:

> The standards that we set for our censors must make a substantial allowance in favour of freedom, thus leaving a vast area for creative art to interpret life and society with some of its foibles, along with what is good.

The next judgement relied upon by the petitioner is in the case of Ramesh v. Union of India. That was a decision concerning a TV Serial by name of *Tamas*, which showed the communal tension before the partition of India.[8] The question before the court was with respect to 'U' (Universal) Certificate granted by the Central Board of Film Censors. A dispute was raised with respect to certain scenes in the film and the effect thereof on common men. In para 13 of the judgement, the Apex Court referred to the judgement of Vivian Bose J. in the case of Bhagwati Charan Shukla v. Provincial Government reported in AIR 1947 Nagpur 1. The court quoted with approval the observation of the learned judge that 'the effect of the words must be judged from the standards of reasonable, strong-minded, firm and courageous men, and not those of weak and vacillating minds, nor of those who sense danger in every hostile point of view'.

The Petitioner has lastly relied upon a recent judgement of a Full Bench of this Court in Anand C. Dighe v. State of Maharashtra reported in 2002 (1) BCR 57. That was a matter concerning a play in Marathi by the name *Mee Nathuram Godse Boltoy* (I am Nathuram Godse Speaking)[9] which sought to explain the actions of Nathuram Godse who murdered Mahatma Gandhi. The Government of Maharashtra in the exercise of its powers under Section 95(1) of the Code of Civil Procedure, 1973 had declared that every copy of that play and its translation in Gujarati or any other language shall stand forfeited to the government.

In para 19, the Full Bench observed as follows:

> The Government in the present case seems to have acted in the wake of the criticism voiced against the play and of the sense of outrage of those who believe that the play unfairly criticizes the Father of the Nation. The Father of the Nation holds a position which is *sui generis* in the nation. The nation owes its freedom to his relentless struggle for independence from a foreign power. His message of peace and non-violence should provide

> a beacon to these troubled times. But it is important to realize that there are eternal values on which the constitution of a democracy is founded. Tolerance of a diversity of viewpoints and the acceptance of the freedom to express those whose thinking may not accord with the mainstream are cardinal values which lie at the very foundation of a democratic form of government. A society wedded to the Rule of law, cannot trample upon the rights of those who assert views which may be regarded as unpopular or contrary to the views shared by a majority. The law does not have to accept the views which have been expressed by the petitioner in the play in order to respect the rights of the petitioner as a playwright to express those views. Respect for and the tolerance of a diversity of viewpoints is what ultimately sustains a democratic society and government. The right of the playwright, of the artist, writer and of the poet will be reduced to husk if the freedom to portray a message whether it be in canvas, prose or verse is to depend upon the popular perception of the acceptability of that message. Popular perceptions, however strong, cannot override values which the constitution embodies as guarantees of freedom in what was always intended to be a free society.

Before we conclude, we would like to record the oft-stated proposition that an issue may be one but there are many facets of looking at it. It is quite possible that the persons in authority today may feel that what they see is the only correct facet of it, though it may not be so. It is only in the democratic form of government that the citizens have the right to express themselves fully and their viewpoints towards various events which are taking place around them. By suppressing certain viewpoints, it is not only the propagator of the viewpoint who suffers, but it is society at large and equally the people in authority who suffer. This is because they fail to receive the counter-view which may eventually lead to immense damage to society due to an erroneous decision at the hands of the persons in authority, in the absence of the counter-view. That apart, the freedom of speech and expression is important not merely for the consequences that ensue in the absence thereof, but since the very negation of it runs as an antithesis to basic human values, instincts and creativity. It is high time that persons in authority realize the significance of the freedom of speech and expression, rather than make and allow such attempts to stifle it.

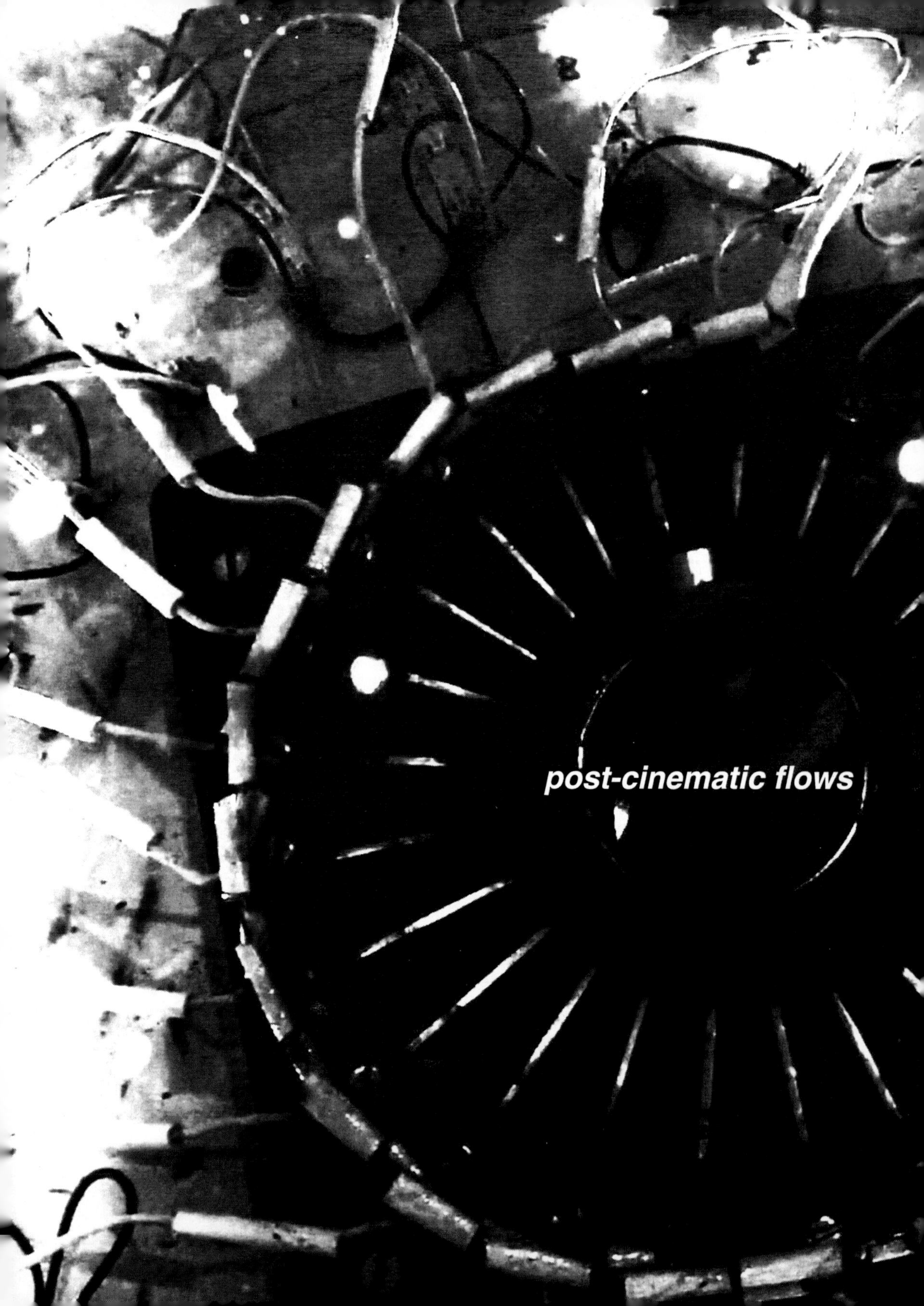
post-cinematic flows

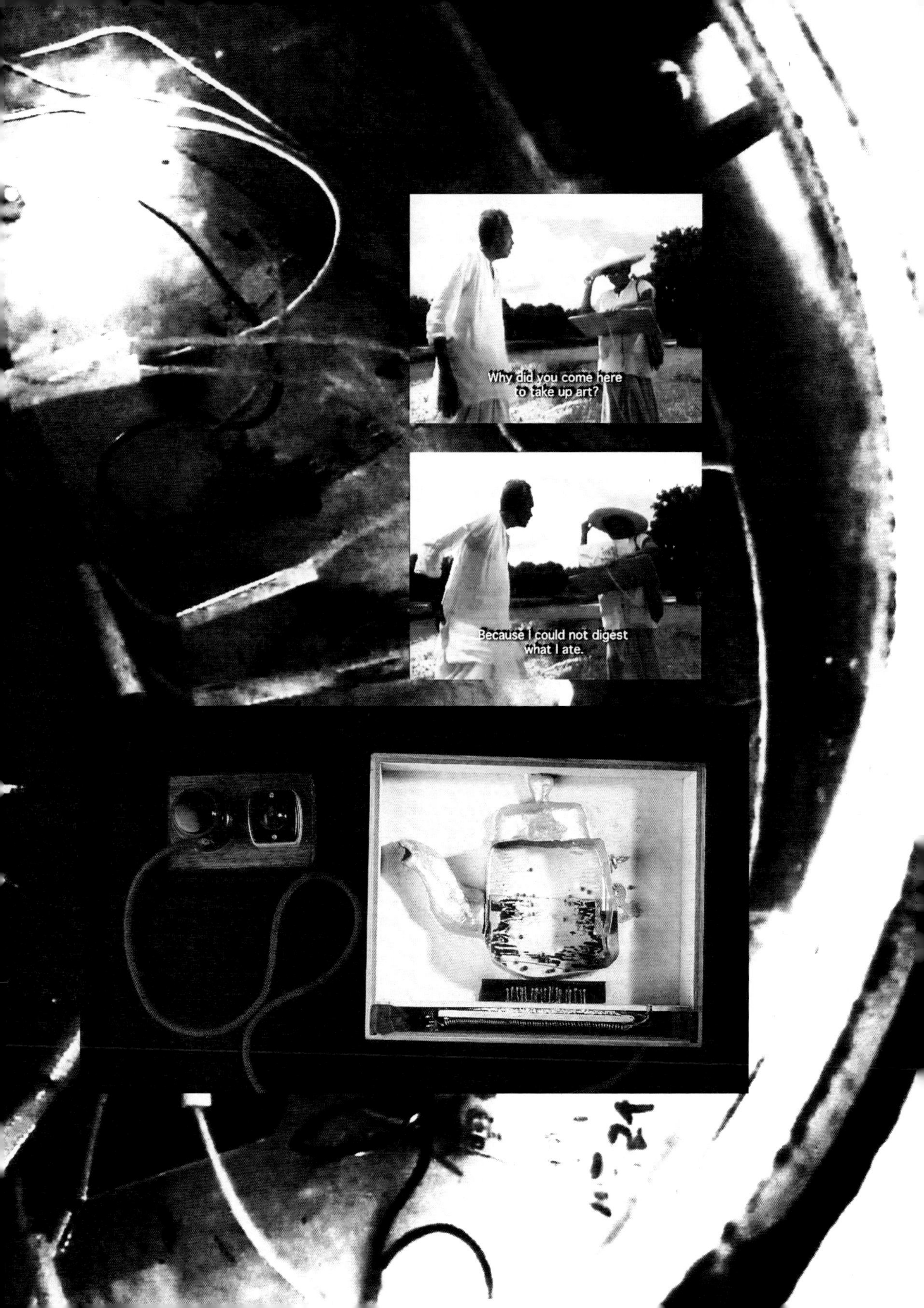
Why did you come here
to take up art?
Because I could not digest
what I ate.

'The more cinema leaks out of the theatre, the more anxieties get created about the proper domain of the circulation of filmic materials.' Artist and curator Jeebesh Bagchi's invitation to cinema studies to 'take to the streets' inaugurates the third section of this assemblage, where the cinema transforms into the threatening 'fecund copy', presaging the digital turn in the moving image. Bagchi's text, written in the form of a series of notes as he highlights the dispersed infrastructures of the cinematic image, is in the context of Sarai's *Publics and Practices in the History of the Present* (PPHP) project at the Centre for the Study of Developing Societies (CSDS), Delhi, and its examination of informal, often illegal, urban infrastructures through an archive of research notes, interviews, documents, photographs, publicity materials and ethnographic observations.

This material was made available in Hindi (*Media Nagar* 01 and 02) and in English in the Sarai Readers (e.g. Media Researchers @ Sarai, 'Complicating the City: Media Itineraries', in Monica Narula, Shuddhabrata Sengupta, Jeebesh Bagchi, Geert Lovink and Lawrence Liang, eds, *Sarai Reader 05: Bare Acts*, Delhi: Sarai, 2005).

Originally presented at the 2005 seminar, 'Currents in Indian Popular Cinema: Liberalization and After', at the Department of Film Studies, Jadavpur University, Kolkata, and published in *Journal of the Moving Image* (2006). Reprinted with permission of the author and publishers.

Keywords

Jugaad Aesthetics, Made in China, Pirate Networks, Tactical Media: See Keywords (pp. 326–44).

Images

pp. 212–13: Montage of modified stills from *Squeeze Lime in Your Eye* (dir. Avijit Mukul Kishore, 2017, digital video, colour). The inset image on p. 213 is from Ritwik Ghatak's incomplete film, *Ramkinkar Baij: A Personality Study*, on the Santiniketan sculptor, which he had started filming in 1975. After 2011, this footage was shared on YouTube by multiple sources. Kishore's film on the new media artist Kausik Mukhopadhyay presents a similar 'personality study' of the artist who broke new ground by giving cheap, ordinary, quotidian objects new life in his artwork, in installation form.

p. 219: Photograph by Rakesh Kumar Singh, as part of the PPHP project at Sarai, CSDS.

p. 220: Montaged signages promising low-tech *jugaad* and 'repair shops', with the ubiquitous anti-piracy warning signs on CDs and VCDs, and a street musician performing covers of copyrighted songs. Inserted with a frame from *Squeeze Lime in Your Eye*. Stills from *Squeeze Lime in Your Eye*, courtesy Avijit Mukul Kishore.

JEEBESH BAGCHI **2005**

15 The Cinematic Object After the 1990s

We are surrounded today by an ever-expanding relay of cinematic images and sounds. The walls of India's cities become a screen on which cinematic materials get a rough-and-ready exhibition, with layer upon layer of peeling posters. Portable images of popular heroes and heroines adhere on vehicles. The intense ubiquity of film music becomes part of the aural environment. The cinema develops an animated and active life outside the darkness of the cinema hall.

We encounter filmic materials through television broadcasts, magazines, newspaper articles, websites, advertisements, fan club publicity material, promos, clips, trailers, countdowns, production stills, memorabilia, radio, tapes, CDs, CD covers, VCDs and DVDs. Cinema and cinema-derived materials form an extended sensory envelope. The ringtone trill on mobile phones brings yet another annotation to our mediatized experience of cinema culture.

The more cinema leaks out of the theatre, the more anxieties get created about the proper domain of the circulation of filmic materials. These notes focus on such anxieties, and on how people live with them. They specifically investigate how the filmic object is transformed through the modes of its circulation. They also, more generally, investigate the influence of the filmic object on our perception, in the sensorial field created by the extended presence of cinema in our cities.

I offer these notes as a kind of montage of effects, punctuated by jump-cuts in the form of images and annotations – fragmentary provocations for further research, and as an invitation to film theory to hit the streets of our cities, and spend some time there.

The Space of Circulation and Dispersion

I will begin with a consideration of a composite image:

At first glance, we see two men sitting in what appears to be a 'shack', a somewhat temporary construction, making amplifiers and tape recorders. Rakesh's notes inform us that it is taken in Angooribad, one of the teeming quasi-illegal settlements that also constitute the industrial underbelly of metropolitan Delhi. The image takes us in different directions:

> i) Here are two people located in a web of multiple social relationships. They are migrants into the city from the countryside. They may be tied to each other in a kinship (or in an imagined kinship) relation. They could be *ustad* and *shagird* (master and apprentice, in an artisanal sense). They may also be linked in an entrepreneur and wage-worker relationship, and they could be neighbours.
>
> ii) The 'shack' or the *kaccha jugaad* (improvised structure) of the workshop expresses a fragile tenure on space built through a negotiation based on rent, risk, security and trust. All these are temporal qualities characteristic of the urban form that has evolved over a long period of time in places like Angooribad. At present, given the current onslaught of the judicial apparatus on a variety of urban forms in Delhi (and in all our cities, generally), this fragile shack stands in direct contravention of legal orders concerning urban land usage.[1] It stands in the metaphorical line of sight of an approaching bulldozer.
>
> iii) This space has negotiated electricity and water for itself through a protracted set of negotiations with the municipal administration. A calibrated set of manoeuvres with municipal authorities has ensured a clutch of administrative orders guaranteeing a fragile, skeletal infrastructure (in the form of an erratic electricity connection) that could be taken away at any time. For a para-electronics/para-media enterprise such as this, electricity is a vital necessity, and a great deal of social as well as technical ingenuity is employed to ensure its functioning.[2]
>
> iv) There is a local credit economy in place that makes possible the 'financing' of the workshop. This is what enables the para-media entrepreneur to get raw materials, organize production and take products to the market. These credit systems are deeply embedded in economies of trust, reciprocity and risk assessment, and have their own rules and systematic obligations.

v) The two persons are also engaged in a technical world of making electronic goods. They have the skill to read circuit boards, they understand load distribution, they are able to read resistors, capacitors, match impedance, etc. They need to keep upgrading what they know in order to add features. Obviously, they are not running a research and development lab here, but they are part of a network of knowledge workers who hack into circuit designs and then produce 'copied' circuit boards through a process of careful reverse engineering. They innovate on the relation between the circuitry and the casing. This may be, in some case, in contravention of intellectual property (IP) laws, specifically patent law.[3]

vi) For its makers, the casing is an opportunity to interface with the 'popular' culture of the sign. Through the casing, they negotiate a path through the complex labyrinth of the values (or 'brand equity') of signs, logos and marks of provenance. They could be dealing with the manufacture of a brand name (Sony, Philips) or a mark of a 'country of origin' name (e.g. Made in China - many objects ostensibly 'made in China' are actually made in India, just as many commodities thought to be 'made in India' are actually manufactured in China). When these entrepreneurs decide to name the product that they are making as SONY, they stand in direct contravention of the IP laws around trademark protection.

vii) The amplifiers and recorders are a strand in an extensive web that encompasses diverse music cultures, performative practices and production-distribution networks. These include practices central to the work of neighbourhood DJs who perform at weddings, life-cycle rituals, religious functions and social occasions.

viii) This technology-entrepreneurship-performance complex exists within the context of neighbourhood culture that does not constitute separations between the realms of work, home or leisure. The music system itself could be playing materials of all kinds; some of the materials would constitute violations of IP law, some would be construed as indecent and immoral provocations by the morality brigade, and sometimes, as in the case of many popular remix numbers, they would be both. All manner of codes and protocols stand subverted on a daily basis.

ix) The two men working in the shack would probably be sending remittances back home to a rural or mofussil hinterland, and somebody 'back home' would be preparing himself, even as these two work, to make the journey to places like Angooribad, impelled by stories of innovation and enterprise from the big city.

I draw attention to the possibilities that can be teased out of the image to suggest that this - along with Bollywood and the big film and media industries - is also a site of production. The proliferation of remixing, dialect musics and low cost digital production[4] are all part of an underlying infrastructure that gives millions of people access to the cinematic experience. These forms of production are highly dispersed, fragile and uncertain.

There is a danger in letting the dispersal, fragility and uncertainty of these forms of production lead to a premature pronouncement of their inevitable demise. Their contingency in no way postulates their insignificance. The narrative of industrialization that postulates the slow demise of the small in favour of scaled-up production does not capture the social dynamics of this uncertain milieu. The vitality, dynamism, conflict and inventiveness visible in this social world demands a more complex description of the entanglement of technologies, subjectivity and desire.

To cease engagement with these sites of media production is analogous to turning a blind eye to the manner in which the inhabitants of squatter settlements improvise and innovate on issues of infrastructure and access to resources. The practices of habitation are a creative, improvisatory riff in response to the structure of urbanism, just as the informal media entrepreneurs and practitioners are creative and innovative responses to the media environment.

Inhabitants of the incremental city face judicial repression and violence, even as unauthorized media practitioners face the wrath of the IP apparatus.[5] These two kinds of practice - in the domain of habitation, and in media - intersect in the figure of the two artisans working with equipment in a shack. The fragility of habitation is a precondition for the manner in which production can be arranged in this unit. Both stand threatened at the same time and for a similar set of reasons, as high-end institutional capital consolidates and expands into areas hitherto marked by low-scale improvisational informality.

The life of the cinematic object is nourished by lived practices of quotidian urban creativity, in media, in technological improvisation and in architecture. If we want to understand how cinema enters and circulates in our cities, we will have to enter this domain. Cinema is not just something that lives and dies in theatres and multiplexes, or television broadcasts; it has a frenetic life of reproduction and circulation in cheap and affordable VCDs and DVDs that pass from hand to hand, or in screenings in 'shantytown multiplexes' - sheds with benches, DVD/VCD players and projectors - within the 'shadow' city.

This space is riven by conflict, by the spectre of the law, and by the creative energies and technological skills of the majority of the urban population. It is remade, repurposed, repackaged and remixed in a myriad ways. Cinema circulates within this force field. It is subject to different kinds of gravitational pulls emanating from different sources, some of which are legal, others technological,

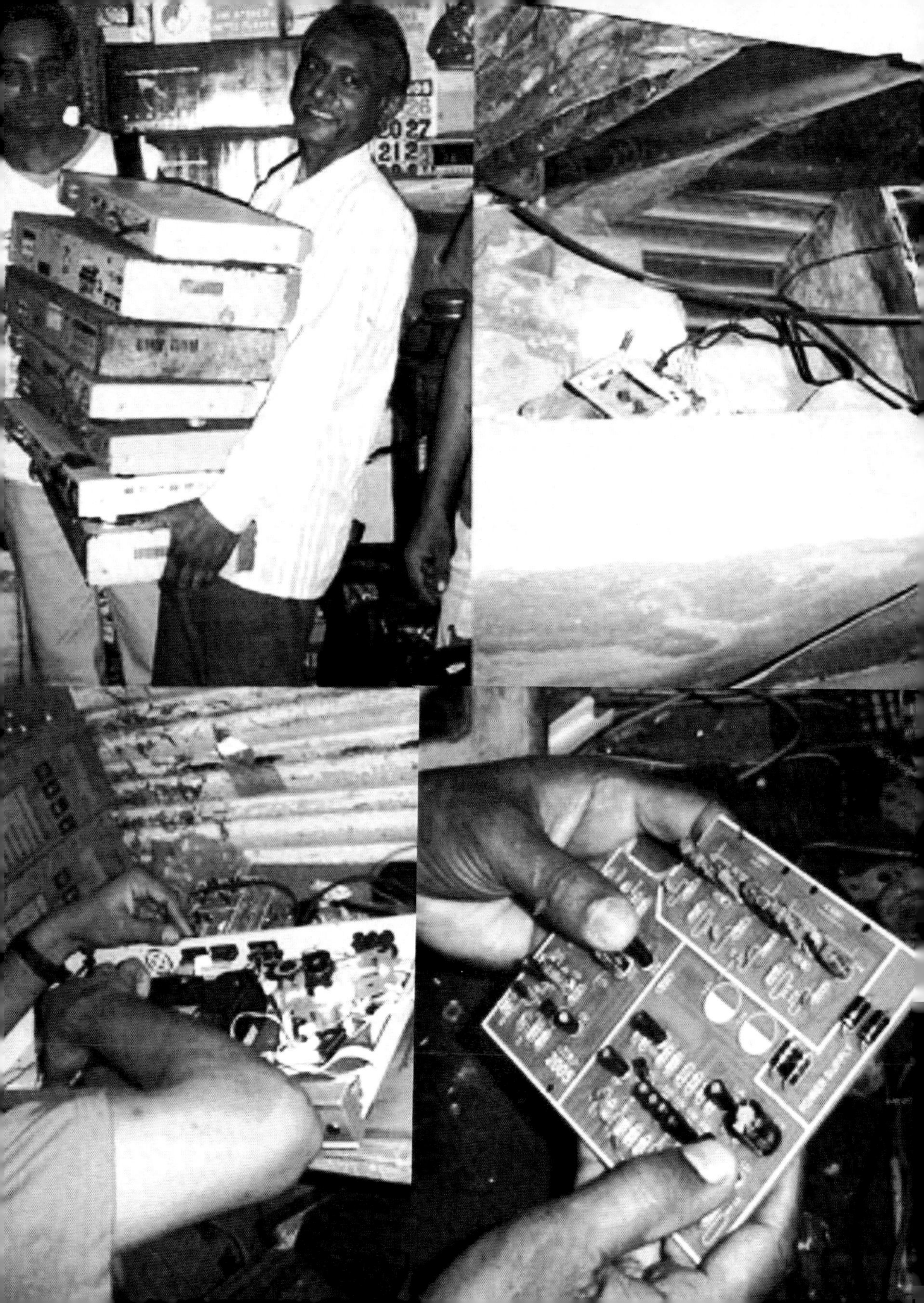

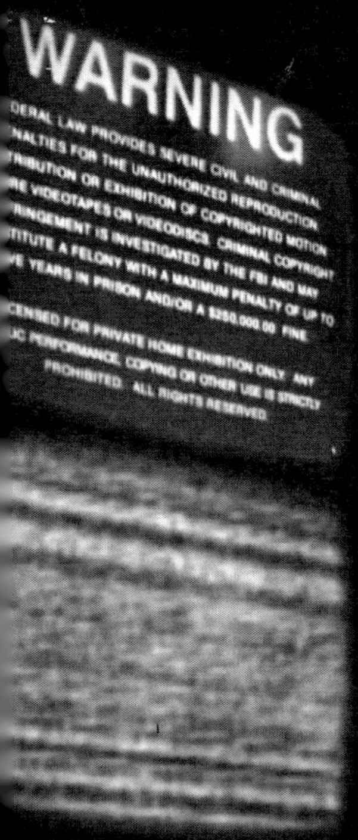
WARNING

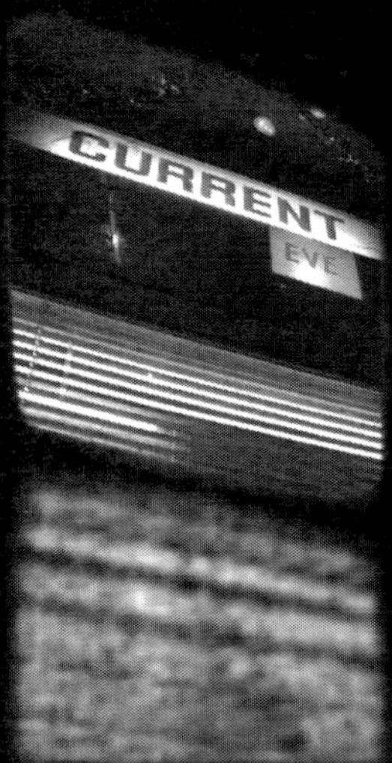
CURRENT
EYE

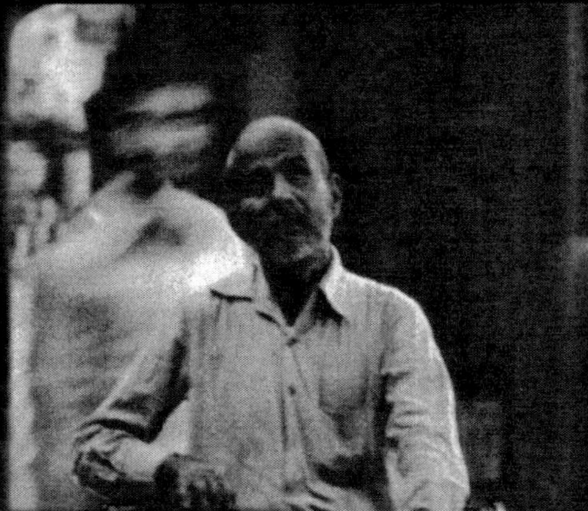

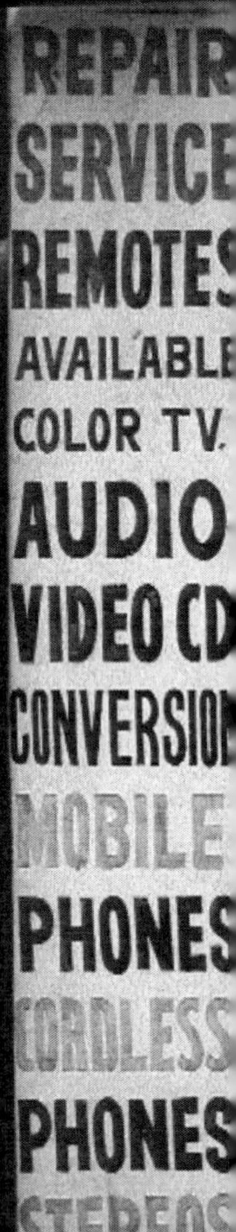
REPAIR
SERVICE
REMOTES
AVAILABLE
COLOR T.V.
AUDIO
VIDEO CD
CONVERSION
MOBILE
PHONES
CORDLESS
PHONES
STEREOS

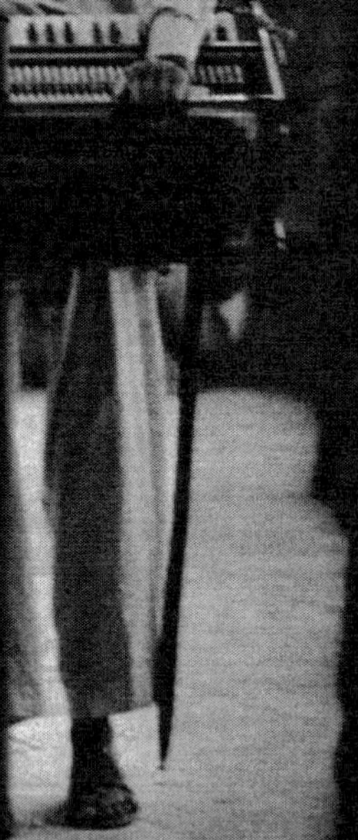

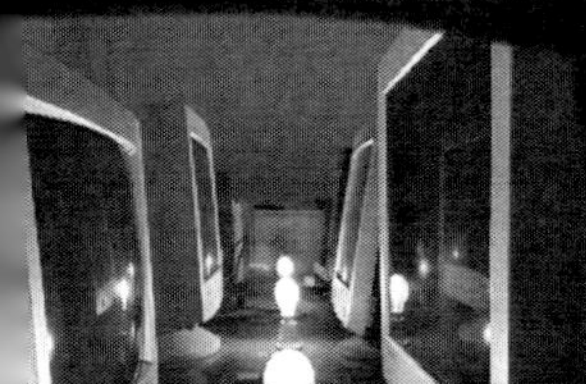

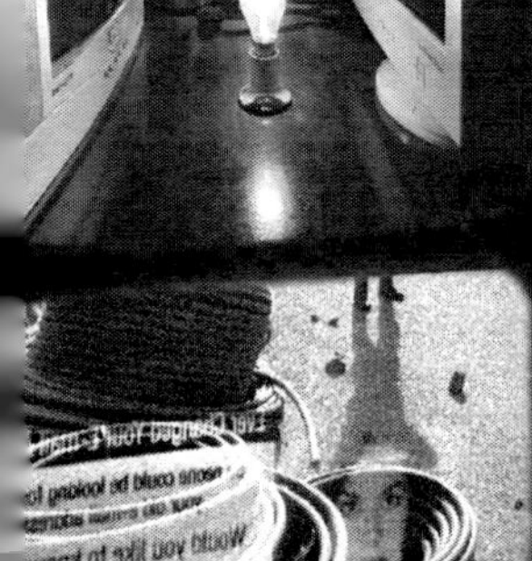

and yet others governed by conventions of practice and taste. Only by locating our enquiries squarely within this turbulent field can we begin to understand the career of images and sounds from the cinema in the lives of most people in our society today.

Cinematic Envelopes and Prohibitory Signs

The objects that originate in the workshop described at the start of this essay, contribute to the intense acceleration of cinematic material in urban spaces. This accelerated dispersal of images and sounds produces a new sensorium of cinema. But this ever-expanding sensorium is also marked by a master sign that speaks to us in the language of prohibition.

Here, I would like to introduce another image: the familiar frame of the prohibitory sign that restricts the circulation of a film.[6] This is an image that we have all grown accustomed to from our experience of watching DVDs, be it in the comfort and privacy of the home, alone or with friends and family, or in a film-theory class in the university.

This sign prohibits certain social and creative practices. These social and creative practices are allied to the para-technologies of mass media that we saw in the earlier image. This is the world of the neighbourhood CD, tape and VCD shop or library, which now dots every imaginable urban settlement, including squatter habitations and shantytowns. The ubiquity of these means is made possible by the low cost and the ease of use of current technologies of duplication, ripping (copying), remixing, publishing, and the digital manipulation of images and sounds.

These factors make such activities viable and attractive – for remunerative as well as creative reasons – and because they fulfil a growing need for media, especially in contexts that we would otherwise consider underprivileged. This is what locates vast swathes of the shadow media industry in squatter settlements and other illegal habitations where the majority of the working urban poor live in India.[7] The frame of prohibition in the DVD seeks, in actual fact, to prohibit an entire domain of possible social practices with images and sounds. We could say that it actually seeks to censor the majority of media practices in the urban environment.

The ramifications of this prohibition are significant:

> i) It prohibits the copying of the encoded digital content within this material object. Copying of digital content is the easiest technological act in the contemporary. It is only through massive police, penal and pedagogic forms that the authenticated version will be kept afloat, and the 'unauthorized' circulation contained.

ii) It prohibits the transmission of encoded digital content through cables and other forms. The transmission of content through various wired networks will inevitably become more and more ubiquitous. Technological blockages, barriers and policing, inevitably become the way of controlling this ubiquitous relay.

iii) It prohibits a creative re-appropriation of the encoded digital content. More and more people have the resources and capacity to work with the digital content that surrounds us. This prohibition, however, makes repurposing a grave offence. Many legal battles will, therefore, be fought with regard to content repurposing. The critical issue will be our ability to argue for 'appropriation' of content that envelops us so as to be able to comment, critique, praise or even just to quote. In a media environment that continuously relays images from diverse locations and sources, one dominated by gigantic players, this ability to 'appropriate' will have critical bearing for democratic social practices.

iv) It prohibits and makes illegitimate the act of congregation around 'cinema' - a practice that has been associated with cinema from its inception. It is asking us to re-imagine the nature of what can be a legitimate cinematic public.[8] By banishing - or at least constricting - congregation and bringing it under the sign of legitimacy and illegitimacy it is rewriting the multiple practices associated with cinema.

One image echoes another. A text frame in a DVD resonates with the opening page of a legal affidavit. We could see them form a thickening layer of legality, an encrustation of the law on the life of the cinematic image.

The Fecund Copy, Ownership and Territoriality Blues

This is a court affidavit of a case brought up by the biggest global media corporations in combination against a small video library operator. The petitioners are Time Warner, Columbia Pictures, Disney, MGM Studios, Paramount, Tristar, Twentieth Century Fox and Universal, against Arun Kumar Gupta, proprietor of a music shop called *Lamhe*, in Greater Kailash in Delhi. What threat could such an opponent pose to this gargantuan corporate coalition? Sections 28 and 29 of the affidavit seek to answer this question in the following manner:

> 28. Even a single sale or rental of a film by the Defendant is capable of causing irreparable injury and damage to the Plaintiffs. The

> single film can act as a plate from which several thousands of other pirate prints can be prepared. If the print reaches the hand of a cable network, even a single telecast on a network is capable of reaching several million homes all over India. The potential for damage is immeasurable and irreparable.
>
> 29. Unauthorized sale and distribution of films by unscrupulous parties such as the Defendant result in reduced viewer-ship at cinema halls and theaters, which additionally results in huge losses to the Government exchequer by way of collection of taxes, including entertainment taxes.

This is an affidavit. Documents presented in court are like actors. They have to perform, and be performative, in their effect on the court proceedings. It should not surprise us that the language of the affidavit has a hyperbolic register, that the account it offers us is performatively exaggerated. But even if we discount its somewhat breathless quality, we are still left with a strange, paralysing anxiety that hovers around the digitally encoded material object (the CD or DVD) that holds and transports the cinematic material all around us.

The persistently multiple practices of production, distribution and circulation stand in direct confrontation with the claims to ownership and the distribution of social surplus between the state and the production sites that the state deems 'legitimate'. The CD/DVD of uncertain provenance ruptures this space of imagined homogeneity, and the supposedly seamless web of production, consumption, returns and surplus distribution that capital always want to build its world with. A spectre threatens the media industry...

If today, we, as practitioners, theorists and students of the cinema, are engaged in the task of rethinking the envelope of the cinematic around us, of trying to understand the reality of the dispersion of access to cinema and the parallel reality of dispersed property and prohibition, we have no choice but to realize that we are being compelled to negotiate a peculiar and thorny conjunction that may transform both the social life of cinematic objects as well as the image-world of the cinema. This is going to be, and in fact already is, a transformation marked by a high degree of conflict. A conflict that is going to envelop all of us.

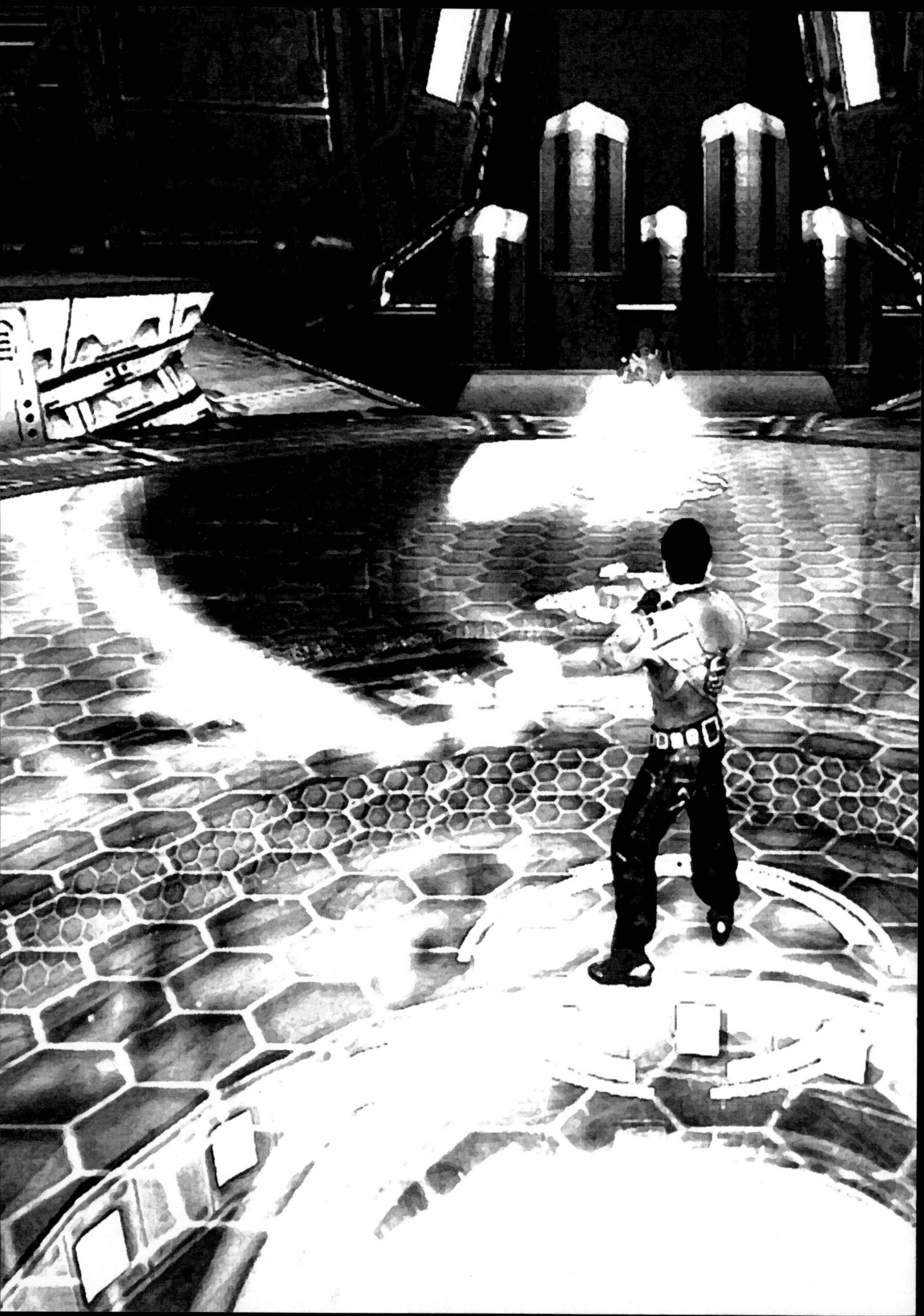

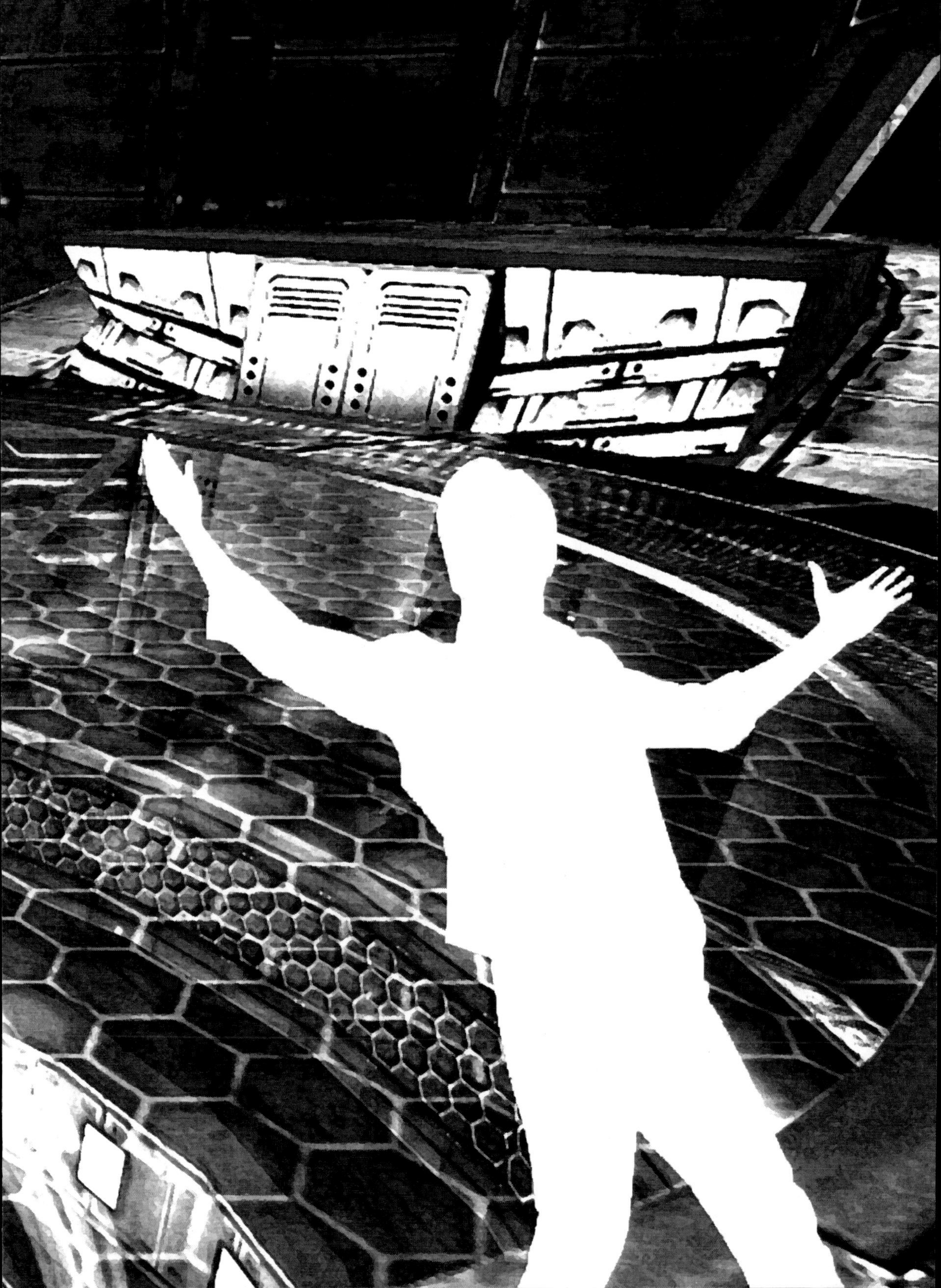

In the early 2000s, as the film industry went digital, the question of 'what next' for the cinema, and especially for the cinema's megastars, took a strange turn in Indian film. The great leap forward was virtualization into superhero status as the cinema itself came closer to online gaming. However, it appeared that something was holding it back. The very cultural memory that had made the cinema possible was now restraining it from its flight of fancy. Analogue cultural memory, and the refusal to forget, play a strange role in an India that is itself on the cusp of digitization.

This text was first presented under the title 'My Name is Khan and I'm a Star' at the international conference on 'Shahrukh Khan and Global Bollywood', University of Vienna, September–October 2010. A different version was published as 'SRK, Cinema, and the Citizen: Perils of a Digital Superhero', in Rajinder Kumar Dudrah, Elke Mader and Bernhard Fuchs (eds), *SRK and Global Bollywood*, Delhi: Oxford University Press, 2015. The original essay is reprinted here with the permission of the author.

Keywords and Names

Ayodhya, Bollywood, (Saeed Akhtar) Mirza, Mumbai Realism, Rajnikant, (Karan) Johar, (Shah Rukh) Khan: See Keywords (pp. 236–44).

AIILSG: All India Institute of Local Self-Governance.

Chopra, Yash (1932–2012): Pioneered the blockbuster before inventing the classic Bollywood film formula of lush romances for global export.

Dhasal, Namdeo (1949–2014): Marathi's best-known dalit poet, who wrote extensively on the city of Bombay.

Girangaon: Former 'mill district' defining the city's late colonial economy and its communist-led working-class movement. Now known for the makeover of its factories into malls for high-end consumerism.

Hyperstardom: When the star becomes larger than the film, forcing the cinema itself to spill over into allied economies.

KRVIA: Kamla Raheja Vidyanidhi Institute for Architecture, Mumbai.

MHADA: Maharashtra Housing and Area Development Authority.

My Name is Khan (dir. Karan Johar, 2010): Bollywood production starring Shahrukh Khan, set entirely in the USA, and seeking to make common cause between Muslims and African-Americans.

Patwardhan, Sudhir (b. 1949), painter known for a form of photorealism specific to Mumbai-based content.

PIL: Public Interest Litigation.

Rajni jokes: Rajnikant's superstardom also circulates via memes and jokes emphasizing his 'god-like status', ungoverned by the laws of the natural or social worlds.

Ra.One (2011): Expensive superhero film presented as a technological breakthrough with a highly promoted game on Sony Playstation 3.

Images

pp. 224–25: Collage of the *Ra.One* video game and the iconic SRK gesture.

pp. 231, 236, 242–43: Digital images of paintings from the *Gentricity* project by artist Ranjit Kandalgaonkar and architects Aditya Potluri and Saurabh Vaidya, under the 2006–07 Majlis Visual Arts Fellowship. In Mumbai's inner city areas, archaic rent control policies, negligent landlords and powerless tenants led to an urban crisis with crumbling buildings and a deteriorating environment. The Cess 33/7 policy offered a blanket redevelopment strategy, resulting in further ad-hoc development. A 2004 PIL case, challenged the Maharashtra government and the MHADA, leading to a report by KRVIA's Design Cell in collaboration with AIILSG, examining alternative, sustainable and balanced redevelopment strategies, considering construction cost, real estate value and site-specific sensitivities.

The *Gentricity* project draws upon the hard data, photographic documentation and surveys generated by the KRVIA/AIILSG report. Through collaborative paintings, it captures the informal narratives and on-site complexities, documenting perspectives that the data couldn't accomodate. Images courtesy the artists.

ASHISH RAJADHYAKSHA **2010**

16 SRK, Cinema and the Citizen: What's Next?

Batman, Not Hanuman: We Need the Acceptance

'It is high time we stopped saying it's good enough for a Hindi film,' says Shah Rukh Khan. This *Front Row* discussion on Star World with his usual television interlocutor and biographer Anupama Chopra is slightly more serious than usual for he has a point to make.[1] They are talking about the 'art of being a superhero', and Khan is desperately concerned to show that, firstly, we can create one without condescension, secondly, we have the technology to make superhero films as good as they can in the USA, and thirdly, most important, that we must do it now to keep the Hindi cinema alive. Don't do it and you sink.

'We have the bucks: I have the bucks, I have the infrastructure, Karan Johar has it, Mr Yash Chopra has it[2] – it's ten times cheaper to make a film like this in this country. We just don't have the acceptance.' For Shah Rukh Khan superherodom had to be the next thing: it had to be done so our cinema could survive and could bring back an Indian audience growing up on the English Premier League, the NBA and NFL, and on American superheroes: 'And sad as it may sound, they like Batman more than Hanuman.'

Technology for Khan is all: VFX or visual effects is where the action is since that relates to fantasy untrammelled, and thence to freedom. Technology gives the filmmaker the big canvas, the capacity to experiment.

> I think all of us are still not fantastic enough in our beliefs: the greatest achievement an Indian can have is hope for a Ferrari, not hope for flying to the moon or saving the earth. We are more seeped in reality in India, we have

> smaller issues, we need to have to deal with having a house, a little car, so this fantasia, so to say, or this leap of faith where the superhero is going to save you against Krypton, fly down and save a thousand people, is still too fantastic for us. It's like, *roti, kapda aur makaan* (food, clothes, shelter), once we have taken care of that in films, then comes sports, and so you have a few sports films that have started doing well, and then – finally, it will be just fantasia, just go mad with the fantasy, even in terms of characters. For example, Heath Ledger: he's the greatest superhero we have, I'm not talking about a villain and a good guy and a bad guy, but look at the way he's played it, it's dizzying, it's anarchic, it's dark, it's brooding, it's edgy, it's free. We are somehow not being able to marry this fantastic form that exists which should actually give you freedom of flight or fantasy.

And so, what he is now doing as he tries to give back to the industry something in return for what he has got from it, is nothing less than an art film about superheroes: *Ra.One* (2011, dir. Anubhav Sinha) is, he says, 'an art film in the commercial sphere'.

This essay tries to make something of the desperate anxiety that can be read in the lines of Khan's quotes above. I shall propose that his definition of superherodom relates to a curious situation that Khan is trying to define for himself in India: a situation with some admitted similarities to a superhero but more like that of the character of Trishanku in the *Ramayana*,[3] trapped between heaven and earth, between what the cinema in India used to be and has been, and what Khan thinks the Indian cinema wants to be and can be. What it used to be is a combination of sheer rubbish – 'I was watching a film the other day, I won't name it, and everyone went, '*arre yaar kya* effects *hain*' (what great effects!) – (but) they're rubbish, and not because we can't do better, but because we accept this, *arre theek hai baki* picture *achhi thi* (it's okay, at least the rest of the film was all right) – and fear – of straying out of our familiar zones'. For example, that in India, whatever you do, you have to have a song.

If Khan is right, he has the 'bucks', even though he admits that it's expensive. The main reason to make the flight of fantasy is *not* financial, he is at pains to say: it *has to be done*, if we are to keep Indian cinema alive, to keep it somehow *relevant*.

Why, it is interesting to ask in this great relevance debate, does he pick on *Batman* as the model to follow? On the specific instance of *Batman*, vis-à-vis *Ra.One* there is of course the specific practical fact of the role of the video game to both films. The *Ra.One* game was formally released in October 2011 on the Sony Playstation 2 platform. As in the tradition of film games after *Matrix* and as the

Arkham games especially show, we are meant to get some additional background information here about the kind of weaponry that the good-bad guys bring to bear, but also devices, like (in *Ra.One*) the 'item spawn point', a tool for 'delivering weapons to armies across the globe'. 'This mini-teleportation device is designed for small objects and its mobility helped Ra.One's armed forces recuperate much faster allowing them to win almost every battle', says the kit accompanying the PS3 version.

It is certainly true that the very idea of a Hindi film narrative working with a console in the hand of the moviegoing fan opens up possibilities that take us back into the very history of the Hindi cinema, the reason for why it exists. The pact between fan and star, the role of fans who did more than merely watch, the possibilities of a spectatorial call to action, all get enlivened the moment we speak of a technologically-enabled fan-audience. As *Batman* resonates through 50 years and more of the fanzine, so Khan hopes that *Ra.One* will create in its console-enabled fan a similar historical resonance.

But there is potentially still more to the parallel. Arguably, the real meat in the argument is the fact that all superhero movies and the *Batman* series especially have been required to work within a social memory: of oppression, tyranny, corrupt states, citizen helplessness – all the structures of both everyday life, realist representation and both physical and mental incapacity that gives birth and power to the phantasy.[4] Which leads us to the question: what kind of memory of oppression could determine the Khan-style superherodom? Can we bring into its ambit figures as unlikely as G.One and Rizwan Khan, the autistic protagonist of *My Name is Khan* (2010, dir. Karan Johar)? Is Khan's superhero then trapped at one level in individual incapacity, but at another also within a technologized audience incapable of navigating two of Indian cinema's basic contradictions? This essay proposes that both characters are a literal embodiment of the conflict between a Hindi cinema unable to shed its moorings, trapped, as it were, in cultural memory, and a future that we find almost incomprehensible because these moorings are such that the fantasy is unable to take on a free rein. Khan's 'crisis of acceptance' is thus not necessarily a crisis from the outside. It is not a problem of such mundane things as finances or distribution: it is a crisis from *within the cinema itself*. The essay attempts, finally, to explore with admittedly initial evidence what such a conflict could mean to the actual experience of the gamer within this environment.

My Name is Khan (and I'm a Star)

When *My Name is Khan* was released in 2010 with a major eye on the US market, there was little doubt as to who the Khan referred to was. SRK himself, as perhaps the leading member of the fabled Khan trio,[5] had by then already taken hyperstardom to heights it is unlikely to have ever seen in its cinematic history. This year alone, the already very exclusive Rs 100-crore club gives way to the super-exclusive 200-crore club comprising – with *Jab Tak Hai Jaan* (As Long as We Are Alive, 2012, dir. Yash Chopra) and *Dabangg 2* (2012, dir. Arbaaz Khan) – only these three and no other, not Akshay Kumar, not Ajay Devgn, no one else.[6]

And yet it is another Khan being referred to: the Khan who also asserts that this is his name and that he is 'not a terrorist'. This is clearly a darker Khan, one who takes us back to a quite different attribution to one with such a name.

The story in *MNIK* is well known: San Francisco-based autistic Rizwan Khan travels to meet the President of America so that he can convey to him that though his name is Khan, he is not a terrorist. Khan/Khan recalls his life, initially with his Bombay-based dad, Dilawar Amanaullah Khan, his mother Razia, and his brother, Zakir. Dilawar works for the State Transport workshop in Borivali, and Rizwan accompanies him, learns the trade and can repair virtually anything. This bit of anchoring in Mumbai Realism[7] is important to the story, as we will see below. Years later, when Zakir relocates to the USA, sponsors Rizwan and hires him as a door-to-door salesman for his Mehnaz Herbal Beauty Products, Rizwan meets and marries single mother Mandira Rathod. The two relocate to Banville with Mandira's son Sameer, encounter racial profiling after the 9/11 terrorist attacks, are blacklisted, suffer losses and Sameer gets killed. Mandira blames Rizwan for her plight and asks him to leave while she decides to pursue Sameer's death. Rizwan sets out on his journey to meet the President. On the way, he has numerous encounters that require us to recall various kinds of cultural oppression mainly located in the USA: Hurricane Katrina, Black politics and the nature of domestic migration attached to the road-movie genre.

This cultural undertow – the reference to a cultural memory of oppression, victimhood and terrorization in a cinema that at the same time yearns to break free – continues to be an extraordinary aspect of Indian popular culture. The failure of freedom, so to say, forces the popular to reveal uncomfortable and disconcerting truths that popular culture is usually meant to cover in its fantasy. It forces the popular to turn political, to even take on radical responsibilities unbeknownst to itself. As the subaltern spectator of this kind of cinema is driven increasingly underground in globalized spaces, the knowledge 'you' need to have to be able to understand a Hindi film has become both cinematic and political. This is the knowledge that defines the name Khan: or what it means to have such a name today in the world.

On the other hand, at the other extreme, the name Khan signals another, very Bollywood, anxiety: one of the sustainability of the cinematic hyperstar. What next for Khan after the cinema? Has a star of such size outlived his usefulness? Or rather, has the figure become so large as to become larger than the cinema itself? Although the cinema has been the par-excellence vehicle for creating the movie

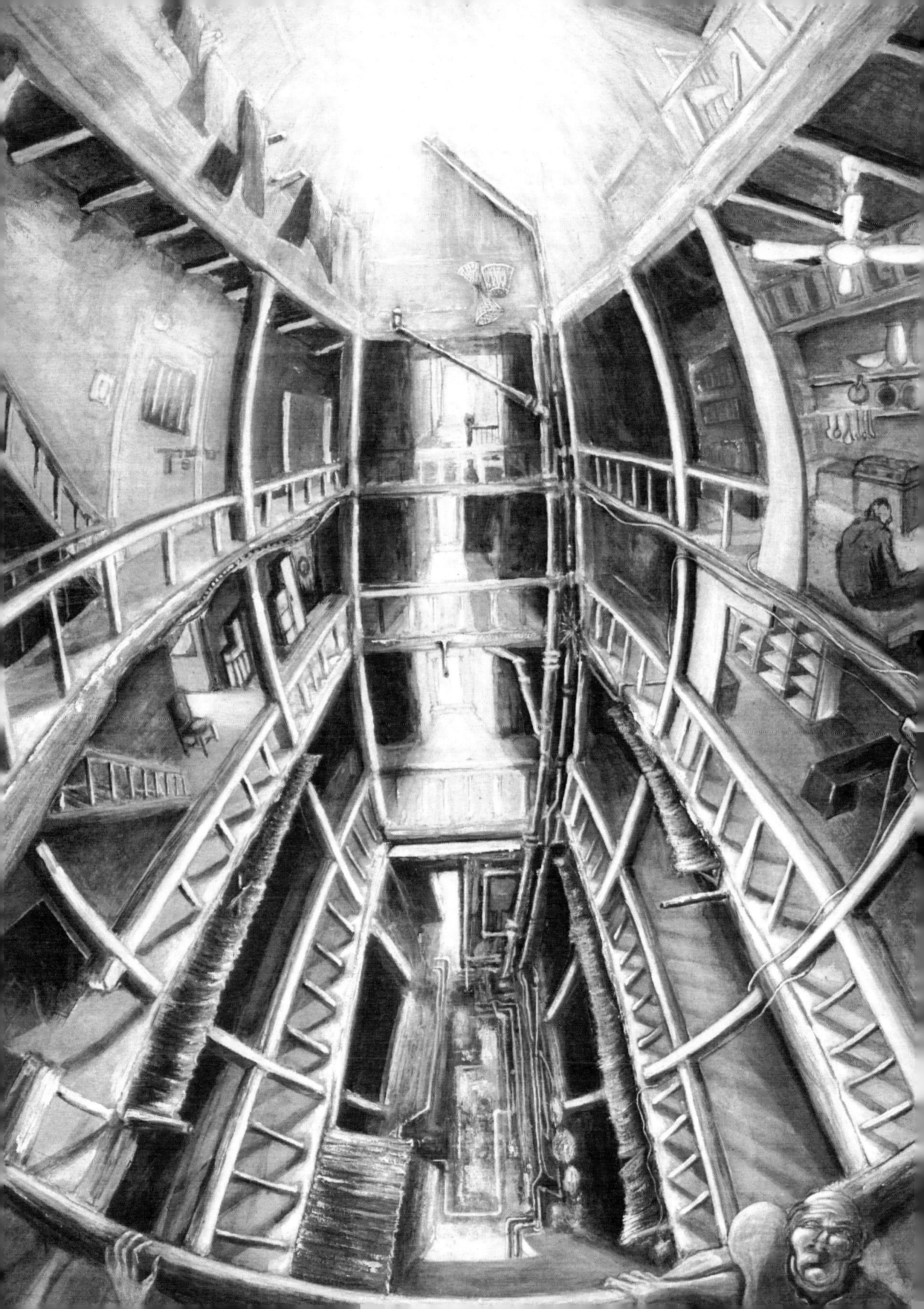

star/superstar/hyperstar, does this over-bloated star now need newer vehicles, new technologies, to survive in this stage of his career?

There is good reason to ask this question at a time in the cinema's global career when people are asking serious questions about the true worth of a star. Anita Elberse,[8] doing a report for the Harvard Business School, points to a similar exclusive club in Hollywood who can command fees of millions of dollars per movie in salaries, perks and profit-participation deals, can have a powerful influence on movie development, and trigger the 'green light' by generating commitments from investors, producers, distributors and exhibitors. But, as things change, she asks, exactly how important are such stars for the success of films? Elberse quotes a 2004 *Forbes* article entitled 'The Myth of Brad Pitt', which did a comparison across more than 200 recent films, revealing that fewer than half of the highest-grossing hits featured an actor who had top billing in at least one hit movie previously. The top three movies of all time – *Star Wars*, *E.T. the Extra-Terrestrial* and *Titanic* – had no stars. This leads her to endorse a well-established belief in the industry that 'it is the movie itself – not the star – that makes the hit'.

Such studies have been threatening for a while now to reverse a mantra of stardom, originally coined by Abraham Ravid's classic study 'Information, Blockbusters, and Stars: A Study of the Film Industry',[9] that 'stars capture their rent': or that the minimum guarantee that stars offer a film is a box-office draw at least equalling the extra cost of hiring them. Ravid claims that although this has been historically true, it has also forced major shifts in the industry: moving from the contract system when stars were owned by studios who then charged the rental to the next stage – when stars shared the property itself – that has itself been now replaced by a considerably more diversified structure, where stars control the intellectual property of the commodity, which relies on sequels and on a range of outcomes that considerably exceed the single film, but also may be seen to be some kind of de-risking strategy by stars to be less dependent only on box-office returns to value their rental worth.

SRK has been perhaps the only Indian hyperstar to make this kind of transition with some degree of planning. There seem to be no reliable indicators of what he is financially worth, but a *Times of India* 21 October 2009 report estimated that his assets were worth Rs 2,500 crore, or almost 10 per cent of the annual total revenues of the Indian cinema as a whole.[10] However, only a small part of this comes from the cinema itself in the orthodox sense: his production outfit Red Chillies Entertainments is majorly invested in VFX (this aspect was especially showcased in *Ra.One*) and of course into both market spinoffs and sport (the Kolkata Knight Riders).[11] *MNIK* itself had tied up to market the core values of the film, its '*Honge kamyaab*' ('We Shall Overcome') line, with Century Ply and Samsonite luggage.

What *MNIK* itself directly shows then, and which I think *Ra.One* can also show, is a particular moment in the contradiction of the career of the star that I think SRK is talking about when he speaks of being conflicted within a cinema of the past and the future: to me, the past is the political undertow of memory that popular culture is condemned to always carry in India, and the future that of a post-cinematic hyperstar both leveraging this memory into diverse outlets but also freeing it from its suffocating narrative bindings in the cinema.

Rajni Power, or, to Keep Browsing, Switch Off Your Internet

> Rajni's email: gmail@rajnikant.com
> When Rajni logs onto Facebook, Facebook updates its status message

Let me take a detour to explore an even larger star than Shah Rukh Khan with an even bigger problem with the cinema. If it is indeed the case that the twentieth century has seen the cinema becoming the par-excellence producer of stardom, are we now in a situation where the cinema is impeding the growth of the twenty-first-century star? Are we seeing a star who is, so to say, trying to be bigger than the cinema itself? Who is like the proverbial Kal-el/Superman's glass ice trapped in the cinema?

Am I the only person to see something curiously tragic in the famous Rajnikant jokes?[12] When the Koodankulam nuclear reactor is to be relocated outside his house since he does not switch on the light but turns the dark off – do we not also perhaps see what this humour is actually saying?

www.desimartini.com/allaboutrajni.htm runs, it claims, on Rajni Power.[13] You are welcomed with much fanfare – Aye Macha! Vanakkam Ayyappam, Welcome, Welcome! Pick one, read on, Macha. You are asked to Pick One from the Man, the Star, the Legend. The Man gives you a curiously unvarnished story of an extraordinarily humble life. He was born the youngest son of Jijabai and Ramoji Rao Gaikwad, who lost his mother aged 5, worked as a coolie and bus conductor.[14] The Legend, on the other hand, comprises almost entirely of the jokes.

Long before I get to any of this, however, something happens that I consider devastating for star power. As soon as you enter the site, it requires you to *first cut off all your external supplies*: your LAN and your wifi. If you don't do it, the site will. Only then does the fanfare begin. I do not have to describe to you, dear reader, what a self-lacerating experience it can be to switch off one's web supplies. Not least when, having enjoyed – if enjoyed is the word – this website, I am instantly brought back to reality, fighting the ultimate fear that some nifty programmer may have changed my settings, as I fight to get the juice back. The people who made this site call it an 'unbelievable spectacle of running a website without the Internet'. The complex algorithm that runs in the back-end, which kicks in as soon as the internet speed is down to zero – the basic premise on which the site and the concept have been constructed – is, he claims, a direct tribute to Rajinikant's larger-than-life image. Unfortunately, when I do reconnect when the site is up, I get a decidedly un-Rajni line, 'Aiyyo! This was unexpected. To keep browsing, switch off your internet'.

Aiyyo! Rajni power, capable of replacing Koodankulam, must therefore be precisely not what it says it is. It is so evidently a statement about *in*ability, maybe tragic failure if anything, of a hyperstar trapped – inside the cinema, now inside my hard disk, deluding himself interminably with the number of guns, flying kicks and bullets he can handle, only pygmified, provincialized by the internet, by atomic energy, by globalization itself. It is so evidently a statement about the *limits* of the cinema: the one medium that through the twentieth century constituted the par-excellence production machine for stardom, now seizing up.

Arming the Spectator

I want to stay for just a little bit longer on this: because I am proposing that something dramatic is going on here. At one level, this business of switching off the net is relatively easily interpreted: the cinema, pioneer of everything grander and larger than life, is being dethroned: dwarfed by an even larger technology. But what, precisely, is 'larger' about the internet? Do we return this to the *Ra.One*-type horror, of a gigantic neural construction run amuck, and which neither Rajni nor Khan can battle anymore because the genie has been now well and truly bottled? (This precise situation obtains in the *Ra.One* game, where in Zone 5 all that G.One has to do is to *run for his life* for 30 seconds). Or is there something else of even greater significance? Can it be that the real act of spillover of cinematic fiction beyond its frames and into the streets has been handed over by the cinema into a radically new vision of narrative? Such a vision, perhaps most directly evidenced in military video games, actually moves into actual reality too, as Eyal Weizman's much-quoted essay on Israeli military manoeuvres in *Frieze* magazine shows.[15] Apparently, in their attack on the city of Nablus in April 2002, Israeli Defence Forces attempted something new that they called 'inverse geometry'. Described in the essay as the 'the reorganization of the urban syntax by means of a series of micro-tactical actions', they worked on the theory that when soldiers defined urban spaces as 'overground tunnels', they could so 'saturate' the urban fabric that very few would have been visible from the air. Such overground tunnels allowed them to move horizontally through walls and vertically through holes blasted in ceilings and floors: a movement named 'infestation' that redefined inside as outside, and domestic interiors as thoroughfares. At stake in all this, says Weizman, was a great deal of theory on urbanism, psychology, cybernetics, post-colonial and post-structuralist theory now taught in military schools.

Of course, both SRK and Rajni can walk through walls. We know that. But if we do take seriously the prior need to switch off the juice, also see this bar on the internet as a threat to *that* spillover? Can this be linked to a further transference of agency that the cinema has already seen, and is now being re-enacted on different platforms? Here, on the internet, and in contrast to ever-larger and more grandiose screen action incarnating the self-image of spectatorial action, we see action at the *other* end, direct spectatorial intervention into the action itself – the possibilities of inverse geometry and infestation and the rest of it most directly evidenced by a once-upon-a-time film spectator now fully armed: first with the zapper, and now a full-scale gaming console with two trigger fingers, the capacity for physical movement and an extraordinary arsenal of weapons to choose from. Today, the Indian superhero's ability to walk through walls fundamentally depends on the skill of the *spectator* to manoeuvre the star-hero through them. If the fan fails, the hero too must.

This *must* have significance for the cinema if the political link between the cinema and everyday life – the signature achievement of Indian film studies – has any salience. If India has provided one basic, foundational, iconic, formulation about the cinema, it is surely this: *cinema stands at the cusp of narrative, apparatus and citizenship*. It is able to provide a uniquely interpellating device in its ability to, first, incarnate the democratic rights of a citizen-spectator as constitutive of the very act of buying a movie ticket, to walk in, sit down and see a movie with full democratic rights, and, second, for the film itself – in *response to the spectator's gaze* – to narratively reaffirm an identificatory/ interpellating pact through conventions of editing, sound mixing and performance. The spectator watched, the apparatus did the work *for him*. No apparatus did this better than that which surrounded the Indian megastar.

Taking this forward, I want to make this suggestion. I believe it is foundational. We see all around us the process of the Indian citizen going digital: with, at least, if not a gaming console, a computer mouse with which to navigate through his rights and act upon his benefits. The best example for this continues to be social networking, which has provoked its own brand of citizen action and direct politics and includes, at once, various candlelight protests, the Arab Spring and Indian anti-corruption activist Anna Hazare.[16] On the other hand, the larger – if more silent revolution – would be transmogrification of states into e-states, requiring all citizens (and sometimes residents) to become digital natives in order to qualify for e-citizen benefits – from PAN cards to gas connections to homeless shelters in Delhi to direct cash transfers to digital land records to insurance to health, and of all the bill payments at Common Service Centres and State Date Centres all

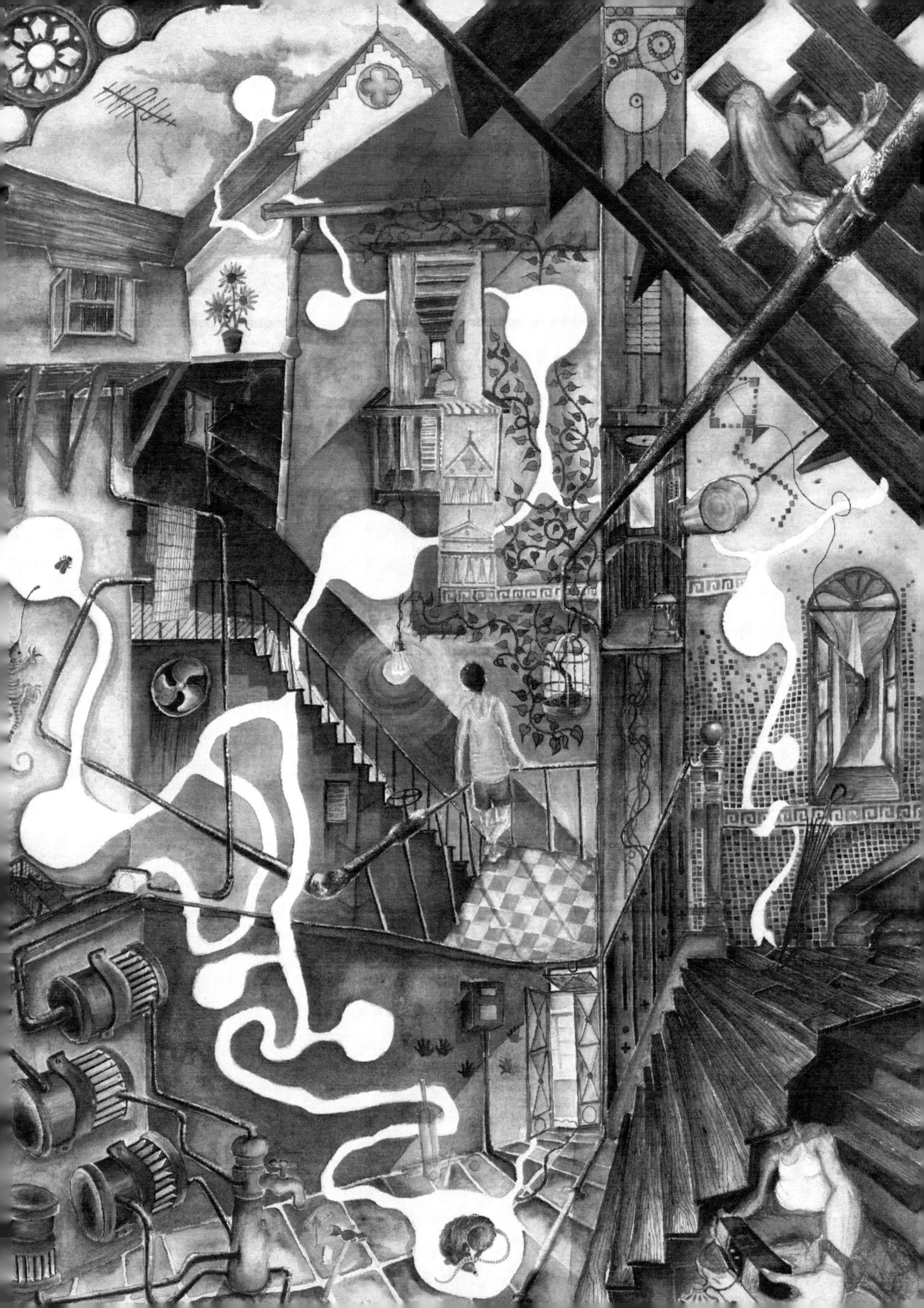

linked through Statewide Area Networks. This half, the aggressive enrolment of India's entire population into a digital ecosystem of governance, further splits into two parts: one, market-driven, includes those seeking to link credit information with bank accounts, in turn with the Public Distribution System, major government schemes including those of employment guarantee, housing and health, and two, potentially draconian plans of surveillance like the proposed National Counter-Terrorism Centre and the NATGRID (National Intelligence Grid) that the Government of India is bent on putting together despite stiff civil-society opposition.[17]

So let me now propose this: what we are seeing now, the opening up of a digital ecosystem of governance, is fully as epochal a development as the original invention of the public sphere that theories of citizenship are likely to survive and indeed take their multi-form identities in the digital ecosystem almost as much as, perhaps even more than, they do in the 'real world'. If *this* is right, and if we expect to have a digital structure as fully laid out as the original public sphere was, it must follow that the process of navigating this space - including knowing where you can be spotted, where you can hide, what you can do, and how you can represent yourself - indeed, all the functions that the denizens of the public domain do today, would find themselves translated *en masse* into the digital ecosystem. If land ownership and credit data - the twin pillars of any self-identity in India - are to be virtualized, as has already happened in astonishingly large parts of the country, it must also follow that digital denizens of this space, including the then cyber-citizens along with cyber-tricksters, cyber-touts, cyber-beggars and cyber-victims, would fully occupy the new cyber-highways, neighbourhoods and alleys, as their originary spaces in the real-life public domain do.

Let me now assume that, for good or ill, we are increasingly part of a digital state. If so, this space must have properties that make it inhabitable, however, such a habitus may be defined. If *this* is right, then digital space must have a *realism* of its own: and perhaps this realism, coming out of the excesses of the cinema, may have very different navigable properties than its now staid ancestor. I am suggesting therefore that a digital *citizen* directly links to the idea of new post-celluloid fictions in which the armed *spectator* plays the key role: and the star, with all his power, mainly works like a puppet at the other end of a long wireless string, one end of which carries the properties of a gaming *console*.

The Back Story: Mumbai

If what we are seeing is a new realism emerging, what would be its memory? Let me now present the denizen of such a digital space - its citizen-navigator - in his profoundly lonely, existential glory, his own private island on *Second Life*,[18] as having one possible ancestry in an equally bombed-out moonscape: in the Hindi cinema, it is the byways and slums of the city of Mumbai. We have repeatedly encountered the mandatory Mumbai back-story of such a hero – once Amitabh Bachchan's Vijay who buys a gigantic multi-storey building in Mumbai to gift to his mother because she once worked as a construction labourer there,[19] and today Rizwan Khan, whose father is working in the Borivali suburb[20] in the State Transport workshop. We encounter it again in *Ra.One* upon the family's return and the problems they have the moment they step out of the airport.

Personally, I have long been fascinated by the presence within Global Bollywood[21] of a particular brand of Mumbai Realism that always somehow grounds it: makes it the grim past that can never be forgotten, however, globalized the glamorous present – and thereby prototypes a remarkable link between cinematic realism in Hindi cinema and what I have elsewhere[22] tried to dub a uniquely Mumbai *territorial realism*. This is not only in obviously Mumbai films like *Shootout at Lokhandwala* (2007, dir. Apoorva Lakhia) or *Mumbai Meri Jaan* (Mumbai My Love/Life, 2008, dir. Nishikanth Kamath); the memory of Mumbai, and locality, local knowledge, even local politics that both attract and repel, are apparently an essential component of the globalized fantasy.

I now further propose that such a Mumbai back-story typically includes a local denizen, even an all-seeing spectator-stalker who is very close to his gaming counterpart as the city produces through local knowledge a*bounded realism*, of the insider, the denizen, the man who walked through his neighbourhood as if he owned it and in that act also claimed for himself the right to *describe* it: a once-upon-a-time-in-the-past gritty realism that becomes essential for producing cultural memory in practically all major globalized Bollywood.

There has historically been a great deal of work done in the spillover of the cinema into spaces outside. In a *longue durée* ancestor to some of the concerns of gaming theory today, as far back as the early 1920s, debates raged on whether movies about bank heists were not, in the final analysis, how-to manuals on the correct way to rob a bank, and whether we were not all learning unsafe sexual habits in addition to losing our eyesight. Since then we have of course had several more sophisticated specific theorizations on the spillover – on how, say, diegetic space can replicate into street architecture or determine, the other way round, the role of horror in capturing certain kinds of urban experience in a way that no other form could. Elsewhere,[23] I have proposed the significance in Indian cinema of the 'cinema-effect', the performance of a specific symbolic gesture prototyped on celluloid but now capable of being replicated everywhere else – to the extent that, for the first time, both technologies (such as gaming) and cultural industries (such as fashion) could 'do' cinema better than the cinema itself could.

Such a denizen of that Mumbai is, for instance, the real-life figure of Marathi

Dalit poet Namdeo Dhasal who walked Virgil-like through the 'Central Bombay's Inferno' (as Dilip Chitre describes him), who *knew* the city, defined himself by the city but literally owned it - or rather *her*, as though she is his 'whore' - by the possession of this knowledge.[24] Dhasal's famous 'Bombay' poem has him saying goodbye to 'her': 'But not before/I will take you/in multiple ways/Not before/I will pin you down/here and now/thus and thus'. Dhasal's use of territorial realism, though spectacular, is by no means unique, and indeed access to such insider realism in the city of Mumbai has become increasingly available to the artist and filmmaker (an early example is Saeed Mirza, but now, via actors like Nana Patekar in Vinod Chopra's *Parinda* (1989), also an entire 1990s generation of Bombay regionalism originating in N. Chandra, Govind Nihalani and even Jabbar Patel films, and later commodified into a larger market in films like Ramgopal Varma's *Satya* (1998).[25]

This was a very particular realism, unique in India, and it alluded to a specific period, a determinate set of political histories and a given set of spaces. The period was the 1970s and early 1980s, the political movements referred to the decade leading up to the landmark 1982 textile strike, the first of two defining political moments that have commonly been seen as having transformed contemporary Bombay (the other being the post-Ayodhya 1992–93 riots),[26] and the space in which it happened was Girangaon (where the city's former textile mills once stood).[27] While the 1982 strike has commonly been seen as Girangaon's 'last stand', since the collapse of the strike also effectively saw the dismantling of the industry itself, both the forms of industrial capital and the histories of state formation and radical-symbolic opposition characteristic of that era continued to be evoked in numerous art practices, particularly in music, poetry and theatre.

'A striker from the 1928 textile strike, parachuted into Girangaon in 1982', writes Raj Chandavarkar,[28] 'would have recognized the same massive, enthusiastic groundswell that drove the leadership forward.' This realism was also, therefore, cast, directly or indirectly, over the time-span of the popular cultures that the working class of Girangaon spawned, as was the larger context within which the 1982 strike mounted its historical significance as it hit at the city's financial elite. And the realism that emerged found itself engaging with foundational questions about the city, its reasons for being (or not being) a part of India: questions that often ran along lines of capital and class rather than region, leading to distinct local variations in India's national imaginary as well as the role of realism in constructing such an imaginary.

Hypervisible Action

A crucial aspect of the politics was a symbolic representation of *this* imaginary, and the most-favoured such representation was that of *spectacular political action* as a particular variant of a *spectacular spectator activity*. Hypervisible action

– the expressive political gesture to which the influential Bombay-based visual artist Sudhir Patwardhan,[29] for example, constantly refers – here goes beyond its usual function of verisimilitude. It reprises, I propose, the *characteristics of a state rationality over a different, expressly political arena* – even going so far as to reconstruct state realism's capacity to embody and to disburse specific rights into an instrument for the exclusive use of an independent citizen/protagonist/ author.

If I am right on all the above, I want finally to suggest it could now be possible to excavate *explicit rights-bearing properties within the symbolic gesture*, whose content, I suggest, reveals shades of social power with startling resemblances to the symbolic domain of a seemingly 'rational' state operation. The political-symbolic gesture derived its formal energy not so much from the radical–ecstatic self-description of the clenched fist, but, rather, from a somewhat specific history of spectatorial imbalance and anxiety arising – I argue – from a particularly 1980s Bombay *legitimation* crisis. Hypervisible political action, in numerous texts in the cinema and the visual arts, functions as a distinct species of the cinema-effect in direct tension with realist textuality, encroaching upon the template of the state's own production of symbolic action.

I mean 'encroach upon' literally here since the political underpinnings often had to do with space. Bombay's political articulations of territory (and the bounded realism policing that territory) have been strident in drawing attention to the hypervisible ambitions of realism as *reclaiming space*: often the very spaces that Article 15[30] of the Indian Constitution names in its prohibition of 'discrimination on grounds of religion, race, caste, sex or place of birth' with regard to access to '*shops, public restaurants, hotels* and *places of public entertainment*; or the use of *wells, tanks, bathing ghats, roads* and *places of public resort* . . . dedicated to the use of the general public' (Constitution of India, Part III, Fundamental Rights: The Right to Equality, 15/2). If the ambitions of such territorial realism were any indication (and we may now no longer limit the instance to Bombay alone), it would appear that political realism would also test out, every step of the way, the rights that such territory embodied for the post-colonial citizen. Its effort to usurp urban realism away from state authentication and into a strategy of *survival-through-description* sharply draws attention to the fact that illegitimate realism often means the illegitimacy of citizenship. A primary right that this particular variant of Bombay realism underpinned was the pragmatic and concretely cognizable right to *shelter*, further equated with the fundamental right to livelihood. For a number of political art practices working on the plane of symbolic realism, the effort is to recast the state's declared 'authenticity-effect' into a new register, to render that effect as an objective urban manifestation, as such realism develops an expressivity via its proven ability to slice through mechanisms that would otherwise render such representations both impossible and illegitimate.

Digital Mediations

If all this is so, and if it is this citizen who is now being digitized, there is surely a role for post-celluloid cinema in *this* new terror-spooked cyberspace: a role similar to the one it had in the era of celluloid. Including the not-so-quaint revisiting of the debate on whether a movie about a bank heist is or is not a how-to manual on the essential facets of a successful bank robbery. It is in this sense that Rajnikant's seeming inability to move his persona into the new virtual domain, the entrapment that I read into Rajni jokes, becomes so tragically significant.

I move to a specific exercise. Digital mediations are increasingly part of everyday life, as actually existing people incarnate their cyborg variants as they both strap on howitzers and drive choppers through dizzying heights, or swipe their credit cards and give their biometrics to an enrolment officer of India's much-discussed Unique Identity for every Indian project.[31] What, as we recognize this fact, if we take the concept of mediation seriously as also having to do with a media*tor*? This could be the local delivery person who brings the digital universe actually to your door – once the hoary character of the postman who also read out letters to their illiterate recipients, and now the 'street bureaucrat' in today's developmental language: the man you actually encounter in an otherwise faceless state. In the cinema, he once was the *benshi*, a species of film-instructor who physically stood between spectator and screen, explaining what the film was about. In the cinema, the mediator has a long history; one that Tom Gunning called the film-instructor,[32] later inducted into the storytelling idiom of cinema, and, we may propose in India, a somewhat diverse and devolved narratorial authority reproduced by many kinds of social mediation.

Such a mediator has resurfaced to a radically new meaning in post-celluloid narrative structures. S/he is not only the bodily consequence of actual individuals putting on various prosthetic or orthotic devices. The category also arises as an entity seemingly capable of mediating a larger problem that digital technologies are presenting across the board to various kinds of meaning-making authority. Traditionally the main carrier of what has come to be dubbed the 'last-mile problem' in India,[33] inappropriate intermediation has often been held as a primary cause for why state benefit does not reach its intended beneficiaries but gets diverted, usually by some middleman. The concept of the last-mile problem is derived from communications theory in addressing the basic question of why a signal does not reach its intended recipient: or when distortions come into play. Often viewed as a principal consequence of corruption, such misdirection is usually sought to be overcome by making an unmediated link between the state as source for the delivery of benefit and the recipient: the best examples being in the phenomenon of direct cash transfers now attached to employment-guarantee

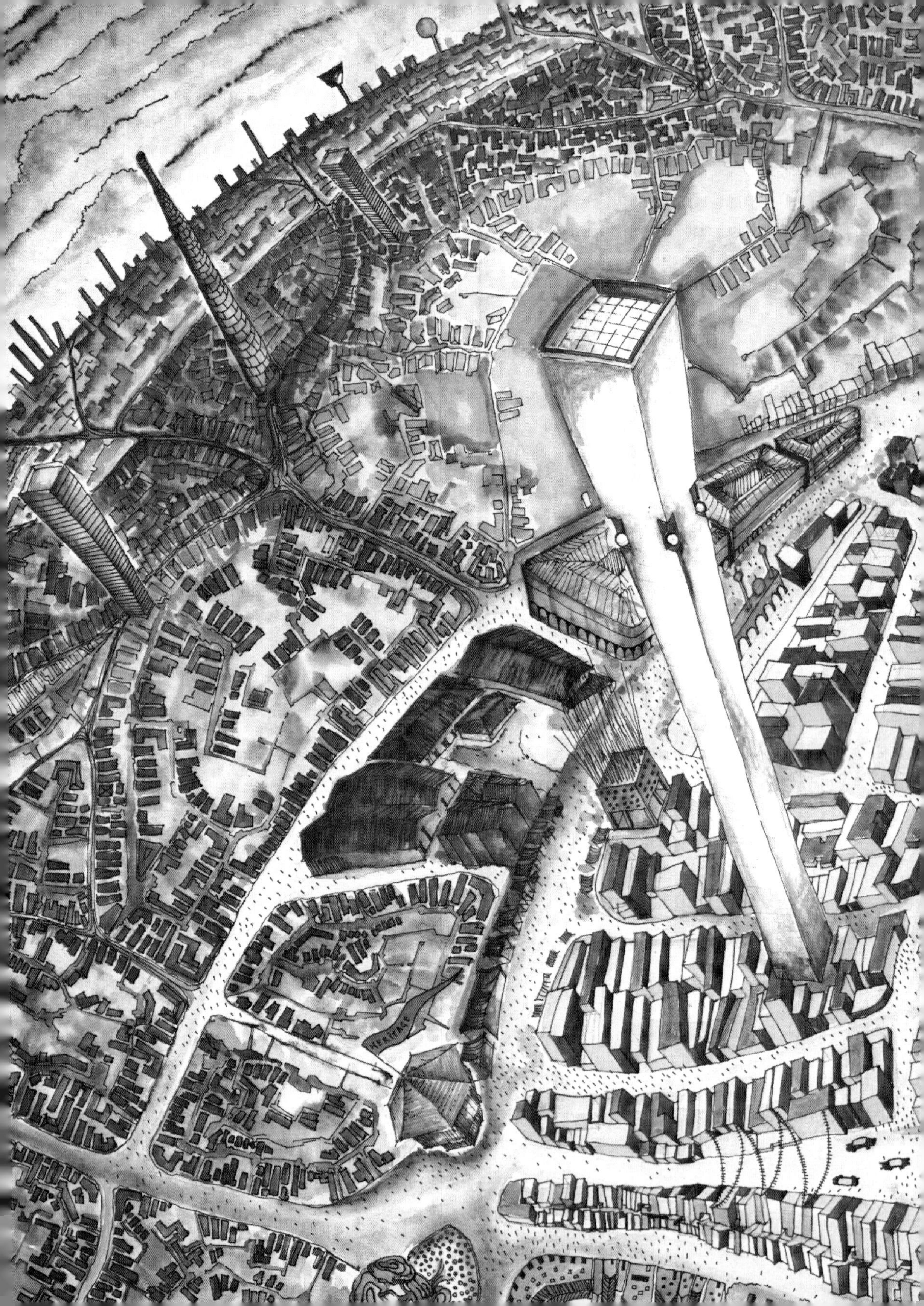
HERITAGE

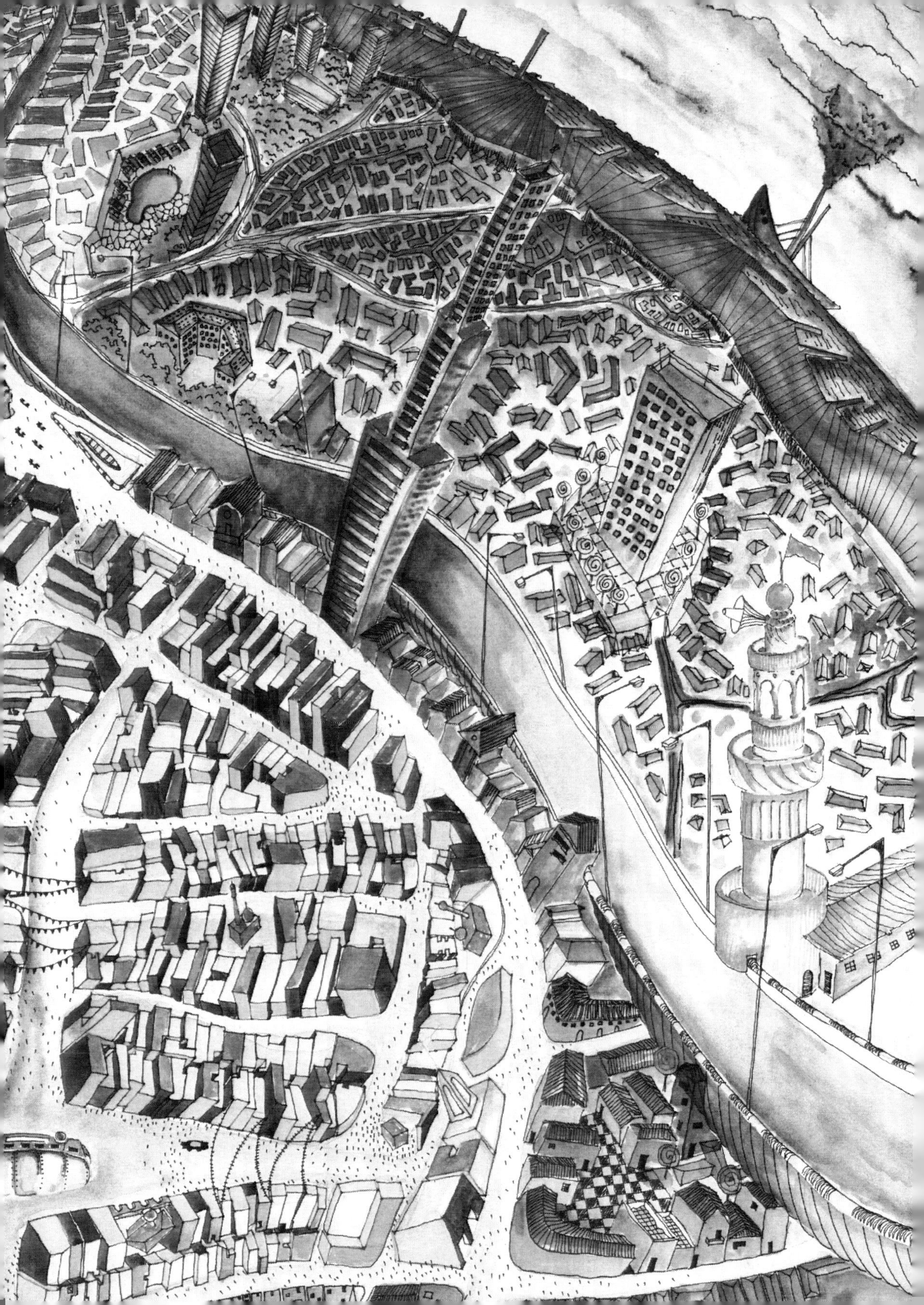

schemes when a state-recognized digital identity is attached to a no-frills bank account and the money goes straight into that account.[34] Such a formulation assumes the middleman as basically the cause of distortion: at worst, personally corrupt, at best, the *cause* of the distortion through his *incomprehension of the message he is meant to deliver*.

Recent modifications being proposed to the Information Technology Act of 2000, which many see as a direct attack on social networking sites, brings matters full circle. A critical rule concerns the kind of 'due diligence' that is to be observed by the mediator of data. This mediation agency now has to notify users of the computer resource that they are not to do any of the many things that 'decent' people should not be doing. Among the things users should not do is to display, upload, modify, publish, transmit, update, share or store any information that belongs to another person. The intermediate agency becomes responsible when the user accesses data that is harmful, threatening, abusive, harassing, blasphemous, objectionable, defamatory, vulgar, obscene, pornographic, paedophilic, libellous, invasive of another's privacy, hateful, or racially, ethnically or otherwise objectionable, disparaging, relating or encouraging money laundering or gambling, or otherwise unlawful in any manner whatever, or which harms minors in any way, infringes any patent, trademark, copyright or other proprietary rights, contains software viruses or any other computer code, files or programs designed to interrupt, destroy or limit the functionality of any computer resource, and so on.

It is one thing to agree, or disagree, as to whether some of these acts are illegal, and quite another to make the mediating agency legally responsible for the data that he is processing; this also has significant political consequences for the entire history of the very concept of mediation. Is a postman legally responsible for the content of the letter that he reads out? Prashant Iyengar of The Centre for Internet & Society has argued that a mediation agency that houses user-generated content, such as say Wikipedia, would need different terms of use from an intermediary such as an email provider such as Hotmail, similar to the liability that a newspaper publisher accrues is different from that accrued by the post office.[35] But wait, what if the intermediary is of a very different generation? What if he is no longer merely your local cable guy or your ISP but is a Google or a Facebook? What, in short, if the user is an unintended mediator? Or, even an ordinary man, who is secretly a heavily armed urban guerilla?

The rules further make it necessary that if intermediaries are informed of any violation, which includes even an email with an electronic signature, they should remove access to such information that is claimed to be infringing or to be the subject of infringing activity, and within 90 days inform the police about such information. This is of course staggering, and Iyengar clearly shows that it is fundamentally unconstitutional. If any person is aggrieved by information posted online, they may seek their remedies – including the relief of injunction – from courts of law, under generally applicable civil and criminal law. Inserting a rule such as this one would take away the powers of the judiciary in India to define the line dividing permissible and impermissible speech, and vest it instead in the whims of each intermediary. This, he says, can only have a chilling effect on debates in the public domain (of which the internet is a part) which is the foundation of any democracy.

Reconsidering Hypervisible Action

This problem is a serious one, it seems, meriting serious action from our armed spectator. If, as we are agreed, the video gamer is almost certainly a direct descendant of the urban guerilla of Mumbai's 1980s realism, how can we imagine today's Dhasal? What would hypervisible political action mean today? Andrew Galloway points out that crucial to any video game is the expressive act, where you select, pick, get, rotate, unlock, open, talk, examine, use, fire, attack, cast, apply, type, emote.[36] What is important is the coupling of an *acting agent* (the player character) and the *actionable object*, which can come in the form of buttons, blocks, keys, obstacles, doors, words, non-player characters and so on. Non-actionable objects are inert scenery, and indeed certain objects are deliberately created as inert masses whereas others are linked to specific functions that can produce action responses.

Imagine a Dhasal walking through Mumbai's metropolis, amid explosions, explaining to his readers which spaces, in his moonscape of a *Golpitha*, are 'inert scenery' and which related to functions that can produce 'actionable objects'. In those days, especially, everyday life realism in Mumbai would all-too commonly be seen as covering up for dark misdeeds: where the more ordinary the view, the more likely that, far from inert, it only hid deep secrets. It is fascinating to imagine the politicized fan-spectator of a celluloid film entering this domain, and perhaps salutary to imagine its reverse – a curious limit, or ceiling, or glass box into which SRK appears trapped within the cinema. We may need to track closely how, say, conventions of editing, sound mixing and shot-taking, the entire cinematic grammar that was associated with spectatorial action, now translates into gaming language.

A curious and significant means by which the hyperstar cuts through the fiction and seemingly addresses the spectator directly is through a hypervisible act: most famously perhaps, Rajnikant's cigarette-throwing gesture or the many gags associated with SRK's *Don* series (2006 and 2011, dir. Farhan Akhtar). If the hypervisible gesture can be seen to find its ancestry in the symbolic political act, can it also show its ability to cut through the maze of civil society to address its beneficiary with the directness that only digital technology can allow? Back in 2002, a furious debate had taken place, in which Lawrence Liang, S.V. Srinivas and I, along with several friends, had virtually fallen out over the famed Rajnikant gesture.[37] The problem was that Rajni had sought to copyright his gesture from the film *Baba* (2002, dir. Suresh Krishna), and the question was whether he, as a movie star with a movie-audience, 'owned' this gesture or not. Was such a copyrighting process – to which adherents of copyleft furiously objected, correctly perhaps, but which they were unable to see as being any different from other forms of corporate copyrighting – not integral to the kind of narrative contract that the movie star established with his audience? Would the radical position, that of attacking the star's effort to copyright his gesture, not threaten to crack open the very edifice of both the political and then the populist gesture, even as these moved into their purely commodified phase? The crucial problem in this was what the gesture implied: a kind of contract that bound spectator and star together; and it was also whether a naïve copyleft position had adequately accounted for the transformation, the *political* transformation, of this gesture from such a contract and into a commodity.

Let me take this to a specific example: the only narrative crisis for an Indian game that I have come across. This is *Ra.One*: an SRK movie that is also a top-down 3D arcade action game available online, on PlayStation 2 and on all Apple platforms. You are the mighty superhero G.One who has to defend the world against the wrath of a surreal creation codenamed Ra.One. G.One not only switches on the dark, he can solidify electricity. The gamer's mission is to survive, and then to destroy Ra.One and his Commanders. The publicity claims that the encounter will include 'epic boss battles, tons of character customization and purchasable weapons, armour and upgrades', and you can also track your unlocked achievements over Game Centre or publish them on your Facebook wall.

It doesn't take more than a few minutes to see that the *Ra.One* game, even if you haven't encountered Batman's Arkham series, is – to use SRK's own language – 'rubbish'. The characters have no depth at all, the arena isn't worked out nor, importantly, the enhancement of power capacity. That the Indian gaming market has fumbled with how to arm an Indian spectator with this kind of armoury – the hypertechnologization, almost overnight, of what used to be no more than the plain act of looking, or at most whistling, or maybe dancing in the dark – such multidimensional functions are not easily technologized – is perhaps understandable. And so a reviewer complains that in the *Ra.One* game you start off with a

> tutorial, where you'd want to keep track or note down what each button does on paper because there's no explanation of the controls via the option menus. Yes. This is a video game in 2011 that decides it's cool to let you fumble your way through it. I think that's the way you're meant to play it because even though each

> button has a specific function, such as ranged and melee attacks or block, the camera doesn't zoom in to the action so you'd rarely know what you're doing without sitting less than a foot away from the screen.[38]

But the Indian spectator can never be taken for granted, and quickly this very review decides that there appears to be a curious and very Bollywood method in the madness since this confusion involves hammering down on your melee and ranged attacks long enough to fill up your, yes, power meter.

> Doing so allows you to unleash a special attack that does an effective job of clearing a room full of baddies. There are *power-ups* that allow you to regain health or enhance your speed, among other things. Certain levels have you trying to survive a rather timid onslaught before the timer runs out. Before you know it, the game devolves into a race to tap your controller long enough to get to a super attack.

These power meters, by which the good guys can recoup are startlingly similar to the kinds of covert knowledge that I had pointed out in the Mumbai instances: streets that you cannot take or ones where there is shelter, spaces where you can hide or where you can top-up. I am less interested in such ways by which the spectator and his screen puppet, the star, than in returning to the crisis that Rajni narratively finds himself in, in having to switch off his own power to generate Rajni Power.

In Conclusion

Is it then that, even as the symbolic modes of meaning production prototyped on celluloid film, which have always in cinema's history tended to spill out into spaces beyond the unstable film frame - the famous Rajni or SRK gestures that were, once, par excellence acts of slicing through cinematic fiction to directly address real-life situations - now finding themselves trapped within some box from which they cannot escape - that, at the same time, we see post-celluloid action marching towards a new brand of citizen empowerment? At once, with machine guns and howitzers, and with biometric data safely ensconced in a state repository?

In this paper, I have tried to address a particular new turn to the concept of cinematic excess, translated into a specific techno-performative crisis that SRK chooses to embody in his new superhero avatar: an avatar that, I think, has the same salience to the very un-superheroic Rizwan Khan as it does to the actual superhero G.One. Khan is correct, I propose in conclusion to speak of both technology and freedom, even as he works out his own economic model for his hyperstardom: both beyond the cinema and within it. The march of cinematic action is, in Khan's work, being virtually driven by a need for narrative exegesis that the traditional apparatus of celluloid simply finds insufficient.

Acknowledgement
I acknowledge with gratitude the help and support of Arun Menon in putting this essay together.

To,

Insurance and Justice department,
Kindom of Ram
Ayodhya

This is to bring to your kind concern that I am Sita, tbe queen of the Kingdom of Ram, d/o King Janaka and lawful w/o King Ram. With due respect, I am writing this letter to you to bring to your notice the incident that took place called 'agnipariksha' which by definition is a material examination of otherwise non-material values of morality and loyalty, tested by fire.

As you are aware, I have successfully stepped through the fire. However,
Ram under the pressure of the public has allowed my name to be tarnished and has bannished me into exile.

This has led to a deep hurt. I claim my insurance on loss of dignity and defamation. I will be waiting for your prompt response. Please have it sent to Valmiki's ashram as I will not be staying at the palacc any longer.

Yours faithfully
Sita

Sita

In 1998, the film *Fire* was cleared by India's Censor Board, two years after it was shown at the Toronto International Film Festival. It created a major public storm for its portrayal of a homo-erotic relationship between sisters-in-law in a traditional, middle-class East Delhi patriarchal joint family.[1] While the domestic Indian response to the film has been discussed, less discussed has been the film's reception in the multicultural political context of the USA. Patel's approach brings together three very divergent stands of analysis: parliamentary debates on the opening up of the insurance industry to foreign investment, political debates around religion and secularism in the 1990s, and public and media reactions to *Fire*. Patel proposes a way of extending our understanding of the individual body to that of the body politic, through a unifying theory of the 'performance and speculation of loss'. She argues that the right to recognition (by the publics of cinema and the nation) is predicated on the *production* of loss.

This text is a new version of the chapter 'Firing Time', originally published in Geeta Patel, *Risky Bodies & Techno-intimacy: Reflections on Sexuality, Media, Science, Finance*, Seattle: University of Washington Press, 2017. This version is published with permission from the author.

Keywords, Names

Ayodhya, Censor Board (CBFC), Sangh Parivar (Vishwa Hindu Parishad, Bajrang Dal): See Keywords (pp. 326–44).

Ghosh, Shohini: Author of *Fire: A Queer Classic* (2010), filmmaker, and member of the Mediastorm Collective, see 166–74.

Karva Chauth: North Indian ritual where wives fast and pray for the longevity of their husbands, popularized by Bollywood neo-traditionalism.

Mehta, Deepa: Indian-born Canadian documentary and fiction filmmaker. *Fire* (1986) was intended as the first of an 'Elements' trilogy, the other films being *1947: Earth* (1998) and *Water* (2005).

NRI (Non-resident Indian): Legal category of Indians living abroad, with special privileges for paying tax and owning property. Since the 1990s also viewed culturally as a class of prosperous, upwardly mobile and politically conservative Indians separated historically from indenture and working-class migration.

Parekh, Asha: Former movie star and first female chairperson of the CBFC from 1998 to 2001, responsible for the astonishing clearance of *Fire* without cuts twice over.

Sita: One of the characters in *Fire*, referencing 'the ideal wife' in the *Ramayana*. The censors asked for this character's name to be changed to Nita.

Images

p. 249: Fictionalized insurance claim by Sita against Rama on grounds of attack on dignity and defamation, following the *agnipariksha* (trial by fire).

pp. 254–55: Low-resolution printouts of images from the film being set on fire at the hands of a seemingly heterosexual married woman. A strange challenge encountered while trying to locate high-resolution media images of protests against the film was that none could be found. Stories that had once featured as newspaper headlines had sunk to the archaeological bottom of digital debris. Perhaps they had gone out of search, and had been deleted. The image used here is a staged construction.

All images courtesy Sultana Zana.

GEETA PATEL 2016

17 Firing Time

Act 1: Scene 1: April 7, 1998

The film *Fire* is screened at a small women's college in the United States. Deepa Mehta attends the screening. She has recently returned from Delhi where she has been shooting *Earth* (1998).

A young woman who heads up the college's south Asian student association, stands up. Men, she says, have fared badly in the film. Their depictions are unsatisfactory, the film violates Indian manhood. The filmmaker responds judiciously pointing out her subtle evocations of men in pain. Tightly woven into emotion, the Indian student forestalls the discussion.

Act 1: Scene 2: May 1998

The semester has come to a close at this women's college. Emails are flying around the local circuit, as faculty get ready to leave campus. The donors whose money was used to screen *Fire* as well as other films by women directors have asked to see the films. The daughter of the donor is extremely upset about *Fire*; she says that her money has gone to fund porn, the film is offensive and not what students on a women's campus should be exposed to.

Act 1: Scene 3:

I talk to students about the controversy over showing *Fire* on campus. The students are mainly white, with a sprinkling of Latinas. Despite the conversations that have taken place on the college-networked bulletin board about the film, which prescribes the film's failures, and which they are aware of, these women seem to have escaped the discussions that produce the film's showing as an institutional artifact. And, they say, the head of the Indian student's association dislikes the representations of Indian men in the film. The Indian student is a Non-Resident Indian (NRI) by default. It seems to me that the silence that follows my attempts to continue this discussion signals a retreat – the voice of the designated other has spoken her will, through a speaking of her injury.[2] The discourse of personal injury seems impassable. A conversation about the presumed proprieties of pedagogy, about institutional imperatives bequested through donating institutional capital that simultaneously gifts proper women who must be kept from porn, and who must be educated right, is forestalled before a hurt body of a person. This discussion is forestalled before the violations of community constructed as a violation of an 'ethnic' person by 'bad' representations – not of their own body, but of the bodies of another gender that share community rights. Bad representations of Indian men hurt Indian women in the diaspora. Another sentence slips into the silence – wasn't Deepa Mehta Canadian, not really Indian? Suddenly we are haunted by a struggle in the diaspora, between women in the diaspora, who are in a tensile debate over how the behavior of Indian men (in India) ought to look.

Act 2

November 13, 1998: *Fire* opens in 42 theaters throughout India.[3] It has been reviewed well; the film is touted as one that has won many awards. In a 6 November article in the *Times of India* the film's distributor describes the film as one about masturbation and lesbian interaction. He is also cautious about its prospects for popularity – after all it has no songs. It shows to packed houses, 80–90 per cent full. Several theatres have women-only shows.

The Censor Board, led by Ms Asha Parekh[4], releases *Fire* uncut. It asks for only one change – that the name Sita[5] be changed to Nita. The shift in names articulates an awareness of modern evocations of Indian womanhood that signify through the mythic character Sita. Though this is never said at the time, it becomes a clearly articulated issue as the debate over the film rages.

One week later (Nov 20): A reviewer[6] in the *Times of India* says that *Fire* is about Indian gender politics and 'traditional' values. She believes that though most people know that the film contains lesbians (relationship between two sisters in law) and labels it a lesbian film, this does *Fire* a grave disservice, because it questions 'traditional' values and accepts pluralistic sexual 'choices'. It is an expression of love offered with a dignity and compassion rarely seen in Indian cinema. For the reviewer, though, it is Mehta's location, as a diasporic Indian, which provides her a special sightline that allows a critique of India's myths – why men don't fast on *Karva Chauth,*[7] why Ram does not want Sita after her trial by fire. Critics of the film allege that despite the sharpness of her critique Mehta 'plays it safe'. Mehta apparently does not produce lesbians in the 'tradition' of portrayals by 'real' lesbians in the diaspora, namely Pratibha Parmar and Suniti Namjoshi.[8]

Real lesbians, then, are not housewives; their companionable relationships fall outside marriage (heterosexual). Mehta's lesbians, are instead, two middle-class housewives who walk out of the scene of the domestic – something not likely to happen in India, according to the reviewer, and therefore generated by the desire of a non-resident Indian longing for women's liberation on home ground. Unlike the Indian student in the United States, this reviewer feels that the men in the film are sympathetic characters: in pain and constrained like the women by longings aligned around 'tradition'.

Dec 3: The finance minister, Yashwant Sinha, and Atal Behari Vajpayee, the Prime Minister, have their backs against a wall. The BJP government is bargaining with 'Sangh Parivar'[9] hardliners over measures to allay *swadeshi*[10] fears over the opening up of the insurance industry (now public) to foreign investment.[11] The new bill will permit foreign companies and Non-Resident Indians (NRI) to invest in a hitherto nationally controlled industry.

Dec 3: L.K. Advani, the home minister, assures the Rajya Sabha (Upper House of Parliament) that arrangements have been made to protect Peer Baba Budhan's shrine[12] in Karnataka, which has recently turned controversial. The Vishwa Hindu Parishad and the Bajrang Dal announce that they will lead suicide squads to liberate the shrine from four directions. Like Ayodhya, this is a site of the performance of overlapping beliefs.[13] The shrine, controlled by the Karnataka government, permits Hindus to come here to worship. Groups of Hindu worshippers, given special dispensation by the Karnataka High Court, arrive for three days to observe Guru Dattatreya Jayanti during *Kartik Purnima*[14] Muslims visit the shrine to commemorate the burial of Peer Baba Budhan. When the home minister, Shree Advani discusses the shrine, his statements appear to give Hindus and Muslims equal access to the shrine's past and the property that forms its domain. Muslim Congressmen point out that the shrine is Muslim, and Hindus are 'given permission' to come and pray. The parliament in Delhi is worried about a repeat of the Babri Masjid.

The language that comes to be deployed a year later when the insurance bill is traveling through the parliament haunts the VHP and Bajrang Dal's calls: the language is of franchising. Successful insurance development, a viable insurance industry, is proposed as something that might need franchises. Is this also the case with particular brands of communalism? Property grounds these evocations of communal 'rights' and calls for 'communalized' access. Through a particular call, that seems to repeat itself insistently, property and rights, history and use come to be contested, where once they were merely present in collective use. The Hindu right wing challenges the rights of a community who has religious use of particular pieces of property mandated by a particular rendition of the historical record: claims to use,

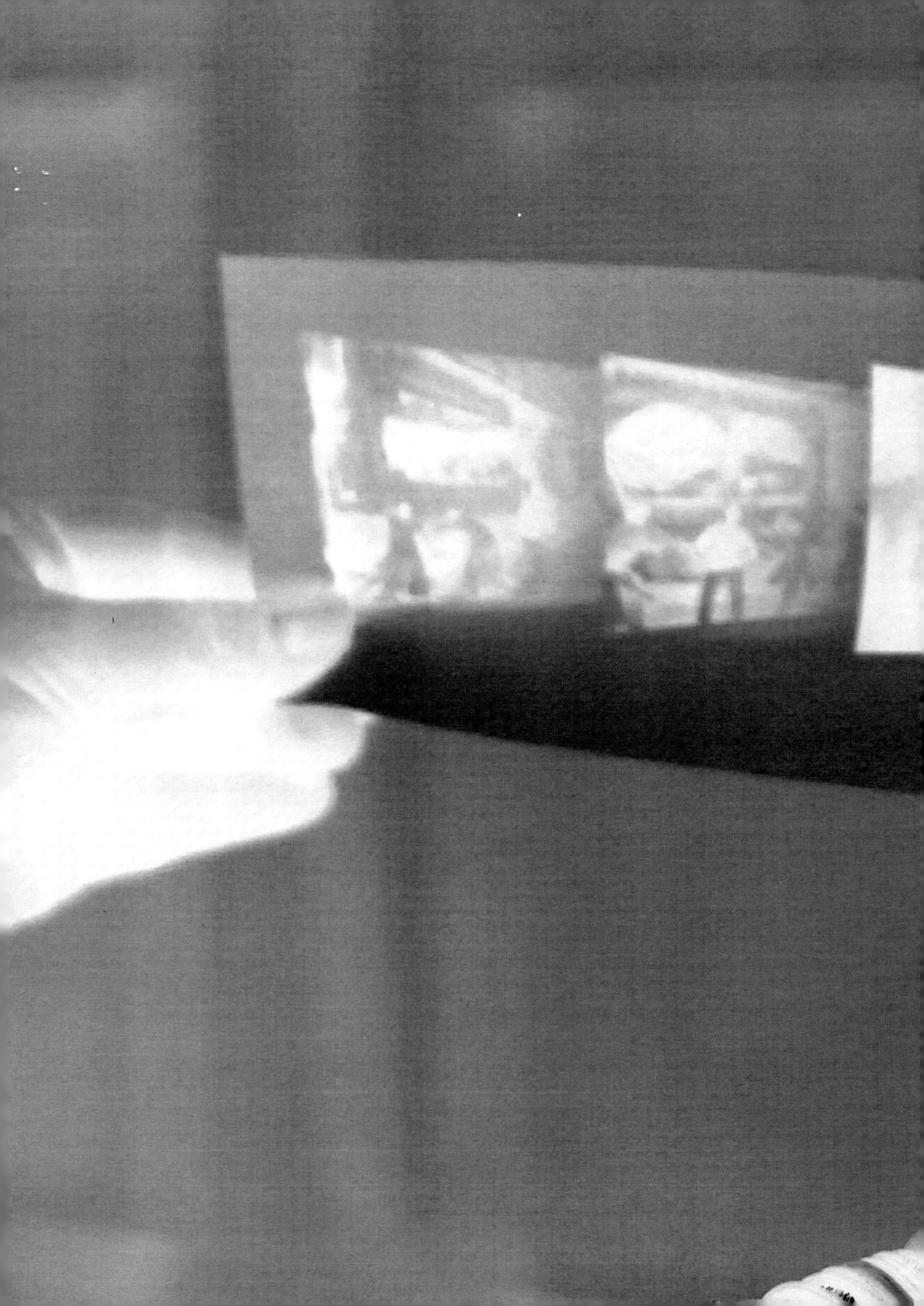

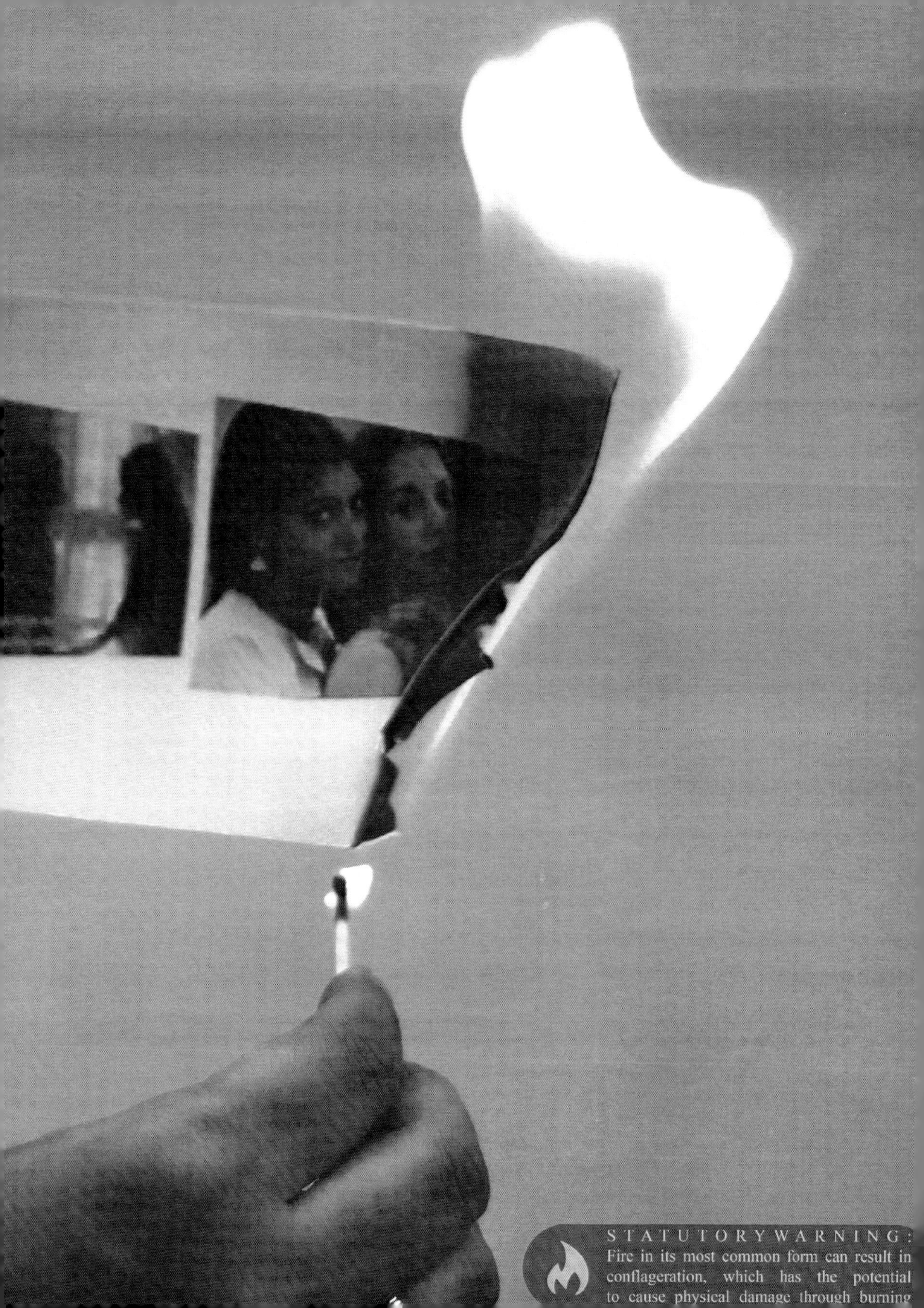
STATUTORY WARNING:
Fire in its most common form can result in conflageration, which has the potential to cause physical damage through burning

rights of access are at stake here. The right-wing challenge to the record, attempts to put to right what they see as use in seizure and a failure to read the historical through the mythic. Nationalism is contested and constituted in the process, who can establish allegiances and accrue political feeling as capital, and how they do it through a re-recording of history. To order up sentimental, nostalgic desiring affiliation to a plot of land, and place that has served, through its monuments, the religious 'needs' of what the Hindu right wing constitutes as one of its others, Hinduness must be produced as violated by the historical violences attributed to Islam.[15]

* * *

Technologies of insurance are about the management of losses that never occurred (and perhaps this is why fraud is such a potent charge when someone comes forward for compensation). Insurance relies on people buying into forms of wholeness that precede losses, where both the losses and wholeness that attends them are sold as commodities that did not exist at one time. Consumers have to be trained to recognize them and participate in and so produce their realness by buying protections for them. That is the paradox of insurance – it is a technology of persuasion that assures you that you will buy into something you had previously never known was there to be attended to. That is its magic, the magic of expanding capital without a concrete product, a tangible thing – to teach the insured to care for something ephemeral and invest in it as something under threat of loss. So also for diasporic communities: the idea of the nation built from the stuff of that comes to stand for 'cultural' immutability. Blood loss: the impingement, the loss that produces the whole as prior, but that whole never actually lives except as the prior which allows the production of the loss. Shared loss – collective compensation for capital invested in the family and the nation that might have (and must have not) been forged assemblages.

Deepa Mehta, presenting her film in the United States, is asked again and again to account for her representations of masculinity – implicit concerns with portrayals of Indianness. The Indian NRI student at the women's college is no exception: she speaks the violations that circulate in the diaspora. In South Asia, neither men nor women seem to have obsessed about masculinity. Instead, the three nodes of incitement, each produced through the other, are: Indianness (not through but by men, and women); women and sexuality; and the freedom of expression in the public sphere. Who has the right to speak for and about 'tradition', to control its production, who has the right to speak for and of women, and who has the right to control public discourse? The public is produced as publics – as innocent watcher, as injured innocent, as mature reader, as critical mass, as being spoken for and as speaking.

Various voices spoke, bringing competing publics into being. In India, in the debates over *Fire*, the publics were coagulated through the 'cultural' which became the magnet around which nationalisms, specifically Indian nationalisms, and Indian citizenship were constituted, even as culture was produced through religious nationalisms. The fiduciary rights that accrued to cultural nationalisms were at stake here, and what was being argued, or spoken for was what genres these nationalisms might assume (Hindu right wing, Hindu left wing, various kinds of secular, sexual through culture, etc.), and which citizens would have access to mandating their shape, controlling them. This speaking resolved itself in appeals to the constitution – to the Supreme Court for a legal resolution on the democratic rights to free viewing and showing that accrue to all citizens, and possibly the constitution for rights under democracy for a particular body of citizens, here lesbians. The right to religious sentiment came to be poised against the right to view, the right to access; an open community of Hindus galvanized as 'all those threatened by damage' against an open community to which all could belong sedimented by a demand for right of free access.[16]

* * *

So what am I *doing* by attending to the serendipity of contiguous political demands, for controlling access to insurance and controlling access to aesthetic objects and that bring insurance policies sold in the diaspora alongside right-wing demands to curb particular sorts of representation? I am deploying several features of insurance to reveal the modalities through which attachments were produced.[17] In an idealized vision of what insurance can mobilize, it pools resources, gathering those who have less access and those who are liable to the danger of loss with those who are safer and more privileged. In the utopian world that insurance theorists sometimes sell, capital is transferred from people with more access to those who have less – we might think of this as the world of the welfare state.

I think of insurance as the form of possibly redistributive capital that offers a way to understand how claims to recognition might be shaped. Recognition itself becomes a kind of demand for redistribution. Competing claims to recognition are *produced* as expectations about redistribution. Recognition through redistribution, protection against loss of value or loss of a good, is deployed by people without access to capital as well as people, such as right-wing Hindu constituencies, who from many vantage points would appear to be given a larger proportion of extant capital but *produce* themselves as always under a state of loss, or subject to past or future deprivation. Access to resources is not about not having access but about *producing* the loss of access as a literal loss; the italicized verbs are necessary here.

Refusals to privatize insurance and to open it up to foreign investment were threaded through the fights over who had proprietary rights over objects that were conceived as prior and that were under threat of loss. This form of protectionism (as valuable and as problematic) is inflected by technologies associated with insurance as an instrument that compensates for losses. To turn to Shohini Ghosh's attentiveness to solidification by proliferation, the unexpected effect of censorship was as true of sexualized communities such as lesbians who gathered together as it was of the idea of the idealized lost world of families, of Hindu 'tradition', of inviolate nation. The right wing understood this. They were thickening into presence what they had constituted as lost – what they might not have realized was that they were also concomitantly shaping what they wanted not to be into being.

* * *

Several things can be observed or become clear in these stagings. Publics can be understood as composed in demand to protections from losses of property vested in a utopian object or past or loss of access to free and easy viewing, whether these publics are made up of more right-wing or more left-wing constituencies in either India or in the diaspora or as Shohini Ghosh has shown as almost macabre collaborations of the right with feminists and left-wing activists in India striving to save women from unseemly (read sexual) representations. Many of these demands were made in the context of losses of capital in other places or shifts in capital, such as losses in elections that preceded the struggles over *Fire* or right and left-wing activists' mandates to restrain promiscuous representational forms when technologies of viewing effloresced in the 1990s.[18] These demands were a kind of transference, a displacement, perhaps even a form of reification (in the networked technological sense of the word) where redistribution and recognition came together.

Nationality traverses borders, finding its definition through religion as culture constituted as a wholeness that never was, and that carries with it the same registers that religious/cultural nationality has when it is defined within India. In both India and the diaspora nationalism is nostalgic. But citizenship breaks away from the territory of the Indian nation-state to be articulated as either global, or as a kind of belonging vested in another, western, nation. This despite, or perhaps because of, the ways that groups whose range of operation is supposed to be India, like the VHP, travel borders to ensure the proper attitudes to Hinduism, and ensure that the appropriate kinds of Hinduism travel as culture outside Indian borders.[19] Cultural capital is invested in religion, and its control is mandated through the body whose investments have been brought to failure. Political capital, or economic capital, is never explicitly marked or marketed, even though it is protected in the ways that we see in advertisements that sell insurance to Indian diaspora communities. Their returns appear only in sidelines – as investments in bodies thought to lose class, or in histories that propose Hinduism as a religion under siege by the political mandates thought to reside in Muslim communities.

It is also clear that bringing *Fire* to the fore to site these discussions aligns them in unexpected ways. It transmutes the body of a person into forms of the body politic. Bodies whose claims are sought in coagulations of feeling around the loss of blood capital invested in nostalgic nationalisms, whether those claims are deposited in technological intimacies in the diaspora or orchestrated in more face to face ones in India. And here, the formal representatives of politicized bodies negotiate traversals: sometimes deliberately, sometimes askance.

The ethics offered by the continuing, and hopefully rancorous disputations around this cultural artifact need to be contextualized by a rigorous demand neither to keep the constitutional body politic as nation in place, nor to keep the body as body violated (and therefore stymieing discussion) in place. The ethics offered by the disputations around *Fire* also need to be attended to in their particularities. That at the very least, multiple, competing, messy, incomplete forms of religiosity should become an axis for an analysis of same-sex sexuality.[20] That the kinds of gestures, modulations, differences that transmute bodies away from abstraction, transmute them in the forms of their beingness produced in locations must be taken into account in matters of policy. All these are modulated by the particular exigencies and urgencies that attend the new state of affairs that pertains following the general elections of 2014 and 2019.[21]

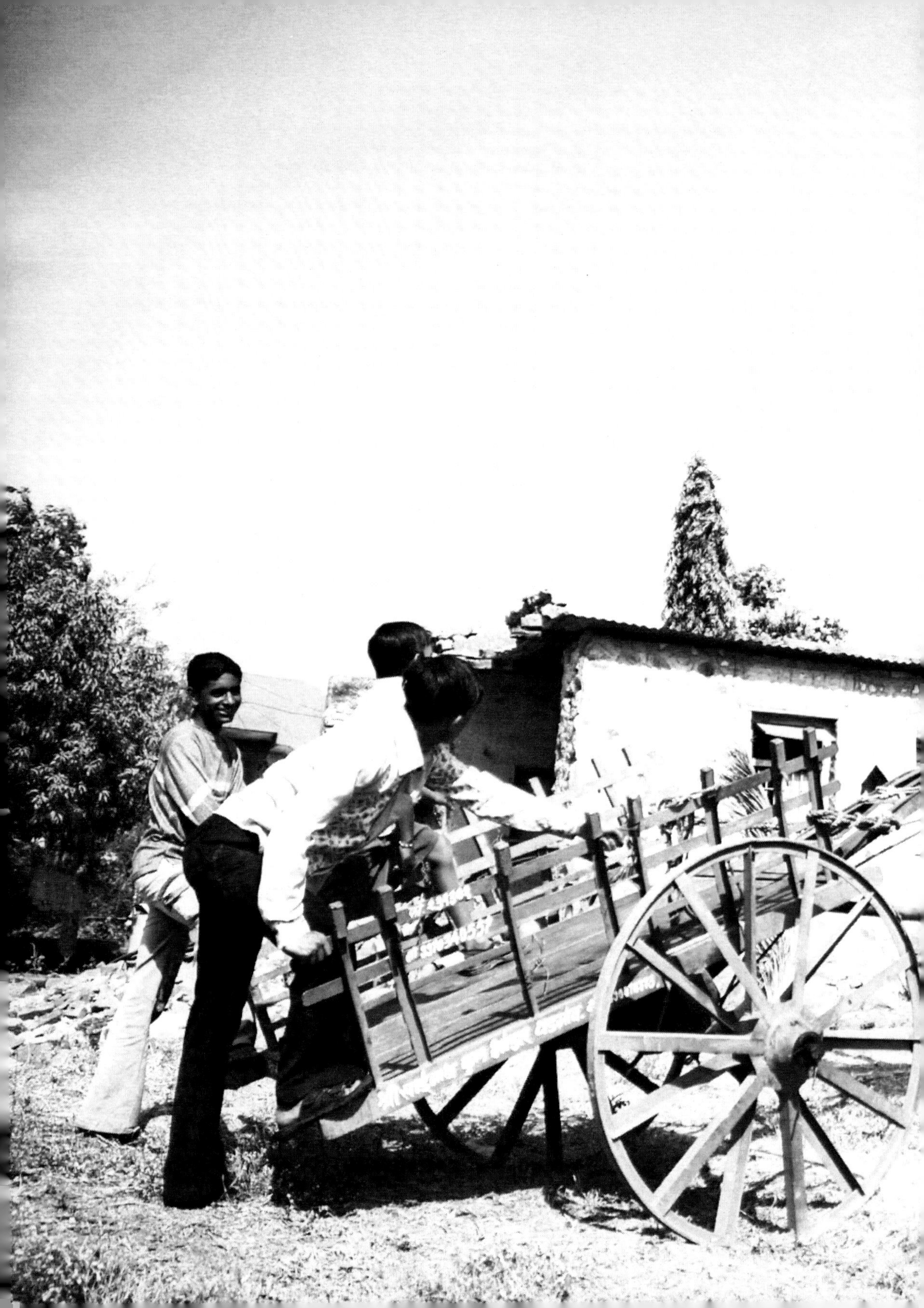

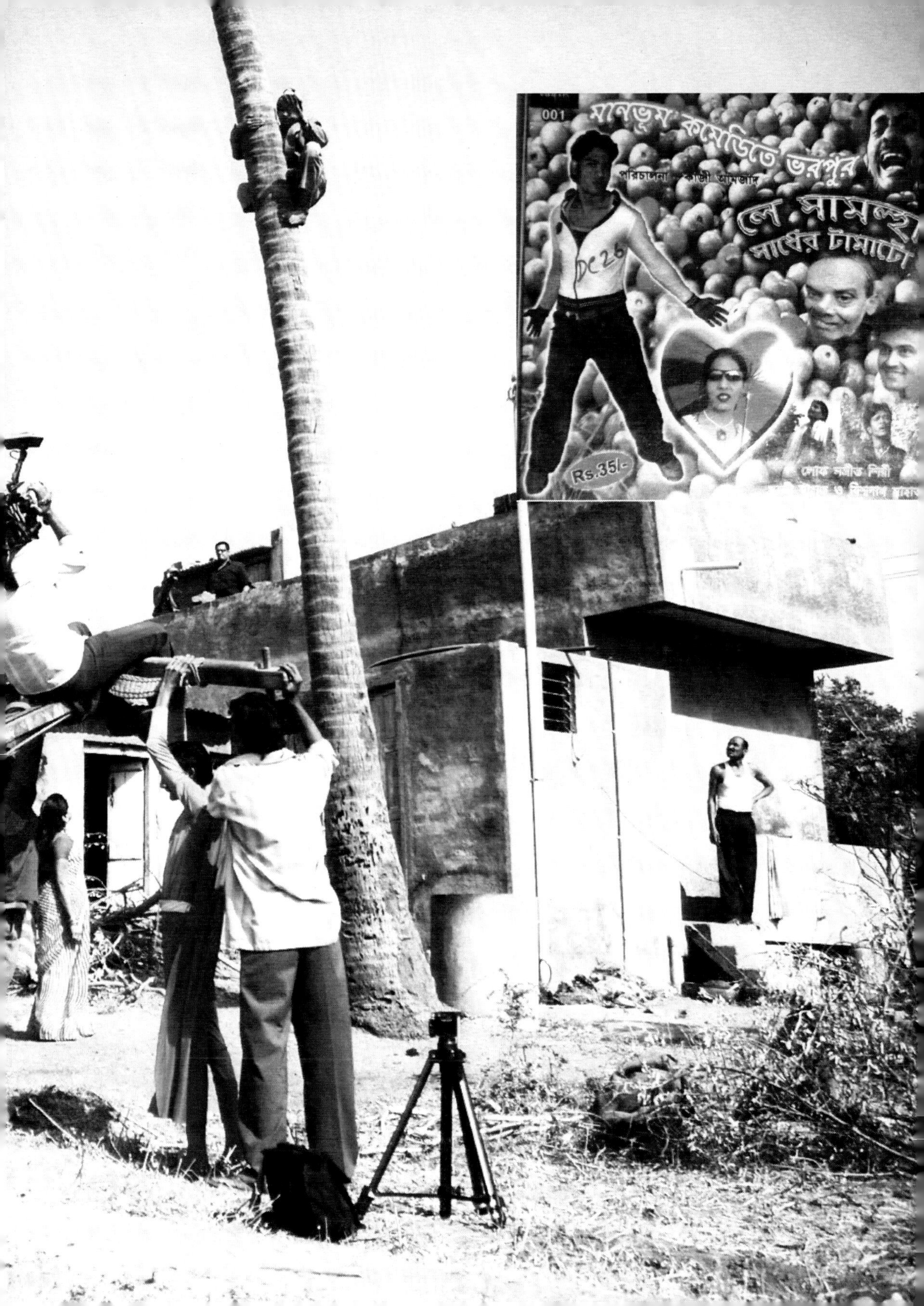
001
মানভূম কমেডিতে ভরপুর
সাধের টামাটো
Rs.35/-

Purulia district, on the edge of West Bengal and known as an epicentre of far-feft activism, is also known as the home of the Manbhum *bhasha* (language), considered the centre of the Bengali nationalist- language movement. Since the 1970s, its location at the borders of three Indian states – Bengal, Bihar and Odisha – makes it at once marginal to centralized metropolitan culture industries and central to another kind of linguistic traffic. An informal low-budget moving image industry today brings new meaning to long histories associated with both the linguistic and political legacies of Manbhum, complicating our understanding of 'regional cinema' beyond the governmentality of official state languages and boundaries. Manbhum also draws attention to the democratizing impulse of informal media through low-cost technologies far removed from the 'national consciousness' of mainstream media.

An earlier version of this essay was published as 'Toward a New Frame for Regional Films: Manbhum Videos and the Other Side of (Indian) Cinema' in *BioScope: South Asian Screen Studies,* vol. 7, no. 1, 2016, pp. 58–79. This version is published with permission from the author and Sage Publications Pvt Ltd.

Keywords, Names

Bhadralok, Jugaad Aesthetics, Malegaon Film, Naxalite, Pirate Networks, Streaming, Tactical Media, Video: See Keywords (pp. 326–44)

Bengali language movement: Campaign to preserve the Bengali language which began in the pre-Independence district of Manbhum and spread to other regions of North East India. Made part of Bihar, it was split into two districts following a long protest on linguistic grounds, with Purulia becoming a new epicentre of state language.

Jhumur, tusu, bhadu: Folk music and performance forms in West Bengal.

Jhumur is sung especially in the tea gardens of Assam. *Tusu* is a musical harvest festival. *Bhadu* is a festival of South Bengal, with origins in the story of a princess called Bhadravati who committed suicide, and involves musical performances by professional and amateur groups.

Santhali, Rajbangsi: Santhali is a tribe in West Bengal and a language spoken by them. Rajbangsi is a language used by several communities in North Bengal, Assam, Bihar and Bangladesh. Santhali music videos and films are produced in Odisha, and are easily available in southern West Bengal. Rajbangsi videos produced in North Bengal and Assam travel to Bangladesh.

Supermen of Malegaon (dir. Faiza Ahmad Khan, 2012): Documentary on the now-famous practice of remaking local versions of Hollywood and Bollywood blockbusters with a near-zero budget, local actors and props, and improvised special effects.

Images

pp. 260–61, 268–69: Stills from the documentary film *Superman of Malegaon* (dir. Faiza Ahmad Khan, 2012) montaged with posters of Manbhum videos. Image credits: Ameet Mallapur. Images courtesy the director.

MADHUJA MUKHERJEE **2016**

18 Toward a New Frame for Regional Films

Manbhum Videos and the Other Side of (Indian) Cinema

Locating Video Cultures

The arrival of cheap DVD players, consumer cameras and cellular phones in India's suburban and rural markets has transformed its media scene.[1] The decline of celluloid has led to a shift within film practices[2] as video cameras and home video systems and, more recently assembled computers, cheap cellular phones and cameras, downloadable software and media files, have created a pool of images that float somewhere amidst the internet, television, and cinema, alongside a viewership that consumes images via multiple platforms.

With this new technology the very nature of the film image (its formats, tonality, textures and lensing) has altered. Such an image operates outside the structures of the film industry, transforming industrial control over production and distribution. It also operates, as this essay will show, in geographically liminal spaces, on the bordering districts of several states and provinces. Video thus accentuates in multiple ways a new *decentering* of media industries. My interest in these videos developed through research conducted at the Media Lab, Department of Film Studies, Jadavpur University.[3] This included a primary survey, entailing collection of material (VCDs) and conducting interviews,[4] followed by documentation of production details. A second phase involved field trips to 'video halls' and production offices.

Manbhum signifies both 'location' and 'language' (including *bhasha* or dialect). The production and consumption of these videos overlap with those produced and circulated across different districts of Jharkhand, Odisha and West Bengal (in Eastern India). Manbhum videos are produced in Purulia and Bankura districts, as well as in Kolkata. They present a new cultural cartography: growing in 'backward' places, they underscore a tussle over borders, languages and cultural homogenization.[5] They reveal a new way to frame the social history of Indian cinema, remapping regional cinemas (usually defined along the lines of official maps) through new technologies and texts.[6]

Bengali film is marked by the production and reception of films and videos in at least three different dialects, along with other languages, including Hindi.[7] Santhali music videos and films are produced in the neighbouring state of Odisha and easily available in the southern part of West Bengal. Rajbangsi videos produced in North Bengal and Assam travel across the borders into Bangladesh. In West Bengal, video functions in a dynamic relationship to political turmoil:[8] for immigrants from North Bengal, primarily from Bangladesh, it is a cheaper medium, easily accessible in addressing marginalization and for narrating a contemporary political–cultural re-figuration. Both Santhali and Rajbangsi video industries support local 'film' festivals in an attempt to legitimatize and institutionalize their practices. While the Santhali script and language has been officially included in the Eighth Schedule of the Indian Constitution,[9] Rajbangsi video cultures are unambiguously connected to political movements for a separate state, and the demands for more power to northern hilly areas.[10] Meanwhile, Nepali-language films in Darjeeling reshape popular Gorkha and Nepali identity.[11] Epsita Halder's research on popular Karbala narratives in the 24 Parganas district of South Western Bengal, demonstrates how media files from the Middle East as well as recordings of local performances and songs, drift among Shia Muslim communities, specifically amongst women, via cellular phones in order to reinvent new Islamic identities.[12] What appears like an explosion of video and digital cinemas may also be regarded as a tool for negotiating cultural identities via new technological forms.

Manbhum videos thus need to be read against the grain of existing cinema histories. This is true across the Global South and spans such unlikely practices as Pashto pornography, Mujra dance video CDs and Bangladeshi videos involving crime stories and folk forms.[13] There is a curious intersection between a global flow of technologies and media texts, genres, styles and shifting patterns of reception that provokes a new historiography for regional film and interrogates the very materiality of cinema.[14]

Recent interest in India's video industries became especially pertinent with the interest in locally produced videos from Malegaon, Maharashtra.[15] Documentaries such as *Supermen of Malegaon*[16] (dir. Faiza Ahmad Khan, 2008) underline how Malegaon's proximity to Mumbai, its cinephilia, its strategic, self-conscious distancing-through-spoofing from Bollywood, have generated a body of videos supported by a self-sustaining distribution network. Around 2007, art filmmakers in Manipur in India's North East began using the same cheap digital technology, circulating in the same digital environment, as popular music videos.[17] South Korean film and TV also have a major popularity in North East India.[18] Political tensions are evident in Bhojpuri cinema between nation and regions, shaping multiple identities including caste, religion, language and location.[19] Local circuits help us to relate transformations at the local level to a different figuration of the region.

The *pran shakti* (life force) of everyday Manbhum culture, in speech, dialect and modes of performance is notably absent in mainstream cultural portrayals. The topography becomes imperative in a Bengal epitomized in cinema as verdant and riverine despite its enormous variations. Such 'vernacular' performances, a performance of the local, turn political in the way they produce - in their very desire to be included in a larger media scene - a counterforce to it.

I shall read the Manbhum videos produced from Purulia district as powerful expressions of political-cultural struggles. They flow outside cinema theatres, beyond both national and global copyright regulations, and deploy narrative and performative techniques different from mainstream narrative forms, subsisting in 'parallel' zones across territories.

The Infrastructure of Manbhum Videos

Manbhum videos came into circulation around 2003-04, usually made with a budget of less than Rs 50,000, mostly between Rs 20,000 and 40,000; they employ local talents, including popular performers from the locality, and often shoot on locations such as local parks, hillsides, lakes, paddy fields, local marketplaces, temple premises and factories, using the houses of crew members or associates for interior shots. They are shot in available light with easily accessible props and locally sourced costumes. While they were initially edited like wedding videos - that is, with two VCRs - they are increasingly being shot with (semi-) professional cameras like the PD 170 or a digital Handycam and edited on PCs on freely downloadable editing software. Every month two to three new videos become available in local tea shops, bazaars and *melas* (fairs), and are often played on screens during long-distance bus journeys.[20]

Production details such as the format, the names of the producers, distributors, technicians and others, and the year/date/time of the production, are often inscribed on the frame, float on the skin of the videos along with the phone numbers of the camerapersons, directors, producers, and so on, as publicity devices to attract new producers, composers and event managers. This practice activates social mobility since many technicians and actors hope to migrate to Kolkata and thus to mainstream Bengali productions. The distribution mechanism of the Manbhum videos functions through informal networks and tends to keep no records about the films or details of the production process.

These videos should be placed in the context of the mass distribution of Bengali music marketed in the all-encompassing 'folk' genre.[21] They reclaim both their cultural products and their audience, by creating channels for existing local musical forms like Jhumur, Tusu and Bhadu.[22] Contemporary Jhumur videos recreate canonical musical forms as trendy Bollywood-style dance numbers.[23] Although some Kolkata-based production houses such as Choice Videos (which also produces Santhali films) play a role, it is local companies in Purulia such as MVM (Malati Video Movies) that control much of the production and distribution,[24] especially with smaller groups and communities, through home-viewing systems, screening on TV sets in local gatherings, clubs and tea shops.

The texts usually display an uneven comic mode. Popular stories, short skits and comic performances are interspersed with song and dance sequences. The comedy emerges from sources like *koutuk naksha* (traditional comic modes) and of course from the everyday. In the absence of any structured plot with a beginning-middle-end, without powerful stars or any (self-conscious) directorial style, the compositions gesture to a shifting, unstable, media assemblage that merges cinema, television, video and file-sharing practices. The porosity of media is complemented by a parallel porosity of cultural and territorial boundaries.

Regional Fantasies: My Favourite Tomato

Le samla sadher tomato (My Favourite Tomato, Kaji Amjad, probably 2009, VCD no. 001) opens with a sequence which involves two drunkards performing in the village, while cows, ducks and cycles cross streets and the video frame. The camera appears to be set up in a village street recording the enactments in a straightforward manner. Often such framing speaks to the portrayal of the place and its people in local TV news. The address is conventionally frontal. The images occasionally involve wide-angle distortions, and the background at times appears bleached out. The said opening sequence is followed by another in which one of the comedians squats next to a well of an ordinary house, which is not a 'set', crying and singing as he washes his clothes. He bursts into a song narrating his woes, as his wife has made him wash clothes. The song is intercut with images of the playback singer performing the same song in open fields. The video *Sadher Tomato* (Favourite Tomato) connects three disparate performances, the comedian duo, the playback singer and the audience either directly watching the performances themselves or watching these videos.

One scene of *Sadher Tomato* opens in a paddy field, offering a curious story of a peasant couple whose young boy is sick. Shot conspicuously through an engaging albeit grainy and unstructured frame, the story then shifts to their house. It transpires that this young boy has not eaten since the previous night. The camera functions like a recorder, involving limited camera movement, though the use of zoom-in and outs is common. A shaman enters, examines the boy and declares that he has been struck by a terrible malady. Nonetheless, this possessed young man quickly recovers as the shaman whispers to him. The shaman enquires, 'Tell me what is on your mind?' To this, he replies, smiling, 'I want a CD player.'[25] The shaman laughs and assures him that he will certainly get one, just as the shaman will get his fees. The shaman exclaims, '[So] this is CD spirit!' This sequence is followed by another in which the father Ali and the young boy buy a VCD player, priced Rs 1,500, along with a VCD for Rs 60 from the local market. We may note that Purulia is neither a vast landscape of plentitude nor an untainted cultural space. Indeed, it is squarely at the crossroads of many borders, and it encounters the circulation of a variety of cultural products, including, as it happens, armaments.[26] Such a 'CD fever' has thus taken root in a place better known as an idyllic village in mainstream cinemas.[27] As the video goes on, it underscores several such subjects encountering social change and contemporary political anxieties, revealed through manifold cultural dialogues.

Another popular video *Huchke niye puchke dili re* (roughly 'You promised but did not deliver' by Swapan Hujuri, VCD no. 016, 2005) also entails comic sequences. It opens in the interiors of a house. While a mirror hangs against a decorative curtain, a teenaged boy hums a popular number ('*Pereet kore ne go sajani/Shomoye chole gele aar to pabi ni*'/'Fall in love my dear/Let not the time pass by'). There is a cut to a composite shot which shows the young lad with his sister who teaches him the entire song. As they break into a dance, the song resonates the 'room tone' in which it was initially recorded. Such soundtracks - involving noises and incongruities - now present a contrasting trajectory to the digitally cleaned soundscape of mainstream cinemas.[28] A single voice is deployed to dub both the mother and the daughter, a curious unsettling of established cinematic aesthetics. Such deployment of sound, although not consciously oppositional, nevertheless includes 'noises' of multiple orders. It draws attention to the conditions of production and to the manner in which sound design draws from live performances and other circuits of consumption. What follows is even more striking. Framed in long shot by a static camera, the boy's father enters the scene and enquires about his studies. Thereafter, the father asks him to frame sentences with the word 'cow'. 'My father is a cow,' replies the young man.

The latter part of the video includes a song without any narrative continuity in which a young man declares his love in a market place. He hums, '*Shampoo chul/khopaye phul*. . . ('She has used shampoo and put a flower on her hair/ she has applied *tika* and powder/she has used *shurma*...[and] colour on her feet and hands [*henna*]).' The scene shifts from the marketplace to a seaside, which acts as a setting for the song sequence, and portrays a group of dancers attempting a Bollywood-style dance number.

Such discontinuities reflect new cultural sites for the political, that are quite distinct from the usual representations of political struggle in Bengal, Bihar and

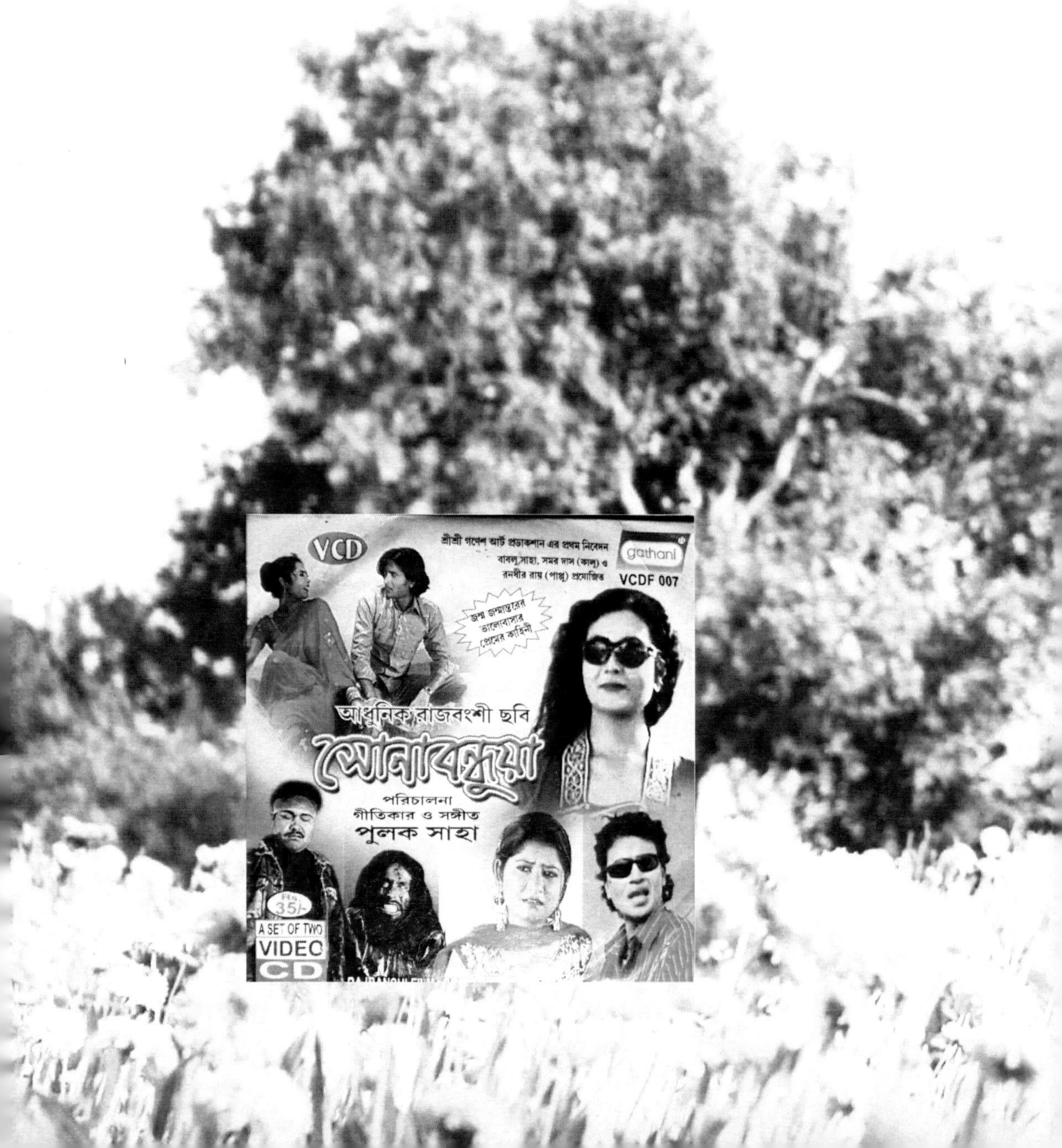
VCD
শ্রীশ্রী গণেশ আর্ট প্রডাকশান এর প্রথম নিবেদন
বাবলু সাহা, সমর দাস (কালু) ও
রনধীর রায় (পাপ্পু) প্রযোজিত
gathani
VCDF 007
জন্ম জন্মান্তরের ভালোবাসার প্রেমের কাহিনী
আধুনিক রাজবংশী ছবি
সোনাবন্ধুয়া
পরিচালনা
গীতিকার ও সঙ্গীত
পুলক সাহা
Rs. 35/-
A SET OF TWO
VIDEO
CD

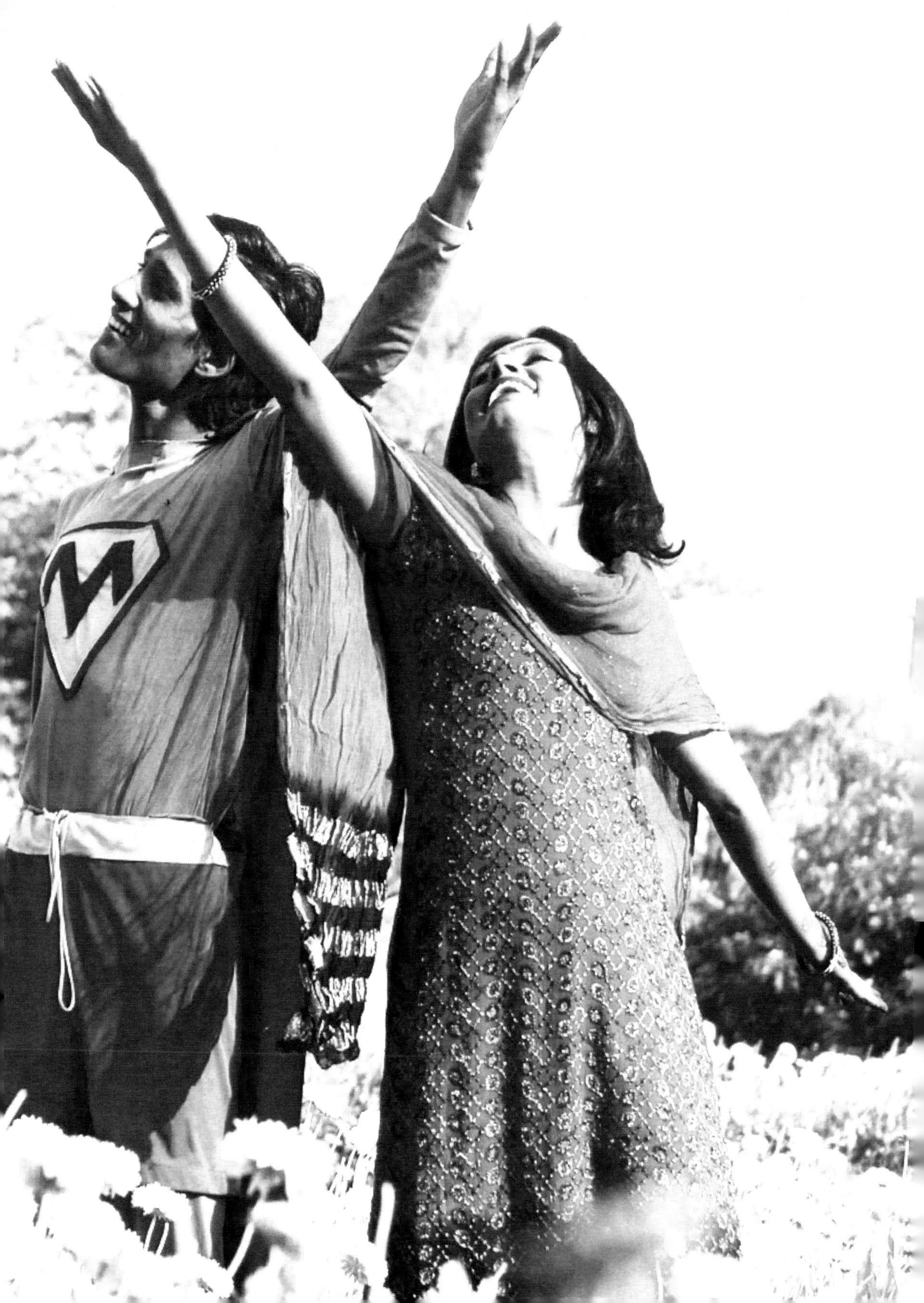

Jharkhand. *Sadher Tomato*, for instance, ends with a sequence that shows people watching videos on a television set and then eating at a feast. Shot in the style of home videos, this appears to be a recording of an actual feast that was likely attached later to the primary video. Such shots of so-called 'backward caste' labourers eating *biriyani* (meat and rice) in an open field are captured against a powerful backdrop of parched land that draws attention to a Manbhum 'everyday' that is a tapestry of documentation and fiction, of actuality and fantasy.

Contexts, Contents and Contested Landscapes

Veteran singer-performer-producer Kuchil Mukherjee and composer-producer Shankar Tara draw our attention to issues of language; specificities of dialect, and popular forms, as well as the processes through which these have been usurped by the more powerful and widely accepted Bengali cultures.

Shankar Tara [ST]: Uttam Kumar was a big artist, yet he failed [to perform the *Manbhum* dialect] though Ajitesh Bandyopadhyay [Indian People's Theatre Association activist, actor], who acted in *Hate Bazare* [Tapan Sinha, 1967] he was from Jhalda [town] he performed beautifully but, now nothing is original[29]
Sadhan Mahato [SM]: Is the situation ['nothing is original'] same in North Bengal [Rajbangsi videos] and Jharkhand [Santhali videos] as in Purulia [Manbhum videos]?
ST: Yes, everywhere what do you expect? These are poor people [the audience], they do not earn more than fifty-sixty rupees [per day], they drink and watch these 'quickies'.

Shankar Tara builds a pertinent argument about the ways in which the Manbhum location and speech has been inauthentically rendered in Bengali films. While attention has been paid to the complex functions of the star persona of Uttam Kumar in the context of post-colonial histories and Bengali modernity,[30] Manbhum videos pose key problems in the way state formation and *bhadralok* hegemony, the domination of the upper-caste Hindu, bilingual, urban, middle classes, have obscured the broader social history of peoples located in Bengal.[31]

Shankar Tara's point about the 'poor' watching 'quickies' may be critically reviewed through Markus Schleiter's work on video nights. In his short commentary about viewership for Santhali films, Schleiter shows how such practices are connected to 'meaningfulness of a 'traditional' dance night, and [how] this has led villagers to celebrate these films as a means of enjoying time together'. 'At the same time,' Schleiter argues that:

> the villagers do expose the enduring nature of 'traditional' dances by comparisons with (the unworthiness of) 'video nights'. As

> such, film watching and 'traditional' practices in a village stand in a *reciprocal reference to each other* [italics added], and such media practice becomes part of supporting 'new media usage' as well as 'traditional' dance forms.[32]

Schleiter's work highlights the contradictory nature of engagements with new media practices. Daisy Hasan too discusses how 'local' media products were at times 'also banned for corrupting local culture'.[33] She notes that film and media experience in Manipur ranges from nationally acclaimed films made by film school graduates alongside ineptly produced music videos.

Return of Mythologies and Narratives of Discontent

Partha Chatterjee in his book *Politics of the Governed* uses Satinath Bhaduri's landmark Bengali novel *Dhorai charit manas* in his endeavour to demonstrate the ways in which political accounts in India are marked by dynamics of heterogeneity. Chatterjee illustrates how:

> Dhorai (Dalit) is uprooted from the narrowness of his home and thrown into the world. The new metalled roadway, along which motorcars and trucks now whizz past ponderous bullock- carts, opens up his imagination. 'Where does this road begin? Where does it end?' [Dhorai] doesn't know. Perhaps no one knows. Some of the carts are loaded with maize, others bring plaintiffs to the district court, still others carry patients to the hospital. In his mind, Dhorai sees shadows that suggest to him something of the vastness of the country. . . .[34]

The virtuosity of Bhaduri's 'modernist retelling of the epic' is compelling, especially because of Dhorai's location and his social position in relation to the vastness of the country. The novel uncovers a glaring absence in Bengali cultural discourse that we may now also attribute to its films: of issues concerning caste and marginalized localities, Dalits and Adivasis as well as Muslim communities.

Exploring the reworking of mythologies within contemporary times appears to be a crucial tool to understand the current political events of Purulia and Bankura. For example, narrative videos like *Desh ta gelo jahanname* (The country has gone to the dogs, by Tota, probably completed in 2010, VCD no. 004) locates mythological stories of Yama (God of death) and his messengers set in the present. This story is interrupted by contemporary song-and-dance sequences, accompanied by phone numbers of producers offering 'stage shows', all the while paralleling the story of the Goddess Durga, her Puja,[35] and the many affairs which the gods have with the locals. The film also uses a television news-reporting style to invoke mythology and to comment on the intensities of present-day politics.

The story of Yama's trip to earth is strung together in television newsrooms which portray Narada[36] (the mischievous sage, traveller, narrator) as a news reporter standing against the backdrop of the Great Wall of China and reflecting on the contemporary scene. He reports how the situation in this world is grave; that the world has become a *jahannam* (hell). 'There is bombing everywhere and landmines are laid all around!' he exclaims, agitatedly. Remarkably, a clip from a Bollywood movie supports this 'report.' Such styles of narration, assembling the 'wonders of the world' and scenes of recent political disorder refracted through Bollywood action films suggest a startling, politically charged media awareness. Eventually, Narada interviews Yama, who is placed against the image of the Colosseum in Rome.

> Narada [N]: Why are you picking up people without intimation?
> Yama [Y]: That's not possible.
> N: During Aila [cyclone, 2009], Tsunami [2004], and other cases.
> Y: That's the fault with the weather forecast.
> N: What about Taj Bengal [Taj Hotel Mumbai attacks, 2008]?[37]
> Y: It takes seven days to arrive at Mumbai from Pakistan by the sea, so, what happened to your Radar? Satellite? Were your men sleeping or were they on leave?
> N: And tell me, those who are making and using bombs or those who are letting them go, why aren't you picking them up?
> Y [stutters and replies]: But I am scared of them. Who knows when they will tie a landmine to my buffalo's tail.

Issues of violence and political disquiet, presented in the comic mode, are broached in a different, epic register, as Narada, Yama and his men encounter the ravaged Mother Earth running through the landscape.

> Mother Earth: Immediately get a permanent solution for me.
> Narada: What's wrong with you, Mother?
> Mother Earth: Can't you see? Shameless creatures! There were riots – and now there are bullets, gunfire, pistols, bombing, I am all wrecked.

Eventually, the film shows the heavens falling apart, and protests growing in Yamalaya (abode of Yama/Hell).

> Ghost [protesting and pelting slogans]: We cannot be picked up without notice. You cannot keep thieves and police in the same cell. The deceased seek justice.
> Narada: How many dead souls are here [protesting]?
> Ghost: Numerous - from Bihar, Bengal, Odhisa and of course Jharkhand. But we are mainly from Bengal, Bankura [neighbouring district]. We will be [eventually] successful if *Ma, maati, atma* [mother, earth, people; italics added] come together. She is everything, we are following her.

Produced around 2010, and paraphrasing the Trinamool Congress election slogan - Ma, Maati, Manush (Mother, Earth, People)[38] - the video participates in the populist political cultures of Bengal.

The video displays a knowing projection of the technology through which it is made: part of the everyday life of its viewers, addressing audiences as technologically mediated and engaged in transactions of media files. It displays technical details, such as phone numbers of the camerapersons, directors and producers, information regarding which camera has been used, along with shots of Yama using a cellular phone or his subordinates recording the events with a Handycam (which eventually fails because the battery has not been charged). While recounting political shifts, the video also narrates the transition from video to digital through its *mise-en-scene* by unmasking a range of technical devices, by drawing attention to the back-projection or by highlighting the special effects. However, Manbhum is not an isolated or unique case. In fact, both *Malegaon ke Superman* and *Out of Thin Air* (dir. Shabani Hassanwalia and Samreen Farooqui, 2009), an ethnographic film about the newly formed digital film industry in Ladakh, producing a handful of feature films and some music videos, emphasize the intense drive for self-projection, and the manner in which marginal groups participate in broader transformations. The showcasing of technological mediation is a key motif in these proliferating local assemblages. Thus, *Desh ta gelo* (The Country is Gone) connects narratives of violence across Bengal, Bihar and Odisha through self-conscious digital strategies; it illustrates how peripheries are positioned through larger technological set-ups like the 'radar' and the 'satellite', even as it gets deprived of such possible links. Through such videos, the margins speak through a new technological awareness about their situation.

Chatterjee notes that 'Satinath Bhaduri's intricately crafted account of Dhorai's upbringing among the Tatmas[39] in the early decades of the twentieth century could be easily read as a *faithful ethnography* [italics added] of colonial governance and the nationalist movement in northern India.' In my understanding, the Manbhum videos achieve similar ethnographic significance, in the ways in which they traverse unexplored rugged territories of Bengal, portray the 'rough and coarse' speech of Manbhum, and present labouring bodies, which remain startlingly absent in middle-class cinemas. In point of fact, the fragmented plots and technological foregrounding of the Manbhum videos may be read as material engagement with our political-cultural histories, not only making visible marginalized experience but also highlighting how such media acts are shared by a wider population.

The Manbhum videos may be understood as a 'sub'-regional media practice, accorded only secondary status because of their locations of production and circulation, and because of their low quality in relation to celluloid and digitally enhanced films. However, they introduce us to new questions with which to frame the historiography of Indian and regional films. Such audiovisual practices, which thrive at the edge of many categories (traditional oral forms, regional films, narrative cinema and music videos, new media practices, industrial structures and viewership) demand innovative research questions. The sprouting of so many industries within the oeuvre of Indian cinema (and across the Global South) demands a new historiographical agenda that incorporates the shifting ground of the media technology which produces and circulates cinema. 'Parallel' media cultures, or what flows boisterously and seditiously alongside larger production conglomerations, even when they have gone unheeded, or will wither away with the advent of newer technological forms, present an alternative historical map of cinema and the mediatized social world of which it is part.

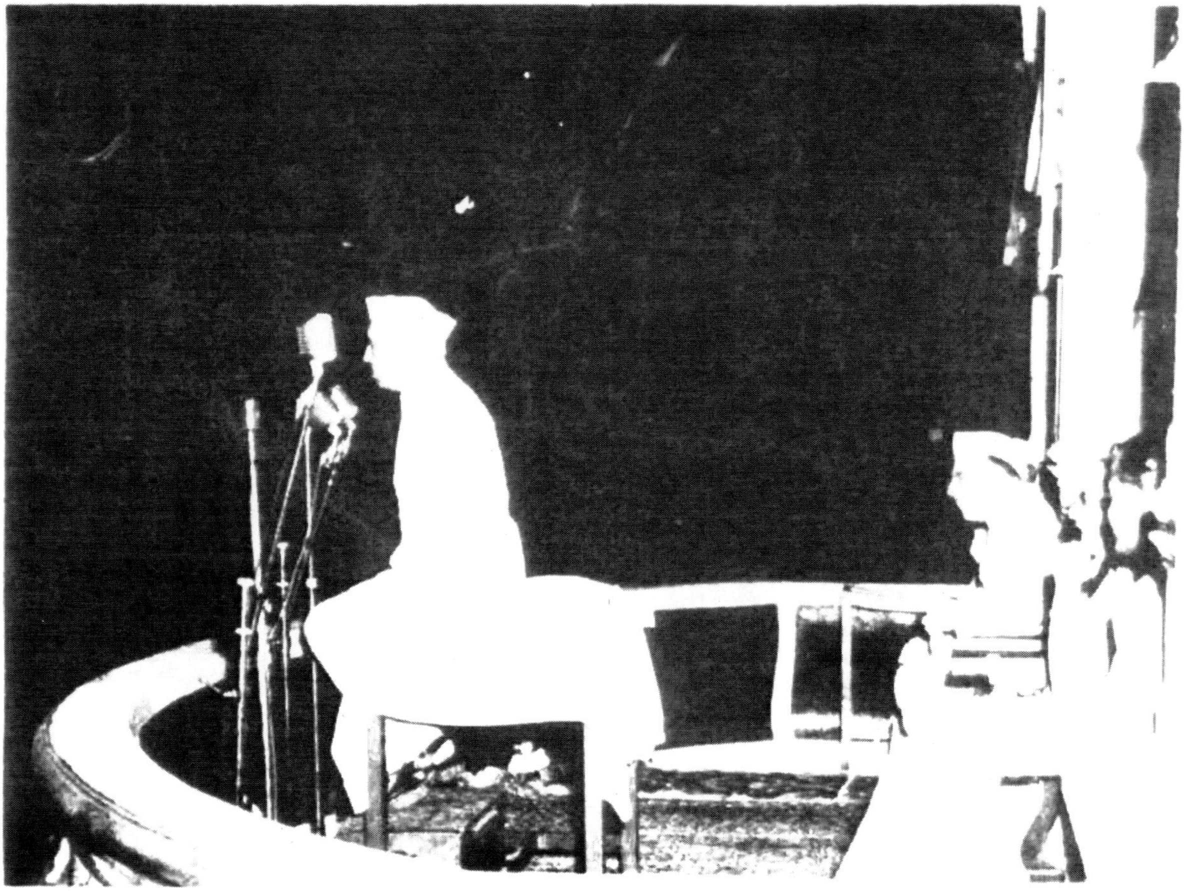

A.P. Formation Day

The state of Telangana has had a long political history associated with radical struggle. A communist-led insurgency in the 1940s led to extreme-left formations such as the People's War Group in the 1960s. These struggles in the 1970s, associated with cultural movements affiliated to different communist outfits, led to a genre of cinema known as 'Red Films'. This essay tracks its afterlife in a new genre of immensely popular music, theatre and cinema, extended to YouTube videos, websites and even dedicated television channels. Some of its stars, including its best-known figure Gaddar, come from older leftist movements. A new generation of 'radical' stars, producers, singers and composers are riding on the popularity of 'Naxalite' films. Telangana was eventually awarded statehood in 2014, but the left has little control over the proliferating mediatized trajectories of repurposed cultural forms.

An earlier version of this text was published as 'Maoism to Mass Culture: Notes on Telangana's Cultural Turn', in *BioScope: South Asian Screen Studies*, vol. 6, no. 2, 2015, pp. 187–205. This version is published here with permission from the author and Sage Publications Pvt. Ltd.

Keywords, Names, Abbreviations

Dalit, Emergency, Jana Natya Mandali, Indian People's Theatre Association, Naxalite, Red Film: See Keywords (pp. 326–44).

CPI (ML): Communist Party of India (Marxist-Leninist).

Gaddar (b. 1949), aka Gummadi Vittal Rao: Poet and iconic revolutionary balladeer associated with the People's War Group until 2010.

KCR: K. Chandrashekar Rao, founder of the Telangana Rashtra Samithi in 2001.

Narayana Murthy, R.: Telugu actor, director, producer, singer and composer, best known purveyor of the 'Red Film' genre.

Narsing Rao, B.: Major artist, filmmaker, poet, actor and producer committed to the Telangana movement.

NTR: N.T. Rama Rao (1923–96), iconic Telugu movie star, director, producer and politician, and Chief Minister of Andhra Pradesh for seven years.

People's War Group: Major far-left political force in Telangana. It merged with the Communist Party of India (Maoist) in 2004.

TPF: Telangana Praja Front (Telangana People's Front), a political party.

TRS: Telangana Rashtra Samithi (Telangana State Council), a political party founded in 2001 by KCR to campaign for Telangana statehood.

TSS: Telangana Samskritika Samakhya (Telangana Cultural Forum), a political party.

Vimalakka: Folk balladeer and social activist who headed the Joint Action Committee for the creation of a separate Telangana state.

YSR: Y.S. Rajasekhara Reddy (1949–2009); popular political leader and Chief Minister of Andhra Pradesh from 2004 to 2009, who was killed in a mysterious helicopter crash.

Images

p. 275: 1 November 1956: Deepavali evening and the formation day of eight states across India; Prime Minister Jawaharlal Nehru addresses Andhra Pradesh's formation ceremony in Hyderabad.

pp. 280–81: Montaged cover of a Gaddar music CD with photo of a headphone-wearing woman at the Bonalu festival.

pp. 286–87: 2 June 2014: Parade Ground, Secunderabad. Workers stand with an image of KCR they have taken down after his signing-in ceremony as Chief Minister of the newly formed state of Telangana.

Image insert on p. 280 courtesy S.V. Srinivas. All other images courtesy Kush Badhwar, filmmaker and artist, who has been researching and working with archives and personal collections of material about the formation of Telangana.

S.V. SRINIVAS

2016

19 The Gaddar Effect

Maoism, Mass Culture and the Legacies of Cinema

The Problem

Since the early 2000s, mobilizations in support of statehood for Telangana have been characterized by the high visibility of cultural forms, and of cultural activists on political platforms. Cultural productions associated with the agitation have left a large footprint on satellite television and the internet, and the political context has created conditions for a hitherto unprecedented revival of folk forms from the region. Curiously, these productions reveal a significant presence of Maoist propaganda from earlier decades: alongside the new visibility of Maoist cultural activists in the statehood agitation.[1] I say 'curious' because many Maoist groups that had once wielded considerable influence in the 1980s and 1990s, have been conspicuous by their absence in undivided Andhra Pradesh from around 2006. This absence is thus especially striking given the hypervisibility of several forms of Maoist propaganda mediated by other forms drawn from mass culture alongside digital technologies and interfaces. Despite the existence of a small sprinkling of online forums and functioning front organizations, Maoists themselves have little or no control over this process. Instead, yesterday's propaganda, detached from the politics that spawned it, has now become dispersed media *content*, acquiring a political significance that has little to do with Maoism itself.

Telugu cinema has had something to do with this re-mobilization and re-signification of propaganda. The complex phenomenon unfolding in Telangana is at once surprising and all too familiar. In southern India, the most visible manifestation of the politics-cinema linkage has been the male film star and his (relatively) big budget vehicle.[2] In Telangana, a specific variant of such political cinema, the genre of the 'Red' or 'Naxalite' film, has played a notable (if modest) role in the emergence of a culture industry driven by the regional political movement. The genre was (and remains) in fact rather marginal to the Telugu film industry in terms of budgets, box office and stars. Nevertheless, its visibility allows us to examine *in situ* a strange afterlife of cinema, as the moving image travels well beyond the cinema hall to other screens and sites of consumption, many of which are now also sites of political action. This overspill offers us new insights into the unexpected ways in which politics and mass culture dovetail in the twenty-first century.

Background

The state of Andhra Pradesh was formed in 1956, merging the Telugu-speaking districts of the former Madras Presidency and the former Hyderabad state (now Telangana). It had faced political opposition from the very beginning.[3] By 1968, the opposition escalated into a full-fledged movement demanding a separate Telangana, in which several protesters lost their lives in police firings.[4] Statehood demands began to gather strength once again in the 1990s.[5] By the end of the 1990s, the Communist Party of India (Marxist-Leninist) People's War – the largest and most influential radical left formation in the country – extended its support to the demand. The agitation continued until late July 2013, when the Congress Working Committee passed a resolution clearing the way for the formation of the Telangana state.[6]

Arguments for statehood in the 1990s only occasionally referred to cultural differences between the state's regions, or the suppression of Telangana's distinctive dialect and other cultural practices. The primary focus then was *underdevelopment*: economic, educational, and employment disparities between the regions, and the uneven distribution of state and natural resources, especially water.[7] This changed in the decade-and-half that followed, as 'sentiment' and culture would come to play a central role in the statehood agitation.

Growing support for Telangana's statehood coincided with the waning influence of Naxalite parties in the region during Y.S. Rajasekhar Reddy (or YSR)'s first term as the chief minister of Andhra Pradesh (2004–09). An observer noted that the military option adopted by the Reddy government succeeded in containing the Maoists by 2006.[8] Naxalite front organizations floated for Telangana's statehood were marginalized shortly afterwards, partly due to political suppression but also, perhaps, due to the growing popularity of a new generation of political parties explicitly dedicated to this single-point issue. Paradoxically however, this did not stop radical left propaganda forms and activists from being seen and heard everywhere in this time.

While I focus here on developments in Telangana, the problem I am trying to define is not limited to the region, but has to do with the porosity between the domains of cultural consumption and mass mobilization. From the 1970s, several studies drew attention to specific forms which flagged this porosity at different points of time.[9] The context I examine here is a particular variant of the larger phenomenon: when film leaks into other forms and moving images begin to be consumed on a variety of screens – a fortuitous leakage, as it turns out, that allows me to move beyond the work of both particular media-cultural forms and political formations, and into a process where I can track continuities and connections between the forms and the formations respectively.

The Cultural Turn

Coinciding with the rising prominence of the Telangana Rashtra Samithi political party (TRS, the Telangana Nationalist Front, established in 2001), statehood demands began to hinge on cultural differences between Telangana and the rest of Andhra Pradesh, specifically on the perceived denigration of Telangana's dialect and culture.[10] A prominent report on Telangana quotes art-house filmmaker B. Narsing Rao make a rather emphatic claim to the region's distinctiveness:

> For me, Telangana is an ethnicity that needs to be understood – we are a people with a language [sic], a culture, dress code, dialect and distinctive food habits. We also have distinctive literary and performative traditions. And a distinct history that goes back 1,300 years. My films tell stories of Telangana[11]

This report highlights humiliation and misrepresentation of the region's culture and the 'disappearance of a composite culture', alongside land, water and livelihood issues, in its account of Telangana politics. Others have made even more forceful accusations. 'The current movement for Telangana is certainly caused not only by economic and political reasons, but also by the *revulsion in the social and cultural spheres*.'[12] This revulsion is a result of the 'regular humiliation of [the] Telangana language, dialects and cultural practices' by the film and media industries dominated by the Kamma caste entrepreneurs from coastal Andhra.[13]

This cultural turn was both reactive and affirmative. The condemnation of misrepresentation and humiliation of the region's dialect and culture was accompanied by the revival and reinvention of tradition as well as construction of new symbols, which for instance included the hitherto non-existent goddess, *Telangana Talli* (Mother Telangana), alongside other folk practices that began to occupy pride of place in the 'Telangana culture'.

Other parts of India, too, have witnessed the large-scale commoditization of folk music, as also the massive growth of the folk as a genre of both music

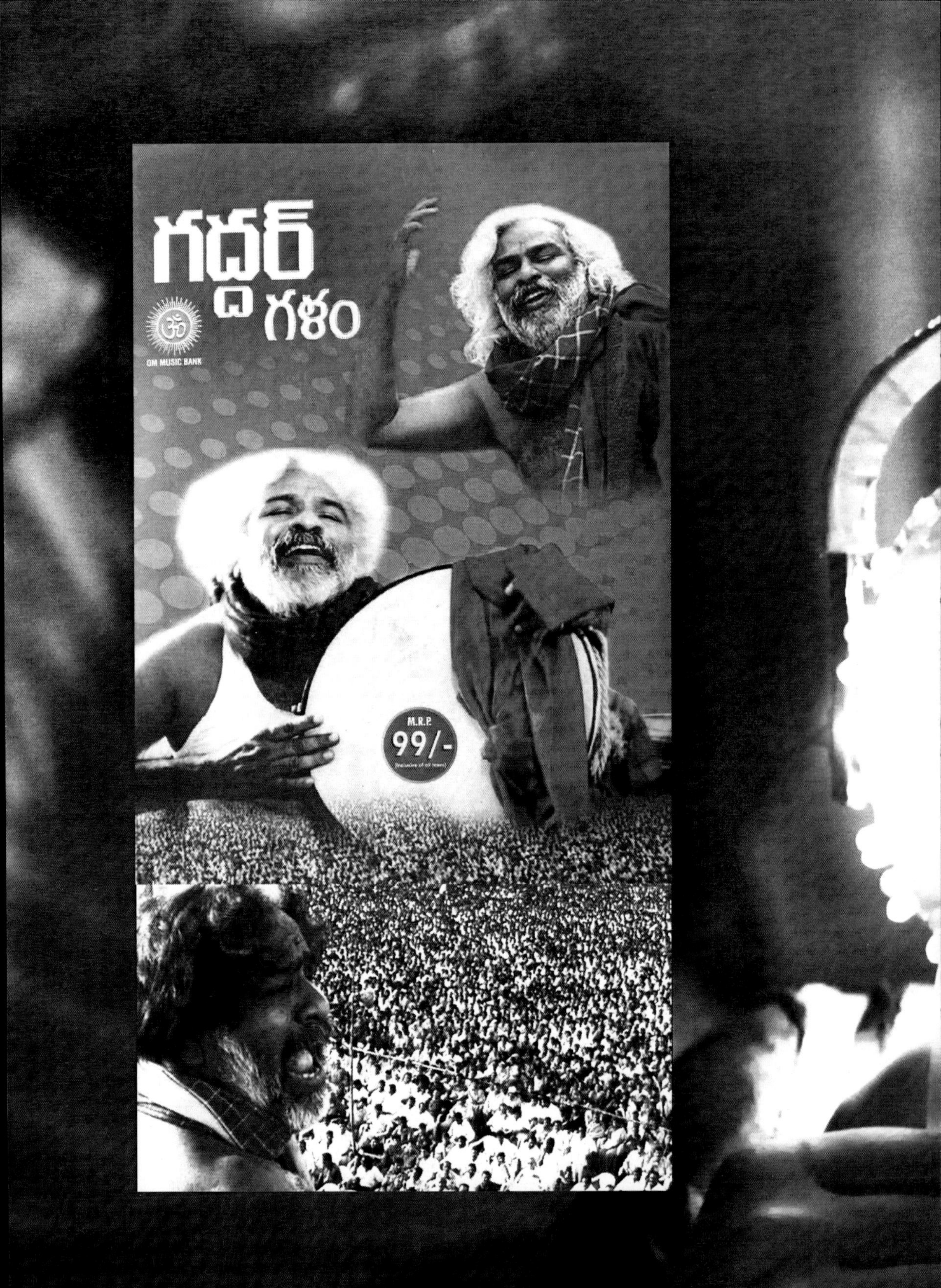
గద్దర్ గళం
OM MUSIC BANK
M.R.P.
99/-

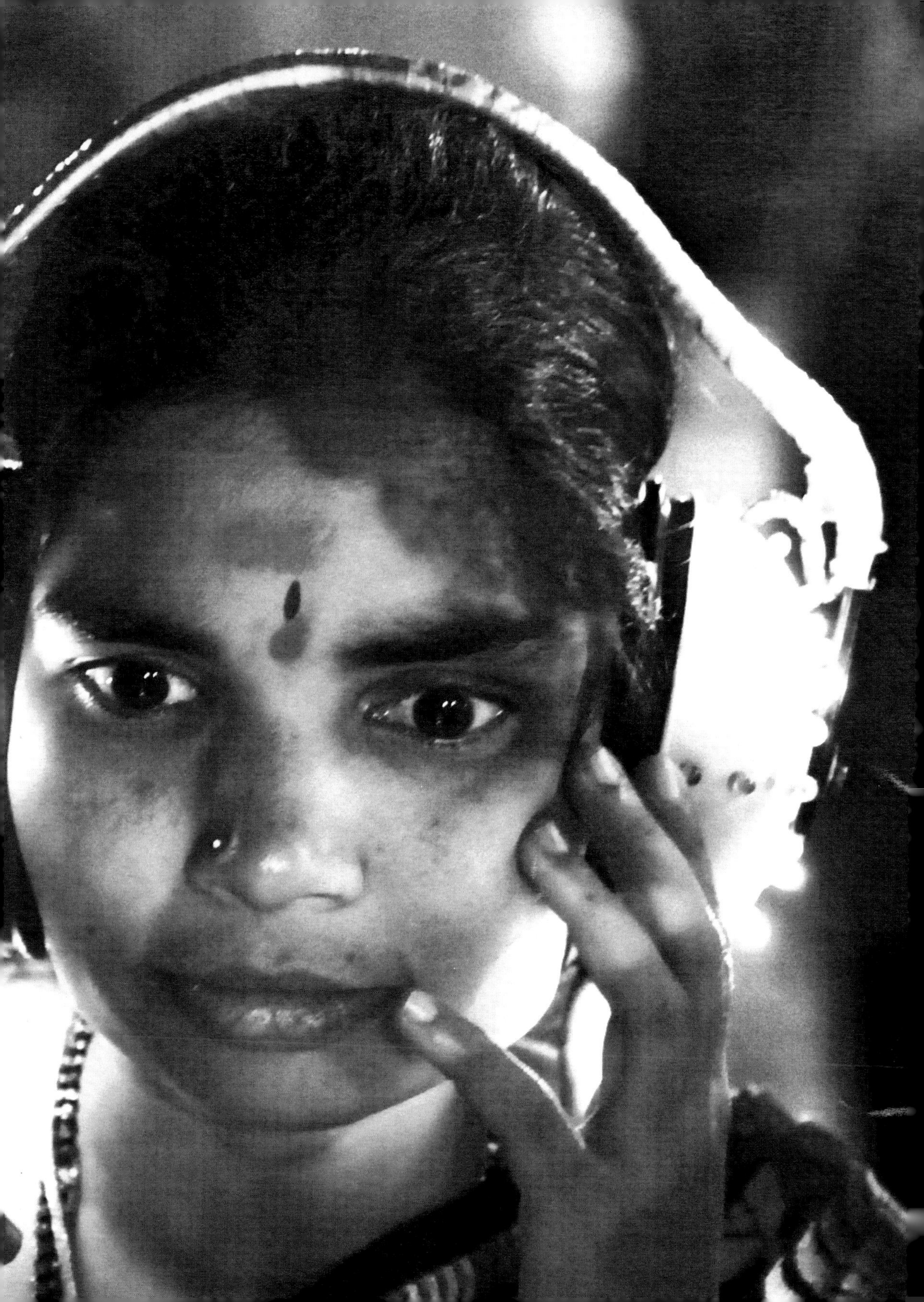

and live performance.[14] Two notable features stand out in Telangana, however. They are, firstly, an appropriation - including adaptation and revival - of folk practices in order to claim a distinctiveness for Telangana's dialect and culture, and thus attributed political connotations, as can be seen in the statement of Narsing Rao cited earlier. And secondly, the sourcing of appropriated folk content for contemporary political mobilization from communist and Maoist cultural activists. The latter move has a long history, going back to the 1940s.[15] It also recalls a manoeuvre by the Telugu film industry in the 1940s and 1950s, which, partly due to the efforts of left-leaning creative workers, also drew on folk forms to claim cultural distinctiveness for the cinema.[16] Now, in the 1990s, its revival served to re-establish a basic popular fact - as one scholar notes: 'The bottom line of the current mobilization is that a significant and visible section of the population has come to believe that there exists a distinct *cultural* region called Telangana.'[17]

Such a 'cultural turn' in the movement has complex linkages with Naxalite activists and the forms they have developed to propagate their party ideologies. For one, the change in the fortunes of left propaganda, and its large-scale adaptation for electronic and digital forms of transmission, was largely unanticipated by the Communist establishment. In 2005, participants of the third state conference of the cultural wing of the Communist Party of India (Marxist–Leninist) 'lamented that the proliferation of television channels had had a negative impact on arts, literature and culture'.[18] Less than five years later, the popular musician-activist Vimala (aka Vimalakka) would be seen performing frequently on private satellite television channels. In March 2014, my search for 'Vimalakka' yielded over 8,000 results on YouTube alone, a majority of these sourced from television channels or uploaded on their official YouTube channels.[19] Vimalakka was not the only performer-activist from the radical left to play a prominent role in the Telangana agitation. The most famous cultural figure of all is of course Gaddar (Gummadi Vithal Rao), the Dalit singer, poet, performer who spent decades propogating the ideology of the CPI(ML) People's War and was the Secretary of the party's cultural wing, Jana Natya Mandali (People's Theatre Group).[20] Gaddar was active as a singer and performer from the late 1960s when he dropped out of engineering college. He would soon be influenced by left writers and cultural activists.[21] He was subsequently attracted to the Naxalite movement, going underground in the 1980s. He was shot and injured - allegedly by policemen in plain clothes - in 1997.[22]

By the early 1990s, Gaddar's public meetings drew more people than those organized by actor-politician N.T. Rama Rao (NTR) at the peak of his popularity, says writer and human rights activist K. Balagopal.[23] He also went on to become one of the key figures in the Telangana movement, credited with organizing massive events in support of statehood, including one in 2008 that witnessed the gathering of some 12,000 poets, singers and cultural activists.[24] He was associated with the CPI (Maoist) front organization, Telangana Praja Front (TPF, Telangana

People's Front, formed in 2010), which he chaired for some years. Of immediate significance for us is the extent of Gaddar's contribution to the popularization of Naxalite propaganda. This prolific composer had some 3,000 songs to his credit and thirty-five audio cassettes of his work were released by 2010.[25]

A key site for the mainstreaming/domestication of radical propaganda was the 'Telangana Dhoom Dham', the name given to song and dance performances in support of statehood. Featuring singers and performers drawn largely from left cultural organizations, the 'dhoom dham' showcased a musical heritage that was explicitly created by the Naxalite movement, and explicitly drew on folk tunes and idioms of the region, thus also reviving a tradition of left propaganda going back to the Praja Natya Mandali (Citizens Theatre Group) in the 1940s. The 'dhoom dhams' were relatively autonomous of direct political control, but performances were often accompanied by speeches by political leaders and public intellectuals. Soon, they became a distinct genre of political-cultural performance.

But it is to Gaddar we have to turn, in order to properly understand Telangana's culture turn, which is not only about the growing prominence of song and dance in a political mobilization but also the centrality of *sentiment*. The Chairman of Telangana Intellectual Forum, made the important observation that the Telangana movement was 'not like any other movement for a separate state in the country. It is a 50-year-old struggle. No other movement has such *emotions and passions*'.[26] He was perhaps implicitly comparing Telangana to the agitation that led to the formation of the Andhra state in 1953.[27] 'Telangana sentiment' is a frequently used English phrase in Telugu newspapers and on television, to refer to both emotional outpouring and popular will alike. Sentiment is an integral part of the Telugu lexicon now, in Telangana as well as Andhra Pradesh.

The impact of the music and performance traceable to the Naxalite movement, to the 'emotions and passions' that have over the past decade emerged as the foundations of the movement, is not to be underestimated. Gaddar's work is striking in this respect. To begin with, the music is deeply moving, so much so that it can come across as dangerously sentimental to researchers who take their Adorno seriously. The literary critic Venkat Rao points out that the lyricist-singer's work is often centered on death, martyrdom and mourning:

> Gaddar addresses the problem of death in the context of what appears to be given: the violent loss, disappearance, or death of loved ones. The work of death or mourning appears in two significant ways in Gaddar's oral writings. On the one hand, the loss, the absence, and the disappearance make the necessity of song absolutely imperative; the song embodies and lays open the imperative of mourning. On the other, the absence or loss is made more radical by turning this impossible condition into

> a situation of possibility: precisely this absence enables Gaddar to forge the signatures of the nameless. The *mnemo signatures Gaddar chisels out are effects of an interminable mourning.*[28]

Death and mourning have been closely associated with the Telangana movement in the recent past with several hundred suicides being traced to the agitation in the past five years. The sheer scale of the phenomenon in the agitation's epicenter at Hyderabad, otherwise globally famous for its information technology (IT) industry, has drawn international media attention.[29] Gaddar is widely traveled in India and is famous among radical left circles across the country. However, partly due to his own efforts to make an impact on the Telangana movement, but also partly because of the manner in which his earlier work has been repositioned as a specific commentary on Telangana (as against on oppressed peoples everywhere), loss and pain are now anchored to the region. In the process, the region itself has come to be marked as the site of 'interminable mourning'. The political subject in this struggle, to use another phrase from Venkat Rao's essay, is 'the bearer of incalculable loss'.[30]

Legacies of Film

Even before Gaddar became something of a mascot for the Telangana agitation, Venkat Rao cautioned against assuming that the performer was merely promoting the party line.[31] Arguably, it is not Gaddar's work alone but cultural artefacts in general that pose the problem of irreducibility because of the sheer excess of their signification, for who can tell how an image or a song will be interpreted? Gaddar is no doubt an *auteur* and a celebrity, albeit one very different from film stars and cricketers. He was never a mere transmitter of his party's agendas. How has his idiom, which reconstituted the folk for contemporary social and political commentary, acquired mobility to become the stuff of live performances, television and YouTube videos?

A good starting point for addressing this question is Telugu cinema, whose contribution to the commoditization of the folk propaganda form that came to be associated with Gaddar is significant. The mediation of Naxalite propaganda by film can be traced to *Bhoomikosam* (For Land's Sake, dir. Tilak, 1974),[32] which featured the Bombay movie star Ashok Kumar alongside Madras industry actors of considerable standing, and also introduced actress-turned-politician Jayaprada to the industry.[33] Tilak was a respected figure in the film industry and spent some years in Bombay as a communist cultural activist, before moving to Madras and Telugu cinema.[34] He drew on the vast pool of actors and creative personnel of the Bombay and Madras industries who had worked with Indian People's Theatre Association (IPTA) in the past. The film itself was a tribute to his Naxalite brother and other 'martyrs' (*amarajeevulu*).

Bhoomikosam inspired several filmmakers in the years to come, and was among the most influential Telugu films of the 1970s.[35] After *Bhoomikosam*, Telugu films made both direct and indirect references to the ongoing Naxalite movement in the state. From the 1980s, coinciding with the spread of the movement in Telangana but without making explicit references to it, a new genre, locally known as *erra* cinema (Red Film) or communist cinema, incorporated symbols, concerns and propaganda associated with the parliamentary left and, simultaneously, depicted violent uprisings against feudal oppressors.[36] Anger and pathos were the driving emotions of the Red Film: anger at the injustices of the exploitative order and pathos engendered by the slain rebel.

From the late 1980s, even as the occasional Red Film continued to be made, a modified version of the genre emerged, making explicit references to the Naxalite movement and lionized revolutionaries as selfless fighters and tragic figures. This came to be known as the Naxalite film (used interchangeably with *erra* cinema and communist cinema). Typically, in the Naxalite film, armed squads of Naxalites are seen performing vigilante actions against landlords, corrupt police officials or politicians and indulging in a variety of populist actions. However, these films were not authorized by Naxalite parties, and were often severely criticized by intellectuals affiliated to them.

Credit for creating this new and modified genre goes to R. Narayana Murthy, actor, director and producer of a majority of these Naxalite films.[37] His efforts earned him the honorific title, 'People's Star'. The genre was launched with *Ardharatri Swatantram* (Freedom at Midnight, 1986). This may have been the first Telugu film to have used the term *annalu* (older brothers, commonly used to refer to Naxalites, members of armed squads in particular).[38] The film features a singer-revolutionary unmistakably modeled on Gaddar, played by T. Krishna, the director of some landmark early 1980s Red Films. The figure of the singing revolutionary would frequently reappear till he became a regular feature of the Naxalite film. Today, Naxalite film is the one genre of Telugu cinema that has widespread acceptance among pro-statehood activists.[39] A minor genre unknown outside Andhra Pradesh and Telangana for decades has now become a major vehicle for celebrity politicians with its capacity for propaganda and popularity with radical trappings.

Narayana Murthy's 1990s films were mainly shot in coastal Andhra and used the Telangana dialect inconsistently, neither of which proved a hurdle for their popularity in Telangana. The turning point of the genre was the success of *Erra Sainyam* (Red Army, 1995) that went beyond Telangana. One of the biggest box office hits in 1995, it attracted big stars, filmmakers, and production houses to his one-man cottage industry. One of the early movers was Dasari Narayana Rao,[40] director of over 100 films and a union minister in the United Progressive Alliance government in 2004. He made the film *Orey Rickshaw* (Hey You! Rickshaw) in 1995, casting Narayana

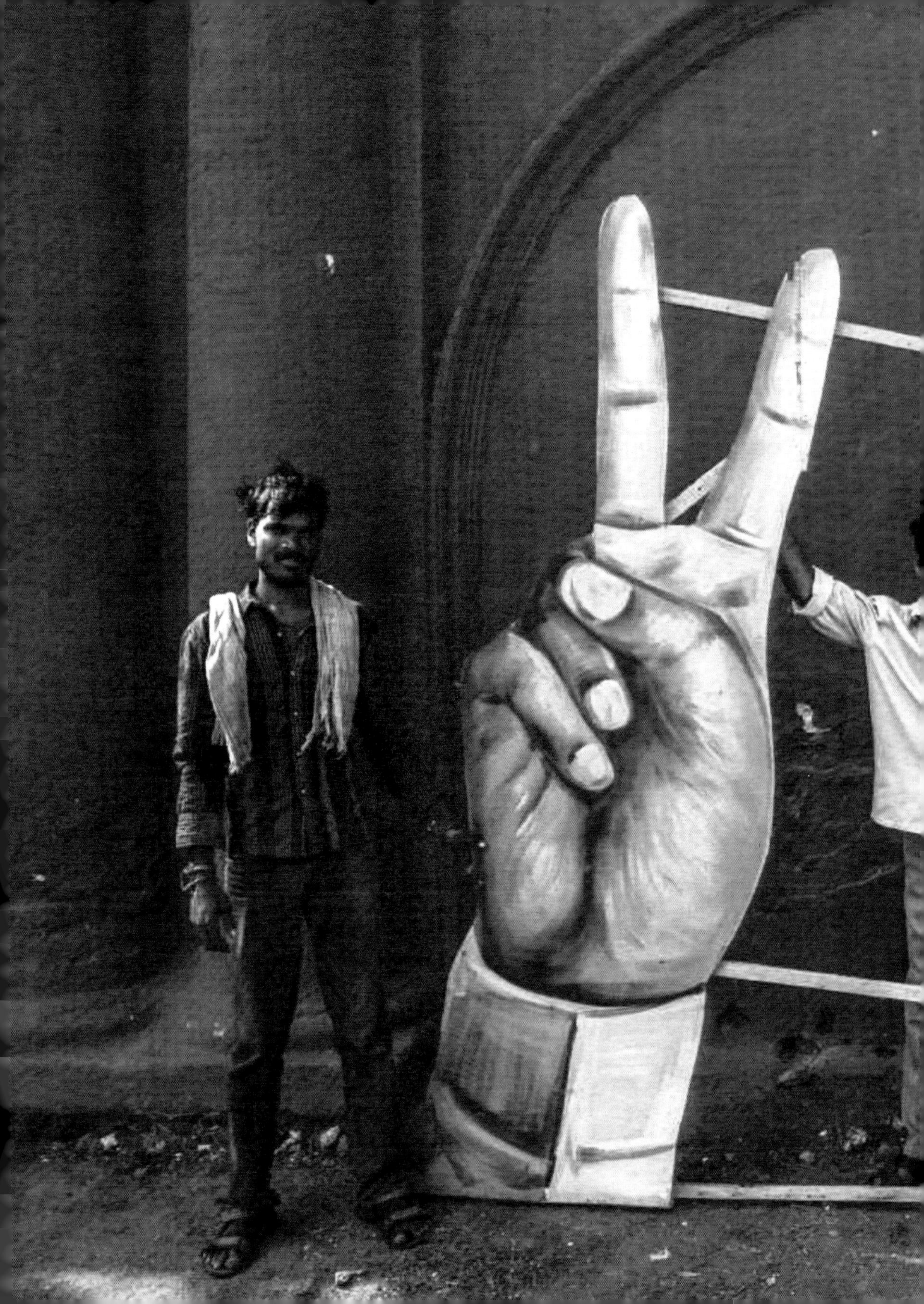

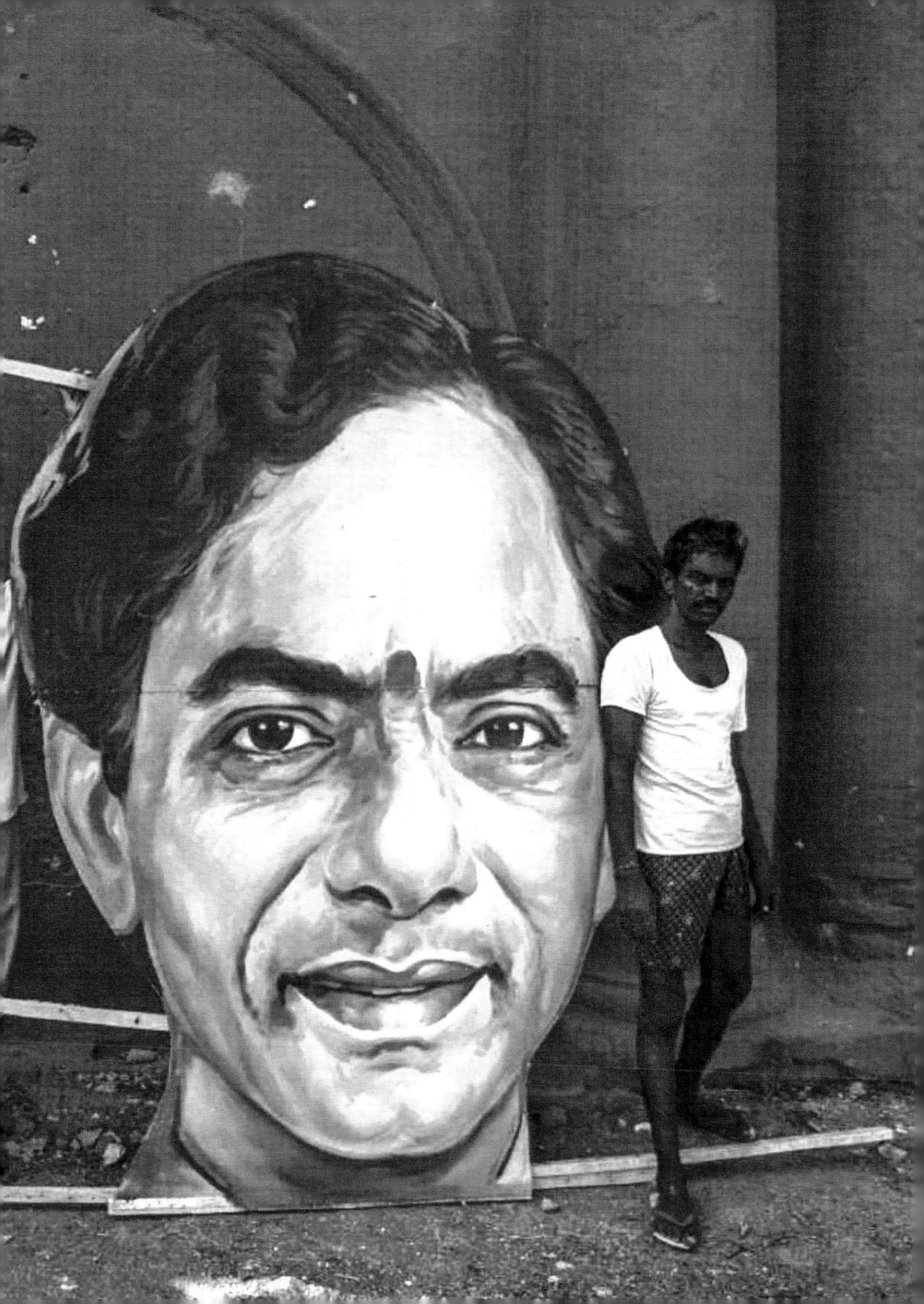

Murthy, who had earlier worked as his assistant, in the lead. The film proved to be commercially successful. The senior director then made *Osey Ramulamma* (Hey You! Ramulamma, 1997), the most famous Naxalite film ever, featuring the major star Vijayashanthi in the lead,[41] and Dasari himself as a Gaddar-like revolutionary singer. As legend has it, people from far-flung Telangana villages hired tractors and trucks to travel to cinema halls screening the film. This film's popularity played no small part in the crossover of Vijayashanthi into politics, first, as an active campaigner initially for the BJP and more recently, for Telangana's statehood.

The appearance of the singer-revolutionary in the Naxalite film from the 1980s was accompanied by another act of appropriation: the genre liberally adapted the tunes and lyrics of popular Jana Natya Mandali and Arunodaya songs.[42] Needless to add, these tunes were, in turn, drawn from or fashioned after folk tunes. Film critics and industry observers are of the unanimous opinion that it is the genre's adaptation of Naxalite propaganda songs that played a big role in its popularity, particularly in Telangana where these songs were already familiar. Audio cassettes of Gaddar and other radical cultural activists circulated widely from roughly 1990, when the ban on People's War was temporarily lifted. They were sold in shops as well as the venues of public meetings organized by the radical left parties and their front organizations. According to a fan website, *Osey Ramulamma* had the second highest audio sales in the Telugu industry till 2009.[43]

The genre's appropriation of Naxalite music was not limited to borrowing existing songs. Major cultural activists of the radical left, including Gaddar and the older Jana Natya Mandali singer, Vangapandu Prasada Rao,[44] were commissioned to write new songs. The practice of commissioning radical left singers and poets to write for films was common among producers of the early 1980s, and it continued into this new era.[45] New writers with radical left activist backgrounds, or from families associated with activist history, emerged. So intimate was the link between the Naxalite film and revolutionary cultural activists that CPI(ML) People's War cited Gaddar's work for commercial films as one of the reasons for suspending him from the party in 1996.[46]

After Cinema

The Naxalite film demonstrated that leftist propaganda could be harnessed to produce and market hybrid musical-entertainment forms for the masses – and that these could, apparently, exist independently of any direct link with Naxalite politics. By the time the first 'dhoom dham' performance was held in 2003, the popularity across Telangana of Gaddar, the individual, and of the Jana Natya Mandali/Arunodaya idiom, was hardly in doubt. Naxalite film had had some role to play in increasing its visibility and popularity alike. Simultaneously, via the 'dhoom dham', there was a dispersal of yet another form of hybrid left propaganda, initially in the form of live stage performances. 'Dhoom dham' performances and artistes became television content from around 2009, when that medium too was drawn into the battle for Telangana.

Padmaja Shaw notes that three pro-statehood channels were launched from Hyderabad in 2009 alone, when the movement intensified on the ground.[47] The immediate cause for the late 2009 upsurge was the hunger strike by KCR from 29 November 2009 and the subsequent announcement by the then Minister for Home Affairs, Government of India (on 9 December 2009) declaring the formation of the Telangana state.[48] On the ground, from November 2009, the spate of suicides in support of statehood added a sense of urgency to the prolonged mobilization, and also led to a spurt in the production of print and audio-visual forms in support of statehood.

On Telugu satellite television, 'dhoom dham' came to refer to a genre of folk performance which did not make explicit references to politics. An anchor with the screen name Racha Ramulamma (Ramya Krishna, notice the reference to *Osey Ramulamma*), speaking in a Telangana dialect, became the host of a new reality show titled 'Teenmaar Dhoom Dham'.[49] All of these developments were by now clearly pointing to a reinvention of folk forms with deeply political content, and thereby playing out a classic nationalist strategy of reinventing tradition, complete with a presiding Mother Goddess (Talli Telangana).

Even as Naxalite propaganda transmogrified into folk revival for television, access to propaganda also increased significantly, for two reasons. First, its circulation was no longer curtailed by fear of police repression that had followed the suppression of Maoism in the state. Second, the digitization of audio and video tapes and sharing of content on Web 2.0 platforms had the effect of assembling a new archive of songs as well as ephemeral live performances. Propaganda was thus *rendered mobile* by both political and technological contexts, and could now travel well beyond its already impressive publics. Much of the access even to 'pure' Naxalite propaganda was mediated by pro-statehood users who turned to Web 2.0 platforms in significant numbers after 2009.

YouTube emerged as an important platform for users who found themselves in a period of heightened political activity. YouTube uploads either tagged as Telangana by users, or popped up in searches related to Telangana, include a fair share of content that is directly drawn from television. Clips of news coverage of events, interviews with Telangana leaders, and performances by Gaddar and Vimalakka, but also 'dhoom dham' participants, are among the most preferred uploads. Political scientist H. Srikanth flags the high visibility of Telangana-related content on old and new media platforms when he says (disapprovingly), 'Easy access to the internet, the growth of online social networks and newspapers, the popularity of websites such as YouTube, and the proliferation of 24×7 television news channels have come in handy for the politicians and ideologues of Telangana.'[50]

As content generated by left cultural organizations finds favour with pro-statehood YouTube users, not the least because of its frequent references to Telangana, entire bodies of work – regardless of actual authorship or content of individual songs – are claimed as 'Telangana songs'. Such content includes Red and Naxalite films to songs saluting the red flag, to processions of peasants and workers (formulaic elements from the early 1980s Red Film) to those that make explicit references to the region.

Accompanying this dispersal – online and offline – are reworkings of original works. Depoliticization is not quite an accurate description of the process, for the dispersal is avowedly in the service of a political mobilization. A particularly telling reworking of Gaddar's work is a video in which the song 'Podustunna Poddu' from the film *Jai Bolo Telangana* plays to an assortment of visuals of Michael Jackson from his music videos.[51]

Between Naxalite propaganda and the Michael Jackson video on YouTube, we have a broad spectrum of media-cultural forms: films, recorded music, live performances, television and user-generated content. The links of such individual artefacts and commodities to Naxalite politics are, at best, tenuous. What then do we make of the hypervisibility of the propaganda and personalities, some of whom continue to be associated with the Naxalite movement?

Gaddar Effect

At issue here is not the prominence of both active and lapsed Naxalite cultural activists in the Telangana movement, but rather what I would like to call the 'Gaddar-effect', as a tribute to the man who played no small role in popularizing an idiom that is now everywhere. While the Naxalite film's role in pushing propaganda well beyond the cultural wings of Maoist parties is notable, the larger phenomenon has remarkable parallels with the fate of the Indian cinema from the late twentieth century. For that reason, it becomes all the more interesting for students of cinema.

Ashish Rajadhyaksha's notion of the 'cinema-effect' is a useful starting point for understanding the problem at hand. The cinema-effect is the substitution of the celluloid medium and the film narrative by 'extra-cinematic productions of a particular kind of symbolic form deriving from what was once filmic content'.[52] The most visible sign of this process is to be found in what Rajadhyaksha terms the 'Bollywoodization of Indian cinema': cinema, once a self-standing entertainment form and industry, is transformed into a relatively minor component of a cultural industry whose constituents include music, television, fashion, food and tourism industries.[53] This transformation in the 1990s 'coincides with a widespread social tendency towards evoking film mainly for the purposes of re-presentation, re-definition or even *evisceration* of the cinema: of reprocessing the cinema in order eventually, to make it available for numerous and varied uses primarily outside the movie theatre'.[54]

Replace the terms 'cinema' and 'cinematic' with Maoist propaganda, and we have a reasonably accurate description of the Gaddar-effect in Telangana. Naxalite propaganda is invoked and quoted, but the end product need not be directly related either to Naxalism or even to propaganda. In this instance, neither the 'star' or icon (Gaddar), nor the form (propaganda), is anchored to the original function.

In many ways, Telangana's linkage between popular culture and politics follows in the wake of political mediation by 'informational' and related cultural commodities, including cinema, during NTR's election in 1983. The expanded reach of print media in the post-Emergency period - for reasons that included rising levels of literacy, availability of new printing technology and localization of content - is well known. Relatively less known was the expansion of the market for cinema in Tamil Nadu and Andhra Pradesh. M.G. Ramachandran's election as chief minister of Tamil Nadu in 1977 coincided with a sharp rise in Madras-based film production in both Tamil and Telugu in the late 1970s.[55] Cinema screens in Andhra Pradesh increased from 892 in 1975 to 1,904 in 1980 and would peak at 3,057 in 1995.[56] NTR's decision to contest the 1983 election was thus preceded by the massive expansion in the film industry across all three regions of undivided Andhra Pradesh.

The role played by the Telugu newspaper *Eenadu* in NTR's successful election campaign has drawn the attention of several researchers.[57] The newspaper was established in 1974 and, according to Robin Jeffrey, did more than just support NTR's campaign: '*Eenadu* and its proprietor Ramoji Rao[58] played a major role in *creating* the Telugu Desam Party . . . .The newspaper - and its rivals - *created the climate in which millions of Telugus came to share a sense that Telugu culture was suffering indignities that required a new political party to rectify*' (emphasis added).[59] *Eenadu*'s circulation increased in the last quarter of 1982, when the newspaper openly supported NTR and adopted a variety of techniques to deride the ruling Congress (I).[60] In 1989, it was the turn of the audio and video cassettes to play 'a significant partisan role'.[61] Today, this is exactly what is being said about Indian television. Evidently, the informational/cultural commodity stands between the party and voter. And the medium is anything but transparent.

The cultural turn was not just about singers on the political platform. The defining term of the most intense phase of the agitation (from 2009) is 'Telangana sentiment'. In its Telugu usage, the phrase 'Telangana sentiment' connotes the expression of popular will that brooks no challenge. The region's people have spoken and that counts for something in a democracy. Anger and pathos are the emotions that drove the movement. The literature, the speeches, and songs offer ample evidence of this.[62] These, let us not forget, are also the signature emotions of Red genres of Telugu cinema. The idioms that Gaddar and his radical left colleagues assembled and perfected were saturated with affect. As the emotions of the Telangana movement came to be directly traceable to Naxalite propaganda, the propaganda itself was rendered into pure melodrama – quite literally all sound and fury.

Gaddar used the phrase *taragani gani* (inexhaustible mine) to describe such people's cultural forms. The popular becomes raw material. Gaddar is the creator of the lost original that now circulates in multiple morphed versions. In this, he also performs an author function, that of authenticating cultural commodities. His name is the tag on songs and images that offers some protection against the terror of uncertain signs, from the digital object becoming completely decontextualized; or a sign of the opening up of multiple possibilities by the transcendence of an earlier (cinematic) form of indexicality – a process that Ravi Vasudevan draws attention to in his discussion of digital simulation.[63] Venkat Rao argues that Gaddar's idiom 'resists translation' and is 'impossible to render into English'.[64] Untranslatability has not rendered the idiom immobile.

Conclusion

Gaddar's makeover as a mass cultural icon was a part of a larger context in which 'regional politics' was no longer predicated on the capacity of language to form or to unify political communities. On the contrary, on both sides of the Telangana divide were Telugu-language speakers, locked in an increasingly bitter contest that went far beyond uncivil behaviour making a splash on national television. Communist and Maoist formations, a significant presence in the territories that became Telangana, had become increasingly marginal politically in the pre-bifurcation of Andhra Pradesh. Their decline coincided with the passing of the celluloid era in what was once the largest market for cinema. Media consumption, for its part, came to be overdetermined by the digital turn, which transformed all analogue forms into free-floating content. Political iconicity became unanchored from its original moorings to rally publics that may have had little use or interest in the political leanings of the icon. The unity of the mass was provisional and its glue was the Telangana sentiment.

Neither the end of language politics nor the post-celluloid turn of cinema suggests that mass mobilization is being replaced by consumption of content. A question thrown up by my material and its contexts of production and circulation is how the examination of media consumption might help us understand today's mass politics. The youths on the streets are, among other things, audiences. The mobilized subject is a consumer and at times also a producer of content. What we are witnessing is not the evisceration of the original or the death of the cinema but the transition to a new situation and the emergence of new locations and modes of publicness.

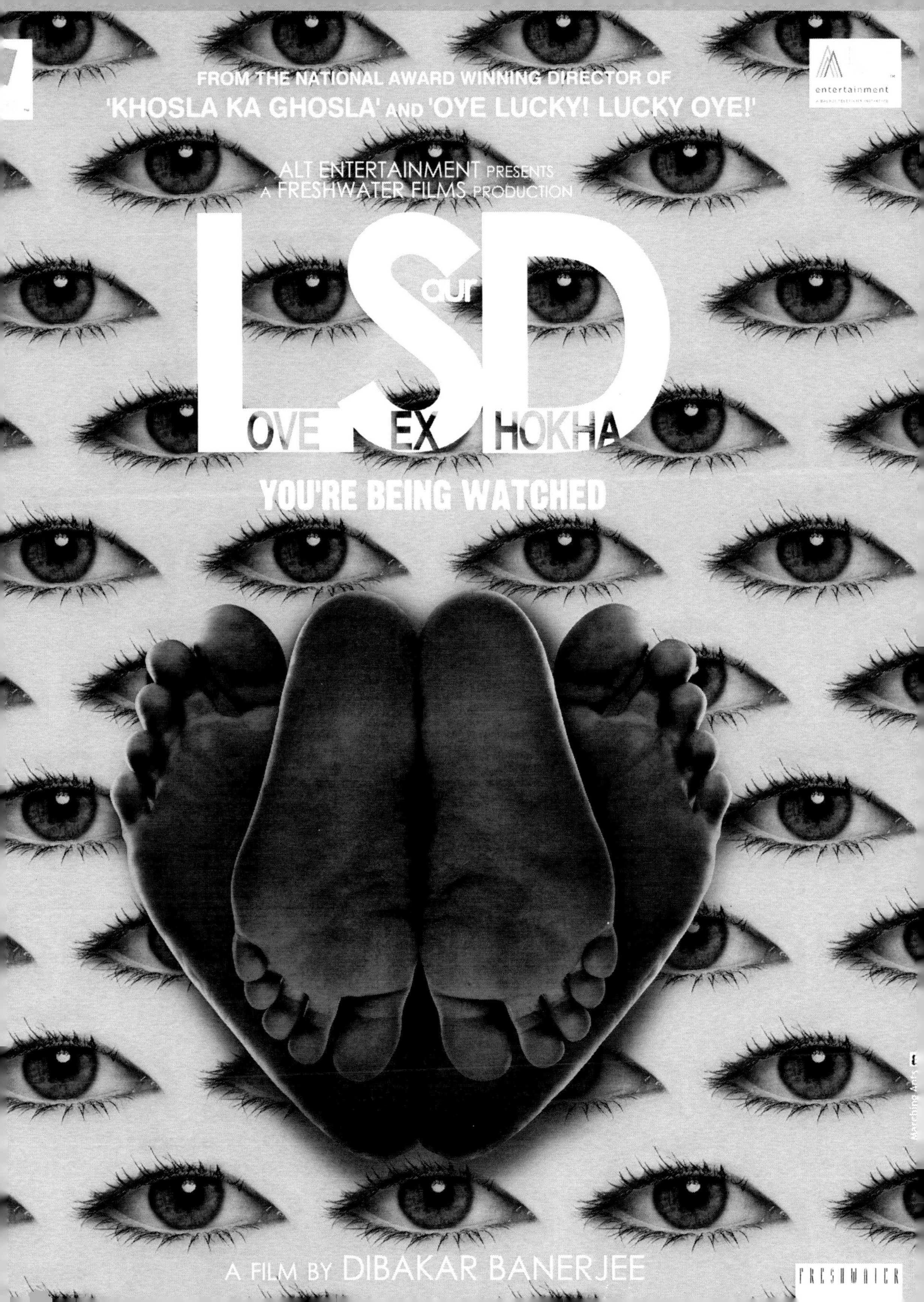
FROM THE NATIONAL AWARD WINNING DIRECTOR OF
'KHOSLA KA GHOSLA' AND 'OYE LUCKY! LUCKY OYE!'
entertainment
ALT ENTERTAINMENT PRESENTS
A FRESHWATER FILMS PRODUCTION
LSD
LOVE SEX aur DHOKHA
YOU'RE BEING WATCHED
A FILM BY DIBAKAR BANERJEE
FRESHWATER

A version of this text was initially presented at a conference in 2012, at the cusp of the wholesale transformation of the moving image on to digital platforms. Legal scholar and media theorist Lawrence Liang takes the question of the transformation back to a retro-futurist moment when technology is about to become something new, and defines that new entirely in terms of what has passed. What is at stake in the post-celluloid world is, he writes, 'as much a question of *our* ontology as it is that of film'. 'When a phenomenon wanes, it also reminds us of the powers it possessed at its peak', he adds. Liang's work in collaboration with Sarai[1] has involved tracking emerging film cultures through the circulation of pirated DVDs across Asia and camera prints circulating on the internet. Here, he draws upon his wider research on copyright and visual culture to raise a more philosophical question about the ontology of the digital image. Looking specifically at the phenomenon of the *digileak* – grainy pornographic images and low-resolution pirated films – he explores what this new body of the cinematic means for our own perceptual conditions of knowing.

Keywords

Copyright Law, Cybermohalla Ensemble, Digitalism, Exploitation Cinema, Intellectual Property, MMS scandal, New Media, Pirate Networks, Pornography, Streaming, Video:
See Keywords (pp. 326–44).

Digileak: Digital data that gets 'leaked out' to be widely circulated and consumed, either by error or deliberately, including low-resolution pornographic videos, incidental footage, grainy sting video footage, muffled sound recordings and poor-quality pirated recordings of film prints.

Love, Sex aur Dhokha (Love, Sex and Deceit, dir. Dibakar Banejee, 2010): The first Indian feature to be shot entirely in the digital format, using guerrilla techniques and different cameras including handycams, night vision cameras, security cameras, underwater cameras and spy cameras. Inspired by the DPS MMS scandal and shot with a shaky, low-tech, fuzzy, unframed aesthetic by cinematographer Nikos Andritsakis.

Mysore Mallige (*The Jasmine of Mysore*, dir. Bharath Murthy, 2007): Well-known remake of a leaked pornographic film featuring two consenting adults filming themselves.

Images

p. 293: Poster of *Love, Sex aur Dhoka* (*LSD*) (2010), digital video, colour. Image courtesy Dibakar Banerjee and Balaji Films.

p. 299: Montage of screen grabs from *LSD*, placed within TV monitor frames.

pp. 304–05: Montage of screen grabs from *Mysore Mallige*. Courtesy Bharath Murthy.

LAWRENCE LIANG 2012

20 From Cinema to the Moving Image and Back

I

Photography and film's emergence as 'new media' at the turn of the nineteenth century unsettled the ontological stability of the visual arts. A century later, we see a similar destabilizing of *film* with the emergence of a wide range of visual practices enabled by *digital* technology. The shift from celluloid to digital – and consequently from its basis in photographic realism to an incipient digitalism – raises a number of questions of the ontological status of film. But is the move from analog to digital as seamless as it appears?

Here, I examine a set of ordinary digital objects, such as leaked videos, which share both proximity and distance from cinema, to pose questions to contradictions internal to the digital moment. I also examine the ethical stakes of the transition from analog to digital, and shall link them to an emerging regime of images in the era of the digital leak.

Jean Luc Godard's *Eloge de l'amour* (In Praise of Love, 2001, French) presents us with an image of cinema as a medium whose time – in Hamlet's words – is 'out of joint'. Godard reverses the normal conventions of shooting the present in colour and the past in black and white, and chooses instead to shoot the present in 35 mm on black and white and the past on video in grainy colour, inviting us to think about how we experience not just the past in cinema, but also the past of cinema. D.N. Rodowick reads the film (and its intriguing title *Eloge* – a curious play on two words: 'eulogy' and 'elegy') for the fading object called cinema. Watching Godard's film on DVD, Rodowick says that you encounter a loss of resolution in the black and white segments of the film while the colour segments appear less saturated and more natural, thereby flattening the past and present into an indistinguishable 'happy medium' of the digital.[2] The struggle of the film's protagonist Edgar to find an artistic form becomes, on DVD, a potentiality in search of a form and medium. The potential of any medium exists here as a virtual existence - between what it can or cannot become. Virtuality is intrinsically marked by an ontological instability, since it expresses itself, not via its being, but via its *becoming*. The unstable domain of the digital moving image - where we see experiments in film, video art and digital objects that have not settled into a stable horizon as yet - is thus a form of becoming that is tied in an umbilical manner to film, even as it attempts to free itself of filmic constraints.[3]

Both the fading past of celluloid and its imperceptible future - where the future of the digital image is tied to the past of film - invites us to consider the history of film in an 'untimely manner'. Nietzsche argues that events can be either followed by mapping their emergence, growth and decline across time, or by going back in another way - to moments that inhabit the event in the process of its becoming. Such an 'untimely' account of the digital moment moves away from the usual progression of old and new, and asks instead *what it would mean to inhabit the space of media as it became new*. We encounter celluloid at the turn of the nineteenth century or the digital at the turn of the twentieth, growing, in Deleuze's memorable words 'both young and old'.[4]

Much before the official versions of Ritwik Ghatak[5] were released in India, I picked up copies of his films from the streets of Beijing. In the course of our work (at Sarai) figuring out pirate cultures, we encountered strange objects like these, all a part of a lively film culture. We weren't sure then whether we possessed an adequate vocabulary to provide an account for such oddities. We began investigating where these pirated DVDs came from, how they were being curated, what histories of labour went into their making.[6] Scholarship on cinema's relationship to the digital moment has excavated new media art or avant-garde practices, but few investigate the changing materiality of film circulation and spectatorship. If we are to make sense of the digital afterlife of cinema, it would be fruitful to turn towards the 'heap of broken images' (in T.S. Eliot's memorable phrase in 'The Waste Land') that make up our everyday digital experience.

The shift from celluloid to digital has transformed production as filmmaking increasingly moves to computer generated images, as well as exhibition, as films are available from the internet to the mobile phone, extending the life of film as commodity. The ensuing transformation in the very idea of the value of a film has gone alongside the devaluing of the classical cinematic experience.[7] All of these diverse positions assume the telos of the move from celluloid to digital, from old to new. Implicit in these positions, then, is an agonistic relationship that analog has to the digital: to competing ideas of filmmaking, to the value of the cinematic experience. What if we were to see the digital moment not just as one that pits the digital against analog, but one in which the digital constantly *battles itself* – where the upgraded digital experience of the ideal image is beset with internal *contradictions* of the digital medium, including its ease of replication and its speed of circulation? Deleuze's famous assertion that the life – or the afterlife – of the cinema depends on its internal struggles with informatics, is nowhere better demonstrated than in the struggle of the digital against what I term as the *digileak*.[8]

The fiction of a seamless flow is vital to the imagination of the business of cinema as it becomes digital. Global regimes from international intellectual property laws to digital rights management, and global anti-piracy initiatives, are all set up in place to shore up this fiction, and to sustain the seamless worldwide flow of film *as film*. Consider for instance, Qube cinema, a new exhibition and distribution initiative responsible for setting up digital cinemas across the country.[9] Their main aim is to bypass the traditional barriers of celluloid prints, including those of film piracy. Satellite linking of cinema halls began about four to five years ago in India, and there are currently around 2,500 digital halls out of 12,900 movie theatres in the country, especially in rural and small-town India. Each film is highly encrypted, watermarked randomly by the projection system, and Qube gets a detailed log of the number of shows of a film, together with show timings, at every hall where their systems are running in the country. When a pirated DVD of the film *Rab Ne Bana Di Jodi* (A Match Made by God, dir. Aditya Chopra, 2008) was seized and brought for investigation, Qube was able to identify, through the watermark, the cinema hall at which the camcorder recording of the film was done – a small cinema hall in Bilimora, a small town in Gujarat, that was screening the film at 3.30 am.[10]

Regardless of its efficacy, as a means for curtailment of piracy, the digital world is actually porous in more senses than one. Camera prints leak out of 'foolproof systems' to dense activity on torrent-sharing websites, many of which release camera prints concurrent with the official release of a film, followed by pre-DVD rips, DVD screeners and finally proper rips. Every once in a while, you have the leaking of a final print even before it is released on DVD. One of the most intriguing leaks in recent times was the Hollywood blockbuster *Wolverine Origins* (dir. Gavin Hood, 2009). The leaked version appeared before the treatment of the computer-generated images had been completed, and serves as a wonderful artifact of our times, for it reveals, more than any finished film can, strings attached to the actor's body, actors merging into their digitally rendered form and digitally fabricated spaces.

Realism and Digitalism

How do we read a text like the leaked *Wolverine*? If the cinema of digital attractions airbrushes the real to hyper-real perfection, the leak invites us to see the conditions of digital production. What happens to our cinematic pleasure when we see 'strings' attached to the body of the actor? It is not as if we did not know that these sequences were shot using computer effects. Most films indeed advertise their special effects. The blockbuster *Ra.One* (dir. Anubhav Sinha, 2011), for example, constantly reminded audiences that it used more special effects than *Avatar* did;[11] DVD specials routinely include the 'making of the film' as a part of the release package. Indeed, it could be argued that one of the most popular film locations is now the famous blue screen. While special effect and background images are well known, the manipulation of facial expressions of actors for particular scenes opens a new bag of tricks: in Michael Mann's *Public Enemies* (2009), a film about the famous bank thief Dillinger, the attempt was to arrive at a stylized clarity of a hyperreal image of the past, both historic but also cinematic, as the film attempted to appeal to audience recall of genre conventions of the gangster film.

Watching the James Bond film *Casino Royale* (dir. Martin Campbell, 2006) on a Blu Ray disc was a strange experience: the image was so clear and sharp that in a scene in which Bond is battered and bloodied, the texture of the blood clearly reveals that it is paint. It was as though Hitchcock revealed to the audience of *Psycho* (1960) at the beginning of the film that he had used chocolate sauce in the famous shower scene to heighten the effect on black and white. Inverting magical conventions, here, the revelation precedes the trick. Even though it is not the eruption of a secret that is at issue here, something strange does happen to us as spectators: a violation of contract between us and the screen. If realism was a contested organizing principle of celluloid seeing, we have a new mode here of organizing perception - one that we might tentatively name *digitalism*. Digitalism serves as a useful reminder that a format is not merely the specific material substrate or medium such as the celluloid filmstrip or a DVD, but the changing material circumstances through which we renegotiate our relationship with, and understanding of, the cinematic phenomenon.

Digitalism is not so much a property of film as conceived by the filmmaker as it is a coming together of both intended and unintended consequences of the movement between mediums, including their 'digileak' versions. Even as digital technology seeks to move us towards a regime of the perfect image and sound, there is a parallel universe in which degraded images and distorted sounds rule supreme. To go there, we need to make sense of the allure of the low-definition image of the camera print: and thence to things like the grainy video of sting operations and amateur pornography, and the barely audible sound recordings of tapped telephone conversations.

Consider the following: Vishal Patel and a few friends were fooling around in front of a webcam, and they decided to play a prank. They used a black marker to paint the spot between their index finger and middle finger, and figured that by positioning their fingers in front of the camera, relying on the graininess of the web cam image they could simulate the image of a naked woman spreading her

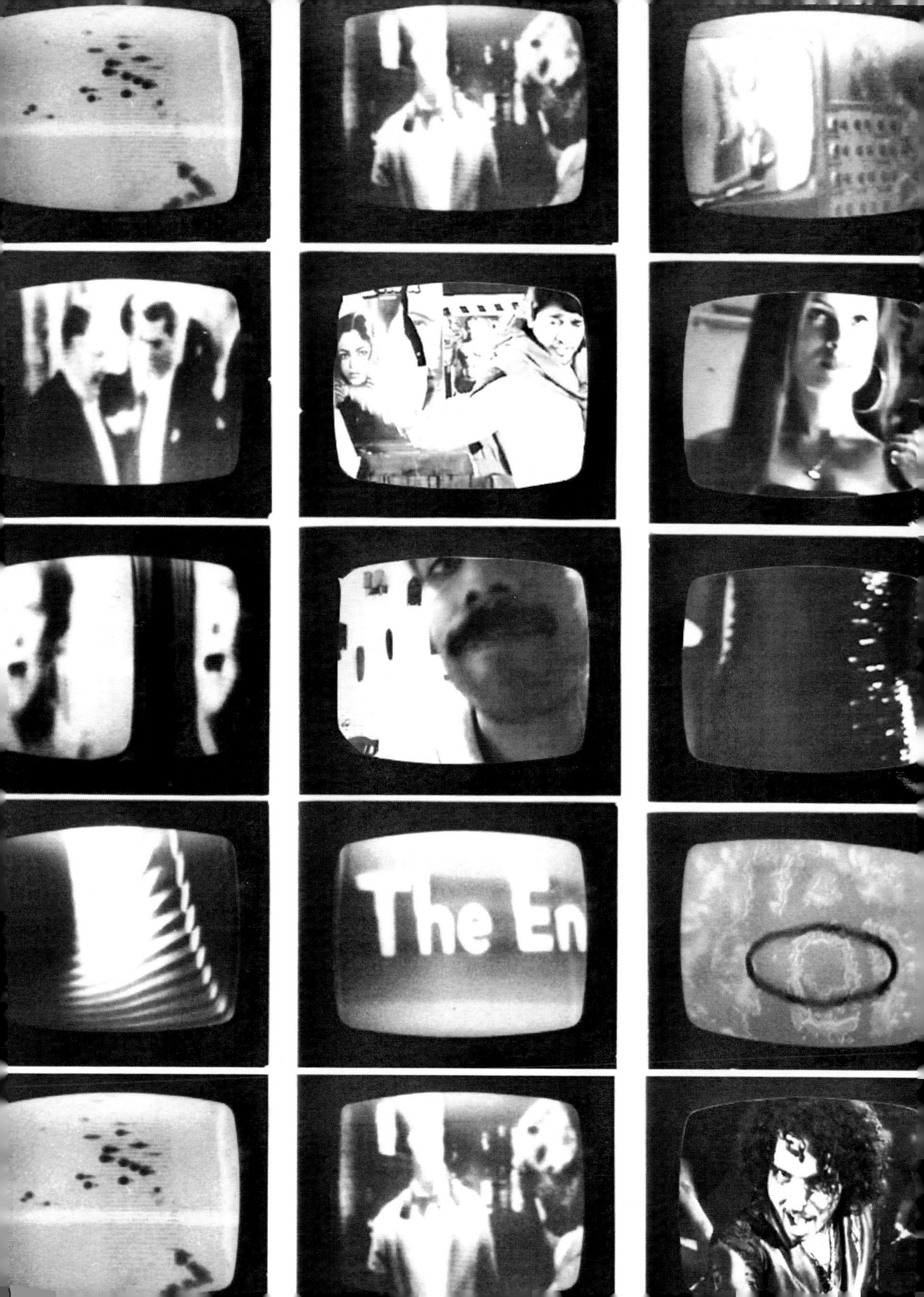
The En

legs. They started webcasting this video and soon had a large following of people chatting with them and requesting them to perform for them.

Why would a bunch of people look at a set of ridiculously grainy images and what pleasures would arise from this form of watching? Given that the internet is filled with high-resolution videos and images of porn, this appears to be more than just the desire for pornography as the desire for sexual content. There was something intriguing about the seductive appeal of the grainy image, which seems to conjure the fiction of 'liveness and the real' as a source of *jouissance*. It almost recalls Jean Louis Comolli's sense[12] of how early visual technology created an intensification of the visible – a new field of the visible as a vision of events, places, and bodies began to be mediated by an optical apparatus that began to see as though in place of the naked eye. There is, as Linda Williams extends Comolli into the area of the hard-core knowledge-pleasure produced by pornography,[13] what she calls a 'frenzy' of the visible – and which I want to call, as I look at pornography on the internet, the frenzy of an 'uncertain real'. This 'real' is specifically referenced through the way cheap digital technologies render a new domain of the private.

A significant part of the pleasure of these images lies in a near-forensic pleasure of figuring out the content of the image, alongside its veracity. Television's turn towards 'reality' shows, live webcam transmissions and analog nostalgia by film makers, all share a common ground – a quest for an unmediated reality. Digitalism seems to exist at the cusp of an inability to believe in the hyper-real, alongside an equally intense *desire for the real* that has become grounded in degraded and unintelligible images, as though the low quality of the image becomes a marker of their indexicality.[14]

Such digital objects – artefacts of an incipient digitalism – are still to find a taxonomy, leave alone an ontology. The puzzle of what is a 'digital object', or a 'digital event', recalls questions of classical film theory that have been out of fashion for some time: they include the various shades of realism, from ontological to perceptual to photorealist.[15] The cinema is indeed the most Hamletian of the arts, constantly plagued by self-doubt, questioning its own being. Its attempts at any stable self-definition seem perennially 'out of joint' because of its parallel life as technology. The ontology of an object is thus brought into heightened focus either when we encounter its astonishing novelty, or when there is a recognition of its own displacement. Both may be useful as we return to the ontology of cinema itself, as a way of finding our way through the digital thicket.

The World Viewed and the Ontology of Film

If the modern condition is to 'know', then the cinema speaks deeply to that condition. Modern subjects, as Cavell argues,[16] are, at one level, freed from moral and epistemological dogma, but then their doubts about the world also become questions of the self in relation to its perceptions. No longer assured of their place in the world, such subjects are provoked into new strategies of self-actualization and self-invention. The modern ethical dilemma is how to regain contact with this world, to overcome our distance from it and restore its 'knownness' to us. A basic problem here is how such subjects bear responsibility for the epistemological and moral consequences of their isolation: and how their quest for meaning is intrinsically tied to encounters with isolated perceptions.

Cinema poses both the condition of scepticism and provides a possible philosophical solution, since it shows us a route back to our conviction of reality. The experience of photography and film makes us 'ontologically restless', Cavell says, but this fundamental perplexity of photographs does not derive simply from the problem of representation. It derives from the curious sentiment that *things absent in time can be present in space*. There is a paradox - of presence and absence - that pervades our experience of the world and of cinema. Films present very different modes of existence to viewing: realism here has less to do with the 'apprehension of likenesses' and very much more to do with our metaphysical contact with a world from which we have become separated.[17]

In such a view, the screen is neither a medium nor a support: rather, it is a barrier, as much conceptual as it is physical - a philosophical situation of a self, divided from the world by the window of perception. We wish for the condition of viewing because it is a way through which we establish and maintain our connection to the world, by having a view of it. Having a 'world view' requires that we believe in the prior existence of the world, even if only in images. Films are precisely not escapist, Cavell argues; rather they are a relief from our private fantasy and its responsibilities. If the reality that film holds before us is that of our own perceptual condition, then it opens the possibility of once again being present to the self - or at least of acknowledging that we may again become present to ourselves. Ontology is now inseparable from that of medium. A medium is that which stands between us and the world as representation. Between the medium as potential and its realization as an art form, lies its self-consciousness - in the manner in which it comes to its awareness about its own artistic possibility. Such a self-consciousness of the medium returns us to our perceptions. We see evidence of this both in the technology of cinema, as well as in cinema's thinking of its own technology: whether of sound (*Singin' in the Rain*, dirs. Gene Kelly and Stanley Donen, 1952), colour (*Pleasantville*, dir. Garry Ross, 1998) or the digital turn (*Matrix*, dirs. Lana and Lilly Wachowski, 1999)

A medium is, thus, unique, because it is not essentialist - because it is both a response to a force that demands such a medium as well as the force itself, which creates a form.[18] The whole of cinematic history, for instance, can be written in ways in which filmmakers have not just discovered the essence of the medium, but sought to extend it, renew it or reinvent its expressive capabilities. Cavell's ontology has less to do with the identity of cinema and more with the ways that films express for us current and future states of being, and return to us our pasts.

And so we ask: if film provided us with a way of encountering our isolated perceptions, what happens to a mode of being that is fundamentally indebted to film, even as film itself fades into wider image-making technologies?

II

The Untimely Digital Object

The past two decades have been, unsurprisingly, marked by dystopic films. *Blade Runner* (dir. Ridley Scott, 1982) and *Matrix* (1999) in Hollywood, *Robot* (dir. S. Shankar, 2010) and *Ra.One* in India, all narratively deal with the post-human, even as their creation deals with the post-analog. I want to up the ante to argue that what is philosophically at stake in the post-celluloid world is as much a question of *our* ontology as it is that of film. As the image moves either into the hyper-real, or downward into the grainy, what is at stake - all over again - is our relationship to our perceptual condition. When a phenomenon wanes, it also reminds us of the powers it possessed at its peak - and for many of us who arrived at our lifelong passion for cinema through film clubs, the pure experience of cinema has always been a theatrical one, and we will always value that even as we discover, crouched over our laptops or watch an LCD projection in a small room, new aspects of film itself and its enduring ability to affect us. But what exactly is lost? What precisely is the cinephile's lament?

What is often believed lost in the cinematic experience is an account of the change in the heightened experience of cinema, and thus of ourselves, for the theatrical experience was a commitment to solitude: to our solitude in a theatre, and also a solitude we shared with others, friends and strangers alike, in the presence of something much larger than ourselves - the screen, or the world.

This play between size and proximity has had an interestingly inverted relationship. In a theatre, one sits shoulder to shoulder with a large number of people staring at a large screen that is far from us. As films moved from the silver screen to our television sets and video, the size of the screen decreased as did our proximity to it. The screen seemed dwarfed, and the number of people we shared this experience with lessened, even as our proximity to those who saw the films with us increased. At the same time, what increased was the relational proximity of the people we watched films with: the intimate space, whether the central spot given to a television in a household or in the space of one's bedroom, also meant a reconfiguring of the intimacy with which we watched films, with a more acute sense of who was next to us, the presence of ambient noise, light, and the possibility of interruptions with phone calls or people at the door.

The body was able to adapt to relatively mobile positions while watching a film and was less restricted than it was in a movie hall. Our backs straightened again when we started watching films on our desktop computers, using mini speakers for amplified sound, and the distance between us and the screen decreased even further. Gone were the mandatory warnings that came from our parents asking us to sit away from the television set lest our eyes get spoilt. But the numbers of those who could sit around a computer screen was considerably lesser than those who could sit around a television set. In fact, in the early days of television in India, TV was a neighborhood ritual with almost everyone landing up, either because a TV serial was showing or an important cricket game. And finally, as it moved to our laptops, the screen gained a spatial intimacy hitherto unimagined, because for the first time we were truly alone with our films, sometimes bringing an epiphanic response which we did not know we were capable of, and at other times, a weary sense of ennui even when watching the most remarkable film.

A recent text by the Cybermohalla ensemble says:

> What is the difference between something being public or becoming *niji* (private) and someone searching for or being in solitude (*ekaant*)? What do we lose when we conceptually confuse between the private and solitude? By associating multitudes with noise and the singular with solitude, do we inadvertently lose out on recognizing the multitude's possibility for solitude? The proliferation of things and things becoming smaller and smaller – do these confuse our discernment of *niji* and *ekaant*?[19]

The passage highlights the centrality of our spatial and corporeal experience of cinema. In considering the movement of film across mediums, we will have to pay attention not just to the ocular experience, but to the *experience of the body*. There are two senses in which I have been using the idea of proximity: the first between bodies and the screen, and the second in the proximity (or distance) between the digital object and cinema. The two are, to my mind, integrally linked.

There is growing evidence that, contrary to the view that the digital turn is also one of disembodiment, the very opposite is true. Mark Hansen argues, for instance, that the phenomenon of digitization demarcates a shift in the correlation of two crucial terms: media and body,[20] and that even as media lose their material specificity, the body takes on an ever-more prominent function as a *selective processor of information*. It is the body's scope of perceptual and affective possibilities, that informs the medial interfaces, so that, with the new flexibility of digitization, a displacement occurs in the framing function of medial interfaces, as they return to the body from whence they originally emerged. On its side, the body – in its encounter with media – becomes a site of indetermination. The cut, in

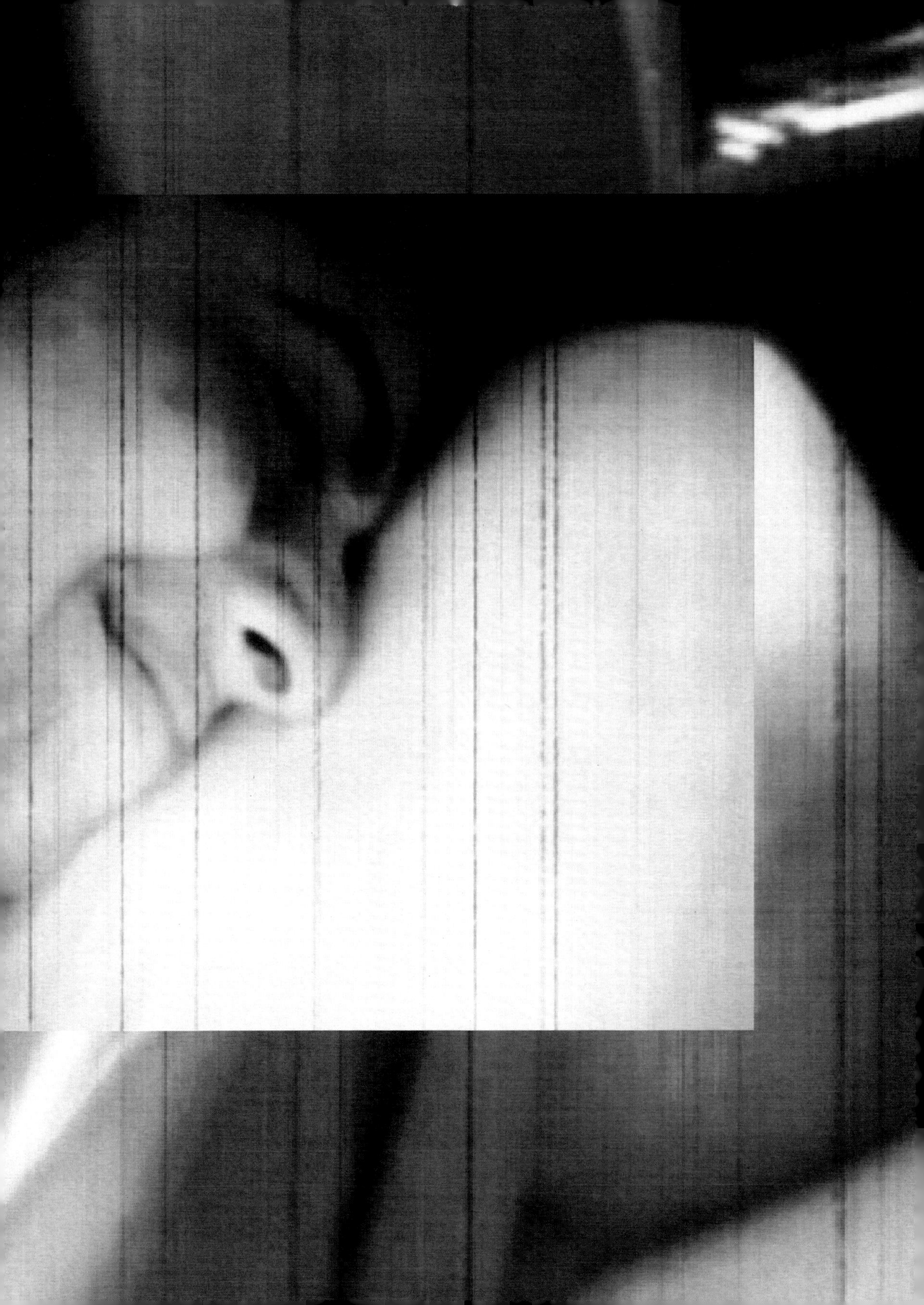

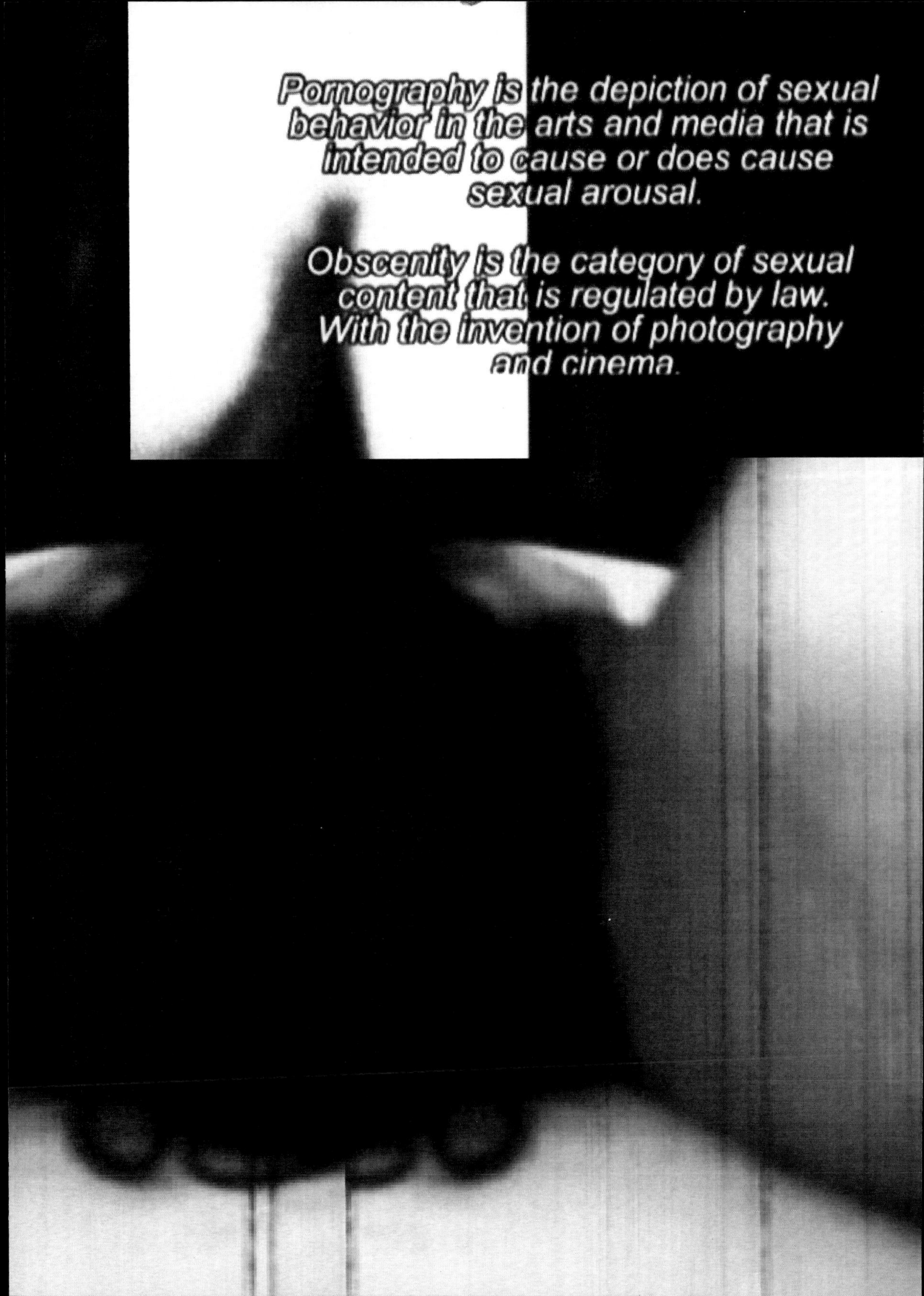
Pornography is the depiction of sexual behavior in the arts and media that is intended to cause or does cause sexual arousal.
Obscenity is the category of sexual content that is regulated by law. With the invention of photography and cinema.

the cinema, is a moment when the body inhabits a space but does not necessarily know what this occupation will entail, says Deleuze.[21] The passage in film from one moment to another is also a passage of the body, and the cinema's powers of affection really lie in its *intensification of duration*, either in surprise or other changes in affective gears. A useful way of thinking of ontology as duration can be found in Kajri Jain's work on the different circuits of value that are embodied in bazaar images of gods.[22] While such images occupy the space of low art and cheap reproductions, they simultaneously gain great ethical value as religious objects. Their true value is revealed in their *circulation*, as 'fleeting constellations between the image, other bodies or objects, and the quality, rhythm and intensity of time at a given moment'.[23]

This proposition is useful when we think of how film shifts across mediums. If we resist the idea that they are mere repetitions, we are compelled to pay closer attention to precisely their *durational ontologies*. When *The Godfather* (dir. Francis Ford Coppola, 1972) travels from the big screen to TV to video, to grainy VCD, DVD and then to the blue ray, or as it moves across different screen sizes, it is of course the same film that moves: Michael Corleone does not turn into a senator in the VCD version. But even as it remains the same film – we may well ask – is it *the same moving image*? In moving closer or further from an ideal form, do its powers or intensities change? How do the perceptual shifts that take place with each movement bring us back to their ontologies? Such questions require closer reading of the moments of a medium, paying attention to what it catches, when it enhances or loses its appeal and intensity, say with 3D or a particular sound technology, such as Dolby digital. Duration here allows us to think through the mobilization of different affects, as we move over the threshold of different mediums, even if the film itself is supposedly unchanged.

Cinema in its classical form offers the body a particular plane of connectivity to sensation: changes in mediums also change connectivity. By moving away from the known and idealized form of cinema, we approach media in an untimely manner: media appear as unstable objects, both less, and more, than cinema. What comes into stark relief is the *persistence of the cinematic*, even as it keeps becoming something else. Historically, the cinema always expressed an ecology of sensations before its codification into narrative, or into discourse. Early motion picture studies and pre-narrative cinema were, for instance, marked by its investment in the body and its possibilities – a woman walking downstairs, a man hurling a disc. If we were to return to this idea, one of the oldest in film, we might now discover how the same moment in a film, as it moves across mediums, also moves us into other *planes of connectivity*.

I have been using the phrase 'ontological proximity and distance' as a way of thinking about what happens to the connectivity of cinema as it becomes a medium. The paradox of horror in the cinema is that, the way that the film acts upon the body is at its most effective when seen in an ideal form (sound, image quality). Yet many people feel they can watch a horror film in a crowd or along with other people, but would not be able to watch the same film alone. Such isolation forces us to contend with what happens when a *medium moves* (its intensity is not so much a guarantee as a constant shift of degree).

One of the most intriguing phenomena in recent years has been the proliferation of the hidden camera - either as the necessary infrastructure of a new discourse of transparency and revelation, via the *sting operation*, or the rise of the sexual MMS scandal.[24] MMS scandals have comprised hidden camera videos when men have secretly taped their sexual encounters, or when a couple has made a video of themselves which has leaked onto the internet. One of the earliest scandals in home video involved an engineering college student and his girlfriend, who taped themselves while on a holiday: the tape leaked, possibly at the time of conversion, and started selling under the name of *Mysore Mallige*: the name becoming in turn a euphemism for leaked sexual scandals. The film was also the inspiration for a number of feature films as well as a documentary titled *The Jasmine of Mysore* (2007) by the filmmaker Bharath Murthy.

There is something both disturbing and compelling about the MMS - perhaps it is disturbing precisely because it is so compelling. We are not quite sure what to make of the images, especially since they do not appear to do the ordinary work of sexual titillation. It seems that what is most disturbing is the uncanny attraction that they hold for us, confronting us with our perversity. 'Even the most refined or perverse among us', says Michael Warner, 'could point to his or her desires or identifications and see that they were public desires, even mass public desires, from the moment that they were the person's desires'.[25]

Most accounts of watching these images capture a basic ambiguity: you can, it was often said, neither look at them nor look away. Bharath Murthy says that these images gave him a sense of the missing reality of other kinds of images found on television and commercial cinema. 'I was immediately struck by the directness of the images', he writes, 'For the first time, I saw an Indian couple having sex in that kind of detail and reality. A new image appeared that had not been there'. It is a strange revelation that 'the pornographic image gave a sense - an understanding - of what we really are, in sort of an obtuse way'.[26] Namita Malhotra writes that

> when looking at material like *Mysore Mallige* and the DPS MMS clip, the affective relation that predominates is indeed that of its 'realness'; for some this produces a sense of fear, paradoxically a ghostly quality to the image and unease. For me it was about the uncanniness of the familiar body, which occupies a similar world to yours that is somehow trapped in a video.[27]

She echoes Murthy in claiming that these images seem to speak to an affect otherwise missing in films.

It is perhaps interesting that it is amateur pornography these days that seems to inspire the most complicated set of affects (unlike the schooled and disciplined and predictable response to cinema) – shocked recognition of yourself and desire to see it again, titillation, boredom but yet unwilling to look away.[28]

What is held back in abeyance in forms of studio- or industry-produced pornography is evident in amateur pornography – a fleshiness that acts on the nerves of the body. This could explain why the affective relation to such material is not entirely about arousal, but about 'something else' that then has to find stories, feelings, meanings and repetitions in other ways.

In 2010, a Hindi film *Love, Sex aur Dhoka* (*LSD, or Love Sex and Betrayal*) (dir. Dibakar Banerjee) articulated this 'something else' in a different perceptual relationship to the moving image. The film narrates three interconnected stories told from the perspective of the home video, the surveillance camera and the hidden camera. Of particular interest is the second segment of the film in which a glib manager of a supermarket seduces a salesgirl who works there, with the intention of filming them having sex. He hesitates as he starts to fall in love with her, but after a fight with the girl in which she tries to draw him away from his illusions of grandeur and reminds him of his 'middle class' status, he goes ahead with recording them having sex and making the video public. *LSD* explores the multiple refractions of the self that have exploded as a consequence of the proliferation of recording technologies from webcams to CCTV and digital cameras to video chat rooms. What these multiple images offer us is a 'blurry, grainy image of the self'.[29]

Watching *LSD* on the screen was already a disturbing experience, both for what one saw on the screen but also for the strange laughter that accompanied one of the most gruesome sequences in the film: that of two runaway lovers getting hacked to death. But what was even more disturbing was encountering the leaked version of the film. *LSD* became subject to its own conceptual prophecies when a leaked copy made it to torrent. It is an eerie experience watching a copy of the film in which you can hear the non-stop commentary of a group of young men urging the protagonist to film his sexual experience and engage in a mock auction bidding for the tape: recalling a real life incident in which an engineering student had put up a leaked sex video of two school students on the equivalent of eBay.[30]

Malhotra's media work on pornography cultures on the internet captures the simultaneity of these versions as well as their haptic appeal by framing these images on a split screen: emulating the interface of the popular video-chat channel Chatroullette.[31] In some places, she introduces a time lag between the videos on the two channels, while in others she introduces contrasting images producing an uncanny relationship between the ideal image of the body that we find in mainstream cinema against the ordinary body of pornography. At one point in the film, she uses Chatroullete to play with the official *LSD* film and its pirate version creating an effect of not one but multiple mirrors and screens.

What happens when screen images – the images of cinema that once offered us an image of the world and ourselves in it – become grainy and blurry? As Jorge Luis Borges remarks in one of his stories, 'mirrors and copulation are abominable, since they both multiply the numbers of man',[32] what seems to be at stake with the multiplication of technologies of image-making is not a *settling of* but a *furthering of* our ontological restlessness. The digital rupture is in the end, says Elsaesser, a *paradox*: for just as it installs the cinema as episteme or as ontology, it does away with cinema as a unique technology of imaging, even as the cinematic persists in the way we frame our visual experiences.[33] If we are not to be lost within the jungle of broken images, or be condemned to watching a cinema both *for* or *of* the blind, as Kafka once imagined, we may have no choice but to pay closer attention to how the displacement of cinema may itself be the grounds on which cinema will have to reinvent itself.

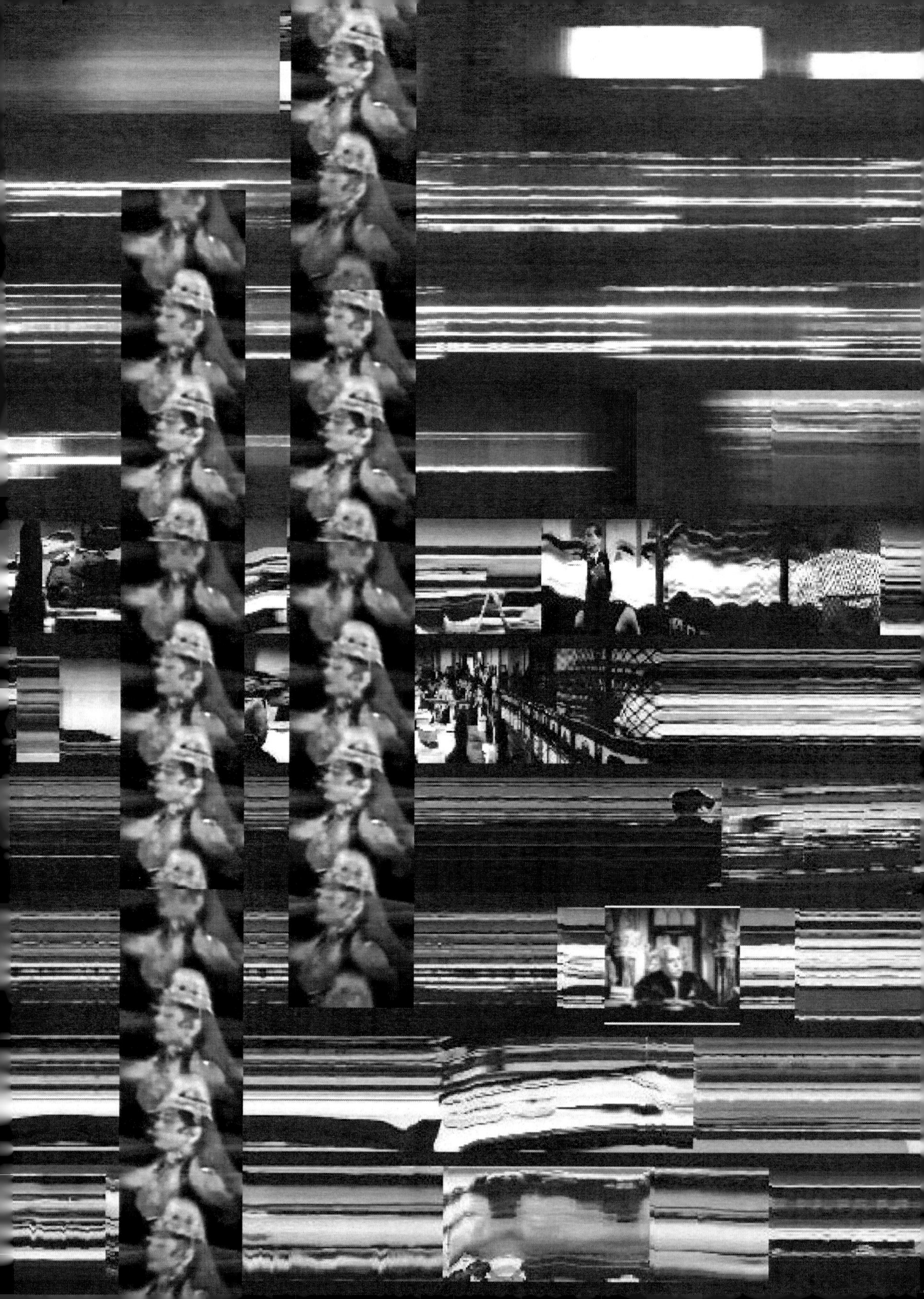

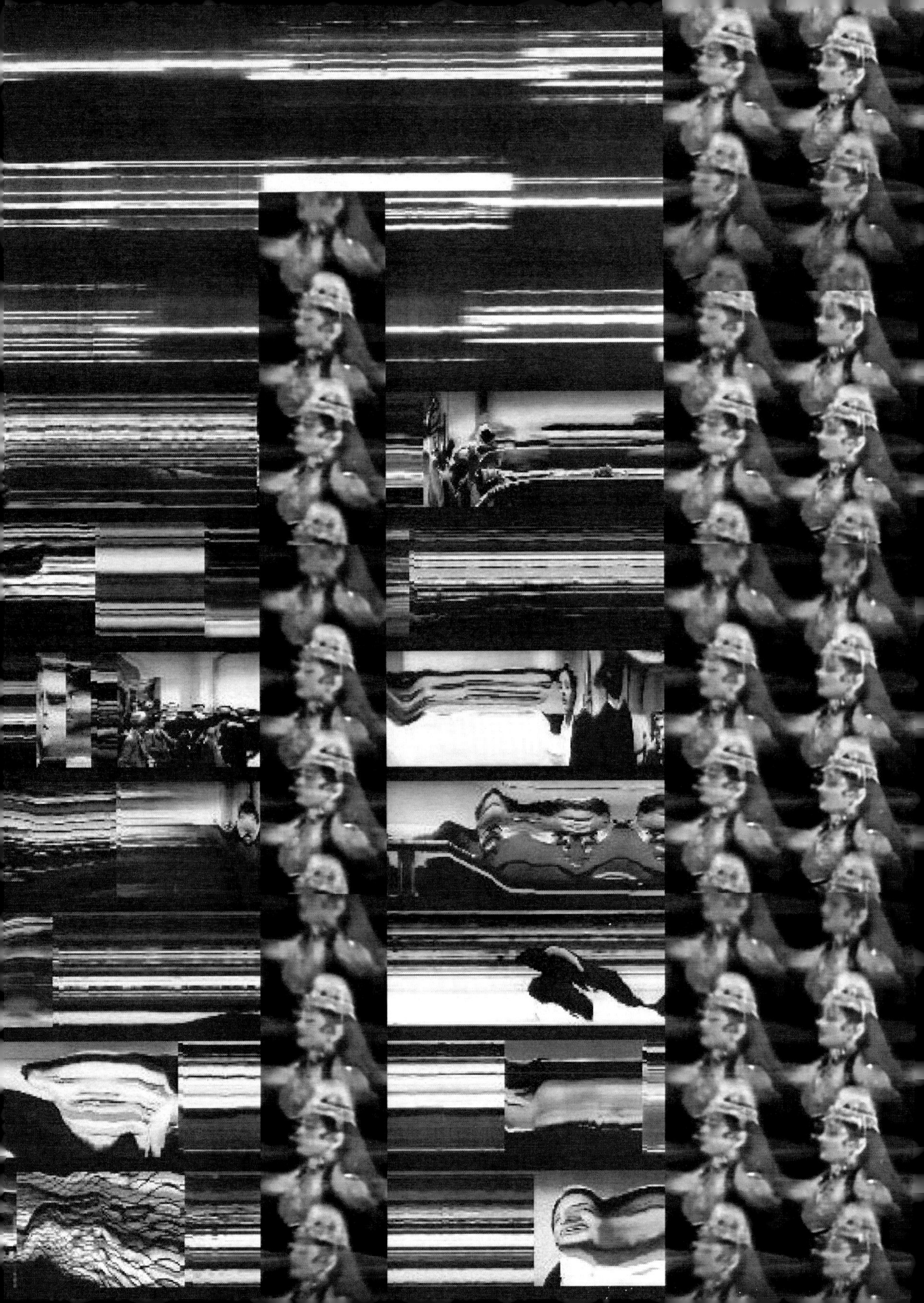

Perhaps the single defining feature of the millennial turn in the moving image was the transformation of the archive that housed it. Across colonial and independent India, the archive had been imagined as a 'fortress' housing valuables, strictly regulating both what and who qualified to enter. Now it had become its mirror opposite: a housing of the ordinary and the copy, a means of dissemination rather than of protection, a condition of 'shared politics and epistemological adventure'. The newly discovered ability of artists to align with coders and archivists to transform the digital archive appeared part of a larger set of possibilities of making aesthetic interventions into older notions of infrastructure, access, ownership, distribution and collectivity.

Ten Theses on the Archive is a manifesto statement assembled in this moment of possibility. It was written in Beirut as a practice roadmap for Pad.ma, a digital archive set up in 2008 as a partnership between Studio CAMP, 0x2620, Majlis, the Alternative Law Forum and Point of View. *Ten Theses* is placed here as an Epilogue, as a reflection on the archive-making and history-writing process explored through the making of this volume. It is an invitation to imagine parallel possibilities, 'to enter the river sideways', as the authors propose.

Keywords, Names, Abbreviations

0x2620: Pronounced 'twenty-six twenty'; a Berlin-based non-profit organization operating at the intersections of art, politics and technology.

ALF: Alternative Law Form, a collective of independent lawyers and legal researchers set up in Bangalore in 2000 for non-profit litigation and advocacy.

CAMP: Critical Arts and Media Practice, a studio for transdisciplinary practice established by Shaina Anand and Ashok Sukumaran in Mumbai in 2007.

Majlis: A legal and cultural centre set up in Mumbai in 1991, working especially on gender issues.

Pad.ma: Public Access Digital Media Archive, set up in 2008.

Point of View: Mumbai-based organization working in the area of gender rights and technology.

Images

pp. 310–11: Mashup of different views of Raj Kapoor's *Awara* (Vagabond, 1951) and K. Asif's *Mughal-e-Azam* (1960) on indiancine.ma. Housed at CAMP, Mumbai, Indian cinema's largest database, with approximately 50,000 listed films and around 10,000 digital prints – or one in five films ever made – available for viewing and annotation, offers multiple 'views' to look at the data resource that was once cinema. Here, the slitscan and keyframes display modes are used.

p. 317: Stills from Rohini Devasher's *Bloodlines* (2009, 45 mins & print), single channel video projected on to fabric. The video installation is inspired by evolutionary biologist Richard Dawkin's theory of cumulative selection. Dawkin asks us to imagine a massive hangar with shelves, occupied by creatures that live and walk the world, and others who are waiting to 'become possible' – much like the 'reserve' of the *Ten Theses* – as soon as their exact genetic sequencing is decoded. Devasher's installation is made out of video feedback achieved by plugging a hand-held camera into a TV monitor to produce a looped optical feed. The image doubles and interferes with itself, producing patterns mimicking those exhibited by physical, biological and chemical systems.

pp. 324–25: Still from *A Gathering at the Carnival Shop* (Mochu, 2015, 35 mins, digital video). Experimental video on the artist K. Ramanujam, founding member of the Cholamandal artists' village established in 1966 in Chennai. The idea of such a village embodied a radical imagination of community, livelihood, artistic practice, distributed resources and relative autonomy from the art market. Beginning with anecdotal conversations surrounding Ramanujam's disappearance in 1973, Mochu responds to the artist's practice with speculations on forgotten materials, decay and immortality.

PAD.MA **2010**

21 Ten Theses on the Archive

1. Don't Wait for the Archive
2. Archives are not reducible to the particular Forms that they take
3. The Direction of Archiving will be Outward, not Inward
4. The Archive is not a Scene of Redemption
5. The Archive deals not only with the Remnant but also with the Reserve
6. Historians have merely interpreted the Archive. The Point however is to Feel it
7. The Image is not just the Visible, the Text is not just the Sayable
8. The Past of the Exhibition Threatens the Future of the Archive
9. Archives are governed by the Laws of Intellectual Propriety as opposed to Property
10. Time is not Outside of the Archive: It is In it

1. Don't Wait for the Archive

To not wait for the archive is often a practical response to the absence of archives or organized collections in many parts of the world. It also suggests that to wait for the state archive or to otherwise wait to *be* archived may not be a healthy option.

This need not imply that every collection or assembly be named an archive, or that all of art's mnemonic practices be once again cast into an archival mould. It suggests, instead, that the archive can be deployed – as shared curiosities, a local politics, or epistemological adventure. The archival impulse could also be recast, for example, to create alliances – between text and image, between major and minor institutions, between filmmakers, photographers, writers and computers, between online and offline practices, between the remnant and what lies in reserve, between time and the untimely. These are alliances, not only against dissipation and loss, but also against the enclosure, privatization and thematization of archives, which are issues of global, and immediate, concern.

The archive that results may not have common terms of measurement or value. It will include and reveal conflicts, and it will exacerbate the crises around property and authorship. *It will remain radically incomplete*, both in content and form. But it is nevertheless something that an interested observer will be able to traverse: riding on the linking ability of the sentence, the disruptive leaps of images, and the distributive capacity that is native to technology.

To not wait for the archive is to enter the river of time sideways, unannounced, just as the digital itself did, not so long ago.

2. Archives are not reducible to the particular Forms that they take

Archival initiatives are often a response to the monopolization of public memory by the state and the political effects that flow from such mnemonic power. But attempts at creating an archive are not necessarily supplementing the memory machine of the state. The state archives are only one instance of the archive. They are not the definition of archives, merely a form. As a particular form, state archives do not exhaust the concept of the archive. The task of creating an archive is neither to replicate nor to mimic state archives but to creatively produce a concept of the archive.

An archive actively creates new ways of thinking about how we access our individual and collective experiences. An archive does not just supplement what is missing in state archives – it also renders what is at present, unstable.

When we subsume the concept of archives to its known form, we are exhausted by it. We suffer from archive fevers and archive fatigue. Contemporary archival impulses attempt to realize the potential of the archive as virtuality, and virtuality in turn challenges us to think through the productive capacities of an archive beyond the blackmail of memory and amnesia.

The production of a concept is a provocation. It is a refusal to answer to the call of the known and an opportunity to intensify our experiences. The archive is therefore not representational; it is creative. The naming of something as an archive is not the end, but the beginning of a debate.

3. The Direction of Archiving will be Outward, not Inward

We tend to think of archiving as the inward movement of collecting things, finding bits and pieces, bringing them together, guarding them in a safe and stable place. The model of this type of archiving is the fortress, or the burning library. This model already provides a clear sense of the limits, or ends, of the archive: fire, flooding, data loss.

Can we think of the archive differently? When Henri Langlois, founder of the Cinémathèque Française, stated that 'the best way to preserve film is to project it', he hinted at the very opposite philosophy of archiving: to actually use and consume things, to keep them in, or bring them into, circulation, and to literally throw them forth (Latin: *proicere*), into a shared and distributed process that operates based on diffusion, not consolidation, through imagination, not memory, and towards creation, not conservation.[1]

Most of today's digital archives seem to still adhere to the model of the fortress, even though by definition, they no longer preserve precious and unique originals, but provide cheap and reproducible copies. These copies can be 'thrown forth' on a much larger scale, and with much greater efficiency, than Henri Langlois – or Walter Benjamin, theorist of analogue reproduction, advocate of its technological potential and critic of its practical political use – would have ever imagined. To archive and to be archived can become massively popular.

The astonishingly resilient archiving practices around Napster or Pirate Bay and the even more virulent promise of actual or imaginary archives far beneath or beyond them – if, for one moment, we could step outside the age of copyright we all inhabit, and fully embrace the means of digital reproduction most of us have at our disposal – not just directly follow the trajectory traced by Benjamin and Langlois, but extend it to a point in the not-so-distant future where we will think of archiving primarily as the outward movement of distributing things: to create *ad hoc* networks with mobile cores and dense peripheries, to trade our master copies for a myriad of offsite backups, and to practically abandon the technically obsolete dichotomy of providers and consumers.

The model of this type of archive, its philosophical concept, would be the *virus* or the *parasite*. And again, this model also allows us to make a tentative assessment of the risks and dangers of outward archiving: failure to infect (attention deficit), slowdown of mutation (institutionalization), spread of antibiotics (rights management), death of the host (collapse of capitalism).

4. The Archive is not a Scene of Redemption

Important as the political impulse of archives is, it is important to acknowledge that archives cannot be tied to a politics of redemption.

A large part of what may be thought of as progressive impulses in historiography is informed by a desire to redeem history through a logic of emancipation. It is the resurrection of the subaltern subject of history, the pitting of *oral* against *written* history and the hope that an engagement with the residual of the archive will lead to a transformative politics.

Benjamin's theses on the philosophy of history has served as an important intellectual reference point for such initiatives. Benjamin says that:

> The tradition of the oppressed teaches us that the 'state of emergency' in which we live is not the exception but the rule. We must attain to a conception of history that is in keeping with this insight. Then we shall clearly realize that it is our task to bring about a real state of emergency.[2]

Benjamin does not hide the redemptive messianic thrust in his thesis: According to him 'Our image of happiness is indissolubly bound up with the image of redemption'.[3] Hope, in this formulation is primarily messianic, 'For every second of time is the strait gate through which the Messiah might enter.'[4] Elsewhere, Derrida writes that 'a spectral messianicity is at work in the concept of the archive and ties it, like religion, like history, like science itself, to a very singular experience of the promise'.[5]

Archival initiatives have unconsciously continued this theological impulse. Their desire to document that which is absent, missing or forgotten, stages a domain of politics which often privileges violence and trauma in a manner in which the experience of violence is that which destroys the realm of the ordinary and the everyday.

Thus if you examine the way that histories of the oppressed are written about, it is as if life is always subsumed under the threat of death, living forever condemned to a shadowy existence under the idea of 'bare life'. The subsumption of life into a condition of bareness is as illusory as aesthetic practices that attempt to redeem experience from the clutches of time and history.

If the archival imagination is to rescue itself from this politics of redemption, it will have to allow for a radical contingency of the ordinary. It will have to engage with 'forms of life' which exceed the totalizing gaze of the state as well its redemptive other. Radical contingency recognizes the possibilities of surprise in the archive, and in the possibility that a descent into the ordinary suspends the urgent claims of emergencies.

5. The Archive deals not only with the Remnant but also with the Reserve

Capitalist production proceeds by isolating the extract from raw materials, producing the remnant, that which is left behind. And the archive, resisting

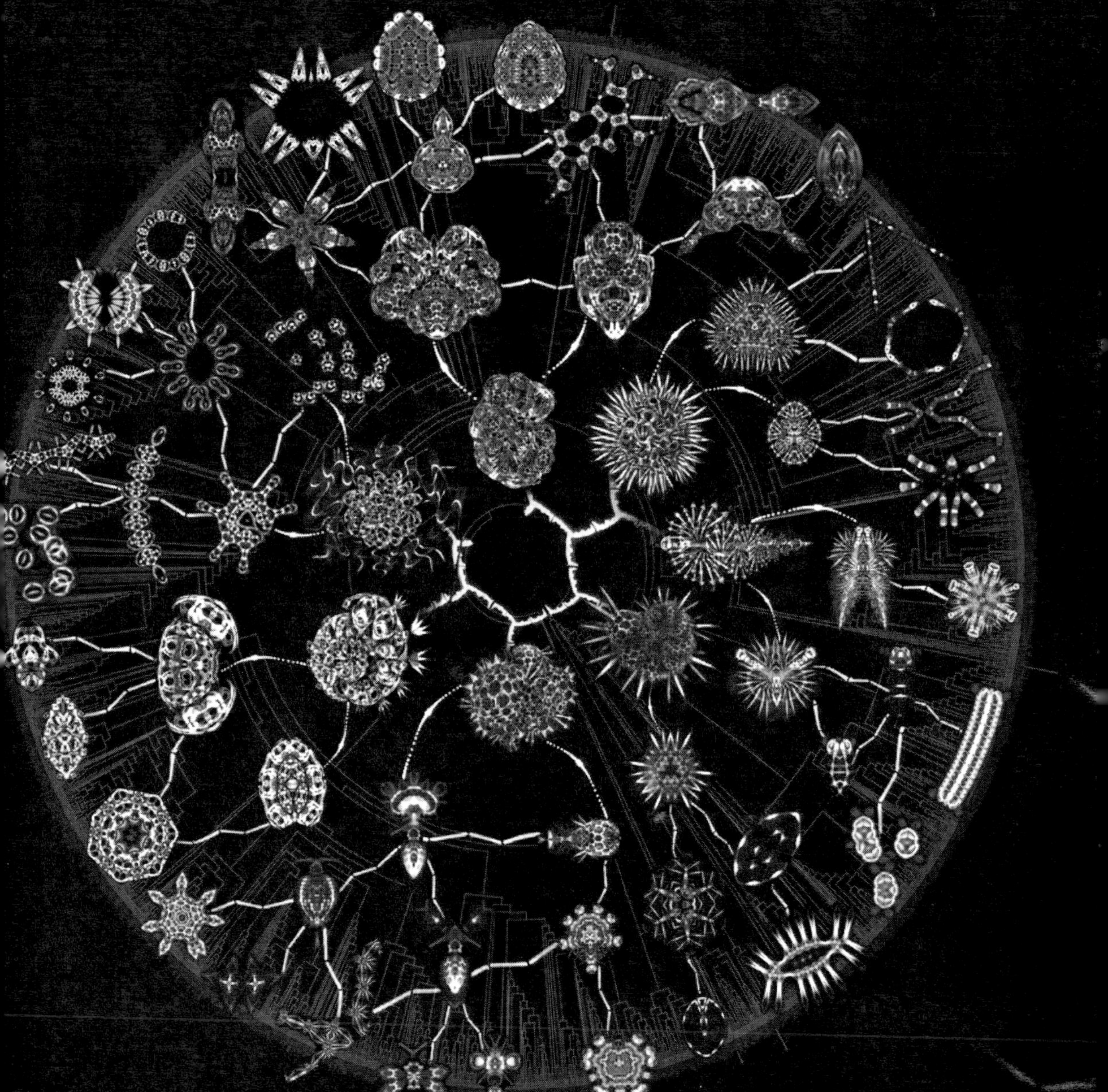

obsolescence, is constituted through these remnants. This is one common view. But there is another place in the contemporary where the role and responsibility of the archive may lie. That is, in addressing the reserve, that which is not yet deployed. And that which, like residue, is cast in shadow.

In surveillance systems, for example, we are forced to rethink the idea of 'waste'. Those millions of hours a day of CCTV images are not just the leftovers of the surveillance machine, they are its constitutive accumulation. They are the mass which waits for the event, and it is this mass that produces the threat.

Following Michel Serres, we could describe this mass as having 'abuse value', something that precedes use value or exchange value.[6] Of course, abuse value and exchange value can change hands. The line between residue and reserve can be unstable. Suddenly, the nuclear arsenal is rendered waste and sold as junk. Our accumulated ideas expire. But to look to the reserve has a strategic value for the archive. It is a way of addressing capital, not only as the production of profit from labour and commodities, but as the accumulation that can be used for speculation, and to extract rent.

The archive in this sense is sympathetic to those practices which sabotage capitalist accumulation, and those which have an interest in the future: in the 'unrealized'.

6. Historians have merely Interpreted the Archive. The Point however is to Feel it.

Archives have traditionally been the dwelling places of historians. The epistemic conceit of history has always been housed in the dust of the archives. But, in the last decade, we have also seen an explosion of interest in archives from software engineers, artists, philosophers, media practitioners, filmmakers and performers

Historians have responded by resorting to a disciplinary defensiveness that relies on a language of the 'authority' of knowledge and 'rigour', in which artists retreat to a zone of blissful aesthetic transcendence. There is something incredibly comfortable about this zone, where history continues to produce 'social facts' and art produces 'affect'. Claims of incommensurability provide a euphoric security that denies conditions of knowing and possibilities of acting beyond that which is already known. To think of the affective potential of the archive is to disturb this 'euphoric security'.

Rather than collapsing into a reinforcement of disciplinary fortresses that preclude outsiders and jealously guard the authenticity of knowledge and experience of historians, or resorting to a language of hostile takeovers by activists and artists, how do we think of the encroachments into the archives as an expansion of our sensibilities and the sensibilities of the archive? Archives are not threats, they are invitations.

Lakhmi Chand, a writer based in the media lab of the Cybermohalla[7] in New Delhi asks '*Kya kshamta ke distribution ko disturb karta hai Media*?' (Does media disturb the distribution of 'capacity' or 'potential'?)[8]

The invitation to think of the ability to disturb the *kshamta* of the archive seems to be marked by a different relation to time. The idea of capacity marks a time: This time is neither in the past nor in the future though they may be related, it is a marker of the present, or exactly where you are.

Anna Akhmatova writes in the *Requiem*:[9]

> In the dreadful years of the Yezhov terror I spent seventeen months in prison queues in Leningrad. One day someone 'identified' me. Then a woman standing behind me, blue with cold, who of course had never heard my name, woke from that trance characteristic of us all and asked in my ear (there, everyone spoke in whispers):
> - Ah, can you describe this?
> And I said:
> - I can.
> Then something like a tormented smile passed over what had once been her face.
>
> 1st April 1957

The question 'Can you describe this' was not a question about the possession of a skill, or even the possibility of language to speak of certain things under certain conditions. It is about a moment or a context that arises in which anyone can be faced with the question of 'Can You'. And they must either answer 'I Can' or 'I Can't'.

How do we think through the ways that archives challenge us to think about the experience of potentiality. To dwell in the affective potential of the archive is to think of how archives can animate intensities.

How do we imagine archival practices as the little practical, experimental and strategic measures that we pursue to expand our sensibilities? The affective potential of archives is therefore both a political as well as an aesthetic question in its ability to activate one's capacity to act, and it is on the very faculty of imagination and possibility that this conflict is located.

7. The Image is not just the Visible, the Text is not just the Sayable

Serge Daney makes a distinction between the *image* and the *visual*. The image is what still holds out against an experience of vision and the visual. The visual is just the optical verification of what we may know already or which may be read or deciphered through reflexes of reading. The image, on the other hand, is alterity.[10]

Jacques Rancière, in the *Future of the Image*, will develop this by saying that images are not restricted to the visible. He will reject the subordination of the image to the text - of material to history and of affect to meaning. He suggests that the commonest regime of images is one that presents a relationship between the sayable and the visible - between image and text, between presence and inscription - a relationship that plays on both the analogy AND dissemblance between them. But, of course, 'this relationship by no means requires the two terms to be materially present. The visible can be arranged in meaningful tropes, words deploy a visibility that can be blinding'.[11]

Rancière thus invents the Sentence-Image. The sentence-image is a form that could appear in a novel, equally as it could appear in a cinematic montage. In it, the sentence-function provides continuity against chaos, while the image-function disrupts consensus.[12]

The sentence-image provides a way to think across the modernist incommensurability of painting, literary works and films, that is, their autonomy. It allows us to acknowledge their appropriations, invasions and seductions of each other. The archive assembles another site where we can conceive, differently or similarly, of the connections and the distance between the functions of writing and of images. It suggests the possibility of art - if art is the alteration of resemblances between the two. With the introduction of software, we have yet another possibility for the disjunct: a third heterogeneity, another possible element of surprise. And perhaps to extend our thesis then: *the software is not just the searchable or the database.*

8. The Past of the Exhibition Threatens the Future of the Archive

What is the relation between memory and its display? Between the archive, 'the system that governs the appearances of statements' and a culture of appearances? In a 2002 essay for the journal *October*,[13] Hal Foster develops three useful stages of the museum as the site of memory in modern art. In the first stage, in the mid-1800s, Baudelaire writes that 'Art is the mnemotechny of the beautiful'. Which with Manet, for example, has become the art of outright citation. Here, art is the art of memory, and the museum is its architecture. The second moment occurs with Adorno's essay, the Valery Proust Museum, which marks a point of suspicion of the museum as the 'mausoleum' of art. *The museum is where art goes to die*. But, it is also the site for a redemptive project of 'reanimation'. The third moment occurs when this reanimation is possible through other means, that is, through Benjamin's mechanical reproduction. The key difference here is between Benjamin's reproduction, which threatens the museum, and Malraux's, which expands it infinitely. For Malraux, it is precisely the destruction of the aura which becomes a basis for the imagination of the museum without end.[14]

But there are 'problems of translation', gaps between Malraux's *Musee Imaginaire*, its English name the *Museum without Walls*, and the concept of a *Museum without End*, that have relentlessly fed many a modernist museum architect's fantasies of endless circulation and views through the glass, even as they offer endless new promises for art's institutional structures and for their relationship with the world. Foster's account of modern western art's archive ends with a split in art itself, between its display function that appears in spectacular form in the exhibition, and its memory function, which retreats into the archive.

The challenge for the archive, which today threatens the exhibition with its own sensual ability to relink and rearticulate these two functions, is how not to end up as a spiral ramp, or as flea market. In other words, how to avoid the tyranny of the two historical 'freedoms': one, the (modernist) formal strategies of audience participation in the spectacle, and two, the (postmodernist) eclecticism in which anything, included and curated, could be accorded 'exhibition-value'. Or we could put it this way: how does the archive avoid the confusion that persists in the exhibition,[15] between accessibility as entertainment and marketing strategy and access as something deeper as something that is 'closer to the question'.

9. Archives are governed by the Laws of Intellectual Propriety as opposed to Property

As the monetary value of the global information economy gains more importance, the abstract value of images is articulated within the language of property and rights. The language of intellectual property normativizes our relationship to knowledge and culture, by naturalizing and universalizing narrow ideas of authorship, ownership and property. This language has extended from the world of software databases to traditional archives where copyright serves as Kafka's gatekeeper and the use of the archive becomes a question of rights management.

Beyond the status of the archive as property lies the properties of the archive which can destabilize and complicate received notions of rights.

They establish their own code of conduct, frame their own rules of access, and develop an ethics of the archive which are beyond the scope of legal imagination. If the archive is a scene of *invention*, then what norms do they develop for themselves which do not take for granted a pre-determined language of rights? How do practices of archiving destabilize ideas of property while at the same time remaining stubbornly insistent on questions of 'propriety'?

Intellectual propriety does not establish any universal rule of how archives collect and make available their artifacts. It recognizes that archivists play a dual role: they act at once as the trustees of the memories of other people, as well as transmitters of public knowledge. This schizophrenic impulse prevents any easy settling into a single norm.

Propriety does not name a set of legislated principles of proper etiquette. Instead, it builds on the care and responsibility that archivists display in their preservation of cultural and historical objects. The digital archive translates this ethic of care into an understanding of the ecology of knowledge and the modes through which such an ecology is sustained through a logic of *distribution*, rather than mere *accumulation*.

It remembers the history of archivists being described as pirates, and scans its own records, files and database to produce an account of itself. In declaring its autonomy, archives seek to produce norms beyond normativity and ethical claims beyond the law.

10. Time is not Outside of the Archive: It is In it

In his history of the book and print cultures, historian Adrian Johns argues against what has traditionally been seen as the 'typographical fixity' which was established by the print revolution.[16] Earlier scholars had argued that scribal cultures were marked by all kinds of mistakes of the hand, and the book was therefore not a stable object of knowledge until the emergence of print technology.

Johns demonstrates the fallacy of this assumption by looking at the various conflicts that erupted with print technology. Far from ensuring fixity or authority, the early history of printing was marked by uncertainty. For Johns, the authority of knowledge is not an inherent quality, but a transitive one. It is a question that cannot be divorced of technologies that alter our senses, our perception and our experience of knowledge.

Rather than speaking about authority as something that is intrinsic to either a particular mode of production of knowledge or to any technological form, Johns' work demonstrates how it would be more useful to consider the range of knowledge apparatuses which come into play to establish authority.

The preconditions of knowledge cannot easily be made the object of knowledge. It is a matter of making evident or making known the structures of knowledge itself, which emerge in ways that provide definitive proof of the imperfectability of knowledge.

Archives are also apparatuses which engage our experience and perception of time. This is particularly true for archives of images since photography and cinema are also apparatuses that alter our sense of time. The traditional understanding of an archive as a space that collects lost time sees the experience of time as somehow being external to the archive itself. It loses sight of the fact that the archive is also where objects acquire their historical value as a result of being placed within an apparatus of time. The imagination of a video archive then plays with multiple senses of the unfolding of time.

Photography and film have a fundamental archival instinct embedded in them.[17] And yet this archival nature is also ridden with paradox because of the relationship of the moving image to the contingent. The presence of the contingent, the ephemeral and the unintended are all aspects of cinematic time, and the challenge of the moving image as archive is the recovery of lost time but within the cinematic.

The recovery of the lost time of cinema and the contingent can be captured through an experience of cinephilia, for what cinephilia names is the moment when the contingent takes on meaning - perhaps a private and idiosyncratic meaning, but one in which the love for the image expresses itself through a grappling with the ephemeral.

The archive is therefore an apparatus of time, but its relation to time is not guaranteed or inherent, it is transitive and has to be grafted. The archive of the moving image grasps this problem in an erotic and sensuous fashion, grafting the experience of time as an act of love.

Negri speaks about the love of time.[18] These two registers, of love - of time, and of cinema - allows us to think about the cinematic and archival apparatus of time, and the way they shape our relation to our time and the time of the image.

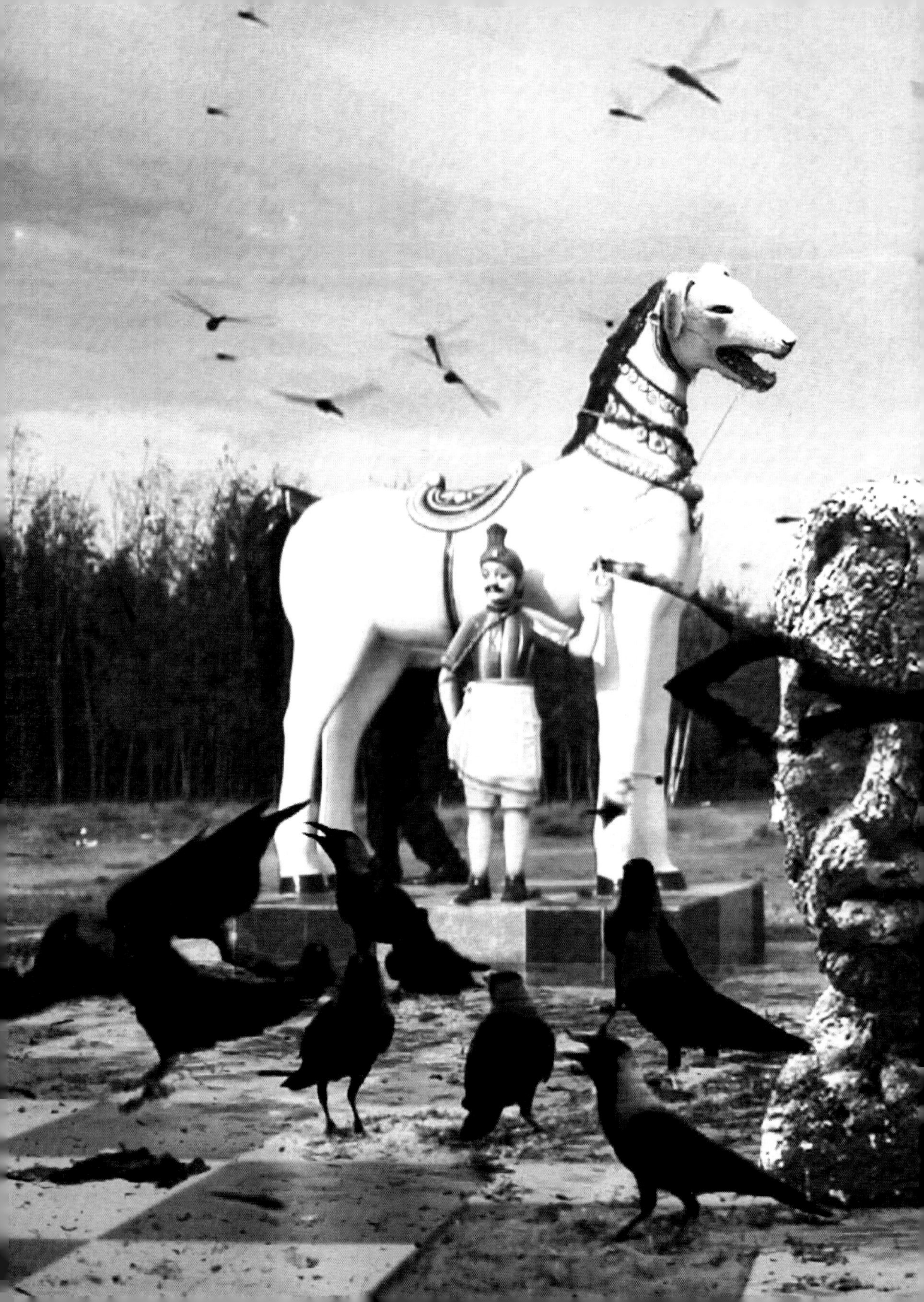

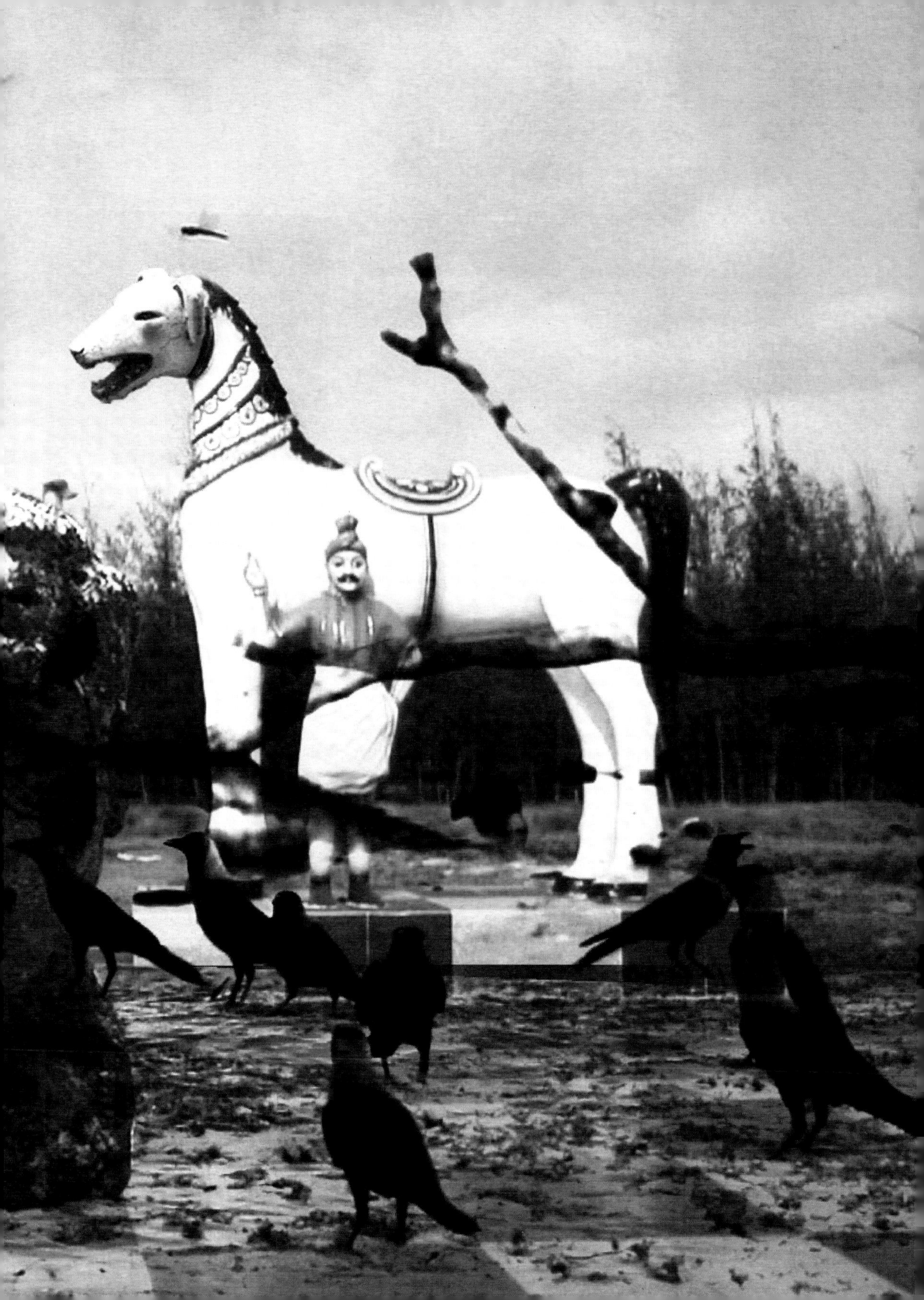

KEYWORDS

Includes names of people, technologies, events, terms and institutions that have specific conceptual significance for this volume. Several are likely to be familiar to readers, but these are being revisited in part as a ready primer, and in large measure to draw attention to how they have been used here and to their shifting and open-ended definitional status.

8 mm, Super-8 mm, 16 mm: **Celluloid** film formats developed by Eastman Kodak. Widespread popular usage in India of 16 mm in the 1960s enabled cinema to turn portable, freed it from the conventional movie theatre in an era preceding **video**, and was an early instance of what later came to be known as **Tactical Media**. 8/Super-8 was occasionally used by artists and amateur filmmakers. Several independent fiction films in the 1980s were shot on 16 mm and blown up to 35 mm. Early documentaries by **Anand Patwardhan** and **Deepa Dhanraj** are in this format. See Amrit Gangar, 'Prayoga' (pp. 102–18), Shohini Ghosh *et al.*, 'Mediastorm: Memories of a Collective' (pp. 166–74).

2002 Gujarat Riots: Riots following a controversial and bloody incident in Godhra, Gujarat, on 27 February 2002, in which 59 Hindu pilgrims returning from **Ayodhya** were killed in a fire inside a railway train compartment. The state-led genocide that followed over the next two months is seen as a turning-point in the history of modern India. The riots are also seen as the first hyper-mediatized political event in modern India, and the site of an unprecedented explosion of independent cinema. See **2002 Gujarat Films**. See Geeta Kapur, 'A Cultural Conjuncture in India' (pp. 120–42) and Shohini Ghosh *et al*, 'Mediastorm: Memories of a Collective' (pp. 166–74).

2002 Gujarat films: Independent documentaries and fiction films made in the context of the political events of the Godhra massacre. Although both **Ayodhya** (1992) and the **Bombay riots** (1993) had been covered by independent documentary, Godhra saw a new era in moving image activism (e.g., the Shared Footage Group set up by two **Film and Television Institute of India** alumni), together with numerous documentaries (e.g., Rakesh Sharma's *The Final Solution*, 2003). Examples include Shubhradeep Chakravorty's series of films between 2003 and 2012, Suma Josson's *Gujarat: A Laboratory of Hindu Rastra, Fascism* (2002), a campaign film for the State Assembly elections, Gopal Menon's real-time documentary, *Hey Ram!! Genocide in the Land of Gandhi* (2002), and Akanksha Damini Joshi's *Passengers: A Video Journey in Gujarat* (2003). See Geeta Kapur, 'A Cultural Conjuncture in India' (pp. 120–42).

Ambiguity: A term with specific cinematic consequences, as a **cinephilic**

engagement with bits of data rather than whole concepts – usually independent of the intention of the filmmaker. Defined by found objects and chance encounters, and with machinic interpretations merging into the blur of tourism and **pornography**. See **Cut-piece**. See Sebastian Lütgert, 'In the Face of Ambiguity, Refuse the Temptation to Guess' (pp. 42–48).

Archive: Although the **National Film Archive of India** has been Indian cinema's official repository, it has globally the smallest holdings in proportion to the total number of films made in India, compared to any similar national repository worldwide. The sheer scale of Indian cinema along with its ephemeral self-imagination pose significant challenges to the very conception of an archive, redirecting the archival impulse into unexpected spaces. Archives of the moving image today include both physical and digital collections, and a significant departure this volume makes is in conceptualizing the archive as a verb rather than as a noun. The archive here is embodied by the archival impulse: processes that transcend collection, classification and preservation, into an expanded imagination of collective action, community and distribution of resources. See Sudhir Mahadevan, 'The Protocols of Film Historiography' (pp. 20–41). See Pad.ma, 'Ten Theses on the Archive' (pp. 310–23), Sebastian Lütgert, 'In the Face of Ambiguity, Refuse the Temptation to Guess' (pp. 42–48).

Artist: Conscious creative selfhood often drawing from the image of the creative genius who transforms alienation and melancholia into sublime beauty, rendered legally visible as the prime beneficiary of the right to freedom of creative expression. Although dominant in Indian modernism and valorized in law, such hypervisible selfhood stands transformed in the context of new media art and technological art that repudiates both originality and individual creativity, emphasizing invisibility and collective practices closer to hacking and maker cultures, and on circulation (see **streaming**). See Section II of this book, titled 'Artist as Citizen'.

Avant-Garde: Art historical term introduced relatively recently into Indian discourse by Geeta Kapur. Set up explicitly in polemic with the modernist conception of the individuated (usually male) **artist**, it expresses a new solidarity with minority practice that pushes the boundaries of the norm and the status quo. See Geeta Kapur, 'A Cultural Conjuncture in India' (pp. 120–42). Sometimes viewed as overdetermined and too easily globalized, several experimental filmmakers have preferred Amrit Gangar's term *prayoga* as a more hospitable concept. See Gangar, 'Prayoga' (pp. 102–18).

Ayodhya: Refers to disputes over the fourteenth-century Babri Masjid site, considered by some Hindus as the birthplace of Rama. On 6 December 1992, a large **Sangh Parivar**-affiliated mob attacked and demolished the mosque. Riots followed in several Indian cities (see **Bombay Riots**). The 1992 episode generated a strong response from sections of civil society and activists, including from artists and filmmakers. Several landmark documentaries were made including **Anand Patwardhan**'s influential *Raam ke Naam* (In the Name of God, 1992).

Benami Finance: 'Unnamed' or anonymous finance using a 'front', a proxy or a non-existent person, banned in 1988 under the Benami Transactions (Prohibition) Act. Such finance had a major impact on several film industries that became conduits for illegal capital movement. In Kerala, 'blade companies', managing remittances from Gulf migrants, defined a cinematic practice of low-brow pornography. Many see a direct link in the 1980s between the economic–aesthetic legitimation of 'good Malayalam cinema' (see **Adoor Gopalakrishnan**) and the crackdown on such finance. See Darshana Sreedhar Mini, 'Disappearance, Desire and Haunting' (pp. 68–87).

Beveridge, James (1917–1993) and Margaret: Documentary filmmakers establishing a direct connection between John Grierson and Indian state initiatives. James Beveridge was Head of Production at the National Film Board of Canada and later Burmah Shell Oil's film production unit in India, helping shape the **Films Division**. Also involved in the 1970s with the Satellite Instructional Television Experiment (SITE). Margaret Beveridge and Anwar Jamal Kidwai (Vice Chancellor of the Jamia Millia Islamia university) developed a proposal for establishing a Mass Communication Research Centre (MCRC). This would become a leading centre for radical student movements and of the video documentary. See Shohini Ghosh *et al.*, 'Mediastorm: Memories of a Collective' (pp. 166–74) and Paromita Vohra, 'Who Is the First Person?' (pp. 175–88).

Bhadralok: Bengali term loosely referencing a 'gentlemanly order' associated with a class of educated, arts-loving elites formed during colonial rule and defining a hegemonic artistic modernism in Bengal. The upsurge in the 2000s of a political (and often **pornographic**) counterculture re-making, re-mixing and adapting classic texts in music, literature and cinema has sometimes been framed as a rebellion against this aesthetic of class-defined taste. See **Rabindranath Tagore**, **Satyajit Ray** and **Ritwik Ghatak**. See Subhajit Chatterjee, 'The Brothers Ghosh' (pp. 49–67).

Bhau Daji Lad Museum: Mumbai's oldest museum established in 1855 in Byculla East as the Central Museum of Natural History, Economy, Geology, Industry and Arts, opened to the public in 1872 as the Victoria and Albert Museum to house a collection of decorative and industrial arts. In recent years it has housed – alongside dioramas showing Indian native types, scenes from the city and countryside, and maps of colonial Bombay – contemporary art including moving image art, that has found new ways to interact with this material, and this history. See Nancy Adajania, 'The Ecologies of Technological Experimentation' (pp. 143–65).

Bollywood: Controversial 1990s term usually to variously describe popular Hindi cinema, all cinema made in Mumbai, or even all of India's cinema. Initially invented as a term of sarcasm by popular local journalism, the term arrived in global usage first with musical remixes after Bally Sagoo's album *Bollywood Flashback* (1994) that used 'dub' strategies to reissue famous Hindi songs. Since then it has become a marketing term for a new era of globalized blockbuster cinema typically associated with filmmakers like **Karan Johar**, further linked to an expanded cinema including ancillary industrial production such as music, fashion, television and gaming. See Sudhir Mahadevan, 'The Protocols of Film Historiography' (pp. 20–41) and Ashish Rajadhyaksha, 'SRK, Cinema and the Citizen: What's Next?' (pp. 227–48).

Bombay Riots: Riots that took place in Mumbai in December 1992 through early 1993, following the 6 December 1992 demolition of the Babri Masjid (see **Ayodhya**). Coinciding with the change in the city's name, this period – including the retaliatory bomb blasts on 12 March 1993 in crowded locations such as the Bombay Stock Exchange – is also seen as having given birth to a new city, signalled by condominium high-rises in former mill-lands, Slum Rehabilitation Areas (SRAs) replacing the former slums and sometimes pavement dwellers. Also widely viewed as the moment when the **celluloid** cinema died, to be replaced by digital info-highways of finance capital (evidenced by special economic zones such as the Bandra–Kurla Complex, a site of the 1993 riots).

CCTV: Closed circuit television used for twenty-first-century surveillance through video technology, which has led to greater state surveillance and increased social monitoring. The technology has been used by numerous artists, for example, by Studio CAMP (founding members of Pad.ma), and in independent and popular cinema such as the film *Love, Sex aur Dhokha* (dir. Dibakar Bannerjee, 2010); see Lawrence Liang, 'From Cinema to the Moving Image and Back' (pp. 293–309). The low-resolution, highly pixilated images generated by CCTV cameras generate a new understanding of the 'truth value' of video images and their aesthetic, termed as the 'poor image' by some theorists.

Celluloid: Analogue film format with an ontology very distinct from video and digital cinema (see **16 mm** and **New Media Art**). The bulk of film theory takes celluloid, a highly combustible substance, as the gold standard, as do film archives in their work of collection, restoration and preservation. Representing cinema with a capital C, it remains a favourite with artists, including several featured in this volume. See Nalini Malani, 'Can You Hear Me?' (pp. 189–200). In 2008, the International Federation of Film Archives (FIAF) redefined celluloid as an 'artefact', like sculpture or any plastic art, a *physical* 'human-eye-readable' entity, to be treated like a 'museum or historic object'. For celluloid's role in representing the ghosts of past history, see Darshana Sreedhar Mini, 'Disappearance, Desire and Haunting' (pp. 68–85), and Kaushik Bhaumik and Desire Machine Collective, 'Death Becomes Her' (pp. 86–101).

Censor Board: Better known as the Central Board of Film Certification (CBFC), formed under the Indian Cinematograph Act, 1952. Its controversial section 5A reproduces the 'reasonable restrictions' on free speech which became a precedent for the notorious section 69A of the Information Technology Act, 2000. Section 6.1, by which the government could effectively overrule a censor certification, was reintroduced in 2020 after the Film Certification Appellate Tribunal was abolished, to create what many see as a 'super-censor'. See Darshana Sreedhar Mini, 'Disappearance, Desire and Haunting' (pp. 68–85), Geeta Patel, 'Firing Time' (pp. 249–59) and 'The Trial' (pp. 201–11).

Cinephilia: Densely theorized term variously described as a passionate interest in films and film criticism, sexual attraction towards cinema, as eulogizing the non-standard and minor, as reverberating with nostalgia and dedication and nothing short of an entire attitude towards life. Sometimes contrasted with *cinephobia* or hatred of cinema, and used to define the Indian state's position. Post video, cinephilic interventions have led to independent, often deeply subversive practices, including trans-genre adaptations, spoofs and spectral hauntings linked to practices like file-sharing, creating memes and repurposing moving images to very different usage. See **Malegaon Film**. See Subhajit Chatterjee, 'The Brothers Ghosh' (pp. 49–67), Darshana Sreedhar Mini, 'Disappearance, Desire and Haunting' (pp. 68–85) and Madhuja Mukherjee, 'Toward a New Frame for Regional Films' (pp. 260–74).

Citizenship: Controversial category that became a political flashpoint with the Citizenship Amendment Act of 2019. The cinema was foundationally implicated in citizenship debates when it was viewed as a major instrument of curbing public order, and cinematic realism received an additional responsibility of producing the gaze of the newly enfranchised citizen subject. This history has taken a new turn with social media and the recent effort to curb free speech in the proposed revision to the Cinematograph Act (see **Censor Board**). See Raqs Media Collective, 'Now and Elsewhere' (pp. 1–14), Kaushik Bhaumik and Desire Machine Collective, 'Death Becomes Her' (pp. 86–101), 'The Trial' (pp. 201–11), Ashish Rajadhyaksha, 'SRK, Cinema and the Citizen: What's Next?' (pp. 224–48) and Geeta Patel, 'Firing Time' (pp. 249–59).

Copyright Law: The Copyright Act of 1952 regulates uses and reproduction of literary and dramatic works, music, art, sound recordings and films. Amendments in 2012 permitted fair use clauses for non-profit and educational purposes. Noted screen writer Anjum Rajabali and the Progressive Writers Group (PWG) within the Film Writers Association fought for writers retaining their right over screenplays and lyrics. Likewise the Indian Performing Rights Society (IPRS) to amend the copyright law to address song remixes. High-profile cases in recent years include petitions filed by large publishers against small photocopying shops and by media conglomerates against local DVD sellers. Ubiquitous anti-piracy warnings seek to maintain an otherwise increasingly blurred distinction between originals and copies. See Jeebesh Bagchi, 'The Cinematic Object after the 1990s' (pp. 212–23) and Lawrence Liang, 'From

Cinema to the Moving Image and Back' (pp. 293–309).

Craft: Usually understood as decorative arts, but commonly inclusive of the wider domain of industrial arts practised by artisans (see **Bhau Daji Lad Museum**). After the introduction of the British style of academic art education, the European distinction between art and craft was extended to the Indian context, and small-scale production of objects of decorative and utility value by specific castes was attempted to be industrialized. However, a hardy tradition of local and handmade craft production continued to thrive across the country, and various (especially female) artists have striven to erase what they see as a false distinction between arts and crafts, and even between artisanal and industrial practice. See Nancy Adajania, 'The Ecologies of Technological Experimentation' (pp. 143–65).

Cut-piece: Term used for small celluloid 'cuts' usually showing **pornography** illegally spliced into censored film prints. See Darshana Sreedhar Mini, 'Disappearance, Desire and Haunting' (pp. 68–85).

Cybermohalla Ensemble: Collective of practitioners and writers emerging from a network of dispersed labs for experimentation and exploration among young people in different neighbourhoods of Delhi. Initiated by Ankur Society for Alternatives in Education and Sarai–CSDS in 2011. Their work has been circulated and shared through online journals, radio broadcasts, publications, neighbourhood gatherings, contemporary and new media art exhibitions. See Jeebesh Bagchi, 'The Cinematic Object after the 1990s' (pp. 212–23) and Lawrence Liang, 'From Cinema to the Moving Image and Back' (pp. 293–309).

Dalit: Preferred term by Babasaheb Ambedkar to describe persons from backward and underprivileged castes in India. The official term is 'Scheduled Castes', as per Schedule 1 of the Constitution. Also known in other official contexts as backward classes and *harijan* (Gandhi's preferred term), subject to several laws and regulations such as the Untouchability Practices Act, 1955, the Prevention of Atrocities Act, 1989 and the Manual Scavengers Act, 1993, among others. Geeta Kapur (in 'A Cultural Conjuncture in India', pp. 120–42) speaks especially of how Dalit writers 'challenge, defy and mock the ideology of the ruling class (and caste), the hegemony of the state and the very legitimacy of the national'. Also see Paromita Vohra, 'Who Is the First Person?' (pp. 175–88) and S.V. Srinivas, 'The Gaddar Effect' (pp. 275–92).

Dhanraj, Deepa (b. 1953): Major **documentary** filmmaker who has been actively involved in the women's movement since the 1980s. Founding member of the **Yugantar Film Collective**, which made three important 16 mm films in the 1980s, now restored by the Arsenal Film Archive, Berlin. Best known for *Something Like a War* (2003), Dhanraj makes her filmed communities active participants in the filmmaking process, addressing workers' rights, sexuality and biopolitics, communal violence, and caste. See Geeta Kapur, 'A Cultural Conjuncture in India' (pp. 120–42) and Shohini Ghosh *et al.*, 'Mediastorm: Memories of a Collective' (pp. 166–74).

Digitalism: Condition of living in a digital culture (e.g., Nicholas Negroponte's *Being Digital*). Lawrence Liang however frames it in the political history of cinematic realism (see **Citizenship**). He speaks of a 'parallel universe' of 'degraded images and distorted sounds' that relate **cinephilia** to 'the allure of the low-definition image of the camera print: and thence to . . . grainy video of sting operations and amateur pornography'. Lawrence Liang, 'From Cinema to the Moving Image and Back' (pp. 293–309),

Documentary: Cinematic form associated for much of India's twentieth century with a state aesthetic (see **Films Division**). Paromita Vohra defines a classic state form (which survived well into the era of independent documentary) as producing a 'disembodied self', a performance by a 'unitary being who had gathered knowledge and then processed it for our benefit into bite-sized bits . . . the one who was speaking knew more than they were telling you and was somehow qualified to speak thus' (see Vohra, 'Who Is the First Person?', p. 179). Independent (i.e. non-state) documentary grows in India only after the **Emergency** (see **Anand Patwardhan**). It is, writes Geeta Kapur quoting **Amar Kanwar**, a direct consequence of a 'crisis in democracy', its different directions after 2002 nothing less than a 'generational change in the nature and pursuit of politics itself' (see Kapur, 'A Cultural Conjuncture in India', p. 131). See **16 mm film**, **VHS Video** and **Streaming**, and **Censor Board**. See also **Deepa Dhanraj**, **Yugantar Collective**, Raqs Media Collective, 'Now and Elsewhere' (pp. 1–14), R.V. Ramani, 'My Camera and Tsunami' (pp. 15–19), Kaushik Bhaumik and Desire Machine Collective, 'Death Becomes Her' (pp. 86–101), Shohini Ghosh *et al.*, 'Mediastorm: Memories of a Collective' (pp. 166–174).

Doordarshan: State-owned television started in 1959, linked to satellite television experiments in the mid-1970s and the launch of colour broadcasting following the Asian Games. Began broadcasting on nationwide terrestrial network from 1982. Part of the autonomous and self-proclaimed 'independent' organization Prasar Bharati since 1997. Subject of significant debates around free speech and the redefined role of the 'people' in the famous Supreme Court judgment which declared that 'airwaves or frequencies are a public property' (*Ministry of Information and Broadcasting vs Cricket Association of Bengal*, 1995). See Shohini Ghosh *et al.*, 'Mediastorm: Memories of a Collective' (pp. 166–74).

Escapement: Time-keeping mechanism that works by transmitting a periodic impulse from the spring to the pendulum of a clock. Purely mechanical time places us in a condition that Raqs Media Collective describes as a 'perennial jet lag'. A shift away from time as a continuum made it harder to surgically separate past and present. 'Clocks . . . rendered a conceptual barricade between each unit, its predecessor, and its follower (which) makes *now* seem so alien to *then.'* See Raqs Media Collective, 'Now and Elsewhere' (pp. 1–14).

Emergency: Usually refers to the episode in Indian history (from 25 June 1975 to 21 March 1977) when Prime Minister Indira Gandhi suspended civil liberties, claiming a 'grave threat' to the very existence of the nation. Since then, there has been growing recognition that Emergency-like conditions have become increasingly possible with other legal mechanisms (such as the Armed Forces Special Powers Act). 1975 was the last effort made by the Indian state to impose a cinematic aesthetic using the twin apparatus of a film financing mechanism for low-budget cinema alongside an active **Censor Board**.

Ephemera in Film: Large domain of the expanded definition of cinema. Includes actual afterlives of celluloid, the retention of film as memory given that actual films are believed to not survive for long in India. Memorabilia such as posters, song booklets and postcards have helped construct Indian film history. In 2013, the Mukul Mudgal Committee set up to make recommendations for a new Cinematograph Act, wanted the definition of 'film' to include (and the **Censor Board** to censor) its video versions, its songs and their lyrics, its advertising material, its item numbers and even its posters. See **Archive**. See Sudhir Mahadevan, 'The Protocols of Film Historiography' (pp. 20–41) and Sebastian Lütgert, 'In the Face of Ambiguity, Refuse the Temptation to Guess' (pp. 42–48).

Exploitation Cinema: B-film genre depicting high levels of sex, nudity, violence and drug usage, which originated in the 1920s and was made popular again in the 1960s and 70s after the relaxation of censorship regulations in Europe and America. Has many sub-genres such as blaxploitation, canuxploitation, carsploitation, sexploitation and splatter films. In India, a popular reference point for low-budget, local films that attempt to marry social reform narratives with titillating footage, or B-film adaptations of cult and classic films. See Darshana Sreedhar Mini, 'Disappearance, Desire and Haunting' (pp. 68–85), Lawrence Liang, 'From Cinema to the Moving Image and Back' (pp. 293–309) and Subhajit Chatterjee, 'The Brothers Ghosh' (pp. 49–67).

Film Advisory Board: See **Films Division**.

Film and Television Institute of India: Film school founded in 1960 (television was added in 1974) along with several other institutions (including the National Film Archive of India and the Film Finance Corporation), envisaged after Independence to regulate Indian cinema. It has produced several of Indian cinema's best known independent filmmakers (**Adoor Gopalakrishnan** and **Mani Kaul**, **Ritwik Ghatak** taught here for a brief period), several well-known actors and mainstream **Bollywood** filmmakers. In 2020, with a slew of new regulations and following several protest movements, the FTII underwent a major transformation that many see as politically and commercially motivated.

Films Division: India's official documentary production unit, established in 1947 with the central objective of documenting important historical events. Known for a distinctive aesthetic style (see Paromita Vohra, 'Who is the First Person?', pp. 175–88) that traces its history to the wartime British documentary through prior institutions, Film Advisory Board (FAB) and Information Films of India (IFI). Also made some experimental short films (see **Pramod Pati**, **S.N.S. Sastry** and **S. Sukhdev**).

Ghatak, Ritwik (1925–1976): Iconic Bengali filmmaker with a largely posthumous reputation for films using mythic elements dealing with the traumas of the partition of Bengal, typically seen as a refugee's counter to entrenched **bhadralok** culture. Active member of the **Indian People's Theatre Association** before he was expelled by the Communist Party in 1955. Taught briefly at the **Film and Television Institute of India**, impacting major independent filmmakers including **Mani Kaul**, **Kumar Shahani**, **Adoor Gopalakrishnan**, **Saeed Akhtar Mirza** and John Abraham. Increasingly seen as something of a spectral haunting and converted into a meme usually referring to his last film, *Jukti Takko aar Gappo* (Reason, Debate and a Tale, 1974) where he plays 'himself'. See Subhajit Chatterjee, 'The Brothers Ghosh' (pp. 49–67) and the still from *Squeeze Lime in My Eye* (p. 213).

Godhra: See **2002 Gujarat**.

Gopalakrishnan, Adoor (b. 1941): Renowned Malayalam film director pioneering its New Wave, sometimes viewed as a clean-up of the Kerala film industry (see **Benami Finance**). Instrumental in establishing Kerala's first film society, the Chitralekha Film Cooperative Society for film production. Known for nuanced representation of Kerala's feudal system and the social transformations following the Land Reform Act of 1970, and for unstinted support to the art-house. See Darshana Sreedhar Mini, 'Disappearance, Desire and Haunting' (pp. 68–85).

Hindutva: Ideology seeking to establish Hindu hegemony with the objective of making India a 'Hindu nation'. A central ploy is vilification of minority religious communities, heightened rhetoric around 'anti-nationalism' and 'urban Naxalism', constructing narratives of historical victimhood, and allusions to an ancient 'golden' civilization awaiting retrieval. See Geeta Patel, 'Firing Time' (pp. 249–59) and Geeta Kapur, 'A Cultural Conjuncture in India' (pp. 120–41).

Intellectual Property: Rights for 'products of the intellect', governed by legislations including the Patents Act 1970, the Copyright Act 1957 and the Designs Act 2000. Expansionist tendencies have led to rearticulation of the 'commons' of knowledge and cultural production, related in turn to a renewed social contract based on P2P and distributary models, similar also to the contemporary archival impetus. See Jeebesh Bagchi, 'The Cinematic Object after the 1990s' (pp. 212–23), Lawrence Liang, 'From Cinema to the Moving Image and Back' (pp. 293–309), and Pad.ma, 'Ten Theses on the Archive' (pp. 310–23).

Indian People's Theatre Association (IPTA): Theatre initiative affiliated to the Communist Party of India, formally constituted in 1943 in the context of the great famine in Bengal, advocating for a theatre that reflected the lived realities of the people for whom it was made. Had a nationwide impact on stage and film, mainly in Bengali, Hindi, Malayalam and Telugu cinemas. See **Ritwik Ghatak**. See S.V. Srinivas, 'The Gaddar Effect' (pp. 275–92), and Shohini Ghosh *et al.*, 'Mediastorm: Memories of a Collective' (pp. 166–74).

Jana Natya Mandali (JNM): The 'People's Theatre Troupe', a popular revolutionary cultural organization in Andhra Pradesh linked to the Communist Party of India. JNM played an instrumental part in Telangana's claims to statehood using folk music and performance idioms. See S.V. Srinivas, 'The Gaddar Effect' (pp. (275–92).

Johar, Karan (b. 1972): Major **Bollywood** film director and media personality. His films are known for lavish production, mega stars, panoramic visuals and a neo-traditional aesthetic emphasizing joint family values amid a hypermodern globalized frame. Regular star-cast includes **Shah Rukh Khan**. See Kaushik Bhaumik and Desire Machine Collective, 'Death Becomes Her' (pp. 86–101) and Ashish Rajadhyaksha, 'SRK, Cinema and the Citizen: What's Next?' (pp. 224–48).

Jugaad Aesthetics: Colloquial term referring to frugal and non-conventional innovations or hacks. Now popular in businesses to denote a clever, low-cost fix symbolizing creativity, the agile response, seen as characteristics of South Asian societies where makeshift solutions are found to challenges of infrastructure and resources. See Nancy Adajania, 'The Ecologies of Technological Experimentation' (pp. 143–65), Jeebesh Bagchi, 'The Cinematic Object after the 1990s' (pp. 212–23) and Madhuja Mukherjee, 'Toward a New Frame for Regional Films' (pp. 260–274).

Kanwar, Amar (b. 1964): Filmmaker and multimedia artist working at the cusp of documentary, art and human rights. Major works include *A Season Outside* (1977), *A Night of Prophecy* (2002), *The Lightning Testimonies* (2007) and *The Torn First Pages* (2004–08). Since *Documenta 11*, has shown increasingly in art museums. See Geeta Kapur, 'A Cultural Conjuncture in India' (pp. 120–42).

Kashmir Insurgency: Ongoing struggle against the Indian state following from the territorial dispute between India and Pakistan since the partition of the subcontinent in 1947. The insurgency in Kashmir began in 1989 due to the absence of local autonomy and grew stronger through the 1990s. The conflict between the Indian military and Kashmiri militants has resulted in the casualty of thousands of civilians and a large number of disappearances of young people. Cinema halls were closed down and converted into military bunkers during the peak of the insurgency: see Kaushik Bhaumik and Desire Machine Collective, 'Death Becomes Her' (pp. 86–101). In 2019, the special protection afforded to the Kashmiri people was revoked with the striking down of Article 370. The state was converted to a Union Territory with reduced autonomy and powers. Everyday violence, curfews and the cutting-off of communication, media and internet has become a normalized condition in the state, which once symbolized an idyllic paradise as depicted in popular Hindi films of the 1960s. See image from Sanjay Kak's iconic documentary, *Jashn-e-Azadi: How We Celebrate Freedom* (2007) on pp. 98–99.

Kashyap, Anurag (b. 1972): Game-changing Indian director, writer, producer, actor and editor, known for gritty realism located in the hinterlands of the Hindi-speaking belt in central India. Considered a cinephilic auteur, known for representations of modern postcolonial India shot on real locations with improvised dialogues, using guerrilla tactics, hidden and hand-held cameras, frequently referencing world cinema. As producer he has supported low-budget, experimental and independent films.

Kaul, Mani (1944–2011): Major figure of Indian art cinema who broke new ground in terms of form and aesthetics. One of the founders of the New Indian Cinema with his debut film, *Uski Roti* (His Bread, 1969). A trained musician in the *Dhrupad* form of classical music, Kaul sought an indigenous film aesthetic drawn from classical aesthetics. He developed a sophisticated theory of the productive friction between absence and presence in the screen image. A student of **Ritwik Ghatak** at the **Film and Television Institute of India**, and subsequently himself a teacher there, he had a major following of student-filmmakers. See Amrit Gangar, 'Prayoga' (pp. 102–19),

Khan, Shah Rukh (b. 1965), aka Shahrukh Khan, SRK: Major Indian movie star, now producer, entrepreneur and cultural icon. Khan's entire career, from his first hits in which he played 'anti-hero' figures to his graduation, at different times, as a romantic and action star, has consistently been associated with path-breaking redefinitions in the industry and in stardom itself. See Ashish Rajadhyaksha, 'SRK, Cinema and the Citizen: What's Next? (pp. 224–48).

Made in China: Term used to refer to popular and often immensely innovative goods, sometimes using fake labels, catering to low-cost economy. Although attacked and delegitimized by the more 'authentic' high-end market, these goods have their own consumers as they often provide high quality at low prices. See Jeebesh Bagchi, 'The Cinematic Object after the 1990s' (pp. 212–23).

Malegaon Film: A unique form of zero-budget cinema, making DIY versions of popular Indian and Hollywood blockbusters on **VHS tape** and now digital formats. Associated with the filmmaker Sheikh Nasir who ran a video parlour, and directed *Malegaon ka Superman* (remaking *Superman*, 2011; see image on pp. 268–69) ten years after his debut film, *Malegaon ke Sholay*, a turning point in the production and distribution of films from Malegaon. See Subhajit Chatterjee, 'The Brothers Ghosh' (pp. 49–67), Darshana Sreedhar Mini, 'Disappearance, Desire and Haunting' (pp. 68–85) and Madhuja Mukherjee, 'Toward a New Frame for Regional Films' (pp. 260–74).

Mirza, Saeed Akhtar (b. 1943): Independent filmmaker and author, known for urban realism in films of social interest like *Salim Langde pe Mat Ro* (Don't Cry for Salim, the Lame, 1989) and television (the 1986–87 tele-series *Nukkad*, depicting the struggles of lower-income class groups in the city of Mumbai). Co-founder of Yukt Film Co-op with **Mani Kaul**, **Kamal Swaroop** and others. Devised an aesthetic style that could be considered as the **Mumbai realism** of parallel or art cinema. Author of several memoirs. Known for his much-cited assertion, reiterated when he was Chairman of the governing council of the **Film and Television Institute of India**, that 'a certain kind of cinema exists because a certain kind of state exists'. See Saeed Mirza, 'How Far Can a Filmmaker Go?' (p. 119).

MMS Scandal: An early 2000s incident involving high school students sharing videos of explicit sexual acts without consent through multimedia messaging services. In 2004 a teenaged boy from a Delhi school filmed a school-mate in a sexual act without her knowledge, and later uploaded it on an online auction site, Bazee.com. See Lawrence Liang, 'From Cinema to the Moving Image and Back' (pp. 293–309).

Mumbai Realism: Politically informed territorial realism linked to neighbourhoods and districts of Bombay. Inspired by **Dalit** poetry in Marathi often producing graphic descriptions of neighbourhoods, and by the landmark judgment of the Supreme Court, *Olga Tellis vs Bombay Municipal Corporation*,1985, giving pavement dwellers the constitutional right to shelter, linking the aesthetic right to describe with the political right to occupy. See **Saeed Akhtar Mirza**, **Anurag Kashyap**. See Ashish Rajadhyaksha, 'SRK, Cinema and the Citizen: What's Next? (pp. 224–48).

National Film Archive of India: Founded in 1964, one of a series of institutions, along with the **Film and Television Institute of India** and the Film Finance Corporation. Set up after a Film Inquiry Committee recommended a state infrastructure to deal with its cinema. With approximately 7,000 Indian films, the NFAI has been Indian cinema's official repository, but it has the smallest holdings in proportion to the total number of films made in India and compared to any similar national repository worldwide. Following a Ministry of Information and Broadcasting plan in 2020 for a rationalization/merger, it is soon to be controversially part of the National Film Development Corporation. See **Archive**. See Sudhir Mahadevan, 'The Protocols of Film Historiography' (pp. 20–41).

Naxalite/Naxalism: Armed struggle started in 1967 by Maoist guerrillas taking the name from the Naxalbari region of West Bengal. Later spread across Chhattisgarh, Bihar, Orissa, Maharashtra, Jharkhand and Telangana. See S.V. Srinivas, 'The Gaddar Effect' (pp. 275–92). See **Mrinal Sen** and **Hindutva**.

New Media Art: Contemporary art made using new forms of media technology. Defies static categorization and changes as new technologies emerge. See **Celluloid**, **Documentary**, **Jugaad Aesthetics**, **Streaming**, **Tactical**

Media, **Torrenting** and **VHS Tape**. See Nancy Adajania, 'The Ecologies of Technological Experimentation' (pp. 143–65), Nalini Malani, 'Can You Hear Me?' (pp. 189–200) and Lawrence Liang, 'From Cinema to the Moving Image and Back' (pp. 293–309).

Pati, Pramod (1932–1975): Experimental documentary filmmaker who developed a posthumous reputation for subversive film, mostly at **Films Division** in Mumbai as the Head of its animation unit. Known for his experimental sound design (usually composed by Vijay Raghav Rao) and bold images, including a split-second 'f*ck censorship' frame in *Explorer* (1968) that has since generated much curiosity and interest (see p. 201).

Patwardhan, Anand (b. 1950): Considered the founder of independent **documentary** in India; initial work on **16 mm**. His films address political issues, growing intolerance, religious violence, nuclear armament, the attack on reason, the Ambedkarite movement and caste-based discrimination. Challenged by the **Censor Board** on multiple occasions in court, fighting for the right to freedom of expression. See Geeta Kapur, 'A Cultural Conjuncture in India' (pp. 120–42), Shohini Ghosh *et al.*, 'Mediastorm: Memories of a Collective' (pp. 166–74) and 'The Trial' (pp. 201–11).

Phalke, Dhundiraj Govind (1870–1944), aka Dadasaheb: Commonly viewed as the 'father of the Indian cinema' and his first feature film, *Raja Harishchandra* (King Harishchandra, 1913), is viewed as marking the birth of India's film industry. A polymath and auto-didact, he trained at the J.J. School of Art, Bombay, and the Fine Arts Faculty in M.S. University, Baroda, subsequently acquiring expertise in architecture, photography, various darkroom printing techniques, engraving, trick-photography and magic. Phalke's films were considered an important contribution to the nationalist *swadeshi* movement emphasizing indigenism. **Kamal Swaroop**'s life-long historiographical quest to resurrect Phalke resulted, among other things, in his speculative experimental documentary film, *Rangabhoomi*, released in 2013, exactly 100 years after Phalke's first film. See Sudhir Mahadevan, 'The Protocols of Film Historiography' (pp. 20–41).

Phantom Films: An independent production house founded in 2011 by **Anurag Kashyap** and three other filmmakers, to foreground the importance of the film director. It sold 50 per cent stake to Reliance Entertainment in 2015. Known for a major track record of edgy mainstream films, such as Vikas Bahl's *Queen* (2014), Kashyap's *Ugly* (2014), Neeraj Ghaywan's *Masaan* (2015) and the Netflix series *Sacred Games* (2018), before it closed down, following allegations of sexual assault, in 2018.

Pirate Networks: Digital networks often set up by copyleft activists who support the idea of 'commons' by way of free and unhindered access to information and knowledge systems. They have played a key role in archiving digital content that either risked negligence in state archives or was inaccessible at an affordable cost. The term 'pirate' itself has been reclaimed to stand for an entire way of life through communities of interest and shared distribution of resources. See Sebastian Lütgert, 'In the Face of Ambiguity, Refuse the Temptation to Guess' (pp. 42–48), Jeebesh Bagchi, 'The Cinematic Object after the 1990s' (pp. 212–23), Lawrence Liang, 'From Cinema to the Moving Image and Back' (pp. 293–309) and Pad.ma, 'Ten Theses on the Archive' (pp. 310–23).

Pornography: Conventionally, audio-visual content intended to provide sexual stimulation, a subject of stringent legal and moral regulation by the state, organized religion and society. Increasingly, however, it relates less to *content* and more to *modes* of leakage or covert circulation, with a social life to data that reveals longer peripheral histories of cinema (see **Ephemera**), video and now **digitality**. See **Cut-piece**. See Darshana Sreedhar Mini, 'Disappearance, Desire and Haunting' (pp. 68–85) and Lawrence Liang, 'From Cinema to the Moving Image and Back' (pp. 293–309).

Progressive Artists Group: Artists' group founded in Bombay in 1947 proposing a clean break with the past (especially in polemic with the influential Bengal School) and with a self-proclaimed desire to introduce modernism into Indian art. Initial links with the Communist Party of India. Founding members include F.N. Souza, S.H. Raza, M.F. Husain, K.H. Ara, H.A. Gade and S.K. Bakre. The group's initial emphasis on oil painting expanded to different mediums and diverse aesthetic influences including lens-based techniques. Husain's documentary *Through the Eyes of a Painter* (1967) and fiction film *Gaja Gamini* (Woman with an Elephant's Gait, 2000), inspired by film star Madhuri Dixit, Tyeb Mehta's (1925–2009) film *Koodal* (1970), along with Krishen Khanna's experiments with photography were significant instances. The painter Akbar Padamsee set up the **Vision Exchange Workshop** in 1968. See Nancy Adajania, 'The Ecologies of Technological Experimentation' (pp. 143–65).

Q (b. 1975), aka Qaushiq Mukherjee: Bengali avant-garde filmmaker and musician, known for the controversial cult film *Gandu* (Asshole, 2010). Central to the countercultural movements challenging **bhadralok** values in the new millennium. See image from the **Rabindranath Tagore** adaptation, *Tasher Desh* (Kingdom of Cards, 2012, p. 57). See Subhajit Chatterjee, 'The Brothers Ghosh' (pp. 49–67).

Rajnikant/Rajinikanth (b. 1950), aka Shivajirao Gaikwad: Tamil superstar reaching iconic stature with an enormous fan-following across India and, astonishingly, in Japan. Popularly referred to as 'Rajni *saar*', a number of jokes and memes have been generated around the superstar as a humorous homage to his 'larger than the universe' persona. See Ashish Rajadhyaksha, 'SRK, Cinema and the Citizen: What's Next?' (pp. 224–48).

Ram Janmabhoomi: See **Ayodhya**.

Ray, Satyajit (1921–1992): Bengali filmmaker and major cultural icon, known for having first brought global attention to Indian cinema with his *Pather Panchal* (Song of the Little Road, 1955). Ray belonged to an upper-class family, studied at **Rabindranath Tagore**'s Santiniketan, was founder of the Calcutta Film Society in 1947, and the creator of many popular characters in Bengali children's literature such as Feluda, the sleuth and Shonko the scientist. See **Bhadralok**. While his films have merited separate analysis, his polemical positions on India's 'New Wave' films and what many saw as covert acceptance of his authorial status by the **Emergency**, present a more controversial history. See Subhajit Chatterjee, 'The Brothers Ghosh' (pp. 49–67).

Red Film: Local Telugu cinema term for a popular genre of radical cinema deriving from Maoist ideology (see **Naxalite**, **Jana Natya Mandali**). Initially a relatively marginal if popular form, through the 1990s it saw mainstreaming as major stars and directors began cashing in on its popularity. See S.V. Srinivas, 'The Gaddar Effect' (pp. 275–92).

Reversal Stock: Photographic film that produces a positive image on a transparent base (also known as diapositive or diafilm) with no negative. Popularly used by artists working with the moving image in the late 1960s. See Nalini Malani, 'Can You Hear Me?' (pp. 189–200).

Sangh Parivar (including Vishwa Hindu Parishad, Bajrang Dal): Umbrella term referring to a range of organizations affiliated to the Hindu nationalist outfit, Rashtriya Swayamsevak Sangh (RSS). These include political parties, religious and militant organizations, and student and workers' organizations which subscribe to a Hindu fundamentalist ideology. See **Ayodhya**, **2002 Gujarat**.

Sastry, S.N.S. (1930–1978): Documentary and short-film maker, and one of the trio (along with **Pramod Pati** and **S. Sukhdev**) at **Films Division** known for making ground-breaking experimental films in the 1960s. Sastry, in particular, was recognized for his use of self-reflexivity, irony and humour in films like *This Bit of That India* (1972), *I Make Short Films* (1968) and *Our Indira* (1973). Paromita Vohra, in 'Who Is the First Person?' (pp. 175–88), writes about Sastry's influence on her own filmmaking practice.

Sen, Mrinal (1923–2018): Major film director from Bengal, known for his affiliation in the 1950s with the Communist Party of India and the **Indian People's Theatre Association**, and his political cinema of the 1970s during the peak of the **Naxalite** movement, especially his trilogy on Calcutta (*Interview*, 1971; *Calcutta 71*, 1972; *Padatik/The Guerilla Fighter*, 1973). His Hindi film *Bhuvan Shome* (1969) is considered to have launched the Indian New Wave. R.V. Ramani's film on Mrinal Sen, *A Documentary Proposal* (2016), shot as a fly-on-the-wall film within the span of a two-hour visit to Sen's house, begins with Sen refusing to be filmed, and ends with him approvingly watching Ramani's footage.

Shahani, Kumar (b. 1940): Noted film director and screenwriter known for films like *Maya Darpan* (1972), *Khayal Gatha* (1989) and *Kasba* (1990). Student of **Ritwik Ghatak** at the **Film and Television Institute of India**, and of the eminent historian D.D. Kosambi, to whom he dedicated his unmade film on the Indian Constitution. Known for his key formulation of the narrative sequence from theories of performance and Indian art, addressing questions of nationalism, indigenous modernism and capitalist commodification. Wrote extensively on cinema and politics, defining the terrain of an independent cinema movement in India.

Sovereignty: Controversial term, increasingly linked to 'security of the state, friendly relations with foreign States [and] public order' (the 'reasonable restrictions' on free speech listed in the Constitution of India) to crack down on dissent. Geeta Kapur ('A Cultural Conjuncture in India', pp. 120–42) proposes the idea of the **artist** as a particular kind of sovereign subject, 'corresponding to but more self-valorizing than that of the citizen-subject', 'both inside the nation and outside the state in their interpretative rendering of the political'. Also see 'The Trial' (pp. 201–11).

Streaming: Multimedia delivered and consumed in a continuous manner from a source, with little or no storage in intermediate network platforms. Although OTT platforms and YouTube dominate the streaming space, it has developed considerable political significance in making circulation central to meaning. See **Tactical Media**, **Torrenting**. See Madhuja Mukherjee, 'Toward a New Frame for Regional Films' (pp. 260–74) and Lawrence Liang, 'From Cinema to the Moving Image and Back' (pp. 293–309).

Street Theatre: aka *nukkad natak*, a popular form of radical theatre. Although practised at times by the **Indian People's Theatre Association**, it took its current shape in the work of theatre activist Safdar Hashmi in the years after the **Emergency**. A key form of **tactical media**, alongside **documentary**, given its lightweight and mobile character. See Shohini Ghosh *et al.*, 'Mediastorm: Memories of a Collective' (pp. 166–74).

Sukhdev, S. (1933–1979): Radical filmmaker who worked at the **Films Division** and became known for his experimental style in the late 1960s and 1970s. Began his career assisting Paul Zils. His documentaries highlighted the sharp disparities of Indian society through avant-garde use of sound and images in, for example, the wordless *India 67* (1968), *And Miles to Go* (1975) and *Nine Months to Freedom* (1975). Daughter Shabnam Sukhdev made a film on him, *The Last Adieu* (2020). See Shohini Ghosh *et al.*, 'Mediastorm: Memories of a Collective' (pp. 166–74) and Paromita Vohra, 'Who Is the First Person?' (pp. 175–88).

Swaroop, Kamal (b. 1950): Experimental filmmaker, graduated from the **Film and Television Institute of India**. Part of the Yukt Film Collective in the 1970s, contributing to its landmark adaptation of the play *Ghashiram Kotwal*. Long-term collaborator of **Mani Kaul**. Experimental debut *Om-Dar-B-Dar* (1988) acquired cult status. In recent years, has been working on the figure of Dadasaheb Phalke. Known for his enthusiastic migration across technological forms, his experimental approach to documentary and fiction, his keen interest in digital cinema (which he likens to a painterly frame), and his fixation with lineage and ancestral lands. See

Sudhir Mahadevan, 'The Protocols of Film Historiography (pp. 20–41), and Kaushik Bhaumik and Desire Machine Collective, 'Death Becomes Her' (pp. 86–101).

Syzygy (1970): Iconic 11-minute b&w silent film made by artist Akbar Padamsee at the **Vision Exchange Workshop** in collaboration with animator Ram Mohan, shot on 35 mm. An abstract film inspired by Paul Klee's pedagogical diagrams, for which Padamsee developed his own mathematical patterns, producing 1,000 drawings on transparent cell animation sheets. See Nancy Adajania, 'The Ecologies of Technological Experimentation' (pp. 145–65), and Nalini Malani, 'Can You Hear Me?' (pp. 191–200).

Tactical Media: Form of media activism privileging strategic interventions in the media sphere. The Tactical Media Network formed in May 1997 was described by its founders David Garcia and Geert Lovink as a 'quick and dirty aesthetic', 'a *vérité* for the 90s', 'never perfect, always in becoming, performative and pragmatic, requiring confidence (that it can) survive intact as it travels from interface to interface'. Its lightweight mobility has since then come to be a central feature in protest art as it moves 'from strategy to tactics', rendering 'the phenomenon of resistance fleeting, ephemeral, and subject to continual morphing' – to 'perform an intervention' which could be the gaining of sudden access to a space, a server or a URL, and then 'just as suddenly to disperse'. See Jeebesh Bagchi, 'The Cinematic Object after the 1990s' (pp. 212–23) and Shohini Ghosh *et al.*, 'Mediastorm: Memories of a Collective' (pp. 166–74).

Tagore, Rabindranath (1861–1941): Poet, writer, composer, artist, philosopher, educationist, social reformer, founder of Visva Bharati university at Santiniketan. See **Satyajit Ray**. Stories and songs by him have been extensively filmed, including by Ray, **Ritwik Ghatak** and numerous other filmmakers; recent experimental work includes **Kumar Shahani**'s *Char Adhyay* (Four Chapters, 1997) and Q's *Tasher Desh* (Kingdom of Cards, 2012, see p. 57). See Subhajit Chatterjee, 'The Brothers Ghosh' (pp. 49–67). In their essay on the 'contemporary' ('Now and Elsewhere', pp. 1–14), Raqs Media Collective refers to Tagore's 1923 China visit in the wake of the May Fourth movement.

Third Cinema: Political film movement in the 1960s and 70s from Latin America, associated, for example, with the manifesto by Fernando Solanas and Octavio Getino rejecting neo-colonialism, capitalism and the Hollywood mode. Furthered by several radical manifestos and low-budget experimental movies in Latin America, Africa and Asia to indicate a geopolitical aesthetic. Influenced Indian filmmakers from the 1970s, e.g. **Mrinal Sen**, and **documentary** filmmakers such as the early Gautam Ghose and **Anand Patwardhan**. See Kaushik Bhaumik and Desire Machine Collective, 'Death Becomes Her' (pp. 86–101).

Torrenting: Serverless file-sharing mechanism through the BitTorrent network accessing files from the devices of other users directly. Largely anonymous, it has become central to the circulation of cinema. See **Digitality**, **Tactical Media**, **Streaming**. See Sebastian Lütgert, 'In the Face of Ambiguity, Refuse the Temptation to Guess' (pp. 42–48) and Lawrence Liang, 'From Cinema to the Moving Image and Back' (pp. 293–309).

Varma, Raja Ravi (1848–1906): Major figure of modern Indian art from the princely state of Travancore, blending European academic art with Indian iconography. His larger-than-life realistic paintings depicting scenes from Indian epics and mythology acquired iconic status, and are considered to have influenced the aesthetic of Indian popular cinema, including film posters. He established a lithographic press in Bombay in 1894, which produced oleographs of Hindu gods and goddesses, and scenes from the Mahabharata. **D.G. Phalke** worked at this press briefly. **Kamal Swaroop** refers to Ravi Varma in describing his own 'collage-making' process in *Tracing Phalke*. See Sudhir Mahadevan, 'The Protocols of Film Historiography (pp. 20–41). A modified version of Ravi Varma's 1898 painting *Satyavan and Savitri* is included in the essay by Raqs Media Collective, 'Now and Elsewhere' (see p. 13).

VHS Tape: Short-lived 1980s technology of analog audio-visual recording magnetic tape cassettes, important for being the first instance of portable shooting, recording and projection of the moving image after **16 mm**. It allowed for the explosion of the cinematic archive with **video** cassette libraries that preceded cable and satellite-driven media globalization.

Video (includes video installations): Analog format whose arrival coincided with the expansion of television and the arrival of cable TV in the early 1980s, also contextualized by the relaxation of import restrictions on **VHS tape** recorders and cassettes. Before the liberalization of the media and television industry in 1991, video had found vibrant life within independent practice. On the one hand, it led to the growth of various local film industries and practices, as shown by Madhuja Mukherjee in 'Toward a New Frame for Regional Films' (pp. 260–74) and S.V. Srinivas, 'The Gaddar Effect' (pp. 275–92); on the other, it enabled experimentation by artists and filmmakers through video installations, raising new questions of spatiality for spectatorship and moving images.

Vikalp: Literally meaning 'alternative', name of a rebel film festival organized in 2004, after the Mumbai International Film Festival introduced new censorship guidelines in the context of the **2002 Gujarat** riots. Since then it has built chapters in several cities across India, with regular screening and discussion programmes curated by documentary filmmakers. See Geeta Kapur, 'A Cultural Conjuncture in India' (pp. 120–42).

Virtuality: The quality of having attributes of something without sharing its real or imagined physical form. The term is used in this volume by Lawrence Liang, 'From Cinema to the Moving Image and Back' (pp. 293–309) and Pad.ma, 'Ten Theses on the Archive', (pp. 310–23), in distinct but related contexts. Liang refers to the ontological instability of the virtual as a process of 'becoming', and Pad.ma refers to it in the context of the potential of the archive as a 'productive capacity.'

Vision Exchange Workshop (VIEW): Landmark workshop set up by painter Akbar Padamsee (see **Progressive Artists Group**) between 1968 and 1972 in Bombay, which resulted in inter-art experiments across mediums. Participating artists included Gieve Patel, Nalini Malani, and filmmakers **Mani Kaul** and **Kumar Shahani**, among many others. Padamsee himself made ***Syzygy*** (1970) and *Events in a Cloud Chamber* (print considered lost). In 2016, Ashim Ahluwalia, director of *Miss Lovely* (2013) (see pp. 68–69), made another film called *Events in a Cloud Chamber* using interviews with Padamsee, footage from 8-mm home videos that Ahluwalia's grandfather had shot, footage from *Sygyzy*, and 'found' footage from the **Films Division** archive, in an attempt to reconstruct this lost film. See Nalini Malani, 'Can You Hear Me?' (pp. 189–200).

Women's Movement: Conventionally associated with the publication of the *Towards Equality* report of the Committee on the Status of Women in India (1974–75) and widespread outrage following the Mathura rape incident (involving custodial rape) in 1974, the movement saw many writers, artists, photographers and filmmakers involved in struggles for women's rights, against dowry, rape, domestic violence, seeking social and legal reform. Iconic cases such as Roop Kanwar's *sati* and the Shah Bano case have been referred to by various authors. **Deepa Dhanraj**, the Mediastorm Collective (see Shohini Ghosh *et al.*, 'Mediastorm: Memories of a Collective', pp. 166–74) and Sheba Chhachhi (see Nancy Adajania, 'The Ecologies of Technological Experimentation', pp. 143–65), all come from this formative history. Also see Geeta Kapur, 'A Cultural Conjuncture in India' (pp. 120–42).

Yugantar Collective: India's first feminist film collective, founded in Bangalore in 1980 by **Deepa Dhanraj**, Abha Bhaiya, Navroze Contractor and Meera Rao. Created pioneering films in collaboration with women's groups across different locations in India during 1980–83. They worked with a group of domestic workers in Pune to make *Molkarin* (1981), documented female factory workers in Nipani for the film *Tambaku Chakkila Oob Ali* (Tobacco Embers, 1982), joined hands with Stree Shakti Sanghatana, a feminist research and activist collective based in Hyderabad, for *Idi Katha Matramena* (Is This Just a Story?, 1983) and with members of the 1970s feminist ecological movement Chipko for *Sudesha* (1983). The significance of Yugantar's films lies in their original collaborative practice before 'participatory video work' or 'community media' became familiar terms, and in being part of India's autonomous women's movement and radical left movements of the 1970s and 80s. See Geeta Kapur, 'A Cultural Conjuncture in India' (pp. 120–42) and the still from *Molkarin* on p. 137.

NOTES AND REFERENCES

Introduction

1 For Babri Masjid, see **Ayodhya** in Keywords, p. 327.
2 See **2002 Gujarat** in Keywords, p. 326.
3 For **Naxals**, see **Naxalite** in Keywords, p. 337.
4 For an in-depth discussion of the cinema of 'prayoga', see Amrit Gangar's interview with Ranjana Ragunathan at https://desistfilm.com/q-a-amrit-gangar-prayoga-possibilities-of-cinema/, accessed 25 November 2021. **Editor's note**: For **avant-garde**, see Keywords, p. 327.
5 Interview of Deepa Dhanraj by Devika Girish, 'Radical Potential', in *Field of Vision*, available at https://fieldofvision.org/radical-potential, accessed 25 November 2021.
6 Interview of Pushpamala N. by Parul Dave Mukherji, in *Voices of Change: 20 Indian Artists,* edited by Gayatri Sinha, Mumbai: Marg Publications, 2010.
7 Pushpamala N. and Clare Arni, *Native Women of South India: Manners and Customs*, exhibition catalogue, New York: Bose Pacia Gallery, New Delhi: Nature Morte and Mumbai: Gallery Chemould, 2004, p. 135. Pushpamala's interview is staged as a parody in which the Phantom Lady is interviewed by a sari-clad journalist, both played by Pushpamala.
8 See Geeta Kapur, 'Dismantling Norms: Apropos an Indian/Asian Avantgarde', in *When Was Modernism: Essays on Contemporary Cultural Practice in India*, New Delhi: Tulika Books, 2000, pp. 398–99; M. Madhava Prasad, 'The Last Remake of Indian Modernity?' in *Pushpamala N.: Indian Lady*, exhibition catalogue, New York: Bose Pacia Gallery, 2004; Susie Tharu, 'This Is Not an Inventory: Norm and Performance in Everyday Femininity', pp. 8–23; Ashish Rajadhyaksha, 'Elimination of Authenticity', pp. 83–85, in Pushpamala and Arni, *Native Women of South India*; and Ajay Sinha, 'Pushpamala N. and the Art of Cinephilia', in Christiane Brosius and Roland Wenzlhuemer, eds, *Transnational Turbulences: Towards a Multi-Sited Reading of Image Flows*, Berlin and Heidelberg: Springer Verlag, 2011, pp. 221–48.

9 For more on Malani, see *Nalini Malani and Arjun Appadurai: The Morality of Refusal*, 100 Notes, 100 Thoughts: Documenta Series 023, edited by K. Sauerlander, dOCUMENTA (13), Kassel, Ostfildern: Hatje Cantz Verlag, 2012; Andreas Huyssen, *William Kentridge–Nalini Malani: The Shadow play as Medium of Memory*, New York: Galerie Lelong and Milan: Charta, 2013; Mieke Bal, *In Medias Res: Inside Nalini Malani's Shadow Plays*, Ostfildern: Hatje Cantz Verlag, 2016; Ashish Rajadhyaksha, 'Spilling Out: Nalini Malani's Recent Video Installations', *Third Text*, vol. 17, no. 1, March 2003, pp. 53–61.

10 For example, see Nancy Adajania, 'Dashrath Patel's Non-Aligned Alignments', in Ananya Vajpeyi, ed., *Inheritances: A Symposium on the Problems and Possibilities of India's Museums*, *Seminar* 659, 2014, pp. 76–81; and Nancy Adajania, 'New Media Overtures before New Media Practice', in Gayatri Sinha, ed., *Art and Visual Culture in India, 1857–2007*, Mumbai: Marg, 2009.

11 Anamika Haksar has an impressive track record in theatre. She studied at the National School of Drama and the Lunacharsky State Institute for Theatre Arts in Moscow (now called the Russian Academy of Theatre Arts), and has directed several ground-breaking productions.

12 For more on the film, read Arvind Rajgopal, 'Postcommunist Aesthetics: A Conversation with Anamika Haksar', *e-flux*, 2021, available at https://www.e-flux.com/journal/120/415811/postcommunist-aesthetics-a-conversation-with-anamika-haksar/, accessed 12 November 2021.

13 Rashmi Sawhney in conversation with Anamika Haksar, Urban Lens Film Festival, 2018, available at https://www.youtube.com/watch?v=MIh1FVXZ9N8, accessed 20 November 2021.

14 Art school established by Rabindranath Tagore. See essays by Raqs Media Collective (pp. 1–14) and Subhajit Chatterjee (pp. 49–67) in this volume for more.

15 Ranjit Hoskote, 'An Indian artist is using discarded household gadgets to create a theatre of dreams and aspirations', *Scroll*, 2 February 2017, available at https://scroll.in/magazine/827777/an-indian-artist-is-using-discarded-household-gadgets-to-create-a-theatre-of-dreams-and-aspirations, accessed 20 December 2021.

16 A 2003 report titled 'Vision Mumbai 2013', drafted by a think tank (Bombay First) consisting of various corporates and the American multinational consulting group McKinsey, laid out a vision for the redevelopment of the city, leading to the Mumbai Transformation Plan 2005. Shanghai's redevelopment plan was taken as a reference model, leading to various controversies, including the proposal to rehabilitate slum-dwellers in low housing schemes in eco-sensitive zones previously marked as No Development Zones (NDZ).

17 For **Cinephilia**, see Keywords, p. 330.

18 Khan's documentary was preceded by Nitin Sukhija's PSBT film *Malegaon ke Sholay* (2005), Ruchika Negi's *Malegaon Times* (2010) and Sudhir Kasabe's *Malegaon Talks* (2012).

19 These three representative positions with respect to the Malegaon films are seen in the work of Lawrence Liang and Ishita Tiwari, Sangita Gopal and Ramna Walia. See Ramna Walia, 'Locating Mollywood: Video industries, inter-regional media networks and the "located mobility" of Malegaon films', in Madhuja Mukherjee and Monika Mehta, eds, *Industrial Networks and Cinemas of India: Shooting Stars, Shifting Geographies, and Multiplying Media*, New Delhi: Routledge, pp. 238–52; Lawrence Liang, 'Piracy, Creativity, and Infrastructure: Rethinking Access to Culture', in Ramesh Subramanian and Eddan Katz, eds, *The Global Flow of Information: Legal, Social, and Cultural Perspectives*, New York: New York University Press, 2011, pp. 54–89; Ishita Tiwari, 'The Discrete Charm of Local Practices: Malegaon and the Politics of Locality', *Bioscope: South Asian Screen Studies*, vol. 6, no. 1, 2015, pp. 67–87; Sangita Gopal, 'The Afterlives of 1970s Hindi Cinema', in Priya Joshi and Rajinder Dudrah, eds, *The 1970s and Its Legacies in India's Cinemas*, London and New York: Routledge, 2014, pp. 120–35.

20 See William Mazzarella, *Censorium: Cinema and the Open Edge of Mass Publicity*, Durham: Duke University Press, 2013.

21 Bagchi's essay addresses a specifically urban context, and is located within larger projects around media aesthetics and infrastructures, particularly the one led by Sarai, but not excluding the large body of compelling work on urbanism generated by designers, artists and architects in Mumbai, Bangalore, Chennai, Guwahati and elsewhere. The term 'shadow city' refers to densely populated parts of a city, where (usually immigrant) residents live in makeshift and temporary structures.

22 This issue has been debated at length by film historians over the years, and in 2010, the *Journal of the Moving Image*, Jadavpur University, published a special issue addressing the condition of film archives.

23 Ashish Rajadhyaksha and Rashmi Sawhney, 'Filmic Afterlives: Considerations on the Uncanny', in S.V. Srinivas *et al.*, eds, *Indian Cinema, Today and Tomorrow: Infrastructure, Aesthetics, Audiences*, special issue of *India International Centre Quarterly*, vol. 47, nos 3 and 4, 2021, pp. 328–41.

Chapter 1 I Raqs Media Collective

1 Julieta Aranda, Brian Kuan Wood and Anton Vidokle, 'What is Contemporary Art? Issue One', *e-flux*, no. 11, December 2009.

2 Rabindranath Tagore, 'First Talk at Shanghai', in *Talks in China*, Calcutta: Visva-Bharati, 1925, quoted in Sisir Kumar Das, 'The Controversial Guest: Tagore in China', in Tan Chung, ed., *Across the Himalayan Gap: An Indian Quest for Understanding China*, Delhi: Indira Gandhi National Centre for the Arts, 1998.

3 Walter Benjamin, *The Arcades Project*, trans. Howard Eiland and Kevin McLaughlin, Cambridge, MA: The Belknap Press of Harvard University Press, 1999, p. 88.

4 Louis Aragon, 'Paris Peasant', in Charles Harrison and Paul Wood, eds, *Art in Theory, 1900–1990: An Anthology of Changing Ideas*, Oxford, UK: Blackwell, 1993, p. 456.

5 Chiu Kin Fung, 'Children of the Walled City', *Asia Literary Review*, 10, Winter 2008, pp. 72–73.

6 M. Ackbar Abbas, *Hong Kong: Culture and the Politics of Disappearance*, Minneapolis: University of Minnesota Press, 1997, pp. 73–74.

7 Chao Lun, *The Treatises of Seng-chao*, trans. Walter Liebenthal, Hong Kong: Hong Kong University Press, 1968. **Editor's note**: Buddhist texts composed by a Chinese monk, Seng Chao (378–413 CE).

Chapter 3 I Sudhir Mahadevan

1 Some time between 1991 and 1994, as a student of Fergusson College, Pune, I made an appointment at the National Film Archive of India (which was located not very far from my college campus) to view Phalke's films. If my memory serves me right, I was given a TV monitor and a video-cassette recorder, and I watched the extant early Phalke films on that monitor. In the course of my viewing, a gentleman came and introduced himself to me as Kamal Swaroop, said that he noticed I was viewing Phalke's films and that he was working on a biography of Phalke. That was my only encounter with Swaroop's work (and him) till now. At the time of writing this, I have not yet seen the movie that accompanies the volume: *Rangabhoomi* (2014), Swaroop's film on Phalke's life (or rather, his translation of his own research into Phalke's life, into images).

2 Kamal Swaroop, *Tracing Phalke: The Man and His Times, 1840–1944*, limited edition, National Film Development Corporation, India, 2013.

3 Ibid. For **Ravi Varma** and **Dadasaheb Phalke**, see Keywords, pp. 343 and 338. Dwarkabai: mother of Dadasaheb Phalke. Usha Mantri: 1930s Marathi and Hindi star.

4 Tehelka TV, *Cinema and Me: Episode 9, Kamal Swaroop*, YouTube, published 22 March 2012, available at www.youtube.com/watch?v=RtxboGynvhM, accessed 24 January 2014.

5 R. Walia, 'Techno-Nostalgia: Colorization of K. Asif's Mughal-E-Azam', *BioScope: South Asian Screen Studies*, vol. 4, no. 2, 2013, pp. 137–58. **Editor's note**: See also, Ashish Rajadhyaksha and Rashmi Sawhney, 'Filmic Afterlives: Considerations on the Uncanny', in S.V. Srinivas *et al.*, eds, *Indian Cinema, Today and Tomorrow: Infrastructure, Aesthetics, Audiences*, special issue of *India International Centre Quarterly*, vol. 47, nos 3 and 4, 2021, pp. 328–41.

6 Ashish Rajadhyaksha, *Indian Cinema in the Time of Celluloid: From Bollywood to the Emergency*, New Delhi: Tulika Books and Bloomington: Indiana University Press, 2009, pp. 77–83.

7 The 'golden age' also emerges in contrast to what Rajadhyaksha calls 'statist-internationalist' histories of Indian cinema. These were histories periodized by Satyajit Ray's art-film classic *Pather Panchali* (1955) and in which nothing of value seemingly existed before Ray, which essentially meant giving short shrift to the entire pre-Independence era of Indian cinema; see Rajadhyaksha, *Indian Cinema in the Time of Celluloid*,

p. 78. The result is the construction of a national cinema tradition while also celebrating Indian cinema's relevance for the history of the art film as a transnational genre (or even narrating that relevance as an implicit precondition for the definition of Indian cinema as a national cinema).

8 **Editor's note**: **Nasreen Munni Kabir**: British Indian TV producer, director and author who has published over fifteen monographs on film personalities like script-writer and poet Javed Akhtar, the 1950s and 60s film star Waheeda Rehman, music composer A.R. Rahman and singer Lata Mangeshkar among others, alongside programmes for Channel 4 including the 46-part TV series *Movie Mahal, In Search of Guru Dutt, Follow that Star* (on superstar Amitabh Bachchan) and *The Inner and Outer World of Shah Rukh Khan.*

9 Rajadhyaksha terms this uneasy relationship 'an unresolved dispute over what [the cinema] was doing, as against what the state thought it was doing (resolved, it seems, only in the 2000s, with the onset of globalization)'. See *Indian Cinema in the Time of Celluloid*, p. 82.

10 **Editor's note**: **Mehboob Khan** (1907–64): Film director and producer known for the magnum opus *Mother India* (1957), earlier helped establish many leading stars like Dilip Kumar, Raj Kapoor, Rajendra Kumar, Raaj Kumar, Sunil Dutt and Nargis. **Bimal Roy** (1909–65) made progressive films on social issues inspired by Italian neorealism in films such as *Do Bigha Zameen* (Two Bighas of Land, 1953). Vasanth Kumar S. Padukone, better known as **Guru Dutt** (1925–64): Actor, director and producer who made classics like *Pyaasa* (Thirsty, 1957), *Kagaz ke Phool* (Paper Flowers,1959), *Sahib Bibi aur Ghulam* (The Master, the Wife and the Slave, 1962).

11 Mainstream newspapers such as *The Times of India* carried reviews of these movies in the pre-DVD (and still early VHS) era that indicates theatrical release.

12 **Editor's note**: Dharam Singh Deol or **Dharmendra** (b. 1935): Popular Hindi film actor of the 1960s, 70s and 80s. Began his career in melodramas, did a makeover in the 1970s into action films, including the hit *Sholay* (Flames, dir. Ramesh Sippy, 1975). *Sholay* also starred superstar **Amitabh Bachchan** (b. 1942), with a tragic love-interest in his real-life wife, **Jaya Bhaduri**. Representative of the rising social unrest among the youth and working classes in the 1970s, Bachchan came to acquire the moniker of 'angry young man', drawn to the lawless underbelly of society. **Zeenat Aman** (b. 1951) is a Hindi film star who was popular in the 1970s and 80s for her roles as a bold and modern woman, in films like *Hare Rama Hare Krishna* (1971), *Yaadon ki Baarat* (Procession of Memories, 1973) and *Hum Kisi se Kam Nahin* (We Aren't Less Than Anyone, 1977). **Hema Malini** (b. 1948): Major movie star, initially in Tamil cinema and then in Hindi cinema. Since the early 2000s, a Member of Parliament.

13 There was the audience familiar with Hollywood conventions (and therefore the songs in the film were removed for the international release, and the title changed to *Raiders of the Lost Stone* – a shameless take on *Raiders of the Lost Ark*, 1981). Then, there was the audience in India that expected some of the amplified emotional intrigue of the melodramatic mode. The movie did well with neither audience.

14 For a review that lambasted the movie, see Dileep Padgaonkar, 'Bhelpuri with Ketchup', *The Times of India*, 10 September 1978, p. 10.

15 For example, an eighteen-million-dollar animation film on Lord Krishna was part of Shah's 2003 plans. Suresh Nair, 'I'm in Bollywood to Make A Difference to Myself', *The Times of India*, 5 August 2003, p. B1.

16 The article titled 'Piracy, Piracy' (playing on the title of the movie) described Shah pretending to be a disinterested customer, listening incredulously and with horror as the London grocery store owner boasts of having already circulated 500 tapes of *Cinema Cinema*. In the ensuing confrontation, the shopkeeper observes that he has provided the filmmaker with free publicity and physically removes Shah from his premises. The report goes on to describe the UK's woefully inadequate piracy laws, and Shah's now destroyed hopes of collecting between thirty and forty thousand pounds in box office receipts for the movie. The movie ran, Shah claims, to packed houses for the first three weeks, and the report ends with Shah's decision to not pursue legal remedies against the shopkeeper because the British cops were already possessed of 'strong anti-Asian feeling'. *The Times of India*, 17 August 1980, p. 5.

17 Ayesha Kagal, 'Opening up Pandora's Box: The Video Wave', *The Times of India*, 17 August 1980, p. 5.

18 Stephen Hughes, 'Mythologicals and Modernity: Contesting Silent Cinema in South India', *Postscripts*, 1.2/1.3, 2005, pp. 207–35, proposes that we see such forms of access as part of a 'living archive' of private collections, state archives, as well as private institutions formed in the public trust specifically in order to collect materials, to acquire film-related collections, and to make these accessible to the public.

19 **Editor's note**: The Edward Theatre was functioning until before the start of the Covid-19-induced lockdown in March 2020.

20 **Editor's note**: **The Cinematograph Committee Evidence and Report** was published in 1928, following a year-long inquiry by the Indian Cinematograph Committee (ICC) established by the colonial government to investigate various aspects of film production, including censorship.

21 **Editor's note**: **Helen Anne Richardson Khan** (b. 1938), of Franco-Burmese lineage, became symbolic of non-familial female desires as the iconic 'Anglo-Indian' cabaret dancer in the 1960s and 70s, until the emergence of a later generation of glamorous actor-dancers like Zeenat Aman and Parveen Babi. See Esha Marjara's film *Desperately Seeking Helen* (1998) and Jerry Pinto's book, *Helen: The Life and Times of a Bollywood H-bomb*, New Delhi: Penguin Books, 2006.

22 For a review of *Cinema Cinema*, see Khalid Mohammed, 'Film Hi . . . Valentine to Show Biz Old Days', *The Times of India*, 15 May 1983, p. 5.

23 **Editor's note**: Pran Sikand Kishore (1920–2013), popularly known as **Pran**, acted in over 350 films, mainly playing either character roles or that of the villain.

24 Mohammad Yusuf Khan (1922–2021), screen name **Dilip Kumar**, acted in over 65 films, including some of the most iconic in Indian film history, such as *Mughal-e-Azam* (The Great Mughal, dir. K. Asif, 1960), *Andaz* (Style, dir. Mehboob Khan, 1949), *Madhumati* (dir. Bimal Roy, 1958) and *Ganga Jamna* (dir. Nitin Bose, 1961) among others. It was his role in Bimal Roy's *Devdas* (1955) that clinched his image as 'the tragedy king' of Indian cinema. **Editor's note**: For more on ***Mughal-e-Azam,*** see essay by Raqs Media Collective (pp. 1–14) in this volume.

25 **Nutan Samarth** (1936–1991) acted in over 70 films in a career spanning four decades; she is noted for progressive films like *Sujata* (dir. Bimal Roy, 1959), *Bandini* (Imprisoned, dir. Bimal Roy, 1963) and *Seema* (Horizon, dir. Amiya Chakravarty, 1955).

26 R. Thomas, 'Indian Cinema: Pleasures and Popularity', *Screen*, vol. 26, no. 3, 1985, pp. 116–31.

27 In this aspect, the movie differs from films like Mark Rappaport's *Rock Hudson's Home Movies*, which Jonathan Rosenbaum reads as a response to the age of video, or to a crisis in the medium of film. See Jonathan Rosenbaum, 'Rock Criticism', available at www.jonathanrosenbaum.com/?p=7158, accessed 4 July 2013.

28 'An archival orphan is like an answer to which the scholar has yet to find the question', notes Frank Kessler in 'Pathé versus Pathé, Exhibit A: Reading an Archival Document', *Film History: An International Journal*, vol. 25, no. 1, 2001, p. 127, an observation that applies with regard to the footage utilized by *Cinema*, provided we acknowledge that the 'answer' here already knows its question, or context. We do know, after all, where these incomplete scenes come from and where they ought to belong. As such, these aren't enigmatic scenes; they are transparent but incomplete ones.

29 Jane Simon, 'Recycling Home Movies', *Continuum*, vol. 20, no. 2, 2006, p. 194.

Chapter 5 I Subhajit Chatterjee

1 Film societies were registered clubs formed mainly by an urban intelligentsia in order to promote and disseminate knowledge of film art. The Calcutta Film Society was formed in 1947, the Federation of Film Societies of India (FFSI) was registered in 1959. See V.K. Cherian, *India's Film Society Movement: The Journey and Its Impact*, New Delhi: Sage Publications, 2016.

2 See Kiranmoy Raha, *Bengali Cinema*, Kolkata: Nandan Publications, 1991; and Chidananda Dasgupta, *The Painted Face: Studies in India's Popular Cinema*, New Delhi: Roli Books, 1991.

3 See Moinak Biswas, 'In the Mirror of an Alternative Globalism: The Neorealist Encounter in India', in L.E. Ruberto and K.M. Wilson, eds, *Italian Neorealism and Global Cinema*, Michigan: Wayne State University Press, 2007, pp. 72–90.

4 For an account of the Bengali film industry and B-grade aesthetics in the 1980s, see A. Nag and S. Bhattacharya, 'The Politics around "B-Grade" Cinema in Bengal: Re-Viewing Popular Bengali Film Culture in the 1980s–1990s', *Acta Orientalia Villnesia*, vol. 2, no. 2, 2011, pp. 13–30. For the political context of Bengali popular cinema in the early decade of this century, see M. Biswas, 'Changing Scene', *Sarai Reader 08: Fear*,

2010, available at http://archive.sarai.net/files/original/d4edbe1 d2815492eb3bfb96f99e08485.pdf, accessed 18 October 2020. Also see mash-up artistes like DJ Bapon, https://www.youtube.com/user/ BostirCheleBapon/ videos, accessed 18 October 2020.

5 See especially *The Bhoot of Roseville* (The Ghost of Roseville, dir. Sanghamitra Chaudhuri, 2010), *Charulata* (dirs. Ghosh Brothers, 2013), *10th July* (dir. Ratul Ganguly, 2014), *Dharshan* (Rape, dirs. Ghosh Brothers, 2014), *Ke Se?* (Who the Hell?, dir. Sougata Biswas, 2014), *Ami Je Tomar* (Truly Yours, dir. Sanjeev Rai, 2014), *Disha* (The Call Girl, dir. Sanjoy Bardhan, 2015), *Achena Bondhutwo* (Unfamiliar Friendship, dir. Rishikesh Mondol, 2015), *Chhip Suto Chaar* (Fishing Rod and Bait, dir. Susanta Saha, 2016), *Piklur Janala* (Piklu's Window, dirs. Anirban and Amlan Majumdar, 2017), *Pornomochi* (The Deciduous Tree, dir. Kaushik Kar, 2018). A rough budget estimate of finished film products suggests that a high-end Bengali potboiler featuring local stars and backed by powerful production and distribution companies would have a budget between 1.5 and 2.5 crore rupees. Budgets of character-centred and therefore less lavish 'new urban dramas' range around 80 lakh rupees rising to a maximum of 1.5 crore rupees. A few independent films made with collaborative effort have occasionally managed to maintain relatively modest budgets between 25 and 70 lakhs. Low-budget films, which I view as a 'homegrown exploitation' sector, usually have significantly lower budgets.

6 **Editor's note**: **Debashree Roy**: Successful popular actress debuting in the early 1980s in Bengali cinema, but also in Bombay and Tamil cinema. Her mother had close acquaintance with several industry personalities.

7 **Editor's note**: **Chapal Bhaduri**: Veteran actor and female impersonator in mainstream folk theatre of Bengal. After retirement, she/he has passionately narrated her/his professional and personal experiences as a queer performer in several documentary as well as fictional films.

8 **Editor's note**: **Chitrabani**: Major institution fostering film education and awareness in Kolkata since the late 1970s. Father P.J. Joseph, to whom, in all probability, the Ghosh Brothers are referring, happens to be the institute's director since 2015. Ironically, Chitrabani's educational vision has been largely analytic and scholarly, operating in sync with the film society movement; it was not, in the normal course, known to engage with amateur, low-brow productions.

9 **Agnidev Chatterjee**: Director of *Charulata* 2011, previously worked in television but is now known for making racy narratives centering on urban female protagonists, themselves crossbreeds between conventional B-grade genres.

10 A small-scale production house located on Lenin Sarani in central Kolkata that specializes in advertising, occasionally venturing into film.

11 **Editor's note**: **Nandan**: Prestigious government-sponsored cultural centre and Kolkata's first multiple-screen cinema complex, located next to the Rabindra Sadan and Academy of Fine Arts, formally inaugurated by Satyajit Ray in 1985. The Left Front government, then at the peak of its success, conceived of Nandan as a site for promoting meaningful, socially conscious cinema. Ticket prices are still government-regulated and it offers a better profit-sharing arrangement than most privately owned theatres.

12 Around 2015, an attempt at making a biopic depicting the early and personal struggles of Satyajit Ray had been stalled by a permissions issue with Ray's son and sole rights owner, Sandip Ray, himself a well-known filmmaker. A low-budget film such as this might well not encounter similar problems.

13 In Tagore's *Nastanirh*, the wary husband Bhupati brings in Charu's sister-in-law Manda to provide female companionship to his lonely wife. There is no hint of eroticism in this relationship either in the original story or in Ray's adaptation, and such a suggestion is presumably blasphemous.

14 A B-grade genre based on supernatural tales about snakes taking human form, that gained popularity during the 1980s and 90s and continues to be showcased intermittently in television serials and regional non-mainstream circuits.

15 The West Bengal Trinamool Congress, which won over the Left Front with wide popular support in 2011, shifted the Chief Minister's and Secretariat office from Mahakaran (Writer's Building) in central Kolkata to a new construction called Nabanna. 'Nabanna' itself refers to an iconic play from India's radical theatre movement, the IPTA. For **IPTA**, see Keywords p. 334.

16 *Autograph* (dir. Srijit Mukherjee, 2010): Successful film in the 'new Bengali urban dramas' genre mentioned in the Introduction, featuring the star Prasenjit paying a tribute to *Nayak* (The Hero, 1966), Ray's film on stardom with superstar Uttam Kumar.

17 **Editor's note**: **Anup Sengupta**: Director of mainstream comedy-potboilers often featuring popular stars in the industry. He is married to Piya Sengupta, daughter of cult actor-director Sukhen Das, known for high-pitched family melodramas in the 1980s.

18 Of these names, except Soumitra Chatterjee (1935–2020), a veteran star who did several minor roles in low-budget films alongside his usual mainstream appearances, the others had close association with the industry, mostly with failed career trajectories leading to their frequent appearances in low-budget fares.

19 The whiplash sounds bear implicit reference to Ritwik Ghatak's sound effects to frame the protagonist Neeta's tragic exploitation in *Meghe Dhaka Tara* (The Cloud-Capped Star, 1960).

20 Till 60 years after Rabindranath Tagore's death in 1941, the Visva-Bharati University at Santinketan, a former brainchild of Tagore himself, ruthlessly controlled copyright over Tagore's entire creative output. In 2001 Tagore's work came into the public domain, leading to a blossoming of cheap publications and myriad appropriations of his music and literature.

Chapter 6 I Darshana Sreedhar Mini

1 Bliss Cua Lim, *Translating time: Cinema, the fantastic, and temporal critique*. Durham: Duke University Press, 2009, pp. 1–2.

2 For instance, the *Maharashtra Herald* article titled 'Soft-porn Film Stopped', dated 9 September 1983, refers to the attempts to disrupt the screening of the Malayalam film *The Crazy Lady* at Odeon Theatre in New Delhi by women's groups and the Delhi Malayali Association, alleging the film to be distasteful to Malayali sensibilities. **Editor's note**: **K.S. Gopalakrishnan** (1929–2015) was a screenwriter, director and producer in the Malayalam and Tamil film industries, known mainly for socially focused melodrama films. **Crossbelt Mani** (b. 1968) is a director and cinematographer in the Malayalam film industry.

3 Navaneetha Mokkil Maruthur refers to the citational practice in the 1980s after the success of *Her Nights* when there was a string of soft-porn films with the term *rathri* (night) in their titles. She reads this as evidence of the impact *Her Nights* had on the emergence of soft porn as a genre. While she does not go in depth into tracking the relationship between *Her Nights* and the emergence of soft-porn as a genre, at another point she also questions the status of soft-porn as a stable category since it is a 'shifting category formed through modes of circulation and exhibition'. Thus, the temporal tension between the industrial and the journalistic usages of the term can be seen in the writings on soft-porn as well. See Navaneetha Mokkil Maruthur, 'Re-viewing *Her Nights*: Modes of excess in Indian cinema', *South Asian Popular Culture*, vol. 9, no. 3, 2011, pp. 276, 297.

4 Interview with directors A.T. Joy (September 2013), Thrikunapuzha Vijaykumar (July 2013), Dubai Mani (August 2013), Nagarajan (production manager, 12 October 2013), Gladys (theatre owner, 10 June 2013) and Shakeela (actress, 14 July 2016).

5 Ratheesh Radhakrishnan writes: 'I suggest that there does not exist an aesthetic or formal or even thematic category called "soft porn" that will be of any analytical value to us. What I mean is that any attempt at studying cinema (and even other forms for that matter) that tries to start from a fixed category of genre as a predetermined and always already constituted category will have to encounter problems that such a fixing throws up. Such a move that is so common among critics and film historians, tries to bank on the common sense about these films and to imagine a universe of texts that could be, without much difficulty, clubbed together.' See Ratheesh Radhakrishnan, 'Soft Porn and the Anxieties of the Family', in Meena T. Pillai, ed., *Women in Malayalam Cinema: Naturalizing Gender Hierarchies*, Hyderabad: Orient Blackswan, 2010, pp. 194–215.

6 Interview with Nagarajan (production manager) on 12 October 2013, in Chennai.

7 This is very similar to the cut-piece phenomenon in Bangladesh that has been studied by Hoek. Lotte Hoek, *Cut-pieces: Celluloid Obscenity and Popular Cinema in Bangladesh*, New York: Columbia University Press, 2013.

8 For instance, *Aadyapaapam* (dir. P. Chandrakumar, 1988) provides a good example of how this circumvention was possible. This film was an early precursor to soft-porn films, utilizing the image of Adam and Eve to deal with issues of human sexuality, and was also the first Malayalam film to show a woman naked. The film had direct releases in four languages – Kannada, Tamil, Malayalam and Hindi – and was a huge box-office hit.

It had only three scenes with dialogues. Shot in the forests of Karnataka, it also availed the subsidy worth Rs 1.5 lakhs offered by the Karnataka state government to develop film production in the state. There was another reason why Karnataka was selected as the shooting location. One of the Censor Board members who had agreed to help them with the certification was transferred to Karnataka. Therefore, unforeseen coincidences paved the way to Karnataka being the location. It was a limited crew of twelve members who left for Karnataka in a car and a van (interview with P. Chandrakumar on 27 October 2013 in Thiruvananthapuram).

9 Sreedhar Pillai, 'Magic on the Wane', *The Hindu*, 23 August 2002, available at http://www.hindu.com/thehindu/fr/2002/08/23/stories/2002082300170100.htm, accessed 15 March 2014.

10 Sreedhar Pillai, 'Malayalam Films: The Smut Glut', *India Today*, 15 May 1986, available at http://indiatoday.intoday.in/story/soft-porn-boom-hits-commercial-cinema-in-kerala-like-a-bolt-from-the-blue/1/348454.html, accessed 29 March 2014. Pillai's pronouncements that these films were 'unmindful of censors' present us with a paradox here. While these films certainly did push the boundaries of censor tolerance in terms of sexually charged narratives and imagery, these often emerged as unpredictable moments of sexual flourish through the use of cut-pieces, or would be hidden behind the garb of 'sex-education films'. This latter tendency had its precedent in one of the first sex-education films made by Sasta productions. Co-directed by S. Kumar and P.R.S. Pillai, the film was titled *Cancerum Laingika Rogavum* (Cancer and Sexually Transmitted Diseases, 1981). The film became widely popular as a medical film and was bought by the Department of Health a few years after its release; it also won the Kerala state government special award for a primarily educational and informative short film. It was censored in Madras and was issued the 'S' certificate by a committee which had more than five medical practitioners, but it opened the doors for exploiting the tag of 'sex-education' for a host of titillating films.

11 In India, theatres are broadly divided into 'A', 'B' and 'C' centres. While the A centre, otherwise known as the 'release centre', had the privilege of screening the new films, the 'B'- and 'C'-centre theatres had to wait till the films finished their initial run in the A-centre theatres. There are many factors which culminated in classifying a particular theatre according to these categories, including the nature of seating arrangements, the capacity of the hall and, most importantly, the locality of the theatre. P.V. Shajikumar's short story, '18+', published in *Madhyamam*, was reprinted in *Kidappara Samaram*, Calicut: Mathrubhumi, 2013, pp. 33–44.

12 **Editor's note**: Expert Committee headed by filmmaker Adoor Gopalkrishnan to reform Malayalam cinema with numerous radical and controversial proposals. For **Adoor Gopalakrishnan**, see Keywords, p. 334.

13 The film also streamed for a limited period on *Netflix* and has now been acquired by Zee5.

14 R. Ayyappan, 'Sleaze time, folks!', Rediff, 24 January 2001, available at http://www.rediff.com/entertai/2001/jan/24mallu.htm, accessed 12 August 2014.

15 M.G. Radhakrishnan notes that in 1999, 'as many as 45 films bombed at the box office, with barely 10 reaping good profits [. . .] with an estimated Rs 80-crore loss and an all-time low production of 60 films in the past year (1999) – a steep decline from 120 movies produced 15 years ago – there are few options for producers but to join the smut brigade'. M.G. Radhakrishnan, 'Crippled by failed productions and losses, Malayalam film industry banks on sleaze', *India Today*, 26 June 2000, available at https://www.indiatoday.in/magazine/society-the-arts/films/story/20000626-crippled-by-failed-productions-and-losses-malayalam-film-industry-banks-on-sleaze-777791-2000-06-26

16 Interview with Dubai Mani in Chennai on 20 August 2013.

17 Telephonic interview with Shaji Kumar on 15 June 2014.

18 Interview with Jayesh in Thiruvananthapuram on 3 June 2014.

19 G. Deleuze, *Cinema 2: The Time Image*, translated by Hugh Tomlinson and Robert Galeta, Minneapolis: University of Minnesota Press, 1989, p. 81.

20 The warehouse takes on a quality that Anthony Vidler calls the 'architectural uncanny'. A. Vidler, *The Architectural Uncanny: Essays in the Modern Unhomely*, Cambridge, MA: The MIT Press, 1992, p. 11.

21 Priyaranjan Lal says that the horse imagery is a direct homage to the art of cinema itself, being inspired by Eadwerd Muybridge's famous series of 1878 photographs, 'The Horse in Motion', widely recognized as one of the precursors of the moving image. Interview with Priyaranjan Lal in Kochi on 8 January 2015.

22 Interview with Priyaranjan Lal in Kochi on 8 January 2015.

23 This works a little differently in the story than in the film. The story '18+' offers a neat closure by portraying Father Michael as being cured completely, although he then becomes addicted to soft porn. The film

avoids this ending, opting instead for a more abstract, symbolic ending in which Father Michael wanders among the ruins of an abandoned church on the seashore.

24 Shaji P.V. Kumar, '18+', in *Kidappara Samaram.*

25 In the short story this is portrayed interestingly, by describing a sequence at mass where Father Michael unknowingly utters lines from the dialogues of soft-porn films during the service.

26 The actual lines are: 'Just as Melquíades cured the people of sleep deprivation by revisiting Marcondo, Father Michael regains his health and sanity when Yakoob visits the second day and touches him' (my translation). Shaji P.V. Kumar, '18+', in *Kidappara Samaram*, p. 44.

27 The 'DPS MMS scandal', as it popularly came to be known, was a leaked viral clip that featured two students of Delhi Public School, R.K. Puram, Delhi, having oral sex. The clip was sold on eBay India by an engineering student, resulting in a lawsuit being filed against the CEO of the company for abetting the sale of pornographic material. See Namita Malhotra, *Porn: Law, Video, Technology*, Bangalore: Centre for Internet and Society, 2011.

28 Interview with Thrikunapuzha Vijayakumar in Chennai on 15 July 2013. Vijayakumar, a production assistant-turned-producer based in Chennai, made a string of soft-porn films in the 1980s. He was one of the few producers who had copies of the script, continuity albums and production-related files of his films.

29 Interviews with A.T. Joy (September 2013), Thrikunapuzha Vijayakumar (July 2013) and Dubai Mani (August 2013).

30 For instance, these questions surfaced prominently when Reshma, a soft-porn actress, was arrested in 2007 for alleged 'prostitution' and her interrogation video was leaked on the internet. The discussions that followed centred on how the soft-porn actress illustrated a narrative of moral decline, much like the characters in the films themselves. For an example of such a narrative, see 'The Trials of Reshma' in *Bollywood Journalist* by Soumyadipta Banerjee, 12 January 2016, available at http://bollywoodjournalist.com/2016/01/12/the-trials-of-reshma/, accessed 3 September 2015.

31 Interview with Jayesh in Thiruvananthapuram on 3 June 2014.

32 Interview with Joseph, Babu and Sanal (names changed), patrons of S.P. Theatre, who were invited for a conversation with me by Gladys (10 June 2013).

33 Interview with Nanukuttan on 5 June 2014.

34 Interview with Vasu (name changed) in Chennai on 13 September 2013.

35 Interview with Gladys on 5 June 2013 in Thiruvananthapuram.

36 Excerpts from interview with a group of men in their 50s who frequented S.P. Theatre in the late 1990s.

Chapter 7 I Kaushik Bhaumik and Desire Machine Collective

1 [Christoph von] **Fürer-Haimendorf** (1909–1995): Austrian ethnologist and professor who spent forty years studying tribal cultures in Nagaland, Andhra Pradesh, Telangana and Nepal. His work includes ten books, thousands of pages of ethnographic notes, over 100 hours of 16-mm footage and over 10,000 photographs, much of which is held in the collection of the SOAS archives.

2 **Editor's note**: For the well-known *Roja* debates in *Economic and Political Weekly (EPW)*, see: Tejaswini Niranjana, 'Integrating Whose Nation?: Tourists and Terrorists in *Roja*', vol. 29, no. 3, January 1994, as well as 'Gravity of the State', vol. 29, no. 44, 4 October 1994; M.S.S. Pandian and Venkatesh Chakravarty, 'More on *Roja*', vol. 29, no. 11, 12 March 1994; S.V. Srinivas, '*Roja* in Law and Order State', vol. 29, no. 20, 14 May 1994; Rustom Bharucha, 'On the Border of Fascism: The Manufacture of Consent in *Roja*', vol. 29, no. 23, 4 June 1994; Arun Kumar Patnaik, 'Idealistic Equations', vol. 29, no. 32, 6 August 1994.

3 Paul Virilio, *War and Cinema: The Logistics of Perception*, London and New York: Verso, 1989.

4 **Editor's note**: Physicist Étienne-Jules Marey coined the term chrono-photography referring to a set of photographs of a moving object, taken to record and study motion. He developed a gun-shaped device which took twelve successive photographs on a set of discs, to capture the natural movement of birds in flight.

5 **Editor's note**: **Third Cinema**, see Keywords, p. 342.

6 **Editor's note**: **Leni Riefenstahl** (1902–2003), German director and actress who made Nazi propaganda films, e.g., *Triumph of the Will* (1935), *Olympia* (1938) and *Day of Freedom: Our Armed Forces* (1938), using footage of Nazi rallies.

7 Gilles Deleuze, *Cinema I: The Movement Image*, translated by H. Tomlinson and B. Habberjam, London: Bloomsbury, 2013, p. 105.

8 **Editor's note**: **Karan Johar**: see Keywords, p. 335.

9 **Editor's note**: **Jacque Rivette** (1928–2016), French New Wave filmmaker and editor of *Cahiers du Cinema* from 1963 to 1965, responsible for its transformation from an apolitical publication to a left-leaning journal examining the relationship between politics, society and culture. **Pier Paolo Pasolini** (1925–1975), Italian director and writer. **Kamal Swaroop**: see Keywords, p. 341, and Sudhir Mahadevan's essay in this volume, pp. 20–41.

10 Ashis Nandy, *The Intimate Enemy: Loss and Recovery of Self Under Colonialism*, Delhi: Oxford University Press, 1983.

11 **Editor's note**: ***Dev D*** (dir. Anurag Kashyap, 2009): Independent black comedy based on Bengali novelist Sarat Chandra Chattopadhyay's novel, the extensively filmed *Devdas*, produced by UTV Productions, which also produced the 2004 blockbuster ***Swades***, starring Shah Rukh Khan. The distribution of risk across films by production houses is a standard strategy used in the cultural industries. **Anurag Kashyap**, **Shah Rukh Khan**: see Keywords, pp. 335–36.

12 **Editor's note**: **Jamshedpur**: Town in north India associated with a Tata steel manufacturing plant. Vikramaditya Motwane's debut film *Udaan* (2010) located here was acclaimed for its 'realistic' portrayal of the domestic abuse suffered by two young boys at the hands of their alcoholic father. The film was produced by Anurag Kashyap and Ronnie Screwvala under the UTV banner. *Peepli Live* (2010), Anoushka Rizvi's debut film, was hailed for its 'realistic' representation of the plight of India's farmers and the media's disinterest in rural stories. Journalist P. Sainath had drawn attention to the plight of the farmers, particularly reporting the increase in farmer suicides post economic liberalization in the 1990s.

Chapter 9 I Geeta Kapur

1 In his work on pre- and post-Independence India, Partha Chatterjee (in *Nationalist Thought and the Colonial World: A Derivative Discourse?*, London: Zed Books for the United Nations University, 1986) characterizes the nature of state formation that has occurred in the aftermath of a national struggle for Independence as that of a national state, distinguishing it from the European concept of the nation-state.

2 A consolidated frame of reference for the period 1992–2002 was foregrounded in the exhibition entitled 'Ways of Resisting' curated by Vivan Sundaram for SAHMAT (Safdar Hashmi Memorial Trust), a major Delhi-based platform enabling artists and intellectuals to articulate their social concerns and participate in the larger public sphere of the country.

3 I refer to literature produced by the lowest members of the Hindu caste hierarchy who have assumed the term Dalit (the oppressed) as a sign of their estrangement and defiance. The radical interrogation in Dalit literature of the presumptions of universality in India's constitutional values – of democracy, modernity, secularism – puts unprecedented pressure on what a culturally validated aesthetic could possibly mean in the deeply divided social life of India, as indeed on the national political formation itself. An account of this (almost) century-long, incomparably powerful literary movement is outside the scope of this essay.

4 For example, the late **Bhupen Khakhar** (1934–2003), who produced a remarkably unique iconography for gay sexuality. See also feminist articulations by artists and photographers using a wide range of materials and strategies: these include **Nalini Malani**, **Rummana Hussain**, **Navjot Altaf**, **Nilima Sheikh**, **Dayanita Singh**, **Pushpamala N.**, **Sheela Gowda**, **Anita Dube**, **Sheba Chhachhi** and **Sonia Khurana**. There are also key feminist works produced by theatre practitioners and filmmakers, and together this output marks, quite literally, the full stretch of the vanguard for cultural practice in India. **Editor's note**: See Nalini Malani, 'Can You Hear Me?' (pp. 189–200) and Nancy Adajania's essay on Sheba Chhachhi, 'The Ecologies of Technological Experimentation' (pp. 143–65), in this volume.

5 India's lofty tradition of auteur-based, modernist and avant-garde cinema is well known. The limits of sovereign-subjectivity are tested by the oeuvre of filmmakers as diverse as Satyajit Ray, Ritwik Ghatak, Kumar Shahani, Mani Kaul and Adoor Gopalakrishnan. **Editor's note**: For **Satyajit Ray**, **Ritwik Ghatak**, **Kumar Shahani**, **Mani Kaul** and **Adoor Gopalakrishna**, see Keywords, pp. 326–44.

6 The **Raqs Media Collective** trio, located in Delhi, have developed a theory and practice of documentary/video/new media art. Through their preferred tropes of migration/displacement, marginality/surveillance, they function across the transcultural zone of global art. Other young artists, mainly from Mumbai, use video and computer imaging to convert extended allegories of subversion into punctual purposes. Notable among them was Tushar Joag (1966–2018), one of whose projects was to devise means to 'facilitate' the common commuter of the Indian metropolis in navigating life in the city. Shilpa Gupta has been manipulating electronic and digital forms to parody local consumer complicity in the perpetuation of global greed. **Editor's note**: See the essay by Raqs Media Collective, 'Now and Elsewhere: The Problem and the Provocation', pp. 1–14, in this volume.

7 Marshall Berman, *All that is Solid Melts into Air: The Experience of Modernity,* New York: Penguin Random House, 1988.

8 **Editor's note**: See note 12.

9 Sudipta Kaviraj, 'The Imaginary Institution of India', in P. Chatterjee and G. Pandey, eds, *Subaltern Studies VI,* Delhi: Oxford University Press, 1992, p. 33. **Editor's note**: Also reproduced in *The Hunger of the Republic*, volume 1 of the *India Since the 90s* series, pp. 25–52.

10 For an update on Patwardhan's films, see http://www.patwardhan.com. For an early contextualization of his film practice, see Anand Patwardhan, 'Waves of Revolution and Prisoners of Conscience: The Guerilla Film, Underground and in Exile', MA thesis, Department of Art History and Communications, McGill University, Fall 1981. Patwardhan has seen himself, and been seen by film theorists like Paul Willemen (see Jim Pines and Paul Willeman, eds, *Questions of Third Cinema,* London: BFI Publishing, 1989), as continuing to contribute to the famous debate initiated by critics and filmmakers Fernando Solanas and Octavio Getino, titled 'Towards a Third Cinema', *Cinéaste*, vol. 4, no. 3: Latin American militant cinema, Winter 1970–71, pp. 1–10. Other references to Patwardhan include: Sean Cubitt, 'Interview with Anand Patwardhan', *Framework*, vols 30–31, 1986; Robert Crusz and Priyath Liyanage, 'Interview with Anand Patwardhan', *Framework*, vols 38–39, 1992; Miriam Sharma, 'Anand Patwardhan: Social Activist and Dedicated Filmmaker', *Critical Asian Studies*, vol. 34, no. 2, June 2002.

11 For a polemical discussion of liberationist cinema in the Third World, see the collection of essays in Pines and Willemen, eds, *Questions of Third Cinema.* **Editor's note**: For **Third Cinema,** see Keywords, p. 342.

12 See Amar Kanwar, *Notes for A Night of Prophecy,* University of Chicago: The Renaissance Society, 2003; Anne Rutherford, '"Not Firing Arrows": Multiplicity, Heterogeneity and The Future of Documentary', Interview with Amar Kanwar, *Asian Cinema*, vol. 16, no. 1, Spring 2005; Ida Kierulf, *Amar Kanwar – Portraits*, catalogue, Oslo: Fotogalleriet, 2005; Marit Paasche, 'Strong Political Filmportraits', *Aftenposten*, October 2005; Jerry Saltz, 'Worlds Apart – A meditation on Separation: Amar Kanwar Walks the Border between India and Pakistan', *Village Voice*, February 2004.

13 Ravi Vasudevan compares the two documentarists in 'Selves Made Strange: Violent and Performative Bodies in the Cities of Indian Cinema 1974–2003', in Indira Chandrasekhar and Peter C. Seel, eds, *body.city: siting contemporary culture in India,* Delhi: Tulika Books and Berlin: House of World Cultures, 2003. For a full discussion of the two documentarists, see Vinay Lal, 'Travails of a Nation: Some Notes on Indian Documentary', *Third Text*, vol. 19, no. 2, March 2005, p. 83.

14 **Editor's note**: Realism, Modernism and Avant-Garde are used here as art historical terms, although their relevance extends beyond the visual arts into literature, theatre and other allied fields. For the Indian provenance and trajectory of these terms, see Geeta Kapur, *When was Modernism: Essays on Contemporary Cultural Practice in India*, New Delhi: Tulika Books, 2000.

15 **Editor's note**: **Bombay films**: Term used to refer to commercial films made in Bombay, which in recent years have also popularly come to be known as 'Bollywood' films.

16 Indian film studies provide highly developed theses on contemporary cultural production and related ideologies of society and state. See, for example, Ashish Rajadhyaksha, 'The Bollywoodization of the Indian

Cinema: Cultural Nationalism in a Global Arena', *Inter-Asia Cultural Studies,* vol. 4, no. 1, April 2003; 'Visuality and Visual Art: Speculating on a Link', in Chaitanya Sambrani, ed., *Edge of Desire: Recent Art in India,* exhibition catalogue, Asia Society Museum/Queens Museum of Art, 2005; 'Rethinking the State after Bollywood', *Journal of the Moving Image*, no. 3, Kolkata: Department of Film Studies, Jadavpur University, June 2004; and *Indian Cinema in the Time of Celluloid: From Bollywood to The Emergency*, New Delhi: Tulika Books, 2009. See also, M. Madhava Prasad, *Ideology of the Hindi Film: A Historical Construction,* Delhi: Oxford University Press, 1998; Ravi Vasudevan, ed., *Making Meaning in Indian Cinema,* Delhi: Oxford University Press, 2000. Essays by Ravi Vasudevan relevant to this subject include: 'An Imperfect Public: Cinema and Citizenship in The "Third World"', *Sarai Reader 01: The Public Domain,* Delhi: Sarai/CSDS and Amsterdam: SONM, 2001; and 'Selves Made Strange: Violent and Performative Bodies in the Cities of Indian Cinema 1974–2003', in Chandrasekhar and Seel, eds, *body.city.*

17 As used most tellingly in Roland Barthes, *Mythologies*, St. Albans, Herts. (UK): Paladin, 1973.

18 Apropos the word 'film', I must clarify that I am not using an exclusively medium-based distinction between those using celluloid and those using electronic and digital media. This means, in effect, that I am not making a foundational difference between mediums on the basis of indexicality; not restricting relational 'truth' between image and material reality to photochemical reproductive processes of the photograph and film. A relative difference will be indicated at points where it seems relevant to the argument.

19 The question of truth-value and witness accounts in the documentary genre is elaborated by Mark Nash, 'Experiments with Truth: The Documentary Turn' and Okwui Enwezor, 'Documentary/Vérité: The Figure of Truth in Contemporary Art', in *Experiments with Truth*, exhibition catalogue, Philadelphia: Fabric Workshop and Museum, 2005.

20 The 'new' is placed in contrast to the early or 'classical' documentary which developed in the 1920s and 1930s in the Soviet Union and Britain (with their respective communist and conservative agendas respectively for nation-building). If the ideology of early documentary corresponds to the full spectrum of the modernist project, the new documentary (post the 1960s), by its very chronology, engages with a critique of the national–modern compact. See Michael Renov, *The Subject of Documentary*, Minneapolis: University of Minnesota Press, 2004, pp. 134–35.

21 Renov, for example, attributes a major role to structuralist and post-structuralist thought, and, more broadly, to cumulative theoretical interventions post-1960s 'that challenged certain fundamental bulwarks of Western thought'; and he sees film- and video-makers since the 1980s as having pursued 'similar matters in their artistic practice, constructing historical selves that are nonetheless sites of uncertainty rather than coherence'. Renov, *The Subject of Documentary*, pp. 104 and 109.

22 **Editor's note**: **Madhusree Dutta**: Documentary filmmaker and activist, co-founder of feminist legal collective Majlis, made *I Live in Behrampada* (1993), set in a Muslim neighbourhood affected by the riots in Mumbai in 1992–93, and *Seven Islands and a Metro* (2006).

23 **Editor's note**: **Baul singers**: Devotional and mystical singers from both Hindu and Muslim communities in Bengal.

24 **Editor's note**: **Deepa Dhanraj**'s *Something Like a War* (1991), see images on pp. 166–67; also see **Yugantar Collective** in Keywords, p. 344. Surabhi Sharma, Reena Mohan, Shohini Ghosh: major figures in the women's documentary film movement as filmmakers, curators and film teachers. Ghosh was a member of Mediastorm (see 'Mediastorm: Memories of a Collective', pp. 166–74 in this volume). See Paromita Vohra, 'Who is the First Person? On Making Documentaries', pp. 175–88 in this volume.

25 Susan Sontag, *Regarding the Pain of Others*, New York: Picador, 2003.

26 See Michael Hardt and Antonio Negri, *Empire*, Cambridge, Mass.: Harvard University Press, 2000.

27 I take for granted the fact that there has always been an interface between art as *artisanal* practice (object-oriented and auratic, signatured or otherwise expressive) and *the technology of vision provided by the lens* (photography and film, video and the digital). This interface became, as we know, a major trope for theorizing visual modernity on the basis of a conceptual/semiotic divide between the original work of art and its reproducible doubles. I am referring, of course, to Walter Benjamin. From the 1960s, and especially with the emergence in the 1970s of a (feminist-led) conceptual (anti-)aesthetic, a re-vision of documentary material in the form of the photograph and, more broadly, lens-based work, takes place in western art history. Thereon, the major entry of experimental video pulls art practice into the realm of the moving image.

28 Renov, *The Subject of Documentary*, p.106.

29 There is a ubiquity of electronic and digital media post celluloid, and it may be simpler to refer to these in a hyphenated compound: *moving-image/media-practices*. For extended sets of definition and the terms of aesthetic discourse on what should strictly constitute 'new' media technology, see Lev Manovich, *The Language of New Media*, Cambridge, Mass.: The MIT Press, 2001.

30 Andre Bazin's foundational contribution to the concept of realism in cinema informs his entire work; for his preferred position, see Andre Bazin, 'An Aesthetic of Reality: Cinematic Realism and the Italian School of Liberation', in *What is Cinema?*, vol. 2, Berkeley/Los Angeles: California University Press, 1971.

31 Renov, *The Subject of Documentary*, p. 139.

32 Fredric Jameson's chapter, 'Video: Surrealism Without the Unconscious', in his book *Postmodernism, or, The Cultural Logic of Late Capitalism* (London: Verso, 1991), characterized experimental video as offering a random play of signifiers, as providing a master trope for psychic fragmentation, and indeed as a medium constitutionally incapable of documentary value, as it is, at the same time, structurally bereft of memory. This characterization is supplemented and critiqued, among others, by Michael Renov, *The Subject of Documentary*, pp. 137–38 and 142.

33 In addition to Lev Manovich's *The Language of New Media*, it is interesting to refer to an intensely interactive debate supported by the Sarai New Media Initiative, Delhi. See *Sarai Reader 03: Shaping Technologies,* Delhi: Sarai/CSDS and Amsterdam: SONM, 2003; and *Sarai Reader 04: Crisis/Media,* Delhi: Sarai/CSDS and Amsterdam: SONM, 2004.

34 While this is not the place to elaborate on the outburst of experimental video and video installation art by Chinese artists within and outside China in the last decade, it is relevant to my argument to mention those extraordinary examples of self-inflicted violence, of aggressive sexuality, of the comic grotesque, of macabre forms of mortality, that characterize the Chinese avant-garde, illustrating the deeply visceral response to a national–global frisson. A brief selection of texts on recent Chinese art include Gao Minglu, ed., *Inside Out: New Chinese Art*, exhibition catalogue, San Francisco/New York, Berkeley/Los Angeles: San Francisco Museum of Modern Art/The Asia Society Galleries/ University of California Press, 1998; Caroline Turner, ed., 'The Spectre of Being Human', in *Art and Social Change: Contemporary Art in Asia and the Pacific*, Australian National University, Canberra: Pandanus Books, 2005.

35 For example, Bill Viola's masterly oeuvre of video installations dating from the 1970s wherein he consistently thematizes the body/self, and in radical contrast, Bruce Nauman's tragic-comic performative video, *Shit in Your Hat-Head on a Chair* (1990).

36 I highlight the point by selecting some examples of artists/filmmakers working with the moving image framed within the white cube of the art space as a black-box (multi-projection) installation. Consider how a change in context, technology and medium, how a reorientation of narrative and a changed protocol of spectatorship, complicates the representational politics of class, colour, race and ethnicity in Stan Douglas's *Le Detroit* (2000); Isaac Julien's *Frantz Fanon: Black Skin, White Mask* (1996) and its two-screen video installation, *Fanon S.A.* (1997–2004); William Kentridge's animation films such as *Monument* (1990), *Mine* (1991), *Felix in Exile* (1994); Steve McQueen's *Western Deep* (2002) and *Carib's Leap* (2002); Willie Doherty's *Non-specific Threat* (2004); Jayce Salloum's multi-projection, *Everything and Nothing and Other Works,* from the 'Ongoing Project', Untitled (1998–2005). Consider how the theme of gender, frequently tuned to surreal modalities – erotic and introvert – is manoeuvred through multiple looped and sequestered projections in Kutlug Ataman's *Four Seasons of Veronica Read* (2002) and, in sheer contrast, in Araya Rasdjarmrearnsook's *Reading for Corpses (*2002).

37 See Mark Nash, 'Art and Cinema: Some Critical Reflections', in *Documenta 11, Platform 5: Exhibition Catalogue*, Ostfildern-Ruit: Hatje Cantz Publishers, 2002. Speaking about the phenomenon of the black box in the white cube, Nash refers to the extensive and ongoing interpretative work on (video) installations by the art theorist Boris Groys.

38 Consider just two examples: Chantal Akerman's multi-monitor piece investigating the conditions of 'illegal migration' on the Mexico–US border, *From the Other Side* (2002), and Eyal Sivan's and Michael Khleifi's *Route 181* (2003), unravelling the history of imperialism in West Asia through a four-hour journey along the undefined border between Israel and Palestine.

39 Enwezor, 'Documentary/Verite', p. 103.

40 Okwui Enwezor, 'The Black Box', in *Documenta 11, Platform 5*, pp. 42–55.

41 **Editor's note**: **Documenta 11**, curated by **Okwui Enwezor**, was game-changing at many levels. In addition to challenging and dismantling the hegemony of the western art world, its protocols and assumptions, it stirred up an intellectual debate around artistic practice in many parts of the global South including India. This led to a sharp recalibration of art and its relationship to critical thought, alongside drawing international attention to the work of artists like photographer and environmental activist Ravi Agarwal, Amar Kanwar and Raqs Media Collective.

Chapter 10 I Nancy Adajania

1 The founding members of the Progressive Artists Group formed in 1947 were F.N. Souza, S.H. Raza, K.H. Ara, M.F. Husain, H.A. Gade and S.K. Bakre. The name of the group was modelled on the Progressive Writers Association, a left-wing literary group founded in 1936. This stemmed from Souza's brief association with the Communist Party of India; however, the Progressives were largely apolitical. **Editor's note**: See **Progressive Artists Group** in Keywords, p. 339. For more, see Yashodhara Dalmia, *The Making of Modern Indian Art: The Progressives*, New Delhi: Oxford University Press, 2001.

2 **Editor's note**: **Festivals of India**: The first Festival of India was held in the UK in 1982, and in subsequent years, editions were held in North America and Europe. The Festivals have drawn major criticism on grounds of commoditizing art for the 'western' market, and using art to further diplomacy and trade relations.

3 **Editor's note**: **Vivan Sundaram**, see Keywords, p. 144. For more on Nalini Malani, see her essay 'Can You Hear Me?' (pp. 189–200) in this volume.

4 **Editor's note**: **Ranbir Kaleka** and **Baiju Parthan**, see Keywords, p. 144.

5 See Nancy Adajania, 'New Media Overtures before New Media Practice in India', in Gayatri Sinha, ed., *Art and Visual Culture in India 1857–2007*, Bombay: Marg Publications, 2009.

6 **Editor's note**: All these artists were members or associates of the Bombay Progressives, except for Nalini Malani. For **Progressive Artists Group**, see Keywords, p. 339. For more on the experimental photography, film and video work of these artists, see Adajania, 'New Media Overtures Before New Media Practice in India'. Also see Nancy Adajania, 'Spillovers and Subterfuges: Krishen Khanna's Photographic Adventures', in *Krishen Khanna '95*, London: Grosvenor Gallery and New Delhi: Artoholics, pp. 68–71.

7 **Editor's note**: **Dashrath Patel**, see Keywords, p. 144.

8 Nancy Adajania, 'Dashrath Patel's Non-Aligned Alignments', in Ananya Vajpeyi, ed., 'Inheritances: A Symposium on the Problems and Possibilities of India's Museums', *Seminar*, 659, 2014, pp. 76–81.

9 Adajania, 'New Media Overtures Before New Media Practice in India'.

10 Ibid. **Editor's note**: ***Syzygy*** (1969), see Keywords, pp. 341–42.

11 Adajania, 'Dashrath Patel's Non-Aligned Alignments'.

12 **Editor's note**: See **Women's Movement** in Keywords, p. 344.

13 Two campaigns that galvanized feminist groups of the late 1970s were the campaign against dowry-related violence, and the landmark nationwide feminist mobilization organized around the case of Mathura, a young girl who had been gangraped by policemen at a police station in Chandrapur, Maharashtra, on 26 March 1972. The case was a milestone in that it shifted the onus of proof from the victim to the accused. The feminist struggle led to an amendment of the Criminal Procedure Code and the Indian Penal Code.

14 **Editor's note**: **Amrita Chhachhi**: Professor of Gender and Development Studies at the International Institute of Social Studies, Erasmus University, Netherlands.

15 **Editor's note**: **Stree Sangharsh**: Feminist group established in 1979 in New Delhi, initially to protest dowry deaths through the medium of street theatre.

16 **Editor's note**: **Jogi Panghaal**: Designer who graduated in Product Design from NID in 1977.

17 **Editor's note**: **Saheli**: Started as a crisis intervention centre in Delhi (1981) and campaigned against the forced sterilization programme initiated by the government during the Emergency years, 1975–77, and on issues of violence against women.

18 The other founding members of Jagori were Abha Bhaiya, Gouri Chowdhry, Jogi Panghaal, Kamla Bhasin, Runu Chakraborty and Manjari Dingwaney. See Jagori, *Living Feminisms, Jagori: A Journey of 20 Years*, New Delhi: Jagori, 2004, p. 2.

19 Radha Kumar, *The History of Doing: An Illustrated Account of Movements for Women's Rights and Feminism in India, 1800–1990*, New Delhi: Kali for Women, 1993, p. 114.

20 Ruth Vanita, who co-edited (with Saleem Kidwai) the anthology *Same-Sex Love in India: Readings in Literature and History* (New York: St. Martin's Press, 2000), bemoans the fact that an important aspect of her life – lesbianism – had to 'remain private' and that, on this issue, 'the personal did not become political' for women within the movement until much later in their lives. See Ruth Vanita, 'More Lives than One', in Ritu Menon, ed., *Making a Difference: Memoirs from the Women's Movement in India*, New Delhi: Women Unlimited, 2011, p. 35.

21 Sheba Chhachhi in conversation with Nancy Adajania, 1 April 2013.

22 Sheba Chhachhi, 'Sheba Chhachhi', in Pooja Sood, ed., *The Khoj Book: 1997–2007, Contemporary Art Practice in India*, New Delhi: Harper Collins, 2010, pp. 238–43. **Editor's note**: *Sati*: Ritual of widow immolation on the dead husband's pyre followed by some communities in India in the nineteenth century, revived in the twentieth century. Shakti: a manifestation of feminine energy. For **Khoj**, see Keywords, p. 144.

23 Personal conversation with author, 1 April 2013.

24 A.K. Ramanujan's translation of Devara Dasimayya's poem, in A.K. Ramanujan, *Speaking of Siva*, Harmondsworth: Penguin, 1973, p. 110. **Editor's note**: **Jater Ma** and **Kotwal** are names of female ascetics.

25 **Editor's note**: **Bhadramahila**: Bengali term referring to affluent and educated women from the upper middle classes.

26 A.K. Ramanujan's translation of Akka Mahadevi's poem, in Ramanujan, *Speaking of Siva*, p. 134. **Editor's note**: **Veerashaiva** is a term long synonymous with the Lingayat religion based on Shiva worship, established by the poet-saint **Basaveshwara** during the eleventh century in north Karnataka. Poet and philosopher **Akka Mahadevi**, belonging to the first generation of Basaveshwara's followers, is remembered as a feminist icon and rebel figure among the pantheon of medieval saint-poets.

27 Based on her conversations with Sheba Chhachhi, Chitra Padmanabhan provides a context for the renunciates at the Kumbh Mela: 'The Kumbh is not meant for ritual alone; it is a meeting place for ascetics who also get sadhu identity cards from the government. Once the Kumbh is over, the women ascetics revert to a largely autonomous and mobile life connected through a network of ashrams, sacred sites and events.' See Chitra Padmanabhan, 'Wild Mothers', *Tehelka*, 1 October 2008.

28 **Editor's note**: An **akhada** is a place of practice, the same word used for places of *kushti*/martial arts training and Hindu monasteries. **Mahant Mira Puri** has been known for her political ambitions. See Sheba Chhachhi, 'The Householder, the Ascetic and the Politician: Women sadhus at the Kumbh Mela,' *India International Centre Quarterly*, vol. 29, no. 3–4, 2003, pp. 224–34.

29 **Editor's note**: **Sadhvi Rithambara** is a member of the RSS and Sangh Parivar, founder of their women's wing, Durga Vahini, and currently a sitting member of the Indian Parliament. She has been acquitted of her role in the demolition of the Babri Masjid as well as for her many incendiary speeches against the Muslim community. For the Ram Janmabhoomi agitation, see **Ayodhya** in Keywords, pp. 327–28.

30 Sheba Chhachhi in conversation with Nancy Adajania, 1 April 2013.

31 **Editor's note**: **Garuda**: Mythical eagle-like hybrid bird in the Hindu, Buddhist and Jain faiths; the favoured vehicle of Lord Vishnu.

32 Stuart Cary Welch, *Imperial Mughal Painting*, New York: The Metropolitan Museum of Art, 1978, ill. no. 27 with note.

33 **Editor's note**: *Tutinama*, 'Tales of the Parrot', is a fourteenth-century series of 52 Persian stories which remain well-known through their many illustrations, including the 250 miniature illustrations commissioned by Akbar. The Persian text was redacted from a twelfth-century Sanskrit anthology titled *Sukasaptati*.

34 Sheba Chhachhi in conversation with Nancy Adajania, 7 September 2007.

35 **Editor's note**: **Baul music**: Heterodox mystic folk singing and practices from Bengal.

36 For a discussion of Lalan Fakir's song and its symbolic valency, set into a discussion of Rabindranath Tagore's relationship with the Bauls, see Gayatri Chakravorty Spivak, 'Tribute to the Poet from a Middle-class Girl', available at http://tagore150toronto.ca/gayatri-chakravorty-spivak-tagoretribute/, accessed 9 September 2013.

37 Sheba Chhachhi in conversation with Nancy Adajania, 7 September 2007.

38 Sheba Chhachhi in conversation with Nancy Adajania, 1 April 2013.

39 **Editor's note**: **National Institute of Design**, see Keywords, p. 144.

40 Sadanand Menon, 'In the Realm of the Visual: Five Decades (1948–1998) of Painting, Ceramics, Photography, Design by Dashrath Patel', in *In the Realm of the Visual*, exhibition catalogue, New Delhi: National Gallery of Modern Art, 1998. **Editor's note**: **Sadanand Menon** is a cultural critic, professor of journalism and writer, with major contributions to contemporary arts, theatre and dance.

41 Adajania, 'Dashrath Patel's Non-Aligned Alignments'.

42 Sadanand Menon, 'Visual Thinker' (Obituary), *Frontline*, vol. 27, no. 26, December 2010, pp. 18–31.

43 In a parallel development, during the early 1990s, the painter Nalini Malani, one of the pioneers of new media art, created a palimpsestual narrative in *Alleyways Lohar Chawl* by inviting the viewer to walk through a pathway of mylar film sheets.

44 **Editor's note**: **Meena Kumari**, see Keywords, p. 144.

45 **Editor's note**: *48°C Public.Art.Ecology*: Nine-day festival of public art situated in and around Delhi. Each artwork interrogated the complex environment of the city, and eight key sites of cultural and/or historical significance were selected to exhibit works by twenty-five artists including Sheba Chhachhi.

46 **Editor's note**: According to Hindu mythology, Lord Krishna was fed poison or poisoned milk by the demoness Putana, due to which his skin turned a nocturnal blue, which is how he is represented in popular culture.

47 As the Situationist philosopher Guy Debord ('Introduction to a Critique of Urban Geography,' in *Situationist International Anthology*, translated by Ken Knabb, Berkeley: Bureau of Public Secrets, 1989) writes, the 'psychogeographical' research 'on the arrangement of the elements of the urban setting, in close relation with the sensations they provoke . . . must be constantly corrected in the light of experience, by critique and self-critique'.

48 Sheba Chhachhi in conversation with Rhana Devenport at Govett-Brewster Art Gallery, as part of the exhibition 'Sub-Tropical Heat: New Art from South Asia', 12 July 2012.

49 **Editor's note**: In 1855, Lord Elphinstone established the Central Museum of Natural History, Economy, Geology, Industry and Arts. In 1858, George Birdwood was appointed its curator, and a committee comprising him, Dr Bhau Daji Lad (1822–1874, physicist, antiquarian, Sanskrit scholar) and Jaganath Shankarseth (1803–1865, educationist and philanthropist) was set up to raise money for a new museum. This museum was opened in the vicinity of Byculla zoo in 1872, and in 1975 was renamed the **Dr Bhau Daji Lad Museum**. See Keywords, p. 328, for more.

50 Tasneem Zakaria Mehta, *The Restoration and Revitalization of Dr Bhau Daji Lad Mumbai City Museum*, Bombay: Dr Bhau Daji Lad Museum Trust, 2009, pp. 24–28.

51 Ibid., p. 32. **Editor's note**: **George Birdwood** (1832–1917): British naturalist and writer.

52 **Editor's note**: ***Itbari Khan ke Haath*** is a work made by Sheba Chhachhi during a 1999 Khoj residency, exhibited in what used to be the home of a feudal landlord after whom the Modinagar area (where the exhibition was held) got its name. The exhibition paid homage to the hundreds of retrenched workers who were once employed in factories in and around the area. The title of the work came from an image of Itbari Khan, an erstwhile worker, photographed holding his old factory identity card.

53 **Editor's note**: **Mahadev Vishwanath Dhurandhar** (1867–1944): Noted Indian painter and postcard artist from the British colonial era. His illustrations of women of that era doing their daily chores are especially popular.

54 Govind Narayan, *Mumbai: An Urban Biography from 1863*, with a foreword by Gyan Prakash, edited and translated by Murali Ranganathan, London: Anthem Press, 2009.

Chapter 11 I Shohini Ghosh, Sabina Kidwai, Shikha Jhingan, Ranjani Mazumdar, Sabeena Gadihoke, Charu Gargi

1 **Editor's note**: **Anwar Jamal Kidwai**: Founder of the MCRC in 1962, and the sixth Vice Chancellor of Jamia Millia Islamia.

2 **Editor's note**: **James Beveridge**, see Keywords, p. 168.

3 **Editor's note**: ***Hamara Shaher*** (Bombay, Our City, 1984), see Keywords, p. 168. Also see Geeta Kapur's essay, 'A Cultural Conjuncture in India: Art into Documentary', pp. 120–42 and *Bombay High Court: Shri Anand Patwardhan vs. the Central Board of Film Censors, 2003*, pp. 209–11, in this volume.

4 **Editor's note**: **Shah Bano**, see Keywords, p. 168. **All India Muslim Personal Law Board**: Legally recognized authority for sanctioning conventions based partly on the Quran and on cultural practices of Muslims in India, officially recognized and consulted by Indian courts as well as the government for dealing with issues involving cultural and social issues related to Muslims in India. The Board has a much-criticized stand on 'triple talaq' or legal separation through unilateral announcement by men, an already controversial issue made more so when it was declared illegal in 2019 by the BJP-ruled government.

5 **Editor's note**: **Muslim Women's Bill**, see Keywords, p. 168.

6 **Editor's note**: **Mike Pandey**: Documentary filmmaker and producer specializing in wildlife and environmental films, also known in Delhi for loaning equipment for independent film work.

7 **Editor's note**: **Chunri** is a long piece of cloth placed on the *sati*'s ashes, and **Mahotsav** is a celebration/festivity. This rite is performed twelve days after the *sati*'s death, and is a stark contrast to the solemnities of rituals performed after the death of the husband or of a man.

8 **Editor's note**: **Sati Sthal**: Memorial location for women who have committed *sati*.

9 **Editor's note**: **Jat**: An upper-caste agricultural and martial community in several states across northern India.

10 **Editor's note**: A temple devoted to the mother-goddess Sati.

11 **Editor's note**: **Vidya Rao**, classical musician; **Kajal Ghosh**, music composer and activist; **Kalindi Deshpande**, women's rights activist.

12 **Editor's note**: **Safdar Hashmi**, see Keywords, p. 168.

13 **Editor's note**: **H.K.L Bhagat** (1921–2005): Politician of the Congress party, known to be politically close to Indira Gandhi, and widely believed to have been responsible for instigating the anti-Sikh riots of 1984 and for the killing of Safdar Hashmi.

14 **Editor's note**: **Indira Gandhi**: Prime Minister of India from 1967 to 1984 (barring the years 1977–80 when her government was voted out of power following the Emergency she imposed in 1975–77), assassinated by her Sikh bodyguards in retaliation for her coming down heavily against the Khalistan movement or Sikh insurgency in the 1980s. In 1984, after the assassination of Indira Gandhi, mobs in Delhi killed a large number of innocent Sikhs, a historical episode often compared to the state-supported genocide against Muslims in Gujarat in 2002.

15 **Editor's note**: **Ram Janmabhoomi/Babri Masjid/1992**: Political movement by the Hindutva right wing in the 1990s. See **Ayodhya** in Keywords, p. 327, for more.

16 **Editor's note**: ***Chabutara*** literally means a raised platform; but in this context, it refers to the small platform created inside the mosque.

17 **Editor's note**: **Bhagalpur riots** of 1989: Discussed in some detail in Gyanendra Pandey, 'In Defence of the Fragment', in Ashish Rajadhyaksha, ed., *The Hunger of the Republic*, Volume 1 of the *India Since the 90s* series, New Delhi: Tulika Books, 2021, pp. 54–85.

18 **Editor's note**: **Madan Gopal Singh**: Scholar and theorist, also known as a composer, singer, lyricist and writer.

19 **Editor's note**: For **Godhra**, see **2002 Gujarat riots** in Keywords, p. 326.

Chapter 12 I Paromita Vohra

1 **Editor's note**: **Renuka Shahane**: Film and television actor, known for playing domestic roles of mothers and sisters in feel-good romances.

2 In 1939 the British government in India decided to harness the power of propaganda by setting up the Film Advisory Board (FAB), which produced the Indian News Parade. Producing mostly war films, the FAB also made the occasional documentary about 'Women of India' and other such lofty topics. It thus became compulsory for cinema halls to show 1,000 feet of government-approved footage before the main feature. **Editor's note**: **FAB**: See Keywords, pp. 176, 333–34.

3 B.D. Garga, *From Raj to Swaraj: The Non Fiction Film in India*, New Delhi: Penguin Viking, 2007, p. 130.

4 **Editor's note**: **Ezra Mir**, see Keywords, p. 176.

5 **Editor's note**: The Indian economy was governed after Independence by a five-year economic planning mechanism. Jawaharlal Nehru was its architect as the first Prime Minister of India.

6 **Editor's note**: **Burmah Shell**: A petroleum company that operated in India and had a monopoly for a long time, set up a film production unit to make industrial and other films. See Ravi Vasudevan, 'Film and Visual Publicity at Burmah Shell 1920s to the 1950s', CSDS, DigiPAPERS, 2020, available at https://www.csds.in/uploads/custom_files/1604642781_DigiPaper%2001%20Ravi%20Vasudevan.pdf, accessed 15 May 2021. Documentary filmmaker James Beveridge was posted as Executive Director of this unit, producing about forty films in the four years of its operations. On the Mass Communication Research Centre (MCRC) at Jamia Millia Islamia, see Keywords, p. 168; also see Mediastorm, 'Memories of a Collective', in this volume, pp. 166–74.

7 **Editor's note**: **James Beveridge**: See Mediastorm, 'Memories of a Collective', in this volume, pp. 166–74.

8 **Editor's note**: **MCRC**, see Keywords, p. 168.

9 **Editor's note**: **Emergency**, see Keywords, p. 333.

10 **Editor's note**: **Jahangir Bhownagry,** popularly known as Jean Bhownagry, was Director of the Films Division (FD). For more, see **Films Division** in Keywords, pp. 333–34.

11 **Editor's note**: **Wolf Koenig** (1927–2014): Canadian director, producer, animator, cinematographer and pioneer of the documentary genre of 'Direct Cinema' at the Canadian Film Board.

12 Quoted in *Cinema Verité: Defining the Moment* (film), dir. Peter Wintonick, National Film Board of Canada, 1999.

13 Mauri Alioff, 'Camera Eye: Peter Wintonick's Cinema Verite: Defining the Moment', *Take One*, 1999.

14 *A Search for the Feeling of Being There*, dir. Richard Leacock, 1997.

15 **Editor's note**: **Pramod Pati, S. Sukhdev, S.N.S Sastry**: See Keywords, pp. 338–41. For **Films Division**, see Keywords, pp. 333–34.

16 **Editor's note**: **Anand Patwardhan**, **Deepa Dhanraj**, **Yugantar Collective**: See Keywords, pp. 326–44. Also see Geeta Kapur, 'A Cultural Conjuncture in India: Art into Documentary', in this volume, pp. 120–42.

17 **Editor's note**: **Third Cinema**, see Keywords, p. 342.

18 Madhu Bhushan, 'Art and Activism: A Dialogue With Deepa Dhanraj', *Deep Focus* vol. 1, no. 3, 1988, pp. 32–33.

19 Ibid., p. 33.

20 Mani Kaul, the personal essay films of Ruchir Joshi, and later, the political essay films of Amar Kanwar; the use of intimate biographies as history by Reena Mohan and Sameera Jain; films incorporating theatrical performance and the theatre of performance by Madhusree Dutta – to name just a few styles that emerged. **Editor's note**: **Films Division**, see Keywords, pp. 333–34. For more on these, and on Ruchir Joshi, Reena Mohan and Madhusree Dutta, also see Geeta Kapur, 'A Cultural Conjuncture in India: Art into Documentary', in this volume, pp. 120–42.

21 Paromita Vohra, 'Separation Anxiety: The Schisms and Schemas of Media Advocacy', in Shamillah Wilson, Anasuya Sengupta and Kristy Evans, eds, *Defending our Dreams*, London: Zed Books, 2005, pp. 201–09.

Chapter 13 I Nalini Malani

1 Wislawa Szymborska, 'Nothing Twice', in *Map: Collected and Last Poems*, translated and edited by Clare Cavanagh and Stanisław Barańczak, Boston: Houghton Mifflin Harcourt, 2015.

2 **Editor's note**: ***Notebook*** (2018–), animated posts made on iPad and regularly uploaded on Instagram @nalinimalani.

3 **Editor's note**: **Vision Exchange Workshop**, see Keywords pp. 343–44. For more on Padamsee, see Nancy Adajania, 'The Ecologies of Technological Experimentation: Sheba Chhachhi's Multimedia Environments', in this volume, pp. 143–65.

4 **Editor's note**: **Charles Correa** (1930–2015): Architect and urbanist seen as the founder of modern architecture in independent India, and bringing radically new ideas to urban development and planning.

5 **Editor's note**: **Nandan Kudhyadi**: Eminent documentary filmmaker.

6 **Editor's note**: **Johan Pijnappel**: Art historian and author of several texts on Nalini Malani and Indian video art.

7 **Editor's note**: ***Memory Record/Erase*** (1996), single channel, stop motion animation of painted watercolour image.

8 **Editor's note**: **Anuradha Kapur**: Eminent theatre and performance art director, formerly Director of the National School of Drama, New Delhi.

9 **Editor's note**: **Alaknanda Samarth**: Theatre and film actor, known particularly for her strong women-centric experimental and collaborative work with visual artists and filmmakers.

10 **Editor's note**: **Satyadev Dubey** (1936–2011): Renowned playwright, producer, actor and director in theatre and cinema.

11 **Editor's note**: ***City of Desires*** (1992): Major site-specific exhibition at Gallery Chemould, Mumbai.

12 **Editor's note**: ***Medeamaterial*** (1993): Theatrical collaboration with Alaknanda Samarth at Max Mueller Bhavan, Mumbai, based on texts by Heiner Mueller, in part bringing *City of Desires* into a performance space.

13 **Editor's note**: ***The Job*** (1996): Theatrical production with Anuradha Kapur based on a short story by Bertolt Brecht at the Experimental Theatre of the National Centre for Performing Arts, Mumbai. **Ritu Talwar**: Actor and graduate of the National School of Drama.

14 **Editor's note**: Ashish Rajadhyaksha, 'Video, Art, Medeamaterial', in *Nalini Malani: Medeaprojekt,* Bombay: Max Mueller Bhavan, 1997, and '"Spilling Out": Nalini Malani's Recent Video Installations', *Third Text* 062, vol. 17, no. 1, March 2003.

15 **Editor's note**: **Ram Mohan** (1931–2009): Indian animator and design educator who began his career at the Cartoon Film Unit of the Films Division of India, Mumbai.

16 **Editor's note**: ***Syzygy*** (1969): Short film by multimedia artist Akbar Padamsee, who led the Vision Exchange Workshop (VIEW) between 1969 and 1974. For more on the film, see Adajania, 'The Ecologies of Technological Experimentation: Sheba Chhachhi's Multimedia Environments', in this volume, pp. 143–65.

17 **Editor's note**: **Amrit Gangar**: Film scholar, writer, critic, curator, and founding theorist of 'Cinema Prayoga', a concept and practice of experimentation developed by a group of independent Indian filmmakers. See 'Prayoga', in this volume, pp. 102–19.

18 **Editor's note**: ***Remembering Toba Tek Singh***: Malani's first multimedia and multichannel video installation, using four projection videos with twelve monitors in twelve tin trunks, on a floor with mirror reflecting material.

19 **Editor's note**: ***Gamepieces*** (2003–09), four-channel video/shadow play on six rotating Lexan cylinders; Unity in Diversity (2004), single channel video play, projected in gilt frame; ***Mother India: Transactions in the Construction of Pain*** (2005), five-channel video play; ***Remembering Mad Meg*** (2007–17), four-channel video/shadow play with light projectors on eight reverse-painted rotating Lexan cylinders; ***In Search of Vanished Blood*** (2012), six-channel video/shadow play with five rotating reverse-painted Mylar cylinders.

20 **Editor's note**: ***Stains*** (2000), stop motion animation using watercolour paint.

21 **Editor's note**: **Kalighat painting**: Nineteenth-century form of painting that developed in Calcutta, characterized by bright colours and bold outlines, depicting science from everyday life.

22 **Editor's note**: ***Blind Man's Bluff***, ***Megalomania I and II***, ***Dystopia***, ***Ubu Roi***, ***Hysterical Bird***, ***Heart-Earth-Art*** and ***Nothing Twice***: All works part of the *Notebooks* series of animations made on the iPad.

23 Walter Benjamin, 'On the Concept of History', in *Walter Benjamin: Selected Writings (Vol. 4, 1938–1940)*, edited by Eiland and M.W. Jennings, translated by Harry Zohn, Cambridge: Harvard University Press, 2003.

24 Hannah Arendt, *The Human Condition,* Chicago: Chicago University Press, [1958] 1998.

25 Szymborska, 'Nothing Twice'.

26 Kim Turcot DiFruscia, 'Listening to Voices: An Interview with Veena Das', *Altérités*, vol. 7, no. 1, 2010, p. 139.

The Trial

1 See Neville March Hunnings, *Film Censors amd the Law*, Sydney: Allen and Unwin, 1967, p. 227; and F.D. Berthold and H. von Hartleib, *Filmrecht: Ein Handbuch*, München, Berlin: C.H. Beck, 1957, p. 215.

2 **Editor's note**: The Film Certification Appellate Tribunal (FCAT) was abolished in 2021 under the Tribunal Reforms Act. Further, the government proposed amendments to the 1952 Cinematography Act, whereby a certificate granted by the CBFC could be retrospectively revoked, through a state order for re-examination of films. Both interventions evoked strong opposition from filmmakers, who rightly saw the state stepping in as a 'super censor'.

3 **Editor's note**: ***Hutatma*** in Hindi and Marathi means 'martyr'. The Martyrs' Square or Hutatma Chowk is the most significant public space in the city of Mumbai for public meetings and protests.

4 **Editor's note**: **Bhai Sangare** was one of the leading voices of the Dalit Panther movement, which was begun by Dalit activists and writers like Namdeo Dhasal, J.V. Pawar, Arun Kamble and Raja Dhale in Mumbai in the 1970s.

5 **Editor's note**: This refers to the trial explosion of an atomic bomb at Pokharan during the tenure of Prime Minister Atal Bihari Vajpeyi in 1998. The atomic blast was subject to a great deal of debate in the media, and severe criticism from public intellectuals and activists.

6 **Editor's note**: **Buddha Jayanti** is the day celebrated annually as the day of the birth as well as the enlightenment of Gautama Buddha.

7 **Editor's note**: **Rama**, **Shankar** and **Vishnu** are names of Hindu gods.

8 **Editor's note**: See excerpts from the judgement (pp. 203–08).

9 **Editor's note**: The tele-series *Tamas* (Darkness, 1988), directed by Govind Nihalani, was challenged in court by Ramesh Dalal for propensity to cause communal riots. The tele-series is based on a 1974 novel of the same title by Bhisham Sahni, and depicts the clashes between Muslim Punjabis and Hindu Punjabis leading to the partition of India. The court examined the petition and dismissed it, allowing *Tamas* to be serialized.

Chapter 15 I Jeebesh Bagchi

1 **Editor's note**: Illegal land usage here refers to temporary or permanent structures built without the sanction and clearance of the relevant urban development authorities – in this case, the 1962 Delhi Master Plan.

2 This is how a vast majority of urban spaces self-organize their infrastructure needs. Solomon Benjamin's study of Delhi's Vishwas Nagar is a sophisticated description and analysis of these processes of incremental urban growth. See Solomon Benjamin, 'Touts, Pirates and Ghosts', in Monica Narula *et al.*, eds, *Sarai Reader 05*, p. 242. **Editor's note**: See also *Cities Untold: Stories, Negotiations and Imaginations over Space*, edited by Solomon Benjamin and the Frozen Fish Collective, Volume 4 in the *India Since the 90s* series (forthcoming).

3 **Editor's note**: **The Patent Act of 1970** (amended most recently in 2005) grants protection to inventors by way of patents for goods and processes that pass legal scrutiny on grounds of novelty, significant departure from existing products/processes and bonafide use, and in turn controls copies and counterfeits.

4 **Editor's note**: The availability of cheap recording technologies resulted in the growth of music production in several Indian languages and dialects, initially in the form of cassettes, and subsequently as digital music shared and circulated through pen drives or via the internet. The Haryanvi and Bhojpuri languages, for example, saw a flourishing music industry as a consequence of cheaper production technologies. See R. Tripathi, 'Music Mania in Small-Town Bihar', *Economic and Political Weekly,* vol. 47, no. 22, 2 June 2012; and 'The Artist as Entrepreneur: Talent, Taste and Risk in Haryana and Bihar', in A. Athique, V. Parthasarthy and S.V. Srinivas, eds, *The Indian Media Economy, Volume I: Industrial Dynamics and Cultural Adaptation*, New Delhi: Oxford University Press, 2017, pp. 197–213.

5 **Editor's note**: In 2006, the Supreme Court of India ordered all commercial activity that was 'non-conforming' to be sealed and closed down, affecting livelihoods of thousands of small traders and service providers operating from areas not designated as 'commercial' in the 1962 Delhi Master Plan.

6 **Editor's note**: Refers to the customary warning against film piracy in the DVD format.

7 **Editor's note**: For more on the 'shadow media industry', see Ravi Sundaram, *Pirate Modernity: Delhi's Media Urbanism*, New Delhi: Routledge, 2010.

8 **Editor's note**: The flammable properties of nitrate film caused fire accidents and led to the 1909 British legislation of the cinematograph, making it mandatory to have a license for screening a film. This gradually led to the censorship of film content and the regulation of the cinema's audiences or publics, seen as ideological subjects.

Chapter 16 I Ashish Rajadhyaksha

1 *The Front Row*: 'SRK talks about his favourite Superheroes', available at http://www.youtube.com/watch?feature=player_detailpage&v=tk5slpwlJv4#t=937s, accessed 9 November 2013. All quotes attributed to Shah Rukh Khan here are from this conversation. Khan is speaking to his biographer, film journalist and television anchor Anupama Chopra.

2 **Editor's note**: **Yash Chopra**, see Keywords, p. 226; ***Karan Johan***, see Keywords, p. 335.

3 Trishanku: Mythical king from the *Ramanaya*, known mainly for being suspended somewhere between heaven and earth for his indecision.

4 See especially the work of psychiatric experts H. Eric Bender, Vasilis K. Pozios and Praveen R. Kambam on the mental health conditions of Batman, The Hulk and Spiderman, in David Moye, 'Super Shrinks Psychoanalyze Superheroes', *AOL News*, 22 July 2010, available at http://www.aolnews.com/2010/07/22/super-shrinks-psychoanalyze-superheroes/, accessed 9 November 2013.

5 **Editor's note**: **Khan trio**: Refers to the three superstars of Hindi film of the 1980s–90s, Aamir Khan, Salman Khan and Shah Rukh Khan. All three are for different reasons pathbreaking figures in Indian film, at a time when Hindu majoritarianism has been on the rise in India.

6 *Jab Tak Hai Jaan* (As Long as We Are Alive, 2012, dir. Yash Chopra), major Shah Rukh Khan production; *Dabangg 2* (2012, dir. Arbaaz Khan), iconic Salman Khan film. Akshay Kumar and Ajay Devgn are both major Hindi film stars, but do not match the power of the Khan trio.

7 **Editor's note**: **Mumbai Realism**, see Keywords, p. 337.

8 Anita Elberse, 'The Power of Stars: Do Star Actors Drive the Success of Movies?', *Journal of Marketing*, vol. 71, no. 4, 2007, pp. 102–20, available at http://www.people.hbs.edu/aelberse/publications/Elberse_2007.pdf

9 S. Abraham Ravid, 'Information, Blockbusters, and Stars: A Study of the Film Industry', *The Journal of Business*, vol. 72, no. 4, 1999, pp. 463–92.

10 'Shah Rukh Khan's net worth is 2500 crore', *Times of India*, 21 October 2009, available at http://timesofindia.indiatimes.com/videos/celebs/Shah-Rukh-Khans-net-worth-is-2500-crore/videoshow/5146155.cms, accessed 9 November 2013.

11 **Editor's note**: Red Chillies Entertainment (https://www.redchillies.com/), Shah Rukh Khan's production house, known for multiple projects across the creative economy, especially focusing on special effects. Kolkata Knight Riders, a cricket franchise owned by Red Chillies playing in the major Indian Premier League cricket tournament.

12 **Editor's note**: **Rajnikant jokes**, see Keywords, p. 339.

13 **Editor's note**: Ironically, the original content of the website is not available any longer.

14 **Editor's note**: This refers to Rajnikant's humble origins and his life before he became a film star.

15 Eyal Weizman, 'The Art of War', *Frieze*, issue 99, 2006, available at http://www.frieze.com/issue/article/the_art_of_war/, accessed 5 August 2020.

16 **Editor's note**: **Anna Hazare** (b. 1937): Indian social activist known for his anti-corruption crusade, used to figurehead the rise of the Aam Aadmi Party in Delhi.

17 Both NCTC and NATGRID have been pet projects of the Government of India, usually attributed to former Home Minister, P. Chidambaram. Both have been branded as sequel instruments for state intelligence gathering and have had trouble getting implemented following major political resistance.

18 **Editor's note**: ***Second Life***: Game and online virtual world that provided a full-scale virtual identity, economy and existence.

19 *Deewar* (The Wall, 1975, dir. Yash Chopra): Famous vigilante film set in the 1970s. The hero Vijay, played by Amitabh Bachchan, buys a building which we see glinting on his dark glasses as he utters the immortal Salim–Javed dialogue: '*Aaj se bees saal pehle meri maa ne yahan eente uthayin thi. Aaj mai use yeh building tohfa dene jaa raha hoon.*' (Twenty years ago, my mother lifted bricks here as a labourer. Today I am going to gift this building to her)..

20 **Editor's note**: **Borivili**: A suburban area of Mumbai, and an important station on the local metropolitan railway network.

21 **Editor's note**: The Mumbai-based HIndi film industry in the early 2000s.

22 Ashish Rajadhyaksha, *Indian Cinema in the Time of Celluloid: From Bollywood to the Emergency*, New Delhi: Tulika Books and Bloomington: Indiana University Press, 2009.

23 Ibid., pp. 84 ff.

24 This iconic poem on Bombay is translated as 'Mumbai, Mumbai, My Dear Slut', and discussed in Vidyut Bhagwat and Sharmila Rege's essay, 'Bombay in Dalit Literature', in Sujata Patel and Alice Thorner, eds, *Bombay: Mosaic of Modern Culture*, Delhi: Oxford University Press, pp. 113–25. **Editor's note**: Dilip Chitre (1938–2009), avant-garde Marathi and English poet and author.

25 **Editor's note**: **Mumbai Realism**, see Keywords, p. 337.

26 **Editor's note**: **Ayodhya**: Site of the Mughal mosque destroyed by right-wing Hindutva forces claiming it to be the birthplace of the god Rama. See Keywords pp. 327–28.

27 **Editor's note**: **Girangaon** (or Mill City), the location for Bombay's famous textile mills between the 1860s and 1980s. See Keywords on p. 226 for more.

28 Rajnarayan Chandavarkar, 'From Neighbourhood to Nation: The Rise and Fall of the Left in Bombay's Girangaon in the Twentieth Century', introductory essay for Meena Menon and Neera Adarkar, *One Hundred Years, One Hundred Voices: The Mill Workers of Girangaon: An Oral History*, Calcutta: Seagull Books, 2004, p. 67.

29 **Editor's note**: **Sudhir Patwardhan**, see Keywords, p. 226.

30 **Editor's note**: Article 15 of the Indian Constitution secures citizens from any sort of discrimination by the state, on the grounds of religion, race, caste, sex or place of birth.

31 **Editor's note**: Refers to the UIDAI, or Unique Identification Authority of India, started in 2009, to provide every single Indian a unique biometric identifier.

32 Tom Gunning, *D.W. Griffith and the Origins of American Narrative Film: The Early Years at Biograph*, Urbana: University of Illinois Press, 1991. *Benshi*: Japanese tradition of live offscreen actor narrating and sometimes emoting characters from silent cinema.

33 The 'last-mile problem', a concept drawn from communication studies describing signal decay, has been widely adopted by the Indian developmental discourse as the key problem for the Indian state: how to ensure that benefit actually reaches its beneficiary. See Ashish Rajadhyaksha, *The Last Cultural Mile: An Inquiry into Technology and Governance in India*, Bangalore: Centre for Internet & Society, 2010, available at http://cis-india.org/raw/histories-of-the-internet/last-cultural-mile.pdf

34 This refers to the controversial 'Direct Cash Transfers' scheme implemented by the Government of India in 2012–13, where the government directly pays out employment guarantee benefit into people's bank accounts.

35 Prashant Iyengar, *Privacy and the Information Technology Act — Do we have the Safeguards for Electronic Privacy?* Bangalore: Centre for Internet & Society, 2011, available at http://cis-india.org/internet-governance/blog/privacy/safeguardsfor-electronic-privacy, accessed 9 November 2013.

36 Alexander Galloway, *Gaming: Essays on Algorithmic Culture*, Minneapolis: University of Minnesota Press, 2006.

37 **Editor's note**: **Rajnikant** was known for several swaggering 'gestures', such as flipping a cigarette in the air; see Keywords, p. 339. One specific gesture of a closed fist with an open thumb and little finger for the film *Baba* (dir. Suresh Krissna, 2002) was sought to be copyrighted, and imitators were warned not to copy him. An intense debate took place on this effort to copyright an action in a discussion thread on the Sarai site. The thread does not exist any longer. For a reference to the debate, see Lawrence Liang, 'Conceptualizing Law and Culture', *Seminar Magazine*, 525, 2003, available at http://www.india-seminar.com/2003/525/525%20lawrence%20liang.htm, accessed 9 November 2013. Also see Lawrence Liang, 'From Cinema to the Moving Image and Back', pp. 293–309, and S.V. Srinivas 'The Gaddar Effect: Maoism, Mass Culture, Cinema', pp. 275–92, in this volume.

38 Rishi Alwani, 'Review: Ra.One: The Game', *Indian Video Gamer*, 30 October 2011, available at http://www.indianvideogamer.com/reviews/review-ra-one-the-game, accessed 9 November 2013.

Chapter 17 I Geeta Patel

1 Shohini Ghosh, *Fire: A Queer Classic*, Vancouver: Arsenal Pulp Press, 2010. See also, Ratna Kapur, 'Too Hot to Handle: The Cultural Politics of *Fire*,' *Feminist Review*, vol. 54, 2000, pp. 54–64; Brinda Bose, 'The Desiring Subject: Female Pleasures and Feminist Resistance in Deepa Mehta's *Fire*', *Indian Journal of Gender Studies*, vol. 7, no. 2, 2000, pp. 249–62; Mary John and Tejaswini Niranjana, 'Mirror Politics: Fire, Hindutva and Indian Culture', *Economic and Political Weekly*, vol. 34, no. 10/11, 6–19 March 1999, pp. 581–82.

2 As Lauren Berlant has pointed so clearly in their recent work, her injured self will win out. See Lauren Berlant, 'Poor Eliza', *American Literature*, vol. 70, no. 3, 1998, pp. 635–68. By inviting me to the University of Chicago to speak, Lauren helped me initiate the analyses here.

3 'Film "Fire" Opens', *Times of India*, 13 November 1998.

4 **Editor's note**: **Asha Parekh**, see Keywords, p. 250

5 **Editor's note**: **Sita**, see Keywords, p. 250

6 Anon, 'That Burning Feeling,' *Times of India*, 20 November 1999.

7 **Editor's note**: ***Karva Chauth***: see Keywords, p. 250.

8 **Editor's note**: **Pratibha Parmar**: British Indian filmmaker, known for her political documentaries and her activist work in the global feminism and queer rights movements. **Suniti Namjoshi**: Canadian Indian poet and feminist writer. See *The Fabulous Feminist: A Suniti Namjoshi Reader*, New Delhi: Zubaan, 2012.

9 **Editor's note**: **Sangh Parivar**, see Keywords p. 340.

10 **Editor's note**: **Swadeshi** means nationally 'home grown'; refers also to the early twentieth century political movement to boycott foreign imports.

11 N. Chandra Mohan, 'Sangh Parivar Twists Government's Arm on Insurance Bill', *The Times of India*, 3 December 1998.

12 **Editor's note**: **Baba Budangiri**: Shrine in the Chikmagaluru district of Karnataka in south India, named after the seventeenth-century Sufi saint Baba Budan (said to have brought coffee to India). Made controversial in recent years with political and religious tension around its status as a syncretic shrine, and claims by the Hindu right wing to the land.

13 **Editor's note**: **Babri Masjid**: See **Ayodhya** in Keywords, p. 327.

14 **Editor's note**: **Kartik Purnima**: Hindu festival celebrated on the fifteenth lunar day of the Kartik month of the Hindu calendar.

15 'Human Rights Violations Against Hindu Minorities in Various Countries', www.hindunet.org/human_rights/ focuses on genocide against Hindus by Muslim in Kashmir, Pakistan, Bangla Desh and Fiji. The website includes a 'Hindu Genocide Museum.'

16 Very similar constellations are being formed in 2011–12 around social media. Though right-wing Hindus emphasize loss and damage in their arguments (perceived violations of Indian, read Hindu, culture), constituencies who are arguing for the right of free viewing, arguing against curtailment of content on social networking sites, have an implicit sense of loss scripted into their rationales. For them the loss is of a kind of utopian free movement, access and freedom of expression. Kavita Philip and Ward Smith suggested that I look at Fred Turner's monograph, *From Counterculture to Cyberculture: Steward Brand, the Whole Earth Network and the Rise of Digital Utopianism* (Chicago: University of Chicago Press, 2006), for the political economy of the language of utopian communitarianism on the net.

17 In Nancy Fraser's language, I have turned to insurance as a form of capital that can be conceived of as a kind of redistributive mechanism. Nancy Fraser, *Scales of Justice: Reimagining Political Space in a Globalized World*, New York: Columbia University Press, 2009.

18 Ghosh, *Fire: A Queer Classic*.

19 In the diaspora the VHP can be seen as a privatized insurance carrier that substitutes for the state, even though Mahajan voices the state, and even though in India the right-wing combine of which the VHP is a member pursues its goals both through the state and independently of it.

20 See Ghosh, *Fire: A Queer Classic*, pp. 113–99, for a careful analysis of *Fire*'s enunciations of religion and the debates around iconography and belief.

21 **Editor's note**: **The General elections of 2014 and 2019** saw the Bharatiya Janata Party (BJP)-led National Democratic Alliance (NDA) come to power for two consecutive terms. These electoral verdicts marked an unprecedented phase in Indian political history, with a majoritarian right-wing government stoking communal conflict, politicizing all independent institutions of state and judiciary, bypassing constitutional requirements, and aggressively pushing the agenda for a Hindutva nation. See Abhrajyoti Chakraborty, 'India's Leading Filmmaker Has a Warning', *The New York Times*, 1 December 2020, available at https://www.nytimes.com/2020/12/01/magazine/india-documentary-anand-patwardhan.html, accessed 3 December 2020.

Chapter 18 I Madhuja Mukherjee

1 See D.N. Rodowick, *The Virtual Life of Film*, Harvard: Harvard University Press, 2007; Ravi Sundaram, ed., *No Limits: Media Studies from India*, New Delhi: Oxford University Press, 2013, in particular Ravi Vasudevan's 'Notes on Contemporary Film Experience: Bollywood, Genre Diversity and Video Circuits', pp. 199–223.

2 Anand Pandian, in his paper '"No Blue": On the Colour of Sensation in Tamil Cinema', discussed processes of the making of the Tamil film *Quarter Cutting* (2010) at The Many Lives of Indian Cinema Conference, Centre for the Study of Developing Societies, Delhi, January 2014. Pandian mentioned that this film was in all probability the 'last' Tamil film to be shot on celluloid and worked on a specific kind of colour saturation, which is remarkably different from digital films.

3 **Editor's note**: **Jadavpur University** established the first Film Studies department in India in the 1990s. Its Media Lab has supported research on local film cultures in Kolkata and West Bengal and created a digital media and film archive.

4 Interviews of Shankar Tara (composer) and Kuchil Mukherjee (singer–composer) conducted by Sadhan Mahato.

5 By 'backward' community, I am referring to the official category used to identify groups for government welfare support.

6 For example, Ratheesh Radhakrishnan critiques the framing of the regions through language, culture and geography, and discusses the tussle over the unification of Kerala and the dynamics of 'aggregation and disaggregation'. See Radhakrishnan, 'Thiruvithamkoor, Malabar, Kerala: Speculations on the Regions in "Regional Cinema"', *BioScope: South Asian Screen Studies*, vol. 6, no. 2, 2015, pp. 126–244.

7 Hindi films like *Piku* (2015, dir. Shoojit Sircar) and *Kahani* (Story, 2012, dir. Sujoy Ghosh) were not only extensively shot in Kolkata, there was substantial involvement of the Bengali film industry in terms of both cast and crew. These films were accepted as 'Bengali' films by the press because the directors were Bengalis, but more importantly because the industry considered these as their productions.

8 For an official record of political unrest, see *West Bengal District Gazetters, Puruliya* (1985). However, such videos are in no way connected with contemporary political movements, and are actually disapproved of by left parties and political activists.

9 The Eighth Schedule of the Indian Constitution lists the languages officially recognized by the Indian state. At present, there are twenty-two languages in this list.

10 As evident from the work done by Tanusree Dey, research student, 2000–15, Department of Film Studies, Jadavpur University.

11 **Editor's note**: The **Gorkha language** is spoken in hilly areas of North Bengal, Sikkim and Assam. The Nepali language is primarily spoken in Sikkim, but a sizeable section of tribals in North Bengal use Nepali.

12 See http://www.indiaifa.org/epsita-halder.html, last accessed 19 August 2015.

13 See Ali Nobil Ahmed, 'Contemporary Pashto Porn Film and Cinema Culture', paper presented at the Media Morphologies: Infrastructures and Technologies in Art, Cinema and Popular Culture Conference, Rotterdam, 2011. Farida Batool, 'The Mujra Dance Video CDS: Its Production, Content and Masculine Desire in Present day Pakistani Popular Culture', paper presented at the Association of Social Anthropologists Conference, Jawaharlal Nehru University, New Delhi, 2012. Lotte Hoek, 'Unexpected Digital Cinema of

Bangladesh', unpublished paper, 2015. **Editor's note**: **Mujra**: A dance form performed by courtesans which originated in Mughal India.

14 Moreover, Vasudevan analyses the 'formal constraints of territorial polities' during the 1940s and 1950s, and discusses the 'possibilities for cultural flow beyond the territorial state'. See Ravi Vasudevan, 'Geographies of the Cinematic Public: Notes on Regional, National and Global Histories of Indian Cinema', *Journal of the Moving Image*, vol. 9, 2010, pp. 94–117.

15 **Editor's note**: **Malegaon film**, see Keywords, p. 336.

16 Faiza Khan's 2008 documentary was instrumental in drawing widespread popular attention to the Malegaon film industry. Drawing upon interviews with various Malegaon film workers, Khan shows the 'making of' these low-budget spoof films using documentary realism.

17 Daisy Hasan, 'Talking Back to Bollywood: Hindi Commercial Cinema in the North-East', in Shakuntala Banaji, ed., *South Asian Media Cultures: Audiences, Representations, Contexts for Arguments on the Mediated Scene*, London and New York: Anthem Press, 2010, pp. 29–50.

18 Neikolie Kuotsu, 'Architectures of Pirate Film Cultures: Encounters with Korean Wave in "Northeast" India', *Inter-Asia Cultural Studies*, vol. 14, no. 4, 2013, pp. 579–99.

19 Ratnakar Tripathy, 'Bhojpuri Cinema: Regional Resonances in the Hindi Heartland', *South Asian Popular Culture*, vol. 5, no. 2, 2007, pp. 145–65. **Editor's note**: **Bhojpuri** is a language spoken in the state of Bihar. In the last few decades, Bhojpuri cinema has emerged as a major cultural industry, especially popular among migrant workers from Bihar consuming video content on their mobile phones. The Bhojpuri film industry now has an established star system, as well as other well-oiled ancillary networks such as advertising contracts.

20 My own experience comprises viewing these videos inside the bus (during a trip to Jhalda town in 2012) and during night shows in shops which also operate as 'video halls'.

21 **Editor's note**: A generic folk aesthetic involving music, dance and ethnic attire, agnostic to local specificities.

22 **Editor's note**: **Jhumur**, see Keywords, p. 262.

23 See Sangita Shresthova, *Between Cinema and Performance: Globalizing Bollywood Dance*, Michigan: ProQuest, 2008.

24 Likewise, the widely held theatrical form *jatra,* which is enormously popular across rural areas, is in fact produced by companies located in the city, and also involves well-known film stars.

25 The 'CD' (compact disc) player is a standalone mechanism attached to television sets, through which discs are played. This appliance is still used in many rural and suburban sectors. The Manbhum films also show people watching films on television connected to a View CD player.

26 Moreover, in recent times, Purulia has been in the news for gathering and circulation of arms and huge quantities of ammunition.

27 A recent mainstream Bengali film, *Proloy* (Destruction, 2013, dir. Raj Chakraborty), based on a true story, was shot extensively in the interiors of Purulia and deployed local dance forms in the climax. The film narrates a plot about rape and revenge.

28 See Sarrazin's (2014) analysis of *Roja* (1992, dir. Mani Ratnam), A.R. Rahman's sound design and new digital sonic cultures of Bollywood. Natalia Sarrazin, 'Global masala', in Gregory D. Booth and Bradley Shope, eds, *More than Bollywood: Studies in Indian Popular Music*, New York: Oxford University Press, 2014, pp. 38–59. Nevertheless, Sneha Khanwalkar, the music director of *Gangs of Wasseypur* (Parts 1 and 2, dir. Anurag Kashyap, 2012), has used the digital recorder and mixer in a reverse way by mixing disparate noises, sounds of local instruments and voices of untrained singers to produce a heavily treated soundtrack.

29 **Editor's note**: **Uttam Kumar** (1926–1980): Cultural icon and renowned Bengali film actor (and director, producer and singer). **Ajitesh Bandyopadhyay**: Prominent Bengali theatre actor, and a member of the Indian People's Theatre Association (IPTA). For **IPTA**, see Keywords, pp. 334–35. **Jhalda**, the town where he was born, is in Purulia district. **Tapan Sinha** (1924–2009): Prominent Bengali and Hindi film director, whose best known film, *Hatey Bazare* (The Market Place, 1967), is located in the Birbhum district.

30 ***Bhadralok***: See Keywords, p. 328.

31 For a study of the ways in which middle-class cinema was canonized, see Moinak Biswas, 'The Couple and Their Spaces: *Harano Sur* as Melodrama Now', in Ravi S. Vasudevan, ed., *Making Meaning in Indian*

Cinema, New Delhi: Oxford University Press, 2000, pp. 122–42, and Madhuja Mukherjee, 'Of Bhadramohila, Blouses, and "Bustofine": Reviewing Bengali High Culture (1930s–40s) from a Low Angle', in Clara Sarmento and Ricardo Campos, eds, *Popular and Visual Culture: Design, Circulation and Consumption*, Cambridge: Cambridge Scholars Publishing, 2014, pp. 145–66.

32 Markus Schleiter, 'India's "Indigenous" Cinemas', *IIAS News Letter* 67, 2014, http://www.iias.nl/sites/default/files/IIAS_NL67_1011.pdf, accessed 6 August 2015.

33 Hasan, 'Talking Back to Bollywood', p. 33.

34 Partha Chatterjee, *The Politics of the Governed: Reflections on Popular Politics in Most of the World*, New York: Columbia University Press, 2004, pp. 112–13. ***Dhorai charit manas*** roughly translates as 'Dear Dalit Man', and was originally published between 1949 and 1951 by the author Satinath Bhaduri.

35 **Editor's note**: **Durga**: The fierce form of the protective mother-goddess is widely worshipped in Bengal as the slayer of the buffalo-demon Mahishasura. In September/October (the Hindu month of Ashvin), a ten-day festival called 'pujo' or 'Durga pooja' is held to worship the goddess, involving wider cultural events and social gatherings. See Tapati Guha-Thakurta, *In the Name of the Goddess: The Durga Puja of Contemporary Kolkata*, Delhi: Primus Books, 2015.

36 **Editor's note**: **Narada**: Mythological character known for his ability to cause minor conflicts, generally found in ancient literature but not quite 'heroic' or 'divine' in status. **Yama**: God of death in Hindu mythology.

37 **Editor's note**: A series of terrorist attacks were carried out in Mumbai between 26 and 29 November 2008 by members of the Lashkar-e-Taiba. One of these was at the Taj hotel in south Bombay.

38 **Editor's note**: The Trinamool Congress is among the major political parties in West Bengal, currently headed by Mamta Banerjee, the controversial and populist Chief Minister of Bengal, with a penchant for the show of muscle force.

39 Chatterjee, *The Politics of the Governed*, p. 11. **Editor's note**: **Tatma** is a caste traditionally associated with the weaving communities of Bihar and Jharkhand.

Chapter 19 I S.V. Srinivas

1 **Editor's note**: See ***Naxalite*** in Keywords, p. 337.

2 **Editor's note**: The five states of southern India – Tamil Nadu, Karnataka, Andhra Pradesh, Telangana and Kerala – where collectively the largest number of films are produced, historically has had a close nexus between cinema and politics. Popular actors across these states have achieved superstardom leveraging their screen image to launch extremely successful political careers, including as long-standing chief ministers. By extension, fan clubs have doubled up as vote banks for political parties. See Dhamu Pongiyanan, *Film and Politics in India: Cinematic Charisma as a Gateway to Cinematic Power*, Bern: Peter Lang, 2015; M. Madhava Prasad, *Cine-Politics: Film Stars and Political Existence in South India*, Hyderabad: Orient Blackswan, 2014.

3 The States Reorganization Commission (est. 1953) had opposed the merger of the two regions, as had political representatives of the Telangana region. See Gautam Pingle, 'The Historical Context of Andhra and Telangana, 1949–56', *Economic and Political Weekly*, vol. 45, no. 8, 2010, pp. 57–65.

4 See Hugh Gray, 'The demand for a separate Telangana state in India', *Asian Survey*, vol. 11, no. 5, 1971, pp. 463–74.

5 Keshav Rao Jadhav notes that two student organizations dedicated to the cause were formed around 1991. Jadhav, 'Towards a History of the Telangana movement', in S. Simhadri and P.L. Vishweshwer Rao, eds, *Telangana: Dimensions of Underdevelopment*, Hyderabad: Centre for Telangana Studies, 1997, pp. 5–14.

6 The Andhra Pradesh Reorganization Act was passed in February 2014 and the new state came into being in June 2014.

7 Responding to the imminent creation of Uttarakhand, Jharkhand and Chhattisgarh, political scientist Pradeep Kumar included Telangana in his list of regions whose statehood demands were *not* based on cultural identity, and said, 'With the passage of time, sentiment for language and culture has given way to the urge for speedier economic development.' Pradeep Kumar, 'Demand For New States: Cultural Identity Loses Ground to Urge For Development', *Economic and Political Weekly*, vol. 35, no. 35–36, 2000, pp. 3078–82.

8 K. Srinivas Reddy, 'The Maoist challenge', *India 2006: A Symposium on The Year That Was, Seminar* # 569, January 2007.

9 See Robert L. Hardgrave Jr., 'Politics and Film in Tamil Nadu: The Stars and The DMK', *Asian Survey*, vol. 13, no. 3, March 1973, pp. 288–305; M.S.S. Pandian, *The Image Trap: M.G. Ramachandran in Film and Politics*, New Delhi and London: Sage Publications, 1992; M. Madhava Prasad, *Cine-politics: Film Stars and Political Existence in South India*, Hyderabad: Orient Blackswan, 2013; Arvind Rajagopal, *Politics After Television: Hindu Nationalism and the Reshaping of the Public in India*, Cambridge: Cambridge University Press, 2001.

10 Political scientist M. Kodanda Ram, a key leader of the Telangana agitation and Chairman of the Telangana Political Joint Action Committee (T-JAC), argues: 'Apart from exploiting the resources of Telangana for the benefit of the Andhra region, there has been a process of marginalization of Telangana dialect and culture.' See M. Kodanda Ram, 'Movement for Telangana State: A Struggle for Autonomy', *Economic and Political Weekly*, vol. 42, no. 2, 2007, p. 93.

11 Quoted in Kalpana Kannabhiran, Sagari R. Ramdas, N. Madhusudhan, S. Ashalatha and M. Pavan Kumar, 'On the Telangana Trail', *Economic and Political Weekly*, vol. 45, no. 13, 2010, p. 70.

12 V. Anil Kumar, 'Why Telangana, Why Now?' *Economic and Political Weekly*, vol. 42, no. 9, 2007, p. 791; emphasis added.

13 The Telugu film industry has been repeatedly criticized by other academics and political activists alike for its role in denigrating the region's people and their culture. See, for example, Rama S. Melkote, E. Revathi, K. Lalitha, K. Sajaya and A. Suneetha, 'The Movement for Telangana: Myth and Reality', *Economic and Political Weekly*, vol. 45, no. 2, 2010, pp. 8–11. **Editor's note**: **Kamma entrepreneurs**: Dominant form of financial entrepreneurship belonging to the affluent Kamma community from coastal Andhra Pradesh.

14 Ratnakar Tripathy notes that in both Bihar and Haryana, a large number of singer-performers are mining vast repertories of folk music, often fusing it with Hindi film songs but also non-Indian sources, for their livelihood. Ratnakar Tripathy, 'The Artist as Entrepreneur: Talent, Taste and Risk in the Music Industries of Haryana and Bihar', paper presented at the international conference on 'India at Leisure: Media, Culture and Consumption in the New Economy', New Delhi, organized by Centre for Culture, Media and Governance, Jamia Millia Islamia, and School of Arts, University of Waikato, 10–11 February 2015.

15 **Editor's note**: Radical practices in music and theatre go back to the early 1940s when the **Indian People's Theatre Association** (IPTA, Keywords, pp. 334–35) was formed with affiliated movements in different regions. In Telangana this was the Praja Natya Mandali (Citizens Theatre Group). Practices of leveraging folk music and tunes for political mobilization continue, as seen in the Dalit movement with Kabir Kala Manch (music repertory) and Sambhaji Bhagat (poet and musician), or as seen here with Gaddar in the Telangana movement.

16 This and other parallels between the movement for a separate Andhra state in the 1950s and the Telangana movement over the past decade will remain unexplored in this article for reasons of focus and space. I have discussed cinema's importance for Andhra Pradesh from the 1950s at some length in S.V. Srinivas, *Politics as Performance: A Social History of The Telugu Cinema*, Ranikhet: Permanent Black, 2013, pp. 51–108.

17 Anant Maringanti, 'Telangana: Righting Historical Wrongs or Getting the Future Right?' *Economic and Political Weekly*, vol. 45, no. 4, 2010, pp. 33–38.

18 Arunodaya Samskritika Samkhya, Staff Reporter, 'Youth Asked to Revive People's Art and Literature', *The Hindu*, 14 November 2005. Krishna Chaitanya Allam, a pro-statehood YouTube user, states that till late 2009, there wasn't much Telangana-related activity on YouTube (email to the author dated 16 February 2014).

19 For example, the programme on Vimalakka aired on 7 April 2013 by TV5 News, titled 'Mee Patanai Vastunna' (I Come to You as Your Song), is available on the television network's YouTube channel, http://www.youtube.com/watch?v=V5swGIBqn28, accessed 29 August 2015.

20 **Editor's note**: **Gaddar**, see Keywords, p. 276; **Jana Natya Mandali**, see Keywords, p. 335. A 'Gaddar Special' episode too was aired on TV5 News, http://www.youtube.com/watch?v=I_hEJYvKxI0, accessed 29 August 2015.

21 Venkat Rao, 'Writing Orally: Decolonization From Below', *Positions*, vol. 7, no. 1, 1999, pp. 253–54.

22 M.S. Shanker, 'Revolutionary Poet Gaddar Survives Murderous Attack', *Rediff on The Net*, n.d., accessed 29 August 2015.

23 K. Balagopal, 'Chenna Reddy's Spring', *Economic and Political Weekly*, vol. 25, no. 12, 24 March

1990, pp. 591–95. **Editor's note**: **K. Balagopal** (1952–2009) was a noted human rights activist and lawyer, very active in the civil liberties movement in Andhra Pradesh.

24 This was organized under the aegis of the Telangana Samskritika Samakhya (TSS, Telangana Cultural Forum) and the Telangana Joint Action Forum (T-JAC). *Andhra Jyothi*, 5 February 2008; *Garjinchina Kalakarulu* (Telugu), *Andhra Jyothi*, Bangalore edition, p. 3. TSS was floated by Gaddar. A brief report on Gaddar's press conference in the run up to the event is available at http://great-telangana.blogspot.com/2008/02/gaddar-calls-peoples-movement-for.html, accessed 29 August 2015.

25 P. Kesava Kumar, 'Popular Culture and Ideology: The Phenomenon of Gaddar', *Economic and Political Weekly*, vol. 45, no. 7, 2010, p. 63.

26 P.L. Vishweshwer Rao, in 'Telangana Replacing Andhra, At Least on Boards', *Indo-Asian News Service* (IANS), 13 August 2011, http://ibnlive.in.com/news/telangana-replacing-andhra-at-least-on-boards/175415-3-67.html, accessed 29 August 2015; emphasis added.

27 **Editor's note**: The transition from Princely states and colonial Presidencies to **linguistic states** in the 1950s included the creation of the Telugu-speaking state of **Andhra Pradesh**, which was achieved in 1953 after violent public agitations following the death of Potti Sreeramulu (freedom fighter and revolutionary, 1901–1952), who died while on a hunger strike in demand of separating Andhra Pradesh from the erstwhile Madras Presidency.

28 Venkat Rao, 'Mnemosigning: Ecstasies in Pain', in Rajeswari Sunder Rajan, ed., *Signposts: Gender Issues in Post-Independence India*, New Delhi: Kali for Women, 1999, p. 360; emphasis added.

29 See, for example, Lydia Polygreen, 'Suicides, Some for the Separatist Cause, Jolt India', *The New York Times*, 30 March 2010.

30 Rao, 'Mnemosigning', p. 368.

31 Rao, 'Writing Orally'.

32 **Editor's note**: ***Bhoomikosam*** (For Land's Sake, dir. Tilak, 1974): Telugu commercial hit and the first to portray far-left politics. Story of a village's liberation was made with left political parties, and dedicated to the filmmaker's brother killed in a police 'encounter' in 1972.

33 **Editor's note**: **Ashok Kumar** (1911–2001): Major Hindi movie star. **Jayaprada**: Indian film actress in Hindi and Telugu cinema who later joined politics as a member of the Telugu Desam Party in 1994.

34 **Editor's note**: **K.B. Tilak** (1926–2010): Independence activist, film director and producer. **IPTA**, see Keywords, pp. 334–35.

35 For a detailed discussion of the film and its lasting influence on Telugu cinema, see Srinivas, *Politics as Performance*, pp. 206–15.

36 For more on the 1980s Red Films and their significance, see ibid., pp. 360–84.

37 Katragadda Murari, ed., *Telugu Chalanachitra Nirmatala Charitra 1931–2005* (Telugu), Hyderabad: The Telugu Film Producers' Council, n.d., pp. 270–73.

38 K. Balaji, 'The Naxalite Film', paper presented at the 'Workshop on Telugu Cinema: History, Culture, Theory', Hyderabad, organized by the Anveshi Research Centre for Women's Studies, Hyderabad and Centre for Study of Culture and Society, Bangalore, 13–16 August 1999.

39 'Errajenda Errajenda' (Red Flag, Red Flag), an adaptation of the Jana Natya Mandali song for the film *Cheemala Dandu* (Army of Ants, dir. Narayanamurthy, 1995), is listed under the category of 'Top Telangana Songs' on the pro-Telangana website, telanganadosti.com. Interestingly, the lyrics of this song do not make any references to Telangana; see http://www.telanganadosti.com/player/songs/Telangana%20Songs/ERRAJENDA%20ERRAJENDA.mp3, accessed 29 August 2015. Also found on the website are songs by Gaddar, Vimalakka and Goreti Venkanna.

40 **Editor's note**: **Dasari Narayana Rao** (1942–2017): Director, producer, actor in Telugu and Hindi cinema and television. His films addressed social inequalities. He was elected as a Rajya Sabha (Upper House of Parliament) member in 2006.

41 **Editor's note**: **Vijayashanthi**: Actress, producer and politician who has acted in close to 200 films in the Telugu, Tamil, Malayalam, Kannada and Hindi languages, and is known as the 'action queen of Indian cinema'. She started her political career with the BJP in 1998, later starting her own political party which merged with the TRS, followed by a stint with the Congress and a recent return to the BJP in 2020.

42 **Editor's note**: The Naxalite movement had splintered into different units and **Arunodaya** was the cultural wing of the faction driven by the CPI(ML) New Democracy.

43 Posted by 'srinivasmahima' on 20 February 2009, http://nagfans.com/.

44 **Editor's note**: **Vangapandu Prasada Rao** (1943–2020): Poet, lyricist, actor and one of the founders in 1972 of the Jana Natya Mandali, the cultural outfit of the People's War Group. He has written more than 400 songs, of which some have been translated into several Indian languages.

45 The popularity of songs scripted by Gaddar in *Orey Rickshaw* was noted by a reviewer in a radical journal: Premchand, '*Orey rickshaw*: chivariki migilchindi emiti' (Telugu), *Prajasahiti*, January 1996, pp. 29–31.

46 M.S. Shanker states that Gaddar was suspended for 'amassing huge wealth using the militant outfit's name'. The actions cited by the party included the establishment of a private school on three acres of land and, in the journalist's words, 'writing lyrics for Telugu films made on revolutionary themes'. See Shanker, 'Revolutionary Poet Gaddar Survives Murderous Attack'.

47 Padmaja Shaw, 'Profit for Power or Power for Profit?: The State of Television Industry in Andhra Pradesh', paper presented at the symposium on 'The Indian Media Economy: New Perspectives from New Zealand', Raglan, New Zealand, hosted by The Faculty of Arts and Sciences, University of Waikato, Centre for Culture Media and Governance, Jamia Millia Islamia, and Centre for Study of Culture and Society, 25–26 February 2014.

48 TRS has repeatedly claimed that the turning point in the movement for statehood was KCR's fast. For an elaboration of the claim, see Special Correspondent, 'KCR's fast a defining moment: TRS', *The Hindu*, 30 November 2013.

49 Lalith Singh, 'An Anchor's Distinct Ride to Fame', *The Hindu*, 8 April 2013.

50 H. Srikanth, 'Construction and Consolidation of the Telangana Identity', *Economic and Political Weekly*, vol. 48, no. 45–46, 2013, p. 41.

51 The video in question is titled 'Podustunna Poddumeeda Song by Michael Jackson' and was uploaded by a user with the handle 'krishnakishore', https://www.youtube.com/watch? v=-vMIad5wDHM, accessed 29 August 2015.

52 Ashish Rajadhyaksha, *Indian Cinema in The Time of Celluloid: From Bollywood to Emergency*, New Delhi: Tulika Books, 2009, p. 100.

53 Ibid., pp. 51–83.

54 Ibid., pp. 99–100.

55 For production figures, see Ashish Rajadhyaksha and Paul Willemen, eds, *Encyclopedia of Indian Cinema*, New Delhi: Oxford University Press, 1999, pp. 31–32. **Editor's note**: **M.G. Ramachandran** (1917–1987) was a film star, politician and founder of the All India Dravida Munnetra Kazhagam (AIDMK) party, serving as Chief Minister of Tamil Nadu from 1977 to 1987. His exceptional ability in leveraging stardom to build a political base was a trend-setter in what Madhava Prasad terms as 'cine-politics'. Madhava Prasad, *Cine-Politics: Films Stars and Political Existence in South India*, Hyderabad: Orient Blackswan, 2014.

56 Srinivas, *Politics as Performance*, p. 35.

57 See Robin Jeffrey, *India's Newspaper Revolution: Capitalism, Politics and the Indian-Language Press*, third edition, New Delhi: Oxford University Press, 2010.

58 **Editor's note**: **Ramoji Rao** is a film producer, media entrepreneur and head of the Ramoji Group, which owns the largest film production facility, Ramoji Film City, in Hyderabad. The Ramoji Group's business extends across film, television, food, hotels, education and print media.

59 Jeffrey, *India's Newspaper Revolution*, p. 77.

60 For a detailed discussion of *Eenadu*'s techniques, see Uma Maheswari, 'Anti-Arrack Movement, Prohibition and After: *Eenadu*'s Strategic Support and Silence', *Journal of Arts and Ideas*, vol. 32, no. 3, 1999, pp. 73–85, and Srinivas, *Politics as Performance*, pp. 305–60.

61 Jeffrey, *India's Newspaper Revolution*.

62 See, for example, the collection of poems titled *Quit Telangana*. One of the poems, written by Udugula Venu and addressed to the opponents of Telangana statehood, is titled 'Bastards' and ends with the line (in English), 'Bastards, Go to Hell'. Singidi Rachayitala Sangham, *Quit Telangana* (Telugu), 2011, pp. 18–19, http://www.scribd.com/doc/46460845/Quit-Telangana-Singidi-Rachayitala-Sangha, accessed 10 January 2013.

63 Ravi Vasudevan, *The Melodramatic Public*, Ranikhet: Permanent Black, 2010, p. 210.

64 Venkat Rao, 'Risking Spaces: The Politics and the Pain of Singing', in Simon Charsly and Lakshmi Narayan Kadekar, eds, *Performers and Their Arts: Folk, Popular and Classical Genres in Changing India*, New Delhi: Routledge, 2006, pp. 197–214.

Chapter 20 I Lawrence Liang

1 **Editor's note**: **Sarai**: Programme at the Centre for the Study of Developing Societies (CSDS), New Delhi, a platform for research and reflection on the transformation of urban space. See https://www.csds.in/sarai, accessed 23 December 2020.

2 D.N. Rodowick, *The Virtual Life of Film*, Massachusetts: Harvard University Press, 2007, p. 90.

3 Amit Rai in his work on Bollywood, for instance, argues that it makes more sense to think of Bollywood as a complex media assemblage in which filmic affects are produced through various interactions of film as technology, as text and as social practice. See Amit Rai, *Untimely Bollywood: Globalization and India's New Media Assemblage*, Durham and London: Duke University Press, 2009.

4 Gilles Deleuze, *Control and Becoming: A Conversation Between Toni Negri and Gilles Deleuze*, 2011, https://thefunambulist.net/law/philosophy-control-and-becoming-a-conversation-between-toni-negri-and-gilles-deleuze, accessed 18 June 2021.

5 **Editor's note**: **Ritwik Ghatak**, see Keywords p. 334.

6 See Ravi Sundaram and Lawrence Liang, 'India', in Joe Karaganis, ed., *Media Piracy in Emerging Economies*, Social Sciences Research Council, USA, 2011, pp. 339–98. See also Ravi Sundaram, *Pirate Modernity: Delhi's Media Urbanism*, New Delhi: Routledge, 2009. Thomas Elsaesser proposes a reconstruction of film history via an alertness to its immersion within *other* technological forms – including electricity, automobiles, aviation, telephones and the phonograph, scientific and medical apparatus, surveillance and military apparatus, sensory/motor apparatus, and finally, censoring/monitoring apparatus. Thomas Elsaesser, *Film History as Media Archeology: Tracking Digital Cinema*, Amsterdam: Amsterdam University Press, 2016.

7 Jonathan Rosenbaum, *Goodbye Cinema, Hello Cinephilia: Film Culture in Transition*, Chicago and London: University of Chicago Press, 2010.

8 **Editor's note**: **Digileak**, see Keywords, p. 294.

9 https://www.qubecinema.com/#, accessed 30 November 2020.

10 See Nupur Jain, 'Anti-Piracy Enforcement Efforts Made by the Bombay Film Industry: A Report and Assessment of Present Ideas and Practices', unpublished paper on file.

11 **Editor's note**: For more on *Ra.One* see Ashish Rajadhyaksha, 'SRK, Cinema and the Citizen: What's Next?' in this volume, pp. 224–48.

12 Jean Louis Comolli, 'Machines of the Visible', in Teresa de Lauretis and Stephen Heath, eds, *The Cinematic Apparatus*, New York City: St. Martin's Press, 1980.

13 Linda Williams, *Hard Core: Power, Pleasure and the 'Frenzy of the Visible'*, Berkeley: University of California Press, 1999.

14 Elsaesser suggests that the digital is not merely the technology of signal conversion and data transmission, but also a 'moment of cultural rupture'. He seeks to disarticulate the cinematic apparatus in its historical dimension and to rearticulate it across its many entertainment and non-entertainment practices, to reveal practices in their diversity but also *our* digital perspective on them. He suggests that the cinema may well have ceased to be important because of this particular cinematic apparatus of camera, projector, screen and auditorium, and instead, become digital culture's internal reference point. See Elsaesser, *Film History as Media Archeology*.

15 It is not surprising that the digital moment has also been accompanied by a return to various figures of classical film theory including Bazin, Epstein and Balazs. See, for instance, Dudley Andrew, *What Cinema Is!*, United Kingdom: Wiley-Blackwell, 2010; Malcolm Turvey, *Doubting Vision: Film and the Revelationist Tradition*, New York: Oxford University Press, 2008.

16 Stanley Cavell, *The World Viewed: Reflections on the Ontology of Film*, Enlarged Edition, Cambridge, Mass.: Harvard University Press, 1979.

17 Ibid.

18 D.N. Rodowick, *Reading the Figural, or, Philosophy after the New Media*, USA: Duke University Press Books, 2001.

19 Nikolaus Hirsch and Shveta Sarda, eds, *Cybermohalla Hub*, Berlin: Sternberg Press, 2012. **Editor's note**: **Cybermohalla Ensemble**, see Keywords, p. 331.

20 Mark Hansen, *New Philosophy for New Media*, New York: Routledge, 2004.

21 Gilles Deluze, *Cinema 2: The Time Image*, Minneapolis: University of Minnesota Press, 1985.

22 Kajri Jain, 'More than Meets the Eye: The Circulation of Images and the Embodiment of Value', *Contributions to Indian Sociology*, no. 36, 2002, pp. 33–70.

23 Ibid., p. 67.

24 **Editor's note**: Incidents involving the non-consensual sharing of sexually explicit videos through multimedia messaging services (MMS) led to **MMS scandals** (see Keywords, p. 337), especially as many of these involved sexual acts among high school kids. One of the most infamous of these MMS leaks was a video circulated by a student of the Delhi Public School in 2004.

25 Craig J. Calhoun, ed., *Habermas and The Public Sphere*, Massachusetts: The MIT Press, 1992, p. 386.

26 Bharath Muthry, quoted in Namita Malhotra, *Porn, Law, Video Technology*, Bangalore: Centre for Internet and Society, 2011.

27 Ibid., p. 127.

28 Ibid., p. 115.

29 Ibid., p. 73 .

30 **Editor's note**: A teenage oral sex video was leaked by the 17-year-old boy involved in the act, which caused a scandal when it was put up for auction in 2004 by an engineering student from a prestigious college, on Baazee.com, the Indian equivalent of eBay. (For MMS scandal, see Keywords, p. 337.)

31 A play on Russian roulette, Chatroulette allows people to have randomized video chats with strangers. More often than not people just surf a series of videos randomly, and a majority of the people who participate in Chatroulette are either masturbating or watching people masturbate.

32 Jorge Louis Borges, 'Tlon, Uqbar, Orbis Tertius', in *Labyrinths: Selected Stories and Other Writings*, New York: New Directions, 1962.

33 Elsaesser, *Film History as Media Archeology*.

Chapter 21 I Pad.ma

1 Henri Langlois, cited in Richard Roud and François Truffaut, *A Passion for Films: Henri Langlois and the Cinematheque Francaise*, Baltimore: The Johns Hopkins University Press, 1999.

2 Walter Benjamin, 'On the Concept of History', in *Walter Benjamin: Selected Writings (Volume 4: 1938–1940)*, edited by Eiland and M.W. Jennings, translated by Harry Zohn, Cambridge, Mass.: Harvard University Press, 2003, p. 392.

3 Walter Benjamin, *Illuminations: Essays and Reflections*, edited by Hannah Arendt, translated by Harry Zohn, New York: Schocken, 1969, p. 254.

4 Ibid., p. 264.

5 Jacques Derrida, 'Archive Fever: A Freudian Impression', translated by Eric Prenowitz, *Diacritics*, vol. 25, no. 2, Summer 1995, p. 27.

6 Michael Serres, *The Parasite*, translated by Lawrence R. Schehr, Minneapolis: University of Minnesota Press, 2007, p. 75.

7 **Editor's note**: **Cybermohalla Ensemble**, see Keywords, p. 331. Lakhmi Chand was one of the participants in this project and a contributing author to the book *Trickster City: Writings from the Underbelly of the Metropolis*, translated by Sarda Nanda, New Delhi: Penguin Books India, 2010.

8 Lakhmi Chand, Cybermohalla Ensemble, 'No Apologies for the interruption' (Translated by Shveta Sarda), CSDS: Sarai, New Delhi, 2010.

9 Anna Akhmatova, *Requiem*, translated by A. S. Kline. See http://www.poetryintranslation.com/PITBR/Russian/Akhmatova.htm#_Toc322442229, accessed 30 September 2014. **Editor's note**: **Anna Akhmatova** (1889–1966): Russian poet, author of *Requiem*, a critique of the terror and violence unleashed during Stalin's regime.

10 Serge Daney made the distinction in numerous articles and on radio, recapped in 'Before and After the Image', *Cahiers du Cinema*, April 1991. See http://home.earthlink.net/~steevee/Daney_before.html/, accessed 21 October 2014.

11 Jacques Ranciere, *The Future of the Image*, translated by Gregory Elliot, London: Verso Books, 2007, p. 7.

12 Ibid., p. 46.

13 Hal Foster, 'Archives of Modern Art', *October*, vol. 99, 2002, pp. 81–95.

14 **Editor's note**: **André Malraux** (1901–1976): French art theorist and novelist, appointed by the Charles de Gaulle government as Minister of Information (1945–46), and subsequently as Minister of Cultural Affairs in 1959, considered the museum as a modern and potentially democratizing and inclusive site of art, and explored the idea of *musée imaginaire* – 'the imaginary museum' or 'the museum without walls', which is a collection of all major works of art represented in our imagination. His ideas have often been leveraged by supporters of digital archives and collections.

15 Irit Rogoff, quoted in 'The Implicated: Reflections on Audience', Artconcerns.net, archive available at http://www.zoominfo.com/p/Irit-Rogoff/405885605/, accessed 21 October 2014.

16 Adrian Johns, *The Nature of the Book: Print and Knowledge in the Making*, Chicago: University of Chicago Press, 1998.

17 See Mary Anne Doane's reflections on the relationship between photography, cinema and the archive. Doane, *The Emergence of Cinematic Time: Modernity, Contingency, the Archive*, Cambridge, Mass.: Harvard University Press, 2002.

18 Antonio Negri, *Insurgencies: Constituent Power and the Modern State*, translated by Maurizia Boscagli, Minneapolis: University of Minnesota Press, 2009.

ACKNOWLEDGEMENTS

The book owes everything to its contributors, who indulged the editing of their original texts and images for inclusion in this volume. To all the authors, filmmakers and artists who trusted us with their work: 'thank you' for the generosity.

I am grateful to Indu Chandrasekhar and the entire team at Tulika Books for their valuable inputs through the process of editing this volume, and for their calm patience. My admiration for Tulika's spirited contribution to the world of publishing has only grown.

To Gauri Nagpal, for designing this book across time-zones and continents: a big thank you for the ever-smiling composure, and for sustaining a lively enthusiasm over a long period of time and multiple iterations.

Thanks to Chen Yun and the Moonchu Foundation for making this series possible, and for the exciting promise of seeing this volume published in Chinese some day.

Credit is due to Ankita Sahoo, Anisha Jain and Kavita Bhardwaj – my students at Christ University – who helped with preliminary research towards this volume in its very initial stages.

To Ashish Rajadhyaksha, for inviting me to be part of the audacious imagination of the *India Since the 1990s* series: I feel greatly privileged and lucky. 'Thank you' is too small an expression, but nonetheless, for being a friend, colleague and guide, *go raibh maith agat*, and cheers to our Coleraine friend, Paul Willemen.

This book took shape during a period of great transformation in my personal life. Much love to friends and companions who were ever present, with food, song and good cheer. And to my parents, G.N. Devy and Surekha Devi, for everything.

My son Ishaan calls this 'the book with cool images'. To him, and to my students who have never seen a VHS tape, in memory of an analogue world.

Rashmi Devi Sawhney
Bangalore, April 2022

Rashmi Devi Sawhney is an academic, curator and co-founder of VisionMix, an international platform for artists, filmmakers and researchers. She writes on cinema and the visual arts, and has held posts at the Jawaharlal Nehru University, the Dublin Institute of Technology, and the Srishti Institute of Art, Design and Technology. She is currently Associate Professor in Film and Cultural Studies at Christ University, Bangalore. Her work has been published in English and Marathi. Her curatorial projects include *Future Orbits* and *Video Vortex XI*, both collaterals of the 2016–17 Kochi-Muziris Biennale, and *Loss and Transience*, Hong-gah Museum, Taipei, 2021.

Cover image

Montage of images from: Deepa Dhanraj's film *Molkarin* (1981); Prime Minister Jawaharlal Nehru's address on the occasion of the formation ceremony of Andhra Pradesh in Hyderabad in 1956; Sheba Chhachhi's *Sathyarani, Staged Portrait* (1990); and Vipin Vijay's *Video Game* (2005). Charulata's all-encompassing gaze surveils these images (*Charulata*, dir. Satyajit Ray, 1964).